Studies in Eighteenth-Century Culture

VOLUME 10

Studies in Eighteenth-Century Culture VOLUME 10

EDITED BY *Harry C. Payne*
Colgate University

PUBLISHED *for the*
AMERICAN SOCIETY FOR EIGHTEENTH-CENTURY STUDIES
by THE UNIVERSITY OF WISCONSIN PRESS

Published 1981

The University of Wisconsin Press
114 North Murray Street
Madison, Wisconsin 53715

The University of Wisconsin Press, Ltd.
1 Gower Street
London WC1E 6HA, England

First printing

Printed in the United States of America

LC 74–25572
ISBN 0–299–08320–9

Editorial Readers for Volume Ten

Contents

Preface

The philosophers and critics of the eighteenth century made the love of variety an acceptable—indeed admirable—part of the culture of Europe and America. The *esprit systématique* allowed for tolerance and free criticism in ways the *esprit de système* did not. Hence it is only appropriate that a volume designed to represent the best of the activities of our society show such variety. No particular system guided the selection of papers for the volume by me and the small army of readers. Our standards were excellence of performance of the task chosen by the author and interest of the subject to a wide range of readers. The results, I think, show that the society is very much alive in its quest to stimulate new thought on its chosen century.

Though no pre-ordained formula guided selection for this volume, I would very roughly divide the papers into four groupings. First, "method." Phillip Harth raises the problem of method in his presidential address, arguing for the relevance of history to literary investigation. And Barbara Stafford, in her Clifford Prize–winning essay on "singularity," best illustrates the rewards of an interdisciplinary, historical approach to a problem of aesthetics.

Second, what might be called "the career of ideas." These papers illustrate the various transformations of individual ideas valued by the eighteenth century as the century ran its course. Roger Hahn discusses in a provocative way the attempts to bring together love of science and respect for mechanical arts in France. Thomas Kaiser and Jeremy Popkin show the difficulties and sometimes unexpected mutations which the philosophes' political ideals experienced in the hard times of revolution. Peter Briggs shows how Locke's psychology served the needs and helped redefine the methods of satire. Jack

Fruchtman illustrates a discovery now becoming important in discussion of the late Enlightenment—the apparently strange amalgam of visionary and republican politics. Bruce Tucker shows how religion and Enlightenment could and did join forces in Puritan America. And John Sitter suggests an interesting conjunction of Humean psychology and the creation of a new "poetics of conversion." Taken together these essays suggest that there is no static formula for "eighteenth-century culture." Rather, individual ideas were formulated, joined, redefined, and changed in surprising ways by individuals and groups. If ideas exist to help people organize their world, then the world is too diverse to allow any formula to work.

Third, what I would call simply "re-readings." These essays stand at the center of the volume in part because their method stands at the center of the study of the eighteenth century, or any century for that matter. Ultimately the cultural history of an epoch must be built from the shrewd reading and re-reading of its central and influential texts. Here we have fine examples of that central task: John Fischer on Gay; Stuart Peterfreund on Blake; Michael Cartwright on Diderot; Marlis Mehra on Goethe; Hamilton Beck on Sterne and Hippel; Charles Scruggs on Phyllis Wheatley; Robert Day on Smollett; Toby Olshin on Austen; Mark Hulliung on Montesquieu; William Siebenschuh on Boswell and Johnson. What they have in common is that they offer new and sometimes surprising perspectives on central figures of the eighteenth-century story. They prove that, without resort to modish devices, the important authors still have much to offer to those who read with care and insight.

Fourth, and last, what might be called "new frontiers." The last group of essays contains perspectives on themes which have become increasingly important in our studies: medicine, family, and women. No century is ever permanently staked out. New methods and new concerns of the present open new ideas about the past. This is proof not—as some would have it—of the subjectivity of our history but of its unclosed richness. Concern about the gritty side of life, opened by new schools of social history, inform the fine essays of Ruth McClure, Louis Greenbaum, and Barbara Schnorrenberg. Lawrence Stone's new work on the family suggested previously unasked questions for Laura Curtis to bring to Defoe's domestic conduct manuals. And the new questions legitimately raised by the women's movement have opened new ideas for Ellen Pollak on Pope, Judith Lawrence-Anderson on Richardson, and Jean Kern on women novelists.

The problem with any such grouping, though, is that it might guide the reader too much and close out other ways of viewing selection. Suffice it to say that the essays can be read together in a variety of ways. The essays of Briggs and Sitter provide two case studies in the influence of the new psychology on aesthetics. Olshin's essay on Austen's view of medicine surely benefits from the background provided by McClure and Schnorrenberg. And so on. What I offer, then, is not the classic French garden of the seventeenth century with its rigid patterns but, rather, an eighteenth-century English garden of winding paths and surprising prospects. The volume shares with both gardens, I hope, the love of what is well constructed and clearly conceived.

There would be no volume at all without the help of many people. I must thank especially my editorial readers, listed at the front, who provided expertise in areas (of necessity many) where I had little. They performed their task with thoroughness, critical acumen, and wit. Ronald Rosbottom, executive director of the society, provided advice and support in a variety of ways. Roseann Runte, editor of volumes seven through nine, gave much-needed advice to a fledgling editor. Rosalie Hiam, secretary to the History Department at Colgate University, did a large variety of chores for the volume with unfailing accuracy and good humor. Debora Hoffman, a student assistant, did much of the preparatory work for the index. Above all, I want to thank the authors themselves for their constant co-operation and excellent scholarship.

HARRY C. PAYNE

Colgate University
October 1979

Studies in Eighteenth-Century Culture

VOLUME 10

Clio and the Critics

PHILLIP HARTH

At this meeting in Atlanta, we are celebrating the tenth anniversary of the founding of the American Society for Eighteenth-Century Studies. Its purpose, as we know, is to foster communication and cooperation among scholars in various disciplines engaged in the study of eighteenth-century culture. In keeping with this purpose, the principal business of the Society is, and I imagine always will be, to afford its membership of experts in various single disciplines the opportunity, through its meetings and its publications, of exchanging information with other experts in other disciplines, in this way overcoming the isolation of their own particular specialty by learning of other aspects of eighteenth-century culture which lie beyond their expertise, but not beyond their interests.

What I want to talk about this morning is a recent trend in the study of eighteenth-century English literature—my own particular specialty—which began at about the time this Society was founded and has continued over the past decade to grow along with the Society. This trend reflects an interest that not all or even most of our members may personally pursue, but that a society such as ours also exists to foster. In the last ten years there has been a phenomenal growth of studies of eighteenth-century English poetry which are not only historical but interdisciplinary, in the sense that they transcend the boundaries between the different historical disciplines to which we have grown accustomed and bring several of them to bear on the understanding of this poetry.

We can see just how remarkable this change has been if we recall what has been happening recently in the study of Alexander Pope's poetry. Before 1969, most books on Pope's poetry were not, by any stretch of the imagination, historical or interdisciplinary studies. They were, with very few exceptions, studies of Pope's poetic workmanship, his couplet art or use of allusions, and the verbal meaning of his poems. In their choice of subject, they shared a determined effort, under the influence of the New Criticism, to provide an intensive study of Pope's poetry essentially free from considerations of its time and place, or of its non-literary relations.

The Garden and the City, which appeared in 1969 with the subtitle *Retirement and Politics in the Later Poetry of Pope*, heralded an abrupt change in the direction of Pope studies. It was followed in rapid succession by a series of books bearing such titles as *Pope and the Context of Controversy*, *The Social Milieu of Alexander Pope*, *Alexander Pope and the Arts of Georgian England*, *Pope's Once and Future Kings: Satire and Politics in the Early Career*, and showing signs that what had begun as a movement has ended as a stampede.

I have cited books on Pope's poetry as a striking example of this changed direction in studies of eighteenth-century English poetry, but other examples would serve just as well: in Dryden studies, for instance, the turning point occurred a year earlier than in Pope studies, and we can perceive the same contrast between earlier books on Dryden's imagery or technique and later books on his poetry with such titles as *Contexts of Dryden's Thought*, *Politics and Poetry in Restoration England*, and *Dryden: The Public Writer*.

I am not suggesting, of course, that the founding of this Society in 1969 was responsible for this abrupt change in the direction of studies of eighteenth-century English poetry, but it seems clear that the nearly simultaneous occurrence of these two events reflects an important growth of interest in historical and interdisciplinary study.

The reasons for this change are probably complex, but two of them stand out. In the first place, the kind of study associated with the New Criticism, rigorously limited to such information about language and technique as could be extracted from an exclusive examination of poetic texts, was reaching a state of exhaustion by the end of the sixties. By that time, for example, over two dozen articles had appeared offering New Critical explications of *The Rape of the Lock*, and there are natural limits to the number of times the same operation can be performed on a poem without causing fatal post-surgical complications. A second reason was a growing dissatisfaction with the artificial limits imposed on literary study by the New Criticism, a dissatisfaction that was fed by natural curiosity about other aspects of eighteenth-century poetry besides those revealed by an exclusive attention to the text. This is a subject to which I shall want to return.

A cynic might mention a third reason as the most compelling cause of all shifts in direction taken by literary studies: the fact that critical fashions change. Our cynic would assert that most practical criticism is written under the impetus of a prevailing critical theory, that these theories have their vogue like anything else, and that as soon as one theory has finally waned and been replaced by another, a new kind of practical criticism inevitably follows in the wake of the latest theory. Our critic would be right about the past but wrong about the present. The nearly exclusive concern before 1969 with the language and technique of eighteenth-century poetry unquestionably reflected the enormous popularity of New Critical theories about the proper subject of criticism. But the present interest in historical and interdisciplinary studies of eighteenth-century poetry is certainly not following recent fashions in literary theory. This is a time when theory and practice have parted company.

There are two ways of describing the new directions in literary theory we have witnessed during the last decade. The more comprehensive way, which usually starts with a lament about the plight of criticism today, describes a situation in which a harmonious school of theorists and practical critics owing their undivided allegiance to the New Criticism lies in ruins, while alongside it has risen a Tower of Babel from which issue the competing claims of Structuralism, poststructuralism, mythography, hermeneutics, phenomenology, and speech-act theory. A more straightforward way of describing the change of fashions in literary theory takes account only of the prevailing winds in the critical climate and notes that the New Criticism has had its season and that Structuralism has now arrived, borne on a fair wind from France.

Recent historical and interdisciplinary studies of eighteenth-century poetry ignore both new fashions and old in literary theory, as do many studies in other literary fields as well today. This indifference to literary theory is causing concern to a number of observers who have pointed to the growing rift between literary theory and practical criticism as a phenomenon of the seventies. On one side of the gulf, many critics, under the influence of Structuralism, define their goal as literary theory rather than the interpretation of particular works and advocate a metacriticism which takes criticism itself rather than literature as its subject. But as Wolfgang Iser recently observed, theory "must have its foundations in actual texts, for all too often literary critics tend to produce their theories on the basis of an esthetics that is predominantly abstract, derived from and conditioned by philosophy rather than by literature—with the regrettable result that they reduce texts to the proportions of their theories, instead of adapting their theories to fit in with the texts."[1] And on the other side, practical critics get on with their job in a world which has no time for theory, and even an active distaste for it. The editor of *Contemporary Literature* introduced a recent collection of essays seeking *Directions for Criticism* by remarking, "It is the very appearance on the American scene of French criticism, with its passion for technology and philosophic abstraction, that has, if anything, increased the horror of all theory among practical critics."[2] What is remarkable about recent historical and interdisciplinary studies of eighteenth-century poetry, however, is that they manage for the most part not only to ignore fashions old and new in literary theory, but to act in tacit defiance of those theories. For if there is one common bond between the New Criticism and Structuralism—it may be the only one—it is their shared anti-historical bias.

When intrinsic criticism made its appearance on the American university scene in the mid-thirties, it first attracted attention by the assault its advocates mounted against the historical study of literature. By its very nature, this campaign took the form of an attack on a very unbalanced kind of interdisciplinary study in which the investigation of literature in English departments was all too often subordinated to some other discipline, being treated as simply one more set of documents yielding evidence concerning social or religious or political or intellectual history. The reformers had no animus against history, as long as it was confined to history departments. What they objected to was the fact that English departments were neglecting their proper business of treating poems in their character as works of art. "It is not criticism but history or sociology," R. S. Crane protested, "when we read imaginative writings for what they may tell us about the manners or thought or 'spirit' of the age which produced them," while John Crowe Ransom declared in disgust that "English might almost as well announce that it does not regard itself as entirely autonomous, but as a branch of the department of history."[3] The remedy they adopted, not surprisingly, was to erect newer and sturdier boundaries between the academic disciplines and to make English studies independent of the others.

This crusade against the historical and interdisciplinary study of literature created for a while an uneasy alliance between the two principal branches of intrinsic criticism in this country, the Chicago Critics and the New Critics. But the fruits of victory, which were re-

markably fast in coming, brought, as they often do, an early end to
the alliance, and each group went its own way, developing a mutual
antagonism in the process. Crane, the founder of the Chicago Critics,
became increasingly concerned at the sharp antithesis which had
been created between history and criticism, and turned his attention
in the 1960s to the possibilities of creating a new and more balanced
synthesis of the two which he called "historical criticism." The New
Critics, on the other hand, went on to develop a theory of literature
which conferred unprecedented autonomy on the poetic work: isolated from the subject matter of other disciplines by the unique character of its language, and from the historical moment in which it
originated by its ontological status as a hypostatized object floating
in a timeless world. The New Criticism never, in fact, lost sight of its
polemical origins in a protest movement against the historical and
interdisciplinary study of literature. This accounts for the negative
character of so much New Critical theory, which not only discouraged but positively prohibited an entire range of interests and activities that might have brought criticism into some kind of new relationship with history. Indeed, by creating a whole new vocabulary of
heresies and fallacies, the one set regulating beliefs, the other practices, the New Critics sometimes suggested that they looked on
themselves as guardians of an orthodox faith who must maintain a
vigilant watch against those who were not only whoring after strange
gods, but trying to worship them with polluted sacrifices.

Structuralism made its first real impact in France in the early and
mid-sixties as part of a temporary alliance of diverse groups of critics—the *Nouvelle Critique*—who were in revolt against the historical
study of literature which dominated the French university scene.
These various critical schools were far more disparate than the different groups of intrinsic critics in America ever were, and they really
had little in common beyond their united determination to root out
the kind of erudition which passed for literary criticism in the French
universities. To anyone familiar with the struggle between criticism
and history in America in the mid-thirties, the polemics of a Roland
Barthes acting as a spokesman for the *Nouvelle Critique* in the mid-
sixties carry a distinct note of *déjà vu*. There was the same complaint
that the academic study of literature was being carried out by biographers and source-hunters who were interested only in the discovery and accumulation of historical facts (the word for this was now
"positivism"), the same charge that such studies inevitably treated
literature in relation to something extrinsic to itself (the word for this
was now "analogy"), the same call for an intrinsic study of literature

which would take account of its own proper character (the word for this was now "immanence").[4] And if Lowes had served as a scapegoat for the New Criticism a generation earlier, Lanson now played the same unhappy role for the *Nouvelle Critique*. No wonder that to some American observers of the French scene at that time, *Nouvelle Critique* was but old New Criticism writ large.

It was nothing of the sort, of course, and when Structuralism, freed from its tactical alliance as part of the *Nouvelle Critique*, reached these shores later in the sixties, there was no need—nor even an opportunity—to use it to flog a dead horse which in this country had long since been decently buried. Instead, it was welcomed as a replacement for an exhausted New Criticism, and it was its differences from its predecessor rather than its similarities that accounted for its immediate popularity. Structuralism, which derives its methodological patterns from other disciplines such as linguistics and anthropology, and which treats the poetic text synchronically as part of the common domain of discourse, or *écriture*, has challenged the lateral autonomy of literature insisted upon by the New Critics. And, by setting itself different objectives from those of the New Criticism—the conditions of meaning rather than meaning itself, an understanding of the operation of structural patterns and semiotic conventions rather than an exclusive attention to the interpretation of individual works— Structuralism is striking out in new directions. But at the same time, Structuralism posits an ontological discontinuity which offers a far more serious challenge to the historical study of literature than was ever posed by the New Criticism. The New Critics banished history from the discipline of criticism for programmatic reasons; they still believed in the possibility of historical study and conceded its right to exist as long as it kept to its own disciplinary boundaries. But Structuralism turns its back on an irretrievable past and demands a total immersion in the present.

Jonathan Culler has recently declared that "if there is a crisis in literary criticism it is no doubt because few of the many who write about literature have the desire or arguments to defend their activity."[5] There is some justice to this frequent Structuralist gibe at most forms of practical criticism in America today. It is also true, as another Structuralist, Tzvetan Todorov, has pointed out, that "no literary scholar can avoid adhering to some theory of literature. . . . One can only choose between being conscious of his theory or not; and there are many more chances of making the theory better if you are aware of it."[6] But debate is only profitable between antagonists who at least share some of the same premises. The situation dividing most practical critics today from the Structuralists and post-structuralists is that the former cannot find a common ground across which they can carry on a dialogue with those who espouse a radically skeptical epistemology. And that may be the real crisis in literary criticism today.

For this reason, we cannot carry on a fruitful debate over the legitimacy and importance of historical and interdisciplinary criticism with those who deny history, distract attention from individual literary works, and discourage practical criticism, but only with those groups—unreconstructed New Critics, archetypal critics who as early as the fifties emerged in competition to the New Criticism, American disciples of the Geneva School—who share a common interest in traditional literary studies but remain suspicious of new historical directions which flout long-cherished beliefs.

The recent popularity of historical and interdisciplinary studies of eighteenth-century English poetry is sometimes described, by observers who should know better, as a "return to history" or a "revival of historical study," as if it were a regressive trend dictated by some kind of mindless nostalgia for the twenties. It is nothing of the kind. There is genuine progress in the learned disciplines, however slow. The academic reforms carried out by the New Critics as well as the Chicago Critics have left a permanent legacy in the establishment of literary study as a discipline in its own right which considers literary works in their proper character as works of art. If the barriers between the disciplines are now being lowered once more, it is because the study of literature, having won its independence, is no longer in danger of being submerged by history. Those who today object to or seek to limit the scope of historical and interdisciplinary studies of literature are not still fighting the battles of the thirties against a departed generation. They recognize that these recent studies claim to be enhancing our understanding of literature, not subordinating it to some other discipline, but they believe that such claims are misguided or, at best, exaggerated, and they have given their doubts repeated expression. If the distance between literary theory and practical criticism is ever to be shortened, these objections cannot simply be ignored while we pursue our own concerns in a happy state of indifference. They need to be honestly met and successfully answered if we want to establish the validity and importance of the historical and interdisciplinary study of eighteenth-century English poetry, not as an exclusive pursuit which denies the legitimacy of textual explication, or the pursuit of archetypes, or the exploration of authorial consciousness, but as an alternative line of inquiry which can make a significant contribution to our understanding of eighteenth-century literature of a kind outside the province of these other critical pursuits.

The first of these reservations about the historical study of literature admits it by the back door, but confines it permanently to the backstairs. One of the most thoughtful and articulate spokesmen for the New Criticism today, René Wellek, has repeatedly defended it in recent years from the charge that it "denies that a work of art can be illuminated by historical knowledge at all," and he has invariably gone on to specify the single respect in which the New Critics do in fact accept and even welcome "the relevance of historical information for the business of poetic interpretation. Words have their history; genres and devices descend from a tradition; poems often refer to contemporary realities."[7] In other words, on the assumption that literary study is concerned only with "the business of poetic interpretation," Professor Wellek restricts the use of history to such textual considerations as the historical meanings of words, the development of literary conventions, and the identification of allusions. This is the blind alley into which an exclusive concern with poetry as a tissue of verbal meanings has led literary study. It is an inevitable corollary of the New Critical doctrine of the autonomy of the literary work, as emerges when Professor Wellek goes on to explain that "literary study differs from historical study in having to deal not with documents but with monuments. A historian has to reconstruct a long-past event on the basis of eye-witness accounts, the literary student, on the other hand, has direct access to his object: the work of art." We can readily concede that the physical existence of a literary text— its "monumentality"—gives an initial advantage to the literary student over the historian who is trying to reconstruct an event. But a monument is simply the tangible outcome of an event whose causes and contemporary significance still await reconstruction. A cathedral, a statue, a painting are also monuments, but an art historian would rightly protest at being denied the use of documents on the grounds that all the pertinent information stood before him.

If the first objection conceives of historical study too narrowly, the second envisions it so broadly that it is dismissed as lying beyond our reach. To deal with this objection we can turn to a quite different quarter. J. Hillis Miller, writing in 1966 at a time when he was a supporter of Georges Poulet, Jean Starobinski, and the other members of the Geneva School, advocated their sensible view that "the essential context of any passage is everything else its author wrote. The meaning of a text can be defined only in terms of the system of relations which ties it to the patterns of an *oeuvre*."[8] This is a promising starting point for literary study, but for Professor Miller it is a final goal which represents a golden mean between two equally undesirable extremes. On one side, he would agree that the New Critic, by limiting himself to the text of the poem, does not go far enough. "The more completely he cuts the poem off from its mesh of defining circumstances," he writes, "the less he can allow himself to say about it. The poem means only itself, and any commentary falsifies it by turning it into something other than itself." Yet on the other side, to seek help "from books read by the author, or from the social and historical milieu in which it came into existence, or from the tradition to which it belongs" is to court an opposite danger. "Where," he asks, "does the context of a poem stop? Its relations to its surroundings radiate outward like concentric circles from a stone dropped in water. These circles multiply indefinitely until the scholar must give up in despair the attempt to make a complete inventory of them." What Professor Miller is describing is not a context, but a Serbonian Bog. Many a study of the "background" or "milieu" or "world picture" of a literary work has foundered in just such a wilderness of remote, tangential relations. Because a wilderness is by its very nature unmanageable, those who have wandered in such regions have tried to impose some order on them by seeking some homogeneous principle or characteristic of the age which is supposed to be present in all its varied manifestations (we may call this essentialism), and which is supposed to dictate the purpose and meaning of any individual work of that period (we may call this determinism). But we have long since abandoned these fruitless attempts to "make a complete inventory" of all the contiguous circumstances which may have some remote bearing on a literary work. Certainly they are not to be found in the studies of Pope, and Dryden, and other eighteenth-century poets which have been characteristic of the last decade or so. The principle of relevance governing these investigations has been suggested in each case by the character of the particular poem in question. Instead of trying "to make a complete inventory" of all those tangential relations in which any poem stands to its historical milieu, these studies have pursued only those specific historical circumstances in which the poem originated, to which it is an immediate response, and which serve to explain the poet's choice of materials, the principles of construction by which he made them into an artistic whole, and the purpose for which he created his poem. In the case of Dryden's *Annus Mirabilis* or some of Pope's poems of the 1730's these historical circumstances have been political, in the case of *Religio Laici* or *The Hind and the Panther* religious, in the case of *An Essay on Man* philosophical, and in the case of some of Pope's other poems landscape gardening and related movements in the sister arts. It is this limitation in these studies to immediately relevant historical circumstances which accounts for the recent popularity of the term "context"— when it is not simply used as a fashionable shibboleth.

This current concern with genetic and teleological considerations is of course anathema to all those—New Critics, archetypal critics, and Structuralists alike—who, on different grounds, share an anti-intentional bias. In 1968 W. K. Wimsatt, who, if he denied the uses of history to the critic, was also a literary historian whose memory is honored by all of us who are interested in the eighteenth century, returned, a quarter of a century after the event, to the assault he and Monroe C. Beardsley had launched against "The Intentional Fallacy," re-entering the debate, as he said, to take notice of those "focuses of recent literary criticism" in which this fallacy had once again appeared. Examining the issue retrospectively from the vantage of the late sixties, Wimsatt was able to add two newer groups of intentionalists to the biographers and source-hunters who had been the original target in the early forties. He now included, with perfect consistency, those critics who, "wishing to throb in unison with the mind of the artist," seek out "his other poems, his essays, letters, and diaries, his thoughts and feelings"—alluding of course to Professor Miller and the other disciples of the Geneva School—as well as those critics who wish to know "as much as possible about his historic context."[9] In the face of these new movements, Wimsatt saw no reason to modify his original position, which he now reiterated in an updated version: "The design or intention of the author is neither available nor desirable as a standard for judging either the meaning or the value of a work of literary art." We might as well begin with the notion that the design or intention of the author is not available, since the issue of whether it is desirable must remain an academic question in more than one sense if it is in fact unavailable. "The search for the author's generative intention as context of the poem," Wimsatt went on to explain, "is a search for a temporal moment which must, as the author and the poem live on, recede and ever recede into the forgotten, as all moments do. Poems, on this theory of their meaning, must always steadily grow less and less correctly known and knowable; they must dwindle in meaning and being toward a vanishing point."

But that is precisely the reason why the historical study of poetry is so necessary. It is these temporal moments, shared by the poet's contemporaries but ever receding, which the pursuit of a historical context tries, as much as possible, to recover for a later generation of readers. The counsel of despair which holds that "the search for the author's generative intention" is a fool's errand is not unique to certain modern theories of literature. It is familiar to historians in many other disciplines who have encountered the same resistance to such investigations as applied to any form of art. To doubts whether we can ever recover these receding temporal moments, Sir Ernst Gombrich has given the only possible reply: "The answer of common-sense is surely that we can understand some better, some worse, and some only after a lot of work. That we can improve our understanding by trying to restore the context, cultural, artistic, and psychological, in which any given work sprang to life, but that we must resign ourselves to a certain residue of ignorance." It is only by such efforts, he concludes, that we can gain the "enrichment that comes from an understanding, however dim and imperfect, of what a great work of art is *intended* to convey. . . . What matters is only that we should not surrender our sanity by losing our faith in the very possibility of finding out what a fellow human being means or meant."[10]

The latter part of Professor Gombrich's remarks, in which, having affirmed his belief in the possibility of discovering the artist's intention, he goes on to speak of the enrichment it will bring to our understanding of the work of art, brings us to the second of the anti-intentionalist reservations I have mentioned: their denial that it is even desirable to seek the design or intention of the author by trying to restore the historic context of the work. This too is a direct corollary of the theory that a poem is "a separately existent and in some sense autonomous or autotelic entity," to quote one of the more carefully worded formulas in which this theory is expressed.[11] In other words, the design or intention of the author always terminates in the production of the poem itself, and is not to be sought outside the poem. For the sake of variety, let us examine this hardy perennial in the words of one of the leaders of another school of criticism, Northrop Frye. Writing in 1957, Professor Frye anchored his archetypal criticism firmly and explicitly to anti-intentionalism. He justified his position by declaring that "a poet's primary concern is to produce a work of art, and hence his intention can only be expressed by some kind of tautology. In other words," he continues, "a poet's intention is centripetally directed. It is directed towards putting words together, not towards aligning words with meanings. . . . What the poet meant to say, then, is, literally, the poem itself."[12]

The answer of common sense to such a theory is that, if it were to be recast as a descriptive statement about the intention of some poets in some poems it would pass well enough, but that as a universal proposition—the form in which it is invariably presented—it flatly contradicts our experience as readers widely familiar with eighteenth-century English poetry. The proper response to this kind of non-empirical dogmatizing is not to adopt the slipshod mental habits of so many modern literary theorists who formulate holistic definitions of poetry which defy common experience as well as common sense. No doubt, some poems are autotelic, including a fair share of eighteenth-century poems, and any attempt to recover the context of these poems would only yield the kind of incidental information Wimsatt and Beardsley once described as "how or why the poet wrote the poem—to what lady, while sitting on what lawn, or at the death of what friend or brother."[13] But we also know—and as students of the eighteenth century we are in a particularly favorable position to know this—that many other poems, including a good share of the most important poems of our period, are nothing of the kind. These satires, occasional poems, poetic essays, and polemical poems are not autotelic but heterotelic, since they were not only occasioned by external circumstances, but written with the purpose of influencing their audience's attitudes toward these conditions. This audience, which shares the same moment in history as the author, has shared his banishment from the free-floating world of the poem created by modern critical theorists, for once the autonomous poem is made free of its origins, it is also made independent of its destination.[14] But to view public poems in their proper character we must restore them to a social dimension in which the audience to whom they are directed and whom they seek to influence is an essential consideration, without which we cannot understand them as works of art differing from natural objects precisely because they reveal the presence of human design. It is ironic that anti-intentionalism, introduced into modern criticism as a means of insuring that poems would be considered in their character as works of art, has succeeded instead in obliterating the specifically artistic character of public poetry.

A public poem, isolated from the circumstances which occasioned it, the artistic intention which produced it, and the audience to whom it was directed, is a monument stripped of its recognizable features as a product of human activity. The very metaphors for a poem made popular by modern criticism to enforce the theory that literary study deals with monuments—the verbal icon, the well-wrought urn—ought to remind us that a poem, viewed in this light exclusively, is what Keats called another such monumental urn: a Cold Pastoral. Historical and interdisciplinary studies can show us some of these poems in another light, as the acts of real poets in a real world, addressing real men and women. With their help, the study of literature can become once again what it may otherwise forget to be: a truly humanistic discipline.

NOTES

1 This essay was the presidential address delivered in Atlanta, April 19, 1979. *The Implied Reader* (Baltimore: The Johns Hopkins University Press, 1974), pp. xi–xii.
2 L. S. Dembo, "Prefatory Note," Murray Krieger and L. S. Dembo, eds., *Directions for Criticism: Structuralism and Its Alternatives* (Madison: University of Wisconsin Press, 1977), p. viii.
3 Crane, "History versus Criticism" [1935], *The Idea of the Humanities and Other Essays Critical and Historical* (Chicago: University of Chicago Press, 1967), II,3–24; Ransom, "Criticism, Inc." [1937], *The World's Body* (New York: Charles Scribner's Sons, 1938), pp. 327–50.
4 "Les Deux Critiques," *Modern Language Notes*, 78 (1963), 447–52.
5 *Structuralist Poetics: Structuralism, Linguistics, and the Study of Literature* (Ithaca, N.Y.: Cornell University Press, 1975), p. vii.
6 "Structuralism and Literature," Seymour Chatman, ed. *Approaches to Poetics* (New York: Columbia University Press, 1973), p. 156.
7 "Literary Theory, Criticism, and History" [1960], *Concepts of Criticism* (New Haven: Yale University Press, 1963), pp. 1–20.
8 "The Antitheses of Criticism: Reflections on the Yale Colloquium," *Modern Language Notes*, 81 (1966), 557–71.
9 "Genesis: A Fallacy Revisited," Peter Demetz, Thomas Greene, and Lowry Nelson, Jr., eds., *The Disciplines of Criticism: Essays in Literary Theory, Interpretation, and History* (New Haven: Yale University Press, 1968), pp. 193–225.
10 "André Malraux and the Crisis of Expressionism" [1954], *Meditations on a Hobby Horse and Other Essays on the Theory of Art* (London: Phaidon, 1963), pp. 78–85.
11 W. K. Wimsatt, "Battering the Object: The Ontological Approach," Malcolm Bradbury and David Palmer, eds., *Contemporary Criticism* (London: Edward Arnold, 1970), p. 62.
12 *Anatomy of Criticism* [1957] (New York: Atheneum, 1970), pp. 86–87.
13 "The Intentional Fallacy" [1946], W. K. Wimsatt, *The Verbal Icon: Studies in the Meaning of Poetry* (Lexington: University of Kentucky Press, 1954), pp. 2–18.
14 For a typical expression of this view, see Reuben A. Brower, *The Fields of Light: An Experiment in Critical Reading* [1951] (New York: Oxford University Press, 1962), p. 19: "The 'person spoken to' is also a fictional personage and never the actual audience of 'you and me,' and only in a special abstract sense is it the literary audience of a particular time and place in history."

Toward Romantic Landscape Perception: Illustrated Travels and the Rise of "Singularity" as an Aesthetic Category

BARBARA MARIA STAFFORD

"*C'est, je crois, chez ces voyageurs qu'une anthologie consacrée au sentiment de la nature au XVIIIe récolterait la plus riche moisson.*"[1]

During the second half of the eighteenth century, the travel book came to reproduce landscape in which the strong sense for the individuality and substance of natural phenomena rendered human figures insignificant.[2] This study will trace the complex development that led to the visual apprehension of natural objects as lone and strikingly distinct. The dominant natural configuration, demanding immediate respectful attention, became a potent feature of scientific travel literature and created an aesthetic category of its own: that of singularity. The distinctive taste for the singular, for the odd outcropping, the characteristic section of terrain, may be seen to emerge from a number of eighteenth-century concerns: the art-versus-nature controversy, the fascination with *lusus naturae*, the delight in minerals, metals and crystals, the desire to plumb the genesis of forms, the aesthetic influence of geology and the recrudescence of animism as a vital force in Enlightenment philosophy.

Throughout the eighteenth century the travel book was one of the primary and most international literary genres, and it was so appealing that almost every writer of consequence worked in that mode.[3]

From the *Art Quarterly*, n.s., vol. I, no. 1. Reprinted by permission.

17

Concomitantly, by the mid-eighteenth century, we find that in descriptive poetry the subject-matter is frequently a particular aspect of nature or a specific geographical region.[4] It can be demonstrated that not only such literary forms, but artistic expression as well, were influenced by the real travel report with its emphasis on meticulously describing what one sees. The bent for topography and for experience in general relates to the Lockeian idea of knowledge: the sequential accumulation of particulars collected from multifarious but verifiable objective reality. Readers of non-fiction voyage literature were dependent on it not only for facts about a world growing larger and very interesting but also for entertainment, since it provided both adventure and a sense of the marvelous.[5]

Many of the voyages of the second half of the century were scientific in nature—those by Byron, Wallis, Carteret and Cook, for instance. The official published journals and their accompanying atlases demonstrated that science and sentiment did not necessarily follow divergent paths.[6] The magnificent illustrations for geological, mineralogical and biological treatises had already indicated earlier in the century that science and art could be associated to a degree unparalleled since the Renaissance.

"Cette fascination de l'esprit opérée par les objets matériels"

One can chart the evolution taking place within the descriptive and visual language used to depict nature by focussing on the exchange of identity and function that occurs between natural object and artifact. At the beginning of the century Addison inaugurates the habit of viewing the natural object as artifact: " . . . yet we find the works of nature still more pleasant the more they resemble those of art . . ."[7] Conversely, artificial works receive a greater advantage from their resemblance to such as are natural. This mode of describing landmarks as if made by the sculptor or the architect can be found in travel accounts. Le Gentil discusses the horizontal strata of a rocky plain on the Ile de France in the following manner: " . . . mais elles sont si bien faites; que l'on diroit que les pierres auroient été moulées les unes sur les autres, & posées par l'art à côté l'une de l'autre . . ."[8] Or again: the mountains of the island "qui offrent un plateau sur leur sommet sont toutes massives comme si elles étoient pavées en dalles de pierre, qui prouve encore une sorte d'arrangement . . ."[9]

As we have remarked, Addison discovered, in the manner of the

Far Eastern masters, that, by a singular reversal, nature is full of works of art and art is full of natural curiosities.[10] By an extension of this thought, Piranesi was wont to metamorphose immense antique ruins into natural monuments: the Colosseum, seen from a bird's eye view, looks like the gaping crater of some extinct volcano, and a Roman cryptoporticus resembles an *arco naturale*.[11] Later, Goethe describes Strassburg Minster as an organic work of nature[12]; more generally, he sees art in terms of quasi-natural images and the making of art as an analogy for natural creation.[13] By the second half of the eighteenth century, nature no longer displays Addison's "negligent order" that seems the result of chance, but embodies a valid order of its own.

In fact, the natural object becomes the true work of art. The aesthetic object is hoisted by its own petard, that is, by the *topos* that it resembles nothing so much as a living being, a concept developed by many writers in the eighteenth century but, particularly, by Diderot. In the *Rêve de d'Alembert*, Diderot draws the distinction between a statue by Falconet and a man, an animal and a plant. The former possesses an inert sensibility, the latter two an active sensibility. Diderot imagines that the two can be breached through assimilation. In his imagination he pulverizes Falconet's sculpture, transforms it into humus and grows vegetables with it! Plants are nourished by the earth, and Diderot is nourished by the plants. As might be expected, d'Alembert is enchanted by this witty fable: "J'aime ce passage du marbre à l'humus, de l'humus au règne végétal, et du règne végétal au règne animal, à la chair."[14] Diderot has shown—in this parody of the Great Chain of Being—that what is really alive is nature, and that the latter is ultimately superior to insensate art because it endures, whereas the block of marble is proceeding to its dissolution.

In the same spirit Robinet, Diderot's contemporary, heaps scorn on art and contrasts it unfavorably with nature:

> L'art taille les matériaux qu'il veut employer: il les arrange les uns à côté des autres, ou les uns sur les autres, il les engraine, il les soude, il les cimente. *L'homme a trouvé les loix de la méchanique, mais d'une méchanique artificielle & toute extérieure . . . mais toutes ses machines sont inorganiques,* & les vastes édifices où il est comme perdu, sont *des masses sans vie,* sans jeu, sans action. *Au contraire, tout vit dans la Nature,* tous les Êtres qu'elle produit sont essentiellement organiques . . .[15] (my italics)

In short, works of art do not grow, they are formed piece by separate piece; consequently, they are dead and lack the energy of nature's constituent parts (Fig. 1). This paean is far removed from Akenside's disparagement of "the forms which brute, unconscious matter wears. . ."[16]

Science is also responsible for the reversal which saw objects that had usually been considered triumphs of art and artifice humbled when compared to nature's works. The microscope located difformity and imperfection in man's work, contrasting it with the fineness and subtlety of nature's.[17] The influential biologist Charles Bonnet speaks of plants and animals as machines quite superior in structure to those of art. In fact, salts and other crystals are no less perfectly organized than an obelisk or portico.[18] Works of art, then, are only imitations of those of nature, hence their fascination is soon exhausted.[19] To survive, art follows the cue: it no longer *seems like* but literally *is* nature. So late rocaille ornament grows out of the earth and becomes a natural monolith;[20] cabinet makers admire the images of hermits, lions, crocodiles and birds that exist, pre-formed, in the veneers they use to ornament desks and commodes.[21]

The eighteenth century raised the question more rigorously than any epoch before as to whether a work of art's being man-made is a necessary condition of its being a work of art; and it is in this period that the natural object acquires the status of being an artifact without the exercise of craftsmanship. We will see that being an artifact is largely a matter of its history, that is, of how it came to have certain of its properties.[22]

"Or shall we rather say, that the great power which contrived and made all things . . . artfully throws the flexible liquid materials of the fossil kingdoms into various figures, to draw the attention of mankind to his works."

Since antiquity man has been interested in images whose formation is due to a natural mechanism. Pliny tells us that the world is not smooth and polished like an egg but carries engraved within it the innumerable shapes of all things.[23] In the eighteenth century the taste for such *mirabilia* was largely replaced by a pan-European fascination with the hieroglyphic or cipher writing of nature.[24] Legible figures were perceived everywhere; specific forms could be discerned in stones, in ice, in crystal.[25]

For Addison, the "accidental landskips" or the *lusus naturae* found in trees and rocks were neither absurdly complete, as they appeared to Alberti, nor simply an illustration of *fortuna*'s strange powers, as they seemed to Pliny.[26] Neither *scherzo* nor freak, the sport of nature is a profound source for the pleasures of the imagination, since it yields the impression that the universe is no mere fortuitous concourse of atoms and, again, proves that the spontaneous hand of nature can produce something equivalent to artifacts "without any help from art."[27]

Addison's delight was typical, and it was further fed by mineralogists. The case of the popular *lapides literati* and of graphic granite offers an entrée into the prevalent eighteenth-century conception that nature literally writes about its own history—a notion quite unlike that held by Alberti or Leonardo, who believed that chance images were not objectively present but must be read into the material by the artist's imagination. Graphic granite could be found in a few areas as far-flung as Corsica, Siberia and Egypt[28] (Fig. 2); it was thought to record a mineralogical language which revealed the internal grammar of nature. The name was given to a rare variety of stone which, when cut, revealed a singular arrangement of quartz crystals whose configuration resembled Hebrew or Arabic letters. The Scottish geologist Hutton even compared them to runic writing. For the scientific traveller, the patterns of the cracks and their distinctive shapes serve to pinpoint the precise moment of their formation within the tumultuous history of granite's development.[29]

Pietra fiorentina was similarly thought to preserve the history of the world, buried as it was in the earth after the Flood.[30] After praising the wonderful crumbling ruins of towers and ramparts or the stretches of forest visible in Florentine stones, the Abbé La Pluche concludes that "les pierres & les métaux nous ont réellement conservé l'histoire du monde."[31]

But above all, fossils, *petrefacta* or figured stones came to be viewed as the ultimate corroboration, as authentic monuments of a history written by the "plastick power of nature."[32] In 1718, Jussieu found sedimentary rocks with exotic plants impressed on their surface and read therein not climatic change but cataclysm. Somewhat later, Fontenelle became convinced—after studying the figurated stones popularly called "Ammon's Horns"—that the Indian Ocean once covered Europe. Leibniz also took them seriously, denying that they were freaks of nature. The belief that they were due to the Noachian Flood was firmly established, lasting until the end of the eighteenth century,[33] and fossils came to be viewed as relics of particular significance, specimens left by a world without man.

"Les rêveries de la terre"

The traveller's delight in rupestral sites—conspicuous by their "otherness," remoteness from all human interests—is typified by the amateur and professional mineralogist's exploration of subterranean caverns.[34] In the second half of the eighteenth century the mine takes on a new artistic life in travel accounts, which emphasize not the deeds of men but those of timeless nature. This idea was presaged by the Jesuit from Fulda, Athanasius Kircher, whose *Mundus subterraneus* (1664, 1665) presented a picture of the motionless earth that generated objects: when mountains rose, the cavities left behind were filled with earth containing seminal principles. Such fetid, dark, underground places provided the natural setting for the unfolding of a chthonic, satyric drama: that of the regrowth of minerals.[35]

Both voyager and artist were attracted to this hidden netherworld by its telluric energies.[36] When the Swiss speleologist Carl Lang embarked on an expedition to explore all the famous mines and caverns of his day it was not to chronicle the horrors of the miner's lot. Instead, he descends into

> Hallen und Kammern, die der Ruhe geweiht sind, worin die Peitsche des Sklaven-Aussehers nicht tönt, wo die Natur in stillen Majestät gebaut hat, und wo der Mensch nichts findet, als Stoff zum tiefsten Nachdenken . . .[37]

In the Petersberg, in Maastricht, our traveller gazes at an endless labyrinth of singular ("seltsam") rock masses illuminated by torchlight. As he ponders these wonders he does not see the toiling miners but is aware instead of being enclosed by a vast tomb burying an infinite succession of organisms.

Like Pope, who earlier wanted to place all the minerals of his grotto at Twickenham in their several natural strata much as in a mine or an actual quarry,[38] Lang and other travellers saw the cavern as representing a shrine to great nature. In the eighteenth century the Renaissance view of the grotto as possessing something static, outside of time, which removes man from the midst of appearances and inserts him into the more authentic core of reality,[39] coexists with a more dynamic geological awareness of the process of mineral formation.[40]

Crystals offer the perfect paradigm of petrified form, which, at the same time, strives to bring forth beauty. These animistic implications were not lost on the traveller. In 1744, Peter Martel reports from the

Ice Alps in Savoy that "crystal is a stone which, in my opinion, is produced by a gentle vegetation, and not by congelation . . ."[41] Robinet's hypothesis of its nature envisages a "lapidary sap" that insinuates itself into the pores of plants and shells, congealing the solid parts into stony substance.[42] The new crystallography of Romé de l'Isle (1783) succeeded in classifying minerals according to their basic shapes, geometrically and mathematically discovering their hidden structure (Fig. 3). One of the more popular aspects of his study was the discussion of the crystalline molecules that compose a variety of stalactites. Among his principles is the axiom that the more a crystal approaches its primitive form the less multiplied are its facets and the more planar and rectilinear are they; whereas the more a crystal distances itself from its elementary form the more it approaches the curved line.[43] Hence the taste for stalactites—composed of more or less formless aggregates—which resemble "grapes," "mushrooms" or "cauliflowers," that is, singular petrifactions revealing nature's prodigality of highly evolved forms.

It is significant that, in the eyes of a Neoclassicist such as Kant, crystals in general and stalactites in particular represent only a partial attainment of formal beauty.[44] On the contrary, it is precisely the fact that they are never schematic models of rigid perfection but remain captivatingly individual material specimens which delights the Pre-Romantics.

In 1749, Maillet revived the cosmogony of Thales, claiming that everything rose from the sea. Consequently not only the "chamber'd earth" but "sea-caves" were perceived to house wonders from the mineral kingdom. One aspect of this extension of interest was the geological controversy of the 1770s,[45] which led to far-reaching aesthetic repercussions when it was demonstrated that prismatic basalt was the result of submarine eruptions (Fig. 4). In addition, the Abbé La Pluche spoke for current biological thinking when he speculated that many marine plants were, in fact, only petrifactions composed of alternating layers of salt and tartar. Even coral was thought to resemble the stalactites attached to the ceilings of certain caves, and, typically, it was the traveller who first drew attention to its beauty. Le Gentil says:

> . . . Rien n'est en effet plus agréable que ces parties de plaisir lorsque la mer est tranquille, & que le temps est beau; on voyage au milieu d'une forêt de coraux de toutes sortes de couleurs, dont la tige est toute hors de l'eau; il y a des temps ou vous voyez les polipiers sortir de leurs demeures sous la forme de panaches ou de lon-

gues aigrettes; on rencontre les plus beaux poissons par la variété de leurs couleurs, des champignons de mer, etc. Le fond est en outre tapissé d'oursins de différentes espèces . . .[46]

Flinders examined the evolution of coral reefs in Australia and described their progress towards petrifaction when, upon the death of these "animalcules," they leave behind "this monument of their wonderful labours . . ."[47]

From the extraordinary and curious Mexican filtering stone which "grows" naturally,[48] to shells,[49] metals, minerals, and crystals: all such phenomena were perceived as hybrids, mixed beings undergoing wonderful transformations, illustrative of the epochal changes of matter.

"Chaos is come again"

There is an aspect of nature in eighteenth-century art which owes considerably to science, namely the derivation of forms from natural structures and processes and, more subtly, the search for a fundamental morphology. The problem of the origin of forms became a significant aesthetic question because it was also the key concern of the mechanistic materialism of the times: in which philosophy they were accounted for only by different combinations of material atoms.

The distinguished French physicist Carra defined matter as the collective destination given to all solid parts of the universe dispersed in space. "Sans la matière, l'espace ne seroit qu'un désert absolu & éternel . . ."[50] The primary quality of matter is solidity, and its secondary quality is form. Romé de l'Isle maintained that there is nothing in nature which is not characterized by an essential individual figure over which chance holds no sway, "car la MATIÈRE NE PEUT EXISTER SANS FORME . . ."[51] If I may anticipate my argument, we will see that this position is crucial for the emergence of a new conception of chaos.

Carra's view of matter is predicated on the eighteenth-century conviction that the external world is the real world. In this conceptual context the heightened awareness of natural objects produces sublime sensations. It is in this regard that Hamann envisions the astonishment experienced by primitive man as, with the *fiat lux*, nature appears and the savage senses for the first time the sudden presence of *things*.[52] One can draw a parallel between the immediate impact made by the world of the eighteenth-century voyager, unveiled for the first time to European eyes, and the shock ascribed to early man as the earth is created in front of him. This event assumes the stature of myth by virtue of its revelatory value. At the moment of visual genesis things are charged with their full significance; subsequently they appear so to us only in privileged instances.

The theme of the birth of forms of specific things finds its antecedent in the history of art in the taste for the *non-finito*. This late Renaissance concept carries overtones both of forms being united with nature in an amorphous state of incompletion, of the *macchia*, and of figures torn from matter—hence, newly perceived—in which they had formerly been drowned.[53] The age-old tension between morphous and amorphous, which offers the possibility of a "coincidentia oppositorum," poses the problem of how a well-constituted order disengages itself from shapeless, primitive matter. The question is as hoary as the myth in which it is told that, after the Flood, Deucalion and Pyrrha threw stones over their shoulders and that these gradually acquired form.[54]

Coexisting with the desire for the emergence of (artistic) form is that of its submergence. Thus Bernard Palissy ornamented his grottoes with herms conceived in a rustic style which, literally, were made to coincide with nature: when cut open they were through and through "toutes pleines de quoquilles."[55] During the Baroque age, the case of emergence can be documented in sculptural configurations intended to be seen rising into view from out of a landscape or site. Conversely, instead of implying the aesthetic ordering of the terrain, these anthropomorphic land masses, anamorphoses or "optical phantoms"[56] can suggest, equally, the hermetic concealment of images well integrated with matter.[57] The seventeenth century was transfixed by—but left open and commended to the eighteenth century—the pressing question of the nature of matter: Was it a protean uniform substance shared both by man and natural phenomena, by organic and inorganic nature alike?[58]

The bipolar tendency of the eighteenth century, its inclination to react defensively against what another part of it is attracted to,[59] can best be seen in how it was torn between the taste for formed and the taste for unformed matter. Thus, as we have seen, crystals could be described as "figured bodies from an unfigured mass"[60]; fossils were indebted for their forms to "les traits qui y sont empreints": earth's particles were shaped by "des moules ou des matrices dans lesquels une partie de la matière même des couches a prise différentes formes"[61]; subterranean regions were given a physiognomy by miners; the pyramidal striving of mountains was seen in opposition to the amorphous density of their mass.[62] Even Alexander Cozens' chaotic "blot," with its disposition to figure, or topiary art, with its peculiar animation of box and yew, is predicated on a strange metamorphosis that turns the unformed into the formed, or, in the case of the latter—taking Ovid as paradigm—transforms the structured human into unconstructed trees and flowers.[63] Simultaneously, one can trace a movement away from such clear-cut readability towards loosely expressive form. The ruin is a prime example of matter disburdened from the servitude to artifice.[64] With the demise of art, material recovers a life of its own, the life of matter now rooted and become part of its site.

From the Renaissance until the eighteenth century, in art, chaos is typically defined as brute matter, that is, without form or figure. According to Michelangelo the *non-finito* is the original state of chaos, by which he means shapeless primitive matter and its association with the fourth element, earth.[65] The eighteenth-century notion of chaos goes counter to the intellectual image of nature, but it is a rich concept, not the Biblical nothingness, the "néant" from which the creator drew all things.[66] The term chaos contains overtones of warlike conflict, of Burkeian enthusiastic forces in nature directed against reasonable definition.[67] It hints at masculine, virile sublimities in opposition to the feminine charms of the ordered.[68] One might say that chaos is nature in its most stringently and purely primitive (Doric) form bearing the least marks of human incursion. All these terms underscore the new-found positive aspects of those parts of nature which are vast, misproportioned or "torn and mangled" by Palladian standards. Chaos has form, form of a special kind which existed before the overlay of sophisticated cultures. The explorer Eyles Irwin thrills at the sight of the "Desarts of Thebais":

> On each side of us were perpendicular steeps, some hundred fathoms deep. But the traveller's attention seems to be purposefully diverted from the danger, by the magnificent objects which surround him. Here he sees pointed heaps of the brightest crystal, that dazzle the eye with their glittering lustre: while ever and anon above his head, tremendous to behold! columns of the finest granite, rent from the mountain, seem ready to bury him beneath their tottering weight. On every part is such a wild confusion of hanging precipices, disjointed rocks, and hideous chasms, that we might well cry out with the poet "Chaos is come again." Whoever can tread these rude retreats, without being struck with the sublimest ideas of that Almighty Providence, who presides as well amid the gloom and silence of the desert, as in the noise and gaiety of the city . . . .[69]

Figure 1: A. Laborde, *Le Château de Plessis-Chamand.*
From *Nouveaux jardins de la France*, 1808, Pl. 67.

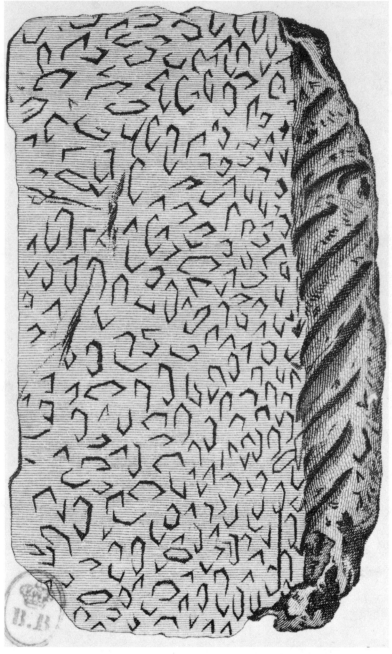

Figure 2: E. M. Patrin, *Granit graphique de Sibérie.*
From *Histoire naturelle des minéraux* I, an IX, p. 101.

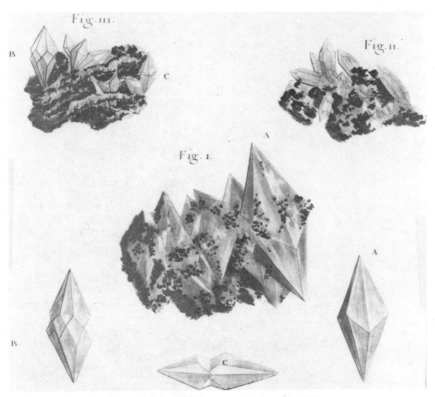

Figure 3: Fabien G. Dagoty, *Grouppes et Cristaux*.
From *Le règne minéral*, 1785.

Figure 4: A. Laborde, *Roches de basalte (Château de Rochemaure)*.
From *Voyage pittoresque de la France*, 1787–, II, Pl. 3.

Figure 5: R. Hentzi, *Mont Saint Gothard*.
From *Vues remarquables des montagnes de la Suisse*, 1785, Pl. II.

31

Figure 6: R. Hentzi, *La grosse pierre sur le glacier de Vorderaar.*
From *Vues remarquables des montagnes de la Suisse,* 1787.

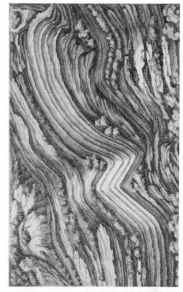
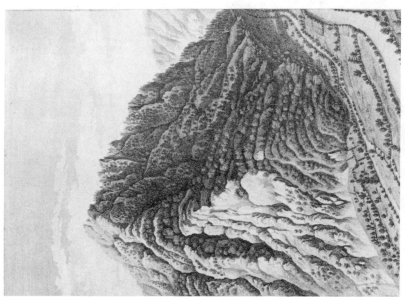

Figure 7: A. Laborde, *Dessin d'une forme singulière de bancs de rochers de schite calcaire.* From *Voyage pittoresque de la France,* 1787–, II, Pl. 7.

Figure 8: J. B. Robinet, *Priapus Pedunculo Filiformi.*
From *De la Nature*, 1766, IV, p. 44.

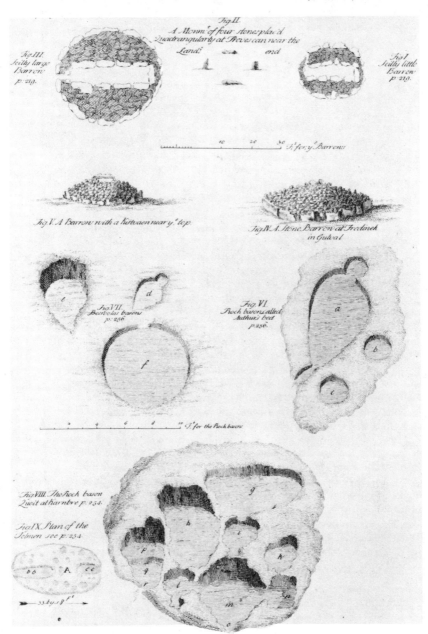

Figure 9: W. Borlase, *Rock Barrows, Antiquities, Historical and Monumental of the County of Cornwall*, 1769, Pl. XX.

Figure 10: J. Nieuhof, *Suytjeen: The Mountain of the Five Horses' Heads.*
From *Embassy . . . to China*, 1669, p. 55.

36

Figure 11: W. Borlase, *Dolmen, Antiquities, Historical and Monumental*
of the County of Cornwall, 1769, Pl. XIII.

37

Figure 12: J. B. Fraser, *Bheem Ke Uder.*
From *Views of the Himala Mountains*, 1820, PI. VII.

38

Figure 13: G. H. Bellasis, *The Column Lot, Fairy Land, Sandy Bay.* From *Views of Saint Helena*, 1815, Pl. 6.

Figure 14: D. Raoul-Rochette, *La Roche Ohistein à l'entrée de la vallée d'Oberhasli.* From *Lettres sur la Suisse*, 1823, I, Pl. 21.

Figure 15: W. Alexander, *Profiles of the Heysan Islands on the Coast of China.* From *Lord Macartney's Embassy . . . to China,* 1792, no. WD960, p. 42.

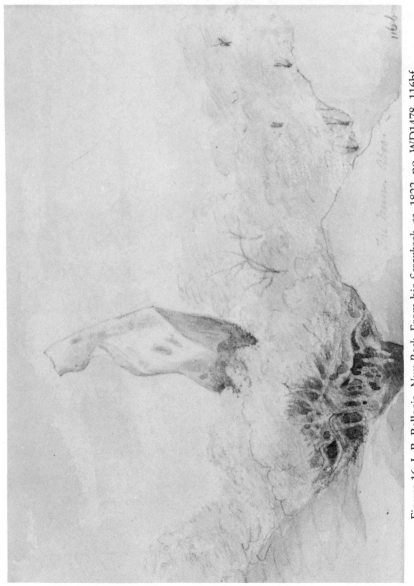

Figure 16: J. B. Bellasis, *Nun Rock*. From his *Scrapbook, ca.* 1822, no. WD1478, 116bf.

Figure 17: A. Laborde, *Vue des rochers appellés les têtes-d'Engin.* From *Voyage pittoresque de la France,* 1787–, II, Pl. 14.

43

Figure 18: L. F. Cassas, *Nahr Qâdes*.
From *Voyage pittoresque de la Syrie*, 1797, Pl. 62.

Figure 19: T. Anburey, *Northern Entrance of Gundecotta Pass*. From *Hindoostan Scenery*, 1799, Pl. 7.

45

Figure 20: R. H. Colebrooke, *Prospect of the Country near Mooty Tallaow.*
From *Twelve Views of Places in the Kingdom of Mysore,* 2nd ed., 1805, Pl. 3.

Figure 21: R. Hentzi, *Seconde chute du Staubbach en hyver*.
From *Vues remarquables des montagnes de la Suisse*, 1785, Pl. 6.

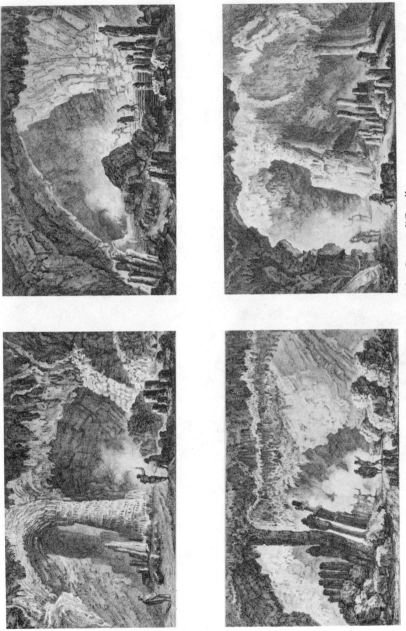

Figure 22: A. Laborde, *Vues des Grottes d'Osselles.*
From *Voyage pittoresque de la France*, 1787–, I, Pl. 6.

Figure 23: Anonymous. *Ice Grotto in the Glacier des Bossons.*

Figure 24: W. Alexander, *Singular Rock*

From *Lord Macartney's Embassy . . . to China*, 1792, no. WD959, p. 52.

Figure 25: J. F. Janinet, *A Vien [sic] of the Needle Rochs [sic] from the Back of the Isle of Wight*, no. 190.

51

The new aesthetic sensibility behind Irwin's rapture is based on a taste for the endless, the remote, the mysterious aspects of nature, suggestive of unseen forces. A taste for chaos is a taste for the primal substructure of a rebarbarized nature antedating human history; it represents the archetypal beginning of things occasionally still brought to life by the descriptions of perceptive travellers.

In particular, the image of the water of chaos is one of the most potent visual symbols found in the second half of the eighteenth century. Romé de l'Isle says that if we closely examine the enormous chains of granite mountains we soon notice that they are nothing but a confused mass of crystals, each with its distinctive form, suspended in the "eau du chaos."[70] Once separated in a liquid, these crystals are determined to be reunited and form a solid mass. From antiquity well into the eighteenth century theories were seriously propounded to show that crystal was born of water.[71] We have seen that it was Maillet who, in the mid-eighteenth century, revived the doctrine of Thales and proclaimed the universal reign of ocean.[72] A vital urge, a will to form originally was thought to rise from primeval fluid much as a not-unrelated ascendant spirit soars in granite mountains and juts to columnar needles in basalt cliffs.

It is within this context that one should note the frequency with which the Alps and other rugged mountain ranges are visualized as petrified oceans with peaked prisms for waves (Fig. 5). Bourrit describes the Mer de Glace of Montanvert as a wrathful frozen sea that captures the image of nature as it must have looked upon emerging from chaos.[73] Raoul-Rochette perceives the Grindelwald as covered by enchanting forms "dont l'aspect est semblable à celui des vagues irritées d'une mer orageuse."[74] (Others imagined it as a huge creeping Saurian monster.) Mercier finds glaciers to be rich in metamorphosis, frozen agitation,[75] and Hentzi extols the infinitely varied structure of their towers of ice.[76]

This imagery suggests, in addition, that the world of the high mountains is one of the few places where metamorphosis is rapid enough to be perceptible. Snow, wind and ice constantly erode old forms and give birth to new ones. By analogy, the metaphor of the ocean was transferred to ruins, so that columns rising from the chaotic debris of the Temple at Selinunte could be visualized as landmarks "qu'en mer elles servent de renseignement aux pilotes . . ."[77]

Nature and the world of man gone to earth in ruins is essentially mobile, subject to continuous change. This immense metamorphosis is akin to the fertile powers of chaos which, far from being nothing, guarantee that matter is never annihilated but constantly revivifying itself and changing form.[78]

"Beyond the reach of any historical monument"

Geology confirmed that change is everywhere: man could trust in nothing, not even the solid earth. The recent Lisbon earthquake revived memories of other mammoth alterations in the face of the globe: Smyrna, Pompeii, Herculaneum, Lima.[79] While famous cities lay razed, travellers were astonished to witness nature in the act of giving birth to land: in 1707 islands rose in the Grecian Archipelago, and in 1720 some others emerged in the Azores. Voyagers to the Pacific Ocean like Bougainville and Cook frequently commented upon the abrupt emergence of sandy atolls in an otherwise empty sea. The convulsive movements of nature brought forth with equal suddenness boulders in the midst of glacier fields and cliffs in the vicinity of volcanic sites (Fig. 6).

The quarrel among the disciplines as to the supremacy of human history or nature was fed by geology. History, under the cool scrutiny of a Montesquieu or a Voltaire, was seen as a stage full of human conceits and developments without moment; whereas nature, perceived by the sciences, was colored by an underlying attitude of deepest awe for its majesty and significance.[80] Infused by this spirit, Diderot in the *Salon* of 1767 was led to muse on the melancholy effect produced by Hubert Robert's paintings:

> . . . Qu'est-ce que mon existence éphémère en comparaison de celle de ce rocher qui s'affaisse, de ce vallon qui se creuse, de cette forêt qui chancelle, de ces masses suspendues au dessus de ma tête et qui s'ébranlent? . . .[81]

Earlier, we noted that travellers brought back reports concerning minerals and metals that proffered literal transcriptions of the earth's history. Rock strata equally were thought to form the annals of our globe. Consequently, matter in its state of chaos was believed to possess a character, a physiognomy, qualifying it to have a bonafide history preserved in the records of geology. In fact, the study of human history was usurped by that of natural history, with all that the latter implied in terms of the action of irresistible titanic forces during the passage of aeons.

But natural history does more than simply ape the conventions of human history, it embodies the late-eighteenth-century quest for *origins*. Geological events belong to "a period indeed much beyond the reach of any historical monument, or even of tradition itself."[82] This leit-motif is sounded frequently during the second part of the century and beyond. The study of nature "carries you back beyond all historical records,"[83] so that even "un petit caillou de nos rivières est plus ancien que les pyramides de l'Égypte."[84] Or, in the words of the Abbé de Lille—thought to be a particularly apt inscription for a boulder—"sa masse indestructible a fatigué le temps."

Such reflections on chronology presuppose an acute awareness of the varieties of time: rectilinear time versus time immemorial, that is, human time versus natural time.[85] The latter represents duration, and in such a continuum, as Mercier observed, even ancient ruins of art are "que de hier" in comparison with the primeval singularities of nature.[86] Or, in the words of Laborde's reflection: "Mais que sont les tems historiques en comparaison de ces grands changements que démontrent l'étude & l'examen des hautes montagnes?"[87]

The concept that true history is natural history emancipates the objects of nature from the government of man. For the idea of singularity it is significant, as we shall see, that geological phenomena— taken in their widest sense to include specimens from the mineral kingdom—constitute landscape forms in which matters dynamic history finds aesthetic expression. The result is that "Temples built with earthly hands confer no glory upon God; but are unstable monuments to man's vanity . . . The Kosmos alone is the true temple of God . . ."[88] And what is the cosmos but "ces blocs [de granit] et leurs débris . . . ces vénérables vestiges des antiques monumens de notre globe . . ."[89]

This epic view of nature, "which makes thoughtless man become thoughtful," combined the sensitive study of surface phenomena with a search for deep structure. Whether in the Jura or in the Dauphiné the traveller was struck by the disclosure of internal form.

> On rencontre à chaque pas des rochers dont les couches boulev-
> ersées d'une façon terrible offre encore l'image des convulsions d'un
> monde primitif; les uns redressées presque verticalement, les autres
> ployées à angles vifs; et toutes, bien qu'assises et affermies depuis
> de siècles, semblent être dans un mouvement perpetuel . . .[90]
> (Fig. 7)

By the close of the eighteenth century two trends were evident in geology: a theological evolutionary theory taught that things progressed, emerging from God, and a dynamic historical theory taught that things developed from themselves.[91] Paradoxically, from this double-pronged study a view of the earth emerged which showed it to be a vast cemetery of artifacts and, at the same time, geologically and biologically alive, that is, both tomb and organism. The concept of metamorphosis or revolution—borrowed from human history—tied the two together: the history of the earth is one of transformations of matter in a single, enduring substance.

So it is not surprising that, from 1760 on, scientific travellers to the High Alps, such as Saussure and Deluc, tried to identify a particular site with a historical moment in the development of the world's landscape. The famous orologist of Geneva thinks in cosmic terms from mountain tops, he feels the convulsive life of the earth stirring through its geological formations and finds an eternal order in periodic chaos.[92]

The final stage in the historicizing of nature sees the products of history naturalized. In 1789, the German *savant* Samuel Witte—basing his conclusions on the writings of Desmarets, Deluc and Faujas de Saint-Fond—annexed the pyramids of Egypt for nature, declaring that they were basalt eruptions; he also identified the ruins of Persepolis, Baalbek, Palmyra, as well as the Temple of Jupiter at Agrigento and the Palace of the Incas in Peru, as lithic outcroppings.[93] His statements represent the logical terminus of the eighteenth-century dream of man losing himself in the immensity and the violence of natural forces. It was this profound desire that permitted the confounding of history with nature.

"Comment une matière brute peut-elle donner la naissance à des êtres animés? Oui, je vis, & les mondes que je renferme vivent."

For the Pre-Socratics, the earth was conceived as alive in all its parts: minerals, metals, stones, all possessed a vital force and grew like the cosmos.[94] Man existed within the ambience of this burgeoning nature. The world was regarded as animate until the Renaissance; thereafter, during the seventeenth century, the old hylozoistic fallacy gave way to the idea of the world as mechanism devoid of both intelligence and life.[95]

However, in the eighteenth century certain Pre-Socratic ideas were revived. For example, the "Knorpelstil" of the late Renaissance, which vivified inorganic forms—and which has been interpreted as an expression of pan-psychism—exerted a strong effect on the formation of the Rococo.[96] Earlier, we noted that Maillet returned to the doctrine of Thales and saw everything born from the ocean's flux. The *philosophe* De l'Isle de Sales expounded the Pythagorean idea of the world as a dynamic "colosse organisé."[97] At the close of the century, the mysterious Fabre d'Olivet—influenced by the vivid reports produced by travellers to India—discoursed eloquently about metempsychosis and related it to the ancient dogma of universal animism.[98] But the French were not alone in thinking that nature no longer resembled Newtonian inert matter. Wieland and Herder—exponents of Idealism—found the universe to be sentient, a living and moving organism. Erasmus Darwin in his *Loves of the Plants* (1789) again filled the universe with quasi-sexual forces reminiscent of Empedocles' war between love and strife.

Putting Darwin aside for the moment, it can be said that an alternate animistic current arises in England and that its source is Locke. His famous hypothesis that God could have endowed matter with the faculty of feeling and thinking had considerable success during the course of the eighteenth century.[99] Unlike the old belief in an *animus mundi*, this view denies that the material universe is permeated by mind; rather, it is matter itself which changes, moves. Some thirty years later Diderot, in his struggle to break with Descartes and the mechanistic tradition in France, develops the argument that matter is in constant transformation. He constructs a material monism which is in opposition to the metaphysical pantheism of a Spinoza, who claimed that there was no being outside the one substance of the universe.[100] For Diderot there is also only one substance, but it is matter, and sensibility is an essential quality of that matter: "Il faut que la pierre sente."[101]

Diderot's concept of self-motion residing in matter is probably derived from the influential psychology of Leibniz. The German philosopher emphasized the dynamic community of all monads ranging from the human soul down through the vegetable kingdom to the monads of apparently inorganic substances.[102] Diderot comes to see the universe as process, as an organic unity of discrete particulars functioning in a way that is no longer mechanistic. He follows up on the ambiguity inherent in Leibniz's monadology which suggests that the three traditionally distinct realms of nature are not easily kept separate. In fact d'Alembert is made to say: "Tout animal est plus ou moins homme; tout minéral est plus ou moins animal; tout plante est plus ou moins animal. Il n'y a rien de précis en nature . . ."[103]

Like Diderot, the biologist Bonnet envisaged a Great Chain of Being, an uninterrupted succession of grades descending from the highest to the lowest forms and mobilized by imperishable germs. Bonnet, despite himself, immortalized the difficulty of distinguishing among the three kingdoms of nature by focussing on the polyp controversy, which mesmerized the second half of the century. The polyp aroused perplexity because scientists were uncertain as to whether it was plant or animal: "les Polypes sont placés sur les frontières d'un autre Univers, qui aura un jour ses Colombs & ses Vespuces."[104] If such ambiguity is found at the border between animal and plant (Fig. 8), what enigmas await us at the zone between vegetable and mineral?

The nature which emerged from the microscope was superabundant, lavish, prolific; it "swarmed," "heaved" with life.[105] This delightful instrument demonstrated how apparently dead particles were, in reality, animate substance: " . . . Un nouveau monde se dévoileroit à nos yeux; la Nature devenue transparente ne céleroit plus sa marche: ses ateliers & ses laboratoires seroient ouverts . . ."[106] Significantly, Bonnet and Robinet were writing of their lively discoveries—extending the topography of vision, in effect—at the time when major scientific expeditions were getting under way: those of Bougainville (1761–68), Wallis-Carteret, James Bruce and Cook (1768). It is no wonder that such "research" produced vitalist ruminations and led to the spectacle of travellers watching rocks grow, clams sprout and the earth secrete many hybrid forms. Mercier—praising Cardano and Paracelsus to the detriment of Newton—rhapsodizes: "Les minéraux s'engendrent, les pierres croissent . . . une vertu générative s'insinue dans les rochers les plus durs: une mine a son organisation, comme le chêne qui se balance au sommet des montagnes."[107] In sum: mineralogists attribute the formation of fossils to *semina*, and crystals to "germs," thus assuming they possess sexuality.[108] Still-life painters show how shells and corals mimic flowers. Voyagers like the sober Jesuit Frézier—citing Palissy for support— insist that the phenomenon of silver or copper daily renewed underground is no fable.[109] Conversely, just as islands and metals can be born, Robinet declares that rocks can die.[110]

These convictions are predicated on an axiomatic belief in the potency of the earth's core; this faith simultaneously denies the existence of the inanimate and ensures that expression is intrinsic to all natural forms.[111] Needless to say, such a thesis runs counter to much of Western aesthetics, which, since Greek antiquity, put forward life as a fundamental principle of art and posited the impossibility of beauty residing in inorganic objects—the metals, minerals, the "singularities" of this paper.[112] This attitude is best summed up by a dictum issuing from the French Academy: the artist's task is to "donner la vie à des choses inanimées"; to imprint life "sur une matière insensible . . ."[113]

In the eighteenth century, on the other hand, beauty or, better, sublimity of the inorganic is founded on the denial of its inanimateness; it is not based on the "pathetic fallacy" or the imposition of human liveliness—via empathy—onto rigid, cold and in themselves unlovely things.[114] This alternate aesthetic development—whose existence this study tries to demonstrate—finds its analogy in the natural symbolism used by pre-Classical art. In the latter, landscape features are sometimes seen as "living stones," the recognizable images of organic creatures[115]—a primitive custom which did not escape the attention of Borlase[116] or Quatremère de Quincy[117] (Fig. 9).

Similar ideas could be found in non-Western cultures and were fostered by seventeenth- and eighteenth-century travellers to the Far East. John Nieuhof, through his *Embassy to China* (1669), disseminated the topographic, geomantic system of Fong Chouei which purported to reveal the inner, hidden essence of nature based on the assumption that everything that lives has a sign; through this terrestrial scheme the Chinese interpret the configuration and position of hills and mountains as if they were planets.[118] By means of these accounts, Nieuhof and Kircher communicated the Taoist view of nature as an organism whose living materials man regarded with awe[119] (Fig. 10).

What links the two types of eighteenth-century animism discussed here with certain aspects of primitive and non-Western aesthetic traditions is the presupposition that the qualities of matter do not exist in the abstract. Landscape perception is bound up with a sentient earth that finds expression in specific vital forms, in singularities.[120]

"Singular figures of earth"

The revival of animism during the Enlightenment coincided, perhaps paradoxically, with the new theories put forth by Newton encouraging the attribution of supernatural characteristics to the physical world.[121] Simultaneously, as we have seen, scientific and pseudo-scientific discoveries made by perspicacious travellers showed the earth to be a *plenum formarum* full of wonderful, one might even say divine, things. This return of emphasis to the perception of the world—now revealed to be nothing short of miraculous—is related to the Empiricist model of the mind—no ideas are innate, all arise from sensation and reflection. But there is more than one way of seeing objects. One has to distinguish between the matter of simple seeing, where the object prompts us to perceive a specific form, and cases where no well-established ways of perceiving exist. In the latter instance, the sudden access of visual meaning is equivalent to discovery.[122] This mode of perception is endemic to a period that valued the factual, that doted on meticulous observation, that dwelled on experience.

Writers frequently distinguished between being a mere tourist and being a serious traveller: the former gives general impressions, whereas the latter conveys particular information about the region. Hence the recurring exhortation that the study of natural history should be carried out *in situ*, among specific objects, in order for the beholder to "saisir cette physionomie, cette manière d'être . . . propre & caractéristique à chaque substance . . ."[123] This visual scrutiny requires a concomitant linguistic development in which words lay stress on the ocular examination of things. Thus, at an early date we find Addison extolling the "new," prompted by Longinus' use of the word "extraordinary," meaning the marvelous, prodigies, events that cause wonder.[124] Unlike the Mannerist fascination with "stupore," suggesting astonishment rather than true admiration,[125] for the thinkers we are discussing not only provide a cure for ennui, but represent a sudden leap to visual recognition.

The age of the Baroque bequeathed to the eighteenth century the coupling of the concept of sublimity with that of simplicity.[126] We have already observed that geology was thought to reveal nature's history through the character of individual formations. By the mid-eighteenth century, this rise of interest in the simple, the singular, is linked to the taste we have just mentioned for suddenness of response as a criterion of aesthetic value, a permutation on the older category of immediacy.[127] Thus Burke:

> A sudden beginning or sudden cessation of sound of any considerable force, has the same [sublime] power . . . whatever either in sights or sounds makes the transition from one extreme to the other easy, causes no terror; and consequently can be no cause of greatness . . . It may be observed that a single sound of some strength, though but of short duration, if repeated after intervals, has a grand effect . . .[128]

Burke's view may be contrasted with that of Price. In the 1790s, the "sudden" makes its appearance as an attribute of the Picturesque.[129] But Price—or Gilpin, for that matter—mean sudden change within a whole view considered as one entire piece, not the configuration of a single object.

This difference also holds true when Gilpin mentions "singularity." It constitutes part of a whole amalgam which includes roughness or ruggedness of texture, variety, irregularity, chiaroscuro and the power of the forms of nature to stimulate the imagination.[130] Singularity—as we are interpreting it here—is rooted in the phenomenal world, which possesses its own vitality, vividness and intensity. This concept is equally distinct from an Alisonian Associationism—which by definition wanders away from the object—and a Wordsworthian Romanticism—which transmutes the object. Both deny nature any capacity to evoke emotion independently of human qualities that matter suggestively represents.

The view of "singularity" which emerges from Picturesque theory coexists with such other late eighteenth-century aesthetic categories as the "piquant"[131] and the "bizarre"[132]: all three function as antidotes to visual boredom.

By contrast, the motif of singularity used in travel accounts is distinctly more serious in nature. It relates to the voyager's being engrossed in what he sees to such a point that the obliteration of his own identity results. The fusion with the singularity beheld is a riveting of the mind to its object in a passonate identification with it.[133] Not only is this distinct from Associationism's lack of external focus and Romanticism's withdrawal into the interior, it also differs from the tenacious Renaissance view of the role of *fantasia* whereby partial forms found in the external world, forms which in their totality do not make up any one thing, suggest something new.[134]

When the traveller is suddenly absorbed, when he looks *at*, not *over*, the natural object, he is no longer a merely bemused spectator of the varieties of the Picturesque, rather, he cannot become anything except what he beholds. Absorption, emerging from this kind of experiential scrutiny, goes hand in hand with an object's being a simple, distinctive mass.

The reverse effect of absorption is expansion. The Sublime stretches the soul, and "infinity has a tendency to fill the mind . . ."[135] Again, this is not empathy but, rather, perceiving suddenly, through sagacious insight, the essential character and reality of the object itself, through a special form of absorption that occurs only when the object is isolated. Thus Faujas de Saint-Fond can speak of "un grand rocher noir taillé à pic et comme isolé, qui avoit fixé mon attention . . ."[136] It was science that trained the voyager to develop such an intense focus on the manifold of things.

Our travellers succeeded in uprooting the sturdy prejudice against particularity fostered by the taxonomic concept of ordering the arts— that is, by the ordering of disorderly particulars into a unified structure of generalization.[137] Penetrating scientific observation and the ardent description of actual topography produced a change: illustrations of "unified" views yielded before those of immensely charged single fragments.[138] On that score it is interesting to hear Diderot berate Joseph Vernet's rhetorical alpine views: "Pourquoi donc ces Alpes sont-elles informes sans détail distinct, verdâtres et nébuleuses . . ."[139]

Unlike a Patinir,[140] a Rosa[141] or even a de Loutherbourg, who went to Switzerland and perceived only fantasy rocks, the scientific traveller became totally absorbed in singularities that combined rarity with remoteness or primitiveness—these qualities made them all the more singular. Witness the rise of interest in rude, undressed stones, which are made to contrast with fertile land clothed by agriculture.[142] The *paysage riant* forms a foil to the uncultivated, uncivilized *rocher brut*. Borlase laments that as mankind grew fond of embellishment it moved away from the mysterious, simple isolation of immense natural forms to ornament, which was employed "to dress up the naked stone . . ."[143] (Fig. 11). Others describe the high Alps as a "desert" where granite is "entirely stripped of verdure," where the surroundings are made impressive by "the abrupt, and . . . naked appearance of the rocks . . ."[144] Nor were travellers to the East disappointed: Elliott and Fraser (Fig. 12) found sections of the Himalayas to be "naked and stony,"[145] Johnson said Table Mountain on the Cape of Good Hope consisted of "naked fragments of rock"[146] and Bellasis was stunned by Saint Helena's "wild nakedness"[147] (Fig. 13). These explorers had seen nature unembellished and, for them, it no longer required softening with a generalized decoration, it did not need "un air paré."

Three persistent types of singularity (of the *singulier*, the *seltsam*) can be identified in travel accounts stemming from the second half of the eighteenth and the early nineteenth centuries: the "morceau," the piece or sample of natural history; the "amas," the lump or heap; and the fragment. The illustrated voyage frequently placed emphasis on single blocks, pieces of crystal, specific pinnacles. Thus for Faujas de Saint-Fond a grotto of volcanic origin represents a "superbe morceau." At the Château of Rochemaure he admires not the ruins of art but, instead, is "stupefied" by "*une* butte basaltique, . . . *une* masse aussi étonnante, aussi isolée, ainsi penchée sur un plateau volcanique"[148] (Fig. 4). Earlier we noted how Frézier "saw" minerals and metals grow: near the Pampas of Paraguay he discovered mines containing just such "morceaux" of copper.[149] Raoul-Rochette apostrophizes a singular upright stone that rises in a Swiss meadow: *"ce bloc éternel sera encore en possession du champ où l'on a jeté les révolutions du globe"*[150] (Fig. 14). In the Malouine Islands, Dom Pernety's attention is arrested by *"une* de ces pierres qui formoit une table d'un grand pic . . ."[151]

Mariners left records indicating how these singularities offered delightful relief to the monotony of a long sea voyage (Fig. 15). The habit of running traverse did something to alleviate the effects of the ocean's flatness and insured that nature provided monuments: "all forms assuming, bold-upright-grotesque . . ."[152] While coasting off of Cape Leopold, Ross discerned "a very remarkable conical rock . . . it was named Princess Charlotte's Monument, after our lamented Princess . . ."[153] A less elegiac monument was sighted in 1785 by the Daniells on their voyage to India by way of China. The "Assess Ears" are two gigantic pillars of granite "towering above the clouds that float on the horizon."[154]

The overland traveller was equally smitten by the natural monument viewed not vaguely "out there" but with the more immediate intensity of being actually *en face* the singular natural specimen. Caspar Wolff, following the course of the Lauteraar Glacier, was struck by the massive boulders strewn along its shores, which he interpreted as "des monumens des ravages causés par des chutes . . ."[155] Appositely, Bourrit comments on "ces énormes monumens de la vétusté de l'Univers" seen emerging from the chaos of surrounding ice.[156] Sometimes these monuments appear to be human (Fig. 16). In France, Laborde was fascinated by "des figures quelquefois fort singulières." Among them were the so-called "Heads" of Engin (Fig. 17). " . . . Tantôt on croit y voir des représentations d'animaux dont les corps sont entiers ou mutilés; tantôt des têtes d'hommes nues ou coëffées; en-fin une multitude de blocs différemment contournés . . ." In Spain, he admired the unique cones of Mont Serrat, the sugar loaves composed of "rochers à figures expressives et rébarbatives."[157]

Cassas prided himself on having survived longer than any traveller before him in the wilderness of Syria. He made numerous sketches of the monumental pyramidal rock, pierced by a tunnel-like hole, found in the region of Nahr Qâdes, because, as he tells us, he was "enchanté [par] des aspects singuliers"[158] (Fig. 18). Malte-Brun praises the "Devil's Bridge" or natural bridge in Switzerland and relates it to such other singular wonders as the hellish cavern described by Dante.[159] James Bruce, struggling across the Great Desert, gives another, more utilitarian, reason why all these enduring formations—detached from their ambient—are worthy of being called monuments: " . . . These are all landmarks of the utmost consequence to caravans in their journey because they are too considerable in size to be covered at any time by the moving sands . . ."[160]

Singularities need not always be homogeneous monuments. As we have noted, they can also consist of lumps and heaps which visually add up to a single, definitive shape (Fig. 19). Faujas de Saint-Fond describes the curious effect caused by a subterranean volcanic explosion. The thrust of the lava produced hanging tatters ("lambeaux") of granite "dans des positions singulières . . ."[161] Mungo Park, trekking through Africa, comments on singular white quartz, "large lumps of which were lying all round; no other stone to be seen . . ."[162] Colebrooke captures in Mysore the endless rock heaps of the Droogs (Fig. 20). Alpine travellers never fail to mention "ces vastes amas de neiges . . .," or "un seul amas de glace . . ."[163] (Fig. 21).

Rock grottoes often fall into this category because of dripstone formations that pique curiosity. At Mont Serrat, flowstone forms flower bunches and other heaped-up petrifactions. In the grottoes of Osselles, Laborde muses on the constant clustered transformations caused by the "lapidary sap" as it filters through the limestone (Fig. 22). But ice caverns—from the point of view of metamorphosis—were thought to be the more striking phenomenon. Diaphanous drapery, transparent mounds: "toute cette féerie change en un clin d'oeil. Un rayon de soleil suffit pour faire évanouir ces fragiles merveilles . . ."[164] (Fig. 23). Even amid the everlasting ice of the Arctic wastes, Captain Lyon was dazzled by the ephemeral clusters: "the silvery icicles, which formed a beautiful contrast with the shaded part of the ebon grotto behind them . . ."[165] And Pallas, enduring the rigors of a Russian winter, illustrates the singular, but fleeting, effect of rain frozen on trees forming a forest of crystal.[166]

Finally, the singularity could be regarded as a self-sufficient fragment detached from former lumps (Fig. 24). Topographical descriptions enhanced the view of rock formations as ruins, that is, forms which had been complex in the past but which through erosion had achieved a new simplicity. Thus, fragments of basalt assume new and distinctive columnar, spherical or needlelike forms, the result of a violent geological shock suffered by the primitive mass. They become potent relics, valiant remnants, and the still-remaining stub is eroded towards final annihilation (Fig. 25). At Thebes, Browne compares "the rough and lofty rocks of granite and porphyry" to the once mighty city: both are going down into the immensities of the desert.[167] The ambiguity between ruin and sketch, between ancient whole and single nascent form can be gauged by the frequency of the image of the city in ruins found in descriptions of glaciers. Out of the chaotic heaps of ice which "représentent les ruines d'une ville" arise new and singular fragments.[168] Similarly, the naturally pierced rock fragment at Tavannes, Switzerland, could be considered worthy—even in the days of the Romans—of being classed among the ruins of their Empire.

This study has traced the cultivation of taste for the natural phenomenon as singularity, a taste originating in scientific and quasi-scientific concerns and given definitive shape by travel accounts from the second half of the eighteenth century.

As Captain Cook reminds us, for the eighteenth century, discovery was the greatest pleasure. And it has been the purpose of this essay to show that the *taste* for discovery, fed by nature's endless succession of specimens, was as important an aesthetic category as the Picturesque; indeed, it was its rival. It is appropriate to observe in concluding that such singularities infiltrate nineteenth-century Romantic landscape painting. The lone natural object is conspicuous in the works of Constable,[169] Girtin, Turner and, particularly, Friedrich. Friedrich's rock masses, oak trees, caves and chasms need not be interpreted as human surrogates[170]: on the contrary, his isolated, detached monoliths should be placed within the vitalist aesthetic tradition—emerging from the illustrated voyage—that valued the natural singular. One might refer to this tradition as that of a "neue Sachlichkeit" in which the regard for the specifics of nature produces a repertory of animate particulars. The variety of natural detail comes to be compacted into an essential motif, a visual symbol not of something beyond itself but located in the matter of things themselves.

NOTES

I would like to thank the American Council of Learned Societies, which awarded me a Grant-in-Aid for the Summer of 1976. It enabled me to complete the research for this article and to gather photographic material for a book I am preparing on the topic of the illustrated voyage and the shaping of Romantic landscape perception. In addition, I am particularly grateful to the generosity of Mrs. Mildred Archer, Keeper of Prints and Drawings, the India Office Library, London, her staff, and to Dr. William Archer; without their encouragement and helpfulness this study would not have been written. Mr. Roger Quarm, Assistant to the Keeper of Prints and Drawings, the National

Maritime Museum, Greenwich, also aided my work. This article owes much to the excellent collection of travel material held by the Bibliothèque Nationale and The British Library. Finally, I thank Jerrold Lanes for his belief in the value of my work, his support of it, and his astute suggestions.

1 P. van Tieghem, *Le sentiment de la nature dans le préromantisme européen*, Paris, 1960, p. 98.

2 J. Barrell, *The Idea of Landscape and the Sense of Place 1730–1840: An Approach to the Poetry of John Clare*, Cambridge, 1972, p. 2. Barrell points out that the use of the word "landscape" meaning a tract of land "considered with regard to its natural configuration" came into use in the mid-eighteenth century.

3 G. P. Parks, "The Turn to the Romantic in the Travel Literature of the Eighteenth Century," *Modern Language Quarterly*, XXV, 1964, pp. 23–26. This paper will argue against Parks' thesis, which claims that natural wonders appearing in travel accounts were ordinarily described in plain, unvarnished language.

4 M. Rostvig, *The Happy Man: Studies in the Metamorphoses of a Classical Ideal*, 2nd ed., New York, 1971, II, p. 195.

5 P. G. Adams, *Travellers and Travel Liars, 1600–1800*, Berkeley, 1962, p. 223.

6 T. M. Perry and D. H. Simpson, eds., *Drawings by William Westall, Landscape Artist on Board H.M.S. Investigator during the Circumnavigation of Australia by Captain Matthew Flinders R.N. in 1801–1803*, London, 1962, p. 23.

7 J. Addison, *The Works*, London, 1804, II, p. 367. *Spectator* 414.

8 J. B. J. Le Gentil, *Voyage dans les mers de l'Inde fait par ordre du roi à l'occasion du passage de Vénus, sur le disque du soleil, le 6 juin 1761 & le 3 du même mois 1769*, Paris, 1779, II, p. 641.

9 Ibid., p. 644.

10 H. Focillon, *The Life of Forms in Art*, 2nd ed., New York, 1948, p. 33.

11 R. Bacou, *Piranesi, Etchings and Drawings*, Boston, 1975, pp. 154, 183. These plates date from 1776 and 1766 respectively.

12 W. D. Robson-Scott, *The Literary Background of the Gothic Revival in Germany*, Oxford, 1965, p. 91.

13 H. Bauer, *Architektur als Kunst: Von der Grösse der idealistischen Architektur-Ästhetik und ihren Verfall*, Probleme der Kunstwissenschaft, Berlin, 1963, I, p. 139.

14 D. Diderot, *Le rêve de d'Alembert*, Paris, 1951, p. 11. The *Rêve* was written in 1769 but only published in 1782 in the *Correspondance littéraire*. For a discussion of the "statue animée," see J. L. Carr, "Pygmalion and the *Philosophes*, The Animated Statue in Eighteenth-Century France," *Journal of the Warburg and Courtauld Institutes*, XXIII, 1960, pp. 239–255.

15 J. B. Robinet, *De la nature*, Amsterdam, 1763–1766, IV, pp. 111–112.

16 M. Akenside, *The Pleasures of Imagination*, 3rd ed., London, 1744, I, pp. 526–529.

17 M. H. Nicolson, *Science and Imagination*, Hamden, Conn., 1976, pp. 207–209.

18 C. Bonnet, *Contemplation de la nature*, 2nd ed., Amsterdam, 1769, I, pp. 236–237.

19 C. C. Sturm, *Reflections on the Works of God in Nature and Providence for every Day of the Year*, new, rev. ed., trans. Adam Clarke, London, 1818, I, p. 377.

20 H. Bauer, *Rocaille, zur Herkunft und zum Wesen eines Ornament-Motivs*, Berlin, 1962, pp. 52–53. Bauer discusses the evolution of natural ornament during the late Rococo. In the works of W. Baumgartner (1740s) and G. L. Crusius (1752–1764) the ornamental is naturalized.

21 L. Bourguet, *Traité des pétrifications avec figures*, Paris, 1742, p. 67.

22 G. Iseninger, "The Work of Art as Artifact," *British Journal of Aesthetics*, 13, 1973, p. 9.

23 H. Damisch, *Théorie du nuage pour une histoire de la peinture*, Paris, 1972, p. 53.

24 M. Thalmann, *Zeichensprache der Romantik*, Heidelberg, 1967, p. 30.

25 J. F. Henckel, *Flora Saturnis, Die Verwandschaft des Pflanzen mit dem Mineral-Reich*, Leipzig, 1722, pp. 551–557.

26 H. W. Janson, "The 'Image made by Chance' in Renaissance Thought," *De Artibus Opuscula XL: Essays in Honor of Erwin Panofsky*, Zurich, 1960, p. 255.

27 Addison, *Spectator* 592.

28 E. M. Patrin, *Histoire naturelle des minéraux*, Paris, an IX, I, pp. 100–102.

29 B. Faujas de Saint-Fond, *Essai de géologie ou mémoires pour servir à l'histoire naturelle du globe*, Paris, 1803–1809, II, p. 179.

30 J. F. Henckel, *Unterricht von der Mineralogie oder Wissenschaft von Wassern, Erdsäften, Saltzen, Erden, Steinen und Ertzen*, Dresden, 1747, pp. 32–33.

31 Abbé La Pluche, *Le spectacle de la nature, ou entretiens sur les particularités de l'histoire naturelle*, Paris, 1785, III, p. 399.

32 J. P. Breynii, *Epistola de melonibus petrefactis Montis Carmel vulgo creditis*, Leipzig, 1722, pp. 9–11. Breynius discusses melon stones and other "petrified fruit" that "grow" in fields.

33 K. B. Collier, *Cosmogonies of Our Forefathers: Some Theories of the Seventeenth and the Eighteenth Centuries*, New York, 1968, p. 447.

34 P. M. Schuhl, "La machine, l'homme, la nature et l'art au XVIIIᵉ siècle," *Corso internazionale di alta cultura*, IX, ed. V. Branca, Venice, 1970, p. 117.

35 E. H. Gombrich, "The Renaissance Theory of Art and The Rise of Landscape," *Norm and Form: Studies in the Art of the Renaissance*, London, 1966, p. 119. According to Vitruvius, caves were part of the setting for a satyric scene.

36 H. Winkelmann, *Der Bergbau in der Kunst*, Essen, 1958, p. 338.

37 C. Lang, *Gallerie der unterirdischen Schöpfungswunder und des menschlichen Kunstfleisses unter der Erde*, Leipzig, 1806(?), I, p. 26.

38 B. Boyce, "Mr. Pope, in Bath, Improves the Design of his Grotto," *Restoration and Eighteenth Century Literature*, ed. C. Camden, Chicago, 1963, pp. 144–151 ff. In late 1739 and early 1740, Pope went to Bath to take the waters. Although he had "finished" his grotto *ca* 1725, now, in Bristol

and Bath amidst rocks and talk of minerals and quarries, he conceived it anew as a cavern place with all the minerals in their correct positions. It should also be noted that on this trip Pope met the Reverend William Borlase, antiquarian, scientist, painter—of whom more later in this paper.

39 E. Battisti, *L'antirinascimento*, Milan, 1962, pp. 183–184. See in particular chapter VI, "La magia degli elementi."

40 R. A. Aubin, "Grottoes, Geology, and the Gothic Revival," *Studies in Philology*, XXXI, 1934, p. 414.

41 P. Martel, *An Account of the Glaciers or Ice Alps in Savoy in Two Letters*, London, 1744, p. 83.

42 Robinet, *De la nature*, IV, p. 203.

43 M. Romé de l'Isle, *Cristallographie; ou description des formes propres à tous les corps du règne minéral, dans l'état de combinaison saline, pierreuse ou métallique*, 2nd ed., Paris, 1783, I, p. 94. This lavishly illustrated work contains over five hundred figures by Desfontaines, engraver to the Comte d'Artois.

44 W. von Engelhardt, "Schönheit im Reiche der Mineralien," *Jahrbuch für Ästhetik und allgemeine Kunstwissenschaft, IV, 1958–1959*, p. 67.

45 A. V. Carozzi, "Rudolph Erich Raspe and the Basalt Controversy," *Studies in Romanticism*, VIII, 1969, p. 245.

46 Le Gentil, *Voyage*, II, p. 657.

47 M. Flinders, *A Voyage to Terra Australis; undertaken for the Purpose of completing the Discovery of that Vast Country and prosecuted in the Years 1801, 1802, and 1803*, London, 1814, II, p. 115.

48 J. G. Freüdenberg, *Dissertatio physico-medica de Filtro Lapide*, Giessen, 1702, pp. 14–15.

49 J. P. Minguet, *Esthétique du Rococo*, Paris, 1966, p. 257.

50 M. Carra, *Nouveaux principes de physique*, Paris, 1781, I, p. 84.

51 Romé de l'Isle, *Cristallographie*, I, p. 24.

52 A. Béguin, *L'âme romantique et le rêve: Essai sur le romantisme allemand et la poésie française*, Paris, 1937, I, p. 105.

53 A. Chastel, "Le fragmentaire, l'hybride et l'inachevé," *Das Unvollendete als künstlerische Form: Ein Symposium*, ed. J. A. Schmoll gen. Eisenwerth, Berne, 1959, pp. 84–85.

54 C. Lazzaro-Bruno, "The Villa Lante at Bagnaia," Diss. Princeton 1974, pp. 195f.

55 E. Herget, *Die Sala Terrena im Deutschen Barock*, Frankfurt am Main, 1954, p. 96.

56 *Anamorfosen, Spel met Perspectief*, Amsterdam *Rijksmuseum*, 1975–1976, n. pag.

57 E.-M. Schenck, *Das Bilderrätsel*, Cologne, 1968, p. 167. Schenck relates Arcimboldo's *Male Head* (Coll. A. H. Barr, N.Y.; fig. 164), perceptible in a rocky landscape, to the recondite aspect of the Baroque emblem, its ability to hide the subject. In addition, on the continuing interest in anthropomorphic landscape imagery see B. M. Stafford, "Rude Sublime:

The Taste for Nature's Colossi in the Late Eighteenth and Early Nineteenth Centuries," *Gazette des Beaux-Arts*, LXXXVII, 1976, pp. 113–116.

58 W. Körte, "Deinocrates und die Barocke Phantasie," *Die Antike*, 13, 1937, p. 307.

59 R. Paulson, *Emblem and Expression: Meaning in English Art of the Eighteenth Century*, London, 1975, pp. 76–77.

60 W. Borlase, *The Natural History of Cornwall*, Oxford, 1758, p. 127, and pl. XIII.

61 Bourguet, *Pétrifications*, p. 55.

62 G. H. Schubert, *Ansichten von der Nachtseite der Naturwissenschaft*, Darmstadt, 1967, p. 199. This work was first published in 1808.

63 M. Hadfield, *Topiary and Ornamental Hedges: Their History and Cultivation*, London, 1971, p. 11.

64 R. Ginsberg, "The Aesthetics of Ruins," *Bucknell Review*, XVIII, 1970, p. 91.

65 Battisti, *L'antirinascimento*, p. 180.

66 B. Teyssèdre, *Roger de Piles et les débats sur le coloris au siècle de Louis XIV*, Paris, 1957, p. 68. See the *Lettre du Sieur Le Blond de La Tour à un de sien ami contenant quelques instructions touchant la peinture*, September 4, 1668, published at Bordeaux in 1669. The author bases his argument that painting is divine on such authors as Augustine, Bonaventure and Marsilio Ficino. He concludes: " . . . La qualité de la Peinture est de créer et de produire une seconde fois, ce qui estoit des-jà créé et produit: et ce qui est encore plus merveilleux, *de faire* pour ainsi dire, *quelque chose de rien*, imitant en cela l'Auteur de toutes choses, qui les a *tirées du néant* par une puissance sans seconde" (my italics).

67 P. Hughes, "Landscape, History & Vision: An Approach to Eighteenth-Century Literature," *The Varied Pattern: Studies in the Eighteenth Century*, ed. P. Hughes, Toronto, 1971, p. 165.

68 A. Müller, *Von der Idee der Schönheit: Vorlesungen gehalten zu Dresden im Winter 1807/8*, Berlin, 1809, p. 154.

69 E. Irwin, *A Series of Adventures in the Course of a Voyage up the Red-Sea on the Coasts of Arabia and Egypt; and of a Route through the Desarts of Thebais, hitherto unknown to the European Traveller, in the Year 1777*, London, 1780, p. 310.

70 Romé de l'Isle, *Cristallographie*, I, pp. 80–81.

71 J. Arthos, *The Language of Natural Description in Eighteenth-Century Poetry*, New York, 1966, pp. 130–131. The idea was as old as Plato's notion that minerals were to be classed as waters of a liquid and fusible kind.

72 B. Maillet, *Telliamed, ou entretiens d'un philosophe indien avec un missionnaire françois sur la diminution de la mer, la formation de la terre, l'origine de l'homme*, Amsterdam, 1758, I, p. 106: " . . . Comment n'être pas persuadé que ce globe que nous habitons est l'ouvrage de la mer, & qu'il a été formé dans son sein . . ."

73 M. T. Bourrit, *Nouvelle description des vallées de glace et des hautes montagnes*

qui forment la chaine des Alpes Pennines & Rhétiennes, Geneva, 1783, III, p. 68.

74 D. Raoul-Rochette, *Lettres sur la Suisse*, Paris, 1823, I, p. 47. This work contains handsome lithographs by Villeneuve and Engelmann.

75 H. T. Patterson, "Poetic Genius: Sébastien Mercier into Victor Hugo," *Studies on Voltaire and the Eighteenth Century*, XI, 1960, p. 59.

76 R. Hentzi, *Vues remarquables des montagnes de la Suisse, première partie*, Berne, 1776, p. 11 and pl. 1. This beautiful, but extremely rare, album has a preface by Albert Haller, a natural history commentary by J. S. Wyttenbach and colored aquatints by Caspar Wolff.

77 J. Houel, *Voyage pittoresque des isles de Sicile, de Malte et de Lipari, où l'on traite des antiquités qui s'y trouvent encore; des principaux phénomènes que la nature y offre; du costume des habitans, & de quelques usages*, Paris, 1782, I, p. 28 and pl. 20.

78 Carra, *Nouveaux principes*, I, p. 100.

79 T. D. Kendrick, *The Lisbon Earthquake*, London, 1956, p. 140.

80 J. Huizinga, *Naturbild und Geschichtsbild im achtzehn Jahrhundert, Parerga*, Basel, 1945, p. 166.

81 D. Diderot, *Salons*, ed. J. Seznec and J. Adhémar, Oxford, 1957, III, p. 229, no. 106, *Grande Galerie éclairée du fond*.

82 J. Whitehurst, *An Inquiry into the Original State and Formation of the Earth*, 2nd ed., London, 1786, p. 257.

83 L. Parris, I. Fleming-Williams, C. Shields, *Constable: Paintings, Watercolours & Drawings*, London, 1976, p. 188, no. 311, *Stonehenge* (1836). The following inscription was found on the mount: "The mysterious monument of Stonehenge, standing remote on a bare and boundless heath, as much unconnected with the events of past ages as it is with the uses of the present. It carries you back beyond all historical record into the obscurity of a totally unknown period."

84 J.-H. Bernardin de Saint-Pierre, *Études de la nature, Oeuvres*, Paris, 1818, V, p. 98. The first edition appeared in 1784.

85 R. Assunto, *Il paesaggio e l'estetica, Geminae ortae*, XIV, Naples, 1973, I, pp. 67–68.

86 L.-S. Mercier, *Mon bonnet de nuit*, Neuchâtel, 1785, I, p. 47.

87 J. L. Laborde, *Tableaux topographiques, pittoresques, physiques, historiques, moraux, politiques, littéraires de la Suisse et de l'Italie, ornée de 1200 estampes . . . d'après les dessins de MM. Robert, Perignon, Fragonard, Paris, Poyet, Raymond, Le Barbier, Berthelemy, Ménageot, LeMay, Houel*, etc., Paris, 1777, I, p. lv.

88 H. Huson, *Pythagoron, The Religious, Moral and Ethical Teachings of Pythagoras*, New York, 1947, p. 50.

89 J. J. Wetzel, *Voyage pittoresque aux lacs de Zurich, Zoug, Lowerz, Eggeri et Wallenstadt*, Zurich, 1819, I, p. 130.

90 Raoul-Rochette, *La Suisse*, I, p. 28.

91 H. Rehder, *Die Philosophie der unendlichen Landschaft: Ein Beitrag zur Ges-*

chichte der Romantischen Weltanschauung, Halle, 1932, p. 37.

92 Van Tieghem, *Sentiment de la nature*, p. 169. H. B. de Saussure was a physicist who, for twenty years, visited Chamonix. His *Voyages dans les Alpes* (1779, 1786, 1796) aroused a strong literary interest and were read by more than only scholars. Also see J. A. Deluc, *Lettres physiques et morales sur les montagnes et sur l'histoire de la terre et de l'homme*, The Hague, 1778, p. 127.

The famous geologist, Reader to the Queen of England, shared Saussure's sentiments: "C'est dans les Montagnes sans doute qu'on doit principalement étudier l'histoire du Monde. Outre que les Plaines sont plus altérées par les travaux de l'homme, leur peu d'élévation au dessus du niveau des Mers ne suppose pas des machines aussi puissantes pour les fabriquer & les mettre à sec, que ces masses énormes entassées les unes sur les autres."

93 A. von Humboldt, *Zerstreute Bemerkungen über den Basalt der ältern und neuern Schriftsteller*, 1800(?), p. 38. Humboldt discusses at length how Witte scoured travel accounts. The inscriptions which Chardin and LeBruyn reproduced in their studies of Persia became, in Witte's eyes, indecipherable scoria and zooliths.

94 W. Burkert, *Lore and Science in Ancient Pythagoreanism*, trans. E. I. Minar, Jr., Cambridge, Mass., 1972, pp. 28–38.

95 M. H. Nicolson, *The Breaking of the Circle: Studies in the Effect of the "New Science" upon Seventeenth-Century Poetry*, rev. ed., New York, 1960, pp. 1–2.

96 G. Weise, "Vitalismo, animalismo e panpsichismo e la decorazione nel cinquecento e nel seicento," *Critica d'Arte*, VI, 1959, Pt. I, pp. 385–386.

97 De l'Isle de Sales, *De la nature*, II, pp. 411–412.

98 A. Fabre d'Olivet, *The Golden Verses of Pythagoras*, trans. N. I. Redfield, New York, 1917, pp. 275 ff. This book was first published in 1813. A typical account of metempsychosis and its attendant belief in universal animism is the report of J. H. Grose, *A Voyage to the East-Indies, with Observations on Various Parts There*, London, 1757, p. 297.

99 M. Raymond, "Saint-Martin et l' Illuminisme contre l'Illuminismo," *Sensibilità e razionalità nel settecente*, ed. V. Branca, *VII Corso internazionale di alta cultura*, Venice, 1967, I, p. 47.

100 M. W. Wartofsky, "Diderot and the Development of Materialistic Monism," *Diderot Studies*, II, 1952, pp. 281–286.

101 Diderot, *Le rêve de d'Alembert*, p. 4.

102 G. W. Leibniz, *On the Reform of Metaphysics and on the Notion of Substance, Philosophical Works*, 2nd ed., ed. G. M. Martin, New Haven, 1908, pp. 75–76. This tract first appeared in Latin in 1694.

103 Diderot, *Le rêve de d'Alembert*, p. 70.

104 Bonnet, *Contemplation de la nature*, I, p. 221.

105 Nicolson, *Science and Imagination*, p. 211.

106 Bonnet, *Contemplation de la nature*, I, pp. 31.

107 Mercier, *Mon bonnet de nuit*, I, pp. 21–22.

108 *De David à Delacroix, la peinture française de 1774 à 1830*, Grand Palais, Paris, 1975, nos. 180, 260, 261 and pl. 49. The naturalistic curiosity of the period can be seen in the works of Anne Vallayer-Coster, Spaendonck and, particularly, Berjon.

109 M. Frézier, *Relation du voyage de la mer du sud aux côtes du Chily et du Pérou fait pendant les années 1712, 1713, & 1714*, Paris, 1716, pp. 146 f. " . . . Dans la suite des temps on est venu de refoüiller les mêmes mines, & l'on a trouvé dans le bois, dans les crânes, & dans les os, des filets d'argent qui les pénétroient comme la veine même . . ."

110 Robinet, *De la nature*, I, p. 223. Our *philosophe* cites the case of a bell tower in Derby, England, which became visible from a certain distance; this was not the case a hundred years before. He attributes the change to the lowering of a mountain which formerly intervened between the viewer's line of sight and the church, and the concomitant rising of the mound on which the church stood: "L'un est une preuve manifeste de la dissolution des premières couches montagneuses, & l'autre des reproductions nouvelles de la terre, qui ont rehaussé l'église." In addition, he points out that Santorini did not exist before the time of Seneca and that it continues to "grow" under the feet of its inhabitants. In a similar way, Rhodes and Delos were seen suddenly rising from the sea.

111 M. Watelet, *L'art de peindre: Poème avec des réflexions sur les différentes parties de la peinture*, Paris, 1760, pp. 123–124. " . . . L'Expression s'étend des objets les plus simples, aux objets les plus composés; des corps les moins susceptibles d'action, à ceux qui sont les plus animés; enfin de la matière à l'esprit . . ."

112 T. Takeuchi, "Die Schönheit des Unbelebten," *Proceedings of the 6th International Congress of Aesthetics*, ed. R. Zeitler, Uppsala, 1972, p. 669.

113 Teyssèdre, *Roger de Piles*, p. 66. This constitutes part of the defense for Gerard Van Obstal, rector of the Academy, delivered by Nicolas Lamoignon on December 1, 1667.

114 H. W. Piper, *The Active Universe, Pantheism and the Concept of Imagination in the English Romantic Poets*, London, 1962, p. 4. For students of history and comparative literature the literature on the role of animism and the concept of energy is vast; but this is certainly not the case in art-historical studies. In addition to Piper's work some useful sources are: E. Rothstein, "'Ideal Presence' and the 'Non-Finito' in Eighteenth-Century Aesthetics," *Eighteenth-Century Studies*, IX, 1976, pp. 307–332; L. I. Bredvold, "The Tendency toward Platonism in Neo-Classical Esthetics," *ELH*, I, 1934, pp. 91–119: M. H. Abrams, *Natural Super-Naturalism: Tradition and Revolution in Romantic Literature*, New York, 1971.

115 V. Scully, *The Earth, the Temple, and the Gods: Greek Sacred Architecture*, New Haven, 1962, pp. 19 ff.

116 W. Borlase, *Antiquities Historical and Monumental of the County of Cornwall*, London, 1769, pp. 211–222, pl. XX and pp. 243–256. Borlase, discussing barrows from the Scilly Isles, recalls the custom of making tumuli, that is, heaping materials till they made a hillock over the dead body. "When

the ancients erected stones in order to compose any memorial, there was something expressive either in the number of the Stones of which the Monument did consist, or in the shape of the Stones themselves . . ." Conversely, one can find on the highest hills of Cornwall hollows scooped out from the tops of Logans or Rocking Stones. King Arthur's Bed (pl. XX, fig. vii) is just such an indented surface made to receive the human body. Apparently, men were laid inside the rock to receive lustrations which cured them of disorders.

117 A.-C. Quatremère de Quincy, *Encyclopédie méthodique*, Paris, 1788–1825, III, p. 541.

118 J. Nieuhof, *An Embassy from the East-India Company of the United States Provinces to the Grand Tartar Cham, Emperor of China*, trans. J. Ogilby, London, 1669, p. 269. When the wealthy Chinese intend to erect a tomb "they diligently examine the shape and nature of the Hill for its situation, and are very solicitous to discover a happy piece of Earth: and such they esteem so which has the resemblance of the Head, Tayl, or Heart of a Dragon; which once found, they imagine that according to wish, all things shall go well with their Posterity . . ."

119 O. Siren, *Gardens of China*, New York, 1949, pp. 17 f.

120 J. Grand-Carteret, *La montagne à travers les âges: rôle joué par elle: façon dont elle a été vue*, Grenoble, 1903, I, pp. 11–14.

121 E. Tuveson, "Space, Deity, and the 'Natural Sublime'," *Modern Language Quarterly*, 12, 1951, p. 32.

122 Piper, *Active Universe*, p. 216.

123 Laborde, *Tableaux topographiques*, I, pp. ii.

124 Addison, *Spectator* 412.

125 C. Lamb, *Die Villa d'Este in Tivoli, ein Beitrag zur Geschichte der Gartenkunst*, Munich, 1966, p. 94.

126 W. Stammler, "*Edele Einfalt,*" zur Gerschichte eines Kunst-theoretischen Topos, *Wort und Bild, Studien zu den Wechselbeziehungen zwischen Schrifttum und Bildkunst im Mittelalter*, Berlin, 1962, p. 173.

127 W. Jackson, *Immediacy: The Development of a Critical Concept from Addison to Coleridge*, Amsterdam, 1973, pp. 6 f. I am indebted to Jerrold Lanes for this reference.

128 E. Burke, *Philosophical Enquiry into the Origin of Our Ideas of the Sublime and Beautiful*, New York, 1844, p. 58. See Pt. II, sect. xviii.

129 V. Price, *On the Picturesque*, Edinburgh, 1842, pp. 77–82. Since this article first appeared in the *Art Quarterly*, three essays have come to my attention which have a bearing on my major points: Gerald Finley, "The Encapsulated Landscape: An Aspect of Gilpin's Picturesque," in *City and Society in the 18th Century*, ed. Paul Fritz and David Williams (Toronto: Hakkert, 1973), pp. 197–201; Scott Elledge, "The Background and Development in English Criticism of the Theories of Generality and Particularity," *PMLA*, LXII, 3, 1947, 147–182; and Frederic V. Bogel, "The Rhetoric of Substantiality: Johnson and the Later Eighteenth Century," *Eighteenth-*

Century Studies, 12 (Summer 1979), 457–480. Finley discusses Gilpin's perceptual isolation of that part of a landscape with Picturesque potential. Although encapsulation brings into sharp relief the isolation of the landscape, it requires the reorganization and synthesis of nature's ingredients by the imagination of the traveller. Thus Picturesque encapsulation—with its predetermined pictorial schema—would seem to differ fundamentally from the scientific traveller's discovery of animate particulars. Elledge notes how between 1759 (*Rasselas*) and 1781 (*The Life of Thomson*), Dr. Johnson fell increasingly under the sway of the Scottish critics: Kames, Ogilvie, Campbell, and Blair. Significantly, these laid emphasis on the value of particularizing. Although too many parts in a composition detract from its grandeur and weaken the description, generality can be equally vitiating. However, these writers seem to align themselves with Associationist theory because the happily chosen "single circumstance" or particular is used to summon up a complete image. Finally, Bogel, also speaking of Dr. Johnson, describes the later eighteenth century's fascination with material metaphors and experience—characteristics which corroborate my thesis that the period witnessed the rehabilitation of matter.

130 C. P. Barbier, *William Gilpin, His Drawings, Teachings, and Theory of the Picturesque*, Oxford, 1963, pp. 100–103.

131 H. Burda, *Die Ruine in den Bildern Hubert Roberts*, Munich, 1969, pp. 86–87.

132 Bauer, *Rocaille*, p. 16.

133 W. J. Bate, "The Sympathetic Imagination in Eighteenth Century English Criticism," *ELH*, 12, 1945, p. 156. More recently, Michael Fried has turned his attention to the theme of absorption: see "Absorption: A Master Theme in Eighteenth-Century French Painting and Criticism," *Eighteenth-Century Studies*, 9, 1975–1976, pp. 139–177.

134 D. Summers, "Michelangelo on Architecture," lecture, Department of Art History, University of Virginia, April 8, 1976.

135 K. Viëtor, "De Sublimitate," *Harvard Studies and Notes in Philology and Literature*, XIX, 1937, pp. 264–269.

136 B. Faujas de Saint-Fond, *Voyage en Angleterre, en Écosse et aux iles Hébrides*, Paris, 1797, II, p. 116.

137 Paulson, *Emblem and Expression*, p. 92.

138 R. A. Aubin, *Topographical Poetry in XVIII-Century England*, New York, 1936, p. 57.

139 Diderot, *Salons*, I, p. 229, fig. 82.

140 H. G. Franz, *Niederländische Landschaftsmalerei im Zeitalter des Manierismus*, Graz, 1969, I, pp. 80–83. Patinir's rock monoliths, rock pinnacles, rock openings are fantasies. According to R. A. Koch, *Joachim Patinir*, Princeton, 1968, pp. 19 f., they are constructions based on the artist's personal observation of nature; nonetheless, they defy optical reality.

141 E. W. Manwaring, *Italian Landscape in Eighteenth-Century England*, New

York, 1925, pp. 49 ff. Joshua Reynolds, in his *Lives*, says of Rosa: *"Everything is of a piece*: his Rocks, Trees, Sky, even to his handling, have the *same* rude and wild character which animated his figures" (my italics). Rosa's generalizing is quite distinct from the particularized image which emerges from travel accounts.

142 C. C. L. Hirschfeld, *Theorie der Gartenkunst*, Leipzig, 1779, I, p. 192. Voyage literature reversed the negative attitude towards rude, undressed stones which could be found in landscape gardening theory. For Hirschfeld, naked boulders possessed something unpleasant "in dem sie den natürlichen Charakter der Wildheit und der Wüste an sich tragen, und sind wenig interressant . . ."

143 Borlasc, *Antiquities of Cornwall*, p. 166.

144 M. Cockburn, *Views to illustrate the Route of the Simplon Pass*, London, 1822, MS. text, n. pag.

145 R. Elliott, *Views in the East: Comprising India, Canton, and the Shores of the Red Sea, with Historical and Descriptive Illustrations*, London, 1833, I, n. pag.

146 J. Johnson, *The Oriental Voyager; or, Descriptive Sketches and Cursory Remarks on a Voyage to India and China in His Majesty's Ship Caroline, Performed in the Years 1803–4–5–6*, London, 1807, p. 39.

147 G. H. Bellasis, *Views of Saint Helena*, London, 1815, pl. 6.

148 B. Faujas de Saint-Fond, *Recherches sur les volcans éteints du Vivarais et du Velay*, Grenoble, 1778, p. 271, pl. II (my italics).

149 Frézier, *Voyage*, p. 76.

150 Raoul-Rochette, *La Suisse*, II, p. 40 (my italics).

151 A. J. Pernety, *Journal historique d'un voyage fait aux Iles Malouines en 1763 & 1764 . . . et de deux voyages au Détroit de Magellan*, Berlin, 1769, II, p. 526.

152 Johnson, *Oriental Voyager*, p. 65.

153 J. Ross, *Voyage of Discovery made under the Orders of the Admiralty in His Majesty's Ships Isabella and Alexander for the Purpose of Exploring Baffin's Bay and Inquiring into the Probability of a North-West Passage*, London, 1819, p. 161.

154 T. and W. Daniell, *A Picturesque Voyage to India by Way of China*, London, 1810, pl. 20.

155 Hentzi, *Vues remarquables*, p. 4.

156 M. T. Bourrit, *Description des Aspects du Mont-Blanc*, Lausanne, 1776, p. 142.

157 A. Laborde, *Voyage pittoresque de la France, avec la description de toutes ses provinces*, Paris, 1787–, II, pl. 14. See also his *Voyage pittoresque et historique de l'Espagne*, Paris, 1806, I, p. 13.

158 L. F. Cassas, *Voyage pittoresque de la Syrie, de la Phénicie, de la Palestine, et de la Basse Égypte*, Paris, an VI, II, p. 8, pl. 67.

159 C. Malte-Brun, *Mexico, Early Western Travels 1748–1846*, ed. R. G. Thwaites, Cleveland, 1905, XVIII, p. 378. Also see Hentzi, *Vues remarquables*, pl. 7.

160 J. Bruce, *Travels to Discover the Source of the Nile, in the Years 1768, 1769, 1770, 1771, 1772, and 1773*, Edinburgh, 1790, IV, p. 552.

161 Faujas de Saint-Fond, *Les volcans*, p. 365.

162 M. Park, *The Journal of a Mission to the Interior of Africa in the Year 1805*, London, 1815, p. 53.

163 Hentzi, *Vues remarquables*, p. 7, pl. 6.

164 M. Sherwill, *Ascension du Docteur Edmund Clark et du Capitaine Markham Sherwill à la première sommité du Mont Blanc, les 25, 26, et 27 août 1825*, trans. A. Pelletier, *Mont Blanc*, 1840, I, p. 338. Facing the text on pp. 338 f. Sherwill has interleaved an anonymous eighteenth-century print illustrating one of the ice grottoes found in the Glacier des Bossons.

165 *The Private Journal of Captain G. F. Lyon of H.M.S. Hecla during the Recent Voyage of Discovery under Capt. Parry*, London, 1824, p. 274.

166 P. S. Pallas, *Nouveau voyage dans les gouvernemens méridionaux de l'Empire de Russie dans les années 1793 et 1794*, Paris, 1801, I, 41, and vignette p. 60.

167 W. G. Browne, *Travels in Africa, Egypt, and Syria from the Year 1792 to 1798*, London, 1799, p. 147.

168 Bourrit, *Mont-Blanc*, p. 49.

169 A. M. Holcomb, "The Bridge in the Middle Distance: Symbolic Elements in Romantic Landscape," *Art Quarterly*, XXXVII, 1974, p. 43.

170 H. Börsch-Supan, *Caspar David Friedrich*, Munich, 1973, pp. 29 f.

Science and the Arts in France: The Limitations of an Encyclopedic Ideology

ROGER HAHN

It has become the standard practice among *dix-huitièmistes* to extol the *Encyclopédie* as a great monument to the Enlightenment, the major collective effort of the age which furnishes a concrete embodiment to a glorious ideology. Cochin's dramatic frontispiece commemorates the illumination of the modern Muses by the rays of light emanating from Truth, and successively drawing attention to Reason, Philosophy, Science, and the Arts, while Theology, on her knees, now seeks elsewhere for inspiration.[1] The allegory, which some have interpreted as masonic in inspiration,[2] represents the views of a much larger group of thinkers whose attitudes pervade the era. The *Encyclopédie* has rightly become the symbol for the Enlightenment's yearning for secular learning, for its criticism of established tradition, and for the diffusion of rational knowledge, each ultimately bringing about a transformation of eighteenth-century culture and, in Kant's memorable language, giving mankind the "courage to make use of one's own understanding."

We know, too, that the effort to summarize all useful knowledge and to make it available to a wide-ranging public was masterminded by two of the age's most prominent figures: Jean Le Rond d'Alembert, the ascetic mathematician, equally at home with the rhetoric of salons and the politics at Court, a master at academic speech-making and yet clever in wielding the sarcastic quip; and Denis Diderot, the ambitious provincial artisan's son whose quickness, literary imagination, artistic flair, and deep human sensibility, coupled with an uncompromising sense of independence, pitted him from the outset against the Establishment. In the prospectus of the *Encyclopédie*, in its preliminary discourse, in the explanation of the system of human knowledge, and in hundreds of articles d'Alembert and Diderot offered the elements of an ideology for enlightenment and provided examples of its possibilities for the reform of mankind.

Without wishing to cast any doubt on these accomplishments or on their historic significance, I want to take exception to the standard views often presented about the initial source for this encyclopedic ideology, and about the origins of the encyclopedic project itself. This viewpoint will also force us to raise some questions about the success of the *Encyclopédie* if measured against the intent which originally guided its inception. There is need for such an examination because the praise and adulation heaped on the mammoth enterprise have been so lavish as often to becloud our historic insight. In symbolizing the age, the *Encyclopédie* has been overloaded with the ascription of values that were not necessarily part of the intent of the original organizers; and the two editors' personal stands have been uncritically transferred to the work as a whole without taking into account an independent source for the encyclopedic ideal.

I am particularly concerned by the notion that the *Encyclopédie*, its editors, authors, and publishers were consciously building a *machine de guerre* against organized religion and state authority. That view, in part a reflection of the serious predicament for the editors following the publication of the first volumes, and in part publicized for commercial reasons, was given considerable currency by the overt hostility of established religious authority and the attendant censorship. The anti-philosophic views expressed later by Jacobins reinforced this belief, thereby lending further support to the view that encyclopedists were irreverent plotters against Church and State. Both the right and the left have since taken this view for granted. My intent here is to suggest that the originators of the *Encyclopédie* were less concerned with attacking the Establishment—civil or religious—and more with linking the arts to the sciences through a reorganization of knowledge and a manipulation of information through the word and the picture.[3]

At first glance this does not square well with what we know of d'Alembert and Diderot. On the issue of religion, they both took a dim view of the organized sects of their time, undermined the validity of their historical and ethical foundations, and criticized those thousand ministers of the faith who spread the Gospel through the often imperfect, temporal agency of the Church. With regard to government, both deplored the social injustices fostered and tolerated by various parts of the Establishment, rejected the concept of Divine Right of Kings and mistrusted absolutism. Diderot clashed repeatedly with authority; the less daring d'Alembert contented himself with the displeasure and suspicion of officialdom, but never risked imprisonment. D'Alembert railed against the Jesuits, Diderot flirted with materialism and atheism, and both advocated independence from governmental interference for men of letters. Given these truths, how can one resist accepting the reputation of the *Encyclopédie* as a vehicle critical of the old order, as a veritable *machine de guerre*?

Here precisely lies the difficulty. We have become accustomed to identifying the persons of d'Alembert and Diderot with the enterprise. Clearly they were responsible for its eventual appearance in print. But we have known from documented evidence since 1938 that they were latecomers in conceiving the specific plan for the *Encyclopédie*.[4] The idea was sponsored by a partnership of printers led by André-François Le Breton before Diderot and d'Alembert's serious involvement. Initially the venture was commercially inspired, and some 36,759 livres were already invested before the famous pair took over the editorship.

The original editor from 1746 till October 1747, when he was deposed on grounds of unreliability, was the abbé Jean Gua de Malves.[5] It is in his intellectual universe that we should also seek the original intent of the project. What is immediately noteworthy is that he was neither anti-religious, nor anti-Establishment. On the contrary, Gua de Malves was an abbé of standard (but not excessive) piety, and held posts as Professor at the Collège Royal and as a member of the Royal Society of London and the Paris Academy of Sciences. He had written extensively on the application of Cartesian mathematics, had recently lectured at the Collège on the philosophy of mathematics, on arithmetic, and on Locke's *Treatise on Human Understanding*. He was also a persistent projector of metallurgical schemes to make money, none of which turned out well.[6] Most significantly, it was Gua de Malves, according to his biographer Condorcet, who transformed the publishers' project to produce an augmented translation of the English dictionaries by Chambers and Harris into a true encyclopedia of all knowledge.[7]

We know little more directly about Gua de Malves' philosophic commitments than indicated above. But in tracing the story of his life, I have unearthed what is undoubtedly the source of his conceptions: a small group of young scientists and skilled artisans who met together in Paris two decades before the *Encyclopédie* to promote the union of the arts with science, with the intention of publishing their findings. The resemblance between their plans and those eventually outlined by d'Alembert in the Preliminary Discourse and Diderot in his article "Art" is too striking to be mere coincidence. Moreover, several members of this small and neglected circle either collaborated with the *Encyclopédie* by writing articles, or figure in Le Breton's account book in the mid-1740s. Those who participated in the activities of both groups include Gua de Malves himself, the famous mathematician Alexis Claude Clairaut, the surgeon and later physiocrat François Quesnay, the traveller Charles-Marie de La Condamine, the engraver Jean-Baptiste Michel Papillon, and possibly the chemist C. Habert. The clock-making Le Roy family also figured in both circles, with Julien Le Roy in the 1720s and his son Jean-Baptiste Le Roy writing for the *Encyclopédie*.

The early group to which Gua de Malves belonged while still in his teens has received only passing mention by Franco Venturi and Jacques Proust, but surely deserves more attention.[8] Sometime in 1726, an assembly of Parisian artisans and amateurs of science met in the Faubourg Saint-Germain to share their ideas and inventions with the express purpose of facilitating progress in the practical arts.[9] The group was initiated by an energetic, converted Protestant clockmaker of Huguenot background, Henry Sully, who had settled in France hoping to introduce English watch-making techniques and personnel at Versailles and Saint-Germain.[10] He was thwarted by the jealousy of the French guilds and the instability of economic conditions at the time of the Law affair. Sully also claimed to have invented an accurate time-piece to solve the longitude problem, and managed to have it tested at sea in 1726. That venture also proved to be a failure. Depressed and hounded by creditors, he turned to his confessor and friend, the curé de Saint-Sulpice in Paris, Jean-Baptiste Joseph Languet de Gergy.[11] Together they helped raise funds for the new Church, constructed a meridian line on its floor to establish solar time, and assembled a group of artisans to discuss means of improving their art and their condition. The informal assembly grew to be the Société Académique des Beaux-Arts, nurturing encyclopedic ideals.

The idea was not entirely new. It is likely to have had its distant origins in the meetings of a sub-committee of the Académie des Sciences answering the call of Colbert to produce a detailed "description of the arts and trades" starting in 1693.[12] That group, under the sponsorship of the abbé Jean-Paul Bignon, is probably the same that was mentioned as meeting sporadically in the Galeries du Louvre as late as 1708,[13] and from which the title of the new society was borrowed. Sully and Languet de Gergy revived and transformed the association into a thriving assembly whose character and purpose was specially designed to appeal to those eking out a living from their labor in the artisan quarters near Saint-Germain-des-Prés. Their object was to "perfect the arts with the help of the sciences and thereby to contribute to public utility."[14]

In the collaboration of these two men, Sully and Languet de Gergy, there was a curious mixture of religious fervor, benevolent humanitarianism, concern for the working man, and a deep conviction that progress could be achieved through learning and the exchange of information. Languet de Gergy sponsored the group because it fitted with his ideas of the social utility of Christian charity and the benefits of secular education for the spirit.[15] Sully sparked the Société to assist his fellow-workers and to infuse them with the value that learning might have for their welfare. His personal misfortunes and his familiarity with similar ideas displayed in English circles of Newton's disciples most likely fed his hopes for the possibility of improving artisans' lot through science. It is symptomatic that Sully chose to translate and read David Gregory's essay on the utility of mathematics to the assembly in 1728, shortly before his unexpected death.[16]

The ideology of the Société was outlined in a letter to the abbé Bignon written during the month after Sully's demise by the engraver of maps and teacher of geography, Henri Liébaux, who had assumed responsibility for the association and offered his home on Sunday afternoons for meetings.[17] He indicated that

> . . . la theorie seule n'aloit gueres plus loin qua satisfaire la curiosité, et que la pratique denuée de lumieres de la theorie n'estoit ordinairement qu'une espece d'habile routine que le bonheur du succès n'accompagnoit pas toujours. Cette reflexion luy a fait naitre la pensée de les unir l'une à l'autre en toute occasion persuadée que sans les secours mutuels qu'elles se doivent necessairement donner et dont elles ont reciproquement besoin, elles ne peuvent que rarement et pour ainsy dire par hazard aprocher du point de perfection dont elles sont susceptibles.[18]

The very spelling and wording of the petition, and the accompanying list of participants in the Société suggest a strong utilitarian bent for the association and reveal how solidly founded it was in the class of young, optimistic and aspiring artisans. The list of twenty-five members, not all of whom I have been able to identify, is impressive.[19] Four future Academicians of Science graced the gatherings, including our encyclopedist abbé Gua de Malves, two teachers of the military, Bernard Forest de Bélidor and Jean-Baptiste Clairaut, whose precocious son the mathematician Alexis Claude was already active, and Jean Paul Grandjean de Fouchy, later to be Perpetual Secretary of the Academy, and at this time an inventor of astronomical instruments. The activities and personal associations of these budding scientists reveal the spirit which guided their meetings. Liébaux earned a living as a teacher at the Longpré Academy for young noblemen, as did the elder Clairaut who was at Dugard's school on rue des Boucheries in the Faubourg Saint-Germain.[20] Liébaux was in a family of engravers connected with the Comte de Clermont, who later became the principal sponsor for the Société des Arts. Grandjean de Fouchy was the son of Philippe Grandjean, who played an important part in the reform of French typography sponsored by the Academy of Sciences, and its protector the abbé Bignon participated in the meetings of the academic subcommittee meeting at the Louvre in the 1690s.[21] They had all been under Louis XIV part of circles concerned with improving certain arts by the concentrated use of learning and under the watchful eyes of government officials.

The initial group listed by Liébaux also included Jacques Le Maire, a maker of naval instruments; the English maker of watch springs and friend of Sully, Guillaume Blaky; Enderlin, the Basel inventor of a frictionless pivot; the two brothers Julien and Pierre Le Roy of the clock-making family; and the lawyer for their guild, Pierre-Philippe Andrieu. A few surgeons are also listed, probably those who were locked in a bitter debate with doctors, and claimed to have a solid and independent base for their art without continuing to be subjugated to the medical community.[22] They included the father and son Crestelet-Duplessis who practiced rue du Harlay; and the son of the famous surgeon Jean-Louis Petit who died in 1737 as a young man before he had a chance to realize his full potential.[23] This nucleus of surgeons was to attract later a number of more prominent figures who shared with them the conviction that their art could be raised to a higher status with the infusion of the intensive study of anatomy, quite independently of the guild of doctors. One of the primary results of this type of ferment was the creation in 1731 of the Académie Royale de Chirurgie which was populated in part by members from the Société des Arts.

Another small group consisted of the "directeur particulier" of the Mint, Matthieu Renard du Tasta and his son, and of the Mint's engraver of coins and medals, Joseph-Charles Roettiers. Thomas Germain, of the goldsmith family was also a participant, probably among those who earlier had met at the Galeries du Louvre where he was lodged starting in 1723.[24] A famous dance-master, Pierre Rameau, also dignified the company that clearly included the fine arts along with the practical ones.[25] One can imagine how this exposure to a variety of artisanal activities played on the young Gua de Malves' outlook. The preponderance of craftsmen working in a variety of domains in the Société helped to develop the kind of diversified interest that was to be so prominent in the encyclopedic ideal.

The earliest set of regulations we have for the Société spells this out explicitly. Articles 2 and 3 state that

> 2° Elle s'apliquera a perfectionner les methodes déja suivies et a en inventer de plus propres a unir intimement la theorie et la pratique, afin de rendre celle-cy familiere aux theoriciens et celle-là aux praticiens.
>
> 3° Elle s'atachera principalement a la geographie, la navigation, la mechanique et l'architecture civile et militaire, mais sans negliger pour cela les autres arts, soit utiles, soit purement agreables. Les belles-lettres auront même part a son attention quand ce ne seroit que pour balancer un peu l'austerité et la secheresse des matières ausquelles elle a resolu de sapliquer.[26]

Judging from the composition of members who later joined the Société, that policy remained in effect for its duration. One finds among them lecturers on physics, mechanics and chemistry avid to share their general knowledge, Dr. Pierre Polinière, the abbé Jean-Antoine Nollet, C. Habert and Daniel Jousse, who probably filled out the function of practically-minded theoreticians; the young naval engineer Jean-Gaffin Gallon who was already known in Parisian circles for his talent as a draftsman and a collector of craft lore;[27] the author of a manual for the infantry, Captain Claude Bottée who probably worked with Bélidor at La Fère; and several accomplished artists including Jean-Baptiste Oudry of the Gobelins works, a noted painter; the mapmaker abbé Jean de Lagrive who was later named Fellow of the Royal Society of London; the encyclopedist and wood engraver Jean-Baptiste Michel Papillon; the handwriting expert Sébastien Royllet; the gossip and would-be critic of the arts, the abbé Jean-Bernard Le Blanc, and an architect named Jean Aubert. Among the new makers of instruments or inventors, we find the pilot De Perne; the

Danish astronomer Peder Horrebow; and two opticians Marc Mitou-flet Thomin and Louis Florent Deshais-Gendron, who wrote on eye diseases. Sully and the Le Roy brothers enrolled a number of other clockmakers and artisans concerned with precision instruments, among them the chevalier de Béthune, the abbé Dendelot, Jean-Baptiste Du Tertre, Pierre Gaudron, and Antoine Thiout. Surgeons also joined, and at one time or another included Croissant de Garengeot, Jean Faget, César Verdier, Henri-François Le Dran and the doctors P. Medalon and François Quesnay, who was to become the Secretary of the Académie de Chirurgie and a leading economist associated with the *Encyclopédie*. The list is clearly incomplete, but sufficient to demonstrate the eclectic and practical bent of the Société which, true to its origins, meant to bring about a marriage of science and the arts.

In a later set of regulations eventually printed in 1730, the relationship between particular sciences and crafts was specified. Each of the nine sections of the Société was to have its theoreticians and practitioners.[28] Thus the naval affairs group was to bring together naval engineers, shipwrights and pilots with mathematicians, mechanists, astronomers, hydrographers and geographers. For the fine arts, the plan was to link mechanists and chemists with musicians, goldsmiths, engravers, painters and sculptors. For architecture, there were to be a painter and a sculptor working closely with engineers, architects, geometricians and mechanics. Everything that was useful was worthy of the Société's attention.

Despite the absence of minutes of meetings, we know that the Société des Arts grew in size and formality. Meetings, initially held on Sundays to permit artisans to attend without missing a day of work, were later scheduled for Sundays and Thursdays from 4 to 6 P.M.[29] In 1728, the Comte de Clermont, a great-grandson of the Grand Condé who thrived on military and galant exploits, superseded the curé de Saint-Sulpice as protector and offered his hotel at the Petit Luxembourg for the gatherings.[30] Publicity was given in the *Mercure de France*, the *Mémoires de Trévoux* and the *Journal de Verdun*. The Société emerged from semi-obscurity. Rules of conduct were established; election procedures were promulgated; and membership limits were imposed. The Société took on the aspect of a little Academy, with the presentation of papers, the examination of proposals by ad hoc *commissions*, the opening of prize-winning competitions for two of the most useful inventions of the year, a recording secretary, and even the Société's approval of books about to be published by its members. By 1730, the Société produced a 35-page set of printed regulations with 46 articles, which specified that members were to be given yearly assignments collecting information about the arts and crafts under pain of exclusion if not fulfilled. The plan was to prepare histories of the arts and trades, as recommended by Bacon, and to publish them as *Recueils* which would become "les Archives de la prospérité particulière et publique, et prouveront à tous les siècles futurs, que la Société étoit digne par ses entreprises d'une si haute protection."[31]

Anyone familiar with d'Alembert's Preliminary Discourse will have easily recognized the themes he took up in the *Encyclopédie*. The union of theory and practice, the way in which systematic examinations shake up routines by a consideration of principles, the expected promotion of the stature of artisans through learning, each stood as a major goal of the *Encyclopédie*. It is true that such values were also to be found in dictionaries the new enterprise was meant to supersede, particularly in Antoine Furetière's *Dictionnaire universel* and John Harris's *Lexicon Technicum*.[32] But the close parallels between the Société des Arts' goals and those taken over by the editors of the *Encyclopédie*, and the overlapping membership of the two groups make it eminently likely that the Société played a specific role in shaping the encyclopedic ideology. The Société meant to do more than prepare a succinct compilation of definitions and descriptions; it was to lead a massive cumulative effort destined to record the annals of invention and to instill in its members and the public a spirit of regeneration and progress. Long before the *Encyclopédie* was conceived, the Société des Arts was leading the way in the advancement of the arts.

For all the above, documentation to back up my claims exists. It would be even more conclusive if one could demonstrate positively a link between the gathering of information by the members of the Société and the plates used by Diderot in the *Encyclopédie*. Some circumstantial evidence for this exists. It was Jean-Gaffin Gallon, a member of the Société, who was chosen to edit the first six volumes of the *Machines et inventions approuvées par l'Académie Royale des Sciences*, first announced in December 1733, just when the Société was moving into a state of great activity. Many of the names of inventors in this *Recueil* are associated with the Société.[33] Two decades later, it was another member of the Société, Grandjean de Fouchy, who presided over the issuance of the Academy's *Description des arts et métiers*, whose plates were often very similar to those prepared for the *Encyclopédie*.[34] Several members of the Société also produced treatises that carried out the goals of the Société and were borrowed with or without acknowledgment by the encyclopedists. All of these works—at times following the examples set by "Theater of Machines" literature, and at times fulfilling a function explicitly assigned to the Academy of Sciences by Colbert in 1675—shared a common mission to provide public access to technological information by giving a visual description of machines, honoring the inventive genius of mankind, and prodding him on to better things. It is futile to try to trace influences back to a single source, but many of the historical circumstances point to a link to the Société des Arts.

Repeated reference to the Academy of Sciences also disturbs the simple linear relations I have been trying to sketch linking the Société and the *Encyclopédie*. By introducing this third actor, I can also shift from a discussion of origins to one of the limits of the encyclopedic ideology. Large and ambitious as it was, the Société never succeeded in producing a publication of its own or in markedly advancing the arts by coupling them with the sciences. Moreover, the Société des Arts was aborted in the mid-1730's for reasons peculiar to the politics of French culture. Even the transference of its goals to the *Encyclopédie* and to similar enterprises later in the century failed to turn this Baconian dream into a reality. Some of the explanation for this disappointment derives from the machinations of the Academy of Sciences, which often acted like the abandoned fiancé in a triangular relationship.[35]

The decline of the Société seems to coincide with the Comte de Clermont's aggressive leadership when the group began to advertise its aspirations too loudly. The decision in 1733 to announce the Société's judgment on technological proposals, to award prizes of 300 francs for the finest inventions, and to publish annals of the arts were sufficient to arouse the Academy's jealousy and to galvanize it into action.[36] Colbert had initially given the academicians national jurisdiction in the realm of technology and assigned them a mission which they had somewhat neglected. While they had sporadically acted effectively in private chambers, they produced little in full view of the public. Only Réaumur's writings on steel and iron emerged from the presses in 1722.[37] Scores of machines and inventions, some accompanied by miniature models, had been presented for approval to the official royal body, but after having been privately acknowledged gathered dust in the Academy's archives. The Société des Arts, with the enthusiasm of a younger association eager to make a name for itself, wanted to fill a vacuum by assuming responsibilities which the Academy had eschewed. In so doing, they not only embarrassed the venerable institution, but challenged its authority.

The established royal body moved swiftly to block the progress of the Société, using all the stratagems of an accomplished political actor. First they persuaded the abbé Bignon to reject the Société's wish to be elevated to the level of a royal institution.[38] There are intimations that the Academy also blocked any publication planned by the Société.[39] They then began to co-opt its more prominent members into the Academy, making it clear to the select individuals that allegiance to both societies was unwise. La Condamine, in a letter to Grandjean de Fouchy written years after the fact, relates his embarrassment on being asked to join the Academy and leave the Société.[40] At the time, La Condamine was not merely Director of the Société, but also dependent upon the Comte de Clermont for his military career. He withdrew from the Société and became a professional academician. One by one some members of the Société were picked off: La Condamine in 1730, Clairaut and Grandjean de Fouchy in 1731, Gallon in 1735. Others were made to understand that their future at the Academy would be compromised if they joined the Société or remained in it.

The ruse to smother the Société by stripping it of its most prominent members and adopting its functions was successful. We hear nothing of the Société past 1736.[41] Gallon was hired to publish the *Machines et inventions,* in part undercutting the need for a published *Recueil* by the Société. The Academy also took its cue from the Société and began to speed up its preparation of the long-heralded *Description des arts et métiers* which was eventually forced into the public domain by the publication of the *Encyclopédie* itself. Thus in one of the ironies history is fond of making, the Société achieved its goal posthumously, but without receiving credit for its pioneering efforts. Both the *Encyclopédie* and the Academy benefited from the artisans' untimely attempts to link the arts to the sciences.

Two later attempts to revive associations with essentially the same purposes were also nipped in the bud by the Academy. One was a society for the mechanical arts sponsored by the Le Roy family and Thiout; the other, the Société libre d'émulation created in 1776, but enjoying an even shorter life span than the Société des Arts.[42] Like so many other institutions of the Ancien Régime, the Academy knew that it would survive only by protecting its prerogatives and opposing attempts to usurp its functions. Instead of concentrating on one of the goals for which it was originally instituted, the Academy preferred to concern itself with institutional continuity by maintaining the status quo. Less than a century after its establishment, the Academy became a conservative force in the culture of the Enlightenment.

The situation is symptomatic of a deeper problem affecting Ancien

Régime culture in France. In contrast to the accomplishments of similar associations across the Channel, the French were unable to benefit fully from the Lord Chancellor's views. In England, the Baconian dream of fructifying practice by theory bore fruit. It was responsible for many of the key technological advances that made the industrial revolution possible. Such different improvements as Jethro Tull's seed drill, the Boulton-Watt steam engines, and the Roebuck lead chamber process each owed their success to the acquaintance of their inventors with scientific knowledge and practices. Many other efforts were encouraged by local societies of arts, initially created in Scotland and Ireland, but eventually popular throughout the British Isles.[43] These societies, whose goals were not markedly different from those of the Société des Arts, held periodic meetings, published proceedings, offered premiums for inventions, and helped to provide enlightened artisans with a respectable place in English life. Ultimately the key to industrial success lay in the adoption of new modes of production by entrepreneurs willing to invest in order to make them work. In England, the discovery of new techniques informed by science was ultimately appreciated because it was profitable.

A different setting confronted the Baconian ideology when it crossed the Channel. France was prepared for an intellectual transformation in a cultural manner. The academic system that Colbert had orchestrated under Louix XIV was dependent upon carefully defined cultural territories and jurisdictions, each jealously guarded. Institutional entities, especially those supported by the Crown, became principal objects of concern, often to the detriment of the function they were meant to serve. The French economy was also regulated by protective laws that discouraged the implantation of new techniques in agriculture and manufacturing. Even the guild system mirrored attitudes shared by administrative and commercial leaders, conservative even while proclaiming their effort to maintain quality. Reform, though it was often and deeply desired by some, was difficult to impose from above, and rarely ventured from below by wealthy individuals. Capital was more often invested in the purchase of offices than in the hope of further economic gain.

The French prided themselves—not without reason—on a high degree of cultural refinement which favored the salons, the reading circles, and the production of beautiful books for sumptuous libraries. Even the royal manufactures—the Gobelins works or the Sèvres factory—were looked upon as producing ornaments of culture rather than as commercial ventures. It was normal that a good literary reputation was much preferable to that of a successful inventor or a skilled craftsman. Even the successful financiers turned to culture.[44] Under such circumstances, it was not likely that the union of the arts and sciences would be significant much beyond academic discussion rooms, and the private circles of literate society. Even when this union was consummated, the practical advantages were rarely publicized if they had commercial merit.

In the French context the goals of the Société des Arts and the planners of the *Encyclopédie* meant the reshuffling of the cards of knowledge rather than the improvement of the material well-being of society. There would be a paper juxtaposition of science and the arts which could be best displayed between the covers of handsome books full of beautiful engravings. There would be a widespread propaganda about the significance of this union and a general rhetorical ferment, but not much more. The intended revolution was conceived in cultural terms, not, until the end of the century, on a political or economic level. Because the practical arts have rarely been improved by this essentially polite, but largely literary modification, it is not surprising that the ideology was never effectively put into practice.

To know why would require a new look at the mental and social attitudes dominant in French society. For, despite the well-intentioned statements about the dignity of craftsmen, there persisted a strong current of disdain of artisans, surfacing in various ways as far back as Colbert's regime. At the time when the Academy of Sciences was on the drawing boards, the notion of a Compagnie des arts et sciences which would overlook social and educational distinctions between savants and unlettered craftsmen was consciously set aside for an aristocratic, elitist view of learning.[45] At the Académie Française, a decade or so later, Antoine Furetière's conception of a dictionary which was to include terminology of the arts, crafts and commerce, was shunted aside in favor of the sterile belletristic tradition.[46] In mid-eighteenth century, when the son of Julien Le Roy was admitted into the Academy of Sciences, he was asked to renounce in writing his association with the watch-making guild and his family business.[47] These are but three revealing examples of official culture rejecting situations which would have helped to provide artisans with a respectable place in French society. In England, by contrast, the value of the craftsman and his work was often recognized when it yielded economic advantage.

Ancien Régime France was not ready to follow the Baconian dream to its logical conclusion. It was only after the political revolution— when the educational system became more open to talent, and elitism was seriously challenged—that the artisan was given a chance. French society then took its cue from the English, this time importing ideas and practices that had already borne fruit in the industrial revolution.

I began by chiding *Encyclopédie* scholars who refer principally to the work as a gigantic *machine de guerre*. Considering the impact of the *Encyclopédie* they are justified in concentrating their attention on this aspect. It seems likely that the initial message of the originators of the encyclopedic mentality was superseded when it became clear that the intellectual impact and commercial success of the enterprise would depend upon its reputation as a critical dictionary filled with thinly-disguised attacks on religion and traditional government, rather than as a handbook of practical reform for the arts and trades. In mid-century, France was ready for an intellectual assault on the authority of the Church and the State, but not for a fundamental realignment of technology and science.

NOTES

1 Georges May, "Observations on the Allegory: The Frontispiece of the *Encyclopédie*," *Diderot Studies*, 16 (1973), 159–74. Richard N. Schwab (in *Eighteenth-Century Studies*, 2 (1969), 255) and Walter E. Rex (in "A Propos of the Figure of Music in the Frontispiece of the *Encyclopédie*," forthcoming, in *Acts of the International Musicological Society*) consider that Reason is about to place a bit in the mouth of Theology, to exercise proper control.

2 For a review and dismissal of these views, see Robert Shackleton, "The *Encyclopédie* and Freemasonry," in William H. Barber, ed., *The Age of Enlightenment* (Edinburgh: Oliver and Boyd, 1967), pp. 223–37; and for another view, Dorothy B. Schlegel, "Freemasonry and the *Encyclopédie* reconsidered," *Studies on Voltaire and the Eighteenth Century*, 90 (1972), 1433–60. Cesare Vasoli, *L'Enciclopedismo del seicento* (Naples: Bibliopolis, 1978), and Shackleton's more recent research on the term *encyclopédie*, give one pause to reconsider the issue in a broader perspective.

3 These ideas are suggested but remain undeveloped in Franco Venturi, *Le Origini dell'Enciclopedia*, 2d ed. (Turin: Einaudi, 1963), pp. 14–16, and Jacques Proust, *L'Encyclopédie* (Paris: A. Colin, 1965), p. 27.

4 Louis-Philippe May, "Histoire et sources de l'*Encyclopédie* d'après le registre des délibérations et de comptes des éditeurs et un mémoire inédit," *Revue de synthèse*, 15 (1938), 7–109.

5 Frank A. Kafker, "Gua de Malves and the *Encyclopédie*," *Diderot Studies*, 19 (1978), 93–102.

6 Information about his family's financial dealings is contained in Guy Chaussinand-Nogaret, *Les Financiers de Languedoc au XVIIIe siècle* (Paris: S.E.V.P.E.N., 1970), pp. 62–63.

7 Condorcet, "Eloge de M. l'abbé de Gua," *Histoire de l'Académie Royale des Sciences, 1786* (Paris: Imprimerie Royale, 1788), pp. 68–69.

8 See note 4 above. Reference to the group may also be found in several éloges by Fouchy and Condorcet read before the Académie des Sciences, and in d'Alembert, "Article du Comte de Clermont," *Oeuvres philosophiques, historiques et littéraires* (Paris: Bastien, an XIII), XI, 405–16.

9 In notes prepared for his biography kept in the dossier Grandjean de Fouchy at the Archives de l'Académie des Sciences, Fouchy indicates he became a member in 1726. For more details on the group, see also *Mercure de France* (December 1728), 2893–94, and *Suite de la clef*, 28 (November 1730), 321.

10 Henry Sully, *Règle artificielle du temps*, new ed. (Paris: G. Dupuis, 1737), pp. 389–409.

11 See for details letters of Angélique Delisle to her brother dated 24 January and 7 May 1728 and 17 January 1729, MS 1508, fols. 42v, 43r, 47v, and 49r, Chambre des Députés, Paris.

12 Claire Salomon-Bayet, "Un préambule théorique à une Académie des Arts," *Revue d'histoire des sciences et de leurs applications* 23 (1970), 229–50.

13 André Jammes, *La Réforme de la typographie royale sous Louis XIV* (Paris: P. Jammes, 1961), pp. 6–7 and 33. Jaugeon, one of the members of the original group, was still active in the project in 1718, as is evident by the letter cited in Jammes, p. 36, n. 22. Meetings at the Galeries du Louvre are mentioned in Sully, *Règle artificielle*, p. 407, and in MS fr. 22225, fol. 7r, Bibliothèque Nationale, Paris.

14 Sully, *Règle artificielle*, p. 293.

15 For Languet de Gergy's career, see Raoul Chevreul, "Une belle figure bourguignonne: L'abbé Jean Baptiste Joseph Languet de Gergy (1675–1750)," *37e Congrès de l'Association bourguignonne des sociétés savantes, 1966* (Dijon, s.d.), pp. 45–47. For the ideology followed by Languet in education, see Carolyn Lougee, "Noblesse, Domesticity and Social Reform: The Education of Girls by Fénelon and St. Cyr," *History of Education Quarterly*, 14 (1974), 87–113.

16 Sully, *Règle artificielle*, p. 408. The essay may have been the one cited by Christina M. Eagles, in "David Gregory and Newtonian Science," *British Journal for the History of Science*, 10 (1977), 223.

17 Letter of Angélique Delisle, 17 January 1729, MS 1508, fol. 49v, Chambre des Députés, Paris. Liébaux' home was at the "carrefour Saint-Benoît." Liébaux' letter to Bignon is dated 8 October 1728, and is found in MS fr. 22230, fols, 372 r and v, Bibliothèque Nationale, Paris.

18 "Idée de l'etablissement de la Société Academique des Beaux-Arts, du plan sur lequel elle se propose de travailler et des reglemens quelle croit devoir observer pour remplir ses vues," MS fr. 22225, fol. 7v, Bibliothèque Nationale, Paris.

19 MS fr. 22230, fol. 373r. I have not identified "le Normand, Des Oeuvres, l'abé de Romieu, and Pelays." The *Almanach royal* for 1729, p. 208, lists a Des Oeuvres de la Blanchardière as "avocat au Parlement," but there is nothing to substantiate linking him with Des Oeuvres in the Liébaux list.

20 Liébaux identifies himself as "à l'ancienne Académie de Longpré." Clairaut is listed as a teacher of mathematics in the *Almanach royal* for 1731, p. 313.

21 See A. Jammes, *La Réforme*, passim. In the correspondence between the son of Philippe and Bignon, kept in MS fr. 22229, Bibliothèque Nationale, Paris, there are numerous references to the Fouchy family showing that it was on intimate terms with the abbé Bignon. Fouchy was for many years also in the employ of the Duc d'Orléans.

22 A revealing document was authored by a later member of the Société des Arts, P. Medalon, entitled *Problême Philodemique, si c'est par zele ou par jalousie que ces médecins s'opposent à l'établissement de 5 démonstrateurs chirurgiens dans l'amphitéatre de S. Côme* (s.l., [1725]), pp. 15–17. For a general discussion, see Paul Delaunay, *Le Monde médical parisien au dix-huitième siècle* (Paris: J. Rousset, 1906), pp. 166–80.

23 For Crestelet-Duplessis, see *Almanach royal* for 1729, p. 343; on Petit's son, see Antoine L. J. Bayle, *Biographie médicale* (Paris: A. Delahays, 1855), II, 182–83.

24 Germain Bapst, *Etudes sur l'orfèvrerie française au XVIIIe siècle: Les Germain, orfèvres-sculpteurs du Roy* (Paris: J. Rouam, 1887), p. 38.

25 The list of members includes the name Rameau, without further identification. While it is plausible that this could be the composer Jean-Philippe Rameau who wrote treatises on the application of mathematical principles to composing, an off-handed comment by Angélique Delisle in a letter of 17 January 1729 (MS 1508, fol. 49v, Chambre des Députés, Paris) to a "maistre à dancer de musique" leads me to believe that it was Pierre Rameau, who at this time lived not far, at the Faubourg-Montmartre (*Mercure de France* [December 1728], 2696).

26 "Reglemens de la societé academique des Beaux Arts," MS fr. 22225, fols. 1 r and v, Bibliothèque Nationale, Paris.

27 Already on 2 May 1728, Bignon was writing to Réaumur "Le S. Galon . . . a un grand talent pour le dessein et ne scait pas mal les mathematiques, de manière que si nous revenions à reprendre votre grand ouvrage des arts, il pourroit ne vous y être pas inutile," MS fr. 22234, fol. 178, Bibliothèque Nationale, Paris.

28 *Reglement de la Societé des Arts* (Paris: G. F. Quillau, 1730), article VIII, pp. 7–9.

29 In 1728, "Les assemblées de la societé se tiendront le dimanche apres midy depuis quatre heures jusqua six et cela afin de ne detourner personne des devoirs de son etat" (MS fr. 22225, fol. 10r, Bibliothèque Nationale, Paris); in 1730 the *Reglement*, article XVI, p. 14, specifies regular meetings on both Sunday and Thursday.

30 Angélique Delisle notes in a letter of 14 February 1730 that meetings have been held for three weeks at the Comte de Clermont's "hotel" (MS 1508, fol. 64r, Chambre des Députés, Paris).

31 *Mémoires pour l'histoire des sciences et des beaux arts* (*Mémoires de Trévoux*) (February 1733), 359.

32 Proust, *L'Encyclopédie*, pp. 16–18; and Jean Macary, "Les Dictionnaires universels de Furetière et de Trévoux et l'esprit encyclopédique moderne avant l'*Encyclopédie*," *Diderot Studies*, 16 (1973), 145–58.

33 The announcement of the publication is in *Mémoires de Trévoux* (December 1733), 2196–98. Among those who presented memoirs to the Academy were Gallon, Grandjean de Fouchy, Lemaire, Le Roy, Nollet, Sully, and Thiout.

34 Georges Huard, "Les planches de l'*Encyclopédie* et celle de la Description des arts et métiers de l'Académie des Sciences," *Revue d'histoire des sciences et de leurs applications*, 4 (1951), 238–49; and George B. Watts, "The *Encyclopédie* and the Description des arts et métiers," *The French Review*, 25 (1952), 444–54.

35 Details from a different perspective can be followed in Roger Hahn, *The Anatomy of a Scientific Institution: The Paris Academy of Sciences 1666–1803* (Berkeley: University of California, 1971), pp. 108–10.

36 *Mémoires de Trévoux* (February 1733), 357–59.

37 *L'Art de convertir le fer forgé en acier* (Paris: Michel Brunet, 1722).

38 Amans Alexis Monteil, *Traité de matériaux de divers genres d'histoire*, new ed. (Paris: E. Duverger 1836), I, 41.

39 Pierre Remond de Sainte-Albine, *Mémoire sur le laminage du plomb*, 3d ed. (Paris: Guérin, 1746), p. v.

40 Copy of an undated letter (probably 1766) in MS LI a685, fol. 659 r, Oeffentliche Bibliothek der Universität Basel.

41 *Mémoires de Trévoux*, (November 1736), 2394–2401, which prints a memoir presented to the Société by Le Maire on 2 September 1736.

42 Jean André Lepaute, *Traité d'horlogerie* (Paris: J. Chardon, 1755), p. xxiii; and Ferdinand Berthoud, *Essai sur l'horlogerie* (Paris: J. C. Jombert, 1763), I, xlv-xlvi. See also Arthur Birembaut, "Quelques réflexions sur les problèmes posés par la conservation et la consultation des archives techniques françaises," *Archives internationales d'histoire des sciences*, 19 (1966), 80–81, and Hahn, *The Anatomy*, pp. 110–11.

43 Roger Hahn, "The application of science to society: The Societies of Arts," *Studies on Voltaire and the Eighteenth Century*, 25 (1963), 829–36.

44 A suggestive analysis of this phenomenon is given in Chaussinand-Nogaret, *Les Financiers*, part 5.

45 Hahn, *The Anatomy*, pp. 11–15.

46 See introduction by Alain Rey of Antoine Furetière, *Dictionnaire universel* (Paris: S.N.L., 1978).

47 Dossier Jean-Baptiste Le Roy, Archives de l'Académie des Sciences, Paris.

Enlightenment and Public Education during the French Revolution: The View of the Ideologues

THOMAS E. KAISER

That the social reforms of the French Revolution were inspired in large part by the ideas of the Enlightenment has long been recognized. That the Revolution in turn molded the social ideas of the revolutionaries who carried the banner of the Enlightenment into the political struggles of the 1790s has been much less appreciated, largely because until recently relatively little scholarly attention was paid to the last generation of philosophes. It is the general purpose of this article to reconsider the relationship between Revolutionary politics and the social policy of the late Enlightenment through an examination of the educational program of the group eventually known as the Ideologues (*idéologues*), self-proclaimed champions of the Enlightenment cause and active participants in the politics of the Revolutionary era.[1] The shifting course of their pedagogical notions across the Revolution provides as clear a demonstration as any of the political pressures to which the pro-revolutionary philosophes were subject and their sensitivity to those pressures.

To the Ideologues, grouped around the salon of Mme Helvétius in Auteuil, the Revolution represented an essentially spiritual struggle for the soul of France. As they saw it, the Old Regime had collapsed principally because of its moral and intellectual corruption; those

95

who sought to reconstruct the new order were waging, in Condorcet's words, not a "revolution of government" against a "despot" but a "revolution of opinions and wills" against "error and voluntary servitude."[2] The new society, they held, would never be secure until a new system of education, based upon the principles of enlightened social theory, was established to extirpate "error and voluntary servitude" and to teach citizens the truths that made them truly free. Into their programs for the redesign of French education, therefore, the Ideologues poured their greatest energies and their highest hopes.

What the Ideologues in fact encountered during the Revolutionary decade was a political struggle fraught with dangers, a struggle that would test their stamina and theories to the limit. Three characteristics of the Ideologues' educational program and philosophy would be most affected: first, the degree to which the program was aimed at the removal of social inequalities; second, the degree to which the program would allow for and encourage academic freedom for teachers and students; third, the degree to which the Ideologues would admit to the potential fallibility of the ideas they proposed as the basis for curricula. Concentrating more on principles of argument than on specific proposals for institutional change, this article will show how the Ideologues, prompted by political developments, altered their program in these three respects; the result, it shall be argued, was an educational policy that came to embrace forms of elitism and authoritarianism which the Ideologues at the outset of the Revolution had sworn to destroy.

I

The distinguishing feature of the Ideologue educational program down to the Directory lay in its attempt to provide the means for universal self-emancipation from self-imposed tutelage and at the same time to reconcile the freedom obtained through self-emancipation with social rationality. The lingering doubts which the pre-Revolutionary philosophes harbored with regard to the possibility of universal self-emancipation[3] were swept away by the emergence of a politically significant popular movement, early in the Revolution, that made any so-called "aristocratic" program of education politically unfeasible. With the old academies torn down and the hold of the Church on education broken, most Revolutionaries looked to the state to provide popular enlightenment through a system of public education.[4] The goal of educational policy, like that of social policy generally, was clear—to enable every person "to enjoy the full plenitude of [his] rights,"[5] rights which not only implied freedom from arbitrary interference in life and property, but also, at least by most accounts, some participation in politics and the major business of society. Whereas Turgot, less than twenty years before the Revolution, had proposed in a memo to the king an education for citizenship that would lead men on a rational basis "to cherish your authority" and to "make manifest the obligations they have to society and to your power which protect it,"[6] Condorcet, his disciple, argued that the goal of education could not be to make men "admire" acts of government but to enable men to understand them and to correct them; according to Condorcet, insofar as men did come to "love" the law, it was first necessary that they know how to evaluate it.[7]

The first order of business was to do away with the artificial barriers to truth placed in the way of the ordinary citizen, according to the Ideologues, by the Old Regime; henceforth, truth could not be the private preserve of corporate bodies or privileged clergies—it would become the patrimony of all mankind.[8] With the freedom to acquire truth had to come the freedom to express truth as individuals saw it; henceforth, no regime, no matter how enlightened, could suppress intellectual dissent for purposes of maintaining a socially sanctioned dogma. As Dominique Joseph Garat explained, one might as a result of freedom of expression be "condemned" to listen to the rantings of the "barely enlightened," but ultimately, with the "healthy conflicts of all opinions," France would show that "liberty is strong enough in principles of order and justice to make use of its inner battles . . . to spread in all classes reason, respect for law, arts, and sciences. . . ."[9] The freedom to teach and to be taught, which the Ideologues closely identified with the right of self-expression, was therefore in no way to be abridged. All men, proclaimed Pierre-Jean-Georges Cabanis and Mirabeau, are entitled to teach what they know "and even what they do not know"; society would now have to leave it ultimately up to the individual to choose between truth and the "deceits of ignorance."[10] Education, they contended, was a form of commerce; the state could not legitimately intervene in the relationship between buyer and seller within what to them was literally a marketplace of ideas, any more than it could legitimately interfere in the formation of other commercial contracts.[11]

Yet clearly education was not just any sort of commodity, and if the state could not prevent any legitimate private sale of ideas, neither, thought the Ideologues, was it prevented from undertaking to provide public education, as even the entrepreneurially minded Cabanis and Mirabeau agreed. More, indeed, than just freedom was required; the state had a positive obligation to make education available to all, such that everyone, through the acquisition of *lumières*, would be able to obtain full redemption of their rights. "Public instruction," asserted Condorcet flatly, "is a duty of society with regard to its citizens."[12] The problem lay in determining just what would be taught and how, in insuring that in the educational system of the new order freedom would be maintained at the same time that the schools spread true enlightenment. On the one hand, the Ideologues wanted to avoid creating, and for political reasons argued strongly against, a system of education that smacked of the corporatism of the Old Regime; on the other hand, it seemed absolutely essential that the new educational system teach only that which was in conformity with the truth as established by the highest Enlightenment authorities.

This problem continued to trouble the Ideologues, especially as their programs fell under increasing criticism from the Jacobin left.[13] Condorcet's plan for a hierarchy of academic institutions, descending from a National Society of Sciences and Arts to the primary schools, appeared particularly vulnerable in this regard, the more so since Condorcet had been for many years the perpetual secretary of the much-resented Royal Academy of Sciences. Later, in fact, to be attacked by a fellow Ideologue, Pierre Claude François Daunou, for wanting to create an "academic church,"[14] Condorcet rested the case for his grand program on a subtle argument which was designed to reconcile the elitist tendencies of advanced scientific institutions with the egalitarian elements of early Ideologue political philosophy. Basing his plan on the notion that it was only through the expansion and propagation of truth that society had emerged from the age of barbarism,[15] that truth was, as he put it, "the sole sovereign of free people,"[16] Condorcet was convinced, first, that the furthering of the individual and collective interest required both the accumulation of new truths and the further dissemination of these truths throughout society, and second, that these goals could only be achieved through a system of publicly managed scientific research and popular education. In his plan for a new system of education, great research bodies at the upper levels of the hierarchy were charged with the responsibility of overseeing institutions at the lower levels; such a distribution of authority, Condorcet believed, would insure that there was a percolation of newly discovered truths down through the system, thereby allowing everyone to benefit from the advances made by those endowed with special abilities.

Was this not a prescription for corporatism, a thinly disguised plan which would have led to publicly sanctioned inequality, a program which would once again have placed the people in a state of subjection to a few and created dogmas that all would be obliged to accept as truth? Condorcet insisted that it was not. While he admitted that his plan would not provide everyone with the *same* amount of instruction, men being too different in their life circumstances to allow for a full uniformity of instruction,[17] everyone would, according to Condorcet, receive a *sufficient* quantity of instruction to allow him to conduct his life adequately as an active citizen. It was inevitable, Condorcet believed, that in modern society some would know more than others, but this did not mean that the less informed were in a true state of dependency with regard to the better educated; so long, Condorcet put it, as a person did not need another to do such things for him as read a letter, calculate expenses, and tell him what the law is, that person was free and at least in a juridical sense equal to all other men. "The man," Condorcet wrote, "who knows the four rules of arithmetic cannot be dependent on a Newton to do anything in ordinary life."[18] While denying that he intended to create twenty-four million publicists,[19] Condorcet did envisage a future society in which the ordinary man and the philosopher were "not in any way two different beings, having a different language, different ideas, and even different opinions."[20] To some degree, at least, the people, transformed after a model of the Ideologues themselves, could now participate in the society of enlightened men. So that the inequalities of education would not re-enforce those of wealth and class, Condorcet required that all costs of education be born by the state; anyone with sufficient funds to support himself could rise as high in the academic ladder as his talents would carry him.[21]

But what of the danger of re-creating academic dogmas? In certain respects Condorcet's demand that public instruction confine itself to the teaching of established truth alone[22] suggested the imposition of such dogmas, especially since Condorcet tended to identify truth with what Enlightenment leaders as a group believed to be true.[23] In fact, Condorcet argued, there already existed certain firmly established truths whose required teaching as established fact in no way violated the rights of teachers or students; the number and nature of such established truths was such that Condorcet could propose that the choice of curriculum and books to be used in public primary education rest with a high central authority.[24] At the same time, however, Condorcet made it perfectly clear that he regarded the number of such established truths as extremely small;[25] moreover, no matter how high his hopes were for the reconstruction of knowledge through the application of probability theory, he explicitly denied that complete certainty could be attained in any academic discipline except mathematics.[26] Hence Condorcet explicitly stipulated that, beyond the primary level, instructors would enjoy full academic freedom.[27] Just because public authorities had no right to teach "opinions" as if they were "truths," there could no longer be any teaching corps in the traditional sense. "Create a teaching corps," Condorcet warned, "and you are sure to have created either tyrants or instruments of tyranny."[28] But what if a duly appointed instructor taught what was clearly false? In such a case, Condorcet assured the Legislative Assembly, the scientific community would immediately discredit his lessons and thereby presumably convince such an instructor to revise his lessons,[29] though Condorcet prescribed no mechanism to forcibly remove this *savant imaginaire*.

In sum, Condorcet could defend his plan for the re-organization of French education by arguing that he had reconciled the requirements of science and the public propagation of truth with those of a free and juridically equal society. If the equality to be enjoyed by the people appeared more formal than substantive, Condorcet could hold out the consolation that the people, having received little but good instruction, would be sufficiently enlightened to acknowledge the superiority of great minds, to assent freely to leadership of the most enlightened, and to retain for themselves the right to make judgments affecting their own lives in accordance with their own right reason.[30] While, therefore, certain inequalities would remain, inequalities which pursuit of truth required in the scientific sectors of society and which Condorcet could accept as being consistent with reason,[31] these inequalities would be mitigated by the common enjoyment of the fruits of scientific research and the rough equality of opportunity.

II

However small the chances for enactment of Condorcet's plan might have been before the calling of the Convention in 1792, the political developments of the following two years made it clear that nothing even remotely like this plan had the least chance of passage once the Convention was convened. The drift to the left, the attention and resources required by the war, the inability of political factions to agree even internally on education policy, all worked to discourage those with ambitious programs from even presenting them. Daunou, one of the few Ideologues who could still afford open political exposure after June 1793, rallied to the defense of the modest Lakanal plan, which restricted itself to the creation of a system of primary education overseen by central and local administrative bodies.[32] Decked out in suitably anti-corporatist rhetoric, the plan espoused no particular scientific dogma, permitted wide academic freedom, and recognized the right to operate private schools. Yet, even though modest and carefully introduced, this plan too fell victim to the attacks of the left, particularly once it was revealed that Sieyès had had a hand in its creation. When the Jacobin Jean-Henri Hassenfratz denounced the plan as too "aristocratic," an exasperated Sieyès tried to argue that an administrative arrangement in which bureaucrats supervised public functionaries carrying out tasks judged necessary by the people was not *ipso facto* "aristocratic"; but this explanation never overcame general opposition to the plan.[33]

The political rehabilitation of the Ideologues after the Terror opened up new possibilities for the design of an educational system. The Ideologues once again offered comprehensive programs, which were at first based upon those principles adopted by the Ideologues early in the Revolution. Garat, for example, justified the establishment of the Ecole Normale by arguing that the preservation of democracy required an end to inequalities of *lumières*.[34] Daunou, similarly, in his proposals struck out at the "enormous inequality of *lumières*" that had characterized the Old Regime and continued to afflict French society, just as he re-affirmed the need to allow private schools to function freely and public schools to teach unharassed by higher authorities.[35] His proposals, most of which were incorporated in the law of 3 Brumaire, provided for the creation of primary, secondary, and professional schools as well as for a National Institute and the holding of national festivals. Ambitious as it was, the Daunou plan established less a system of educational institutions than a mere collection, for it contained no provision for a body to regulate and to co-ordinate the new institutions. Flexible to the point that it underwrote anarchy, the plan allowed for improvements based upon "the experience of every [new] day."[36]

In the end, the flow of politics and the need for better organization told against this plan and its underlying principles. In politics, the persistent instability of the Directorial regime, to which most of the Ideologues pledged their support, seemed to demonstrate that the people were not so susceptible to rapid enlightenment as the Ideologues had first thought and that, far from being dependent upon the ever-widening access of the masses to high positions of power and authority, social and political stability required the narrowing of such access. As Cabanis came to formulate it, "all is [to be] done for the people and in the name of the people; nothing is [to be] done by [the people] under their unreflective guidance."[37] As new emphasis was placed upon the degree to which the majority was subject to so-called vicious habits and passions and upon the necessity of repressing these habits and passions,[38] Daunou and his colleagues hastened to push for the limitation of effective control of the state to those possessing sufficient wealth and knowledge to be able to administer in the public good.[39] The Ideologues put forward fresh programs for the surveillance and control of popular political clubs,[40] while they demanded new curbs on the freedom of the press;[41] in short, they turned decisively against the popular movement which they had formerly embraced, even if with reservations. At the same time, the Ideologues as a group turned sharply against the right; while a few of the Ideologues were not wholly satisfied with the successful Fructidor coup of 1797, the Ideologues on the whole were prepared to accept the new Directorial campaign against the so-called royalists.[42] The real question of politics now appeared, as Mme de Staël put it, not whether or not society would be aristocratic, but whether the aristocracy of the future would be drawn from the "factitious" aristocracy of birth or the "natural" aristocracy of wealth and talent.[43]

The second reason for the change in the educational program and principles of the Ideologues was the breakdown in the educational system set up during the first Directory.[44] Though technically under the control of the Ministry of the Interior, the schools were in fact managed by departmental and local officials, who acted without apparent regard to the needs of the system as a whole. Inadequate facilities for the training of lay teachers, shortages of funds for the payment of teacher salaries, shortages of books, classrooms, and supplies continued to plague the new system. The central schools, which the Ideologues counted on to teach future elites in a rigorous encyclopedic course of studies, failed to attract students to courses that had no direct relevance to vocational goals. Problems developed with the professional schools. The Ecole Normale collapsed within months of its opening; the three medical schools, in which the Ideologues took a special interest, proved inadequate to meet current needs and insufficiently rigorous in their testing procedure.[45] What made the failure of the school system of the Republic especially galling—and serious—was the apparent success of private schools, particularly those under right-wing control, which mushroomed all over during the relatively relaxed regime of the first Directory. The possibility that the minds of future generations might belong to the enemies, not the friends of the Enlightenment and the Revolution, prompted the Ideologues to re-examine and to re-invigorate the entire system of public education.

Three salient features of the new Ideologue program may be noted.

First, there crept into the new Ideologue program a new, more pronounced elitism. The Ideologues had never believed that all social inequalities could or should be eradicated, and their early Revolutionary program had surely not been free of elitist elements; but whereas before 1795 the Ideologues had at least looked toward a blurring of social and intellectual distinctions, after 1795 they tended to accept such distinctions as inevitable, and even to build upon them. Antoine-Louis-Claude Destutt de Tracy put it as baldly as any when he began his *Observations on the Present System of Public Instruction* (1801) by laying it down as an ineradicable fact of society that there existed two separate classes of men, the intellectual class [*classe savante*] and the working class, and that each class ought to pursue a different course of instruction.[46] While the Ideologues never advocated such measures as deliberately misinforming the public for its own good, they did begin, in line with the new policy of restricting popular participation in politics, to play down the need to educate the ordinary men in anything more than general vocational skills and the basic duties of the citizen. It was time, François Guillaume Jean Stanislas Andrieux asserted, that the enlightened minority stop trying to remake the masses in their own image; it was time to stop trying to underwrite the education of "simple men," who could at best turn out to be "half-literati" and "quarter-scientists";[47] it was time to train the masses of men, not in a watered-down version of the *Encyclopédie*, but in the methods of particular crafts.[48] In this way society would benefit most, each individual specializing in a particular occupation to which he could devote all his energies. The educational system would thus re-enforce a broadly conceived division of social labor, taking into account that the people, as Andrieux now deemed them, were "moved more by their senses and heart than by their mind and rational capacities."[49] Destutt de Tracy despaired of ever weaning the people from their dependency on popular almanachs for knowledge and could only pray that the writers of these almanachs were enlightened men.[50]

For the Ideologues, the great Revolutionary movement for social equality was now essentially over. Society was no longer to encourage children of the working class to improve their social status through education; they were no longer to be directly consulted in the formation of social policy. Instead, they were to be shunted, after minimal instruction, into the workshops of the nation where they were to remain. Education was no longer to be thought of as a right— increasingly it was thought of as a privilege. Daunou, in the law of 3 Brumaire, reversed his earlier position that education should be free of cost to all students;[51] by the accession of Bonaparte, we are hearing arguments that the poor would not send their children to school even if it were cost-free to them, that the expenses of wide spread public education would be too heavy for taxpayers to bear, that sufficient education for most could be acquired at home.[52]

The second major shift in the Ideologue educational program came with respect to organization; the administrative chaos created by the law of 3 Brumaire set off a strenuous search for ways to eliminate shortages, curriculum irregularities, and the want of general co-ordination. The essential change here was that the Ideologues no longer were willing to leave the education of the national elite to chance, to the whims of individual instructors and administrators; should the nation do nothing more to order from above its various educational agencies, Cabanis warned, it risked losing its republican spirit and the only chance it might have to establish firm republican institutions.[53] Already a year after the passage of the law of 3 Brumaire, Daunou admitted that the law had done more to "recognize the necessity" of an educational system than it had to "specify" it,[54] a sentiment expressed by the Ideologues again and again during the Directory. Cabanis attacked the disorganization of French education, especially medical education, calling for the implementation of a new "total plan."[55] Destutt de Tracy, along with a number of other Ideologues, served on a newly created Council of Public Instructions designed specifically to re-examine the entire curriculum of French education. Students, it was now argued, could not be trusted to choose their own courses because of the danger that in following their so-called caprices they would wind up "completely inverting the order of ideas"; nor could parents be trusted to choose courses for them because their prejudices might blind them to the true logic of learning;[56] and far from encouraging free selection of materials and methods by individual instructors, the Ideologues now pushed for general surveillance of curricula by central agencies of the state. All parts of the system, proclaimed the Council of Public Instruction, "must be related to each other and work towards a common center"; the "nature, object, and scope of each course" would now be determined in detail from above.[57]

But how would this be done and by whom? The call for a better organized system of education resulted in proposals to place control of the system in the hands of an enlightened few, to create just that "aristocracy" which the Ideologues had decried several years earlier. The geographical center of this control was to be, predictably enough, Paris. Cabanis indicated in his plan for the surveillance of the teaching of medicine that it was only Paris which could provide that progressive impetus necessary to energize the grand new system he was planning.[58] Daunou, too, glorified the capital, justifying its national predominance in spiritual affairs by pointing to its concentration of great minds and institutions.[59] "From the Pyrenees to the Alps," proclaimed Garat, "the art of teaching will be the same as in Paris."[60] The people who would run the new system would be enlightened intellectuals, technical specialists, indeed, people very much like the Ideologues themselves. Perched atop the French intellectual world in their self-created National Institute, the Ideologues now thundered down with renewed vigor against the intellectual chaos which had given "charlatans" new opportunities to peddle their "absurd ideas."[61] With ignorance making what Cabanis considered "frightening progress," it was now time, he thought, to create a system of "normal teaching"; through the direction of such teaching, a single body of "systematic knowledge" could be put together to guide individual instructors in their courses.[62]

The Ideologues never went so far in their lust for concentration and control as to deny flatly the right of private individuals to teach or to attend privately run schools. Yet they shared the concern of the Directory over the phenomenal success of the new right-wing schools, and some Ideologues were willing to sanction measures to be taken against them. Cabanis was particularly outspoken against the effects of private education, insisting, as already noted, that it threatened the life of the Republic. He called for police surveillance of private schools, stating that while he wanted to protect them from undue interference, some intervention was required to prevent charlatans from inculcating the "passions" and "prejudices" of the enemies of the Republic into the minds of the "precious new generation."[63] Cabanis's views were shared by the Ideologue journal, *La Décade*, which editorialized against the government's initial repressive policies not because they were too severe, but because they were too mild; the local surveillance of public schools which the Directory advocated, argued the journal, would not be effective because too often these local authorities seemed "enveloped in the darkness of the fourteenth century"; what was needed, thought the journal, was a constabulary of inspectors chosen "at the center of enlightenment," presumably Paris.[64]

The third major shift in Ideologue educational policy came with regard to the Ideologues' belief in the possibility of attaining certainty in that body of "systematic knowledge" that was to be the basis of the new education. There is no place here to consider the difficult and complex philosophical issues that attended the Ideologues' search for the grounds of scientific certainty[65]; yet it is important to point out that if the Ideologues had maintained their earlier position that certainty was impossible in most disciplines, their mandate for imposing "normal teaching" would have been undercut by the argument that the imposition of any curriculum would very probably mean the imposition of error by public authority. The Ideologues now needed to argue that certainty could be obtained in order to justify the narrowing of academic freedom. Already in 1795, Garat, in proposing the creation of the écoles normales, contended that with Bacon and Locke mankind had found a method to illuminate certain truths in every field of human investigation. Hence he urged that public authority not shrink from engraving into the hearts and minds of the citizenry specific social doctrines which enlightened scholars had established to be true through the use of philosophical analysis. Whereas Condorcet had stressed how much the uncertainty of most human knowledge made illegitimate attempts by public authorities to stipulate a fixed canon of principles, Garat was now insisting that the state underwrite a wide variety of social principles whose truth, Garat affirmed, could never be disproved.[66] Similarly, Cabanis founded his argument for the legitimacy of regulating French medicine through the regulation of French medical education on the demonstration that medicine had become a science which could explain the course of pathological phenomena in terms of laws graspable by the human mind. Were this not the case, he freely admitted, there would be no use trying to regulate medical teaching and practice.[67]

Traditionally conceived, the problem of interpreting the relationship between the Enlightenment and the French Revolution has been one of determining how and how much the Enlightenment prepared the way and guided the course of the Revolution. Without denying the importance of this aspect of the problem, I have tried to suggest in this article that the issue is broader than has customarily been recognized. The experience of the Ideologues indicates that not only did the Enlightenment's pedagogical ideas set the stage for the educational reforms of the Revolution but that the Revolution reshaped the Enlightenment's pedagogical ideas. Seeking first to establish the reign of *lumières* through an alliance with the popular movement, the Ideologues at the outset of the Revolution put forward educational programs to throw open the doors of academe to many who had hitherto been denied entrance, to encourage the diffusion of knowledge among all classes, and to stimulate free discussion of ideas; but once during the Directory the Ideologues came to feel "betrayed" by the popular movement and increasingly threatened politically by the left and the right, they moderated their attempts to spread enlightenment among all social classes, argued for stricter controls on the institutions of education, and tried to narrow the grounds for legitimate philosophical debate. Such a transformation demonstrates that historians attempting to relate the Enlightenment to the French Revolution must reckon not only with the influence of the Enlightenment on the Revolution but also with the influence of the Revolution on the Enlightenment. It remains an open question which influence was the greater.

NOTES

1 See, in particular, Sergio Moravia, *Il tramonto dell'illuminismo: Filosofia e politica nella società francese (1770–1815)* (Bari, 1968), and *Il pensiero degli idéologues: Scienza e filosofia in Francia (1780–1815)* (Florence, 1974); Keith Michael Baker, *Condorcet: From Natural Philosophy to Social Mathematics* (Chicago, 1975); and Emmet Kennedy, *A Philosophe in the Age of Revolution: Destutt de Tracy and the Origins of Ideology*, in *Memoirs of the American Philosophical Society*, 129 (1978). See also Thomas Ernest Kaiser, "The Ideologues: From the Enlightenment to Positivism," (Diss. Harvard 1976). Martin Staum's study of Cabanis is in press.

Older works on the Ideologues as a group include François Picavet, *Les idéologues: Essai sur l'histoire des idées et des théories scientifiques, religieuses, etc. en France depuis 1789* (Paris, 1891); Charles Van Duzer, *Contribution of the Ideologues to French Revolutionary Thought* (Baltimore, 1935); Emile Caillet, *La tradition littéraire des idéologues* (Philadelphia, 1943); Jay Stein, *The Mind and the Sword* (New York, 1961).

2 M.-J.-A.-N. C., marquis de Condorcet, *Oeuvres de Condorcet*, ed. A. Condorcet O'Conner and M. F. Arago (Paris, 1847), VII, 470.

3 Roland Mortier, "Esotérisme et lumières: Un dilemme de la pensée du XVIIIe siècle," and "Les 'philosophes' français et l'éducation publique," *Clartés et ombres du siècle des lumières: Etudes sur le XVIIIe siècle* (Geneva, 1969), pp. 60–103 and 104–13 respectively; Harry C. Payne, *The Philosophes and the People* (New Haven, 1976). See also Gabriel Compayré, *Histoire critique des doctrines de l'éducation en France depuis le seizième siècle* (Paris, 1879), vol. II.

4 For general accounts of the history of education in this period, see Albert Duruy, *L'instruction publique et la Révolution* (Paris, 1882); Augustin Sicard, *L'éducation morale et civique avant et pendant la Révolution (1700–1808)* (Paris, 1884); E. Allain, *L'oeuvre scolaire de la Révolution, 1789–1802* (Paris, 1891); Louis Grimaud, *Histoire de la liberté d'enseignement en France*, new ed. (Paris, 1944), vol. II; M. Gontard, *La question des écoles normales primaires de la Révolution de 1789 à nos jours* (Paris, n.d.); Robert J. Vignery, *The French Revolution and the Schools: Educational Policies of the Mountain, 1792–1794* (Madison, 1965). See also the editorial comments of James Guillaume, editor, *Procès-verbaux du comité d'instruction publique de la convention nationale*, 7 vols. (Paris, 1891–1907).

5 Condorcet, *Oeuvres*, VII, 453.

6 A. R. J. de Turgot, *Oeuvres de Turgot*, ed. Gustave Schelle (Paris, 1913–23), IV, 580.

7 Condorcet, *Oeuvres*, VII, 212 and 477. Condorcet emphasized that all citizens had to understand the consequences of the law or they might be tricked and misled. See Condorcet, *Oeuvres*, VII, 326.

8 The rising resentment against established corporate scientific and artistic bodies in the late eighteenth century is discussed by Robert Darnton in "The High Enlightenment and the Low-Life of Literature in Prerevolutionary France," *Past and Present*, 51 (1971), 81–115. The popular conception of "democratic science" in the early Revolution is discussed by Roger Hahn, *The Anatomy of a Scientific Institution: The Paris Academy of Sciences, 1666–1803* (Berkeley and Los Angeles, 1971), ch. 9.

9 Dominique Joseph Garat, *Considérations sur la Révolution française, et sur la conjuration des puissances de l'Europe contre la liberté et contre les droits des hommes, ou Examen de la proclamation des gouverneurs des Pays-Bas* (Paris, 1791), pp. 17, 35–36, 19.

10 H.-G., comte de Mirabeau, and Pierre-Jean-Georges Cabanis, *Travail sur l'instruction publique* (Paris, 1791), p. 17.

11 Ibid., p. 17.

12 Condorcet, *Oeuvres*, VII, 169.

13 See Vignery, *Schools*.

14 Pierre Claude François Daunou, "Rapport sur l'instruction publique présenté au nom de la commission des onze et du comité de salut public—séance du 23 vendémiaire, an IV," in Guillaume, *Procès-verbaux*, VI, 789.

15 Condorcet, *Oeuvres*, VII, 178–79.
16 Ibid., p. 434.
17 Ibid., p. 199.
18 Ibid., p. 479n.
19 Ibid., p. 327.
20 Ibid., p. 247.
21 Ibid., pp. 490–93. Condorcet also proposed that money be appropriated to provide indigent students with scholarships.
22 Ibid., p. 451.
23 Ibid., p. 362.
24 Ibid., pp. 272, 498.
25 Ibid., p. 208.
26 Ibid., p. 498n.
27 Ibid., pp. 272–73.
28 Ibid., p. 206.
29 Ibid., p. 416.
30 Ibid., pp. 377–78.
31 Condorcet, *Oeuvres*, VI, 659.
32 Joseph Lakanal, "Project de décret pour l'établissement de l'instruction nationale, présenté par le comité d'instruction publique (June 26, 1793)," in Guillaume, *Procès-verbaux*, I, 507–16. Daunou presented his defense of the plan in his *Essai sur l'instruction publique* (Paris, 1793).
33 Emmanuel-Joseph, abbé de Sieyès, "Du nouvel établissement public en France (June 29, 1793)," taken from the *Journal d'instruction publique* and republished in Guillaume, *Procès-verbaux*, I, 574–75.
34 [D.-J. Garat], "Rapport sur l'établissement des écoles normales" (Paris, Year III), in Guillaume, *Procès-verbaux*, V, 156. Though published under Lakanal's name, the report was written by Garat.
35 Daunou, "Rapport—23 vendémiaire an IV", pp. 788–91.
36 Ibid., p. 791.
37 Pierre-Jean-Georges Cabanis, *Oeuvres philosophiques de Cabanis*, ed. Claude Lehec and Jean Cazeneuve (Paris, 1956), II, 475. For more on these developments, see Kaiser, "Ideologues," ch. 3.
38 Cabanis, *Oeuvres*, II, 449n.
39 See the series of articles entitled "Politique—affaires étrangères—affaires de l'intérieur," in *La Décade*, 23 (Year VIII), 126–27, 249–51, 314. The authorship of these articles is attributed to Daunou by Raymond Guyot, "Du Directoire au Consulat—les transitions," *Revue historique*, 111 (1912), 8.
40 Pierre-Jean-Georges Cabanis, "Opinions sur les réunions s'occupant d'objets politiques" (n.p., n.d.).
41 See, in particular, the denunciations of press abuses by Charles François Dupuis, "Discours sur la liberté de la presse" (Paris, Year IV), in which Dupuis argued that freedom of the press during the Revolution had produced more "disaster" than "glory," that the enemies of the Republic would use their right to publish in order "to corrupt the public spirit, to

mislead the people, to enervate republican zeal, to exaggerate the evils that they have themselves created and impute them to the government . . . to foment hatred, to embitter all passions, to nourish all unworthy hopes, to swallow up and to render odious everything which belongs to the republican regime." While using prose slightly less purple than that of Dupuis, Cabanis, Garat, and Mme de Staël all supported restrictions on the press of one kind or another.

42 Jean-Baptiste Say explicitly approved of the law of hostages in "Affaires de l'intérieur," *La Décade*, 22 (Year VII), 188–92.

43 Germaine de Staël, *Des circonstances actuelles qui peuvent terminer la Révolution et des principes qui doivent fonder la république en France* (Paris, 1906), pp. 121, 171.

44 For the following, see Duruy, *Instruction*; Gontard, *Question*; and L. Pearce Williams, "Science, Education, and the French Revolution," *Isis*, 44 (1953), 311–30.

45 Michel Foucault, *Naissance de la clinique: Une archéologie du regard médical* (Paris, 1972), pp. 69–72.

46 Antoine-Louis-Claude Destutt de Tracy, *Observations sur le système actuel d'instruction publique*, in *Elémens d'idéologie*, II (Paris, 1825), 332–34.

47 François Guillaume Jean Stanislas Andrieux, "Opinion de Andrieux sur l'instruction publique dans les écoles primaires" (Paris, Year VI), pp. 3–4.

48 Ibid., p. 18.

49 [F. G. J. S. Andrieux], "Affaires de l'intérieur," *La Décade*, 22 (Year VII), 576. Attributed by Joanna Kitchin, *Un journal "philosophique": La Décade (1794–1804)* (Paris, 1965), p. 126.

50 Destutt de Tracy, *Observations*, p. 375.

51 Law of 3 Brumaire Year IV (October 25, 1795), Title I, Sections 7 and 8. A copy of the law is reprinted in Duruy, *Instruction*, Appendix No. 2.

52 Pierre-Louis Roederer, "Discours prononcé par Roederer, orateur du gouvernement, sur le projet de loi relatif à l'instruction publique (24 Floréal an 10)" (n.p., Year X), pp. 9–13.

53 Cabanis, *Oeuvres*, II, 441.

54 P.-C.-F. Daunou, "Rapport sur l'organisation des écoles spéciales: 25 Floréal V" (Paris, Year V), p. 9.

55 Cabanis, *Oeuvres*, II, 448.

56 "Pièces relatives à l'instruction publique," published in Destutt de Tracy, *Elémens*, II, 315–16.

57 Ibid., p. 318.

58 Cabanis, *Oeuvres*, II, 412.

59 Daunou, "Rapport: 25 Floréal V," pp. 18–19.

60 [Garat], "Ecoles normales," p. 158.

61 Destutt de Tracy, *Observations*, p. 329. Cabanis argued that charlatanism was especially likely to flourish during times of "agitation and upheaval" and could cause the "sciences and the public spirit to take a false direction." *Oeuvres*, II, 434.

62 Cabanis, *Oeuvres*, II, 435–46.
63 Ibid., p. 448.
64 *La Décade*, 21 (Year VII), 382–83.
65 For a discussion, see Kaiser, "Ideologues," ch. 5.
66 [Garat], "Ecoles normales," pp. 155–56. Similarly, Cabanis asserted that "rights, liberty, virtue, happiness" were now determinable by a "veritable science." *Oeuvres*, II, 448.
67 Cabanis, *Oeuvres*, II, 406.

The Newspaper Press in
French Political Thought, 1789–99

JEREMY D. POPKIN

The outbreak of the revolution in 1789 brought with it the real birth of a national political newspaper press in France. Before the convocation of the Estates-General, the government-authorized *Journal de Paris* had been the only daily paper, but within a few months after the deputies assembled in Versailles, dozens of new journals sprang up. They quickly established themselves as the most significant form of political literature in France, and, as a result, political writers of many different outlooks found themselves forced to think about the effects of such publications. The revolutionary period thus saw a number of attempts to analyze the workings of the newspaper press, its relationship to society and its impact on politics. Although the writers of the period differed widely in their attitudes toward the daily press, their clashing observations identified many of the social and political problems that the existence of the newspaper press has continued to pose for liberal and democratic societies ever since.

The French newspaper press had developed slowly before 1789, and there was little theoretical writing on the subject to guide observers during the Revolution. The *Encyclopédie* devoted only a few paragraphs to newspapers, giving far more attention to learned periodicals like the *Journal des Savants*.[1] Lamoignon de Malesherbes, in his unpublished memoranda on censorship policy, took a remarkably broadminded position—he even recommended against prosecution of journalists who printed diplomatic secrets, on the ground that it was up to the government to prevent news leaks—but this recommendation for relaxed press controls was not fully implemented.[2] Such discussion of newspapers as did appear took the form of reports on the press in other countries, especially England. Delolme's influential *Constitution de l'Angleterre* called the newspapers a basic pillar of English liberty. In his extremely idealized description, Delolme made a special point of the English newspapers' ability to bring the whole population into the political process. The electoral system might not be democratic, but the press compensated for this by reflecting the views of the most remote areas and the lowest social classes: "Each individual is informed daily of the state of the nation, from one end to the other; and the communication is such, that the three kingdoms seem to be but one city."[3]

The English example, and, to some extent, the American experience strongly influenced the early revolutionary discussions of newspapers in France after 1789. To be sure, the newspapers were not a central topic of concern in the revolutionary debates; even the vast majority of pamphlets and speeches on freedom of the press lumped newspapers together with books, pamphlets, and magazines. Two significant exceptions, however, were the writings of two French journalists who had some direct experience with newspaper publishing in the Anglo-Saxon world, J. P. Brissot and Charles Panckoucke. Brissot's *Mémoire aux Etats-Généraux: Sur la nécessité de rendre dès ce moment la presse libre, et surtout pour les journaux politiques*, published to justify his own projected paper, was a complex and insightful analysis of the role newspapers could and should play in a democratic society. Brissot's main argument was that newspapers alone could resolve the classic problem of how to establish a democratic polity in a large country. The press would allow the continuous transmission of the public's opinions to their elected representatives, and would also allow the country's intellectual leaders to enlighten that public: ". . .one can teach the same truth at the same moment to millions of men; through the Press, they can discuss it without tumult, decide calmly and give their opinion."[4] Books were obviously too expensive and slow to serve such a function, and the general public could not keep up with the flood of pamphlets: "It has neither the time, nor the means. But a newspaper arrives everywhere at the same instant, is read everywhere; it is read by even the poorest individuals. A hundred thousand people will have read a newspaper, when barely a hundred will have read a pamphlet."[5] This democratically inclusive effect could be achieved because newspapers were so easy to read and so cheap; in passing, Brissot repeated the familiar objection to the English newspaper stamp tax as a "tax on knowledge," designed to restrict readership to the wealthy. In the preface to his *New Travels in the United States and America*, published in 1791, Brissot continued to argue for the widest possible diffusion of the press and the removal of economic barriers to readership: "How quickly would the Revolution be consolidated if the government had the wisdom to allow all newspapers to be posted free of charge."[6]

Brissot's analysis of the press attributed a double function to it: the spread of enlightenment from journalist to public, and the transmission of public opinion from the readership, through the journalists, to the government. He thus identified the two main problems that all succeeding theories of the press have had to deal with: the extent of its influence, and the degree to which it reflects public opinion. He did not explicitly recognize a potential contradiction between influencing public opinion and representing it, although his reference to newspapers as "the only means of instruction for a numerous nation, hindered in its faculties, little accustomed to reading, and seeking to escape from ignorance and slavery," implied that the *vox populi* in its unenlightened state was not worth listening to.[7] Nevertheless, he had two important suggestions for insuring that the journalists reflected public opinion. One was the pressure of competition. He promised that the rivalry between papers would guarantee the eventual triumph of truth, and praised American newspaper readers for refusing to buy long-term subscriptions to publications. In this way, they compelled the journalists to bid for their favor day by day, thereby forcing them to follow public opinion as closely as possible. He strongly condemned newspapers which accepted direct subsidies from special political interest groups and thus insulated themselves from direct popular pressure; their motives could only be counter-revolutionary.[8] Since newspapers could be corrupted, however, Brissot saw the need for a second line of defense to keep them representative of the people's true opinions. He claimed that the nation's elected representatives had the most sweeping powers to suppress counter-revolutionary publications. No one had the right to attack the deputies: "All citizens owe them the greatest respect, since they represent the entire Nation. To outrage them is thus to outrage the Nation itself." Journalists haled before the national assembly should not even have the right to a court trial: suppose a counter-revolutionary judge acquitted one of them![9]

The two ways of regarding the newspapers' political influence which Brissot brought together in his writings—the notion of the press as the people's representative and the notion of it as their instructor—could both be justified by revolutionary principles. As the expression of popular will, the papers served an essential democratic function. But Brissot recognized the difficulty of determining the general will in a country unaccustomed to political freedom and also looked to the press as one tool for shaping the new democratic man without whom the Revolution could not succeed. The major difficulty for both aspects of his theory came from his attempt to combine it with a realistic appraisal of how the market for newspapers functioned. Insofar as Brissot wanted the newspapers to be a means of popular education, he was bothered by the fact that they were commodities which had to be paid for, and that some readers might be excluded from their audience for lack of money. On the other hand, his main suggestion for compelling the press to give its audience's views rather than its editors' relied on the force of the market, which would have been nullified if newspapers had really been distributed free of charge. Furthermore, although Brissot showed a keen appreciation of how economic inequality could limit newspaper readership, he paid no attention to the implications this had for the representative model of the press. But clearly, if only the rich could afford to buy newspapers, then only their views would be represented in the press.

Not all the supporters of the Revolution shared Brissot's optimistic assumption that newspapers could reach the entire population directly. For example, the editors of the *Feuille villageoise*, a paper established by several members of the Idéologue group to enlighten the peasants, expected to reach their audience indirectly; they felt compelled to call on the village curés and local noble landowners to read the paper aloud to their largely illiterate neighbors.[10] They also recognized that the peasants had an extremely limited understanding of politics: among the terms they felt compelled to explain in their first issue were words as fundamental as "frontier." Although they thus recognized the cultural barriers to the spread of newspaper readership, the *Feuille villageoise*'s promoters did not explicitly mention the obstacle caused by the cost of subscriptions.

For those who did not share the democratic faith of Brissot or the Idéologues' conviction that the people could be easily educated, however, the commercial nature of newspapers could appear as a positive feature, guaranteeing their responsibility and an appropriate limitation of their audience. Charles-Joseph Panckoucke, the veteran publisher and newspaper entrepreneur, was a representative of this more moderate political tendency, and his article "Les Journaux et papiers anglais," published in his *Mercure de France* early in 1790, offered a view of the press quite different from Brissot's. Like Brissot, Panckoucke referred more to the English experience than the French; unlike him, he took a more realistic view of the English press, which was not, in reality, anything remotely resembling Brissot's vision of a democratic medium reaching the entire population. Instead, Panckoucke noted that the English daily papers, as opposed to periodicals devoted to education and the spread of enlightenment, were heavily taxed, thereby raising their price and limiting their audience—a tendency he was far from deploring. Furthermore, as Panckoucke pointed out, the English papers derived much of their revenue from advertising, a resource the French revolutionary press tended to neglect. In order to fit in these ads, however, English papers had to expand their format—in this period, they were usually four pages folio, whereas the French papers were at most four pages quarto—and this in turn required large editorial staffs to fill the extensive space. As a result, the English papers were sizable business enterprises with a strong stake in maintaining social order, unlike the one-man operations characteristic of the early French revolutionary press. Panckoucke urged the French legislators to follow the English pattern and adopt a tax policy that would favor industrial rather than artisanal press enterprises.[11] Just as the moderates in the Constituent Assembly wanted a political system that would represent "responsible" opinion rather than the capricious passions of the mob, so Panckoucke wanted a press that would not be immediately swayed by shifts in its readers' opinions. Like Brissot, he saw that the workings of the press market would affect the content of the papers, and he gave an acute explanation of why the French revolutionary press was diverging so rapidly from the English model. But by 1790, it was too late for the revolutionary legislators—divided among themselves in any event—to impose such controls on the newspapers. It was not until the Napoleonic period that the government stepped in to force the press to coalesce into a few large, easily controlled enterprises. The Restoration system of requiring newspapers to post heavy cash bonds was an effort to use monetary pressure to achieve the result Panckoucke had desired, but the very necessity of that system testified to the fact that French papers continued to shun commercial advertising. In this situation, it was a paper's ability to find paying subscribers that determined its prosperity. Throughout the revolutionary decade, much of the debate over the press turned on the implications of this situation, and especially its tendency to make the press reflect the opinions of that select group who had the wealth to afford subscriptions.

The newspaper press was often in the news between 1789 and 1794, but few of the many furious debates of that period addressed the questions Brissot and Panckoucke had raised at the outset of the Revolution. Successive moderate politicans sought vainly for a justification of repressive measures against journalists like Marat, but never managed to define the difference between liberty and "license."[12] Robespierre, on the other hand, developed Brissot's hint that the people's assembly had the power to repel attacks on itself into a full-fledged doctrine of revolutionary government; he clearly believed that the newspapers should serve to prepare citizens for the Republic of Virtue, rather than reflect unenlightened and possibly counter-revolutionary existing opinions.[13] Actual Jacobin policy never achieved the totalitarian rigor implied in Robespierre's doctrine, however; even enthusiastic proponents of the Terror had difficulty abandoning their idealistic commitment to a democratic conception of the press.[14]

When calmer political and journalistic weather returned after Robespierre's downfall in 1794, the debate over the newspaper press resumed on the basis of an entirely different body of experience and ideas from those available to Brissot and Panckoucke in 1789. In the intervening five years, royalist journalists had shown that the papers could be used for the most unenlightened purposes; Marat, Hébert and others had converted them into a tool for populist agitation; and the Jacobins had taken halting steps to transform newspapers into instruments of a dictatorial state. The role of the press was one of the most frequently debated issues in the political assemblies of Thermidor and the Directory, and the topic generated a considerable volume of pamphlet literature, as well as frequent discussions in the newspapers themselves, which continued to thrive as they had in the first years of the Revolution. Much of this literature resembled the earlier revolutionary debates in remaining vague and contradictory, but there were several serious efforts to work out a real theory of the press. Most of this discussion went on among a small group of political writers, many of whom also had direct involvements with the press as newspaper owners, editors, or columnists. In addition, most were members of a single intellectual coterie: Mme. de Staël's circle of friends. Mme. de Staël's personal sympathies, eclectic though they were, embraced neither genuine Jacobins nor devoted royalists, and she had little use for grub-street hacks, even those who had valuable insights into their profession. Within those limits, however, her group included men with widely varying points of view on all major political issues. Her friend Roederer represented one major school of thought; Benjamin Constant, J. B. Louvet, and Pierre Daunou joined Mme. de Staël herself in another camp.

The analyses of the press written between Thermidor and Brumaire did not reflect all aspects of the press's development since 1789. They concentrated, in fact, on the situation created after 1795, as though the confusing spectacle of the early revolutionary years and the Terror had been an irrelevant aberration. In truth, the years from 1789 to 1794 had provided no clear lesson about the effects of the press, and every political party had come out of them with some grounds for believing that press freedom favored its opponents. After 1794, however, a clear pattern of newspaper conduct emerged: the political press shifted strongly to the right. Even the Directory's drastic suppression of counter-revolutionary newspapers in the coup of 18 Fructidor V (Sept. 4, 1797) did not really change this situation.[15] Press analysts therefore had to deal with two main questions: why had the free press, creation of the Revolution, turned against its parent, and what should the republican government do about the situation?

Most contributors to the press debate after 1794 agreed on the answer to the first question. The press turned counter-revolutionary in response to the force of the newspaper market. Unlike Brissot, however, these analysts explicitly noted that this audience did not include the whole *peuple*. Châles, a minor Jacobin deputy and journalist, was among the first to formulate a crude theory linking social class and ideology to explain this phenomenon. He conceded that all visible indications of "opinion publique" had turned against democracy after Thermidor, but he asserted that this "opinion publique" was diametrically opposed to the "opinion du peuple," which remained loyal to the egalitarian principles of 1793. The opinions expressed in the Thermidorian press were those of "the bourgeois aristocracy," whose interests and views could never be the same as those of the vast majority of the population. Rather than hoping, as the *Feuille Villageois*'s editors had, that the upper classes would pass news and ideas on to their inferiors, Châles proclaimed the people's ability to think for themselves.[16]

Although his argument clearly hinted that the press echoed the opinions of the bourgeoisie because only they bought the papers, Châles never made this point explicit. He was content to have shown that the newspapers did not speak for the poorer classes. It was, ironically, the counter-revolutionary movement which now evoked Brissot's image of the newspaper as a democratic medium, reaching all classes of society. The rightwing deputy Barbé-Marbois asserted that "a newspaper enlivens the artisan's dinner, the farmer relaxes with it after plowing his field . . .," and he cited America as proof that regulations such as those imposed on the royalist press were eminently unrepublican.[17] In reality, however, the post-Thermidorian press reached few peasants and artisans. The most original analyst of the press during this period, Pierre Roederer, was only too pleased to concede this fact: his entire defense of the newspapers depended on a demonstration that they represented the views of the wealthy, educated elite to whom he felt national political leadership should be restricted. A well-known revolutionary political figure—member of the Constituent Assembly, close associate of the abbé Sieyès, past master of political ambiguity and future member of Napoleon's Conseil d'Etat—Roederer was also, after 1795, co-owner and editor of the *Journal de Paris*, which had survived as one of the many competing Paris daily papers. He thus knew the problems of political journalism thoroughly. His theoretical analyses of public opinion and the press reflected this personal experience, but they were also part of a genuine effort to incorporate the analysis of newspapers into a comprehensive science of society. Fully versed in the eighteenth-century liberal tradition and in the most sophisticated sociological methods of his day, including the use of statistical data, Roederer was well prepared to provide a more comprehensive theory of the press and its social role than any of his predecessors.

Roederer began by creating a theory of public opinion formation that could account for the visible conservative bias of the press and at the same time answer criticisms like Châles' that this opinion was not that of the common people. He argued that public sentiment did, in fact, arise first among the lower classes, who were the most exposed to the effects of crises requiring government action. But this popular sentiment was little more than a confused grumbling, which had to filter upward along various natural social pathways—from workers to their employers, from domestic servants to their mistresses to the mistresses' husbands—before it could become politically meaningful. Eventually, a rationalized version of this popular sentiment would develop among the country's natural opinion leaders, the owners of property, who formed the basis of political society. These *propriétaires*, scattered throughout the country and in touch with all its problems, would in turn transmit their views to a few *hommes éclairés* whose writings would give the nation's opinion its definitive formulation. The government would then take appropriate action, and the same writers would explain its policy to their readers, who in turn would pass the message along to the lower classes. Despite its rigid schematic quality, Roederer's analysis had some genuine factual basis and it anticipated some of the findings of modern communications studies.[18] More significantly in the short run, it justified Roederer's contention that government policy should be guided by the opinions expressed in the newspapers and other writings most popular among the propertied classes: "Since the expression of the general sentiment and the initiative of opinion belong to the property-owners, since they are its guides and its organs, the government should give all its attention to their interests, to their discourses, to their readings, to the books and newspapers that circulate among them."[19]

Roederer recognized that public opinion could be expressed in other forms besides newspapers, but he also saw that newspapers had some special relationship to political opinion. In his brief but suggestive "Essai analytique sur les diverses moyens établis pour la communication des pensées, entre les hommes en société,"[20] he argued that books took a long time to reach a wide audience, and tended to affect different readers in different ways. Short pamphlets might have more immediate and predictable effects, but they did not have the guaranteed audience of a successful newspaper. "The newspapers," Roederer concluded, "being essentially composed of new and vital things, having a much greater number of readers than books, having them all, every day, at the same hour, in all classes of society, in all public places, being the almost indispensable food of daily conversation, not only act on a much greater mass of men, but they act more strongly than any other form of writing." In this passage, Roederer repeated Brissot's assurance that the newspapers would reach all social classes, but in fact he had observed the fact that Panckoucke had already stressed—namely, that newspapers were a commodity, sold through a market system.[21] Roederer accepted this as the natural means of assuring that public opinion, like the right to vote, would be restricted to the property-owning classes. His condemnation of the printed wall poster, which was "not a commodity; it costs the reader nothing . . . ," shows his position on this question.[22] He and other right-wing writers of the period all agreed that the wall poster, even though it was printed, could not possibly enjoy constitutional protection as a means of expression. Laharpe, the Voltairean turned counter-revolutionary, was simply expanding on Roederer's earlier comments when he explained: "The book or the paper, sold by the bookseller or peddler, speak to the isolated individual and consequently to the reflection; he who posts something up or cries it in the streets speaks to everyone at once, and may raise up 10,000 men in a quarter of an hour."[23] Thus Roederer and Laharpe condemned the wall poster for doing exactly what Brissot had hoped the newspaper would accomplish: bringing the common people into politics, by eliminating the barriers to communications created by poverty and illiteracy. Roederer's theory of the press replaced Brissot's dream of a universal and democratic public with a readership stratified according to wealth, just as the Constitution of 1795 replaced universal suffrage with a franchise limited to the wealthiest taxpayers.

The serious scientific side of Roederer's theory of the press showed in his effort to define a statistical method for measuring opinion. He was among the first to realize the significance of comparative circulation figures, although the ones he himself published during the Directory were probably doctored to prove a political point.[24] Under the early Consulate, he prepared several surveys of newspaper circulation for Napoleon which show an awareness of many of the pitfalls inherent in this form of public opinion measurement. Among other things, he noted that each copy of a paper was read by more than one person, but that this multiplier might differ in different regions. He also tried to analyze the reasons why people subscribed to newspapers in general and why they tended to prefer papers critical of the government.[25]

Roederer's theory of the press marked an abandonment of the democratic writers' assumption that the journalist was qualified to guide his readers along the path of enlightenment. For Roederer, it was the educated and property-owning class as a whole which embodied the intellect of society; the journalist or intellectual had no special claim to consider himself above the landowner or manufacturer who bought his writings.[26] It was embarrassing to have to admit that the journalist was the slave of sales figures, however, and so Roederer tried to elude the logical conclusion of his own argument. He noted that most publications had a division of labor between editor and publisher. The latter might be influenced by vulgar considerations like sales, but the former were men of principle who would prefer to change jobs rather than opinions. In this way, the man of letters' integrity could be preserved without raising the possibility that devotion to truth and devotion to public opinon were potentially incompatible.[27] At the same time, however, this argument threatened to sever the connection between journalists and their readers which justified the use of the press as a measure of public opinion. In reality, though, as Roederer himself knew from his involvement with the *Journal de Paris*, most journalists' income did depend on the sales of the paper they worked for.[28] Other right-wing journalists of the period were quite willing to admit their dependence on their readers, expressed through sales figures. Jean-Pierre Gallais, a popular editorialist who had made at least one political about-face for pecuniary reasons, argued that men in every other profession considered the market for their wares: "Why, then, should the writer for a periodical, a writer who devotes his nights and often sacrifices his comfort to instruct his fellow-citizens, why should he not, without ceasing to be honest and scrupulous, figure out the income of his paper, and count on a monetary reward? It is in not letting himself be stained by ignominious favors or partialities that he maintains his honesty, and not in refusing a salary he has legitimately earned."[29]

Roederer and Gallais not only explained why the press had taken on a conservative tint after Thermidor but accepted that development as perfectly legitimate. Their republican opponents recognized the press's turn to the right, but a reluctance to admit that public opinion had actually turned against a regime which based its legitimacy on the will of the people prevented most of them from offering any convincing explanation of this development, other than the perversity of the journalists. Instead of explaining the reasons for the press's behavior, most republican spokesmen settled for justifying repressive measures to deal with it. They asserted the government's right to suspend constitutional guarantees of press freedom because of "circumstances,"[30] or argued, as Brissot had in 1789, that no one had the right to editorialize against a freely chosen representative government.[31] Often the formulations these orators used seemed flatly self-contradictory to all but the most impassioned. When M.-J. Chénier told the thermidorian Convention that "no political writer . . . had been mad enough to confuse the right to express one's thought without restriction or limitation, a sacred and imprescriptible right, with the privilege . . . of inciting royalism in a republic . . . ," it is doubtful that he convinced anyone except those already converted.[32] It was one of the most genuinely apolitical newsmen of the period, and not a disingenuous counter-revolutionary, who answered this type of argument by observing that "either freedom of the press is nothing, or it is the right to put forward a bizarre, singular and absurd opinion; it is clear that no safeguard or guarantee is needed to say what pleases everyone, or the majority. . . ."[33]

Members of the circle around Mme. de Staël were not content simply to assert that press attacks on the republic were examples of liberty rather than licence, however. They attempted to provide a more convincing explanation for the behavior of the journalists and the newspapers, and a more satisfactory justification for government-imposed press restrictions. Whereas Roederer emphasized the representative function of the press in expressing the opinion of the public, writers like J. B. Louvet, Pierre Daunou, Benjamin Constant, and Mme. de Staël took up the other major theme Brissot had sounded: the journalist's duty to enlighten and guide his public, rather than lower himself to its level. At the same time, paradoxically, these same critics raised serious doubts about the newspapers' ability to perform such an educational function, because of inherent limitations in the medium itself, and they often concluded by endorsing severe press restrictions which foreshadowed the policy of the Napoleonic period.

The notion that journalism was a trade, just like any other, gave the republican critics of the newspaper press an easy opening for an attack on it. The man of letters who ran after patronage and popularity rather than truth had never enjoyed much respect, and all press critics had damned the journalist who took secret subsidies. But Benjamin Constant did not see why catering to a mass public rather than a single patron should excuse the journalist from the charge of venality: "This daily calculation, which makes a paper a source of income, which speculates on subscriptions, which creates such a specific monetary relationship between the reader whose opinion is flattered, and the writer who flatters it, leaves neither the time nor the independence necessary for the composition of useful works." He accused mercenary journalists of "committing every crime, for the miserable daily reward which serves to excuse them from every kind of honest work. . . ."[34] Neither Constant nor any of the other republican press critics of the period, however, offered any other suggestion as to how newspapermen should support themselves.

If they did not really address the economic aspect of the press problem, the republican press critics had more than enough to say about the journalists' proper obligation to society. They were to devote themselves to defending the principles of reason and progress, as embodied in France's republican institutions. Some press critics, like the republican journalist and deputy J. B. Louvet, accused the market-oriented journalists of having created the anti-republican groundswell in the first place, although he gave no explanation for their motives.[35] The more thoughtful republican writers, like Constant and Mme. de Staël, admitted that there were deeper reasons for the reaction against revolutionary principles. According to Constant, the excesses of the Reign of Terror had discredited even such genuine accomplishments of the Revolution as the abolition of the monarchy, the hereditary nobility, and the Catholic Church.[36] Mme. de Staël even admitted that the Revolution in its reforming zeal had gone farther than French society was really prepared to go. Nevertheless, since the Republic represented a higher stage of political progress than the constitutional monarchy for which the country had been genuinely prepared in 1789, she thought it would be wrong to turn back; instead, the public should be educated up to the level of its new institutions.[37] Both Mme. de Staël and Constant agreed that it was the duty of journalists to put aside personal considerations and throw their weight behind the progressive cause.

There was also the question, however, of whether the daily press was even a suitable medium for enlightening the public. In a speech on behalf of a government press bill in 1796, Pierre Daunou, a member of the Idéologue group, argued that the newspapers could not really deal with substantial intellectual issues, and that they therefore should not enjoy the same constitutional protection as more serious forms of literature: one should not grant "impunity for Marat out of respect for Bacon and Montesquieu."[38] Daunou attempted to buttress his position by showing that the chance collection of immediate reactions to specific events printed in the newspapers did not constitute meaningful public opinion. True public opinion developed at the level of general principles; it was "national ideas which the progress of instruction develops, which the lessons of experience confirm, and which, gradually becoming steady and rooted sentiments for a whole people, are in effect the most respectable of human authorities and ultimately the most powerful." This slowly evolving public opinion could not respond to the quickly changing circumstances of daily politics: how could a country the size of France be expected to have "a truly common opinion" on "particular new or complicated questions, on the personalities who succeed each other quickly in politics, on all the obscure incidents and hidden workings of a revolution . . .?"[39] Daunou noted the journalists' own confusion about whether they reflected or formed public opinion of these issues. He urged them to take up their responsibilities to lead the public, but claimed they would never be able to do so through the "ephemeral sheets" in which they were concentrating their efforts. If they really wanted to serve society, they would turn to more serious forms of literature.[40] Benjamin Constant echoed some of these complaints about the shortcomings of the press, particularly the way in which the speed of journalistic writing prevented mature development of ideas: "the necessity of writing every day . . . is the tomb of talent."[41] For writers committed to a reflective and analytic approach to politics, the daily press, with its obsession with current events, was not worthy of serious consideration.

From this point of view, the newspaper's potential—admittedly not realized in this period—of reaching a broad popular audience was simply another argument against it. Roederer, who had a clearer sense of the actual readership, had maintained that the papers were not popular, and that they reached only respectable property-owners. Mme. de Staël, on the other hand, continued to see them as a menace to social order. They were "the common people's only reading," she claimed, and she agreed with both Brissot and Roederer that they had far more political impact than books. Unlike Brissot in 1789, however, she did not consider this a point in the newspapers' favor; instead, it was proof that the papers necessarily had to lower themselves to the level of an uninstructed mass audience which responded more to emotional appeals than to rational considerations. In effect, she applied to the newspapers the same reasoning Roederer and Laharpe had applied to wall posters, arguing that they were used "to agitate with facts" rather than "to propagate ideas," and condemning them accordingly.[42]

This assertion that the newspapers were inherently incapable of transmitting rational discourse because of the nature of their audience supplied a theoretical basis for the republican critique of newspaper freedom that had been developed in numerous speeches, pamphlets and editorials since 1794. Mme. de Staël's friend J. B. Louvet had earlier established the respectable Enlightenment credentials of this position by reprinting a passage from Mably's *Letters on the American States*, in which Mably advised the victorious American republicans that they should ban subversive publications and limit religious freedom. In his text, Mably had spelled out the fundamental elitist assumption behind his advice: "How small is the number of men capable of thinking for themselves and discussing an opinion. The rest are a mass of children. . . ."[43] In his condensation of Mably's work, Louvet carefully omitted this anti-democratic sentiment, but printed the earlier writer's assertion that "the government is made to direct the thinking of such men, as fathers are destined to direct their children whose reason is not yet developed. . . ."[44]

Whereas many of the republican attacks on press freedom during this period depended on the assumption that the principles of the new regime were superior to those of the old, the arguments that the press was unsuitable for reasoned argument and that it necessarily had to lower itself to the level of a mass audience were less obviously biased. This was also true of another argument that Louvet and

Mme. de Staël advanced: that newspapers were inevitably a cause of political disorder. Louvet argued that this subversive attribute of the press had been an asset under the tyrannical monarchy, but that it could not be tolerated now that France had a free government.[45] Mme. de Staël went into the matter in more detail. Drawing on the post-Jacobin period's strong prejudice against collective, as opposed to individual, self-expression reflected in laws against political clubs and collective petitions, she pointed out that "a newspaper and readers are a sort of association . . . ," and that "the newspaper is a continuing action. . . ."[46] As a result, press freedom could not be justified purely in terms of the individual's right to speak; a newspaper was a collective action, and the government consequently had a right to supervise it. "The journals are . . . a public act announcing public events, capable of leading citizens into error about what they should do, being not only the most important part of public instruction, but a means of governing or revolutionizing so powerful that one cannot remove it from the authorities' surveillance."[47] Mme. de Staël's carefully worked out argument provided perhaps the fullest justification of an absolutist press policy since Thomas Hobbes' *Leviathan*, and it corresponded in many respects to the actual practice of the French *ancien régime*.[48] And, like so many other features of her critique of the Directory in 1798, it pointed directly to the policy which Napoleon was soon to implement—over Mme. de Staël's vehement protests, but ironically with the full cooperation of that doughty defender of press freedom, Pierre Roederer.[49]

With Mme. de Staël's argument that the newspapers needed to be controlled because of their capability of reaching and mobilizing a mass audience, the revolutionary attitude toward the newspaper press had come full circle from 1789, when Brissot had argued for press freedom on exactly the same grounds. The reason for this strange evolution lay in the course of the Revolution itself. Brissot's view of the press had depended on the assumption that public opinion and government policy would both follow the clearly defined path of reason. By the time of the Directory, however, public opinion and government policy had diverged—at least, insofar as the public which voted in the elections of 1795 and 1797 and which supported the popular rightwing newspapers was concerned. The press theorists of the period followed divergent paths depending on their own political position. Roederer, tending to side with the counter-revolutionary public, emphasized the representative role of the press; the republicans, siding with the government or at least with the basic principles of the constitution, saw some of the undesirable effects of newspapers more clearly. Of the two, Roederer undoubtedly made the more original theoretical contribution; his work constituted a major step toward the creation of the theory of public opinion. With its attention to statistics and its awareness of possible pitfalls, Roederer's theory was far ahead of its time; much of what Roederer said in the 1790s has had to be laboriously rediscovered by modern sociologists of communications.

At first glance, the republican press theorists of the 1790s do not seem to have contributed as much to the theory of the press. The ability of writers like Mme. de Staël to praise the invention of the printing press, through which "the riches of thought have been, so to speak, democratized, in being put at everyone's disposition,"[50] in the same work in which she demanded tight government controls over one major product of those presses, appears to indicate that this whole body of thought rested on flatly contradictory assumptions— as indeed much of the polemic against press freedom in this period did. If one can no longer accept as "scientific" the assumption that monarchy, nobility, and Catholicism represented absolute evil and the Republic of the Year III, progress, one can still admit, however, that Daunou, Constant, and Mme. de Staël put forward some ideas about the newspaper press which were destined for a long future. Even before the Revolution, some French writers had noted the tendency of the periodical press to lower the level of intellectual discussion, but it was really with the republican critique of the newspapers after 1794 that this assertion was given something of a theoretical basis, resting on the nature of the newspaper itself, with its demand for rapidity, and on the nature of its audience. By separating the issue of newspaper freedom from the more general debate about freedom of expression in general, the republican press critics also laid the basis for the tradition of French press regulation throughout most of the nineteenth century. When Benjamin Constant came to the defense of newspaper freedom in 1814, after his long experience of Napoleonic press control, he found himself, ironically, answering the very argument in favor of special newspaper restrictions that Mme. de Staël had elaborated privately in 1798: that papers needed special controls because of their continuous activity, broad audience, and rapid impact.[51] In practice, Constant's liberal argument lost out, and newspapers remained under special restrictions until the Third Republic. The republican polemicists of the Directory deserve the perhaps dubious honor of having initiated that tradition.

The debates over the press in the revolutionary period succeeded in identifying most of the significant issues raised by the existence of a newspaper press. Brissot, Panckoucke, Châles, and Roederer all raised, directly or indirectly, the issue of the effects of economic pressure on editorial content. Roederer probed the theoretical difficulties of relating the press to public opinion, and laid the bases for a modern sociology of the press. The republicans of the Directory, hostile to the newspapers, made a precocious critique of mass culture which has found many echoes in later periods. It cannot be said, however, that the writers of the 1790s laid the basis for a continuing tradition of theories about the press and the mass media. Instead of becoming a subject of continuous intellectual interest, the newspapers after 1800 became an accepted part of the background of daily life; only the debates over the proper extent of censorship and government control continued to make them a subject of public interest. A German scholar has traced the slow development of press sociology in that country during the nineteenth century; the evolution of French attitudes toward the press remains less well studied.[52] It is all the more remarkable, then, given the paucity of such work after 1800, that the writers of the 1790s, the first generation to see the newspaper press in action, should have made such penetrating analyses of it.

NOTES

An earlier version of this paper was delivered at the East-Central American Society for Eighteenth-Century Studies conference in Pittsburgh, Pa. (Oct. 1978). I would like to thank Jack Censer, Robert Darnton, Elizabeth Eisenstein, Patrice Higonnet, and Daniel Resnick for their criticism and advice.

1 See the articles "Gazette," "Journal," "Journaliste," and "Liberté de la presse," the latter by Jaucourt.
2 Lamoignon de Malesherbes, *Mémoires sur la librairie et sur la liberté de la presse* (Paris: Agasse, 1809), pp. 77–78,85. These memoranda were written in 1759, but not published until the Napoleonic period.
3 Delolme, *Constitution de l'Angleterre*, nouv. ed. (Amsterdam: Van Harrevelt, 1778), pp. 207–8.
4 J. P. Brissot de Warville, *Mémoire aux Etats-Généraux: Sur la nécessité de rendre dès ce moment la presse libre, et surtout pour les journaux politiques* (Paris, 1789), p. 10.
5 Ibid., p. 21.
6 Brissot, *New Travels in the United States and America*, trans. M. S. Vanos and D. Echeverria (Cambridge, Mass.: Harvard University Press, 1964), p. 8.
7 Brissot, *Mémoires*, ed. C. Perroud (Paris: Picard, 1911), II, 179.
8 Brissot, *Mémoire aux Etats-Généraux*, p. 10.

9 Ibid., pp. 52–53.

10 "Avertissement," *Feuille villageoise*, Sept. 30, 1790.

11 C. J. Panckoucke, "Sur les journaux et papiers anglois," *Mercure de France*, Jan. 30, 1790, pp. 223–35. For an analysis of the background to Panckoucke's ideas about the press see the important work of Suzanne Tucoo-Chala, *Charles-Joseph Panckoucke et la librairie française 1736–1798* (Pau: Marrimpouey jeune, 1977), pp. 442–45.

12 The best discussion of these debates is in Alma Söderhjelm, *Le Régime de la presse pendant la Révolution française*, vol. 1 (Paris: Welter, 1900–1901). A typical condemnation of press "abuses" is Malouet's "Motion contre les libellistes" (June 18, 1790), in Victor-Pierre Malouet, *Collection des Opinions de M. Malouet, député à l'Assemblée nationale* (Paris: Valade, 1791), pp. 52–56.

13 Robespierre, speech to Convention, Apr. 19, 1793, in *Oeuvres de Maximilien Robespierre*, ed. M. Bouloiseau and A. Soboul (Paris: Société des Etudes robespierristes, 1938–58), ix, 452.

14 See, for example, Pierre Caron's analysis of the Convention's refusal to vote subsidies to patriotic newspapers in the fall of 1793. Pierre Caron, *Paris pendant la Terreur* (Paris: Klincksieck, 1910), I, 23.

15 On this shift in public opinion and on the endurance of the right-wing press in this period, see Jeremy D. Popkin, *The Right-Wing Press in France, 1792–1800* (Chapel Hill, N.C.: University of North Carolina Press, 1980), chs. 1, 3.

16 Châles, in *Journal des Hommes libres*, 9 Bru. III (Oct. 30, 1794); original in *L'Ami du Peuple* (Lebois, ed.), 6 Bru. III.

17 Barbé-Marbois, speech of 5 Fri. V (Nov. 25, 1796), printed in *L'Historien*, 6 Fri. V.

18 Roederer, in Adrien Lezay, *De la faiblesse d'un gouvernement qui commence, et de la nécessité où il est de se rallier à la majorité Nationale* (Paris: Mathey, 1796), pp. 15–18, 23–24. Roederer claimed authorship of this when he reprinted these sections of Lezay's pamphlet in his *Mémoires d'économie publique* (1797), I, 75. Compare modern research on public opinion and the impact of communications, such as Elihu Katz and Paul F. Lazarsfeld, *Personal Influence* (Glencoe, Ill.: Free Press, 1955), esp. pp. 32–33, where the theory that mass communication works by influencing key "opinion leaders" who in turn influence their communities is stated. Katz and Lazarsfeld did not find, however, that opinion leaders necessarily occupied high status positions in the social structure; from their study of American society, they concluded that "opinion leaders seemed to be distributed in all occupational groups, and on every social and economic level" (p. 32).

19 Roederer, in Lezay, *De la faiblesse*, p. 32.

20 This "Essai" first appeared in Roederer's *Journal d'économie publique*, 30 Bru. V (Nov. 20, 1796), where it was attributed to "a famous Swiss." But Roederer's son printed it among his father's works in Roederer, *Oeuvres* (Paris: Firmin-Didot, 1853–59), VII, 84–87. Its content is certainly consis-

tent with Roederer's other works on the press and public opinion.

21 "Essai," p. 429.

22 Ibid., p. 428.

23 Laharpe, "Du droit des placards," in *Mémorial*, 10 Fruc. V (Aug. 27, 1797).

24 Roederer cited circulation figures of anti-Jacobin papers in his *Journal de Paris*, 29 Plu. III (Feb. 16, 1795) and gave figures for papers of all shades of opinion in *Journal d'économie publique*, 30 Flor. V (May 19, 1797). In each case, the figures he provided proved a point he was trying to make with suspicious neatness.

25 Roederer, Report of Germinal XI (April, 1801), in carton 29 AP 91, Archives nationales, Paris, reprinted most recently in A. Cabanis, *La Presse sous le Consulat et l'Empire* (Paris: Société des Etudes robespierristes, 1975), p. 320. Roederer estimated the multiplier for copies mailed to the provinces as being four readers per copy, and in Paris, from ten to sixty per copy. He gave no grounds for his estimate, which had the convenient effect of giving his *Journal de Paris*, whose readership was concentrated in the capital, a larger estimated total audience than any other paper except the royalist *Journal des Débats*, even though several other papers circulated more copies. In his sketch of reader psychology, Roederer suggested that half read the papers to look after their material interests, a sixth "from simple curiosity," another sixth "from simple malice" and the final sixth "to keep up with conversation." His analysis of readers' motivations is remarkably close to that of the German sociologist Otto Groth in *Die Unerkannte Kulturmacht* (Berlin:W.de Gruyter, 1960–72), II, 280–315.

26 Roederer, in *De la faiblesse*, p. 20. Roederer argued that intelligence depended on social class; although there were some rich dolts, statistically the wealthy were smarter than the poor on the average. Roederer defined property broadly, admitting not only landowners but also merchants, manufacturers, and educated professionals into the category—the latter on the grounds that their cultivated minds constituted a capital. Roederer, *Oeuvres*, VI, 97–98.

27 *Journal d'économie publique*, III, 377–78.

28 Roederer's interest in the *Journal de Paris'* performance can be seen in various documents in carton 29 AP 91, Archives nationales, Paris, in which he disputed his share of the proceeds with his co-owner, Corancez. For other evidence of journalists' dependence on sales for their income, see Popkin, *The Right-Wing Press in France*, ch. 2.

29 *Censeur des Journaux*, 25 Flor. V (May 14, 1797).

30 Jean Debry, *Discours sur l'exécution de l'article 355 de la Constitution* (Paris: Imprimerie nationale, 1796), p. 3.

31 Charles Dupuis, *Discours sur la liberté de la presse* (Paris: Imprimerie nationale, 1796), pp. 10–11.

32 Chénier, speech of 12 Flor. III (May 1, 1795) in *Le Moniteur*, 16 Flor. III.

33 Emmanuel Brosselard, in *Le Républicain français*, 8 Plu. III (Jan. 27, 1795).

34 Benjamin Constant, *Des réactions politiques* (Paris: n.p., 1797), pp. 42, 44.

35 J. B. Louvet de Coudray, *Discours sur la nécessité de mettre actuellement à exécution l'article 355 de la Constitution, en ce qui concerne la presse* (Paris: Imprimerie nationale, 1796).
36 Constant, *Réactions*, p. 35.
37 Mme. de Staël, *Des circonstances actuelles qui peuvent terminer la Révolution, et des principes qui doivent fonder la République en France*, ed. J. Vienot (Paris: Fischbacher, 1906), p. 35. This work, composed some time in 1798, was not published in Mme. de Staël's lifetime.
38 Pierre Daunou, *Rapport fait par Daunou au nom d'une commission spéciale, sur la répression des délits de la presse* (Paris: Imprimerie nationale, 1796), p. 4.
39 Ibid., p. 15.
40 Ibid., p. 17. Daunou's distinction between books, the true vehicles of enlightenment, and newspapers became the theoretical basis for most defenses of the repressive press legislation enacted just after the coup of 18 Fructidor V (Sept. 4, 1797) and renewed in 1798. During the debate over renewal of the Fructidor measures in 1798, the Idéologue Cabanis reiterated Daunou's argument. Assimilating newspapers to "orators who harangue the People in public squares," he also used exactly the same argument that Roederer and Laharpe had applied to justify control of wall posters. (Cabanis, speech of 8 Fruc. VI (Aug. 25, 1798), in *Le Moniteur*, 11 Fruc. VI). In June 1799, during the debate over press freedom which served as the prelude to the next-to-last of the period's coups d'état, the beleaguered Directory's defenders unsuccessfully trotted the argument out once again (Creuzé-Latouche, speech of 23 Prair. VII (June 11, 1799) in *Le Moniteur*, 28 Prair. VII). This time, however, it had apparently lost its persuasive power. The Directory's opponents went back to Brissot's *Mémoire* of 1789 and even to Delolme, as though nothing had happened since then to throw doubt on their optimism. (Duplantier de la Gironde, speech of 22 Prair. VII (June 10, 1799), in *Le Moniteur*, 26 Prair. VII; the neo-Jacobin deputy Dethier had already published excerpts from Brissot under the title *Ombre de Brissot aux législateurs français sur la liberté de la presse* (Paris: Vatar, Dec. 1798). To be sure, many of the deputies who demanded repeal of the Fructidor press law still supported enforcement of an earlier law carrying the death penalty for royalist and "anarchist" propaganda. Garat, speech of 29 Ther. VII (Aug. 16, 1799), in *Le Moniteur*, 2 Fruc. VII (Aug. 19, 1799).
41 Constant, *Réactions*, p. 42.
42 Staël, *Circonstances*, pp. 98, 96.
43 Mably, *Collection complète des oeuvres* (Paris: Desbrières, 1794–95), VIII, 419.
44 Mably, ibid.; reprinted in Louvet's *Sentinelle*, 9 Vend. V (Sept. 30, 1796). The passage appears to have been unearthed by Louvet's legislative colleague Hardy, who cited it in a closed session of the Council of 500 on 6 Vend. V, reported in the *Véridique*, 9 Vend. V.
45 Louvet, *Discours*, p. 6.
46 Staël, *Circonstances*, pp. 96, 99.

47 Ibid., p. 97.

48 See Hobbes, *Leviathan*, Book II, ch. 26, where he discusses the drawbacks of public political debate. On the assumptions underlying old regime press policy, see Lamoignon de Malesherbes, *Mémoires*, p. 97.

49 As a member of the Napoleonic Conseil d'Etat, Roederer helped draft the edict of 27 Niv. VIII (Jan. 17, 1800), which restricted the number of papers in Paris and imposed tight regulation on them. Despite his earlier interest in press statistics, he also composed an article attacking the most popular paper of the day, the *Journal des Débats*, for collecting its readers by maintaining "a continuing scandal which draws everyone's attention. . . ." *Journal de Paris*, s.d., clipping in Roederer papers, 29 AP 91, Archives nationales, Paris. The fact that Roederer, in effect, changed sides on the question of press freedom in 1800 does not detract from the significance of his earlier theoretical contributions. His arguments in favor of freedom for a press representing the interests of property continued to be used by less opportunistic writers, such as Joseph Fiévée in his secret memoranda to Napoleon (see Fiévée, *Correspondance et relations de J. Fiévée avec Bonaparte* (Paris: Desrez, 1836), II, 128). Similarly, the conversion of Mme. de Staël and Constant to a more liberal view of press freedom after 1800 does not change the fact that they had helped lay the bases for the restrictive policies of the Napoleonic and Restoration periods.

50 Staël, *Circonstances*, p. 193.

51 Constant, *De la liberté des journaux considérée sous le rapport de l'intérêt du gouvernement* in *Oeuvres* (Paris: Pléiade, 1959), p. 1259.

52 Otto Groth, *Geschichte des deutschen Zeitungswissenschaft* (Munich: Weinmayer, 1948), covers German analyses of the press from the seventeenth to the early twentieth centuries. Recent French press historians have tended to neglect the development of theoretical analyses of the press in French thought, although there is some material on the subject scattered through the venerable work of Eugène Hatin, *Histoire politique et littéraire de la presse en France* (Paris: Poulet-Massis, 1859–61).

Locke's Essay *and the* Strategies of Eighteenth-Century English Satire

PETER M. BRIGGS

—Attitudes are nothing, madam,—'tis the transition from one attitude to another—like the preparation and resolution of the discord into harmony, which is all in all.

—Tristram Shandy

The examination of human error is the satirist's vocation, and contemporary satirists were well aware of Locke's new views on error relatively soon after the publication of *An Essay Concerning Human Understanding* in 1690. More than a generation ago Kenneth Maclean demonstrated that nearly all eighteenth-century men of letters read the *Essay*; Addison and others sought to popularize some of its tenets, and satirists from Swift to Blake toyed or wrestled with Locke's ideas about sensation, mental habits, the nature of imagination, the potentialities of education, and other matters.[1] My purpose here is not to survey the breadth of Locke's influence, however, but to explore some of its particular complexities: specifically, to ask what difference the currency of Lockean ideas made in satire, both in its down-to-earth technical and strategic aspects and, somewhat more broadly, in its moral ethos. Locke's clear-eyed and quite systematic examination of man's cognitive abilities and limitations had a significant impact upon contemporary discussions of human error and consequently upon the literary practices of satirists.

Locke was primarily interested in urging that man possesses no innate ideas and in showing that all of his thoughts are ultimately

135

traceable to sensations received from the external world. Man receives sensory data from the world and the mind organizes and evaluates those data; the individual understanding works by finding patterns in its sensations, by comparing new data and its previous formulations of experience, by inferring connections among particular instances and general rules from them, by reflecting upon the design of its own experiences. Through such processes, Locke argued, man can eventually arrive at true though limited knowledge of his world; man cannot know everything, but he can know enough to manage his life in a reasonable way.

Several ideas derived from Locke's system attracted both immediate and sustained attention in the literary world. The most important of these, at least from the point of view of moralists and satirists, was the fact that Locke consistently treated human error in terms of specific, identifiable mental failures—that is, perceptual, cognitive, or linguistic failures—rather than in terms of moral failure, a weakness of character or will. A reasonable man would do the right thing unless his reason was deluded (hence the enormous importance of education in Locke's view). Second, Locke's model drew particular attention to understanding as a *process*, not a fixed product; the mind engages in a continuing dialogue, not only with the external world reported by the senses, but also with its own habits and its own past formulations of experience. Third, Locke's critical attention to language as an aspect of understanding treated in a systematic way a problem which had bothered both philosophers and literary writers for some time previously: words, with all their imperfections, were an inevitable intermediary between man and man, between man and the external world, even between man and his own inner reflections; the fallibilities of language and the failures of man's understanding were related and reciprocal.

Two important qualifications are necessary here. Strictly speaking, Locke was not the originator of any of these ideas, though he contributed much to their refinement; he was indebted to a long tradition of skeptical philosophers—Montaigne, Bacon, Descartes, Hobbes, and others—and a large part of Locke's contribution was the critical systemization of possibilities raised by others. It is also important to note at the outset that writers do not really need a philosopher to tell them that human beings can go astray from misunderstanding their world, their perceptions, or their language. It is only necessary to think of *Don Quixote* or Shakespeare's plays to remind oneself that a great deal of literary insight preceded Locke's formulation of the mind's workings, and Locke might well be viewed as systemizing and refining

the theoretical underpinnings of matters which had often been observed in literary practice.

Still, the impact of Locke's *Essay* and the genuine intellectual ex-
citement which it engendered cannot be denied. One need only recall
Addison's *Spectator* essays on "the Pleasures of the Imagination"
(nos. 411–21) to realize the literary importance of the new perspectives offered by Lockean psychology, and certainly some epistemological and psychological possibilities opened up by Locke substantially shaped the century-long discussion of literary sublimity.[2]
Naturally, few readers simply "received" Locke as the new gospel;
most had to assimilate Locke's ideas to an existing literary and ethical
heritage. What one typically finds in trying to assess Locke's reception into literature is a Burkean pattern of marrying new ideas with
older beliefs—even using the new to *support* older ideas which it apparently superseded—and nowhere is this conservative pattern more
evident than in satire.

Philosophers' terminology, methods, and goals often strike the
non-philosopher as overly abstract, opposed to common sense, and
foolish—too much reasoning upon too little matter. Many Augustan
satirists had fun parodying the tone of Locke's *Essay* and offering
reductive interpretations of its methods. Matthew Prior's caricature
of Locke provides a clear instance: "You seem, in my poor apprehension, to go to and fro upon a Philosophical Swing like a Child upon
a wooden Horse always in motion but without any Progress, and to
Act as if a Man instead of Practising his Trade should spend all his
Life in Naming his Tools."[3] Criticisms of this sort need not imply any
very specific response to Locke's ideas, only the feeling that the methodical earnestness and abstraction of his discussion were somehow
ludicrous. But satirists who came to scoff remained to pray when
they discovered that Locke's orderly exposition of how the understanding works offered, *mutatis mutandis*, a detailed and systematic
survey of how the mind could *fail* to work; read in this way, the *Essay*
offered a promising resource for the satirists' own anatomy of human
error.

Of course, it was necessary for the satirists to change Locke's emphasis quite substantially. In spite of the skepticism which shaped his
philosophical methods, Locke was not a pessimist concerning man's
ability to comprehend his experience of the world. Limited by his
senses, the powers of his mind, and the vagaries of language, man
may not be able to know all things, but he can comprehend enough
of the world to know his own good. Locke insists that to pursue
knowledge beyond one's capacities is unnecessary, foolish, and vain:

. . . it will be an unpardonable, as well as Childish Peevishness, if we undervalue the Advantages of our Knowledge, and neglect to improve it to the ends for which it was given us, because there are some Things that are set out of the reach of it. It will be no Excuse to an idle and untoward Servant, who would not attend his Business by Candle-light, to plead that he had not broad Sun-shine. The Candle, that is set up in us, shines bright enough for all our Purposes.

. . . Our Business here is not to know all things, but those which concern our Conduct. If we can find out those Measures, whereby a rational Creature put in that State, which Man is in, in this World, may, and ought to govern his Opinions, and Actions depending thereon, we need not be troubled, that some other things escape our Knowledge.(*Essay* I,i,5–6)[4]

Locke was undisturbed by the fact that man must inevitably see the world from within the confines of his own subjectivity; as an empiricist he assumed that man's subjective ideas would continually be checked and refined by reference to new information reported by the senses. But a darker possibility lurks in the same epistemological model. The Lockean mind can never confront any experience of the external world directly. And if one adds together all of the constraints of man's knowing suggested by Locke—the limitations and fallibility of the senses, the delusive possibilities within words, man's susceptibility to habitual thought in the place of critical thought, the potentiality that the mind itself may err through inadvertence or on the basis of partial and distorted information—one arrives at the possibility that man might be seriously alienated from the world of experience and thus unable to learn consistently from it.

The danger extends still further. Locke defined human knowledge as follows:

> Knowledge . . . seems to me to be nothing but *the perception of the connexion and agreement, or disagreement and repugnancy of any of our Ideas*. In this alone it consists. Where this Perception is, there is Knowledge, and where it is not, there, though we may fancy, guess, or believe, yet we always come short of Knowledge. (*Essay* IV,i,2)

When Locke wrote this definition, he was envisioning a reasonable mind in continual communication with the experiential world. But a possible fallacy seems clear: a mind which is alienated from the experiential world and thus deprived of its checks could still have the *impression* of true knowledge simply by reaching subjective agreement with itself. It is only continual and sanative contact with the real world which differentiates Locke's definition of knowledge from his definition of madness (*Essay* II, xi,13).

And, of course, eighteenth-century satire is filled with characters who are not in dialogue with the world but only with themselves, who have lost their bearings in the real world. Instances spring readily to mind: Swift's Hack in *A Tale of a Tub* or Gulliver toward the end of his *Travels*; the pedants who annotate Pope's *Dunciad* and the critics and collectors who occupy small corners there ("The mind, in Metaphysics at a loss, May wander in a wilderness of Moss"; B *Dunciad* IV, 449–50);[5] Walter Shandy, with all his arcane knowledge and reckless hypothesizing; Blake's Idiot Questioner; and many others. Isolated sensibilities, madmen and fools, existed in life and in literature long before Locke. But Locke's subtle and systematic examination of how the mind comes to terms with the experience of the world—and how it can fail—gave to the satirist a new and sophisticated tool for looking at human error *from the point of view of the erroneous.* The erroneous are not simply weaker or stupider or more vicious than "we" are (they may be that, *too*), but they also see the world in a different way than we do and respond to it accordingly. Tristram Shandy implies this new awareness that error might be rooted in cognitive difficulties when he tries to account for the eccentricity of his father's opinions:

> —The truth was, his road lay so very far on one side, from that wherein most men travelled,—that every object before him presented a face and section of itself to his eye, altogether different from the plan and elevation of it seen by the rest of mankind.—In other words, 'twas a different object,—and in course was differently considered:[6]

Keeping an eye on cognitive processes offered the satirist a number of strategic possibilities previously unexplored or only incidentally explored. Madness from the point of view of the mad is one, but consider another: the traditional satiric *naif*. By well-established convention the function of the *naif* was a relatively simple one: an innocent or outsider, he confronted a new set of circumstances and, by asking "innocent" questions about what he saw, served as a vehicle to expose the inconsistencies and the vices in the situation which were hidden from eyes accustomed to it. Now, however, the *naif* could maintain his traditional role while taking on a new one: he could still ask his innocent questions, but the impact of the answers and the new experience on him could also be explored; he was, after all, a walking *tabula rasa* (or, curiously and paradoxically, sometimes a repository of *idées fixes*), trying to come to terms with new experience and to derive true knowledge from it. His outlook, perceptions, and processes of cognition could become a locus of satire even while his traditional function, exposing what he sees, remained intact: two satires, and a complexly ironical relationship between them, for the price of one. Most satirists preferred protagonists who were sublimely unaffected by their own confusions, who could rise to equal obtuseness another day, and yet the permutations of this kind of protagonist in eighteenth-century satire are practically endless; one immediately thinks of Swift's Gulliver or of Strephon in "The Lady's Dressing Room," but further reflection quickly leads to Pope's Belinda and Fielding's Joseph Andrews and Sterne's Uncle Toby and Blake's innocent children in the *Songs of Innocence and of Experience*.

The same considerations apply in connection with another rich vein of eighteenth-century satire, the examination of the works and characters of the learned. Of course, it was already deeply traditional to satirize the learned for pride and foolishness, for missing common human truths in the narrow-minded pursuit of out-of-the-way "learning": "Professing themselves to be wise, they became fools. . . ." (Romans i,22). But Locke's exposition of the workings of the mind had much to add to that tradition: an explanation of exactly *how* the reasonable and inquiring mind could still miss its objects; a model to explain why narrowing the pursuit of truth could be satisfying—or, at least, self-satisfying; a rationale to explain how the learned could get so lost in language; finally, an explanation of how the learned could still be proud, even surrounded by the products of their foolishness. The lucubrations of Swift's Hack, Martinus Scriblerus, Walter Shandy, and others are permeated by a Lockean awareness of the mind's power to delude itself, multiplying words and fragmenting understanding, all in the earnest pursuit of knowledge. In the same vein, the idea that both the fool and the knave lack self-knowledge, a traditional theme of classical satire, gained new resonance and apparent inevitability in the light of Locke's premise that a man's understanding, like his eye, is unavoidably limited by its own perspective—and, like the eye, least able to turn objective attention upon itself. Many other characteristic themes and strategies of eighteenth-century satire gain a new resonance when one realizes that they imply literary re-creations of cognitive problems discussed by Locke: the importance of perspective and context to understanding; the disjunction of style and content, words and things; the difficulties of establishing shared languages and common values; the predominance of surface over substance. The well-known disjunctiveness of many satiric narratives may even be founded upon a suspicion raised (but not embraced) by Locke, that human experience itself is potentially disjunctive and inevitably at odds with the orderly impulses of man's mind. Locke's analysis of the mind probably did not *cause* any of the new strategies and preoccupations of satire, but it systematically laid bare the materials and perspectives which made them possible.

Another consequence of the satirist's ability to portray error from the point of view of the erroneous is a more dynamic representation of error. Once again, earlier literary examples—Shakespeare's Richard III, Milton's Satan, and many others—pointed the way, but the systematic qualities of Locke's argument combined with his insistence that the mind engaged in a *continuing* dialogue with the world made it possible and perhaps necessary for satirists to approach error in a different way. Most traditional satire had viewed error as a relatively fixed or at most sequential quality; that is, the satiric victim embodied a certain error or set of errors and the process of satire exposed these errors by portraying the victim in a sequence of ever-more-ludicrous or debased postures. The postures changed, as the satirist manipulated his audience's view of the victim, but the errors themselves remained fairly constant. At most, the victim followed the logic of his given error: a man who was overly proud was also likely to be vain, uncharitable, intolerant, uncompromising, and antisocial.

Now, however, the satirist's new-found ability to explore error from the inside, seeing the world from the point of view of the erroneous, allowed a more flexible and dynamic portrayal of error; the *mental habits* of error rather than its outward manifestations in behavior became a principal focus of satire, and a reader was soon persuaded that *whatever* new experience came along, a Gulliver, a Martinus Scriblerus, a Dr. Pangloss, or a Walter Shandy would somehow manage to misconstrue it. It is no accident that the real hero of Pope's *Dunciad* is not Lewis Theobald or Colley Cibber, but a state of mind, Dulness herself; Dulness is not only omnipresent and Protean in her manifestations, but she is also significantly Lockean in her essence:

> . . . Dulness here is not to be taken contractedly for mere Stupidity, but in the enlarged sense of the word, for all Slowness of Apprehension, Shortness of Sight, or imperfect Sense of things. It includes . . . Labour, Industry, and some degree of Activity and Boldness: a ruling principle not inert, but turning topsy-turvy the Understanding, and inducing an Anarchy or confused State of Mind. (B *Dunciad* I, 15n)

Though particular errors are everywhere to be found, the lowest common denominator of all error is mental, and the satirists now had a system and strategy which would allow them to pursue error to her lair.

My point is not that the eighteenth-century satirists either were or eventually became convinced Lockeans. They were opportunists, not converts, and more often than not, they were exposing what they saw as the fallacies of his views, or at least qualifying his relative optimism. They saw the possibility of moral and strategic advantage in Locke's exposition of error, and with both sophistication and control they carefully played off Locke's model of understanding against other models for assessing man's condition.

The easiest model to oppose to *any* philosophical system is "common sense"—we all recall Samuel Johnson kicking a stone to "refute" idealism—and all of the major satirists relied on this ploy. But much more sophisticated juxtapositions were possible. Consider Gulliver's confrontation with the Yahoos in *Gulliver's Travels*.[7] Gulliver, well-meaning and reasonable, quite consistently fails to comprehend his situation for all the predictable Lockean reasons: he is blind to the limitations of his own perspective; he values surface over substance and words over things; though he records his sensations faithfully, his own reflections represent for the most part a long series of uncritical or erroneous inferences. Gulliver's easy and consistent confidence in his own judgments becomes an ironical measure of his total inability to grasp his situation, to find (or even to miss) those larger perspectives and values which would unify and give proportion to the various fragments of his experiences. On the other side, Swift's Yahoos represent a caricature, written from the point of view of conservative Christian morals, of man's total depravity; significantly, we are given no access to their thoughts, but their behavior shows them to be greedy, self-centered, savage, and benighted. When Gulliver concludes that he *is* a Yahoo and sails away from Houyhnhnm-land under a sail made from Yahoo-skins, Swift is in effect combining the intellectual (Lockean) and moral (Christian) notions of man's propensity to err into a new and monstrous formulation: a doubly benighted depravity, both moral and rational. Swift used the same concurrence in "A Modest Proposal," where again the narrator's errors are seen from the "inside." Of course, the example of Gulliver is eventually played off against the goodness and generosity of the Portuguese sea captain, whom Gulliver also fails to comprehend.

Pope's *Dunciad* offers another kind of juxtaposition. Critics sometimes suggest that Pope implied a split attitude toward the Dunces:

on one hand, they are held morally and intellectually responsible for the death of English culture; on the other, they are presented as weak, hungry, foolish, and ultimately pitiable men, narrowed and made desperate by their circumstances, men who are not so much the perpetrators of Dulness as her victims.[8] In fact, Pope is juxtaposing two contemporary (and perpetual) attitudes toward human responsibility. The grand sweep of the text, which implies an unequivocal denunciation of Dulness, all her works and all her minions, is based upon a traditional view of man's moral and intellectual nature; man is a responsible steward in this world and can be held accountable to higher values. However, the initial definition of Dulness, some of Pope's footnotes, and many of the portraits of individual Dunces imply a very different vision: man is narrowed by his perceptions, by his circumstances, by his language, by his entire education; he is alienated from nature, from his fellow-man, from any broad perspectives on his situation; he is sitting in darkness, trying desperately to deal with a situation which he cannot even comprehend. Obviously this is not Lockean man as Locke conceived him but it is Lockean man as Pope interpreted and imagined him: "Son: what thou seek'st is in thee! Look, and find Each Monster meets his likeness in thy mind" (B *Dunciad* III, 251–52). Whatever the collective responsibility of many such creatures may be, they certainly cannot be held individually responsible for the state of the world. I do not mean to portray Pope as a psychologist or sociologist of alienation, covertly siding with the underdog; it seems clear that his primary sympathies lay with those higher values which condemned Dulness and all her works. But the strategy of viewing errors from the "inside" and the "outside" simultaneously, presenting them as countervailing parts of the same story, yields a troubling (and perhaps troubled) double vision of human responsibility. Pope does not underestimate the difficulty of overcoming Dulness, and a significant part of that difficulty is defined in Lockean terms.

Locke's presence in Sterne's *Tristram Shandy* is well known; Tristram's style of thought and writing constitute a caricature of associationism, and he and his relatives repeatedly cite, quote, and burlesque ideas from Locke's *Essay*.[9] Walter Shandy's *Tristra-poedia* was no doubt inspired by the popularity of Locke's essay on the education of children. However, reciting incidental uses of Locke does not capture the full importance of his place in the novel. *Tristram Shandy* is quintessentially a book about man's attempt to give a reasonable and definitive form to his experience of the world—and about the tendency of experience to run counter to man's formulations; the basic

Lockean opposition between mind and world is the central fact not only in Tristram's life, but in Parson Yorick's, Walter Shandy's, and Uncle Toby's as well. Sterne toys with many models of the mind's workings, but the major opposition which structures the novel and its satire is a struggle between only two: on one hand, Locke's ideas of the reasonable understanding of experience; on the other, Don Quixote.[10] The appropriateness of the Lockean model is everywhere apparent: to bring one's life to reasonable shape is fighting against the odds, and Tristram's wry amusement at the perplexities of his own history is founded upon a Lockean awareness of man's inevitable cognitive limitations. Tristram's sententious remark that man lives amongst "riddles and mysteries," that the most familiar things have dark sides which we cannot see into (p. 293), gains in resonance when one realizes that Sterne cribbed the entire passage from Locke's *Essay:*

> He that knows any thing, knows this in the first place, that he need not seek long for Instances of his Ignorance. The meanest, and most obvious Things that come in our way, have dark sides, that the quickest Sight cannot penetrate into. The clearest, and most enlarged Understandings of thinking Men find themselves puzzled, and at a loss, in every Particle of Matter. (IV,iii,22)[11]

Tristram and all the characters who inhabit his world continually project cognitive and verbal patterns upon the common realities which surround them, yet the ordering principles of their world—laughably *and* pathetically—forever elude their grasp.

But Don Quixote is always at Tristram's side to balance this sober awareness of man's inevitable limitations. Tristram pronounces Cervantes his favorite author and invokes Don Quixote to characterize all three of the novel's comic heroes: Walter, Toby, and Yorick. What does the example of Don Quixote offer to Tristram?[12] Don Quixote's view of the world, like Locke's, is premised on a radical subjectivity, but their resemblance ends there. Quixote offers an implicit statement of the positive value of whimsy and fantasy, of sentiment and absurd ideals and imagination; he serves, in other words, as an avatar of another kind of "human understanding," a balance to the austerities imposed by Locke's sober insistence that man must deal with the real world reasonably and as best he can. Only the spirit of Don Quixote can release man from the rigors of rationality and circumstance.

> Gentle Spirit of sweetest humour, who erst didst sit upon the easy pen of my beloved CERVANTES; thou who glided'st (*sic*) daily through his lattice, and turned'st the twilight of his prison into noon-day brightness by thy presence—tinged'st his little urn of water with heaven-sent Nectar, and all the time he wrote of *Sancho* and his master, didst cast thy mystic mantle o'er his wither'd stump, and wide extended it to all the evils of his life—
> —Turn in hither, I beseech thee! (*Tristram Shandy*, p. 628)

Cervantes could rise above imprisonment and physical disability to find freedom and renewal in his imagined creations: the resiliency and faith of both Quixote and Sancho triumph, momentarily yet eternally, over the restrictions imposed by time and circumstance. Perhaps Tristram can be equally fortunate, equally free. He knows that life is a poor fragment indeed, unless one can cultivate humor, imagination, and sentiment to fill out its mental dimensions; "I . . . must be cut short in the midst of my days, and taste no more of 'em than what I borrow from imagination. . . ." (p. 495).

Blake's antipathy toward Locke is too complex to discuss fully here.[13] However, in Blake's world opposition may include true friendship, and he seems to have owed more to Lockean ideas than he imagined: in particular, the notions that human error is fundamentally epistemological, rooted in the ways in which people understand themselves and their world, and that consequently the rectification of error will stem not so much from moral exhortation as from a reexamination of the powers of understanding. Of course, Blake had a conception of "understanding" very different from Locke's. The philosopher's most famous work became in Blake's interpretation "An Easy of Huming Understanding by John Look ye Gent," a metamorphosis which seems to imply that Locke's sensationalism (Look-ye) is too easy and leads eventually to the skepticism of Hume.[14] Throughout his prophetic works Blake repeatedly associates Locke with Bacon and Newton and treats all three as archenemies of inspiration and corrupters of English thought.

In essence, Blake caricatured Locke so as to sharpen a satiric opposition to him: in Blake's poetry Locke appears not simply as an analyst of human limitations but rather as their advocate, a prophet of materialism, rationalism, and other mind-forged manacles. Like Swift, Pope, and Sterne before him, Blake re-creates the Lockean mind imaginatively, seeing error from the inside, in order to identify its limitations. The mind which falls away from the unified vision of eternity finds itself in an alien world, left with only "ruinous frag-

ments of life" and surrounded by "An ocean of voidness unfathomable" (*Book of Urizen* 5:9–11). Blake's Urizen typifies the fallen mind's
failure to discover a ruling principle to organize its sensations; his
view of the world is fragmented, blood-dimmed, phantasmagorical,
a prophetic caricature of Lockean vision.

> And his world teemd vast enormities
> Frightning; faithless; fawning
> Portions of life; similitudes
> Of a foot, or a hand, or a head
> Or a heart, or an eye, they swam mischevous
> Dread terrors! delighting in blood
> (*Book of Urizen* 23:2–7)

The darkened mind is a *tabula rasa* only to an endless concatenation
of torments and chaos is come again.[15]

Blake's opposition to Lockean thought was not always so overt and
ferocious as in *The Book of Urizen*. Although mental limitation seldom
coexists with delight in Blake's world—there are no delicate Sylphs,
no whimsical hobbyhorses—he occasionally satirizes mind-forged
manacles with dry irony and even a certain sympathy. In the *Songs of
Experience*, for example, little boys are taught to rationalize the horrors of their lives rather than to struggle against them:

> There's little Tom Dacre, who cried when his head
> That curl'd like a lambs back, was shav'd, so I said
> Hush Tom never mind it, for when your head's bare,
> You Know that the soot cannot spoil your white hair.
> ("The Chimney Sweeper," 5–8)

The chimney sweeper who speaks is playing a Lockean role, urging
accommodation to existing realities instead of rebellion against them,
but how could he do otherwise? The object of Blake's satire is not
really the little boy but those like Locke who taught him to rationalize
the circumstances which oppress him, or more generally, man's powers of rationalization themselves. Though Locke was an ideological
enemy, Blake owed something to him for the ability to make cognitive
processes an object of satire, to re-create imaginatively the world
seen through the eyes of innocence and of experience.

One further implication of the satirist's post-Lockean ability to portray error from the "inside" should be mentioned. So long as the
satirist views error from the "outside," paying principal attention to
what satiric characters are doing wrong, most satires seem to offer

portraits of vice and madness unleashed maliciously or mindlessly upon the world. However, if one looks more closely at *why* errors occur and exactly *how* the objects of satire go wrong, satire often seems more an exposition of human fallibility, a tale of misperception and muddle-headedness, failed purpose, and miscommunication. Thus Lockean insight into the minds of the erroneous can lead to a potentially more "sympathetic" or generous kind of satire, one less single-mindedly directed toward a final moral judgment: Pope's Belinda and Sterne's Uncle Toby demand a response more multi-faceted and ambivalent than simple moral disapproval. Error is not a fixed quality, Vice or Folly, but a product of specific and complex human limitations. Lockean ways of thinking led to a subtle shift in the moral ethos of satire: if error is essentially or even partly a perceptual and cognitive matter, then the "correction" which satire traditionally supplies must be less strictly moral and more semantic; correcting the confused requires a different posture and a different, perhaps gentler set of strategies than lashing the wicked does.

This important shift also raises a second possibility too broad to be explored here: that is, that the satirist, increasingly sympathetic toward the inevitable fallibilities of men, might turn from satirizing men's errors to satirizing the circumscribed and fatal conditions upon which life is given to man. Sterne implies that man is trapped by dark and unfathomable "riddles and mysteries," and in a satiric fragment addressed "To God" Blake challenges the Master of all circumstances: "If you have formd a Circle to go into [,] go into it yourself and see how you would do." Or the potential satirist might give over satire altogether in favor of a more compassionate approach to man's inevitable difficulties. Here Johnson's Imlac in *Rasselas* may seem a straw in the wind: when Nekayah and Pekuah laugh at the mad astronomer who imagines that he controls the weather, Imlac rebukes them—

> . . . to mock the heaviest of human afflictions is neither charitable nor wise. Few can attain this man's knowledge, and few practice his virtues; but all may suffer his calamity. Of the uncertainties of our present state, the most dreadful and alarming is the uncertain continuance of reason.[16]

My sequence of examples from Swift, Pope, Sterne, and Blake, I think, implies these significant changes. As far as Swift is concerned, to understand human failures, whether moral or cognitive, is *not* to forgive them, and he yokes new intellectual failures to traditional moral ones to yield an even more devastating portrait of man's possible failings. Whether one looks at his early *Rape of the Lock* or the final *Dunciad*, Pope seems to imply a more equivocal position: man is indeed responsible for his moral and intellectual conduct, but the limitations of man's perceptions and comprehension seem somewhat to mitigate, or at least to complicate, a summary moral judgment of him. Sterne responds to the potential conflict between moral and cognitive definitions of error by divorcing moral and intellectual error almost entirely. There are few moral errors in *Tristram Shandy*, and Sterne is left free to transform the mind's Lockean limitations into positive (or at least lovable) virtues: "Every thing in this world . . . is big with jest,—and has wit in it, and instruction too,—if we can but find it out" (p. 393). Blake accepts Locke's position that epistemological errors have precedence over moral ones, then outflanks Locke with an anti-Lockean epistemology: "The tygers of wrath are wiser than the horses of instruction" and "Every thing possible to be believ'd is an image of truth" ("Proverbs of Hell," 44, 38).

Locke and satire, an odd couple married by the opportunism and ingenuity of satirists around 1700, grew old together after 1760. There is no time to survey their decline here; suffice it to say that both yielded to equally subjective but more "feeling" ways of interpreting human experience in psychology, in aesthetic theory, and in literature. There is much in Locke's thought which the satirists never addressed; conversely, the best eighteenth-century satire contains a humor, an energy, an exuberance and complexity which no Lockean background is likely to account for. Still, these disparate traditions of discourse are substantially joined. In assessing man's cognitive powers Locke almost inadvertently provided new grounds for human humility and permanently changed the nature of discourse concerning human error; the satirists, even without wholly subscribing to Locke's views, gave that new discourse an enduring literary form. Their joint legacy requires some explanation, but no apology.

NOTES

1 See *John Locke and English Literature of the Eighteenth Century* (1936; rpt., New York: Russell & Russell, 1962), passim.
2 See Ernest L. Tuveson's important study of Locke's impact upon eighteenth-century ideas of artistic imagination in *The Imagination as a Means*

of Grace: Locke and the Aesthetics of Romanticism (Berkeley and Los Angeles: University of California Press, 1960), passim.

3 From "A Dialogue between Mr. John Lock and Seigneur de Montaigne," in *Literary Works*, ed. H. Bunker Wright and Monroe K. Spears (Oxford: Clarendon Press, 1971), I, 620–21. Prior's four *Dialogues of the Dead*, written around 1721, were not published until 1907, but Pope and others read them in manuscript; see Joseph Spence, *Observations, Anecdotes, and Characters of Books and Men*, ed. James M. Osborn (Oxford: Clarendon Press, 1966), I, 92.

4 Quoted from *An Essay Concerning Human Understanding*, ed. Peter H. Nidditch (Oxford: Clarendon Press, 1975). Further references are noted in the text.

5 Quotations of Pope's poetry are taken from the reduced Twickenham edition of the *Poems*, ed. John Butt (New Haven: Yale University Press, 1963) and hereafter cited by line number in the text.

6 Laurence Sterne, *The Life and Opinions of Tristram Shandy, Gentleman*, ed. J. A. Work (New York: Odyssey Press, 1940), p. 382. Further quotations, taken from this edition, are noted in the text.

7 For a broad and judicious survey of the many modern interpretations of Gulliver in Houyhnhnm-land, see James L. Clifford, "Gulliver's Fourth Voyage: 'Hard' and 'Soft' Schools of Interpretation," in Larry S. Champion, ed., *Quick Springs of Sense: Studies in the Eighteenth Century* (Athens, Georgia: University of Georgia Press, 1974), pp. 33–49.

8 See, for example, Aubrey S. Williams, *Pope's Dunciad: A Study of Its Meaning* (1955; rpt., Hamden, Conn.: Archon, 1968), pp. 77–81.

9 Sterne's indebtedness to Locke has been much discussed in this century, particularly since the publication of John L. Traugott's *Tristram Shandy's World: Sterne's Philosophical Rhetoric* (Berkeley and Los Angeles: University of California Press, 1954); Lodwick Hartley offers a useful summary of modern critical debate on this subject in *Laurence Sterne in the Twentieth Century* (Chapel Hill: University of North Carolina Press, 1966), pp. 22–28, 150. Helene Moglen's study *The Philosophical Irony of Laurence Sterne* (Gainesville, Florida: University of Florida Press, 1975), passim., provides the most thorough and in many ways the most persuasive assessment of Sterne's relationship to Locke.

10 All modern critics have recognized elements of satire in *Tristram Shandy*, particularly satire directed against members of the "learned" professions—philosophers, lawyers, divines, physicians, and others; however, there is no entirely satisfactory account of how thoroughgoing a satire Sterne's work is, principally because there is little critical consensus on the true objects of Sterne's satire. In *Laurence Sterne as Satirist: A Reading of "Tristram Shandy"* (Gainesville, Florida: University of Florida Press, 1969) Melvyn New argues that *Tristram* is in the tradition of Swiftian satire and should be read as a satire of Walter, Uncle Toby, and particularly its confused author; but the earnestness and relative narrowness of New's ideas

of satire leave him little room to recognize that the faults of Tristram and his relatives coexist with comic energies and human virtues too widely felt to be wholly denied. Helene Moglen's *The Philosophical Irony of Laurence Sterne* offers a good account of the full range of satiric materials in *Tristram*, but construes many of these materials as more ironical than satirical; Professor Moglen explores ideas of ironical incongruity to explain the relationship between faults and virtues in Sterne's characters. I think that a recognition of Locke's role in the satirical strategy of the novel helps to resolve many critical difficulties. Basically *Tristram Shandy* offers a satirical anatomy of man's cognitive difficulties in interpreting his world: themes of cognitive confusion unite the "background" characters (lawyers, divines, and so on) with the "foreground" characters, Tristram and his relatives. And Sterne combines a Lockean awareness of the cognitive and verbal dimensions of human error with an implicitly unLockean notion—namely, that men possess an essential nature quite apart from both their experiences and their wrestlings with cognitive difficulty—in order to rationalize the relationship between satirical faults and humane virtues in his characters. Walter Shandy is sympathetic and Uncle Toby is lovable precisely because their cognitive confusions, which are the objects of satire, never quite touch their essential virtues, which are not.

11 This passage apparently had a special significance for Sterne; he borrowed from it, again almost verbatim, in two of his *Sermons of Mister Yorick*: III, iv ("Felix's Behaviour towards Paul Examined") and VII, xvii ("The Ways of Providence Justified to Man").

12 An answer to this question is complicated by the fact that critical interpretation of Cervantes' novel was changing rapidly in eighteenth-century England. Readers early in the century tended to see Don Quixote as a burlesque figure, a crack-brained gentleman who overheated his imagination with chivalric fantasies and was deservedly rebuffed by the good-humored practicality and common sense of the workaday world. Later readers, particularly those inclined toward sentimentalism, saw a new Don Quixote: Cervantes' hero was a misunderstood idealist and altruist, a sincere and superior champion of lost causes, condemned to the taunts of shallow and uncomprehending worldlings. See A. P. Burton, "Cervantes the Man Seen through English Eyes in the Seventeenth and Eighteenth Centuries," *Bulletin of Hispanic Studies* 45 (1968), 1–15, and Anthony Close, *The Romantic Approach to "Don Quixote": A Critical History of the Romantic Tradition in "Quixote" Criticism* (Cambridge: Cambridge University Press, 1978), chs. 1, 2. With characteristic ambivalence Sterne seems to imply some sympathy toward both readings of Cervantes' hero, though in the end he preferred the more "romantic" Quixote.

13 For more extended discussion of Blake's opposition to Locke, see Northrop Frye, *Fearful Symmetry: A Study of William Blake* (Princeton: Princeton University Press, 1947), pp. 14–29, 245–46, 384–85; Peter F. Fisher, *The Valley of Vision: Blake as Prophet and Revolutionary* (Toronto: University of

Toronto Press, 1961), pp. 101–21; George M. Harper, *The Neoplatonism of William Blake* (Chapel Hill: University of North Carolina Press, 1961), pp. 61–76; Kathleen Raine, *Blake and Tradition* (London: Routledge & Kegan Paul, 1968), II, 100–150; Donald D. Ault, *Visionary Physics: Blake's Response to Newton* (Chicago: University of Chicago Press, 1974), pp. 57–70; and many others. Most modern interpreters are principally interested in Blake's epistemological and ontological "arguments" with Locke; however, understanding Blake's opposition to Lockean psychology, including his ability to personify and then caricature a Lockean outlook in his characters, provides an important key to an appreciation of his satiric strategies.

14 From "An Island in the Moon" in *The Poetry and Prose of William Blake*, ed. David V. Erdman (Garden City, N. Y.: Doubleday, 1965), p. 447. Further quotations from Blake are taken from this edition and cited by line number in the text.

Professor Erdman suggests (p. 766) that "huming" should be read as "humming," but "Hume-ing" seems probable, an implicit recognition on Blake's part of Locke's contribution to Hume's epistemology and psychology. Moreover, Hume had published *An Enquiry Concerning Human Understanding* in 1748. Blake's "Gent" (i.e., gentleman) is written over a deletion, possibly "pantryman." Given Blake's own humble origins and social situation, a part of his antipathy toward Locke may have been based upon class attitudes.

15 For further discussion of Blake's visionary caricature of Locke's ideas, see Harald A. Kittel, "*The Book of Urizen* and *An Essay Concerning Human Understanding*," in Michael Phillips, ed., *Interpreting Blake* (Cambridge: Cambridge University Press, 1978), pp. 111–44.

16 Samuel Johnson, *The History of Rasselas, Prince of Abissinia*, ed. Geoffrey Tillotson and Brian Jenkins (London: Oxford University Press, 1971), p. 113. Jean H. Hagstrum relates Johnson's thought to the traditions of Lockean empiricism in *Samuel Johnson's Literary Criticism* (Minneapolis: University of Minnesota Press, 1952), ch. 1. In *The Achievement of Samuel Johnson* (New York: Oxford University Press, 1955, 1970), pp. 121–27, Walter Jackson Bate argues persuasively that Johnson's impulses toward satire were effectively disarmed by his personal compassion and commitment to Christian charity.

Politics and the Apocalypse: The Republic and the Millennium in Late-Eighteenth-Century English Political Thought

JACK FRUCHTMAN, JR.

Until quite recently, the convention of historical scholarship has been that eighteenth-century English political thought and Georgian religious beliefs were two separate and unrelated areas of investigation. In the past few years, a number of important studies have challenged this convention. Convincing works by Clarke Garrett, Margaret C. Jacob, and J. G. A. Pocock on England and Nathan O. Hatch and Henry F. May on America have all in varying degrees set the political debates of the eighteenth century in theological contexts.[1] The present essay seeks to extend the points of some of these earlier works by demonstrating that in late-eighteenth-century England, a mode of millennialist political thought was articulated in the language of the "classical republican" (or "Old Whig," "Country," or "Commonwealthman") tradition. More particularly, the political thought of two late-eighteenth-century Dissenting ministers, Richard Price (1723–91) and Joseph Priestley (1733–1804), exemplified this convergence of classical republicanism and Christian millennialism in a manner which is here referred to as republican millennialism.

Like their Whig predecessors of the late seventeenth and early

153

eighteenth centuries, Price and Priestley believed that English government was infected with corruption where unequal representation, coupled with the overpowering influence of the crown, had led to the establishment of government by a few who had reduced the many to dependence. This dependence had called into question the ability of the ideally autonomous citizen to realize a genuine republican form of government. In so doing, it had also compromised the fragile balance of King, Lords, and Commons (based on the classical paradigm of the one, the few, and the many), which was so necessary for the continued existence of the republic in time.[3]

But there was a broad difference separating the Old Whigs of the seventeenth century and these Dissenters of the late-eighteenth. This difference was principally embodied in their vision of the coming human, political, and social perfection in the millennium through the providential control of history. This vision uniformly both determined and colored the political ideology of Dissent, as expressed by Price and Priestley. As two millennialists deeply immersed in scriptural prophecy, they understood the future course of history and God's control of that history beyond the realm of mortal men.

Republican millennialism gave to these Dissenting ministers and publicists a ready explanation of the true meaning and significance of all political events. It made the historical process itself seem comprehensible, because within an apocalyptic context it was possible to see how progress occurred and what responsibilities fell to the citizenry to ensure that progress to the millennial moment in time when the godly kingdom of universal peace and happiness would be forever established on earth. Moreover, change was to occur in men as individuals as well, and not only in society, as men's individual and collective consciousnesses developed and improved. As a result, men would become prepared for the millennium and the truths which were to be revealed at that moment. For the human mind to be readied for these truths, an open society had to be created which permitted expression and inquiry to be free from the political encumbrances which hindered the mind's advance. Free inquiry and open debate were the very bases of an enlightened educational process.[4] The republican millennialists thus believed that God had delegated to the individual as civic man the responsibility to organize the political forms of government in a republican manner which would be conducive to the mind's progressive development.

For Price and Priestley, the republic and the millennium were never two separate and discreet categories of thought. The arrival of the republic coincided with the inauguration of the millennial period.

The republic was always the ideal goal for men to achieve, for once attained, it meant that they had also accomplished their final liberation. The republic that they were to build was a replication of the classical idea of mixed government with balanced institutions so that man would be a naturally free, virtuous, and autonomous individual. This idea was consistent throughout their writings. But to be a republican in the late-eighteenth century also meant that men at long last could achieve the common good, the *res publica*, but only through the political guarantee of individual liberty. The millennial period with its republic was to usher in the greatest liberation of all: the unchaining of the human mind from outmoded superstitions, political falsehoods, and ungodly beliefs. As the mind neared its full potential to attain true knowledge through its own inherent powers, men would finally learn that the common good (and therefore the millennium itself) was to be realized in the republic.[5]

The constituent elements of republican thought, as expressed in the Country language, had various apocalyptic counterparts. Price and Priestley at times equated liberty, virtue, and the common good with the godly life and with those political conditons that hastened the arrival of the end of time. Oppression, corruption, and slavery, in the meantime, were signs of evil, sin, and the very embodiment of the Antichrist. Corrupt government in general and slavery in particular were both primary blockades to men's achievement of the millennium.[6] Once these disabilities could be overcome, the conditions of life on earth would at last be readied for the last days.

The inseparability of the old Puritan categories of the apocalyptic and eighteenth-century republican discourse, was, then, complete.[7] In the revolutionary experiences of both the American colonies and France, Price and Priestley saw how men could specifically order society in preparation for the end of time. Until these revolutions, however, all they did was to notice the fundamental human political progress of the previous two centuries and to attack the existing corruptions in their own government. After 1776 and especially after 1789, they believed that God's everlasting kingdom of justice and peace was now imminent and that liberty spreading throughout the world had truly cosmic dimensions.

Only in a pure, uncorrupt form of government, namely the republic, could citizens be free to unlock the mysteries of the universal and divine historical plan. Republican government was the sole political arrangement whereby civic man realized his own virtuousness and possessed liberty and godliness to develop his consciousness sufficiently to be prepared for the end of time.[8] Men could only be prepared for this moment in an environment of genuine liberty.[9] Only in this atmosphere could they live a naturally virtuous life. Price and Priestley therefore advanced the idea that the highest political good was liberty, both because it meant the creation of the republic in time and because it led to greatest happiness of the people. But this happiness was never merely political or economic well-being, but rather the means for men to organize the political arrangements which enhanced the prospects for the future kingdom. While liberty and the republic were, then, political goals, to be achieved in time, their achievement also had millennialist implications. As God's instruments, men had the responsibility to ensure the prevalence of liberty on earth and to build the republic. Until all men were free, the forces of evil, the Antichrist, and sin would continue to impede human progress toward the millennium (where the political embodiment of these forces was always in the form of tyranny, oppression, corruption, war).

For these republican millenialists, liberty was not merely an abstract principle. It was fundamentally a practical concept that acted as a scale on which an individual could measure the effectiveness by which particular events and phenomena were leading to republican government. As a classical-republican concept, it was one means to determine the existence of civic virtue: a free man was one who was an independent and autonomous being, one who possessed natural virtue if only from his military and economic stake in society, and one who ultimately should possess the responsibility to participate in governmental decision-making. In a millennialist mode, liberty became the yardstick for measuring human success in the creation of those earthly political and intellectual conditions for the future millennium.

The denial of liberty exhibited itself in many forms. Self-evident to Price and Priestley was the enslavement caused by church establishments and religious intolerance. But these were not merely infringements of political and civil liberty. For the millenialists, state churches and intolerance had to be seen in the larger context of forestalling the moment when Christ's kingdom would be realized on earth. The political and religious disabilities under which the Dissenters had suffered for over a hundred years in regard to the Test and Corporation Acts thus became prime targets for Price and Priestley in this millennialist context. These Acts had barred Dissenters from full participation in decision-making. But even more important, they were sinful, evil, and ungodly because they were indicative of a slavery that bound men's minds. As long as men's minds were enslaved, the millennial kingdom could never be realized.

In one of his many published works on the Acts, Priestley demanded that they be rescinded, not merely because he himself suffered under the disabilities, but because of the larger implications that slavery had in impeding the arrival of the end of time. In 1789, he directly coupled this political and intellectual slavery with physical slavery as a basic hindrance to free government. The mind's enslavement by the established political order should remind men of "the rights of others, especially the common rights of humanity, of which the poor negroes have long been deprived, being treated as brutes, and not as men, and also of the just claims of all men to the rights of a free and equal government." Directly following his linkage of the two categories of slavery, Priestley noted that the special significance of the revolution in France, and with it the sacred blessings of liberty established there, proved the very nearness of the end of time. He cited biblical prophecy to emphasize that now throughout the world, "the voice of the oppressor may every where cease to be heard." If Englishmen helped revolutionary France establish itself, then "we may see the nearer approach of those glorious and happy times, when wars shall cease to the ends of the earth, and when the kingdoms of this world shall become the kingdoms of God and of his Christ."[10]

Price too believed that church establishments were hindrances to God's progressive plan. In 1787 at the dedication of a new dissenting academy, Hackney College, he noted that scripture had taught that before the beginning of Christ's universal kingdom, the world would witness the downfall of the Antichrist. In Protestant historical understanding, the Antichrist had always been associated with the Pope. Both Price and Priestley made this connection throughout their theological and political tracts. But now Price broadened his notion of the Antichrist to include all church establishments. Before the millennium, he said, religion "must lose that connection with civil power which has debased it, and which now in almost every Christian country turns it into a scheme of worldly emolument and policy, and supports error and superstition under the name of it."

Despite the continued existence in England of these political and religious disabilities for the Dissenters, Price believed that he saw definite progress in the world toward the end of such establishments. Soon men would enjoy genuine tolerance in the final state when they would attain that "happy time" when "bigotry shall no more persecute the sincere enquirer, and every one shall tolerate as he would wish to be himself tolerated." In words which directly suggested the convergence of the millennium with the cause of liberty, Price intoned that "when the sacred blessing of liberty" spread over the land, then men would fearlessly profess and practice "that mode of faith and worship which they shall think most acceptable to their Maker." At that moment, those times forecast by Isaiah will come to pass when "the wolf will dwell with the lamb; the leopard lie down with the kid."[11]

With the fervor and for the reasons that they attacked the unwillingness of Parliament to change the laws governing church establishments, Price and Priestley also railed against the slave trade and slavery: Priestley in a 1788 sermon; Price in his 1784 pamphlet of advice to the Americans. In their respective works on this subject, Price and Priestley held that all distinctions between men were only artificial and temporary and that they were but earthly manifestations which would undoubtedly disintegrate in the future state. Everyone was morally obliged to relieve his fellows of whatever distress in which he found them, whether they were Christian, Moslem, or Jewish. The slave trade was peculiarly insidious for Priestley who argued that "it is high time to put an end to it."[12] Price was also shocked by the trade. He noted that "the Negro Trade cannot be censured in language too severe. It is a traffick which, as it has been hitherto carried on, is shocking to humanity, cruel, wicked, and diabolical."[13]

For Priestley, in the future state of the millennium, there would be no such thing as physical servitude, just as he had argued that there would be no intellectual or spiritual servitude in his discussion of the Test and Corporation Acts. For "if we have any faith in history and prophecy, the last age of the world is to be infinitely preferable to any thing that we have yet experienced." The world in its perfected condition was to be "a state of universal peace and happiness, which must, as I have observed, imply the abolition of slavery."[14] Price went farther than Priestley in arguing that it was the obligation of the Americans (and all men for that matter) to abolish "the odious slavery." Thus Price told the Americans that until "they have done this, it will not appear they deserve the liberty for which they have been contending." It would be inexcusable if the United States did not accomplish this task "with as much speed and at the same time with as much effect, as their particular circumstances and situation will allow."[15] Slavery, like the existence of the Test and Corporation Acts, signified the work of the devil (hence, Price's previous reference to the slave trade as "wicked and diabolical").

Abolition of slavery—both physical and intellectual—was, then, God's cause. He used his human instruments to bring about the demise of all forms of slavery. As Priestly noted in his sermon, "God works by instruments; and his instruments in things that respect mankind, are chiefly men." Men should consider themselves "as being workers together with God, in bringing about an improved state of things, in bettering the condition of our species, and extending the just rights of humanity to all our race." In this way, we along with God would "make even this world a real paradise, and fit us for a state of greater glory and happiness in another."[16]

Both physical and intellectual slavery directly affected the life of the individual citizen. It could be seen as a direct impediment to the historical process toward the millennium. But slavery also existed in the larger and broader context of society as a whole, and not just as a problem for the individual. Nowhere was this better illustrated than in the momentous events in both America, following its independence from England, and France, during the revolutionary fervor of the last decades of the century.

Price and Priestley were well aware that evil in the form of injustice, tyranny, and war was a fact of life. But they both believed that although men propagated evil, it always served a higher divine purpose, because God saw to it that men would overcome evil by their own actions and conduct. Priestley wrote, for example, that while men might not always understand why certain natural and political disasters occurred in time, they could learn that the outcome of these disasters was usually for a higher good. In fact, "upon the whole," they "bring about the most happy and desirable state of things." This reversal occurred so many times in history "that the more we study the work of Providence, as well as those of nature, the more reason shall we see to be satisfied with, and to rejoice in, all the fair conclusions we can draw from them."[17] In his present imperfect state of development, man could not fully understand the true implications of world events, but could know them in a general way. There was always a good side to evil. Price once said that "a dark age may follow an enlightened age; but, in this case, the light, after being smothered for a time, will break out again with a brighter lustre."[18]

In this connection, Price and Priestley understood the millennial implications of the situation that existed between the American colonies and England. They believed that the English treatment of America was ungodly. It was evil, and it was unconstitutional because it denied liberty, and it violated the sacred balance of the one, the few, and the many inherent in the English ancient constitution. It was tyranny, pure and simple, and it precluded man's advance toward the millennium. America was, in short, enslaved. By its acts against the colonies, said Priestley, England promoted the king's desire to impose an "absolute despotism" over the Americans. He noted that the Stamp Act by itself had subverted the balance of the constitution, because it confounded "the first and fundamental ideas belonging to the system of different realms subject to the same king, and even introduced a language quite new to us; viz. that of America being subject to England." Indeed, it was again the very embodiment of evil, because this situation was the antithesis of a godly life. When liberty was measured in this context, it was self-evident that freedom had been denied to the Americans: "it is only by justice, equity, and generosity," he wrote, "that nations, as well as individuals, can expect to flourish; and by the violation of them, both single persons and states, in course of the righteous providence of God, involve themselves in disgrace and ruin."[19]

For these same millennialist reasons, Price was moved to comment on what he thought was the truly world-historical significance of the American Revolution. First, he concluded that "next to the introduction of Christianity among mankind, the American Revolution may prove the most important step in the progressive cause of human improvement." The significance of the Revolution was in fact so great that it portended the last age of the world: "the old prophecies be verified," he said, "'that the last universal empire upon earth shall be the empire of reason and virtue, under which the gospel of peace (better understood) shall have free course and be glorified, many will run to and fro and knowledge be increased, the wolf dwell with the lamb and the leopard with the kid, and nation no more lift up sword against nation.'" Indeed, he added that he was convinced that "the independence of the English colonies in America is one step ordained by Providence to introduce these times."[20]

If the liberty achieved by the American colonies at war's end signified to Price and Priestley a major step toward the millennium, then the revolution in France in 1789 made this moment appear absolutely imminent. Some twenty years earlier, Priestley had expressed the feeling that the world was yet "in its infancy," and that it would take hundreds of thousands of years for the human species to be prepared for the end of time.[21] Price too had given no indication in either his tracts on civil liberty or in his advice to the Americans when he thought the projected world reformation would occur. Nor had he given any hint as to when the entire process would terminate in the millennium.

By 1789, however, both were certain that the end of time was imminent. Thus, Price told his fellow members of the Revolution Society in his famous *Discourse on the Love of Our Country* that "we shall enjoy the transporting hope of soon becoming members of a perfect community." He rejoiced in the events in France, and he expected the final moment. Already, he noted, he had lived to see millions of people in America and France set themselves free. "After sharing in the benefits of one Revolution, I have been spared to be a witness of two other Revolutions, both glorious. — And now," he thought that he saw "the ardour for liberty catching and spreading." In an often-cited passage, he revealed, apparently in an ecstatic declamation, his deepest millennial hopes with the words: "tremble all ye oppressors of the world! Take warning all ye supporters of slavish governments and slavish hierarchies." The world was not to be held any longer in darkness. The forces of evil and corruption could not win the struggle "against increasing light and liberality."[22] For Price, the linkage of political reformation with the future development of the world in its course toward the millennium was always present. In this manner, he again made the connection of political progress, liberty, and republican government with the inevitable movement of time toward its apocalyptic termination.

After 1789, Priestley also became absolutely positive that the times in which he was living were indeed special and that they provided the final stage of history before the inauguration of the millennium. Like Price, he thought that he needed only now to watch the final disposition of world history, as political changes were occurring so quickly as to increase the movement of events to their rightful end. In 1790, he wrote to Price to extend his congratulations concerning Price's speech before the Revolution Society. Priestley congratulated him on the success of liberty in France, "and especially on the share that is, with so much justice, ascribed to you, with respect to the liberty of that country and America, and of course all those other countries that, it is hoped, will follow their example." The hatred and dread of revolutions was undoubtedly spreading amongst the kings and their courtiers. But that was for the good, because their power was usurpation, and now "the time is approaching when an end will be put to all usurpation, in things civil and religious, first in Europe, and then in other countries."[23]

In 1794 in a fast sermon entitled *The Present State of Europe Compared with Ancient Prophecies*, Priestley noted that although it was possible for "the storm" to "blow over," he could not conceive of the end of time being "deferred long." Revolution and the upheaval in Europe following it were inevitable as the time drew nearer to the millennium. "May we not hence conclude," he remarked in the closing passage of this sermon, "it to be highly probable, that what has taken place in France will be done in other countries?" The ultimate result would be the "sudden, and most unexpected, coming of Christ."[24] And ten years later in a work published posthumously, Priestley reiterated his belief in the imminence of the millennial period. "If the present commotions in Europe" were the political cataclysms spoken of in the prophetic books of scripture, then the time for the millennium "may be now come." And, he concluded, "we may be looking for the completion of this remarkable prophecy [Daniel] in our own time."[25] For Priestley as for Price, men's actions were consonant with God's historical plan. The achievement of civil and political liberty and the republic awaited men in a future that was nearer than anyone might imagine.

In the political ideologies of Richard Price and Joseph Priestley, the convergence of the two traditions of classical republicanism and Christian millennialism was complete. As the blessing of liberty became sacred, as Price put it, the citizen's striving for this liberty reached cosmic proportions. Price died in 1791 believing that the human task of achieving the millennium was well underway with the events surrounding the revolution in France. Priestley lived an additional thirteen years, and although he encountered a number of personal tragedies and disillusionments, he never abandoned hope of an imminent end of time. In 1794, he left England for America to establish there for himself and for all lovers of liberty a perfect society in which conditions might be made right for the development of the human consciousness. For both men, human achievement of the republic and the liberty which naturally went with it was what ultimately caused them to view as inevitable the movement of time and events toward the final end point in the historical process.

NOTES

1 See Clarke Garrett, *Respectable Folly: Millenarians and the French Revolution in France and England* (Baltimore: Johns Hopkins University Press, 1975); Margaret C. Jacob, *The Newtonians and the English Revolution, 1689–1720* (Ithaca, New York: Cornell University Press, 1976); J. G. A. Pocock, *The Machiavellian Moment: Florentine Political Thought and the Atlantic Republican Tradition* (Princeton: Princeton University Press, 1975); Nathan O. Hatch,

The Sacred Cause of Liberty: Republican Thought and the Millennium in Revolutionary New England (New Haven: Yale University Press, 1977); Henry F. May, *The Enlightenment in America* (New York: Oxford University Press, 1976). For pioneering efforts, see Ernest Lee Tuveson, *Millennium and Utopia: A Study in the Background of the Idea of Progress* (Berkeley and Los Angeles: University of California Press, 1949) and *Redeemer Nation: The Idea of America's Millennial Role* (Chicago: University of Chicago Press, 1968).

2 In addition to Pocock noted above, see Bernard Bailyn, *The Ideological Origins of the American Revolution* (Cambridge, Mass.: Harvard University Press, 1967); idem., *The Origins of American Politics* (New York: Vintage, 1970); Caroline Robbins, *The Eighteenth-Century Commonwealthman: Studies in the Transmission, Development and Circumstances of English Liberal Thought from the Restoration of Charles II until the War with the Thirteen Colonies* (Cambridge, Mass.: Harvard University Press, 1959); Zera S. Fink, *The Classical Republicans: An Essay in the Recovery of a Pattern of Thought* (Evanston: Northwestern University Press, 1945); Isaac Kramnick, *Bolingbroke and His Circle: The Politics of Nostalgia in the Age of Walpole* (Cambridge, Mass.: Harvard University Press, 1968); H. T. Dickinson, *Liberty and Property: Political Ideology in Eighteenth-Century Britain* (New York: Holmes and Meier, 1977).

3 Pocock, *The Machiavellian Moment*, pp. 66–81, 333–60.

4 Like many of their millennialist predecessors, Price and Priestley often cited *Daniel* XII, 4 which proclaimed that as a prerequisite for the millennial times, "many shall run to and fro and knowledge shall increase."

5 Pocock, *The Machiavellian Moment*, p. 403.

6 Hatch, *The Sacred Cause of Liberty*, pp. 22–23.

7 See Bernard S. Capp, *The Fifth Monarchy Men: A Study in Seventeenth-Century Millenarianism* (London: Faber and Faber, 1972); Paul Christianson, *Reformers and Babylon: English Apocalyptic Visions from the Reformation to the Eve of the Civil War* (Toronto: University of Toronto Press, 1978); Christopher Hill, *The World Turned Upside Down: Radical Ideas During the English Revolution* (New York: Vintage, 1972); William Lamont, *Godly Rule: Politics and Religion, 1603–1660* (London: Macmillan, 1969); Peter Toon, ed., *Puritans, the Millennium and the Future of Israel: Puritan Eschatology, 1600–1660* (Cambridge: James Clark, 1970).

8 Robbins, *The Eighteenth-Century Commonwealthman*, pp. 333–53, for Price's and Priestley's roots in the classical republican tradition.

9 See Joseph Priestley, *An Essay on the First Principles of Government and on the Nature of Political, Civil, and Religious Liberty* (London, 1768), in John Towill Rutt, ed., *The Theological and Miscellaneous Works of Joseph Priestley*, XXII (Hackney, 1816–31), 1–144. See also Richard Price, *Observations on the Nature of Civil Liberty, the Principles of Government, and the Justice and Policy of the War with America* (London, 1776), and idem., *Additional Observations on the Nature and Value of Liberty, and the War with America* (London, 1777).

10 Joseph Priestley, *Conduct to be Observed by Dissenters on the Repeal of the Corporation and Test Acts* (Birmingham, 1789), *Works*, XV, 403–4. (Unnec-

essary italicisms have been deleted from Priestley's and Price's quotations.)

11 Richard Price, *The Evidence for a Future Period of Improvement in the State of Mankind, with the Means and Duty of Improving it* (London, 1787), pp. 19–20, 23–24.

12 Joseph Priestley, *A Sermon on the Subject of the Slave Trade* (Birmingham, 1788), in *Works*, XV, 373.

13 Richard Price, *Observations on the Importance of the American Revolution, and the Means of Making it a Benefit to the World* (London, 1784), p. 68.

14 Priestley, *Sermon on the Slave Trade*, in *Works*, XV, 387.

15 Price, *Observations on the American Revolution*, pp. 68–69.

16 Priestley, *Sermon on the Slave Trade*, in *Works*, XV, 387.

17 Joseph Priestley, *Lectures on History and General Policy* (London, 1761–88), in *Works*, XXIV, 438.

18 Price, *Observations on the American Revolution*, p. 5.

19 [Joseph Priestley], *An Address to Protestant Dissenters of All Denominations on the Approaching Elections of Members to Parliament with Respect to the State of Public Liberty in General, and of American Affairs in Particular* (London, 1774), in *Works*, XXII, 493 and 498.

20 Price, *Observations on the American Revolution*, pp. 7–8.

21 Joseph Priestley, *Institutes of Natural and Revealed Religion* (London, 1772–74), in *Works*, II, 365 and 367.

22 Richard Price, *Discourse on the Love of Our Country* (London, 1790), pp. 39–40.

23 Joseph Priestley to Richard Price, Aug. 29, 1790, in Priestley, *Works*, I, Part 2, 79–81.

24 Joseph Priestley, *The Present State of Europe Compared with Ancient Prophecies* (London, 1794), in *Works*, XV, 543, 548–549.

25 Joseph Priestley, *Notes on All the Books of Scripture, for the Use of the Pulpit and Private Families* (Northumberland, 1804), in *Works*, XII, 306–7, 329.

Beyond Reason and Revelation:

Perspectives on the Puritan Enlightenment

BRUCE TUCKER

Despite the immense literature on the religious history of New England, the relationship between Puritanism and the Enlightenment has largely remained unexplored.[1] The reason for this gap in the literature is that historians have found nothing particularly problematic to explain. For although scholars have agreed that ministers "liberalized" Puritanism during the first half of the eighteenth century, they have not perceived the kind of intellectual tension in the thinking of these ministers which might encourage further investigation. Since seventeenth-century Puritans had incorporated science, nature, and reason into their theology, it is argued, their descendants in the eighteenth century welcomed the ideas of the Enlightenment simply as further proof of the validity of their tradition. This process did not involve a rigorous intellectual exercise, moreover, because it took place during a period of "declension" in New England's religious life. During the provincial era ministers and laity struggled unsuccessfully to maintain the high standards of piety set by the founding generation. Because New Englanders were increasingly absorbed in commerce and the task of establishing a permanent society in the New World, the argument runs, they gradually abandoned the zeal for religious purity of earlier generations.[2] Unimaginative and spiritually lax, therefore, the eighteenth-century descendants of the first Puritans accepted the ideas of the Enlightenment without intellectual dislocation.

165

Henry May provided early American intellectual historians with the first effective study of the relationship between Puritanism and the Enlightenment in his book, *The Enlightenment in America* (1976). May resolved the problem of conceptualization by addressing primarily the development of Enlightenment ideas and by subordinating the Puritan tradition to the status of a "matrix" in which the process of liberalization was accomplished.[3] He argued that New England ministers adapted natural religion to the language of their own theology, creating a powerful rational Calvinism which balanced reason with revelation, and piety with intellect. Although Boston liberals and ultra-evangelicals assaulted this moderate Calvinism, he continued, their criticisms merely "served to keep the powerful center properly in balance."[4] Thus in May's history, the ministers engaged in the ancient struggle between reason and revelation and presided over the emergence of a Moderate Enlightenment which prevailed until the radical ideas of Paine and Godwin brought the compromises of the provincial period crashing down.[5]

By portraying the provincial ministers as moderate imitators, however, May avoided the dialectical nature of the process in which neo-Puritans with only limited interpretive options struggled to make sense of their world. Consequently, historians still lack a sense of the intellectual choices available to eighteenth-century ministers and of how they came to integrate Enlightenment ideas with their own legacy. For what purpose and with what level of consciousness did these ministers appropriate and use the ideas of a non-Calvinist alternative that was emerging in England? To answer these questions about the Puritan Enlightenment, historians will have to be sensitive to two problems. First, they will have to understand the political context in which eighteenth-century ministers remoulded their tradition. Secondly, they will have to ask how the Puritan tradition kept functioning, limiting the alternatives of its exponents, despite the circumstances which were pulling it in new directions.

In contrast to May, who began with a description of the different schools of Enlightenment thought, I suggest that the point of departure must be with the peculiar dilemma of the inheritors of the Puritan tradition. It is the nature of this dilemma, and the attempts of two ministers, Thomas Prince and John Barnard, to resolve it that I wish to explain in this paper.[6]

By the beginning of the eighteenth century, third-generation ministers were confronting a crisis of self-identification. The founding generation had removed to New England in the 1630's to secure God's true church from Laudian corruptions, but its leaders had never considered themselves as a people set apart from England. The second generation, overwhelmed by its isolation from the mother country, had imposed a sense of mission on the founders, claiming that the migrants of the 1630's had intended to create a model of the Christian commonwealth for eventual export to England.[7] In sermons of the 1660's and 1670's second-generation ministers created an image of their past in which they saw themselves as the unworthy inheritors of the reformist zeal of their elders.

In the early decades of the 1700's, however, third-generation leaders were beginning to see the mother country as a standard of culture and achievement. The Crown ended sixty years of relative autonomy in 1691 by appointing a governor over Massachusetts, an act which signalled the beginning of New England's transition from a neglected colony to a royal province. Thus as provincials who were intrigued by the intellectual fashions of Augustan England, third-generation ministers could never be as certain as the founders of their Puritan identity. But Puritanism was not a malleable set of beliefs which could easily be adapted to accommodate the new Imperial arrangement or to legitimate the status of an emerging mercantile elite. It existed as a religious tradition with a peculiar history which limited its explanatory possibilities. Eighteenth-century ministers could not totally reject their past, nor could they maintain the rigid ethos of separation bequeathed to them by the second generation. Thus they could not easily reconcile their fascination with the metropolis with their history. Ultimately, however, they were able to integrate the legacy of the founders with the ideas of the English Enlightenment because they too reinterpreted their history, giving it an Anglo-American cast. They participated in the creation of a genuine Anglo-American culture which disintegrated only in the wake of the Revolutionary crisis. To interpret their intellectual effort as a complacent theology of balance, or worse, as evidence of declension, is seriously to misunderstand the significance both of their predicament and of their achievement.

In England at the end of the seventeenth century, Calvinism was being transformed by the work of Locke, Newton, and the Boyle lecturers.[8] For all of the intellectual differences among these figures, they seemed to share the common purpose of purging English Protestantism of sectarianism. With its radical location of authority in the conscience of the believer, Cromwellian Puritanism had led to regicide and the leveling social aims of the sects. In contrast, the followers of Newton and Locke created a political and social ideology which legitimated the structure of power and authority that had emerged from the Glorious Revolution.[9] Rejecting the radicalism of Puritan ideology, these writers attempted to fashion a harmonious political and religious order from a physico-theological base.

The solution of Augustan intellectuals to the problem of order in post-Revolutionary English society was not sufficient for the Puritan provincials because it denied the radicalism of the migration which the third generation cherished in its history. The reconstruction of religious ideas in England and America during the Enlightenment, therefore, involved two different views of the past. In England, the Puritan concept of authority, conscience as opposed to law, was now regarded as a burden which had thrown the country into civil war and revolution. New Englanders, on the other hand, conceived of this part of their tradition as a birthright to be transmitted to succeeding generations. Thus they could not adopt uncritically the views of their English counterparts who were refashioning the Puritan tradition.

At the same time, however, New England ministers were drawn towards the English metropolis with a fascination which transcended the suspicions of the second generation. Both Thomas Prince and John Barnard travelled in England before returning home to settle in the ministry. Prince was born in 1687 and graduated from Harvard twenty years later. In 1709 he set sail with the Barbados fleet and eventually landed in England where he stayed for seven years. At Gresham College he attended lectures on modern science, cultivating an interest which he retained all his life. Almost unrecognizable in his fancy English dress, Prince returned to Boston in 1717 where he served for the next forty years as pastor at the Old South Church. An amateur historian, scientist, and interpreter of English politics, Prince was a major figure in the Puritan Enlightenment.[10]

Historians have frequently noted Prince's curiosity about Newtonian science and English rationalism.[11] It is not simply Prince's experimentation with the ideas of the Enlightenment which requires explanation, but his process of intellectual growth. By 1730, the Newtonian world view had become a crucial part of his cosmology. The political and natural worlds had become almost interchangeable for him, and both proved indisputably that God involved himself actively in the affairs of men and women. Indeed, Prince mused, God was constantly intervening both in nature and politics to sustain equilibrium: "Let but the minutest atom throughout this mighty frame of beings be either placed too near, provided it don't unite, or too far off; it will immediately require a new and amazing force to turn it back to its due point of distance;. . . . By such means as these the lower world is kept from age to age, and without them all things would quickly run into the last confusion."[12] Divine intervention extended into politics, Prince continued, managing human affairs with a self-regulating principle which always overcame disorder. Obviously this is not the rhetoric of an inner-directed individual committed to confronting the political order should it fail the test of conscience. In this instance, Prince was using his understanding of the Newtonian cosmology to develop a perspective on New England's identity as a royal province. Thus his interest in the political ideology of the Newtonians had the effect of transforming his revolutionary tradition into an ideology which acknowledged New England's alignment with England and the settlement of the Glorious Revolution.

How was it possible for a minister such as Prince, schooled in the messianic rhetoric of Puritanism, to adopt a Newtonian view of divine presence? Through the re-interpretation of history, Prince softened the radicalism of his tradition, convincing both himself and his audience that his experimentation merely followed and did not alter his religious training. In a sense, Prince created his own past, and by assessing his contribution to the re-ordering of Puritan history, historians can begin to understand the nature of his society's dilemma and its solution.

Two themes pervaded Prince's historical writing. He espoused an intense filiopietism which served to anchor him rhetorically within the world of the founders. Secondly, Prince anglicized the past, turning seventeenth-century migrants into the earliest heroes of the fight for Anglo-American liberty. In other words, he saw the past through the filter of the Glorious Revolution. This was a view of history thrust upon him by the inexorable logic of the Puritan tradition, under pressure as it was, from larger developments in the reorganization of the first British Empire.[13]

In retrospective sermons, Prince ranged over the achievements of the past, searching for his links with the first American Puritans. His memory filtered out diversity and contention among them, and he portrayed their faith as the "Pure Religion," claiming that "this and nothing else, they earnestly breathed and laboured after. . . ."[14] In this re-ordering of history certain events faded into the recesses of memory, while others took on a renewed salience. Prince almost never mentioned Cromwell's triumphant revolution which had elevated the rule of conscience over venerable institutions. The Glorious Revolution, which had actually wrenched New Englanders from their revolutionary past, figured more significantly. New Englanders,

Prince reported in 1730, "now greatly rejoice in the happy advancement and succession of the illustrious House of Hanover to the British throne in which alone under God, we trust to preserve our Constitution, laws and liberties. . . ."[15] Nor did he recall the bitter debates over polity which had wracked the minds of the founders. Highlighting the unity and completeness of the views of the first generation, Prince adapted the second-generation's myth of New England's origins, and thereby located eighteenth-century New England within the confines of an identity which it had in fact abandoned.

While he charged his rhetoric with visions of a glorious past, however, Prince also wondered about New England's prospects for the future. Third-generation ministers habitually compared the first generation with their own and found themselves wanting. Prince was no exception. "We are now risen up in our father's stead," he wrote, "an increase of sinful men, to augment the fierce anger of the Lord against his people."[16] In the traditional language of the jeremiad, Prince castigated his people for their moral and spiritual failures. But in the same sermon he also cited past signs of divine favor which showed that God had never totally abandoned New Englanders. For over one hundred years New England had suffered the attacks of powerful enemies with only meager defences, he said, and "yet we have greater civil and religious privileges than almost any others." And for Prince, this successful endurance was only the beginning. He urged his hearers to strive for personal reformation and to prepare for a magnificent future. "May we be Emmanuel's land, the people of the holy one of Israel; and may the Lord make us an eternal excellency, a joy of many generations."[17] Thus Prince both chastised New Englanders and encouraged them with enthusiastic visions of recapturing the glory of the Puritan past, a possibility which he thought was entirely within their reach.

Prince based his hopefulness for the future on a new partnership between England and the colonies. Together the mother country and New England, he thought, would lead in the extension of Anglo-Protestant liberties throughout the world. As Prince interpreted New England's history, the causes of England and New England had always been identical. By-passing the self-proclaimed role of the second generation to reform England by example, Prince now returned to the more universal aim of the founders to extend the one true church polity throughout Christendom. The years of exile, which had prevented the founders from realizing their goal, were now over.

Two events in the 1740's, the Great Awakening and the capture of Louisbourg in 1745, seemed to reinforce Prince's highest aspirations for New England. The Awakening confirmed his filiopietism, and he searched the historical record for signs that God had all along intended to rescue New England from its precarious spiritual existence. In Prince's view the progress of mass revivalism was back towards the security and completeness of a mythic past, but only a particular reading of the signs of the Awakening could put it into this light. On the nature of the new birth, for example, Prince obscured the differences between those first-generation ministers who had emphasized the idea of an instantaneous conversion and those who had favored an evolutionary process.[18] Unconsciously he associated the dramatic conversion with all of the founders, thus giving the methods of the revivalists an added authority and confirming their connection with the golden age of Puritan history. In addition, Prince denied that trances or extraordinary visions were a significant feature of the revival, and he minimized the importance of the physical signs of individual conversions.[19] Thus he harmonized experimental religion with his understanding of the past and in so doing, he made revivalism safe for New England.

If Prince's interpretation of the Awakening secured New England within the world of the founders, his reading of the capture of Louisbourg by New England militiamen served to join both New England and Old in a heroic Protestant enterprise. He began his assessment of New England's victory over the French by telling the congregation about the history of Louisbourg and its historically strategic value to Britain. Originally settled by the British in 1621, he told them, Louisbourg had been unhappily ceded to the French by the Treaty of Utrecht in 1713, a decision which Prince described as one of the most regrettable mistakes of the Tory ministry. With its abundance of coal, its spacious harbors and its strategic position, Louisbourg was a valuable colony and the French would undoubtedly have continued to settle there. Mindful of his special covenant with New England and of this particular threat to British hegemony, however, God "was pleased to leave them to precipitate a war upon us." Miraculously, the victory fell to less than four thousand untrained, undisciplined men, surely a sign of divine encouragement for the combined destiny of New England and her mother country.[20]

The capture of Louisbourg was a victory for all of Christendom, moreover, for it marked the beginning of God's plan to extend his Anglo-Protestant kingdom from the Atlantic to the Pacific Ocean, bringing a vast new continent into the fold. In this bold statement of destiny, Prince overcame the isolation of the second generation, for it had conceived of the exodus from England as the only way to secure the Reformation from the hands of its betrayers. Now, in 1746, Prince interpreted British success in international warfare and diplomacy as a fulfilment of the founders' dreams, and he linked New England's destiny to reunion with the mother country.

Prince's rhetoric marked a decisive shift in his understanding of New England's relationship with England. Although anti-popery had always suffused Puritan rhetoric of self-identification, this factor alone cannot account for the transformation in conceptual and expressive styles which allowed Prince to accept a partnership which the second generation had explicitly rejected. His integration of the history of British liberties can only be explained as the fulfilment of the Anglicization of New England culture which had been under way from the mid-seventeenth century. This process had begun for Prince during his visit to England from 1709 to 1717 and continued with his explorations in science, history and theology in the 1720's and 1730's.[21] It reached a point of culmination in the 1740's and 1750's when he began to interpret the whole future of New England's historic mission as part of a larger Anglo-American venture. Prince's hopes for New England, like his theology and history, had become thoroughly anglicized.[22]

Neither Prince's filiopietism nor his view of the first Puritans as harbingers of Anglo-American liberty seem like the stuff of historical writing in the Age of Enlightenment.[23] Prince's re-creation of the drama of God's role in Puritan history, however, actually sharpened his historical vision, enabling him to notice and record details which might have eluded the eyes of an historian guided by less lofty purposes. In his documentary narrative, *Annals of New England* (1755), for example, Prince gathered an immense amount of material. In addition to his use of institutional records and personal journals, Prince requested the assistance of New England ministers in advertisements, asking for reports on the history of their towns. He wanted to know the date of the first settlement, the original Indian name of the town, the names of the first proprietors, the history of land divisions, and data on the erection of public buildings. He also asked for reports on the history of education, accounts of natural disasters, and evidence of remarkable favors bestowed by God upon the people.

What emerged from this project was a detailed, almost day-to-day account of the history of New England from September 28, 1630, to July 2, 1633. Sifting through his sources, comparing dates and checking inconsistencies, he quoted from the diaries of Bradford, Winslow, and Winthrop, church records, court records, and documents pertaining to local and provincial administration. A typical coverage for one month consisted of five or six dated entries recording such events as the arrival of badly needed supplies, deaths, Thanksgiving days, court sessions, council meetings, and encounters with Indians. Having outlined the broad themes of the past in his sermons—the achievements of the founders, the development of British liberties, and the triumph over the French Antichrist—Prince now proposed to write a microscopic history of the personal experiences of New Englanders from the beginning to the present.[24]

In the *Annals of New England*, Prince recorded the larger cultural transformation experienced by his generation in the years between 1700 and 1760. His intense filiopietism drew him back to the authority of the past for his explanation of this new phase of New England's mission. The result was not a single-minded adulation of fanciful characters, however, but a modern rendering of the struggles of the first Puritans against the disorder of the wilderness. A major achievement for a pastor who had begun his career under the shadow of mythic ancestors, the *Annals of New England* demonstrates the modernity of Prince's intellectual perspective. For by the end of his life in 1758, Prince had moved along with his society into the mainstream of British history and culture.

While Prince compiled New England's religious and institutional history, John Barnard offered his understanding of the past in autobiographical form. Barnard was the pastor of a Congregational church at Marblehead, Massachusetts from 1716 until his death in 1770. Born in 1681, he studied at Harvard, and he too traveled and preached in England before settling down in the New England ministry.[25] In 1766 Barnard set out to record his personal experience of the provincial era in the history of New England. Responding to a request from Ezra Stiles for his autobiography, Barnard ranged over the key events in his life, imposing his explanation for the course he had taken. He wove together the strands of his life history with an account of the transformation of Marblehead over a half century, telling a story of success. From a tiny, crude, and undeveloped hamlet, Marblehead had grown into a thriving seaport with all of the comforts and civility of an English town. Barnard fancied himself, moreover, as a prime mover in Marblehead's growth.

In shifting from Prince to Barnard, we move from the act of creating a collective history to the art of personal memory. For Barnard too created a past, a sense of his life as he thought it should have appeared to others in both England and America. In form and content Barnard's autobiography resembled those of his seventeenth-century predecessors. Like Thomas Shephard (1605–49), Barnard included several incidents in which the hand of God had plucked him from the grip of disaster.[26] Thus did a merciful God show his favor to a poor earthly sinner. What is new in Barnard's account of his life, however, is a sense of the intellectual dilemmas faced by Puritan provincials. Striking the pose of a tolerant, slightly bemused figure, Barnard wrote to convince himself and others that he had been loyal both to the Puritan tradition and to the education in civility which he had received in the metropolis. Writing almost defensively, as if he were vulnerable to accusation, Barnard sought in his personal record a measure of assurance about the way he had handled the pressures of provincialism. His autobiography, therefore, offers a second point of entry into the study of the relationship between Puritanism and the Enlightenment in eighteenth-century America.[27]

Barnard devoted one-third of his autobiography to his visit to England in 1709–10. Because he wanted his readers to understand that he counted this experience as one of the most important in his life, he described it in rich detail. With a posture of modesty, Barnard told of his encounters with English people who thought that they knew something about the colonies. One acquaintance, he wrote, seemed to think that all New Englanders were black like West Indians. She also had marveled at Barnard's quick comprehension of English, given that he had only been in the mother country a few months. "I told her," he wrote proudly, "that all my country people, being English, spake the same language I did."[28] By adopting the persona of a misunderstood provincial in the metropolis, Barnard managed to display indirectly the sophistication that he felt he ought to possess. Thus he studded his autobiography with several assessments of himself as an urbane, sophisticated metropolitan, an image which he then denied by ascribing it to English ignorance about the colonies. Using a strategy of assertion and denial from his vantage point in 1766, Barnard managed to conceal the wonder and discomfort which he had felt in England fifty years earlier.

Towards the end of the autobiography, Barnard's reconstruction of his life merged almost imperceptibly into a larger narrative of the principal changes which had transpired in Marblehead since his arrival there in 1716. At that time the militia had consisted of two motley companies of poorly trained, undisciplined men. There had been no artisans worthy of the name, he mused, nor had there been any foreign trade. The inhabitants had been a crude lot, moreover, "as rude, swearing, drunken and fighting a crew, as they were poor."[29]

The fifty years of Barnard's pastorate, however, had witnessed a wondrous transformation. He boasted, for example, that Marblehead's militia now surpassed any other in New England. Marblehead in 1766 was also a thriving seaport, and Barnard hinted that he had played an instrumental role in its economic success. Not long after his arrival in 1716, he remembered, he had realized that the town had marvelous economic potential if only someone would risk an outlay of capital. Because there had been no such adventurous soul about, Barnard had set himself the task of learning the fishing trade from captains of English vessels. Then he had tried to persuade his friends to ship their catches themselves instead of relying on Boston merchants. He had scant success at first, but one successful adventurer soon encouraged others. "From so small a beginning the town has risen into its present flourishing circumstances, and we need no foreigner to transport our fish, but are able ourselves to send it all to market."[30]

As for the manners of the town, Barnard wrote that by mid-century, Marblehead had become a model of polite society. Just as Barnard supposed that he had assumed the polite bearing of his English models, so too, Marblehead had matured. "Whereas not only are the public ways vastly mended, but the manners of the people are greatly cultivated; and we have very many gentlmanlike and polite families, and the very fisherman generally scorn the rudeness of the former generation."[31] Having grown into a replica of the English towns of Barnard's memory, Marblehead had now rid itself of its former churlish ways.

Barnard's portrayal of his own past and of Marblehead's history was hopeful, proud and aggressive, for it was designed to demonstrate how easily he had mastered the challenges of provincial life. He wished to be remembered as an educated gentleman who had brought culture and enterprise to a backward town. In his presentation of his public self, moreover, Barnard cultivated the image of a man who was above the foibles of provincial society and at the same time untainted by the pretensions of the metropolis. And his magnetic style easily draws the reader into believing that Barnard had led his town in the triumph of civility over the precarious and God-centered world of earlier generations.[32]

Taken at face value, Barnard's autobiography records the liberalization of the Puritan tradition. But if it is read as an exercise in self-assurance, an attempt to convince himself that he had been both a loyal Puritan and a sophisticated Englishman, a different interpretation of the relationship between Puritanism and the Enlightenment may be considered. Barnard had invested much of his intellectual energy in resolving the tensions between the tradition in which he had been schooled and the increasingly anglicized nature of New England culture and society. Yet in his autobiography he obscured both the conflict and the process of resolution, claiming that he had not diverged from the faith and practice of his seventeenth-century mentors. In sermons and in a major statement of New England theology in 1750, Barnard tried to demonstrate the compatibility of Lockean sensationalism and empiricism with Puritan theology.[33] But in a sense, he "protested too much." For the traces of defensiveness in the autobiography form a central motif in Barnard's theological writings. Barnard harbored a subterranean reservoir of doubt about his Puritan identity with which he struggled all of his life. In his final evaluation of his career, he denied others access to his personal strategy of accommodation, preferring instead to maintain the air of a detached, calm and rational observer. Rich in the details of the making of a Puritan provincial, Barnard's autobiography, like Prince's history, testifies to the troubled yet creative character of intellectual life in early eighteenth-century New England.

In their writings in the 1750's and 1760's, Prince and Barnard completed a process in the reinterpretation of Puritan history which they had begun early in their lives. The past, which had once been the foundation of New England's uniqueness, gradually emerged from their reflections as the basis for a new partnership with England. Judging from their careers, the provincial period was a time of intense cultural insecurity and strenuous intellectual activity during which ministers led New Englanders back into an Anglo-American perception of themselves. The Puritan legacy was so deeply entrenched in New England culture that even in the early eighteenth century it still formed the outermost boundary of conceptualization. In the act of reconstructing that past, ministers helped to resolve their crisis of identity. Scholars who wish to continue the study of the relationship between Puritanism and the Enlightenment will have to focus on the creation of Anglo-American culture in its own right, for this is a topic which can no longer be studied as the tapering off of Puritanism or as the beginning of a uniquely American identity. We must try to recover, therefore, the dilemmas of the neo-Puritans even if they seemed to resolve them without difficulty. Or, to conclude with an insight from Claude Lévi-Strauss, we must now try to understand "not how men think in myths, but how myths operate in men's minds without their being aware of the fact."[34]

NOTES

1 Notable exceptions are Peter Gay, *A Loss of Mastery: Puritan Historians in Colonial America* (Berkeley: University of California Press, 1966); Perry Miller, *Jonathan Edwards* (New York: Meridian Books, 1965); G. Adolph Koch, *Religion of the American Enlightenment* (New York: Meridian Books, 1968); Conrad Wright, "Rational Religion in Eighteenth-Century America," in his *The Liberal Christians: Essays on American Unitarian History* (Boston: Beacon Press, 1970).

2 The "declension" thesis was best summarized by Perry Miller in the following sentence. "Puritanism failed to hold later generations largely because the children were unable to face reality as unflinchingly as their forefathers." Miller, *The New England Mind: The Seventeenth Century* (Cambridge, Mass.: Harvard University Press, 1939), 37.

3 Henry May, *The Enlightenment in America* (New York: Oxford University Press, 1976), xiii.

4 Ibid., 65.

5 This paradigm is not peculiar to May. See Joseph Haroutunian, *Piety Versus Moralism: The Passing of the New England Theology* (New York: Harper and Row, 1970); Alan Heimert, *Religion and the American Mind from the Great Awakening to the Revolution* (Cambridge, Mass.: Harvard University Press, 1966); James W. Jones, *The Shattered Synthesis: New England Puritanism Before the Great Awakening* (New Haven: Yale University Press, 1973).

6 For the purposes of this essay, "third generation" refers to the cohort of ministers who were born in the 1680's and 1690's and began their careers during the second decade of the eighteenth century. I have followed the development of their careers more elaborately in "The Founders Remembered: The Anglicization of the Puritan Tradition in New England, 1690–1760" (Diss. Brown 1978).

A second term which requires clarification is "the Puritan tradition." I agree with critics of Perry Miller that Puritanism in the seventeenth century did not exist in a monolithic form and that there was considerable diversity among contemporaries in their definitions of religious faith and practice. I have used the term "Puritan tradition" to refer to the sense of the past created by eighteenth-century ministers. It is hoped that by investigating the fabrication of the past by ministers of different religious persuasions in New England, we can begin to understand the problem of the transmission of Puritan ideas over time in all of its complexity.

7 Perry Miller suggested that the sense of mission originated in the first generation of settlers in New England. Robert Middlekauff has argued convincingly, however, that it was the second generation which "invented" the myth of New England as a model for England. See Perry Miller, "Errand into the Wilderness," in his *Errand into the Wilderness* (New York: Harper and Row, 1964), 1–15; and Robert Middlekauff, *The Mathers:*

Three Generations of Puritan Intellectuals, 1596–1728 (New York: Oxford University Press, 1976), ch. 6.

8 On this topic, see G. R. Cragg, *From Puritanism to the Age of Reason* (Cambridge: Cambridge University Press, 1966); John Redwood, *Reason, Ridicule and Religion: The Age of Enlightenment in England, 1660–1750* (Cambridge, Mass.: Harvard University Press, 1976); Margaret C. Jacob, *The Newtonians and the English Revolution, 1689–1720* (Ithaca, New York: Cornell University Press, 1976).

9 Margaret Jacob develops this argument at length in *The Newtonians*. For a similar treatment of Locke's religious ideas, see Richard Ashcraft, "Faith and Knowledge in Locke's Philosophy," John W. Yolton, ed., *John Locke: Problems and Perspectives* (Cambridge: Cambridge University Press, 1969), 194–223.

10 On Prince, see Clifford K. Shipton, *Sibley's Harvard Graduates*, vol. 5 (Cambridge, Mass.: Harvard University Press, 1937), 341–68.

11 See Theodore Hornberger, "The Science of Thomas Prince," *New England Quarterly*, 9 (1936), 26–42; and John E. Van de Wetering, "God, Science and the Puritan Dilemma," *New England Quarterly*, 38 (1965), 494–507.

12 Thomas Prince, *Civil Rulers Raised Up by God to Feed His People* (Boston, 1728), 13.

13 Borrowing from Jack P. Greene, I have used the word "Anglicization" to denote a "strong disposition among the colonists to cultivate idealized English values and to seek to imitate idealized versions of English forms, institutions, and patterns of behavior." See Greene, "Search for Identity: An Interpretation of the Meaning of Selected Patterns of Social Response in Eighteenth-Century America," *Journal of Social History*, 3 (1970), 206. See also, John Murrin, "Anglicizing an American Colony: The Transformation of Provincial Massachusetts" (Diss. Yale 1966).

14 Thomas Prince, *The People of New England Put in Mind of the Righteous Acts of the Lord* (Boston, 1730), 24.

15 Ibid., 35.

16 Ibid., 36.

17 Ibid., 48. On the jeremiad, see Sacvan Bercovitch, *The American Jeremiad* (Madison, Wis.: University of Wisconsin Press, 1978).

18 David Hall, *The Faithful Shepherd: A History of the New England Ministry in the Seventeenth Century* (New York: W. W. Norton, 1974), 251.

19 Thomas Prince, *An Account of the Revival of Religion in Boston, in the Years 1740–1–2–3* (Boston, 1744), 19, 28.

20 Thomas Prince, *Extraordinary Events the Doings of God* (Boston, 1745), 18–19. For a persuasive analysis of the impact of military conflict on millennial ideas in New England, see Nathan O. Hatch, *The Sacred Cause of Liberty: Republican Thought and the Millennium in Revolutionary New England* (New Haven: Yale University Press, 1977). My argument builds on Hatch's point that New England ministers hailed the defeat of the French as a sign that the millennium was close at hand. My own analysis is in-

tended to explain how ministers integrated this development in their thinking with Puritan history. The pattern of Anglicization began much earlier than Hatch suggests, and was the result among ministers at least, of their reinterpretation of history.

21 See Tucker, "The Founders Remembered," chs. 2 and 3.

22 Prince expounded on this theme in several other sermons. See his *God Destroyeth the Hope of Man!* (Boston, 1751) and *A Sermon Delivered at the South Church in Boston, New England August 14, 1746* (Boston, 1747).

23 Peter Gay offers this critique of Puritan historical writing in *A Loss of Mastery*. My assessment of Prince's talents as a historian owes much to David Levin's lengthy review of Gay's book in *History and Theory*, 7 (1968), 385–93.

24 Thomas Prince, *Annals of New England* (Boston, 1755). This book was a sequel to Prince's *Chronological History of New England in the Form of Annals* (Boston, 1736).

25 On Barnard, see Clifford K. Shipton, *Sibley's Harvard Graduates*, vol. 4 (Cambridge, Mass.: Harvard University Press, 1933), 501–14. Barnard's autobiography is reprinted in *Massachusetts Historical Society Collections*, 3rd. ser., 5 (Boston, 1836), 177–243.

26 See Michael McGiffert, ed., *God's Plot: the Paradoxes of Puritan Piety, Being the Autobiography and Journal of Thomas Shephard* (Boston: University of Massachusetts Press, 1972), 33–77; and Barnard, "Autobiography," 180–83, 193–94, 210–12.

27 For a limited commentary on Barnard's career, see Larzer Ziff, *Puritanism in America: New Culture in a New World* (New York: Viking Press, 1974), 286–88.

28 Barnard, "Autobiography," 200.

29 Ibid., 240.

30 Ibid., 240–41.

31 Ibid., 240.

32 Thus Ziff mistakenly portrays Barnard as a genteel moralist. See Ziff, *Puritanism*, 286–88.

33 John Barnard, *Janua Coelestis: or the Mystery of the Gospel in the Salvation of a Sinner, Opened and Explained* (Boston, 1750); and *A Proof of Jesus Christ, His Being the Ancient and Promised Messiah* (Boston, 1756).

34 Claude Lévi-Strauss, *The Raw and the Cooked*, trans. John and Doreen Weightman (New York: Harper and Row, 1969), 12.

A Poetics of Conversion in Mid-Eighteenth-Century England

JOHN SITTER

I want to offer and try to illustrate a few propositions about the perceived role of memory in mid-eighteenth-century English poetry. The first of these is, as the title suggests, that religious conversion becomes the model, usually secularized, for what ought to happen in a poem. A second proposition is that the dramatization of conversion replaces traditional historical material in much of the experimental poetry written from the 1740s onward and figures largely, though mostly unconsciously, in ideas of "pure poetry" which begin to emerge in this period and which sometimes continue into our own. A third proposition is that the various kinds of conversion treated in the poetry reflect both the interest in intensity of experience and disruption of behavior on the part of the Evangelicals (whom for the moment we can group together as the "New Light" Brigade) and interest in the problem of belief or conviction evident in the work of Hume. And proposition four is that it is easier to describe how these developments parallel each other than to explain why they do.

Anyone wishing to make a case for discontinuity in literary history following the "Age of Pope and Swift" is likely to turn to Joseph Warton, whose poetry in the 1740s and criticism in the 1750s demonstrate a self-conscious desire to break—quickly—with the immediate poetic past, which means primarily Pope. Warton's odes of 1746 are intended, he says, to help turn poetry away from the late fashion of moralizing in verse and "into its proper channel," and his *Essay* on

Pope a decade later works out in more detail the idea that Pope and poetry—the highest poetry—are not the same. At one point in that *Essay*, Warton argues that the epic, *Brutus*, which Pope projected but never wrote, would have been a failure:

> . . . it would have appeared . . . how much, and for what reasons, the man that is skillful in painting modern life, and the most secret foibles and follies of his cotemporaries, is, THEREFORE disqualified for representing the ages of heroism, and that simple life, which alone epic poetry can gracefully describe; in a word, that this composition would have shown more of the *Philosopher* than the *Poet*.[1]

This passage is interesting for several reasons, not least of which is the fact that it is entirely in the subjunctive: Warton, like many contemporary critics, rises to his highest rhetoric when unencumbered by an actual text. Interesting for our purposes is Warton's assumption that what disqualifies Pope for the highest kind of poetry is his modernity; Warton views Pope, in other words, as too much *in* history to rise above it. "For Wit and Satire are transitory and perishable, but Nature and Passion are eternal." Warton would not interpret his own remarks as I have just done; in fact, he says that poetry is likely to be better if it is "grounded on true history." But his examples—*Oedipus, Lear, Romeo and Juliet*, as well as Pope's own *Elegy to the Memory of an Unfortunate Lady*—suggest that Warton has in mind stories based on distant, obscure, or private history. Anything recent, documentable, and public is likely not to have "poignancy" enough.[2]

The opposition of satire and true poetry represents more than the triumph of sentimentalism as that is usually understood. Since satiric poetry is nearly always highly historical poetry, the battle is in large part over whether poetry should be factual or manifestly fictional. A similar desire to divorce poetry from history appears in the first line of the first poem in Warton's *Odes* when, in the ode *To Fancy*, fancy is saluted as the "parent of each lovely muse." This is of course the traditional role not of fancy but memory, communal memory, the literate name for which is history. One can argue that the idea of memory as mother of the muses is merely a relic from pre-literate societies, retaining little of its force in a literate culture, particularly one in which printed books are increasingly common. But clearly it is an important conception for Dryden and Pope, both of whom take seriously their roles as historians of their own times, and one finds the connection between poetry and historical memory taken quite seriously, for example, by Goldsmith in *An Enquiry into the Present State of Polite Learning* (1759).

This is merely one of several opinions which link Goldsmith more closely to the early Augustans, however, than to many of his own generation. We might, in fact, use Goldsmith and the Wartons antithetically here. One of the signs of decadence in modern Italian poetry for Goldsmith is its departure from mimesis: "Poetry is not longer among them the imitation of what we see, but of what a visionary might wish."[3] Goldsmith is talking about idealized pastorals at this point, but the statement might also describe many of the odes addressed to personifications from 1745 on written by Gray, Akenside, and Collins, as well as the Wartons. Indeed Thomas Warton the younger summed up what seemed to him most distinctive about the poetry of his own day in almost exactly the same terms—and most approvingly. In a manuscript essay recently published in part by David Fairer, Thomas Warton wrote: "The principal use which the antients made of poetry . . . was to imitate human actions and passions, or intermix here and there descriptions of Nature. Several modern authors have employed a manner of poetry entirely different from this, I mean in imitating the actions of spirits, in describing imaginary scenes, and making persons of abstracted things, such as Solitude, Innocence, and many others."[4]

Solitude and Innocence are not, as we will see, accidental examples, for if there is one characteristic situation for what Warton goes on to call this "Romantic Kind of Poetry" it is that of a poet in solitude expressing or seeking radical innocence. The quest for radical innocence, whether achieved or still imminent, constitutes the characteristic "plot" of these poems, a conversion plot, in which the poet, and sometimes everything else, is taken out of the old historical order and made the chosen son (or people) of the principle of purity being addressed. In Gray purity tends to mean death, the collision between history and poetic purity being fatal, as in *The Bard* most spectacularly, but just as decisively in the *Elegy*.

If we think for a moment of Gray's *Elegy* and Swift's *Verses on the Death of Dr. Swift* as two poems on the same theme, the death of the poet, we have a shorthand way of recalling the distance separating the dominant voice of the early 1730s from that of the late 40s. Swift does assume a position of moral superiority for himself and even some isolation as a result of it, but Innocence and Solitude are the last things he would attach himself to. The humor of the poem and of much of what we think of as characteristically "Augustan" poetry is a way of dealing with, a way of remembering, the Fall—simply recognizing it in playful moods and, in more militant attitudes, confronting its effects. That they have no fall to remember is all that excuses Swift's Houyhnhnms for their otherwise unpardonable lack of humor.

The conversion poems of the next generation are not all so fatal for the subject as Gray's, but they are equally intent upon excluding—as unpoetic—conversational irony, self-implication, or playfulness; they are much less tolerant of these qualities than the apparent model for sober conversion, *Il Penseroso*, which after all is a somewhat playful debating exercise. The atmosphere tends to be hushed and critical, not necessarily melancholy but if cheerful, earnestly so, single-mindedly so. In this atmosphere three types of conversion poem can be distinguished at mid-century, though the categories often overlap:

1. Salvational poems, that is, poems which involve the adoption, after a period of error, of views necessary for salvation.
2. Vocational conversions, that is, poems dramatizing or recalling the poet's *call*, his dedication to poetry and/or his decision to become the votary of a value seen as essential to poetry.
3. Cultural conversions, that is, poems which announce the sudden transformation of the whole culture (England or perhaps the entire West) into something fundamentally different, operating on new principles, in accord with new but universally shared values, entering a harmonious era.

Salvational conversions are central to three of the notable long poems in the middle years of the century: *Night Thoughts* (1742–45), Akenside's *The Pleasures of Imagination* (1744), and *The Castle of Indolence*, (published in 1748). In *Night Thoughts* there is a sort of double conversion—of the free-thinking Lorenzo to orthodoxy and the speaker's own movement from 'Complaint' to 'Consolation.' In *The Pleasures of Imagination* the youthful poet perplexed in doubt is suddenly translated into a state of harmony where Virtue and Pleasure are reconciled. *The Castle of Indolence* is the most suggestive for our purposes because it points to how the claims of public orthodoxy (not necessarily religious claims per se) and poetic vocation can come into conflict. Officially the saving conversion of that poem takes place when the poet-speaker and his associates are rescued from their bowers of blissful indolence by the Knight of Arts and Industry and his rousing minstrel, Alexander Pope. But the Castle is not only an enthralling place, it is a very persuasive objectification of the poetic imagination, a metaphor for creativity and reflection in general (vs. the foolishness reflected in the "Mirror of Vanity" within the Castle). It is more like Tennyson's *Palace of Art* than Spenser's *Bower*, so that its repudiation is more problematic, more costly, than the triumph over lust.[5] I will return to this conflict between salvational and vocational claims in a moment.

Vocational poems would include any number of lyric poems, primarily odes, which proceed by invocation and apostrophe to focus attention on the poet's relation to the muse, fancy, the "poetical principle" or some other unworldly quality, and which either enact or re-enact the sudden turning toward the imaginatively sacred and away from the profane. In addition to several odes of Collins, Joseph Warton, Akenside (especially *To the Muse*, *To the Evening Star*, and the longer *Hymn to the Naiads*), we might include here Thomas Warton's *Pleasures of Melancholy* and Joseph's *The Enthusiast*, in which the speakers detach themselves from most of the ambition, strife, commerce, in fact most of the social life around them, in order to be votaries of something purer, more innocent, unitary.

If we allow that cultural conversions can be dystopian as well as utopian, then our list would include the *Dunciad* and the virtueless England of the end of *The Enthusiast*, as well as more optimistically apocalyptic visions like Collins' *Ode to Liberty* ("Thou, Lady, thou shalt rule the West!"), or *To Mercy* ("Thou, thou shalt rule our Queen and share our / Monarch's throne!"), Thomson's *Liberty*, with its "prospect" of the English futurescape. The common element here is the sudden, radical transformation of the society into something not only desirable but single—everything under "one sway," and presumably unchanging ever after; like the convert's soul, born out of time into eternity.

The kind of change experienced is both deeper and more sudden than conventional processes of education, maturation, or changing one's mind. William Law in his so-called "mystical" phase, that is, about a decade after his most famous book, *A Serious Call to a Devout and Holy Life* (1729), contrasted the mere "Act of Memory upon something that is *absent*" with the genuine "inward Change" of the soul or "new State of our Existence" in God: "And the least Stirring of this inward principle, or power of life, is of more value than all the Activity of our Reason, which is only as it were a Painter of dead Images, which leave the Heart in the same State of Death, and Emptiness of all Goodness in which they find it. Therefore, listen to the voice of Grace, the Instinct of God that speaks and moves within you; and instead of forming dead and lifeless Images, let your Heart pray to God". Law's next work, in 1739, was an extended treatise on the subject of "new birth" (*The Grounds and Reason of Christian Regeneration*) and over and over he stresses the importance of an intense "sensibility," an entire and "inward sensation," not rational assent, as constituting true belief.[6]

I mention Law here, rather than Wesley or Whitefield, because he is generally a more interesting writer and because his vocabulary is often close to Hume's. The comparison would have displeased both parties, but Hume as well as Law tends to describe belief as a sudden conviction, a momentary experience of intensity (in Hume's terms an intensity which more or less converts an idea into a sensation). In fact, by the time of the second *Enquiry* (1751), Hume's description of the operation of "taste," where more and more mental activity seems to be located, sounds like Warton on Fancy—taste has "a productive faculty, and gilding or staining all natural objects with the colours, borrowed from internal sentiment, raises in a manner a new creation"—and in fact it sounds like Hume himself on "superstition" ten years earlier, that faculty which "opens a world of its own, and presents us with scenes, and beings, and objects, which are altogether new."[7] What I want to suggest here is simply that toward the mid-century neither the fideist nor the skeptic were conceiving of belief as a matter of mere rational assent; the sudden conviction, which is another way of saying a miniature conversion, becomes the model for the act of belief. It is just possible that Hume's famous conclusion to the infamous chapter "Of Miracles"—that Christianity not only must have been attended by miracles at its beginning but cannot be believed at present without one—is at some level less ironic than usually supposed; for in Hume's psychology belief, any belief, is virtually miraculous.[8]

The quest for intensity and the enactment of critical turning-points in the poems are often ways of denying, or attempting to deny, the significance of memory and the continuous past. (Stephen Dedalus' sense of history as "nightmare" is one which I believe first begins to emerge in the mid-eighteenth century.) Essentially, the distinction between public and private memory becomes accentuated, so that praise of memory is likely, as in Shenstone's *Ode to Memory*, to mean private memory, recollections of innocent childhood (which is also something of a period invention: cf. John Scott's *Ode to Childhood*). When public memory—either in the form of recent history or official orthodoxy—enters the poetic world it usually breaks up the poem, just as Thomson's Knight breaks up the Castle.

In the terms I have been using, this conflict can be seen as one between competing conversions; that is, many of the poems, including some promising ones, fall apart or end abruptly when salvational and vocational conversions are set against one another. For example, *The Enthusiast* by William Whitehead is nearly a miniature or epitomized version of *The Castle of Indolence*. The first half of the poem recounts a visionary moment in May when the poet was moved to profess, in "unbidden lay," his devotion to nature, contemplation and "serenest solitude." The second half of the poem consists of the voice of reason reminding him of his social obligations and that "man was made for man." Having been first converted to the "poetic" or vocational world, the speaker must then be converted out of it. The distrust of poetry implied here and in *The Castle of Indolence* figures again in Joseph Warton's ode *Against Despair*, where similarly the first half of the poem contains a lively and at least conventionally persuasive exploration of melancholy pressures, which are then suddenly revealed to belong to a past mood (*merely* a memory), since cancelled out by the voice of Patience. And we find it again in Thomas Warton's *The Suicide*, where the speaker identifies with the despair of the suicide, who is imagined as somewhat like the poet as seen by the swain at the end of Gray's *Elegy* and who in fact had vainly "sought the powers of sleep" in terms similar to Warton's own poem *To Sleep*. The speaker even begins to build a poetic shrine to him, when he is suddenly reproved by a voice from the clouds for the "specious" poetry he has bestowed on the "foul self-murderer." But to most ears this official dismissal is likely to sound more specious than the better part (in both senses) of the poem.

A last and more poignant example of this confict is Thomas Warton's *Written at Vale-Royal Abbey in Cheshire*, more poignant because in its evocative attempt to reconstruct by effort of historical imagination the meaning of the ruins the poem is on its way to being one of the best of the period, when Warton suddenly loses faith in his vision and in poetic vision generally: "Thus sings the Muse . . . ," but we need to pardon her: "Her fairy shapes are tricked by Fancy's pen: / Severer Reason forms far other views, / And scans the scene with philosophic ken" . . . and so on, to the praise of "new civilities" and the modern "social plan."

But the most deeply troubling instance of the conflict between the claims of conversion to poetic vocation and moral salvation is the spectacle of William Collins, unquestionably the most promising of the young poets, repudiating his early poems at about the same time he was last glimpsed by Johnson carrying only a small bible, "such as children carry to school."

The preoccupation with conversion-models of truth in the period represents an unusually strong interest in regarding as "poetic" moments of intensity and innocence, an unusually strong sense of public memory as public guilt (and correspondingly, of private memory as childhood purity), and an unusually strong concern with validating conviction on the instantaneous strength of feeling—what Hume would call its "liveliness" or "vivacity" or "force." Or, as William Law would put it, in the "life . . . or living Sensibility of the Thing that is known . . . ; so far as our Life reaches, so far we understand, and *feel*, and know, and no further. All after this, is only the Play of our Imagination, amusing itself with the *dead Pictures* of its own Ideas."[9]

The only one of my original propositions which I am confident of having demonstrated here is that it is easier to see how these developments in evangelicalism, skepticism, and the new aestheticism of the mid-century coincide than to say why they do. There is no evidence at all, for example, that any of the mid-century poets were impressed by the Methodist convulsions becoming prominent from the late thirties on—though possibly we could argue for the Calvinist impress upon Hume's thought, which is not just irreligious but Protestantly irreligious. Nor is there any evidence that the economic crisis of 1738 which Halevy long ago used to help explain the evangelical eruption directly affected the poetry of the 1740s. And we may do well to emulate the circumspection of Samuel Monk, who cautions against taking his description of the sublime as a "sort of Methodist revival in art" very literally.[10]

But perhaps it is useful to see the shift of emphasis in the mid-eighteenth century from the rhetorical features of the Longinian tradition toward its affective and expressive concerns as representing much of what it seems to have meant for Longinus himself, a counterforce to the "apathy" or "half-heartedness" of everyday life (ch. 44). The sublime poetic in this aspect is compensatory, in a self-consciously post-heroic and affluent period, not for a lack of grandeur but a lack of conviction. In the "conversion" poems, as in evangelical practice and Humean description, an increasing reliance on the intensity of the instant of belief suggests a dramatic weakening of faith in any larger structures of certainty. For the intellectual history of the period this convergence is significant primarily for what it suggests of a general condition. For the more strictly literary history of the period—a history necessarily narrower but also "longer," in its concern with the development of conventions—the greatest import of this poetic phenomenon is its effect upon the literary contract, what Wordsworth was to describe as the "promise" or "expectations" aroused in different eras by the "exponent or symbol" of verse (Preface to *Lyrical Ballads,* 1802). From the mid-eighteenth century on, one of the range of implicit promises tendered by poetic form has been the experience of conversion.

NOTES

1 *An Essay on the Writings and Genius of Pope* (London, 1756), pp. 280–81.
2 *An Essay*, pp. 253–54, 333–34.
3 *Enquiry*, in *Collected Works*, ed. Arthur Friedman (Oxford: Clarendon Press, 1966), I, 276–77. For other of Goldsmith's "Augustan" remarks on the desirable connection of poetry with history and memory cf. I, 263–64 and 269.
4 "The Poems of Thomas Warton the Elder?" *Review of English Studies*, n.s., 26 (1975), 287–300, 395–406; see pp. 401–2 for the MS fragment.
5 For a recent reading which argues against finding ambivalence in the poem, however, see Donald Green's essay, "From Accidie to Neurosis: The Castle of Indolence Revisited," in Maximillian E. Novak, ed., *English Literature in the Age of Disguise* (Berkeley and Los Angeles: University of California Press, 1977).
6 *The Works of William Law*, reprinted for G. Moreton, 9 vols. (New Forest, England, 1892–93), V, 60–61, 93–94, 140–45, 161.
7 Hume, *Enquiries Concerning Human Understanding and Concerning the Principles of Morals*, ed. L. A. Selby-Bigge, 3rd. ed. rev. P. H. Nidditch (Oxford: Clarendon Press, 1975), p. 294; cf. Conclusion to Book One of *A Treatise of Human Nature*.
8 The chapter "Of Miracles" is Section X of the *Enquiry Concerning Human Understanding*; of particular interest here is Anthony Flew's work, *Hume's Philosophy of Belief* (New York: Humanities Press, 1961).
9 *The Spirit of Prayer* (1749–50) in *The Spirit of Prayer and The Spirit of Love*, ed. Sidney Spencer (Cambridge: James Clarke, 1969), pp. 115–16; cf. *Works*, V, 19–20, 89–94.
10 *The Sublime: A Study of Critical Theories in XVIII-Century England* (repr. Ann Arbor: University of Michigan Press, 1960), p. iii.

Never on Sunday:
John Gay's The Shepherd's Week

JOHN IRWIN FISCHER

One's first reaction to John Gay's *The Shepherd's Week: In Six Pastorals* is likely to be frustration; nothing in the poem seems to work properly, starting with the title. A week, after all, is seven days long, yet this poem boasts only six eclogues and omits the Sabbath. Gay's "Proeme" explains: "ours being supposed to be Christian shepherds," they are "then at church worship."[1] This explanation merely begs the question. One still does not know why Sunday was omitted: is church worship ineffable, unimportant, unpastoral, all of the above, or none? The only certain conclusions one can reach are these: Gay wishes to emphasize his omission of a Sunday eclogue and does not wish to tell us why he omitted it.

Such frustration is not an occasional effect of *The Shepherd's Week*; it is continuous, and even the poem's minutiae are confounding. For example, at the conclusion of his poem Gay appends "An Alphabetical Catalogue of Names, Plants, Flowers, Fruits, Birds, Beasts, Insects, and other material things mentioned in these Pastorals." The "Catalogue" is obviously a swipe at index-lovers, but it is also disturbing to anyone who likes order at all, for it is alphabetical, but not quite. Selections from the list of words catalogued under the letter "C" suffice to show the problem. "Calf," "Capon," "Carr," "Cat," "Cicily," and "Clover-grass" begin the list in proper alphabetical order. "Cloddipole" follows "Clover-grass," however, and is itself followed by "Churn," "Colworts," and "Clumsilis." The entire list ends

191

with "Cuckow," "Cur," "Cyder," and, finally, "Corns." While always somewhat alphabetical, the list exhibits no regular pattern of distortion; it is a perfect foil to linearity: imitating order and simultaneously defying it.[2]

Critics are usually orderly folks, while Gay's poem is an unusually disordering performance; consequently, one result of most modern efforts to read the poem is that those efforts illustrate sharply the poem's radical alinearity. These efforts can be classed under two heads: those that portray the poem as fundamentally parodic and those that portray it as a "straightforward, accurate, and at times moving rendition of rural actuality."[3] Of the readings that stress the parodic elements in *The Shepherd's Week*, Hoyt Trowbridge's "Pope, Gay, and *The Shepherd's Week*" is, justly, the most widely known.[4] Trowbridge demonstrates that much of the parody in *The Shepherd's Week* echoes the implied criticism in Pope's *Guardian* 40 of Ambrose Philip's *Pastorals* and Thomas Tickell's articles on the nature of pastoral. Trowbridge's arguments are strong, but, as Patricia Meyer Spacks notes, his conclusions are overstated. If, as Trowbridge maintains, Gay's purpose in *The Shepherd's Week* "is to reveal the artistic fatuity of Tickell's pastoral theory and Philip's practice,"[5] then Gay overshot his mark. For Sir Richard Blackmore, Thomas D'Urfey, and Spenser's E. K. are also satirized in *The Shepherd's Week*, along with, perhaps, Spenser himself, Theocritus, Virgil, and even Pope. In fact, just because Gay launches so many satiric darts in this poem, many readers have supposed he has no single butt at all.

For such readers, what counts about the poem is its fidelity to rural life, especially to the ubiquity of labor in such a life.[6] This view of the poem, like Trowbridge's, has its strengths: Gay's shepherdesses do tie sheaves, drive hogs, milk cows, and even arrange to have those cows serviced; the shepherdesses, that is, seem more to live on Hesiod's farm than in Epicurus's garden. Even here, however, the matter is not clear cut. For example, Gay's milkmaids "with soft stroakings milk the Cow" ("Friday," 118, l. 154), but cows are in fact only grumblingly lactiferous and, as Charles Beckwith points out, "a milkmaid quickly develops the grip of a blacksmith."[7] Thus, Gay's shepherdesses, like his shepherds, are both here and there; they are representatively rural but also artificial, just as they are vaguely Hesiodic but also very pastoral. Like the poem in which they appear, they defy simple definition.

Implicitly, at least, many readers of *The Shepherd's Week* have recognized this fact. Professor Trowbridge remarks the delightfulness of Gay's shepherds; Professor Spacks acknowledges the strength of

Trowbridge's arguments, but neither critic suggests what happens if both their positions are equally right. What is a poem that is at once a specific parody, a general parody that undercuts the specific one, and no parody at all but rather an account of rural actuality that is also highly artificial? Some answers to this question can be developed by exploring the qualities of traditional pastoral verse using techniques designed to cope with twentieth-century literature of the absurd. These techniques work, I think, because in *The Shepherd's Week* Gay really has "hit the true spirit of pastoral poetry,"[8] and that spirit itself is, in some ways, absurd.

I am not the first to note a connection between pastoral verse and modern literature of the absurd. In *The Green Cabinet*, a very attractive treatment of Theocritean pastoral, Thomas G. Rosenmeyer discusses an analysis by Jean-Paul Sartre of Albert Camus's *L'Etranger*. Sartre is engaged in describing Camus's narrative technique.

"Are we not dealing here," he asks,

> with the analytic assumption that any reality is reducible to a sum total of elements. . . . If in describing a rugby match I write: "I saw adults in shorts fighting and throwing themselves on the ground in order to send a leather ball between a pair of wooden posts," I have summed up what I have seen, but I have intentionally missed its meaning. . . . [M. Camus] slyly eliminates all the significant links which are also part of the experience. . . . Each sentence is a present instant . . . separated by a void from the following one. . . . The world is destroyed and reborn from sentence to sentence. . . . M. Camus and many other contemporary writers . . . like things for their own sake . . . [preferring] these short-lived little sparkles, each of which gives a bit of pleasure, to an organized narrative.[9]

As Rosenmeyer remarks, "several things [in Sartre's analysis] command attention, notably the emphasis on brief, disconnected sentences; the stress on things rather than the relations between them; the reluctance to project into them feelings and modes of existence that are analogous to human feelings and modes; and the perception of a world that is not continuous, but a series of discrete units, each to be savored for its own sake." And Rosenmeyer continues:

> The artlessness affected by the pastoralist has much in common with the novelist's attempt to capture the absurdity and beauty of things . . . in pastoral the accent is on separation and dispersal, not on unity . . . almost every Theocritean or Virgilian pastoral is best analyzed as a loose combination of independent elements. It is left

to the listener to weld the parts together in his imagination if he so
wishes. . . .[10]

The rightness of Rosenmeyer's insight is readily confirmed. Take
the character of pastoral song contests in Theocritus and Virgil: sometimes one shepherd wins, sometimes the other, sometimes the con-
test is a draw. In no case, however, is it possible certainly to determine the grounds on which the judgment is made. The attempt
causes one to delight in the poem, and, perhaps, to memorize it, but
the attempt yields no answers. Like Gay's omission of Sunday, and
his wacky "Alphabetical Catalogue," ancient song contests put to one
that question from Ionesco's *The Bald Soprano* which Martin Esslin
took as the motto for his book, *The Theatre of the Absurd*: "What is the
moral"? And, like *The Shepherd's Week* in its entirety, ancient pastoral
gives Ionesco's answer: "That is for you to find out."

Historically, there are good reasons why the spirit of ancient pastoral should resemble the spirit of modern absurd literature and why
both should be reflected in Gay's *The Shepherd's Week*. As William Berg
points out in his study, *Early Virgil*, the birth of pastoral poetry coincided with a period of unusual turmoil within the Greek political
world. "The old *polis*, the traditional Greek community, lost its integrity. No longer capable of self-determination, it had gone limp in the
grip of Macedonian generals and their successors. Bureaucratized
and cosmopolitan, it ceased to seek self-expression in the voice of its
poets."[11] In one of his earliest poems Theocritus catches the spirit of
this time for us:

> Who in this day and age will cherish the poet's good word?
> I know not. Gone are the heroes who loved old-fashioned praise
> for deeds well done: overwhelmed are they by greed.
> (Everyone keeping his hands in his pockets, a sharp eye out
> for coin, won't scrape the tarnish to make a donation;
> instead, a ready lecture: "Charity begins at home."
> "Wish I had some myself." "The gods will pay the poets."
> "Homer's enough for all; who wants to hear another now?"
> "The best of poets is he who costs me nothing."
> (XVI, 13–21, tr. Berg)

All this sounds familiar, of course; the mood it describes is one of the
seasons of the human year, and men have suffered its climate many
times. That is why it need not startle us to suppose that what Theocritus learned in the weather of his time, Gay may have learned in
the weather of his, and many a writer has learned in the weather of
our own.

Primarily, what Theocritus learned was a knack of disengagement; that is, he invented the pastoral, a form built to turn in on itself, beginning with its language. Of course, everybody knows that Theocritus wrote his idylls in Doric rather than the more expected literary dialects, but, for reasons Gay's readers will immediately grasp, I particularly like A. E. S. Gow's explanation of Theocritus's Doric proceedings. Having reminded us that Doric was one of the two broad divisions of the Greek language and spoken with pronounced variations from one end of the Greek world to the other, Gow, with considerable exasperation, tells us that not only did Theocritus "use concurrently Doric forms not found together in any variety of spoken Doric," but he also "uses forms which are not Doric at all, some epic and attributable to the meter in which he writes, and a few seem to be rather Aeolic than Doric. . . . In short, Theocritus's dialect is artificial, peculiar to himself, and not consistent even in his own usage. He is not writing native Syracusan, nor is he imitating those who have written it before him . . . Nor again is he trying to reproduce the dialect of a particular place. . . . There are, therefore," Gow concludes, "no external criteria by which his Doric can be tried."[12]

Doubtless, Theocritus's Doric is frustrating to an editor, but Gow's description of it is delightfully suggestive to us. Like a modern abstract painter, Theocritus simply thickens his medium so that it no longer flows into the outlines of a subject but becomes itself an object for examination. This is what happens in absurd literature, too. Ionesco tells the story of how he learned English: "I set to work. Conscientiously I copied whole sentences from my primer with the purpose of memorizing them. . . . [Suddenly, though,] a strange phenomenon took place. I don't know how—the text began imperceptibly to change before my eyes. . . . The very simple, luminously clear statements . . . fermented . . . expanded and overflowed."[13] That overflow produced *The Bald Soprano*, in which Ionesco found in the foreignness of English what Beckett found in the foreignness of French, that beyond the accustomed track of one's native language there is a realm of gaiety, sometimes as frightening or grotesque as Theocritus's cyclopic shepherd, but always liberating.

Now I must drop the other shoe: having quoted Gow on Theocritus's Doric, I must quote Gay on Gay's own English. Gay begins his description with a flourish.

> That principally, courteous Reader, whereof I would have thee to be advised, (seeing I depart from the vulgar usage) is touching the Language of my Shepherds; which is, soothly to say, such as is neither

> spoken by the country Maiden nor the courtly Dame; nay, not only
> such as in the present Times is not uttered, but was never uttered in
> Times past; and, if I judge aright, will never be uttered in Times
> future. It having too much of the Country to be fit for the Court; too
> much of the Court to be fit for the Country, too much of the Lan-
> guage of old Times to be fit for the Present, too much of the Present
> to have been fit for the Old, and too much of both to be fit for any
> time to come ("Proeme," 92, ll. 67–75).

To be sure, this hilarious description can be explained into sobriety
by referring it, through Spenser, to the quarrel between Pope and
Philips about the decorum of pastoral rhetoric. And it is likely that
Gay's games with language began with that quarrel. Thus, in "Tues-
day, or The Ditty," Marian's complaint, beginning "Ah woful Day! Ah
woful Noon and Morn," parodies those complaints, in Philip's second and fourth pastorals, that Pope had already sent up in *Guardian*
40. Nevertheless, though any number of such parodies are directed
at Philips in *The Shepherd's Week*, collecting them fails to establish a
significant account of the language of the poem because the parodies,
once collected, refuse to gel. Philips hardly emerges from *The Shepherd's Week* as a character whose literary activities threaten language,
or religion, or civilization itself in the way that, say, Shadwell's acts
seem to threaten all three in Dryden's *Mac Flecknoe*. Rather, Gay's
parodies of Philip's work are casual; they blend with his parodies of
other pastoralists and with a kind of word play that is not specifically
parodic at all. Supplying us with Chaucer's second and vulgar meaning of the word "queint" ("Monday," 99, l. 79n.), or with a zany ety-
mology for the word "dumps"—"from dumpling, the heaviest kind
of pudding, though possibly from Dumops, an Egyptian king"
("Wednesday," 104, title note)—or with a self-erasing usage report on
the word "ken"—"This word is of general use, but not very common,
though not unknown to the vulgar" ("Wednesday," 107, l. 89n.)—
Gay is scarcely parodying anyone in particular, he is just thickening
the soup. Of course, in doing so he laughs at all of us who want
parodies to be meaningfully particular, and etymologies to be helpful, and who believe that language, religion, and civilization are
stable enough ever to be threatened by anything. Wanting and believing such things we enter Gay's work condemned to struggle
against its nature until, at last, we, too, learn to laugh.

Not that *The Shepherd's Week* is just a bit of mischief. In his
"Proeme" Gay states his purpose in writing it plainly enough: "It is
my purpose, gentle Reader, to set before thee, as it were, a picture,
or lively landscape of thy own country . . . even as Maister Milton

hath elegantly set forthe the same" ("Proeme," 91, ll. 33–35). Of course, like everything else in *The Shepherd's Week*, the lines Gay chooses from "Maister Milton" in order to illustrate his own purpose come across the net with lots of spin; they are those that compare Satan, as he enters the Garden to provoke man's fall, to "one who long in populous City pent,"

> Where houses thick and Sewers annoy the Aire
> Forth issuing on a Summer's Morn to breathe
> Among the pleasant Villages and Farms
> Adjoin'd, from each thing met conceives delight;
> The Smell of grain or tedded Grass or Kine
> Or Dairie, each rural Sight, each rural Sound.
> ("Proeme," 91, ll. 37–43)

By quoting these lines, Gay reminds us of Satan's character and, I think, warns us about our own. Milton's Satan is perhaps the most linear character in English literature. Save this once, he never knows what it is (borrowing Sartre's phrase again) "to like things for their own sake." Even in this scene he does not willingly delight in Eve or the garden; he is merely overtaken by the beauty of what he sees and so stands, for a moment, "stupidly good." In *The Shepherd's Week*, Gay gives us the chance to do better than Satan. If, demonically, we begin by attempting to alphabetize his "Catalogue," we can end by laughing at his joke, enjoying the sound of his words, and being reminded of the lines from which they come. Similarly, if we begin by tracing his parodies in search of an argument, we can end by being reintroduced to some literature that is great by any standard, and much that is at least pleasant. Finally, if we attempt to discover among Gay's six pastorals something like the complex symmetrical relationships between Virgil's ten, we can discover not only what the poem's title should have told us, that *The Shepherd's Week* really is a poem at sixes and sevens, but also that the poem's pleasures reside not in systems but in things like Hobnelia's spells, Colin's sex-teases, Susan's bonny speed, and the Silenus-like but more modest visions of Bowzybeus. If we learn from "each thing met" in the poem to "conceive delight," we have found the point of *The Shepherd's Week*.

Better still, in finding delight in the particulars of Gay's poem, we recover something at least of the pastoral spirit. As we noted earlier, Theocritus created the pastoral in a linear age: greedy, turbulent, filled with ambition. The Slender Muse of his idylls represents a swerve away from that age; she portrays an alternative vision of human life in which not wealth, nor conquest, nor even virtue constitute the good, but only pleasure. Much has happened to the pastoral since Theocritus first conceived it in delight, and most of what has happened obscures the way the form originally opposed not only the values of the age that gave it birth but also the achievements of earlier, bigger, and more holistic Greek forms. Perhaps Virgil did more to tame the pastoral than any other poet. First, he used pastoral as a means toward epic, blurring the way that, in Theocritus, its achievement opposed that of the bigger forms. Also, he yoked together the pastoral and the georgic, mingling thereby the shady pleasance of pastoral song with the sun-drenched, sweaty fields of Hesiodic labor. Finally, he gave his shepherds gods and made them pious. Seen from such an angle, Virgil nearly wrote anti-pastorals,[14] and that is why it is useful, as a final gauge for measuring *The Shepherd's Week*, to notice how much of Virgil's influence Gay either rejects or subverts.

First, there is the matter of tone; unlike the ambitious, nervy Virgilian tautness of Pope's pastorals, Gay's *Shepherd's Week* simply sinks into itself in laughter and delight. Gay is not "practicing up" in his eclogues to write an epic or anything else; instead, like that of Theocritus, his devotion to the Slender Muse was life-long. Further, despite Professor Spacks's opinion that a work ethic is central to *The Shepherd's Week*, Gay displays some hostility to the Hesiodic field in his eclogues. In Hesiodic verse, work is a subject and man is often subservient to that work; in pastoral verse, like *The Shepherd's Week*, men and women are the subjects, and, though they may do tasks, they are always free. To see how clearly Gay chooses a pastoral and Theocritean vision rather than a Hesiodic and more Virgilian one, we need only remember that the calendar, to which a wise laborer must always submit, is a Hesiodic, not a pastoral device. Of course, as part of the process that altered pastoral vision, calendars came back into the English pastoral tradition by way of Spenser. But Gay, feeling them to be alien there, not only shrank his calendar to a week and then lost one day of that but finally refused to tie his poems to the days he kept. As he wryly explains: "of many of Maister Spencer's Eclogues it may be observed; though months they be called, of the said Months therein, nothing is specified; wherein I have also esteemed him worthy mine imitation" ("Proeme," 92, ll. 64–66).

In one way only, then, does Gay follow Virgil's lead in *The Shepherd's Week*: in the matter of the gods Gay performs a trick he might have learned from Virgil's eclogues. Here, too, perhaps the best first way to describe this trick draws not on Virgil but on twentieth-century literature of the absurd. For example, during the night that separates the first and second acts of *Waiting for Godot* several things change: a tree that was barren sprouts four or five new leaves, and Gogo's boots, which fit him abominably in Act I, seem to have been exchanged for or transformed into boots that fit well in Act II. Neither Didi nor Gogo make much of these alterations; they happen during the night, and Didi and Gogo care about the days, during which they wait for Godot. Only we, the audience, are left to wonder at the end of the play how these changes came about.

Often enough, absurd literature does make us suspect the presence of spirits. At the conclusion of Ionesco's *The Chairs*, as the human audience begins to exit from the theatre, we find the following stage direction: "We hear for the first time the human noises of the invisible crowd: these are bursts of laughter, murmurs, shh's, ironical coughs. . . . All this should last long enough for the audience—the real and visible audience—to leave with this ending firmly impressed on its mind."[15] Or again, after the violence that concludes Pinter's *The Room*, we are forced to recognize that, despite Rose's protestations, her room is vacant after all, and that therefore the voice that announced its vacancy early in the play was a prophetic one. In each of these cases, and they can be easily multiplied, the very process by which drama of the absurd uproots a rational world also produces a sense of the numinous: take the world to pieces, these plays suggest, and the pieces may well grow mysterious.

Because the pastoral idylls of Theocritus take a world to pieces, too, they could produce a similar effect, but they do not. In fact, Theocritus actually seems to have suppressed this element of his invention; like that of Epicurus, his universe has gods, but they do not count for much in the day-to-day scheme of things. Thus even Daphnis, whose name reflects the divine origin of song, goes to the stream (that is, dies) without Orphic overtones: "The waters closed over him whom the muses loved, nor did the nymphs mislike him" (*Idyll I*, 140–41). Flux, beautiful but not divine, is the stuff of Theocritus's idylls.

One need hardly say that Virgil alters all this in his eclogues: of his Daphnis Mopsus says, "God, he is a god, Menalcus" (*Eclogue V*, 64), and there is always the "Divine" eclogue itself. Nevertheless, though Virgil's pastorals are inspirited, we must record their divinity carefully. Mopsus's line about Daphnis suggests the problem: "God, he was a god, noble Memnius" (*De rerum natura*, 5.8 tr. Berg) is what Lucretius says about Epicurus, who had freed men from fear of the gods; thus, Mopsus's line lives between what it claims and what it recalls. Generally, the numinous in Virgil's eclogues is just as bland as that; present in his pastorals as leaves grace Beckett's tree, Virgil's

numinous quality almost never argues anything, nor proves anything, but is just there.

The numinous in Gay's *The Shepherd's Week* is like that, too; so for
some readers, who find a sense of spirit only in "grave points . . . of
churchly matter and Doubts in Religion . . . to great Clerkes only
appertaining" ("Proeme," 91, ll. 56–57), there will be no numinous
quality in *The Shepherd's Week* at all. But in Gay's "rural" as well as
Spenser's "rumbling reed" there are haunted passages enough, I
think. My favorites are actually a complex of passages. At the conclusion of his "Prologue," Gay credits Bolingbroke with the suggestion
that *The Shepherd's Week* should be annotated and published. At the
same time, though, Gay warns Bolingbroke against the charms of the
poem he has called into print.

> Let not Affairs of States and Kings
> Wait, while our *Bowzybeus* sings.
> Rather than Verse of simple Swain
> Should stay the trade of *France* or *Spain*,
> Or for the Plaint of Parson's Maid,
> Yon Emp'ror's Packets be delay'd,
> In sooth, I swear by holy *Paul*,
> I'd burn Book, Preface, Notes and all.
> ("Prologue," 95, ll. 89–96)

It is possible, of course, to read this passage in a straightforward way
as a characteristic instance of Gay's modesty about his work. Even
read straightforwardly, however, the passage does manage to testify
to the subversive power of pastoral verse: ministers of state must be
warned against its seductive alinearity. Also, read in this fashion, the
last two lines of the passage—"I swear by holy *Paul* / I'd burn Book,
Preface, Notes and all"—pose a problem: why holy Paul? Charles
Beckwith remarks that the phrase may be explained either by the
exigencies of rhyme or by the fact that St. Paul is the patron saint of
commercial London's cathedral, and Beckwith may be right.[16] There
are other possibilities, however.

Writing to the Corinthians (I:3, 10–15), Paul observes that sooner
or later every man's work shall be burned, at which time it will not
matter as much whether the work is of gold and survives, or of stub-
ble and burns, but whether the man himself shall be saved. There are
several reasons for believing that as Gay wrote the last two lines of
his "Prologue" this passage may have been running through his
mind. First, at just about the same time he composed *The Shepherd's
Week* Gay was also writing two short poems on the transience of all

earthly works, and it is certainly possible that there was some carry-over from one literary project to the other. Further, there is at least one other passage in *The Shepherd's Week* itself that calls the Pauline scripture to mind. In his "Proeme," after identifying his language as being of a kind that never was, is not now, and never will be, Gay remarks that "in this my Language, I seem unto myself, as a *London* Mason, who calculateth his Work for a Term of Years, when he build-eth with old materials upon a Ground-rent that is not his own which soon turneth to Rubbish and Ruine. For this point, no Reason can I alledge, only deep learned Ensamples having led me thereunto" ("Proeme," 92, ll. 76–80). Of course, this passage, too, can be dis-cussed without reference to Paul; at one level, the "deep learned En-samples" Gay refers to are only, parodically, Philips, Spenser, and imitative pastoralists generally. Nevertheless, in the text already mentioned, Paul, too, discusses foundations. All men's work shall be tried by fire, Paul says, but men themselves shall be saved if, like Paul, "the wise masterbuilder," they lay a right foundation: "for other foundation can no man lay than that is laid, which is Jesus Christ." In the midst of London's squabbles, political and pastoral, a shadowy reminder of Paul's admonition to the divisive Corinthians would at least not be inappropriate.

All this sounds very serious for *The Shepherd's Week*, perhaps too serious. Before deciding Paul is not present in this passage, however, or in the lines from the "Prologue" cited above, it is worth remem-bering that this passage leads into the final paragraph of the "Proeme."

> But here again, much Comfort ariseth in me, from the Hopes, in that I conceive, when these Words in the course of transitory Things shall decay, it may so hap, in meet time that some Lover of *Simplicity* shall arise, who shall have the Hardiness to render these mine Ec-logues into such more modern Dialect as shall be then understood, to which end, Glosses and Explications of uncouth Pastoral Terms are annexed. ("Proeme," 92, ll. 81–86)

Of course, this whole paragraph is ironic on several levels, but per-haps its final irony rests in Gay's knowledge, shared with Paul, that nothing can be more "simple" than to believe that anything can last that is made of words shaped to the transitory things of this world.

Such knowledge is neither unpastoral, nor outside the ken of ab-surd literature. What would be both unpastoral and outside absurd vision would be Paul's voice ringing too clearly through *The Shepherd's Week*. That is hardly a danger. The final lines of the "Prologue" probably are informed by Paul, but one cannot prove that, just as one cannot prove that when old Bowzybeus breaks into the Hundreth Psalm in the "Saturday" eclogue he is doing more than singing by rote a very famous set piece. To be sure, the words of the psalm happily summarize what I think is the final point of *The Shepherd's Week* "Know ye that the Lord He is God, it is He that hath made us and not we ourselves, we are His people and the sheep of his pasture." But amidst the crazy quilt of Bowzybeus's chant, we cannot prove the centrality of this psalm, and that is as it should be. The pastoral breaks our sense of a humanly rational world, and it sometimes points beyond itself toward something numinous. But it does no more. Gay's "Contemplation on Night," the second of his poems on transience, ends this way: "The Stars shall drop, the Sun shall lose his flame, / But thou, O God, for ever shine the same" (89, 53–54). But these lines forecast the apocalypse. *The Shepherd's Week*, written a few months later, ends with just a sunset over drunken Bowzybeus. "The Pow'r that Guards the Drunk, his Sleep attends, / 'Till, ruddy, like his Face, the Sun descends" ("Saturday," 123, 127–28). There is not even a sequent sunrise. For, as we said at the beginning of this essay, tomorrow is Sunday, and Sunday, though mentioned, never dawns in *The Shepherd's Week*.

NOTES

1 *John Gay, Poetry and Prose*, ed. Vinton A. Dearing and Charles E. Beckwith, 2 vols. (Oxford: Clarendon, 1974), I, 92, lines 62–63. All quotations of Gay's work are from this edition and will be identified hereafter by page and line number in my text.
2 Admittedly, one cannot prove that the disorders in Gay's index are intentional, but, because eighteenth-century professional English indexers recognized basically the same standard of indexing as ours—letter-for-letter-to-the-end-of-the-word—and because Gay himself sometimes observes this standard, his gross violations of it are probably no accident. See G. Norman Knight, "Book Indexing in Great Britain. A Brief History," in L. M. Harrod, ed., *Indexers on Indexing* (New York: R. R. Bowker, 1978), pp. 9–13.
3 I borrow my two headings, as well as the description for one of them, from Patricia Meyer Spacks's *John Gay* (New York: Twayne, 1965), p. 32. For a less-dichotomized summary of scholarship on *The Shepherd's Week* see Aldina Forsgren, *John Gay: Poet "of a Lower Order"* (Stockholm: Lagerström, 1964), pp. 106–13. I know of no major essays on *The Shepherd's*

Week published very recently: however, three essays on *Trivia* have influenced me: Martin Battestin, "Menalcas' Song: The Meaning of Art and Artifice in Gay's Poetry," *Journal of English and German Philology*, 65 (1966), 662–79; Arthur Sherbo, "Virgil, Dryden, Gay, and Matters Trivial," *PMLA*, 85 (1970), 1063–71; and Diana S. Ames, "Gay's *Trivia* and the Art of Allusion," *Studies in Philology*, 75 (1978), 199–222.

4 *Modern Language Quarterly*, 5 (1944), 79–88.

5 Ibid., p. 88.

6 The emphasis on labor is most strongly marked in Spacks's argument; see pp. 33–40.

7 *John Gay: Poetry and Prose*, II, 523, l. 4n.

8 *The Beauties of English Poetry*, ed. Oliver Goldsmith, 2 vols. (London, 1767), I, 133.

9 J. P. Sartre, *Literary and Philosophical Essays*, trans. Annette Michelson (New York: Criterion Books, 1955), pp. 37–40.

10 Thomas G. Rosenmeyer, *The Green Cabinet: Theocritus and the European Pastoral Lyric* (Los Angeles: University of California Press, 1969), pp. 46–47.

11 William Berg, *Early Virgil* (London: Athlone, 1974), p. 7. Translations of Virgil's eclogues are from this text.

12 *Theocritus*, ed. A. E. S. Gow, 2 vols. (Cambridge: Cambridge University Press, 1952), I, lxxiii. Unless otherwise marked, translations of the *Idylls* are from this text.

13 "Lorsque j'écris . . . ," *Cahiers des Saisons*, 15 (Winter 1959). Reference in Martin Esslin's *The Theatre of the Absurd* (New York: Doubleday, 1961), pp. 86–87.

14 Two qualifications are required here. First, if by "pastoral" one means an exquisitely balanced, intricately imagined "proving ground for the development of [Virgil's great] themes and figures" (William Berg, *Early Virgil*, p. 190), then, obviously, Virgil's poems are not anti-pastorals. In any case, I certainly am not arguing that Virgil's pastorals are less than magnificent. Second, the distinctions that I make between Theocritus's pastorals and Virgil's are not the ones Gay or his contemporaries consciously made. As J. E. Congleton demonstrated almost thirty years ago in his *Theories of Pastoral Poetry in England* (Gainesville: University of Florida Press, 1952), in the English "Pastoral War" Theocritus became the ideal of the rationalist school because of his supposed realism, while Virgil became the ideal for the neoclassicist school because of his assumed elegance, neatness, simplicity, and delicacy. Both schools, as Congleton recognized, tended to narrow the achievements of both poets; guided by recent criticism, I have reframed some of the differences between the two in order to illuminate Gay's achievement in *The Shepherd's Week*, but I have not attempted a detailed account of either Theocritus's or Virgil's pastorals.

15 Eugene Ionesco, *Four Plays*, tr. Donald M. Allen (New York: Grove, 1958), p. 160.

16 *John Gay: Poetry and Prose*, II, 521, l. 95n.

Blake and Newton:

Argument as Art, Argument as Science

STUART PETERFREUND

There has been a good deal of discussion recently, by George S. Rousseau and others, about the status of the relationship between literature and science as modes of discourse.[1] Interestingly enough, much of what has been written about literature and science has been focused on the relationship of the two modes as viewed in the context of the eighteenth century, when the relationship of the two, clearly defined or otherwise, seems to have been the strongest. Problems with defining the status of the relationship seem to have arisen from the variety of its "surface" manifestations. These range from the implicit relationship of Book III of *Gulliver's Travels* to *Philosophical Transactions of the Royal Society*, so astutely perceived and documented by Marjorie Hope Nicolson,[2] to the highly explicit relationship of Blake's *Milton* to Newton's *Principia*, with which this essay will be principally concerned. But before entering into the substance of the discussion, it would seem proper to raise a question begged by the preceding remarks: on what basis or common ground may literature and science be discussed, with the purpose of understanding their relationship?

One answer to this question is that literature and science may be viewed as artifacts of rhetoric—as arguments, in other words. One who begins from such a view proceeds in the study of the relationship between literature and science with the understanding that, when any argument, either literary or scientific, speaks to the issues raised by another argument with the goal of overturning that other argument, the critical argument in question proceeds from a rhetorical position no less well defined and interested than that of the argument it seeks to overturn. Seen in this perspective, the General Scholium of the *Principia* differs from the "conversation" of the "Visionary forms dramatic" that takes place at the end of Blake's *Jerusalem*[3] not so much in terms of what it argues for as in terms of its refusal to acknowledge its status as argument—with the corollary refusal to acknowledge that what is being said, or argued for, must ultimately be reflexive to the interested position of the person mounting the discussion. Newton, for example, having disposed of the Cartesian model of vortical planetary motion, is not content to rest on his calculations, nor is he content to regard those calculations as evidence brought forth in support of his argument. Instead, by disclaiming any personal interest in elaborating the model of the solar system based on the principle of elliptical rotation, Newton is able to deny that there is any argument on his part in the first place, averring instead that "this most beautiful system of the sun, planets, and comets, could only proceed from the counsel and dominion of an intelligent and powerful Being."[4] This "Being," happily enough for Newton, is also the source of the language and rhetoric that Newton "discovers" for the purpose of propagating his (His?) celestial mechanics, just as Newton "discovers" the system of mechanics itself. Blake's Four Zoas, by way of contrast, do not discover, in their use of language, the space and time that are the parameters of Newton's system. Rather, the Zoas are seen "Creating Space, Creating Time according to the wonders Divine / Of Human Imagination." The consequence, which would be an abhorrence to Newton, with his allied conceptions of absolute time and absolute space, is the "variation of Time & Space / Which vary according as the Organs of Perception vary."[5]

To be sure, many of the eighteenth-century writers active before the 1790's, when Blake came to intellectual and artistic maturity, recognized the rhetorical and ontological status of Newtonian argument, *as argument*, and they evinced a shared concern about the full significance of that argument and the limits to which it might be made, by analogy, to serve in other fields of inquiry. Writers as far apart in politics as Addison and Pope and as far apart in temperament as Desaguliers and Doctor Johnson all had something to say about the impact of Newtonian mechanics and optics and the implications to be derived therefrom. These responses have already been dealt with in several fine studies, including book-length treatments by Nicolson, Richard B. Schwartz, and Margaret C. Jacob,[6] and need only be mentioned here in passing to emphasize the crucial difference between Blake's response to Newton and the responses of English writers before him. Addison, Pope, Desaguliers, Johnson, *et al.* may have disagreed over the extent to which Newtonian physics could, by argument from analogy, be used to help see the "subjective" aspects of the universe in an orderly manner. But these and other writers of the eighteenth century were of one mind concerning the "objective" truth of Newtonian physics *per se*. Pope may have taken issue with Addison over how far Newtonian argument might be extended in the areas of perceptual psychology and political economy, but both writers agreed on the paramount importance of the physics itself to Western thought. And although Johnson may have placed less emphasis on the discovery of physical truths than on the discovery of moral and religious ones, he still considered Newton a model of scientific thought and conduct.[7] Up to Blake's time, the response of eighteenth-century literature to Newtonian science is unanimous in its belief that Newton's mathematics and physics are fully disinterested, inductive, impartial, and authoritative. It is only in the question of how far Newtonian thought might be extended into other spheres of inquiry that there is any real debate.

For Blake, however, the painful and oppressive conditions of human existence, which he viewed as being in part descended from the "reasonable" assumptions of Newtonian physics, translated into Newtonian metaphysics and implemented as social policy, meant that there was something wrong with the physics itself. Blake seems to have understood, as we now do, that the metaphysics might precede the physics as well as follow from it. Accordingly, Blake undertook the critique and demonstration, whose record is to be found throughout the Prophetic Books, especially in *Milton*, a critique and demonstration anticipatory, in the essentials, of the insights set forth by relativity physics concerning the space-time continuum and other matters in the latter physics' correction of the Newtonian model of the universe.[8]

Lest it be objected, however, that the present strategy is to turn Blake into an *ur*-Einstein, the point should be made that Blake's insights about, and critique of Newtonian physics—indeed, his critical responses to many of the language-bound activities of the age—owe a good deal to his grasp of the nature and function of language, as well as of the way in which one reads that language. Blake's senses of language and reading depend upon his understanding that all texts, as the artifacts of specific individuals writing in specific contexts of time and place, are rhetorical, or argumentative, and that the situation could not be otherwise, since all language is produced by individuals speaking from positions more or less clearly defined, but always definite.[9] Accordingly, there is no such thing as disinterestedness, only concealed or dissembled interest; no such thing as pure induction, only induction with a concealed or impure hypothesis, usually disguised as an "axiom" or "truth"; no impartiality, only imperfectly revealed partiality; and no authority, only usurped freedom.

Blake's idea of language has been discussed at some length previously by Robert F. Gleckner and this writer. These discussions emphasize that fallen humanity uses a fallen language that is at best partial in its grasp of phenomena and at worst tyrannous in its insistence on the authority of that partial grasp.[10] But neither of the discussions deals with the relationship between language and reading, or with the role of reading as an instrument of language reform. Blake has a vision of how language functions when properly used, and that vision is closely tied to his idea of how one should read. Before turning to the way in which Blake reads and responds to Newtonian language specifically, it might be helpful to develop an understanding, in general terms, of the relationship between language properly spoken and reading properly practiced.

Blake's most complete account of language properly spoken is found at the end of *Jerusalem*, in his rendering of the "conversation" dealt with briefly above. The Four Zoas

> conversed together in Visionary forms dramatic which bright
> Redounded from their Tongues in thunderous majesty, in Visions
> In new Expanses, creating exemplars of Memory and of Intellect
> Creating Space, Creating Time according to the wonders Divine
> Of Human Imagination, throughout all Three Regions immense
> Of Childhood, Manhood & Old Age [;] & the all tremendous unfathomable
>   Non Ens
> Of Death was seen in regenerations terrific or complacent varying
> According to the subject of discourse & every Word & every Character
> Was Human according to the Expansion or Contraction, the Translucence or
> Opakeness of Nervous fibres such was the variation of Time & Space
> Which vary according as the Organs of Perception vary.
>
>   (98.28–38)

The language spoken by the Four Zoas creates what it refers to rather than merely describing something thought to have been created previously. "Exemplars of Memory and of Intellect," up to and including space and time themselves, are created in the course of such speech. But the overall qualities of any given "Exemplar" are entirely reflexive to the qualities of the speaker in question: "Human Imagination," the speaker's age, "the subject of discourse," and the variables having to do with differences in "the Organs of Perception" from speaker to speaker. In a "conversation" of the sort described by Blake, no one speaker lays claim to, or is accorded, the authority that would make that speaker's position the only "right" or "reasonable" one among other "wrong" or "unreasonable" alternatives. Authoritative meaning under such circumstances is comprehensive meaning, which takes the form of a living body of utterance, augmented by each additional utterance but never completed by it. Thus the sense of the verb *redounded*, as Blake uses it, meaning in the context of *Jerusalem*, pl. 98, "to add, yield, cause to accrue" (*OED*, VIII.309).[11]

In order to use language as the Four Zoas do at the end of *Jerusalem*, it is necessary to relinquish the coercive authority implicit in point of view and usually identified in Blake's lexicon as *selfhood*. Selfhood is Blake's cardinal sin, replacing the more usual pride and posing a threat to the individual far greater than might be posed by pride alone, since selfhood is an amalgam of pride and of deceit that denies the existence of that very pride, a powerful amalgam indeed. As Albion faces the prospect of putting off his selfhood, for example, he comments on the powerful bond between pride and deceit, a bond which gives the resultant selfhood the power of a mighty army.

> O Lord what can I do! My Selfhood cruel
> Marches against thee deceitful from Sinai & from Edom
> Into the Wilderness of Judah to meet thee in his pride.
> (96.8–10)

Albion must put off selfhood in order to be united with the paragon of selfless energy, Jesus. The goal of doing so is one proposed by Blake for all of creation in the Greek epigraph to *Jerusalem*, μόνος ὁ Ἰεσοῦς (one in Jesus), and describes as occurring at the end of the epic, when the triumphant "All Human Forms identified" is pronounced and those forms are described as "Awaking in his [i.e. Jesus's] Bosom in the Life of Immortality" (99.1, 4).

As Enitharmon notes slightly earlier in the poem, the putting off of selfhood must necessarily entail the repudiation of Bacon, Newton, Locke, and others like them—those who worship a "natural" order they both have created and have refused to take responsibility for creating.

We shall not die! we shall be united in Jesus.
Will you suffer this Satan this Body of Doubt that Seems but is Not
To occupy the very threshold of Eternal Life. If Bacon, Newton, Locke,
Deny a Conscience in Man & the Communion of Saints & Angels
Contemning the Divine Vision & Fruition, Worshiping the Deus
Of the Heathen, the God of This World, & the Goddess Nature
Mystery Babylon the Great, the Druid Dragon & hidden Harlot[,]
Is it not the Signal of the Morning which was told us in the Beginning?
(93.19–26)

How does one go about repudiating those who champion the empirical mode of observation and the argument by induction, while at the same time worshiping the horrible Antichrist under its several names and guises? Blake's answer is that one reads the texts produced by these and other usurpers—all texts, for that matter—in what he calls the "infernal or diabolical sense." This reading strategy is described in *The Marriage of Heaven and Hell*.

The speaker of Blake's mixed media polemic has just shown an "Angel" that the Gospels, although written by men of genius about a man of genius,[12] have been misread consistently because of the interpositions of the priesthood in the reading process. These interpositions have perverted Christianity, until it has become an organized religion along typically tradition-bound lines.

. . . a system was formed, which some took advantage of & enslav'd the vulgar by attempting to realize or abstract mental deities from their objects; thus began Priesthood.
Choosing forms of worship from poetic tales.
And at length they pronouncd that the Gods had orderd such things.
Thus men forgot that All deities reside in the human breast. (pl. 11)

In the sense that both are attempts to exercise spiritual sovereignty in the name of an absent, originary "other," priesthood and selfhood are synonymous. Both are interested points of view that pretend to disinterestedness, calling on "Jehovah," "Nature," or suchlike to bear witness to the impartiality with which they hold sway. Both priesthood and selfhood are in fact argumentative positions that deny the existence of any argument whatsoever, in light of their self-image of authoritativeness and permanence.

Priesthood and selfhood have their antithesis in the authentic voice of religious vision, that of the prophet. The nature of the antithesis is made clear in Blake's account of a "dinner conversation" with Isaiah and Ezekiel, in which Blake asks the two prophets why they should not be charged with the same crime of selfhood attributed to the priests. Isaiah answers that he "was then perswaded, & remain[s] confirm'd; that the voice of honest indignation is the voice of God, I cared not for the consequences but wrote" (pl. 12). Thus emerges the doctrine of "firm perswasion," which furnishes a useful gloss on Blake's statement, also in *The Marriage*, "that all deities reside in the human breast" (pl. 11). As a state of mind, "firm perswasion" is characteristic not only of Isaiah and Ezekiel, but of the Four Zoas at the end of *Jerusalem* as well. In such a state, the fact that language is always argument, always coming from an interested position, is openly acknowledged, and the creative, verbal energy liberated by that very acknowledgement is of a magnitude comparable to that of the Zoas as they create and recreate space and time in their respective images. Blake inquires as to the potential for such energy through the acknowledgement of one's interested position, and Isaiah tells him that there is no reality without that acknowledgement.

> Then I asked: does a firm perswasion that a thing is so, make it so?
> He replied. All poets believe that it does, & in ages of imagination this firm perswasion removed mountains; but many are not capable of a firm perswasion of any thing. (pl. 12)

Reading in "the infernal or diabolical sense" proceeds on the understanding that the primary difference between prophecy (inspired poetry) and the literature of doubt ("philosophy," "rational discourse," "dogma," etc.) is that the former affirms, even celebrates, its "perswasion," or interested position, while the latter denies the very existence of such a position. Blake's venture in reading, then, is to "converse" with the text in order to locate and identify the human form responsible for producing it and its point of view. This venture is made clear in *The Marriage* and even clearer in Blake's Annotations of various authors, where his designedly *ad hominem* stance is aimed at producing from behind his words the writer who has refused to take full responsibility for the substance and implications of his text. "Conversing" in this context is Blake's reading strategy for prophecy and the literature of doubt alike, for the locus of rhetorical interest in each is alike in its need for elaboration and clarification. Blake therefore reads prophecy and the literature of doubt in precisely the same way, and in each case he fully acknowledges the status of his own discourse in the process of doing so. With specific reference to Blake's reading of Newton, it should be noted that Blake's adversary position is not held with the hope of "destroying" Newton. Blake acknowledges the power of the scientist's intellect; moreover, he wishes to "save" the intellect in much the same way that he wishes to "save" Milton's creative genius: by having both Newton and Milton acknowledge that their texts are the creations of a self-interested position, then having them cast off the selfhood that ordains and disguises the self-interest inherent in the position.

Blake does indeed "save" Newton in much the same way that he "saves" Milton. In the case of the latter, the process of this "salvation" is clearly chronicled in the brief epic that bears his name. In the case of Newton, however, the process is less clear, being carried forward by means of what might be termed "Christian association": the use of Christlike, visionary avatars, whose putting off of selfhood is done both for their own good and, by example, for the good of others. Milton functions as one such avatar for Newton, as does Albion, who functions in this capacity for Milton and Newton alike. Near the end of *Jerusalem*, shortly after Albion has confronted Jesus and participated in the "Mysterious / Offering of Self for Another" (96.20–21), the time of the fallen world ends, and all those immured in that time reappear in their eternal forms. "The innumerable Chariots of the Almighty appeard in Heaven / and Bacon & Newton & Locke, & Milton & Shakspear & Chaucer" (98.8–9).

Salvation of the sort Blake practices and preaches depends upon criticism, the sort of "Opposition" that "is true Friendship" (*MHH*, pl. 20). Blake's criticism of Newtonian physics is one instance among many of Blake's friendly opposition to what he conceives of as being deluded thinking. At this point it is time to turn to an examination of Blake's criticism of Newton, in order to see how well the former understands the latter's physics and metaphysics. If Blake's criticism is to be considered cogent, it may only be so if his understanding is equal to Newton's, in much the same way that the unceasing "Mental Fight" that Blake announces in *Milton*, 1.13, must occur between equally matched antagonists if it is to be successful in redeeming them from error.

The evidence for Blake's having read widely and deeply in Newtonian literature is extensive, both in Blake's own writing and in discussions of it by Donald D. Ault and F. B. Curtis, among others.[13] There is accordingly no need to reargue the issue of Blake's degree of familiarity with Newtonian thought. What does need to be argued, however, is that Blake's reading of Newton led him to focus on the *Principia* as much if not more so than on the *Optics*, the primary source of Newtonian thought for Blake, according to Ault and Nicolson before him.[14] The importance of Blake's knowledge of the *Principia* for the creation of *Milton* will be demonstrated in the discussion below. A general reason for such having been the case may be ventured at this point, however. The reason "that the English poets who wrote about science in the eighteenth century put greater emphasis on the *Principia* than on the *Optics*," according to William Powell Jones, is that "the poets knew . . . that Newton had mathematically demonstrated the order of the universe. . . . They used this idea over and over in numerous variations, not only when they mentioned Newton by name but when, in their illustrations of various branches of science they devoted more space to celestial order . . . than to the physics of light and color."[15] It is precisely on this issue of celestial order—where ideas of it come from and what force they ought and do have—that Blake confronts Newton. Blake's understanding is that such "celestial order" is in fact the order of Newton's mind, projected outward and argued for subtly but powerfully for the purpose of compelling the very consensus of opinion commented on by Jones above.

As Blake assesses it, the net effect of the Newtonian argument in the *Principia* is to create the universe in Newton's image, an act of creation for which Newton refuses to take responsibility, assigning it instead to a God with whom Newton and no one else is able to communicate on an intimate, father-son basis.[16] It is in response to this Newtonian move and all the implications to be derived from it that Blake frames the narrative of *Milton,* in which the poem's namesake must fight off not only the implications of the Newtonian model of the universe, but also the implications of the continuing cast of mind that is always ready to fabricate such models. That cast of mind may be viewed in the context of a tradition that embodies it, a tradition known as the *prisca sapientia,* or *prisca theologia,* and recently discussed by Ault in relation to Blake.[17] This tradition of ancient, or pristine wisdom, or theology is what Blake has in mind when he derides "The Stolen and Perverted Writings of Homer & Ovid: of Plato & Cicero. Which all Men ought to contemn" (pl. 1). Milton's goal in condemning this ancient tradition, as all ought to, according to Blake, is to be reunited with his "emanation," Ololon, who represents space just as Milton represents time. Ololon, for example, is described as being "Sixfold" (2.19), a multiple unique to her in all of Blake's number symbolism, at least in part because Blake associates her spatialized being with Newton's conception of the "six primary planets."[18] Seen in a larger frame, the reuniting of Ololon with Milton is but one in a series of similar reunions, including those of Enitharmon with

Los, Vala with Luvah, and Jerusalem with Albion, the overall purpose being to reunite fallen time, which Blake sees as being male,
with fallen space, which Blake sees as being female and somehow
being "generated" by time. Out of this multiple reconstitution of the
space-time continuum Blake hopes to see established conditions under which space and time, energy and matter, approach identity at
the speed of light itself.[19]

But any such reconstitution must begin with a taking stock of what
conditions are like in the fallen world and how they have come to
pass. Blake does so in *Milton* by retelling the story of the Creation,
which he had told several times previously, for example in *The Book
of Urizen* and *The Four Zoas* (1794, 1797). Implicit in such a retelling is
the awareness that the Creation and Fall have been as fully multiple
as the reconstitution that corrects them must be. For Blake, the story
of the Creation is the story of a fall into finitude, brought about by
the sort of God Newton talks about in the General Scholium of the
Principia. Creation in *Milton* begins when Los, Blake's avatar for all
poets and prophets, is unable to "identify" Urizen, whom Ault associates with Newton,[20] such "identification" being a matter of giving
Urizen an eternal form or an eternal name.

> Los siezd his Hammer & Tongs; he labourd at his resolute Anvil
> Among indefinite Druid rocks & snows of doubt & reasoning.
> Refusing all Definite Form, the Abstract Horror roofd. stony hard
> And a first Age passed over & a State of dismal woe!
>
> (3.7–10)

Urizen's "Refusing all Definite Form" cuts at least two ways, given
the Newtonian background of *Milton*. On the more obvious level,
Urizen is Newton's God, "utterly void of all body and bodily figure"
(p. 545). But on a subtler level, Blake's description—or non-descrip-
tion—goes right to the core of the Newtonian argument. Blake senses
the relationship between the attributes of Newton's God and the habits of Newton's thought. "Refusing all Definite Form" is also a gibing
reference to Newton's claim to "frame no hypotheses" (p. 545). Blake,
who by his own account knew how to read Latin tolerably well by
1803,[21] seems to have in mind a pun on the Latin original of Newton's
statement about framing hypotheses: *"hypothese non fingo."*[22] "I frame
no hypotheses" is an adequate translation of the Latin, but it is by no
means the only adequate one. *Fingo*, which may mean *to form* or *to
frame* in the sense usually understood of Newton, may also have

other meanings of interest in light of the present discussion. Two other translations of the verb are possible on the basis of the definitions of the Latin root, which discuss it in terms "of the plastic art, *to form* or *fashion by art . . . to mould or model*, as a statuary," and "with the access. notion of untruth, *to alter, change,* for the purpose of dissembling."[23]

The net effect of such a pun is to show that Newton's God and Newton are one and the same, and that a God who refuses definite form is the creation of a man who dissembles about the fact that he has created God in his own image and refuses to acknowledge the responsibility for exercising the creative initiative that would lead him to do so, since by the standards of such a mind being found out would mean being caught lying, not caught in the act of creating art. This particular set of circumstances accounts for Urizen's continual disavowal, here and elsewhere throughout the Prophetic Books, of form. It also accounts for the confrontation that occurs later in Milton proper, in which Milton marches against Urizen at the River Arnon and attempts to give him form through the sculptorly act of moulding to his formless bones the red clay of Succoth (pls. 19–20). Urizen must realize his own full presence, of body as well as of mind, before he can experience the full presence of the God he creates—and realize that such a God is only as powerful and good as its creator. The applicable text, from Blake's "The Everlasting Gospel," is "Thou art a Man God is no more / Thy own humanity learn to adore" (pp. 52–54, ll. 75–76).

A far cry from the Four Zoas who, at the end of *Jerusalem,* freely create space and time in their own images with dazzling rapidity, Urizen/Newton denies responsibility for creating what is "out there," much as Newton before him had denied responsibility for the hypothesis that placed God, invisible, at the center of a universe composed of very visible, very dead, atomistic matter. Somehow, even though he wishes to disavow any knowledge of, or responsibility for it, creation—or anti-creation—of a universe of dead matter centered by a materialistic sun possessed of invisible force(s) is a direct result of Urizen's refusal to assume form. After the "first Age," in which Urizen is characterized as "Refusing all Definite Form,"

> Down sunk with fright a red round Globe hot burning. deep
> Deep down into the Abyss. panting: conglobing: trembling
> And a second Age passed over & a State of dismal woe.
>
> (3.11–13)

Because he disavows any responsibility for voluntarily creating a centered, materialistic universe, Urizen suffers the fate of all Blake's self-denying artificers who refuse to take responsibility for their creations: the process appears to be reversed, and the created appears to have created the creator. Nor will the creator correct this misapprehension, owing to his ulterior motives. Thus Urizen/Newton postulates a universe that is centered by "a round red Globe hot burning," denies responsibility for doing so, and instead appears to become what he beholds, his organs of vision appearing to have been formed by the sun at the center of that postulated universe, when that sun in fact has been looked into place by eyes that do the bidding of a will. And that will exercises a *fiat* every bit as powerful, within its own sphere, as the first such *fiat: fiat lux.*

> Rolling around into two little Orbs & closed in two little Caves
> The Eyes beheld the Abyss: lest bones of solidness freeze over all
> And a third Age passed over & a State of dismal woe.
> (3.14–16)

The "creation," which is in fact a fall into a state of fragmented materialism, continues apace. Urizen/Newton's failure to assume responsibility for framing the first hypothesis causes the division of the creative consciousness into a fragmented, materialistic world "out there" and five contracted senses with which to perceive it. Stunned momentarily by doubt, Los believes that the "creation" taking place "out there" has a spiritual as well as a material reality. His doubt leads to Los's recapitulation, willy-nilly, of the fall of Urizen into generation. With no sense, momentarily, of his own creative energy, no sense that voids and absolute space exist only for those who do not fill them with plenitude by perceiving *through* them to the infinite, Los becomes fearful. As Blake elsewhere notes, "One thought fills immensity" (*MHH*, pl. 8.36). But when fear leads the individual to cease thinking creatively, the process reverses and immensity fills the thinker. In this particular case, instead of Los filling the void, the void fills Los, fragmenting him into the fallen categories of Newtonian space and time.

> Terrified Los stood in the Abyss & his immortal limbs
> Grew deadly pale: he became what he beheld: for a red
> Round Globe sunk down from his Bosom into the Deep in pangs
> He hoverd over it trembling & weeping. suspended it shook
> The nether Abyss in tremblings. he wept over it, he cherish'd it
> In deadly sickening pain: till separated into a Female pale

As the cloud that brings the snow: all the while from his Back
A blue fluid exuded into Sinews hardening in the Abyss
Till it separated into a Male Form howling in Jealousy.
                                                                    (3.28–36)

The "Female pale" is of course Enitharmon. She is "pale," as is Los, because of an act of self-deception fundamental to the process of "creation" in which both are involved. When the void fills and fragments Los, it causes him to fragment into his likeness. Paleness in Blake usually connotes desire restrained or repressed.[24] In restraining his creative energies, Los does not totally abdicate his role as a creator—not any more than Urizen/Newton does, in fact. Instead, Los creates Enitharmon in the image of his restrained desire—pale creator, pale creation. His "trembling & weeping" are also symptomatic of the creative drive sublimated, and these symptoms are likewise passed along in the creation of a female who shakes "the nether Abyss in tremblings."

The creation/fragmentation that occurs leads Los to believe that he and Enitharmon are separated by some insurmountable obstacle, a "Male Form howling in Jealousy." Like Enitharmon, however, this male form is the creation of Los's own mind and body, and is separated from Los when, because of fear, he refuses to do anything to halt or control the fragmentation. In this particular case, the spectre that is created bears a striking resemblance to Newtonian absolute space, a resemblance that is hardly accidental. The idea of "A blue fluid . . . hardening in the Abyss" is derived from at least two of Newton's concealed axioms concerning the nature of space. The first of these states *"That the centre of the system of the world is immovable"* (p. 419),[25] that is, that absolute space is rigid. The second of these states that "the matter of the heavens is fluid" (p. 549). The fact that the *locus maledictus* of Los's activity is described alternately as an abyss or a void has to do with Newton's description of absolute space as being *"void of resistance"* (p. 68). Space, absolute or otherwise, of course appears to be blue to the earthbound observer.

Los assumes, as Newton seems to assume, that all the materialistic fragmentation he encounters is "really" going on "out there," that is, that it arises because of an external, "natural" cause that is responsible for all instances of fragmentation, perceived as external, "natural" effect. In doing so, Los is only being "reasonable," in the sense of following the line of logic laid down by Newton in the "Rules of Reasoning in Philosophy" that preface the third book of the *Principia*.[26] The result of Los's being "reasonable" on the basis of his assumptions is bitterly humorous. Believing the cause to be external and doubting his ability to stem the fragmentation, the deluded Los makes fragmentation the law of the universe, using a distinctly Newtonian style of inductive reasoning to do so. And in his longing and lusting after Enitharmon as a discrete being forever fragmented and apart from him, Los participates in the further fragmentation of the universe, by begetting on Enitharmon children who add to the force of the "selfhood explosion," by means of which the universe is populated with discrete little bodies, which are, at least in this context, Blake's visionary rendering of what is implied by Newton's corpuscular theory of matter. A corpuscle is, in the root sense of the Latin, a little body. The irony underlying the whole of Los's project is that he causes additional fragmentation in the very attempt, albeit a deluded one, to end the process by somehow transcending and comprehending what is already deployed in the depths of spectral, rigid, absolute space.

> Within labouring. beholding Without: from Particulars to Generals
> Subduing his Spectre, they builded the Looms of Generation
> They Builded Great Golgonooza Times on Times Ages on Ages
> First Orc was Born then the Shadowy Female: then all of Los's Family
> At last Enitharmon brought Forth Satan Refusing Form, in vain
> The Miller of Eternity made subservient to the Great Harvest
> That he may go to his own Place Prince of the Starry Wheels
>
> (3.37–43)

The reference to the idea of moving "from Particulars to Generals" is Blake's gibing allusion to Newtonian inductive method and summary of it as it, for example, *generalizes*, in the "Rules of Reasoning in Philosophy," about the *particular*, or particle-like nature of matter. The third of the rules would seem to be the one Blake has explicitly in mind. By the use of inductive method, Newton concludes, in the third Rule of Reasoning dealing with matter, that "the hardness of the whole arises from the hardness of the parts, we therefore justly infer the hardness of the undivided particles not only of the bodies we feel but of all others" (p. 399).

Satan's refusal of form is a trait that helps the reader trace his lineage back to Urizen/Newton, as indeed Los and Enitharmon do later in *Milton*, when they discover that "Satan is Urizen / Drawn down by Orc & the Shadowy Female into Generation" (10.1–2). The fact that Satan is the last-born of Los and Enitharmon's children is significant, in the sense that his birth indicates that the limits of "particularization," of fragmentation, have been reached. As the "Miller of Eternity," Satan, who is also the most finely-ground grist of his "mill," has witnessed, both in the creation of his own body and that of the world as the body-image he sees from it, the matter of the fallen world divided as finely as it can be divided. Henceforth, in Blake's theatre of visionary action, the forces of particularization and fragmentation are to be made "subservient to the Great Harvest," made to look inward into living, visionary space, rather than outward into dead, Newtonian space. In so doing, all "human forms" will be "identified" and will therefore be able to put off that corpuscular identity which is selfhood. Under such circumstances, seemingly dead corpuscles will be perceived as actually being living seeds, which throw off their dead husks to become grapes and grain, which in turn throw off their individual identities, in the winepress and the mill, to become wine and bread, which in turn give up their identities in a massive and progressive Eucharist. Ultimately, all of creation becomes the flesh and blood of one body, the one seen at the end of *Jerusalem* walking "To & fro in Eternity as One Man reflecting each in each & clearly seen / And seeing . . . " (98.39–40). The task of bringing this Eucharist to pass is the task of all of Blake's visionary avatar-heroes, Milton, Los, and Albion among them.

Until such a putting off of selfhood is made to occur, however, Satan presides over all that is to be annihilated, known as the world of the Ulro, an "*ul*timate *ratio*" of dead particles acted upon by blind forces, both particles and forces in fact being reflexive to the wills of their self-effacing, self-deceiving creators. Satan's "own place," the very phrase commenting on the solipsistic nature of such a place by echoing Satan's speech in *Paradise Lost*,[27] is that of the presiding spirit, "Prince of the Starry Wheels." This title is yet another gibing reference to the Newtonian model of the universe, in which planets, moons, and comets revolve around "fixed stars" in circular or elliptical orbits, making their motion seem wheel-like. The proprietary role connoted by the phrase "own Place" should also serve to indicate that Satan, rather than being merely the superintendent of these "Starry Wheels," is their creator as well.

The particularization and fragmentation of the universe will never be more complete in any of Blake's other poems than it is at the end of the third plate of *Milton*. It is at this point that affairs begin to reverse, with the recognition, by Los, of Satan's true identity: the latter is the Supreme Being Newton refers to in the General Scholium, the God Newton creates in his own image through the use of concealed hypotheses and assumptions, all the while denying the existence of these hypotheses and assumptions and asserting that the will has no role in promulgating his view of the matter. In a flash of *insight*, Los identifies his multifaceted, yet unitary enemy as Satan/ Newton/the God of Natural Religion/Locke's God revealed by Reason/Urizen.

> O Satan my youngest born, art thou not Prince of the Starry Hosts
> And of the Wheels of Heaven, to turn the Mills day & night?
> Art thou not Newtons Pantocrator weaving the Woof of Locke[?]
> (4.9–11)

The identification of Satan as "Newtons Pantocrator" is a direct reference to the General Scholium, in which Newton has occasion to talk of a "Being" who "governs all things, not as the soul of the world, but as Lord over all; and on account of his dominion he is wont to be called *Lord God* παντοκράτωρ, or *Universal Ruler*; for *God* is a relative word, and has a respect to servants; and *Deity* is the dominion of God not over his own body, as those imagine who fancy God to be the soul of the world, but over servants" (p. 544). The relevance of the idea of "Newtons Pantocrator" in a poem about Milton has to do with Blake's critique of Milton's allegiances in *Paradise Lost*, given in full in *The Marriage of Heaven and Hell*, pl. 5. In that critique, Blake argues that Milton mistook the real Satan, in all of his dissembling humility, for God, who was actually immanent not in Heaven but in the energy of the fallen angels and in the realm of art they created by dint of that energy. The reason that Milton, Los, and Blake himself are all walking about in the "Eternity" (1.16) that frames *Milton* is to begin the task that culminates in the announcement of "All Human Forms identified" at the end of *Jerusalem*. The first step of that task seems to entail calling a pantocrator a pantocrator, thus identifying covert selfhood.

In one important sense, though Milton may have initially been deluded in his allegiances, he saw clearly enough that the Fall was fortunate. For it did lead Adam to turn his gaze from the outer world, which begins to fragment at the very moment that the angels fall, to the inner world, which may be retained as a paradise inviolate, notwithstanding the vicissitudes of "natural," external change. Adam and Eve do have to experience the selfhood that comes from the eating of forbidden fruit in order to realize the limits one faces in attempting to look outward for coherence. The outer world is a realm of fragmentation and particularization; it is the Hell depicted by Milton in Book II of *Paradise Lost*.

> . . . many a Frozen, many a Fiery Alp,
> Rocks, Caves, Lakes, Fens, Bogs, Dens, and shades of death,
> A Universe of death. . . .[28]

Outward lies a "Universe of death"; inward lies something else entirely. Surrounded by that universe as the result of eating the forbidden fruit, Adam, at the behest of Michael, looks inward and sees the deeds of all time spread out before him. As the result of this perception, Adam realizes the delusory nature of fallen time and fragmentation, and he heeds Michael's injunctions in the hope of possessing "A Paradise within . . . happier farr"[29] than the materialist Paradise he is about to leave.

Insight plays the crucial role in Adam's realization, as it does in the realizations of Milton, Los, and Blake. Jehovah the tempter must get *into* Adam and Eve, be ingested as the apple in what is essentially an "anti-Eucharist," in order to force them to look *outward* with his point of view and see the fragmentation that he sees. Similarly, Urizen must get *into* Milton, Satan must get *into* Los, and Newton must get *into* Blake, the last of these, at least, by means of reading, which is but another form of ingestion, witness Blake's reading of/dining with Isaiah and Ezekiel in *The Marriage*. But whereas Isaiah and Ezekiel are "wholesome," in the sense that their "firm perswasion" on issues vouchsafes against the possibility of any deception on their part, Urizen, Satan, and Newton are not "wholesome," in the sense that they do practice deception in the name of reason. One of Blake's "Proverbs of Hell" is to the point: "All wholsom food is caught without a net or a trap" (*MHH*, pl. 7.13). The nature of the "poisonous" reason in question is to impose, with few or no symptoms, an alien point of view on the victim, under the guise of being "natural," thus substituting the selfhood of the "poisoner" for that of the "poisoned" and "killing" the "poisoned" individual, as is the case in "A Poison Tree."[30]

Accordingly, when Los "identifies" Satan, or when Milton and Blake do the same thing to Urizen and Newton, respectively, two steps are involved. The first of these has to do with the recognition that the figure "identified" is only seen to be *outside* because he has "poisoned," or gotten *inside*, his victim. Los sees Satan as "Newton's Pantocrator" because Satan has managed to put that "Pantocrator" *inside* Los by "poisoning" him, either with food for the body or food for the mind, if in fact a distinction can be made between the two in the world of symbolic action of Blake's poetry.

The second step involved in "identifying" Satan has to do with replacing the "poison" of another selfhood imposing its views on its victim with the healthy food of self-nurture. Only by this means can one freely create the world in one's own image and then merge in full plenitude and likeness with that image.

Thus it is, at the point when fragmentation has reached its utmost limit and Satan is "identified" by Los that Blake, by means of a marvelous transposition, is able to turn the dead and potentially "poisonous" Newtonian corpuscles into living seeds of the life of humanity to come. At a later point in *Milton*, Los will be able to proclaim the plenitude of those seeds, harvested as grain and grape, the stuff of bread and wine, flesh and blood. "Fellow Labourers! The Great Vintage & Harvest is now upon Earth / The whole extent of the Globe is explored" (25.17–18). But at the outset of the struggle in *Milton*, the outcome seems very much in doubt. The seeds of the humanity to come must be made to grow, which means that they must be regarded and responded to as though there were a life force within their apparently lifeless exteriors, a life force in need of liberation and nurture. Only in such a manner can the collective power of the life force within be revealed, and only in such a manner can that collective life force merge so as to liberate its full apocalyptic energy, "To go forth," as Milton does at the end of the poem bearing his name, "to the Great Harvest & Vintage of the Nations" (43.1).

NOTES

1 The present essay grows out of a discussion and dialogue begun with George S. Rousseau in the meeting of the Literature and Science section of the 1978 MLA convention, where I delivered a paper entitled "Visionary Semantics: Blake, Newton, and the Language of Scientific Authority," currently in circulation. Rousseau himself delivered "Literature and Science: Decoding the State of the Field" in a special session convened to discuss the implications of his paper and the papers of those presenting in the section for new and future directions in literature and science. Rousseau's paper, slightly reworked, appears as "Literature and Science: The State of the Field," *Isis*, 9 (1978), 583–91. In it, he claims that the current vogue of structuralist and post-structuralist approaches to the history of ideas have rendered traditional approaches to literature and science moribund, if not obsolete. For example, the rise to prominence of Michel Foucault, "all of whose books inherently deal with literature and science," had the result of repelling "most serious students then [i.e., in

the sixties] . . . and had the further effect of transforming old categories, in a sense rendering them obsolete. The question for someone writing about science and literature changed from 'what type of critic are you?' to 'how much self-consciousness do you have about your methodology?'" (p. 589). This essay constitutes a response to Rousseau's gloomy portrayal of the field and, it is hoped, one conceptual approach to the field that can arrogate to itself the close analysis of rhetoric that is at the heart of the structuralist and post-structuralist methodologies, while at the same time dealing with recognizable scientific and literary texts in a manner that is plausible, if not wholly conventional. In its original form, the essay was presented at a seminar chaired by John Neubauer and entitled "Conceptual Approaches to Literature and Science in the Eighteenth Century." The seminar was convened at the 1979 meeting of ASECS, held in Atlanta.

2 See *Science and Imagination* (Ithaca, N.Y.: Cornell University Press, 1956), ch. V, "The Scientific Background of Swift's *Voyage to Laputa*," pp. 110–54.

3 *The Poetry and Prose of William Blake*, ed. David V. Erdman, commentator Harold Bloom (Garden City, N.Y.: Doubleday, 1965), pl. 98, ll. 27 ff. Subsequent references to Blake will be to this text, and will appear in the text of the essay, cited by plate, plate and line, or page and line, as appropriate.

4 Newton's conception of absolute space is made clear in Book I, Section II, of the *Principia*. The passage quoted in the text of the essay may be found in *Sir Isaac Newton, Principia*, trans. Andrew Motte, rev. Florian Cajori, 2 vols. (Berkeley and Los Angeles: University of California Press, 1934), p. 549. Subsequent references to the *Principia* will be to this edition and will be made by page number only in the text of the essay. The rationale for omitting the volume number is that the Cajori edition uses running pagination, even though it is printed in two volumes. Newton's conception of absolute time, i.e., a framed, six-thousand-year Biblical chronology, is made clear elsewhere, in *Observations on the Prophecies of Daniel and the Apocalypse of St. John in Two Parts*, 2 vols. (London: J. Roberts, 1733).

5 See note 4 for Newton on absolute space and time.

6 See Nicolson's *Newton Demands the Muse: Newton's "Opticks" and the Eighteenth Century Poets* (Princeton: Princeton University Press, 1946); Schwartz's *Samuel Johnson and the New Science* (Madison: University of Wisconsin Press, 1971); and Jacob's *The Newtonians and the English Revolution, 1689–1720* (Ithaca, N.Y.: Cornell University Press, 1976).

7 On Pope and Addison, see *Newton Demands the Muse*, pp. 123–64. On Johnson, see *Samuel Johnson . . . Science*, pp. 59–93.

8 A fuller elaboration than can be made here has been made in my "Blake on Space and Time," forthcoming in *Science/Technology and the Humanities*. Briefly, it might be noted that the Four Zoas, as they approach the condition of instantaneous change at the end of *Jerusalem*, also approach the condition of light, under circumstances in which the newly merged cate-

gories of space and time become one and the same, existing in a contin-uum. The energy exhibited by the Four Zoas, which appears as consum-ing fire to the fallen and as delight to the redeemed, is derived from the ability of the "matter" of the Zoas to change instantaneously—with the speed of light, in fact. The space-time continuum Blake is describing in his visionary way, a continuum in which energy is liberated by matter moving at the speed of light, is, in its essentials, very close to the contin-uum described by Einstein in his world-shaking equation $e = mc^2$.

9 For a good and pithy restatement of this position for a modern critical audience, see Stanley E. Fish, "Normal Circumstances, Literal Language, Direct Speech Acts, the Ordinary, the Everyday, the Obvious, What Goes without Saying, and Other Special Cases," *Critical Inquiry*, 4 (1978), 625–44.

10 For Gleckner's discussion, see "Most Holy Forms of Thought: Some Ob-servations on Blake and Language," *ELH*, 41 (1974), 555–77. My "Vision-ary Semantics" is discussed in note 1.

11 The sense is that of a corpus, the term used by linguists to describe a body of utterances made and recorded diachronically, as opposed to the total number of possible utterances in the language deployed synchronically. See Claude Lévi-Strauss, *Le cru et le cuit* (Paris: Plon, 1964), especially the conclusion. See also Jonathan Culler, *Structuralist Poetics* (Ithaca, N.Y.: Cornell University Press, 1975), pp. 43 ff.

12 *The Marriage of Heaven and Hell*, pls. 22–23, makes as much clear. Accord-ing to Blake, "The Worship of God is. Honouring his gifts in other men, each according to his genius." And "if Jesus is the Greatest man, you ought to love him in the greatest degree." The Gospels were written by those who loved such a "man of genius," and thus the Gospels exhibited the genius of those who wrote them.

13 See Ault's *Visionary Physics: Blake's Response to Newton* (Chicago: University of Chicago Press, 1974); his "Incommensurability and Interconnection in Blake's Anti-Newtonian Text," *Studies in Romanticism*, 16 (1977), 277–303; and Curtis's "Blake and the 'Moment of Time': An Eighteenth-Century Controversy in Mathematics," *Philological Quarterly*, 51 (1972), 460–70.

14 See *Visionary Physics* and *Newton Demands the Muse*.

15 *The Rhetoric of Science: A Study of Scientific Imagery and Ideas in Eighteenth-Century English Poetry* (Berkeley and Los Angeles: University of California Press, 1966), p. 97.

16 For a full discussion of this "father-son" relationship, see Frank E. Man-uel, *A Portrait of Isaac Newton* (Cambridge, Mass.: Harvard University Press, 1968), pp. 23–35, 51–67.

17 See "Incommensurability and Interconnection," cited above. See also J. E. McGuire and P. M. Rattansi, "Newton and the 'Pipes of Pan,'" *Notes and Records of the Royal Society of London*, 21 (1966), 108–43, also cited by Ault, p. 277n.

18 Newton begins by talking of the *"five primary planets, Mercury, Venus, Mars, Jupiter, and Saturn"* (p. 403), then proves that the earth exhibits similar properties of motion, talking finally of the six in the General Scholium, p. 543.

19 See note 8.

20 *Visionary Physics*, pp. 96–140.

21 In a letter to his brother James, dated January 30, 1803, Blake writes that he goes "on Merrily with my Greek & Latin . . . as I find it very Easy . . . " (in *Blake*, ed. Erdman, p. 696).

22 For a fuller discussion of Newton's meaning and his dilemma, see Colin Murray Turbayne, *The Myth of Metaphor* (1962; rpt. Columbia, S.C.: University of South Carolina Press, 1970), pp. 44–45.

23 *Harper's Latin Dictionary*, eds. Charlton T. Lewis and Charles Short, rev. ed. (1879; rpt. New York: Harper Brothers, 1907), p. 750.

24 The connotation is consistent and of long standing, going all the way back to Blake's earliest preserved writings. See, for example, the Ossianic fragment "then She bore Pale desire," contemporaneous with *Poetical Sketches* (1783), in *Blake*, ed. Erdman, pp. 437–39.

25 For Ault's comments, see *Visionary Physics*, pp. 155–56.

26 These rules, found on pp. 398–400, attempt to standardize the causes of apparently similar phenomena, the covert motivation being to move toward a view of the universe in which formal cause and efficient cause proceed from one and the same source—God.

27 "The mind is its own place, and in it self / Can make a Heav'n of Hell, a Hell of Heav'n" (II.254–55).

28 Ll. 620–22.

29 XII.587.

30 The speaker of that poem puts his selfhood into the seemingly selfless task of tending a tree, rather than confronting the friend who angers him. As the result of his choice of strategies, the tree produces an apple which, like the apple in the Garden, is a deceptive form of selfhood.

> And I waterd it in fears,
> Night & morning with my tears:
> And I sunned it with my smiles,
> And with soft deceitful wiles
> (ll. 5–8)

When the speaker's friend steals, and presumably eats, the apple, he is seen to be "outstretched beneath the tree" (l. 16)—"dead," in the sense of having been deprived of his free and autonomous selfhood. For the speaker, now "inside" his erstwhile friend, has taken over that selfhood. Without the full Gothic trappings, the concept seems very much like that of the vampire, interest in which grew and evolved during the late eighteenth and nineteenth centuries. On the other hand, Blake may be viewed as being caught up in the same currents of thought that led Sade to write of the utter possession of one individual by another. See Michel Foucault, "Language to Infinity," in *Language, Counter-Memory, Practice: Selected Essays and Interviews*, trans. Donald F. Bouchard and Sherry Simon (Ithaca, N.Y.: Cornell University Press, 1977), pp. 53–67, esp. 60–63, 65–66.

Diderot's Connoisseurship: Ethics and Aesthetics of the Art Trade

MICHAEL T. CARTWRIGHT

The place of Art in Society, and the strictures placed by certain social values on the function of Art, gave rise to very considerable problems in Diderot's mind, but one principle remained constant. Art, insofar as it can be abstracted from the vehicles of its expression, leads to the noble ideals of Beauty, Truth, and Goodness. As a theoretician and as a critic, Diderot's guiding motive was an elevation of Taste, both individual and public, leading to entirely beneficent understanding of the processes of the creative imagination.

This very simple formula reflects in only the most general way the complex ramifications of the enquiry that has followed Lester Crocker's seminal work on subjectivism and objectivism in Diderot's aesthetics.[1] It underscores a basic moral attitude which cannot be challenged, but which does indeed admit of interesting questions and interpretations if one cares to examine in detail certain functions of Diderot as critic of the plastic arts. For painting and sculpture, although they stimulate aesthetic enjoyment of the most elevated kind, are tinged with a danger inherent in their very material nature. They are objects, presented for our contemplation and, since they bear the indelible mark of the human presence, they arouse the desire of annexation and possession. A work of literature, of music, or of the theatre can only be possessed through the shared medium of print or performance. The literary and the performing arts are there-fore "purer" in a moral sense that Diderot would perhaps have been reluctant to admit, but which is easily deduced from a number of his pronouncements.

I have chosen to approach this question through the notion of con-noisseurship because "connoisseur" is a title that Diderot would not have refused, and at the same time it offers a challenge to the way in which he perceived himself as a critic.

A few matters of definition are indispensable. In the middle part of the eighteenth century, the terms "amateur" and "connaisseur" were used to some extent indiscriminately, but in the *Supplément* to the *En-cyclopédie*, Marmontel elaborates upon the meaning of the former term to give it an almost entirely pejorative cast: "la foule des ama-teurs est composée d'une espèce d'hommes qui, n'ayant par eux-mêmes ni qualités, ni talents qui les distinguent, et voulant être dis-tingués, s'attachent aux arts et aux lettres, comme le gui au chêne, ou le lierre à l'ormeau." The definition of "connaisseur" is consider-ably milder: "en fait d'ouvrages de peintres, ou autres qui ont le des-sein pour base, (connaisseur) renferme moins l'idée d'un goût décidé pour cet art, qu'un discernement certain pour en juger." The author here is Landois, but one may suppose a general semantic distinction by which "amateur" implies the self-appointed expert whose taste depends at best upon the whim of fashion and who, at worst, has the presumption and the necessary force of patronage to dictate the technique of the artist. In the preliminary remarks to the *Salon* of 1767, which appear to have inspired Marmontel's article, Diderot ful-minates against the "race des amateurs," and not so much against their pretensions as against the way in which they "s'interposent entre l'homme opulent et l'artiste indigent; . . . font payer au talent la protection qu'ils lui accordent, qui lui ouvrent ou ferment les portes; qui se servent du besoin qu'il a d'eux pour disposer de son temps; qui le mettent à contribution; qui lui arrachent à vil prix ses meilleures productions; qui sont à l'affût, embusqué [sic] derrière son chevalet."[2]

In this way the artist's livelihood is decided, not by real merit, but by arbitrary judgement based upon social privilege, either real or as-sumed. Diderot expands his argument to criticize the injustice of the lowly status given to painters, and it is clear that he himself shares responsibility, although unwillingly, in this act of judgement. As a preliminary to his criticism of the *amateurs*, he describes how the art-ist Oudry sold a picture of a dog to d'Holbach and refused to go back upon his contract even when other would-be buyers offered double the agreed price. Oudry's reported words are: "Non, monsieur non. . . . Je suis trop heureux que mon meilleur ouvrage appartienne à un homme qui en connaisse le prix. Je ne consens à rien. Je n'accepterai rien; et ma chienne vous restera."[3]

This is an ideal transaction, moral in every sense of the word, even in its recounting. If we recall for an instant the words of Landois, it will be clear that the connoisseur is one who judges with accuracy and impartiality: the critical stance to which Diderot aspired. However, included in it is the notion of *prix* considered also as a monetary value, and of judgement that leads to acquisition.

Diderot's discomfort when faced with the duality of this situation can be seen in his reactions to the eighteenth-century *amateur par excellence*, the comte de Caylus. Everyone remembers that Diderot supplied the acid epitaph,

> Ci-gît un antiquaire acariâtre et brusque,
> Oh qu'il est bien logé dans cette cruche étrusque.

In fact, Diderot's hatred of Caylus is based upon distinctions of class and upon personal jealousy rather than upon any clearly documented evidence of Caylus's incompetence or injustice. Jean Seznec has defined the rivalry felt by Diderot, who wished to be a friend and an adviser to artists, as was Caylus.[4] Diderot had not made the essential pilgrimage to Italy, as had Caylus, of course, and there can be little doubt that Diderot *philosophe* viewed with mixed feelings at best, the fact that Caylus's house was decorated with elaborate displays of original antiquities. Inspiring as they doubtless were, the engravings of works by Poussin that hung on the walls of Diderot's study were indeed engravings, and the work in which they are catalogued, the *Regrets sur ma vieille robe de chambre*, is dominated by a rhetorical style and such a tirade against the evils of luxury that we should, I think, be on our guard against interpreting Diderot's moralism on the exact level at which he takes such obvious pains to state it. There has at most times been a very close correlation between patronage and artistic production. Despite his criticisms of the "goût des Fermiers Généraux," Diderot was certainly aware that, without this market, French art of his time would have been poorer, national prestige would have been lower, and, in fact, the freedom of expression of the artist would have been considerably limited. Throughout his writings on Art, Diderot turns, sometimes with remarkable disingenuousness, to the models of Antiquity, but by an unfortunate irony it was this very Antiquity that Caylus, and of course, his successors, made every effort to document and to re-create with scientific precision.

In his essay "The Transformation of Art into Culture," Rémy Saisselin has shown how the *philosophes*, in their fight against Art as an aristocratic privilege, with "collecting, cupidity, love, greed, study, scholarship, imitation, play, style" as its motivating forces, were anxious to channel artistic expression towards education and the improvement of mankind.[5] The taste for bourgeois realism was an outcome of this new sensibility, but so too was the tendency to see the work of art as an article to be catalogued and preserved. The word "museum" becomes current during the course of the eighteenth century, and there is born with it the high-minded spirit of curatorship. Caylus exercised a diligent curatorial function: his greatest crime was his aristocratic indifference to expertise other than his own, and the deployment of sufficient wealth to acquire those artefacts of past civilizations he found significant.

In accepting the task of the *Salons*, Diderot was also assuming a role of authority, not merely for an assessment of the contemporary works exhibited at the Louvre, but for the body of art history into which his observations would necessarily be integrated. It seems impossible to believe that he was entirely unconscious of this function of his criticism which, furthermore, could not be undertaken without points of reference, antecedents and comparisons. Gita May has given a list of old masters mentioned frequently by Diderot, and an equally interesting catalogue of important painters of both the recent and the distant past of whom he seems to have been ignorant.[6] Some of the latter were indeed known to the eighteenth-century public, and the former are headed by Raphaël, Rubens, Poussin, Rembrandt, Le Sueur, and Van Dyck. All these are "safe" names with which Diderot's readers were most likely familiar, either through direct observation or through much-repeated description and discussion. Professor May concludes that Diderot's historical references are hardly innovative and that his taste was very much the general taste of his time. There are indeed moments in the *Salons* when it seems that Diderot is repeating a critical observation at second hand, since the name of a painter is dropped into a description and, once a parallel is made, the subject is abandoned. This is not to suggest that he pretended an expertise that he did not possess. He was fully aware that his connoisseurship would always be incomplete without a wider range of comparisons upon which he might draw. However, his traditionalism and his reticence were perhaps conditioned too by his knowledge that the very history of art was establishing itself through the ethically and morally doubtful forces of ownership.

In the second of the Andrew W. Mellon Lectures on the History of Art, 1978, Joseph Alsop has spoken of art collecting as the "basic element in a larger system of phenomena; and in this system, art collecting, art history and an art market are the irreducible triad."[7] He points out that, since Vasari, the Western tradition of art history has been built upon the *authentication* of works by a specific artist. This has bestowed upon them canonical excellence from which a currency, a market value, cannot be dissociated.

At the moment when Diderot turned his attention to art criticism, this process was well advanced, although it was by no means as absolute as it is today. An art market existed, and there were individuals such as Mariette and Lazare-Duvaux who exercised a function that we may recognize as dealership.[8] However, they did not, through systematic personal acquisition, evaluation and re-sale, organize a trade. In practically all cases, acquisition was made through direct negotiation with the artist. Moreover, the price asked for a commission—and this was particularly true of portraiture—could vary wildly with the rank of the purchaser and the moment of the sale. It must not be forgotten either that the second half of the eighteenth century was marked by a steadily increasing rate of inflation and that then, as now, there was every incentive to invest in material objects of high quality.[9] Diderot disapproved of ostentatious displays of wealth; at the same time he was forced to admit that the taste of his time was the taste which all Europe sought to imitate or to import directly. Furthermore, the very existence of the Salons could hardly fail to stimulate a wider appetite for works of art, particularly amongst those social classes which were rapidly achieving the financial power necessary for prestigious collecting.

It is hardly surprising that Diderot's feelings were mixed when he stepped into this turbulent stream, and he did so warily. As Virgil Topazio has shown, the *Correspondance littéraire* and the *Salons* produced by Grimm provided a very adequate model of the form that Diderot's reporting should take.[10] There is, however, an air of hesitation in the *Salons* of 1759 and 1761, and an air of mockery which cannot be attributed entirely to initiation and an unfamiliar genre. It is as if the official, academic nature of the occasion were being acknowledged and then almost immediately disregarded. The subscribers to the *Correspondance littéraire* are being given the aristocratic privilege of a personal but often irreverential account of an event which they themselves cannot attend, but of which they must be made to feel a part. This strain of confidentiality runs throughout the *Salons* and it forms, of course, the basis of the literary readability for which they are so much praised. Without placing in jeopardy the significance of this quality, it does seem possible to claim that Diderot became swiftly attached to it in a way that stultified the potential of his critical knowledge. I am not suggesting that for each painting or sculpture described he should have indicated a price evaluation, but that his references could have been wider and his observations more acute. If we limit ourselves to the strictly contemporaneous, it seems not unreasonable to ask why we are not given a wider account of the *scène de genre* in the work of Chardin, or why the drawings of Greuze, to which Diderot must surely have been attracted since he was an admirer of Greuze's sketches for finished paintings, are not discussed. That these works were not always seen at the Salon is not really a sufficient reason, since Diderot's art of digression was more than capable of assimilating them.

In fact, the *Salons* are cast early in a mould of general reference that demanded some knowledge of painting on the part of the reader, and that guaranteed the largest possible measure of liberty for the author. The very many ways in which this liberty was used are, of course, remarkable, but even the most intensive modern analyses of the *Salons* lead back to literary themes.[11] It may be argued that the very nature of painting in the eighteenth century renders this inevitable. I am suggesting that Diderot adopted a style of narrative that placed his art criticism in a particular mode where questions of authentication, patronage and ownership, and with them, wider historical implications, could be kept to a minimum.

When a material and commercial consideration does arise, it strikes us as coming from an almost alien set of values and references. In the *Salon* of 1765 there is, for example, a passage where the expertise of the dealer Mariette is compared with that of a jeweller who may distinguish from the smallest detail the identity and value of a precious stone.[12] This in turn leads to a discussion of engraving, which became a collector's passion in the eighteenth century, since it offered the ultimate refinement in the appreciation of authentication and graphic detail. As a corollary, it should be remembered that collections of engravings were generally not displayed but catalogued in drawers and folders, becoming a variety of semi-secret currency in their own right.

It is significant that after the prodigious effort of the *Salon* of 1767, Diderot's interest in the genre flags appreciably. Yet his interest in works of art and the function of the artist continues until his death with unabated vigour. It is as if, with the obligation of composing the *Salons* reduced, and finally dispersed, Diderot feels able to concentrate his attention upon specific problems where well-developed expertise was a necessity. At the end of the 1760s and during the 1770s his accumulated experience bears fruit in a way that points to what is almost a distinct category of aesthetic ideas, one that is marked by an intense interest in questions of technique, and by direct participation in the business of acquiring works of art. This activity of Diderot's later years hinges upon his friendship with the sculptor Falconet and the role of agent that both men played in securing paintings for the collections of Catherine II.

The Diderot-Falconet correspondence is significant to our purpose here, not so much for the theme of posterity as for the way in which it led to a sharpening of Diderot's critical faculty. For Falconet was no easy acquaintance in the manner of Chardin or Michel Van Loo, patiently explaining his art as best he could to the enthusiastic man of letters. In his *Observations sur la Statue de Marc Aurèle*, Falconet rejects utterly the value of "literary" judgements and sets himself against "appreciations which have little to do with the actual form and craftsmanship of the individual work under consideration."[13] At the same time he was a model of diligence and probity, accepting only half the sum offered for the execution of the statue of Peter the Great in St. Petersbourg.

Diderot, intrigued by Falconet's honesty and obstinacy, recognizing the sculptor's talent, cannot admit that his own literary sensibility should be dismissed so lightly. The famous letter of 2 May, 1773, a reply to the *Observations*, is an impassioned analysis of the expertise of both artist and *littérateur*. However, in the middle of it there arises the interesting admission that perhaps the dealer in pictures acquires, through the experience of earning his livelihood, a critical faculty of a wholly superior variety:

> Rémy, Ménageot, Collin ne sont ni peintres, ni statuaires, ni littérateurs. Ils sont de purs et simples commerçants en tableaux. Cependent ils en jugent mieux qu'aucun peintre, littérateur ou artiste; et si le littérateur fait hausser les épaules au peintre, et si le peintre en rit, le peintre fait hausser les épaules au brocanteur, et le littérateur rit à son tour. Est-ce que le brocanteur s'entend mieux en dessin, en couleur, en magie de clair-obscur qu'aucun de nous? — Aucunement; mais il a passé quarante ans de sa vie à voir, à comparer, à acheter, à vendre. Ses connaissances sont le résultat de son temps, de sa fortune.[14]

This may be read as an example of Diderot's belief in the powers of specific perfectibility, but it is also a vindication in part of the role that he had played to such good effect two years earlier when he had helped to acquire the Crozat collection for Catherine. This task, and the other commissions undertaken from the time of the Gaignat sale in 1768, may be followed through the Roth-Varloot edition of Diderot's correspondence, with the essential complement of the inventory of letters from the Tronchin Archive brought to light by Jean-Daniel Candaux.[15]

Even with the modest prosperity of his old age, Diderot could not become a collector in his own right, but as an agent for a patroness as demanding as Catherine, and especially when he could act with the encouragement of such knowledgeable friends as Grimm and Falconet, he became a more complete connoisseur than one could ever imagine from the evidence of the *Salons*. After the Gaignat sale he expresses unabashed pride in having secured the cream of the collection:

> J'ai acquis à la vente Gaignat, pour Sa Majesté Impériale, cinq des plus beaux tableaux qu'il y ait en France: un Murillo, trois Gérard Dow, et un J.-B. Vanloo. La somme est assez forte, quoiqu'elle soit très au-dessous du mérite de ces morceaux.[16]

In the same letter to Falconet he does not hesitate to press for speedy settlement of his expenses and to suggest that a credit placed at his disposal could assure more interesting purchases. In August 1767, and again in May 1769, he transmits the information that La Live de Jully is suffering a mental illness and that the Empress should negociate immediately a *private* purchase of his collection.[17] This tactic was an extremely important one since it protected the buyer from the notorious vagaries of the public market, and notably from the machinations of the "amateurs." For this very reason the help of the brothers Tronchin, and particularly that of the conseiller François, is enlisted for the spectacular *coup* of the Crozat sale in 1771. Between January of that year and July 1772, the multiple exchanges of communication between Diderot, Grimm, the Tronchins, the Prince Galitzine and Falconet are filled with the particular enthusiasm of evaluation, negotiation, the drawing up of a complete catalogue of the treasures to be acquired. After much feverish activity, the Crozat-Thiers family settled for a sum of 460,000 livres, in January 1772.[18] Three months later, and in the light of another large, but this time public sale, they were able to judge how astute Diderot had been. On 17 April, 1772, he writes to Falconet:

> On vient de finir la vente des tableaux de M. de Choiseul. Le départ de ceux du baron de Thiers pour Pétersbourg, la concurrence de M. de Laborde et de Mme du Barry, et d'autres causes qui tiennent à la personne de M. de Choiseul, ont fait monter cette vente à un prix exorbitant. Cent cinquante tableaux ont été achetés 444,000 livres, tandis que nous en avions eu, trois mois auparavant, cinq cents pour 460,000 livres. Aussi les héritiers du baron de Thiers jettent-ils feu et flammes.[19]

The exploit was a complete success, and it appears to have given Diderot a satisfaction that whetted his appetite for more. Four years after the Crozat sale he informs Grimm that a number of the most famous Parisian collectors have died and that there could hardly be a more opportune moment for Catherine to make even further additions to her store of pictures. The quality of the works that will shortly become available is of the highest, and international competition (a factor upon which Diderot is now well informed) is at its lowest. "Ainsi," he writes, "voilà pour cinq à six millions de tableaux à l'encan, et tous à la fois; et dans un moment où il n'y a point d'acquéreurs ni en France, ni en Allemagne, ni en Angleterre."[20]

There is, of course, no absolute moral judgement to be made on these activities. Diderot himself is clearly proud of them. After the Crozat sale he announces to Falconet with a note of pride:

> Je jouis de la haine publique la mieux décidée, et savez-vous pourquoi? Parce que je vous envoie des tableaux. Les amateurs crient, les artistes crient; les riches crient. Malgré tous ces cris et tous ces criards, je vais mon train, et le diable s'en mêlera, ou incessamment je vous expédierai toute la galerie Thiers.[21]

The export of works of art serves as a criticism of the established order and of the corrupt financial institutions upon which it is based. In the cause of enlightened knowledge, whether it be transmitted through philosophical discourse or aesthetic appreciation, political frontiers have no real meaning. The dispersal of part of a national patrimony was seen, in 1770, as a regrettable but inevitable result of national weakness.

In these ultimate pronouncements of Diderot as art critic there is, as one might expect, a definite strain of fatalism, but there is also a tonic sense of realism. Having enumerated the great collectors who have died in 1776, he confronts the question of the market value of a painting with complete lucidity:

> Un tableau considéré en lui-même, quelque beau qu'il soit, n'a pourtant qu'une certaine valeur au delà de laquelle son prix est de pure fantaisie. Ce prix de fantaisie n'a point de limites. Il dépend absolument du nombre, de la richesse, de la vanité, de la jalousie, et de la fureur des amateurs. Or j'ai beau tournoyer dans Paris, je n'y vois aucun millionnaire enthousiaste des beaux-arts.[22]

To reach this state of understanding and, within its moral imperfections, to build a satisfying moral aesthetic, was clearly no easy task for Diderot. The gradual acceptance of the function of connoisseurship provided a very considerable step along the way.

NOTES

1 Lester G. Crocker, *Two Diderot Studies: Ethics and Aesthetics* (Baltimore: The Johns Hopkins Press, 1952).
2 Diderot, *Salons*, ed. Jean Seznec and Jean Adhémar (Oxford: Clarendon Press, 1957–67), III, 55.
3 Ibid.
4 Jean Seznec, *Essais sur Diderot et l'antiquité* (Oxford: Clarendon Press, 1957), pp. 79–96.
5 Rémy G. Saisselin, "The Transformation of Art into Culture: From Pascal to Diderot," *Studies on Voltaire and the Eighteenth Century*, LXX (1970), 193–218.
6 Gita May, *Diderot et Baudelaire, critiques d'art* (Geneva: Droz, 1957), p. 53.
7 Joseph Alsop, "Art History and Art Collecting," reprinted in *The Times Literary Supplement*, July 28, 1978, pp. 851–53.
8 Maurice Rheims, *La Vie étrange des objets* (Paris: Collection 10:18, 1959), pp. 96–106.
9 Jean Fourastié, *Documents pour l'histoire et la théorie des prix* (Paris: Armand Colin, n.d.).
10 Virgil W. Topazio, "Art Criticism in the Enlightenment," *Studies on Voltaire and the Eighteenth Century*, XXVII (1963), 1639–56.
11 The most significant recent example is the study by Michael Fried, "Absorption: A Master Theme in Eighteenth-Century French Painting and Criticism," *Eighteenth-Century Studies*, vol. 9 (1975–76), no. 2, pp. 139–77.
12 Diderot, *Salons*, II, 225.
13 H. Dieckmann and J. Seznec, "The Horse of Marcus Aurelius: A Controversy between Diderot and Falconet," *Journal of the Warburg and Courtauld Institutes*, 15 (1952). For a full account of the Diderot-Falconet friendship,

see Anne Betty Weinshenker, *Falconet: His Writings and his Friend Diderot* (Geneva: Droz, 1966).

14 Diderot, *Oeuvres complètes*, ed. Roger Lewinter (Paris: Club français du Livre, 1969–73), X, 1028–29. The Roth-Varloot edition of Diderot's *Correspondance* has been usefully integrated into the Lewinter edition. All further references will be made to this source.

15 Jean-Daniel Candaux, "Le Manuscrit 180 des Archives Tronchin," *Dix-Huitième Siècle* (1970), no. 2, pp. 13–32.

16 Diderot, *Oeuvres complètes*, VIII, 835.

17 Ibid., VII, 547–48; VIII, 850.

18 For the sale contract, see Diderot, *Oeuvres complètes*, X, 874.

19 Ibid., X, 901.

20 Ibid., XI, 1169–70.

21 Ibid., IX, 1007–8.

22 Ibid., XI, 1170.

The Art of Landscape Gardening
in Goethe's Novel
Die Wahlverwandtschaften

MARLIS MEHRA

When Goethe's third novel *Die Wahlverwandtschaften* appeared in 1809, it immediately gave rise to controversy and criticism. One aspect, which provoked negative comments from Goethe's contemporaries, was the importance given to landscape gardening. Some critics declared that the very subject of landscape gardening had become too prominent in the novel.[1] Others maintained that Goethe had incorporated his own experiences in improving the Park of Weimar without molding them into an integrated and artistic whole.[2] The most severe criticism in this respect was voiced by the Austrian playwright Franz Grillparzer in 1841 who, although he held *Die Wahlverwandtschaften* in high regard, disliked the importance given to gardening activities in the beginning of the novel:

> Was in diesen Wahlverwandtschaften am meisten stört, ist gleich von vornherein die widerliche Wichtigkeit, die den Parkanlagen, kleinlichen Baulichkeiten und dergleichen Zeug, fast parallel mit der Haupthandlung, gegeben wird. Es ist als ob man ein Stück aus Goethes Leben läse, der auch seine unvergleichlichen Gaben dadurch zum Teil paralysiert hat, daß er fast gleichen Anteil an derlei Zeitverderb wie an den wichtigsten Angelegenheiten seines eigentlichsten Berufes nahm.[3]

239

From our present point of view this negative criticism from Goethe's contemporaries seems quite astonishing, because later critics have usually considered the gardening as well as the landscape descriptions a significant part of the novel's intricate symbolic design.[4] The interpretations by Walther Killy, Keith Dickson, and H. G. Barnes have shown, moreover, how well integrated with the development of the plot and the characters—either as a setting for the action, as a means of psychological insight into the characters and their developing love relationships, or as a technique of foreshadowing future events—the gardening and landscape descriptions really are.[5] On closer examination, therefore, much of the criticism by Goethe's contemporaries has proved to be groundless. Yet the question remains: why did they tend to perceive the treatment of landscape gardening in this novel so negatively? Since their opinions were based on subjective impressions rather than on a methodical literary analysis which relates specific features of the work to the entire structure, the gardening descriptions may have seemed obtrusive because they conveyed so much obvious cultural information. Already K. W. F. Solger pointed out in his well-known letter about *Die Wahlverwandtschaften* that the novel contained so much that was in fashion at that time, such as the art of landscape gardening, the love for medieval art, and the representation of tableaux vivants.[6] Solger also noticed the artistry with which these matters were treated but which other contemporary critics failed to see. They may have considered the cultural documentation of the novel as unnecessary ballast, as unmolded subject matter, as pure "Stoff," if we may apply Schiller's aesthetic terminology here.[7]

Most critics of *Die Wahlverwandtschaften* have concentrated their analyses on the symbolic significance of the setting and the descriptions of nature rather than on the gardening descriptions *per se*. To my knowledge, there is no interpretation dealing specifically with their historical and cultural context as well as their symbolic implications. In the present study I propose to fill this gap. I proceed specifically from the gardening and not from the landscape descriptions and attempt to situate the old gardens and the new landscape park, depicted in Goethe's *Wahlverwandtschaften*, in their historical and cultural context. Contemporary descriptions of existing landscape gardens in Weimar, Wörlitz, Hohenheim, and Seifersdorf are used as references and the historical development of the English gardening movement, in England as well as in Germany, provides the necessary cultural background.[8] From such a historical comparison the unique features of the garden descriptions in Goethe's novel should clearly emerge and allow us to draw well-founded conclusions about their symbolic implications.

In order to examine the charge made by some contemporaries that Goethe had incorporated his own experiences in landscape gardening in his novel, let us briefly consider his involvement in improving the Park of Weimar. Upon his instigation, the park was gradually transformed into an English landscape garden during the period from 1778 to 1797. Goethe took an active part in these projects only at the very beginning, while he was living in his cottage in the Park of Weimar, where he also designed his own gardens. Later on, after his return from Italy, he only served as an advisor, especially when the "Roman House" was built in the park under his supervision during the Duke of Weimar's absence. Thus, Goethe's active involvement was limited largely to the late 1770's and the early 1780's. During this time, a rapid change in gardening fashions took place in Germany, for the formal and geometrical French garden style was quickly superseded by the free and irregular English manner of landscape gardening. Many formal French gardens were now destroyed to make room for the new English landscape gardens, which were laid out everywhere in the sentimental fashion of the time. Garden designers strove to create great contrast and diversity, because they wanted to express a variety of emotions and moods. Serene and pastoral scenes were designed to alternate with sombre and melancholic ones, thus evoking emotions of joy as well as of sadness, solitude, death, and grief.[9] Graves, urns, and memorials to dead family members and friends now became popular garden decorations. The erection of such a memorial was Goethe's first attempt at landscape gardening. In a mood of Wertherism, a young lady of the court, Christel von Lassberg, had drowned herself in the river Ilm in January 1778. Her body—with a copy of Werther in her pocket—was found near Goethe's garden house and pulled from the river by his servants. To commemorate her death, Goethe had a number of steps cut into the rocks above the river Ilm and a stone bench set up so that one might view the path where Christel had last walked and contemplate the place where she had drowned.[10] This spot was called "die Felsentreppe."

Although still in the sentimental and melancholic gardening fashion of the late 1770's, Goethe's second contribution to the Park of Weimar had a more joyous origin. As a surprise present for the Duchess Luise, Goethe had a hermitage constructed on the shore of the river Ilm near the "Felsentreppe." In an essay entitled "Das Luisenfest," he later described how he and his friends, disguised as monks, received the Duchess and her court there for the celebration of her nameday on July 9, 1778. To evoke a melancholic mood, the artificial ruin of a cloister with a chapel was added in the background. This spot, therefore, became known as "das Luisenkloster." The hermitage itself was a rustic little hut made of wood and bark and covered with a thatched roof. It was remodelled in 1784 and from then on called "das Borkenhäuschen" (the bark hut).[11] In 1786, a "Gothic House" was erected near the "Felsentreppe" and the "Luisenkloster" so that these three spots now formed a harmonious sentimental unit.

From these initial attempts the Park of Weimar grew slowly along the river Ilm toward the village of Oberweimar, until, in 1787, it extended continuously from the palace to the village.[12] The natural beauty of the landscape with its winding river, sloping meadows, pretty shrubs, and stately trees provided the sole basis for the park's picturesque effects. No drastic changes were made in the topography of this river landscape: no large earthmoving operations took place for the erection of artificial hills and valleys, no vast damming projects for the creation of an artificial lake. Perhaps the meagre finances of the Duchy of Weimar did not permit such ambitious projects as were popular elsewhere in England and in Germany. It is also possible, however, that a strong preference for the natural beauty of the landscape prevented them. In comparison to other German landscape gardens, therefore, the Park of Weimar distinguished itself by its close adherence to the natural features of the landscape, its great simplicity, and its tastefulness. With its few decorative buildings and simple design, it followed the guidelines of a leading English garden artist, Capability Brown (1715–83), who preferred the quiet natural beauty of lakes, streams, meadows, shrubs, and clumps of trees to intricate designs and excessive decoration.[13]

This was, however, unique in Germany, for the German princes favored more ornate landscape gardens. The Park of Wörlitz near Dessau—one of the earliest and most famous examples of English landscape gardening in Germany—had inspired Goethe and the Duke of Weimar during their visit in the spring of 1778 to create something similar at home. Laid out around a large artificial lake of irregular shape, the Park of Wörlitz was covered with artificial hills and valleys and cluttered with decorative buildings. There were Roman temples, grottoes, and catacombs, an imitation of the Pantheon, a temple of Venus, a reproduction of the Villa Hamilton near Naples as well as medieval hermitages, Gothic chapels, pavilions, and houses. This conglomeration of architectural styles—classical, medieval, and even oriental—was advocated by Sir William Chambers

(1726–96), an influential English garden architect, who wanted to lend variety, contrast, and surprise to the otherwise plain and natural English landscape garden.[14] Wörlitz excluded the oriental style but blended classical and medieval architecture. The Gothic element was rather strong in Wörlitz. Besides medieval chapels and hermitages, there was also a "Gothic House," which served as a residence for the Prince of Anhalt and housed his collection of medieval paintings, stained glass, and other art objects.[15] The English landscape garden at Hohenheim, laid out in 1774, was equally ornate. Here reproductions of Roman ruins dominated the scene. The Gothic element was represented by a Gothic church, whose floor was covered with medieval tombstones. In addition, there was a cloister with a Gothic chapel and a hermitage with the hermit's grave. Hohenheim also contained an oriental mosque and an imitation village with Swiss farmhouses.[16] The Park of Seifersdorf near Dresden, laid out between 1781 and 1792, was closer in spirit to the Park of Weimar. It extended along the course of a winding river whose terrain was left largely unchanged. Its many decorations consisted of rustic huts and hermitages as well as classical temples dedicated to truth, virtue, charity, and the muses.[17] In this contemporary cultural context, represented by Weimar and Seifersdorf on the one hand and Wörlitz and Hohenheim on the other, the new landscape park in *Die Wahlverwandtschaften* must be viewed.

Consider now the description of the setting and the gardens in Goethe's novel. Eduard's and Charlotte's house—"das Schloss," as it is called in the novel—is situated on a hill, surrounded by terraces and old gardens. There are orchards as well as kitchen and flower gardens with greenhouses. The narrator mentions that these old gardens were laid out long ago by Eduard's father. We may, therefore, assume them to be in the formal French style which was popular in Germany until the 1760's. Besides, the terraces leading down to the river, described in Eduard's first walk, were an integral part of French garden design. The assistant from the boarding school, who later visits Ottilie, still admires the old-fashioned beauty of these French gardens with their tree-lined avenues and regular geometric design.[18] Nobody else, however, notices the old gardens. They are left in the care of the gardener, and Eduard and Ottilie visit them only occasionally. Even the narrator's description of them is sparse and dispersed. Because of the rapid change in gardening fashions, formal French gardens were no longer fashionable by the turn of the century, which may be considered the novel's temporal setting. In *Die Wahlverwandt-*

schaften, therefore, all attention is focused on the new English landscape park, which is laid out under Charlotte's supervision. All visitors are immediately taken to see and admire these new English gardens. That English models were indeed followed here becomes evident when the Captain takes over the work from Charlotte. Before continuing the project, he and Eduard consult English handbooks on garden design with descriptions and copper engravings of English parks. These books show layout plans of English estates and sketches of the landscape in its original state as well as sketches of the artistic improvements which were made to enhance the beauty of nature.[19] The Captain then proceeds to adapt these English models to the topography of the existing German locality.

While the narrator mentions the formal French gardens surrounding the palace only in passing, he constantly directs the reader's attention to the new English landscape park by describing several walks that the main characters and their visitors take in it. This dynamic narrative device permits him to show the gradual expansion of the park and also to reveal its various scenes in succession. The first walk shows the topography in general. The English landscape park, located on a hill across from the palace, is separated from it by the village and the river. Two paths lead down from the palace across the river on each side of the village. The path on the left divides into two branches on the other side of the river which encircle the new landscape park. One of these runs across the churchyard straight toward the rocky cliff near the top of the hill; the other—a little further to the left and not so steep as the first—winds in gentle curves through shrubs and bushes also to this point. Where both paths meet, a bench is set up so that the wanderer may rest and admire the view. Then the path climbs upward over steps and platforms to the "moss hut," a rustic little hermitage at the foot of the rocky cliff, representing the first centre and focal point of the new landscape park. Here significant decisions are made and important actions take place, until, with the gradual expansion of the park, the pleasure house on top of the hill takes over this function. The "moss hut" has been artfully placed in such a way that the view of the village with its church below, the valley with its river, trees, and meadows on the right, and the palace with its formal terraced gardens across, form picturesque views through the windows and the door which give the impression of landscape paintings in a frame.[20]

Designers of English landscape gardens always sought to include beautiful views of the surrounding countryside as picturesque effects in their garden design. They placed benches, pavilions, and pleasure houses at vantage points from which these views could best be admired. Garden walls were therefore eliminated. Moreover, English landscape architects tried to arrange the scenery of the park itself into a composition similar to that of a landscape painting. They sought to compose a series of pictures with the elements of nature just as landscape painters did on their canvases. It is not surprising, therefore, that great painters like Salvatore Rosa, Claude Lorrain, and Nicolas and Gaspar Poussin exerted a powerful influence on the English landscape movement and such early English garden artists as Charles Bridgeman and William Kent.[21] In referring to the views from the "moss hut" as "Bilder, welche die Landschaft gleichsam im Rahmen zeigten," the narrator of *Die Wahlverwandtschaften* makes a direct allusion to the aesthetic theory of landscape gardening which such well-known aestheticians as Johann Georg Sulzer, C. C. L. Hirschfeld, and Immanuel Kant related to the aesthetic principles of landscape painting.[22] The narrator also seems to adopt this technique of composing picturesque views by using the elements of nature according to the aesthetic principles of landscape painting in his landscape descriptions. The most striking example of this is the view from the pleasure house on top of the hill overlooking the three ponds which are later combined into an artificial lake. Here wooded hills, steep rocks, a deep forest gorge with a cascading mountain brook and an old mill form a truly picturesque effect reminiscent of the heroic landscapes of Claude Lorrain or Jacob van Ruysdael, both of whom Goethe admired very much.[23]

In describing the new English landscape park, the narrator of *Die Wahlverwandtschaften* places special emphasis on the clever layout of its winding paths with their resting places and beautiful views. In the third walk, when Eduard and Charlotte take the Captain through the park, he notices every beautiful spot which has been made more visible and enjoyable through the skillful arrangement of the footpaths.[24] The aesthetic effect of English landscape gardens depended largely on such picturesque scenes that were arranged as a scenario along irregular winding paths.[25] Contrast, variety, surprise, the avoidance of symmetry and artificiality—in fact, the concealment of art—were desired effects that English garden designers tried to achieve. Only in motion, while walking, riding, or driving, could the beauty of an English landscape park be discovered, since it did not depend on a fixed perspective as the geometrical French garden, but on different and constantly changing vantage points. The narrator also uses this dynamic device in the novel to acquaint the reader with various scenes in the park, whose beauty, however, is never described in detail but only evoked through brief remarks or indicated through its effect upon the visitor. The climax in this respect is reached by the impression which the new landscape park makes upon the travelling English nobleman, who is presented as a connoisseur of English landscape gardening and who includes the beautiful scenes of the finished park in his collection of such drawings.[26] This incident can only be interpreted as a high compliment to the new landscape park which seems to have become a successful artistic creation.

The narrator of *Die Wahlverwandtschaften* presents the activity of landscape gardening explicitly as a form of art.[27] This is in concurrence, of course, with contemporary aesthetic theory. He refers to the new landscape park several times as "die neue Schöpfung"—a term which implies artistry. Although Charlotte's first efforts in creating an English landscape park are described with a touch of irony as mere dilettantism, the narrator does not rule out the possibility of creating a true work of art in this genre. In fact, he strongly suggests that the Captain with his superior knowledge and skill might be capable of performing such a task. In contrast to Charlotte, who goes about her work haphazardly and without a prior conception of the whole design, the Captain begins his work like a professional landscape artist by making a thorough survey of the grounds and by drawing a detailed map of the entire estate.[28] Since he proceeds from a conception of the whole, his work has a greater chance of achieving artistic unity. The Captain is also fully aware of Charlotte's mistakes and criticizes her sharply for her dilettantism. He points out that she relies too much on trial and error and on a step-by-step procedure which consists merely of embellishing certain favorite places in the park.[29] In his opinion, she lacks the boldness to remove obstacles and to make changes in the terrain which are necessary for the creation of a unified work of art in landscape gardening. Because Charlotte does not have the artistic imagination to envision the final aesthetic effect of the park, her work must remain dilettantish. The Captain, on the other hand, seems to possess all the qualities that Charlotte lacks. He corrects her mistakes and completes the project successfully. Finally the finished landscape park appears to be an accomplished work of art, deserving the admiration of the travelling English nobleman, who is deliberately portrayed as a connoisseur of English landscape gardening. The Englishman considers the picturesque views of this park worthy of being included in his collection of drawings made with the help of a camera obscura. The artistic reproduction of the park's beautiful scenes gives it final approval as a work of art and ranks it among the noteworthy landscape gardens of its time deserving admiration and emulation.[30]

If we compare the English landscape park described in Goethe's *Wahlverwandtschaften* with existing contemporary landscape gardens described in Hirschfeld's *Theorie der Gartenkunst*, several unique features emerge. First of all, the location of the new park is highly unusual, for it does not surround the palace but is located far away on the other side of the village and the river.[31] English landscape gardens were usually laid out along a winding river as in Weimar or around an artificial lake of irregular shape as in Wörlitz and included the house either as their centre or as their focal point at one end. This is not the case in Goethe's novel. Here the new landscape park remains a totally separate entity, centered around the moss hut and related only to the pleasure house on the hill and the Gothic village church with its graveyard. The palace, still surrounded by its formal French gardens with their terraces and tree-lined avenues, their orchards, flower and kitchen gardens, is visible only in the distance. This unique location, which draws such a sharp dividing line between the palace and the new landscape park, must express the author's intention and, therefore, also have symbolic implications.[32] From this setting, the old and the new are perceived not as harmoniously integrated but as distinctly separate and disharmonious. Viewed symbolically, the palace with its old-fashioned gardens represents the social order of the eighteenth century, the *ancien régime*, the spirit of the Enlightenment, which in its aesthetics combined beauty with utility and rationality. The new English landscape park, on the other hand, represents the free spirit of Romanticism with its rejection of these values, its love of freedom, its aversion to artificiality, and its closeness to nature based purely on aesthetic considerations.[33]

In actuality, the French and English gardening styles were often harmoniously integrated or existed side by side in Germany, where the gardening revolution did not go as far as it did in England. Here French gardens were usually eliminated in favor of the new irregular landscape gardens. England's leading garden artist from 1750 to 1783, Capability Brown, was known for his merciless destruction of all French gardens, terraces, and tree-lined avenues. He would place the house on a vast expanse of lawn, surrounded only by winding paths, shrubbery, single trees, and clumps of trees which had to be specially planted. Orchards, kitchen and flower gardens were moved far away and hidden from view. No utilitarian considerations were allowed to interfere with the aesthetic beauty of the landscape park. Germany's leading theorist of garden art, Hirschfeld, disagreed on this point with his English colleague and insisted on the preservation of symmetrical, architectural French gardens near the house. He believed that the sudden transition from the symmetry of the building to the complete irregularity of the English landscape garden was too harsh a contrast.[34] In Weimar, therefore, the French gardens, called the "Welsche Garten," and the tree-lined avenues of "der Stern," located between the palace and the English gardens, were preserved. In Wörlitz, the house was surrounded by lawns, shrubs, and trees in the English manner on the lakeside, but on the east and west sides the old tree-lined avenues were retained. The setting in Goethe's *Wahlverwandtschaften*, therefore, reflects to some extent the state of affairs in Germany; yet a harmonious integration of the old and the new gardens, which designers tried to achieve, is deliberately avoided in the novel. In England, Capability Brown's successor Humphry Repton (1752–1818), who was the leading garden designer from 1790 to 1818, blended the French and the English styles successfully.[35] He achieved a harmonious synthesis between the geometric French garden close to the house, surrounded by a wall, from which the irregular English landscape park then extended. In Germany, Fürst Pückler-Muskau became the leading proponent of this mixed gardening style.

Other features of the landscape park described in *Die Wahlverwandtschaften*, which distinguish it from many contemporary English landscape gardens in Germany, are its close adherence to the natural characteristics of the landscape and its utter simplicity. In this respect, of course, it resembles the Park of Weimar. With the exception of the artificial lake on the other side of the hill, no drastic changes are made in the natural terrain of the landscape. Only the layout of the footpaths requires some grading, levelling, and the removal of rocky edges in certain places to make their winding curves flow with greater freedom and ease. Compared with the actual practice of landscape gardening at that time, when large earthmoving operations, damming projects, and the rerouting of streams were not uncommon, the changes effected in the novel are truly minimal. A desire to preserve the natural features of the landscape as much as possible can be discerned as the prevailing attitude. Many interpretations of the novel, therefore, go too far in stressing the violence done to nature by the landscaping activities and the complete arbitrariness of the changes.[36] The artificial lake is intended to restore the pristine beauty of the valley, because it had been there originally. The combination of three insignificant ponds into a large artificial lake, which was almost considered a necessity for an English landscape garden, would have been advocated by any competent landscape designer at that time.

Considering the cultural context, however, another feature of the park is more unusual: its utter simplicity and the sparseness of decorations. The moss hut and the pleasure house on top of the hill are the only decorations mentioned within the confines of the park; the Gothic village church and its graveyard are adjacent to it. In comparison to the parks at Wörlitz, Hohenheim, and Seifersdorf, this austere simplicity is striking indeed.[37] Even the Park of Weimar, famous for its frugality, had many more decorations. In the narrator's description of the landscape park in *Die Wahlverwandtschaften*, we therefore detect a strong tendency towards abstraction, a reduction to the bare essentials. All concrete details, either personal or cultural, have been completely eliminated. The narrator only mentions what is necessary for the setting or the action. In his interpretation of the novel, Eberhard Mannack also notices this lack of color, contour, and concrete detail in the park descriptions. He points out the narrator's preference for general rather than specific terms.[38] In spite of that, the gardening descriptions in the novel have great authenticity, which they derive from Goethe's thorough familiarity with the practical and aesthetic principles of landscape gardening. Their descriptive style is based on knowledge, not on sense impressions and reflects Goethe's strong belief that artistic style should be knowledgeable and penetrate to the essence of things.[39]

Viewed from the cultural context of contemporary landscape gardens, the complete absence of neoclassical monuments in the landscape park of the novel is utterly remarkable. When we consider that the period of German Classicism had barely passed with Schiller's death in 1805 and that most contemporary German landscape gardens blended neoclassical and Gothic architecture harmoniously, the omission of these elements is most unusual. The existing decorative features of the landscape park in the novel—the hermitage, the graveyard, and the Gothic church (no hint is given about the architectural style of the pleasure house on top of the hill)[40]—have their origin in the sentimental, pre-romantic period of the 1770s and reached great popularity again after 1800 during the age of Romanticism. The narrator of *Die Wahlverwandtschaften*, therefore, chose to give the new landscape park a highly unified setting, which had nostalgic overtones, evoking the past period of sentimental melancholy. At the same time, it must have seemed quite contemporary in 1809, because of the prevailing fashion of Romanticism. Goethe's early experiences in changing the Park of Weimar into an English landscape garden—the erection of the memorial to Christel von Lassberg and the construction of the hermitage with its cloister and chapel—seem to have been incorporated in this artistically transformed description. All the elements selected project the dominant mood of death and melancholy. The deliberate avoidance of any neoclassical decorations and the pronounced preference for sentimental, pre-romantic features lend a strong dose of death symbolism to the novel's setting. Neoclassical monuments, so cheerful and serene in mood, would have clashed disharmoniously with this predominantly melancholic atmosphere. In his book on the theory of garden art, Hirschfeld points out that a hermitage would be totally out of place in a cheerful pleasure garden. He advises that hermitages should only be placed in gardens near a monastery, a chapel, a graveyard, or in simple and serious gardens of a melancholic nature.[41] Three out of these four conditions are met in Goethe's novel. In reality, these rules were not applied so strictly. Yet hermitages, chapels, and graves often formed a separate unit in the park, as was the case in Hohenheim and also in Weimar, where the memorial to Christel von Lassberg, the hermitage, the artificial ruin of the cloister, and the "Gothic House" were all located in close proximity. The neoclassical decorations erected during the 1790's—a statue of Pan, a bas-relief of Triton, three pillars representing the ruin of a classical temple, and the Roman House— so different in mood and style, were all placed far away.

In our deliberations so far, we have simply assumed the "moss hut" to be a hermitage without explicitly proving the point. The narrator uses the term "die Einsiedelei" (hermitage) once in referring to the "moss hut," when he describes Charlotte's emotional upheaval after she has learned about the Captain's possible departure.[42] In her grief, Charlotte seeks refuge, solitude, and consolation in the "moss hut." However, there is also cultural and biographical evidence to back up our assumption. How striking the resemblance between the "moss hut" in the novel and the hermitage in the Park of Weimar really is, will become evident from a description of the "Luisenkloster" in Hirschfeld's book *Theorie der Gartenkunst*:

> Das Kloster ist eine kleine Einsiedeley, mit einer Kapelle am Ilma-Fluß. Man kommt durch Wege dahin, die sich durch Felsen schlängeln, bald Gewölbe sind, bald zu lichten Plätzen werden, und mit ihrem öden, wilden Anblick, hie und da angebrachten Höhlen und Sitzen, eine Vorstellung von den berühmten Felsengängen der sinesischen Gärten geben können. Unten schleicht der Ilm-Fluß in seinen schattigten Ufern, und oben erblickt man die künstlichen

Ruinen eines weitläufigen Gebäudes. Die Einsiedeley und Kapelle
sind mit Moos und Baumrinde bekleidet.[43]

There are striking similarities in the appearance and location of the
"moss hut" in the novel and the hermitage in the Park of Weimar.
Both are located in a lonely area surrounded by rocks, one on a hill
and the other on the shore of the river Ilm. The hut in the novel must
be covered with moss, leading to the name "moss hut," while the hut
in the Park of Weimar was covered with moss and bark and, therefore, called "bark hut" (das "Borkenhäuschen"). But the parallel goes
further. The nameday of the Duchess Luise was celebrated on July 9,
1778 in the "bark hut" shortly after Goethe had it constructed. In the
novel, Eduard's and the Captain's nameday is also celebrated in the
"moss hut" shortly after its completion. In transforming the Park of
Weimar into an English landscape garden, the construction of the
hermitage was one of Goethe's first projects. Similarly, the "moss
hut" stands at the very beginning of Charlotte's landscaping activities
in the novel. Goethe obviously incorporated his own experience
here, but stripped of all personal and unique features; it, therefore,
appears general and typical. In order to conceal its origin further, he
also transferred the action of constructing the hermitage and arranging the celebration from a male (himself) to a female fictional character (Charlotte).

The other decorative features of the new landscape park in the
novel, the Gothic chapel with its graveyard and tombstones, which
Charlotte includes among her landscaping projects, have received a
great deal of attention in the secondary literature. Charlotte's embellishment of the graveyard is usually seen as an irreverent and arbitrary act.[44] Viewed from the historical perspective, however, it was
very much part of the cultural context at that time. In Wörlitz, for
example, the graveyard surrounding the Gothic village church was
also landscaped and decorated with monuments, mottos, and garden
seats, enclosed by hedges, to give it an aesthetically pleasing appearance.[45] It was probably included among the landscaping projects
there, because of its proximity to the palace and the park, and because it added the desired melancholic effect. In Hohenheim, genuine medieval tombstones were used to cover the floor of the neo-
Gothic chapel in the park. The antiquary's interest in medieval art,
which led to its collection and restoration, had originated in England
earlier in the eighteenth century and spread as part of the English
gardening movement to Germany in the 1770's, where a love for
Gothic park decorations soon became prevalent. Charlotte's efforts to

display the old tombstones and to have the Gothic village church restored by the architect, therefore, do not surprise us. What is surprising, is the mood evoked by her beautification. All aspects of death and sentimental melancholy are carefully avoided here. The former sombre graveyard has been transformed into an aesthetically pleasing, even cheerful place. All the graves have been levelled and the ground has been planted with various kinds of colorful clover. This is in complete contradiction to Hirschfeld's recommendations for the beautification of cemeteries, which he classifies as "melancholic gardens," devoid of cheerful scenes, shiny bodies of water, and pleasant lawns.[46] He advises that dark coniferous trees should be planted singly or in groves in cemeteries to evoke emotions of sadness and mourning. Monuments and mottos should stimulate the visitor to melancholic sentiments and contemplative thoughts. A cemetery should give a sombre and solemn impression. Charlotte's embellishments do exactly the opposite: the colorful clover and bright linden trees project a mood of peaceful serenity. Life and art here prevail over the traditional mood of death and melancholy. We may either interpret this innovative treatment of the cemetery as an early expression of a new trend which was to develop later in the nineteenth century—the landscaping of cemeteries as English gardens[47]—or we may view it as an aesthetic device which softens the tragic impact of the novel's conclusion. The beauty of art here transcends the horror of death. The same aesthetic principle also applies to the artistic decoration of the chapel, which later becomes Ottilie's and Eduard's burial place.

Let us now return to the questions that were raised in the beginning. How did Goethe incorporate his own experience of landscape gardening in the novel and what are the symbolic implications of the gardening descriptions?

Evidently Goethe drew heavily on his initial attempts of changing the Park of Weimar into an English landscape garden by selecting exactly those elements that he needed to project the dominant mood of death and melancholy in his novel. According to Hirschfeld's principles, the new landscape park in *Die Wahlverwandtschaften* can only be classified as a melancholic garden, for it is simple in design and contains a hermitage, a Gothic church, and a graveyard as its sole decorations. Probably Goethe deliberately unified the setting of this landscape garden in order to intensify its symbolic significance. His later landscaping activities, involving the erection of neoclassical monuments, therefore, have left no trace in the novel. Besides, the cheerful and serene nature of such neoclassical decorations would have destroyed the predominantly melancholic effect.

In their tone and manner, Goethe's gardening descriptions are kept general and typical; they are completely devoid of all personal and unique details. Concrete visual impressions have also been carefully avoided. These descriptions derive their authenticity from a thorough knowledge of the practice and aesthetics of landscape gardening and evoke only such essential features that enable the reader to complete the picture of the new landscape park in his imagination.

In discussing the purpose of his novel with Riemer on August 28, 1808, Goethe stated that his intention was to portray social relationships and their conflicts symbolically in the novel. In doing so, however, he avoided any direct reference to actual events of his time such as the French Revolution or the Napoleonic Wars in which Eduard participates. Instead Goethe may have found the innocuous garden descriptions convenient for providing the necessary historical background, because the rapid change of garden fashions in the 1770's may be linked symbolically to the political and social upheaval of the time. As the life-style of the *ancien régime* finally succumbed to a new and more liberal outlook on life, so also the formal French garden style with its preference for rigid symmetry, geometric design, and complete subjugation of nature gave way to the free manner of English landscape gardening with its new appreciation of nature and its complete rejection of restraint, artificiality, and symmetry. The social and historical implications of this gardening revolution are briefly discussed by the "Gehülfe" and Charlotte, who perceive this rapid change of gardening styles as an expression of the "Zeitgeist." The "Gehülfe" also believes that sentiments, attitudes, opinions, tastes, and prejudices are equally conditioned by the movement of time leading to severe generation conflicts. Such social relationships and their conflicts are mirrored in the novel not only in the rapid change of garden fashions but also in the harsh clash of traditional and new attitudes towards love, passion, marriage, and divorce, which is at the centre of the novel's plot.

If we draw a symbolic parallel here between these conflicting social forces and the setting of the novel, then the palace with its antiquated French gardens, laid out by Eduard's father, quite obviously represents the older tradition of the eighteenth century. Similarly Eduard's and Charlotte's previous marriages, arranged to increase their wealth and social status, represent the typical "mariages de convenance" of eighteenth-century aristocrats. Eduard and Charlotte, therefore, still have their roots in this older tradition but are also inclined towards

new values, as is indicated by Charlotte's dabbling in English landscape gardening and Eduard's romantic predilection for heights and
wide open spaces. Although Eduard still cares for the tree nursery
and the old kitchen and flower gardens of his estate, he dislikes the
confinement of these walled gardens—as well as that of the moss
huts—and always initiates walks to the other side of the hill where
forests, cliffs, ponds, and an old mill form a picturesque romantic
landscape. Eduard is generally considered a romantic character ruled
by feeling, impulse, and passion. After falling in love with Ottilie, he
also readily adopts the new attitude towards marriage and divorce,
based on the view that love and passion are the sole reason for marriage and that any union no longer conforming to these standards
might as well be dissolved. Eduard is able to convert Ottilie temporarily to this point of view and even succeeds in swaying the Captain's and Charlotte's more traditional outlook momentarily. Ottilie,
whose conformity to traditional values is at first expressed by her
confinement to the house and its household duties later begins to
adopt Eduard's preferences and ideas. She, therefore, determines the
location of the pleasure house on the hill in such a way that it over-
looks the romantic landscape and that the palace with its old gardens
remains hidden from view. When Eduard considers the possibility of
divorce and remarriage, he envisions himself travelling with Ottilie
and assigns the palace with its formal gardens to the Captain and
Charlotte, who are generally regarded as more traditional characters,
ruled by reason and moderation and endowed with the moral virtues
of the Enlightenment.

Thus the constellation of the four characters in the novel is linked
symbolically to different spatial spheres which correspond to their
views and attitudes towards traditional and new values. This clash
between tradition and innovation, which leads to the irreconcilable
conflict of the novel concerning love, marriage, and divorce, is symbolically represented by the two spatial spheres of the setting: the
palace with its antiquated French gardens on the one side and the
new English landscape garden, with its hermitage, its pleasure
house, and its extension towards the romantic landscape on the other
side of the river. These two units, which are divided by the village
and the river, form two distinctly separate entities that appear never
bridged over, directly connected or harmoniously integrated. Thus
the disharmonious juxtaposition of the old and the new gardens in
the setting is symptomatic of the irreconcilable conflict between traditional and new social attitudes in the novel.

NOTES

1 Wilhelm Grimm and Friedrich Heinrich Jacobi, cited in Hermann Bitzer, *Goethe über den Dilettantismus* (Bern: Herbert Lang Verlag, 1969), p. 69.
2 Wilhelm von Humboldt in a letter to his wife, dated March 6, 1810. Bitzer, pp. 69 and 121.
3 Franz Grillparzer, *Sämtliche Werke* (Munich: Carl Hanser Verlag, 1964), III, 772–73: "What is most annoying in Goethe's *Elective Affinities* is the distasteful importance given from the very beginning, together with the development of the main plot, to landscape gardening, the construction of petty buildings, and similar things. One seems to be looking directly at a part of Goethe's life, who partially paralyzed his incomparable gifts by taking the same interest in such diversions as in the most important matters of his proper vocation" (translated by the author).
4 Richard Beitl, *Goethes Bild der Landschaft* (Berlin, 1929). Kurt May, "Goethes 'Wahlverwandtschaften' als tragischer Roman," *Jahrbuch des Freien Deutschen Hochstifts* (1936–40), 139–58. Eva Neumeyer, "The Landscape Garden as a Symbol in Rousseau, Goethe, and Flaubert," in *Journal of the History of Ideas*, 8 (1947), 187–217. Wolfgang Staroste, "Raumgestaltung und Raumsymbolik in Goethes 'Wahlverwandtschaften,'" in *Etudes Germaniques*, 16 (1961), 209–22. Eberhard Mannack, *Raumdarstellung und Realitätsbezug in Goethes epischer Dichtung* (Frankfurt am Main. Athenäum Verlag, 1972), pp. 163–94.
5 Walther Killy, *Wirklichkeit und Kunstcharakter: Neun Romane des 19. Jahrhunderts* (Munich, 1963), pp. 19–35. Keith Dickson, "Spatial Concentration and Themes in 'Die Wahlverwandtschaften,'" in *Forum for Modern Language Studies*, 1 (1965), 159–74. H. G. Barnes, *Goethe's Wahlverwandtschaften: A Literary Interpretation* (Oxford: Clarendon Press, 1967), pp. 71–85.
6 K. W. F. Solger, "Über die Wahlverwandtschaften," in *Goethes Werke*, Hamburger Ausgabe (Munich: Verlag C. H. Beck, 1977), VI, 637.
7 Friedrich Schiller defined this term in his essay, *Über die ästhetische Erziehung des Menschen in einer Reihe von Briefen*, ed. Wolfhart Henckmann (Munich: Wilhelm Fink Verlag, 1967).
8 Contemporary descriptions of notable English landscape gardens in Germany as well as in England can be found in C. C. L. Hirschfeld's five-volume work *Theorie der Gartenkunst* (Leipzig: M. G. Weidmanns Erben, 1779–85). Dieter Hennebo and Alfred Hoffmann also provide much useful information in their three-volume work *Geschichte der deutschen Gartenkunst* (Hamburg: Broschek Verlag, 1963). The development of the English gardening movement is outlined by Edward Hyams in *Capability Brown and Humphry Repton* (New York: Charles Scribner's Sons, 1971), Isabel Wakelin Urban Chase in *Horace Walpole, Gardenist* (Princeton: Princeton University Press, 1943), and Marie Luise Gothein in *A History of Garden Art* (New York: Harker Art Books, 1966).

9 Cf. Hennebo and Hoffmann, *Geschichte der deutschen Gartenkunst*, vol. III, *Der Landschaftsgarten*, pp. 40–42. C. C. L. Hirschfeld also describes this tendency in his *Theorie der Gartenkunst* and Renate Krüger in her book *Das Zeitalter der Empfindsamkeit* (Vienna and Munich: Verlag Anton Schroll & Co., 1972), pp. 56–91.

10 Wolfgang Huschke and Wolfgang Vulpius, *Park um Weimar* (Weimar: Hermann Böhlaus Nachfolger, 1955), p. 34.

11 Huschke and Vulpius, pp. 35–36.

12 Ibid., p. 38.

13 Edward Hyams, *Capability Brown and Humphry Repton* (New York: Charles Scribner's Sons, 1971). In his essay "Über die Englischen Gärten," published in 1807, Johann Georg Jacobi also condemns excessive decorations and advocates a simple, natural beauty for English landscape gardens. Johann Georg Jacobi, *Sämmtliche Werke* (Zurich: Orell Füssli und Compagnie, 1819), VII, 13–52.

14 William Chambers, *Plans, Elevations, Selections, and Perspective Views of the Gardens and Buildings at Kew in Surrey* (London, 1763). William Chambers, *Dissertation on Oriental Gardening* (London, 1774).

15 Hennebo and Hoffman, III, 75–77.

16 Ibid., pp. 81–87.

17 Ibid., pp. 99–107.

18 *Die Wahlverwandtschaften*, in *Goethes Werke*, Hamburger Ausgabe (Munich: Verlag C. H. Beck, 1977), VI, 417. Hirschfeld and Hennebo use the term "regelmässige Anlagen" only in referring to geometrical French gardens.

19 *Die Wahlverwandtschaften*, pp. 287–88. The narrator gives us no hints here about which English handbooks on garden design the Captain and Eduard may have consulted. Hirschfeld, whose work was known to Goethe, gives many descriptions of English parks but no copper engravings of their picturesque scenery. Capability Brown did not publish any books on garden design. Humphry Repton, however, was very well known in Germany because of his many publications: Humphry Repton, *Sketches and Hints on Landscape Gardening* (London, 1794); Humphry Repton, *Observations on the Theory and Practice of Landscape Gardening* (London, 1803); Humphry Repton, *An Enquiry into the Changes of Taste in Landscape Gardening* (London, 1806); Humphry Repton, *Fragments on the Theory and Practice of Landscape Gardening* (London, 1816). Repton had a peculiar method of before-and-after illustration which Goethe also refers to in the novel. The picture would first show the scene as it was originally. By raising one or more cut-out and pasted-in flaps, one could see how the scene would look after the improvements which Repton proposed. Marie Luise Gothein (*A History of Garden Art*, II, 306–7) and Edward Hyams (*Capability Brown and Humphry Repton*, pp. 194–96) believe that Goethe knew Repton's work because he refers to his unique method of illustration. However, I learned at the Staatsbibliothek in Weimar that Repton's books were purchased only after 1809.

20 *Die Wahlverwandtschaften*, p. 243.

21 Isabel Wakelin Urban Chase, *Horace Walpole, Gardenist*, p. 135.
22 Johann Georg Sulzer, *Allgemeine Theorie der schönen Künste* (Leipzig, 1771–74), I, 421. C. C. L. Hirschfeld, *Theorie der Gartenkunst*, I, xiii and 29. Immanuel Kant, *Kritik der Urteilskraft* (par. 51). English writers such as Joseph Addison, Alexander Pope, and Horace Walpole had, of course, pioneered these ideas earlier. Joseph Addison, *Spectator*, No. 414 (June 25, 1712), and No. 477 (September 6, 1712). Alexander Pope, *The Guardian*, No. 173 (September 29, 1713), and "Epistle to Burlington" (1731). Horace Walpole, "On Modern Gardening" (1780).
23 *Die Wahlverwandtschaften*, pp. 259–60. In his conversation with Eckermann of May 2, 1824, Goethe mentioned Ruysdael in connection with the picturesque views of the Park of Weimar. He expressed his admiration for Ruysdael's landscape paintings in his essay "Ruysdael als Dichter," Hamburger Ausgabe, XII, 138–142. In an essay fragment "Landschaftliche Malerei" (Hamburger Ausgabe, XII, 216–220), Goethe analyzes the perfection of Claude Lorrain's heroic landscape compositions.
   There have been speculations whether Goethe had a real landscape in mind when he wrote this description. Drakendorf, Wilhelmsthal, Ziegenberg, and Karlsbad have been mentioned as possible models by André François-Poncet, *Goethes Wahlverwandtschaften* (Mainz: Florian Kupferberg Verlag, 1951), p. 109. Yet none of these contains all the elements mentioned in the novel; therefore, the description is more likely to be a composite picture or a poetic analogy of a picturesque landscape painting.
24 *Die Wahlverwandtschaften*, p. 258.
25 Hennebo and Hoffmann, III, 79 and 124.
26 *Die Wahlverwandtschaften*, pp. 429–31.
27 This hypothesis differs from most interpretations of *Die Wahlverwandtschaften* which condemn the novel's landscaping activities as pure dilettantism. As proof, they usually refer to Goethe's notes on dilettantism (Weimarer Ausgabe, div. I, vol. 47, pp. 299–326) where, under the heading "Gartenkunst" (Garden Art), negative aspects outweigh positive ones. Viewed from this perspective, the gardening activities in the novel appear in a very negative light. Such interpretations, however, fail to acknowledge that Goethe also conceded the possibility of artistry in the garden arts in his notes on dilettantism ("erster Eintritt in die Kunst"), if an artistic form, a beautiful composition, and a transformation of nature into a picture could be achieved. I have tried to show that this actually happens in *Die Wahlverwandtschaften*. Moreover, some negative aspects of dilettantism, mentioned by Goethe in his notes, are deliberately avoided in the novel. There are no playful architectural decorations such as temples, pagodas, grottoes, or cottages that Goethe condemned as "Kartenhaus-Architektur," nor are the other arts made to serve the garden arts in an unworthy manner. The secondary literature on dilettantism (Gerhart Baumann, "Goethe: 'Über den Dilettantismus,'" in *Euphorion*, 46 (1952), 348–69; Ursula Wertheim, "Über den Dilettantismus," in *Goethe-Studien* (Berlin: Rütten & Loening, 1968), pp. 36–64; Helmut Koopmann, "Dilet-

tantismus: Bemerkungen zu einem Phänomen der Goethezeit," in *Studien zur Goethezeit*, Festschrift für Lieselotte Blumenthal (Weimar: Hermann Böhlaus Nachfolger, 1968), pp. 178–209, also fails to distinguish sufficiently between Charlotte's and the Captain's landscaping activities. While Charlotte's work is definitely dilettantish, the Captain's is not. In fact, he criticizes all the aspects of dilettantism in her work and since he is so aware of them, one may safely assume that he does not repeat these mistakes. In his extensive study of dilettantism in Goethe's *Wahlverwandtschaften*, Hermann Bitzer also comes to the conclusion that the finished landscape park, completed by the Captain, can no longer be regarded as an example of dilettantism: "Der erste, auf den die Gegend nach ihrer Verschönerung ihre volle Wirkung ausübt, ist ein englischer Kenner. Indem dieser die Parkansichten aufnimmt, erhebt er die Anlage in den Rang der Vorbildlichkeit. . . . Der rückhaltlose Beifall des Kenners erlaubt es also nicht, die Parkliebhaberei als kleinlichen oder gefühlvollen Dilettantismus, als willkürliche Naturpfuscherei abzustempeln; anfängliche Verirrungen in dieser Richtung hat der Hauptmann gründlich beseitigt" (Hermann Bitzer, *Goethe über den Dilettantismus* [Bern: Herbert Lang Verlag, 1969], p. 80).

28 In his book *Capability Brown and Humphry Repton*, Edward Hyams points out that Repton always began his work with a survey of the estate: "His survey would have entailed the use of a theodolite, the making of notes both written and sketched and the taking of measurements; he would have studied the house thoroughly and walked or ridden over every acre of the estate; . . ." Following this he would have presented "a neatly drawn map of their park, finished in water-colours, and probably keyed. This would have been to illustrate what would have come next, an analysis of the park . . . followed by positive suggestions for the major lines of improvement" (pp. 127–29). The similarities between Repton's and the Captain's methods are striking.

29 Charlotte's procedure resembles that of Christiane von Brühl, who took an active part in the layout of Seifersdorf. Hennebo and Hoffman mentioned "das Häuslich-Enge und keinerlei Verschwendung Duldende" as the main characteristic of this park designed by a woman. Christiane von Brühl also proceeded without a prior conception of the whole: "Also wieder eine Anlage, bei der nicht von einem zusammenhängenden Konzept ausgegangen ist. Je nach Laune und ganz planlos wählte man die schönsten Stellen aus und besetze sie mit Hütten, Denkmälern und dergleichen, während die landschaftlichen Gegebenheiten zumeist blieben, wie man sie fand. Ein punktartiges Vorgehen, das bei vielen Anlagen gebräuchlich war" (p. 100). It must be pointed out here, that Goethe's initial attempts at landscape gardening also correspond to this "punktartige Vorgehen," but his later efforts, bolder and on a grander scale, resemble more the Captain's professional procedure. In the novel Goethe probably looks back at his first landscaping activities with irony.

30 This practice was quite frequent in the eighteenth century. Hirschfeld, for

example, requested that drawings and descriptions of noteworthy landscape gardens should be sent to him for publication in his books and
journals on garden art. There were numerous publications of park descriptions with copperplate illustrations.

31 This location again corresponds to Seifersdorf: "Die Anlagen sind Teil einer ringsum verhältnismäßig offenen Flur und ohne erkennbare Abgren-
zung. Schloß und eigentlicher Schloßgarten stehen in keinem Zusammenhang mit ihnen, sondern liegen in einiger Entfernung beim Ort Seifersdorf"
(Hennebo and Hoffman, III, 100).

32 Mannack also views the palace and the landscape garden as separate entities, as "gesonderte Bezirke, denen es an Zusammenhang mit der wei-
teren Umgebung mangelt" (p. 179). I shall return to this point in my conclusion.

33 Johann Georg Jacobi contrasts these two aesthetic conceptions in his essay "Über die Englischen Gärten." He deplores that all utility is banished
from the English garden, which is devoted only to beauty, and advocates
a return to the earlier combination of beauty and utility.

34 C. C. L. Hirschfeld, *Theorie der Gartenkunst*, III, 12–13.

35 Cf. Edward Hyams, *Capability Brown and Humphry Repton*, pp. 145, 151.

36 Walter Benjamin, in his famous interpretation "Goethes *Wahlverwandtschaften*" (reprinted in *Goethe im XX. Jahrhundert*, ed. Hans Mayer (Hamburg: Christian Wegner Verlag, 1967), stresses the arbitrariness of the
landscaping changes, for which the demonic powers of nature later revenge themselves. Eberhard Mannack also overestimates the transformation of the original landscape by the gardening activities in the novel.

37 Johann Georg Jacobi, who advocates rustic simplicity for English gardens,
also censures the contemporary rage for excessive decorations in his essay
"Über die Englischen Gärten" (1807).

38 *Raumdarstellung und Realitätsbezug in Goethes epischer Dichtung*, p. 169.

39 Cf. Goethe's essay "Einfache Nachahmung der Natur, Manier, Stil," in
Hamburger Ausgabe, XII, 30–35.

40 Judging from the contemporary context, there are only two possibilities
for its architectural style: neoclassical or neo-Gothic. When we consider
the landscaping projects in the novel, however, neo-Gothic seems much
more probable than neoclassical.

41 C. C. L. Hirschfeld, *Theorie der Gartenkunst*, III, 104–5.

42 *Die Wahlverwandtschaften*, p. 314.

43 C. C. L. Hirschfeld, IV, 238.

44 For example, by Walter Benjamin and Eberhard Mannack.

45 Hennebo and Hoffmann, III, 74.

46 C. C. L. Hirschfeld, V, 118–19.

47 A change in this direction is indicated by a publication of 1825: Voit, *Über
die Anlegung und Wandlung der Gottesäcker in heitere Ruhegärten der Abge-
schiedenen* (Augsburg, 1825). In contrast to Hirschfeld, Voit stresses the
serene aspects for the beautification of cemeteries.

Tristram Shandy *and Hippel's* Lebensläufe nach aufsteigender Linie

HAMILTON H. H. BECK

It is nothing new in the field of German literature to compare Laurence Sterne with his imitators in Germany, among them Theodor Gottlieb von Hippel. One recently published work on this topic is Peter Michelsen's *Laurence Sterne und der deutsche Roman des achtzehnten Jahrhunderts,*[1] which corrects a superficial overevaluation of Hippel at Sterne's expense by German scholars from earlier in the century.[2] Michelsen's long overdue revision of their chauvinistic judgments praising Hippel as "deep" and brushing off Sterne as a lightweight nevertheless leads Michelsen—and most other scholars since his work appeared—to a misunderstanding and misrepresentation of Hippel's position.

Hippel once used to be better known, at least in Germany. Kant, who knew Hippel well, praised him as a nuclear thinker ("Centralkopf")—and saw himself forced to state publicly that he was not the author of the *Lebensläufe*, which had been published anonymously and contained popularized excerpts from Kant's lectures. Jean Paul, the other German humorist who is often compared with Sterne, regarded Hippel as his immediate, and worthy, predecessor. Hegel spoke of the "wonderful individuality, freshness and vitality" of Hippel's novel,[3] and the young Karl Marx, when still in Trier, put into verse (in an album of poetry for the future Jenny Marx) some of Hippel's prose translations of Latvian folk songs taken from the second volume of the *Lebensläufe*.

261

The first volume of this novel appeared in 1778, as Hippel was just on the verge of the great successes in his career as a civil servant. Born in 1741 in Gerdauen, East Prussia, he first studied theology at the Albertina University in Königsberg, but later switched to law. Virtually penniless, he supported himself as tutor for the daughter of a noble family. He fell in love with his charge, who apparently returned his affections. But the father put an end to the relationship: his daughter would marry only another member of the nobility. (The "von" in Hippel's name was added years later when Hippel successfully petitioned Joseph II, the Holy Roman Emperor, to renew the family title that had fallen into disuse.)

Hippel was forced to leave, but resolved to overcome the deficiencies of his social background by means of a successful career. He became chief of police, judge, mayor of Königsberg, and Privy Councillor, a post he held until his death at the age of fifty-five in 1796. Hippel never married, though in various radical (and of course anonymous) treatises in the cause of women's rights he always defended the institution of marriage.[4]

Parallel to this public career, however, Hippel followed a semi-public one, where he operated either incognito or under a pseudonym. As a Freemason the by-now-wealthy Hippel, whose name in the Lodge was "Eugenius," founded a stipend for an orphan attending the university and in general was the moving force behind the philanthropical activity of the Lodge.[5]

It is in this spirit of enlightened activity that Hippel's novel should be viewed. His magnum opus was the *Lebensläufe nach aufsteigender Linie*, which appeared in four volumes between 1778 and 1781.

To be sure, Hippel's novel, when viewed as an imitation of *Tristram Shandy*, falls short of its great model. It can be argued that every novel in Sterne's manner is condemned to be the work of an epigone. Sterne, in *Tristram Shandy*, had already stretched the conventions of the novel to the limit. Victor Shklovski has argued that *Tristram Shandy* is *nothing but* a parody of traditional forms.[6] The content of the novel, wrote Shklovski, consists of emphasizing form by means of destroying it.[7] The structure of Sterne's novel is a dislocation and violation of traditional structures, so that none of the techniques of storytelling serves the purpose it had always been made to serve. Shklovski concludes that *Tristram Shandy* is the most typical novel ever written (and Tristram himself jokingly calls it "this book of books," III, 31)[8] because it is made up of typical techniques, conventional elements taken out of their normal context and put into a new and unusual order.

Shklovski surely is one-sided in considering only formal aspects and excluding any consideration of the ultimately moral intent of the work. Of course Sterne's narrator trespasses against all the conventions of storytelling, or follows them only in order to parody them. But the effect of this is, for example, to make the "confrontation with Death," which has a weighty enough ring to it, into but one more of "those whiffling vexations which come puffing across a man's canvass" (OED quotes just this passage from *Tristram*, VII, 16, in its definition of whiffling: "moving lightly as if driven by gusts of wind"). Even the more sentimental episodes (Maria, Le Fever) are not entirely free of parodistic or ironic undertones. Shklovski fails to consider fully the effect of this play, and he is quite wrong in calling Sterne unfeeling ("gefühllos," p. 149). Sterne is criticizing his countrymen's gravity and self-importance as well as their shallow cult of the sentimental. He hopes to improve them through laughter. This is the moral root of Sterne's play, which is not so close to play-for-the-sake-of-play as Shklovski implies.

Shklovski is right, however, in emphasizing that Sterne defunctionalizes forms, in the sense that they cease to serve any purpose other than to reveal themselves for what they are. Sterne thus wants to jar his readers into an awareness of the fictional nature of novelistic conventions. In the words of another critic, "The trouble with Sterne's predecessors, he cannot have failed to see, was that they made segments of life too ordered and too intelligible to be true accounts, connections too simply clear to be credible."[9] Sterne's humorous (and at the same time educational) intent is to vex the reader with the caprices of the narrator, who deliberately raises expectations only in order to disappoint them.

Sterne was so inventive with his technique of dislocating both the reader and traditional narrative techniques that he left little room for any novelists after him to play with these conventions in an original fashion. The inferiority of Hippel's *Lebensläufe* is grounded, however, not solely in the inimitability of Sterne's novel. There are also historical reasons. The differences between Sterne's novels and those of Hippel reflect the different stages of development of English and German literature in the eighteenth century. When *Tristram Shandy* began to appear, English literature was already a literature of international importance. Its influence was particularly strong in Germany, which in the 1750's was just beginning to create a national literature. As Herder wrote in 1796, "Wir wachten auf, da es allenthalben Mittag war und bei einigen Nationen sich gar schon die Sonne neigte. Kurz, *wir kamen zu spät. Und weil wir so spät kamen, ahmten wir nach*[. . . .]"[10] Michelsen develops this point when he writes that the difference between Sterne's urbanity and wit and the crudeness and clumsiness of his followers, translators and imitators in Germany is the difference between high society and provincialism.

Michelsen is right: Sterne's inimitability, Hippel's historical disadvantage, perhaps a lack of talent on Hippel's part, all these reasons help to explain the difference in quality between the two authors' novels. But the most important (and obvious) reason has never been properly evaluated: Hippel's aims were, despite certain similarities, essentially different from Sterne's.

Some of the traditional interpretations of the relationship between Sterne and Hippel have a point when they criticize Hippel's *Laune*. Contemporary critics complained that Hippel's *Laune* failed to be amusing because his allusions were too far-fetched, and therefore unclear—and these critics found the same error in *Tristram Shandy*. Modern critics are more convincing in their argument that Hippel tries for the same effects as Sterne, but is never as successful as Sterne.[11]

It has become typical, however, to explain the stylistic shortcomings and overextended *Laune* of Hippel by referring to his extreme subjectivity. His primary concern, so the argument goes, was to use the novel as a vehicle for presenting his *Ich*. Since the *Ich* is the only real character, all the other characters are but mouthpieces, or puppets, of the author. The *Ich* is furthermore the only constitutive principle, and since Hippel held a chaotic worldview, the work is necessarily formless. Its chaos reflects Hippel's chaotic subjectivity. This criticism was first made by his contemporaries, who accused the author of too little concern for his audience, and it survives in the arguments of those critics who follow Michelsen and accuse Hippel of too much subjectivity.[12] Hippel's contemporaries attributed his faults to Sterne's baneful influence, whereas latter-day critics argue that Hippel, like so many German authors in the eighteenth century, misunderstood Sterne.

And some superficial support for such criticism is to be found in the *Lebensläufe*. Originally the courses of life of the hero, Alexander, then of his father and grandfather were to be told (hence "nach aufsteigender Linie"), but in fact only the hero's life does get told, and that only with some effort. For Hippel, like Sterne, seemed less interested in his semi-autobiographical story than in the long digressions and asides. Rather than tell his course of life Alexander prefers to record the morbid observations of the Count of Death, "ein beson-

derer Mann. Seine Hauptbeschäftigung war, Leute sterben zu sehen."[13] Or Alexander quotes from Kant's lecture notes—which later
gave rise to the suspicions that Kant had written the *Lebensläufe*. Or
Alexander notes down a comic *Leichenabdankung*, a "schmackhafter
Vergleich" of a man's life with a meal (II, 386). Such picturesque
asides tend to support, on the surface at least, the contention that
Hippel was imitating the Sternean, digressive, *launischen*, style.

But *Tristram Shandy* is not just a comic novel, it is also a first-person
novel,[14] and it is this aspect of Sterne's work that can be seen as the
more important for Hippel. *Tristram Shandy*, as Michelsen says (p.
14), had shown how a novel could consist of nothing but digressions.
As Tristram himself writes, "Digressions, incontestably, are the sun-
shine; — they are the life, the soul of reading! — take them out of
this book, for instance, — you might as well take the book along with
them [. . .]" (I, 22, p. 73). Hippel can be considered the first German
author who did not simply imitate this trait of Sterne's but regarded
it as a challenge. Tristram is an example of an omniscient narrator
carried to an extreme: he knows everything about his topic—and has
made it his task to *tell* everything. (Henri Fluchère speaks of Tristram's "determination not to let the smallest particle of reality escape."[15]) Tristram is the most truly omniscient narrator perhaps in all
literature; "nothing which has touched me will be thought trifling in
its nature, or tedious in its telling" (I, 6, pp. 10–11). No fact concerning his life is too slight or too remote for him to track down. "My way
is ever to point out to the curious, different tracts of investigation, to
come at the first springs of the events I tell [. . . .]" (I, 21, p. 66).
Of course this involves him in innumerable digressions, but that is
the situation in which the omniscient narrator who is honest about
his business must necessarily find himself. *Real* omniscience does not
square well with the narrator's sovereign control over his narrative,
in other words, with the *convention* of narrative omniscience. Tristram's obsession with getting to the bottom of things, with arriving
at first causes of events, carries him so far afield that his stated intention of writing his life and opinions becomes increasingly lost from
sight. Tristram is so circumstantial in his account of his birth that he
is never able to relate his life. As Wayne Booth put it, "in a sense
Tristram Shandy is an elaborate evasion of the promise given in the
title."[16] Sterne treats the fiction of the all-knowing narrator as though
it were no fiction but the actual position of the narrator. Such a narrator is incapable of giving his story any form other than that of the
fragment. His story is engulfed by the details of the world to be de-

scribed. Sterne calls the pose of the omniscient narrator into question—he carries it to its logical conclusion, but in leading it *ad absurdum* he puts forward no other narrative pose.

The fiction underlying the first person novel is that the narrator himself is the author of the novel. Until Tristram Shandy the omniscience of this narrator-author was an often—if for the most part tacitly—accepted pre-condition of the first person novel.[17] Sterne made this assumption explicit and in so doing made it problematic.[18] Hippel's novel can be understood as an attempt to deal with this problem, to make the world tellable again after Sterne had shown that omniscience must impede the telling of a story. Hippel's solution is to develop the position of the narrator further.

At the beginning of the *Lebensläufe* the narrator is about to introduce himself but after the first word is abruptly cut short by an imaginary critic: "Ich — Halt!" But the narrator makes his appearance only in order to withdraw from the stage (taking the critic with him) and permit an unmediated confrontation of world and reader. Just as historians are for Hippel necessarily forgers who do not record the past but reinvent it,[19] so too the guiding hand of the narrator is for Hippel a deceiving hand, and one that he banishes from the presentation of the world in the novel. Hippel's radical (and remarkably modern) cure for the Shandean disease of the omniscient narrator run wild is to create the narrator who knows (almost) nothing, but who can speak reliably. The subjectivity of the narrator must necessarily color the perception of reality. Hippel's aim is to reduce this subjective element to a minimum in order to keep the world (and not just the narrator's *impressions* of it) tellable. He wants to present actions, not opinions concerning actions, to paraphrase the quotation from Epictetus which Sterne used as the motto for *Tristram Shandy*.[20] The monolithic narrator of Sterne's work is split into fragments by Hippel, each one of them a miniature monolith—but the sum of their narratives can claim the greatest possible reliability in their presentation of the fictional world. Each one is reliable (as far as he can be), and tells all he knows (but that is necessarily not much).

The narrator Alexander could better be called the editor and copyist. He lets the characters present themselves directly, without interference from the narrator, in that they write letters of advice to Alexander. This technique is used with great frequency in the first volume of the *Lebensläufe*. Thus Alexander's father writes to him on education (pp. 116–9), Mine, Alexander's girlfriend, writes to him (pp. 138–53), and his mother writes him a "Denkzettel" (pp. 179–209). The pages between Mine's letters and the mother's *Denkzettel* are filled completely with the mother's narrative of her husband's background. Alexander interrupts her and abridges her tale only occasionally. Later, at Herr v. G.'s, he wants to make his readers better acquainted "mit den Charakteren dieses hochwohlgebornen curischen Hauses und seiner Art [. . .] oder wie es mir eben einfällt, sie sich selbst bekannt machen lassen. Ich will versuchen, diesen Tag nachzuschreiben [. . . .]" (p. 211). The rest of the volume is taken up with a conversation in the garden of the estate of Herr v. G. The narrator does not suddenly become a playwright, although the printed page looks as though it were taken from a play: each character is identified before his speech by name (Alexander is called "ich"), no one stands above or outside the dialogue. Alexander does not become a dramatist but rather a protocolist.

It is in the following three volumes, however, that documentation replaces narration almost completely. Up until now Alexander has, for the most part, been able to act as narrator because he has been recording his own experiences (experiences that are reminiscent of Hippel's own youth). For much of the rest of the novel this will not be the case. And at the beginning of the second volume Alexander announces his intention not to pretend to an omniscience he cannot have.

Auch selbst, wenn ich im gemeinen Leben erzählen höre, seh' ich—ich sehe den Erzähler steif an, recht, als schien ich es zu bedauern, daß ich diese Geschichte nicht im Original gesehen; ich verlange, der Erzähler soll sie nachhandeln; soll, was und wie es geschehen, leibhaftig zeigen. Je mehr ein Erzähler zu sehen ist, je mehr freu' ich mich, je mehr find' ich die Kopie getroffen. Oft hab' ich gedacht, daß es eine Geschichte geben könne, (ob einen Roman, weiß ich Nicht), wo man nicht höre, sondern sehe, durch und durch sehe, wo nicht Erzählung, sondern Handlung wäre, wo man alles, oder wenigstens mehr sehe, als höre. Man sieht freilich den Erzähler im gemeinen Leben; allein die Wahrheit zu sagen, man hört ihn mehr, und es würd' Affektation seyn, wenn er mehr zu sehen, als zu hören wäre. Ein Erzähler, wenn er im Druck erscheint, wie wenig ist er zu sehen! wie weit weniger, als im gemeinen Leben!—Dergleichen *Geschichte,* wo, wie meine Mutter sagen würde, *gewandelt* und *gehandelt* wird, will man sie eine *redende,* eine *Geschichte mit eigenen Worten nennen,* meinethalben! Daß eine Geschichte *durchweg in Gesprächen,* eine in *Frag'* und *Antworten* ein ganz ander Ding sey, versteht sich. Wären in einer redenden Geschichte auch nur ausgerissene Lebensblätter, wie leicht würden sie zusammenzusetzen seyn. — Man würde dem Leser noch obenein eben hiedurch unvermerkt Gelegenheit zu mehrerer Anstrengung geben, und ihn zum

Mitarbeiter an seinem Werke machen. — Daß ich es bei dieser Geschichte zu diesem Ziel nicht angelegt, bescheide ich mich von selbst,
und ich bin schon zufrieden, wenn mein Lebenslauf nur hier und
da Darstellung enthält, und wenn sich in dem Schlusse des ersten
Bandes die Personen selbst zu erkennen und zu verstehen gegeben.
Rede und *du bist*, könnte das Motto zu diesen Gesprächen seyn; es
liegt eine besondere Natur in der Rede.[21]

This passage is of central importance to Hippel's novel, for it intro-
duces a number of concepts that are fundamental to his understanding of the novel. At the beginning and end of this quotation the narrator expresses his longing for immediacy not just in the novel but
also "im gemeinen Leben." He always values a direct sense impression more highly than information that is second-hand. This is
the principle that underlies his apparently inconsistent remarks on
the relative merits of seeing and hearing. When a story is told in
person ("im gemeinen Leben"), the emphasis is on sight. The best
storyteller should, like an actor, perform and not just relate what he
tells. He should appeal not just to the ear but also to the eye. At best,
however, such a performance is but a poor substitute for the events
themselves, which Hippel would prefer to see as they happened,
without having to rely on someone to report them. When Hippel
praises the narrator as performer, he singles out for praise precisely
that kind of narration in which the narrator does not interpret the
story, but rather recreates it before the eyes of his audience. This narrator draws attention not to himself but to the events, so that he
becomes as it were a transparent medium through which the events
can be seen without distortion.

But this praise of the narrator could easily be misunderstood.
When Hippel says, "Je mehr ein Erzähler zu sehen ist, je mehr freu'
ich mich," it could seem that he advocates that the narrator call attention to himself. To correct any such misunderstanding, Hippel seems
to reverse himself and suddenly consider hearing more important
than seeing, and calls it "Affektation" when the narrator is more seen
than heard. But the thrust of his argument is consistent throughout:
the events themselves are of prime importance, and the narrator is
little more than a necessary evil. The audience should see not the
narrator but see through the narrator to the events. If the narrator's
presence diverts the audience from the story, then they should not
look at him but instead listen to what he says. Indeed this is almost
a necessity when the narrator tells his story not in person but "im
Druck."

The implication for this novel of this concern to emphasize the events at the expense of the narrator is that a work must strive to give at least the illusion of immediacy. Thus a novel should not be "Erzählung," that is, it should not be told, narrated, mediated, rather it should be "Handlung [. . .], wo man alles oder wenigstens mehr sehe, als höre." The narrator's other term for "Handlung" is "Darstellung," which he mentions near the end of this passage. "Darstellung" is perhaps the better term since it suggests the presentation of events as on a stage, whereas "Handlung" suggests more the events themselves, which could be presented any way the author wishes.

The narrator distinguishes between his proposal of a novel as "Darstellung" and experiments such as those undertaken by J. J. Engel with the *Dialogroman*. Probably the narrator has Engel in mind when he speaks of a "Geschichte *durchweg in Gesprächen*, [. . .] in *Frag'* und *Antworten*" and calls it "ein ganz ander Ding." The difference is a fundamental one, though it is only implied in this passage. The dialogue-novel breaks with the conventional novel only in a formal sense. Hippel's narrator, on the other hand, proposes a radical break with novels of the past, for the very elements of his novel cease to be fictive and are rather "ausgerissene [und wieder zusammengesetzte] Lebensblätter."

To be sure, the narrator admits that it is open to question whether or not such a work would be a novel, and he claims to have attained his ideal in this work "nur hier und da." But the *Darstellungsroman* is clearly the goal he is striving for. He recommends such a novel because it forces the reader to participate. The reader, confronted with "ausgerissene Lebensblätter," tries to put them together himself as he reads. By putting them into some context that will make them meaningful for him, the reader is placed in the same position as the narrator-author. In this fashion a community of interests is established between the author and his public such that they can be considered his "Mitarbeiter."

Hippel was prepared to go to great lengths in order to turn his work into "Lebensblätter." In volume II the quotation of documents begins in earnest. These documents and conversations, it must be emphasized, give the impression of being recorded virtually word for word, with Alexander making only minor alterations. "Eine Erzählung, der man das Studirte, das Geflissene, das Geordnete ansieht, ist unausstehlich. — So wie es in der Welt geht, so muß es auch in der Geschichte gehen. — Bald so, bald so" (II, 44). Later he remarks, "Ich bemühe mich auch hier, Lebensläufer zu seyn, und diese Abschrift ist dem Original ähnlich. — Wir fielen von einem aufs andere. Wir scheitelten die Haare nicht. Würd' ich nicht einen Roman schreiben, wenn ich nicht auch von einem aufs andere fallen und die Haare scheiteln sollte? Ein Roman! fern sey er von mir!" (II, 132).

Most of volume II is taken up with the pursuit and death of Alexander's beloved Mine, who is the victim of a conspiracy involving, among others, Herr v. E. (a lecherous nobleman whom Mine refuses to marry), her father, and legal officers of the law courts of Courland and Prussia. The actual narrator of Mine's last days is a clergyman in the Prussian city of L——, "von dem ich dieses alles haarklein habe," as Alexander says (II, 296).

Observations on death, an important subject throughout the *Lebensläufe*, become most prominent after Mine's death. The last pages of volume II and much of volume III, part 1 are given over to the Count of Death, whose life consists of preparing himself for death and observing the deaths of others. One of the patients the Count entertains at his castle is the "Krippenritterin," whose story Alexander retells with the preface, "Ich will ihre Geschichte *in tertia persona* geben, ohne zu bemerken, ob ich die Umstände von ihr selbst oder vom Grafen empfangen" (III, 63).

The speculations of the Count are given much room (about fifty pages), and are only now and then interrupted by the narrator's commentary: "Der Graf hätte so ohne End' und Ziel reden können. Es war Zephyr, den er mir zuwehte — wirklicher Zephyr, sanfte Empfindung, womit er mich anfächelte" (III, 89). "So vortrefflich unordentlich war diese Rede. Es war kein Kunst-, sondern ein Naturstück" (III, 118). "Was ich meinen Lesern von der Wildnißrede gegeben, sollte eine Nachfolge des Originals seyn; ich wollte nicht den Hauch der Natur von der Pflaume wegwischen, sondern so wie sie da ist, mit diesem Naturathem, der mir wie ein Heiligenschein vorkommt, wollt' ich sie [. . . .]" (III, 118).

If the Count's hobby-horse is the subject of death, his counterpart is the clergyman, who is writing a book on transgressions against the Holy Ghost. Their hobby-horses are not antithetical, but their styles are. The clergyman says of the Count's disorderly manner of speculation, "Es ist, sagte er, so etwas Beängstigendes, so was von Todesnoth darin. Eben das, sagt' ich, hat mich entzückt bis zur Halle des Himmels. Dieß in der Rede zu treffen, zu copiren, war unmöglich. — Ich liebe, fuhr der Prediger fort, eine genaue Bindung der Perioden, eine gewisse Baukunst im Vortrage, und so viel Fenster wie möglich in jedem Stock. Zwar halte ich es für keine Sünde wider den heiligen Giest—" and thus he returns to riding his hobbyhorse (III, 137). This passage is significant for two reasons. First, it suggests that the Count's and Alexander's disorderly style is, at least in this section of the work, justifiable on aesthetic grounds. If the lack of order itself has something of death about it, then it is the appropriate vehicle of expression for the mourning and distraught Alexander. Second, this passage also indicates that Alexander will overcome his depression and closeness to death. For it is the clergyman's emphasis on systematization that, for Alexander, is deadening. Alexander's greater sympathy for the living and natural paradoxically leads him to defend the Count, who, for all his preoccupation with death, has more in common with life in his speculations and activities than does the clergyman in his book.

Alexander's return to life takes place in the last volume, near the beginning of which he receives a letter from his father, noting, "Um es authentisch meinen Lesern mitzutheilen, schreib ich es aus dem Original aus, das noch da vor mir liegt" (III, pt. 2, pp. 18–19).

Another narrator is introduced to tell of the mother's death. She had "eine alte Priesterwittwe, anstatt einer Diakonin, zu sich genommen, und *von ihr hab' ich empfangen,* was ich meinen Lesern erzähle, und zwar so, als wär ich Augenzeuge gewesen" (III, pt. 2, p. 39). "Meine Leser wissen, wie sehr ich für eigene Worte bin!" (III, pt. 2, p. 52). Later fifteen pages are taken up with a collection of the mother's maxims and views, utterly without order, simply listed one after the other, giving the impression that the "narrator" has contributed nothing. He merely prints what falls into his hands haphazardly.

In his despair over Mine's death Alexander decides to join the Russian army in the war against the Turks. This episode is ended when Alexander receives a letter from the Empress Catherine the Great raising him into the ranks of the nobility. Thus he is doubly ennobled, both through merit and blood, for, as a letter from his father reveals, Alexander is also a nobleman by birth.

Alexander returns to Courland and woos the daughter of Herr v. G., Tine, whom he had saved from drowning during his first visit at the estate of Herr v. G. in volume II. They are united not only by their love for each other, but also by their love for Mine, in whose honor Tine changes her name so that she too is called Mine. They retire to an estate in the country and Mine gives birth to their son Leopold, as the story apparently comes to an end.

But after turning a blank page (an obviously Sternean technique) the reader finds that the story continues into the present: Leopold dies, Mine is unable to give birth again, and Alexander resolves to leave the estate to dedicate himself, at least temporarily, to some kind of work, not defined, in public service. Thus the work ends as a diary.

The narrator closest to Hippel, the "Ich" of the opening passage, is absent from the work to a significant degree, reports only what he can say with certainty about himself, and otherwise lets the characters speak for themselves in letters, dialogues, prayer, or he retreats behind impersonal documents: protocols of meetings and judicial writings. He appears not at all in the three *Beilagen* A, B and C. "A" follows the death of Mine in volume II, and is a translation of Latvian folksongs into German prose. Most of them deal with the themes of love, nature and death. "B," the counterpart of "A," follows immediately upon it in volume II, and is the *Leichenabdankung* for Mine delivered by the organist in L——. His tolerance of flies parodies that of Uncle Toby: "Kann sie ein so großer Herr, als der liebe Gott ist, in seiner Welt leiden, so können sie doch wohl in meiner Stube seyn? Ich hab' es von einem sehr vornehmen Herrn, der bei einem Feste auch für seine Fliegen und Mücken Wein eingießen läßt, um alles was um ihn lebt und schwebt, zu sättigen und zu tränken mit Wohlgefallen."[22] "C," in the middle of volume III, part 2, is a book of letters written by Alexander's friend Gottfried to Alexander's mother dealing with questions of tolerance for Jews and *Ketzer* in Courland and Königsberg.[23]

In general, Alexander in his role as narrator treats the character Alexander as just one of many characters, his experiences with Mine and Tine are but two of many similar episodes dealing with the problems young lovers face when society and parents, misunderstandings and, sometimes, the lovers' own feelings stand in the way of their marriage. Hippel breaks up Sterne's omniscient narrator into a conglomerate group of narrators, each of them limited to a well-defined area, to be sure, but each one also a narrator who knows all that can be known from that point of view. In this way Hippel achieves what is perhaps his ultimate aim, namely to let the world itself speak directly to the reader with as little interference as possible from an omniscient narrator.

Above and beyond this "invented document" method of composition, however, is a second layer of documentation, one that Hippel works into the novel in a way that shows clearly how deep his concern is to avoid engaging in any falsification: for Hippel not only quoted from invented documents, he also took notes from his everyday life, from conversation, lectures, and judge's bench, and worked them into a first draft. He then passed the manuscript around to a select group of friends for them to make their additions and criticisms. Hippel always had the final word as to what went into the novel, but the work can still legitimately be considered the product of a collective.

After Hippel's death his friends discovered in his papers fragments of conversations he had had with them.[24] Hippel, who was, it must be remembered, chief of police, had the habit of jotting down remarks he thought interesting—complete with the date and name of his conversation partner. It was all intended, obviously, as raw material for future works. Hippel's friends, disillusioned and feeling themselves betrayed, destroyed most of the notes.[25] They should not have been so surprised at what they found, however, since even during Hippel's lifetime it was argued (not, of course, on the basis of documents, but rather because of alleged stylistic similarities) that Lichtenberg, or Leisewitz, or Lenz authored various works of Hippel. Today it is possible only in Kant's case to see to any degree just how much Hippel made use of the words and thoughts of his friends.

This method of composition, one that anticipates twentieth-century montage techniques, is the logical extension of the method of inventing documents. The subjectivity of the narrator, if it cannot be completely eliminated, should be significantly reduced—and not just on the surface, but also as far as possible in the very fiber of the novel.

In summary it could be said that Sterne carries narrative omniscience so far that it turns into ignorance, or better, the inability to tell a story to the end, the inability even to get to the beginning of a story. Hippel, on the other hand, carries the *limitation* of the narrator so far that it turns into an epic technique of its own. As in the case of *Tristram Shandy* the apparent chaos of Hippel's novel is not a result of dilettantism or inability to control the métier, as critics have traditionally maintained, but is part of the intention of the work. Hippel might sometimes look as though he is imitating Sterne, but in essence Hippel runs directly counter to his supposed model.

But questions remain: Could it not be argued that Hippel is trying for Sternean effects with contrary means? Is Hippel any the less an epigone when read as an anti-Sternean? The traditional interpretation of the relationship between Sterne and Hippel clearly needs to be reinterpreted. But how important *is* Sterne's influence on Hippel? Hippel's novel can be understood as a reply to Sterne, but perhaps it is better understood as a reflection of Hippel's personality. F. J. Schneider called the *Lebensläufe* the most faithful reflection of its au-

thor's inner life,[26] but this inner life is itself of course a reflection of
Hippel's situation in a society that was still in many ways feudal. We
have already seen, for example, how the class structure worked
against his relationship with a daughter of the nobility. Hippel's response to this situation was to conform to the system outwardly and
make use of its opportunities for social advancement. Inwardly,
though, he remained closed to the world and created a private sphere
that not even his closest friends could ever entirely penetrate. This
side of Hippel, writing alone until late in the night, always remained
one he deliberately concealed. Only in this way could he be both
effective in public life and true to his inner self.

Hippel always satirized, for example, the snobbery of the landed
gentry, the *Junker*. Nevertheless he renewed the old noble title in his
family name in 1791, since only members of the nobility could own a
Landgut or become ministers of state. But in the *Kreuz- und Querzüge
des Ritters A bis Z*, Hippel's last (and, as always, anonymous) novel
(1793–94), his satire of the false pride of the nobility is even more
biting than when he was not one of them himself.

One of Hippel's most fundamental characteristics is thus his striving to unite contradictory elements. This character trait is not merely
idiosyncratic, however, for it is anchored in the structure of contemporary Prussian society. Hippel's contradictory reactions of criticism
leading to reform (expressed in his anonymously published works)—
and the conformism of his public career, spring ultimately from his
position in the society that was in some ways enlightened and in
others still very much a feudal system.

The impossibility of reconciling such contradictions eventually led
to deformations in Hippel's character. There is an almost schizo-
phrenic quality about his personality: on the one hand Hippel presents himself as the efficient mayor who could lay down his pen
every evening in the certainty that all business had been taken care
of; on the other hand he played the eccentric hermit in his country
house, filled with symbols of death, complete with an imitation
cemetery in the garden.[27]

Hippel's striving for totality, for the reconciliation of contrary elements, is thus a reflection of his social situation. His writings, for
example, belong basically to the Enlightenment; they intend to educate their readers and amuse them at the same time. But what separates his writings from the Enlightenment is the deformed elements
peculiar to him, and in this context his obsession with death is often
cited. An even more important deformation, however, one that gives

Hippel's works (not just the novels) their idiosyncratic form, is that in them the striving for totality takes on a life of its own.

In the *Lebensläufe* Hippel wants to include certain central aspects of life in their entire fullness, especially the process of maturation, the experience of love, of death, and man's reaction to the death of a beloved one. This desire for totality threatens to explode any literary form—except that of the Sternean novel. Thus Hippel takes up and transforms Sterne's techniques according to his own needs. Maybe Hippel is much less indebted to Sterne than has ever been thought before.

NOTES

This essay is a revised version of a paper delivered at the regional meeting of the North East American Society for Eighteenth-Century Studies in Amherst, Mass., 6 October 1978.

1 Peter Michelsen, *Laurence Sterne und der deutsche Roman des achtzehnten Jahrhunderts*. Palaestra. Untersuchungen aus der deutschen und englischen Philologie und Literaturgeschichte, vol. 232. 2nd ed. (Göttingen: Vandenhoeck & Ruprecht, 1972).

2 See for example Johann Czerny, *Sterne, Hippel und Jean Paul* (Berlin: Duncker & Humblot, 1904), and Ferdinand Josef Schneider, "Studien zu Th. G. von Hippels 'Lebensläufen.' 2. Über den Humor L. Sternes und Th. G. v. Hippels," in *Euphorion*, 22 (1915), 678–702.

3 *Aesthetik*, 2 vols. (Berlin and Weimar: Aufbau, 1976), I, 559.

4 Some of these treatises are available at present. The best of the reissued works on this topic is *Über die bürgerliche Verbesserung der Weiber* (Frankfurt a. M.: Syndikat Autoren- und Verlagsgesellschaft, 1977). An annotated (and abridged) translation of this work, under the title *On Improving the Status of Women*, has been made by Prof. Timothy F. Sellner (Detroit: Wayne State University Press, 1979). For a discussion of this edition, see my review in vol. XII of the Lessing Yearbook. The first edition of *Über die Ehe*, in which Hippel still held relatively conservative views on women, has also been reissued (Stuttgart: Deutsche Verlags-Anstalt, 1972). The last edition, in which Hippel's views are much more radical, is available as part of Hippel's collected works, in 14 volumes, which have been reprinted by de Gruyter (Berlin, 1978). Finally, one other work, the underrated *Biographie*, is also available in its original form (Hildesheim: Gerstenberg Verlag, 1977; reprint of the 1801 Gotha edition, which differs from the revised version in the de Gruyter set.

5 Richard Fischer, *Geschichte der Johannis Loge Zu den drei Kronen* (Königsberg in Preussen: Als Manuskript gedruckt, 1910), p. 131.

6 Viktor Shklovski, *Theorie der Prosa*, ed. and trans. Gisela Drohla (Frankfurt a. M.: S. Fischer Verlag, 1966), pp. 131–62.

7 Shklovski says that "Hervorhebung der Form durch deren Zerstörung bildet den Inhalt des Romans" (p. 135).

8 *The Life and Opinions of Tristram Shandy, Gentleman*, ed. James A. Work (Indianapolis: The Odyssey Press, 1940), p. 218.

9 B. H. Lehman, "Of Time, Personality, and the Author. A Study of *Tristram Shandy*: Comedy," in *Essays on the Eighteenth-Century Novel*, ed. Robert Donald Spector (Bloomington: Indiana University Press, 1965), p. 179.

10 Johann Gottfried Herder, *Briefe zu Beförderung der Humanität* (Berlin and Weimar: Aufbau-Verlag, 1971), II, 113.

11 See especially Norbert Miller, *Der empfindsame Erzähler* (Munich: Carl Hanser Verlag, 1968), p. 444. Also H. H. Borcherdt, *Der Roman der Goethezeit* (Urach and Stuttgart: Port Verlag, 1949), p. 60.

12 "Hippels Roman ist wirklich ein Chaos, und das nicht nur hinsichtlich der Form. Er ist das getreue Abbild eines zerbrochenen Weltbildes, mit dem der Autor nicht fertig geworden ist" (Eva Becker, *Der deutsche Roman um 1780* [Stuttgart: J. B. Metzlersche Verlagsbuchhandlung, 1964], p. 215). "[Bei Hippel] sind die Begebenheiten um das erfahrend-erzählende Ich des Helden Alexander alles andere als verbürgte, unbezweifelte Handlungen im Sinne Sternes: Hippels "Lebensläufe" zeigen die Welt als Chaos, dessen dichter, unsicherer Nebel vom Ich nicht zu durchdringen ist" (Miller, p. 292). "Es ist ein extrem subjektivistisches Erzählprogramm, das hier mit Hilfe sternisierender Mittel verwirklicht ist" (Jürgen Jacobs, *Prosa der Aufklärung*: Kommentar zu einer Epoche [Munich: Winkler Verlag, 1976], pp. 206–7).

13 Theodor Gottlieb von Hippel, *Lebensläufe nach aufsteigender Linie, Nebst Beilagen A, B, C* (Leipzig: Göschen, 1860), II, 371. All references are to this edition.

14 See Franz Stanzel, "*Tom Jones* und *Tristram Shandy*," in *English Miscellany*, 5 (1954), 107–48; also *Die typischen Erzählsituationen im Roman* (Wiener Beiträge zur englischen Philologie, 63 [1955]). Stanzel distinguishes between the authorial narrator on the one hand, who, like the narrator of *Tom Jones*, could be considered a chronicler or editor, someone who has only a loose relationship to the events he relates, who tells the story in the third person and is not himself part of the story; and, on the other hand, the personal narrator, who is himself one of the characters in the story he tells, and who speaks in the first person. To account for Tristram, who as a narrator has authorial omniscience yet speaks in the first person, Stanzel invents the type of the first person narrator as well, who is somewhere between the authorial and the personal types of narrator.

15 Henri Fluchère, *Laurence Sterne: From Tristram to Yorick: An Interpretation of Tristram Shandy*, trans. and abr. Barbara Bray (London: Oxford University Press, 1965), p. 40.

16 Wayne Booth, "The Self-conscious Narrator in Comic Fiction before *Tristram Shandy*," in *PMLA*, 67 (1952), 169.

17 Wayne Booth, *The Rhetoric of Fiction* (Chicago: The University of Chicago Press, 1961), esp. pp. 224–26.

18 Narrative omniscience should be on A. A. Mendilow's list of conventions flouted by Sterne when he writes, "Sterne was very deeply interested in the problems these conventions raise, namely the relationship between reality and fictional illusion. Above all, he wished to arouse his readers to the realization that these *are* conventions, that they should not be taken for reality, not even for valid symbols, let alone transcripts of reality. . . ." Mendilow is referring to conventions of plot, chronology and causality in his *Time and the Novel* (New York: Humanities Press, 1972), p. 166. Likewise John Traugott's assertion that "To say that Sterne was self-conscious is, I think, to say little. What he really seems to have wanted is self-consciousness from the reader" applies not just to Tristram's use of rhetoric. See Traugott's *Tristram Shandy's World: Sterne's Philosophical Rhetoric* (Berkeley and Los Angeles: University of California Press, 1954) p. 109.

19 Hippel quotes with obvious agreement his father's view, "Daß einem Sonntagskinde ein Volk aus der Sprache recht aus dem Grunde kennen zu lernen weit leichter wäre, als aus allen Historienbüchern, in die der Geschichtschreiber jederzeit seine eigne Geschichte, seine eigne Denkart und überhaupt sein eignes Ich zu verwickeln und zu verweben pflegt." Th. G. v. Hippel's *Sämmtliche Werke* (Berlin: G. Reimer, 1835), XII, 43.

20 "It is not actions, but opinions concerning actions, which disturb men" (trans. J.A. Work).

21 "Even when in everyday life I hear a story told, I see—I look hard at the story teller, just as though I seemed to regret it that I have not seen the story take place just the way it was; I desire the story teller to reenact it; he should visibly demonstrate what happened and how. The more a story teller is to be seen, the happier I am, the more I find an accurate depiction. I have often thought there could be a story (I do not know whether it would be a novel), in which one would not hear but rather see, see through and through, in which there would not be narration, but rather action, in which one would see everything, or at least more than one heard. The story teller is of course seen in everyday life; but to tell the truth, he is more heard, and it would be affectation for him to be more seen than heard. How little is a story teller to be seen when he appears in print! how much less, than in everyday life! — Such a *story*, in which, as my mother would say, there was *faction* and *action*, could be called a *speaking story*, one *in its own words*, whatever! It is evident that a story told *only in conversations*, in *questions* and *answers*, is quite a different thing. Even if in a talking story there were only pages torn from life, how easy it would be to put them together. — In addition the reader would by this unobtrusive means be given the opportunity to exert himself more and to become a contributing author of the work. — I freely grant that in this story I have not achieved this goal, and I am already satisfied if my course of life contains representation only here and there, and if at the close of the first volume the characters have revealed themselves and made themselves

understood on their own. *Speak* and *ye shall be* could be the motto of these conversations; speech has a nature all its own."

22 *Lebensläufe*, II, 388. See *Tristram Shandy*: "my uncle *Toby* had scarce a heart to retaliate upon a fly. —Go—says he, one day at dinner, to an overgrown one which had buzz'd about his nose, and tormented him cruelly all dinner-time [. . . .] —Go, says he, lifting up the sash, and opening his hand as he spoke, to let it escape;—go poor devil, get thee gone, why should I hurt thee?—This world surely is wide enough to hold both thee and me" (p. 113).

23 *Lebensläufe*, III, pt. 2, pp. 167–86. It is interesting, in considering the role of documents in the *Lebensläufe*, to conjecture on just how much of the work Hippel originally conceived as *Beilagen*. In his first reference to it Hippel calls the work *Lebensläufe* etc. "mit Beilagen A.B.C.D.E.F.G.H." See his letter to Scheffner, no. 67, written at the end of July 1775, in Th. G. v. Hippel, *Briefe*, vol. 14 of *Sämmtliche Werke* (Berlin: G. Reimer, 1828–35), p. 4.

24 See the *Biographie*, pp. 463–65.

25 F. J. Schneider's efforts to recover Hippel's unpublished papers, which included another novel, remained fruitless. See his biography, *Theodor Gottlieb von Hippel in den Jahren von 1741 bis 1781 und die erste Epoche seiner literarischen Tätigkeit* (Prague: Taussig & Taussig, 1911).

26 Ibid., p. 107.

27 *Biographie*, p. 361.

Phillis Wheatley and the Poetical Legacy of Eighteenth-Century England

CHARLES SCRUGGS

Although we have learned a good deal in recent years about Phillis Wheatley's life and literary career, we have rarely attempted to discuss her poetry as poetry.[1] As America's first important black poet, Phillis Wheatley has been treated less as an artist and more as a curiosity. For instance, right at the outset, American responses to her poems remained tied to racial debate. When her first and only book of poetry—*Poems on Various Subjects, Religious and Moral*—appeared in 1773, Abolitionists rushed to herald her artistic efforts as a symbol of deserved equality for the Negro; whereas pro-slavery critics pooh-poohed her poems as objects beneath their contempt.[2] This non-aesthetic approach to Phillis Wheatley continues in our own time. Her art is still a locus for political controversy, but the terms of the argument have shifted. In the 1970s, some feel that Phillis Wheatley has evinced a genuine concern for her race in her poetry; whereas others believe that the slave poet had a low opinion of her fellow bondsmen.[3]

Whenever her poetry has been discussed as poetry, a "Romantic" bias has determined her critical reputation. Even in the twentieth century, criticism of her poetry has been shaped by prejudices inherited from the Romantic period. To listen to her modern critics, "neo-classicism" was the *bête noire* of her brief poetic career. Saunders Redding talks of the "chill . . . of Pope's neo-classicism upon her," and M. A. Richmond complains that "neo-classicism" was responsible for her artificiality. "Neo-classicism," says Richmond, encased Phillis Wheatley within the "tyranny of the couplet" and crushed her talent under "the heavy burden of ornamental rhetoric."[4] The kindest thing that has been said of "neo-classicism" is that it taught her regularity.[5]

Thanks to Donald Greene (*The Age of Exuberance*) and others, we have become somewhat suspicious of the word "neo-classicism." Not only was this word invented by the nineteenth century but the concept itself cannot possibly encompass the richness and complexity of eighteenth-century art. Even when the term "neo-classicism" makes sense within a limited context, no student of the eighteenth century today would treat it as though it were synonymous with the contemporary meaning of "artificiality." In fact, as all students of the eighteenth century know, the word "artificial" presents an interesting historical irony. The eighteenth century ordinarily did not use the word "artificial" in a pejorative sense—although it could be used that way. Usually "artificial" meant "artful, contrived with skill."[6]

That many of Phillis Wheatley's poems are "contrived with skill" is the basis of my argument in this paper. We are told that Phillis Wheatley was a bad poet because she lived in an age uncongenial, even hostile, to the true poetic sensibility. If she had been planted in better soil, such as the fertile ground of the Romantic period, then we would have had a real poet instead of a hothouse flower.[7] Eighteenth-century poetry, these critics insist, was impersonal, stylized, and ornate; and the poetical fashions of this period were dictatorial and absolute. Thus in imitating the literary conventions of her day, Phillis Wheatley wrote poetry which is artificial and insincere. This view is wrongheaded because it fails to understand those literary conventions which it deplores. More precisely, it fails to take into account that eighteenth-century aesthetic thought made a distinction between artifice and artificiality, and not between sincerity and artificiality.[8] Because Phillis Wheatley's critics have refused to recognize the artifice of eighteenth-century poetry, they have not seen the competent craftsmanship of Phillis Wheatley's poems. Not seeing the forest, they certainly cannot be expected to see the trees.

I

When Phillis Wheatley visited England in 1773, she was received there with more fanfare than she would ever receive in her lifetime in America. This reception is significant, because it tells us something about mid-eighteenth-century aesthetic taste. Arriving in London with her owner Susannah Wheatley, this humble young girl found herself courted and lionized by the city's literati. The Countess of Huntingdon became her patron; the former Lord Mayor of London presented her with a copy of *Paradise Lost*; and *Poems on Various Subjects* was actually published in England—primarily owing to Lady Huntingdon's efforts.[9] These events have been described in detail,[10] But no one has told us the reason for such lavish attention given to a lowly slave poet. The answer lies in England's fascination for poets who illustrated the principle of "natural genius." This principle can best be explained by the Latin aphorism, *poeta nascitur, non fit* ("a poet is born, and not made").[11] Although the idea of "natural genius" is at least as old as Pindar, it was given a new interpretation by the middle of the eighteenth century. This interpretation not only helps us to understand the English response to Phillis Wheatley, but it also enables us to see how she could use the idea of "natural genius" to her own poetical advantage.

As was the case with many ideas not his own, Joseph Addison popularized the concept of "natural genius" in the eighteenth century. In 1711, in *Spectator* 160, Addison had distinguished between two kinds of poetic genius. The first kind are those artists "who by the mere strength of natural parts, and without any assistance of art or learning, have produced works that were the delight of their own times and the wonder of posterity." The second kind are artists who "have formed themselves by rules and submitted the greatness of their natural talents to the corrections and restraints of art." Addison claims to make no invidious comparison between the two types of genius, but he does admit that there is something "nobly wild, and extravagant in . . . natural geniuses that is infinitely more beautiful than all the turn and polishing of what the French call a *bel esprit*, by which they would express a genius refined by conversation, reflection, and the reading of the most polite authors."[12] As Addison defined the term, "natural genius" implied an elitist view of the poet; some are born with this divine talent and others are not.

Addison never imagined that the idea of "natural genius" could be applied to a working-class poet. Nevertheless, at mid-century this concept was given a distinctly democratic twist. Some members of the English aristocracy became convinced that among the poor were to be found "mute, inglorious Miltons," who if only given the chance would burst forth in glorious song.[13] Thus poets were seized upon because they were "unlettered," and in the thirty-five or so years before Phillis Wheatley began to write in the late 1760s, we find numerous examples of bards from the lower classes who were patronized by people of position. For example, Joseph Spence sponsored Stephen Duck, the "Thresher-Poet"; William Shenstone, Lady Mary Montague, and Lord Lyttelton encouraged James Woodhouse, the "Shoemaker-Poet"; Lord Chesterfield helped Henry Jones, the "Bricklayer-Poet"; and in little more than a decade after Phillis Wheatley's death, Hannah More took Ann Yearsley under her wing, the poet known as Lactilla, the "Milkmaid-Poet."[14]

Given this atmosphere, it is understandable that Lady Huntingdon became excited over the poetry of a young slave girl.[15] To Lady Huntingdon, this was another example of "natural genius" among the impoverished classes. Furthermore, she knew that others would respond to this new manifestation of the "Unlettered Muse," and she therefore placed a picture of Phillis Wheatley on the frontispiece of *Poems on Various Subjects* in order to call attention to the author's humble station.

The advertisement for Phillis Wheatley's book also emphasized the author's "natural genius." This notice appeared in the *London Chronicle* (September 9–11, 11–14) and in *The Morning Post and Advertiser* (September 13 and 18), and it included a testimonial from people "distinguished for their learning" who "unanimously expressed their approbation of her genius, and their amazement at the gifts with which infinite Wisdom has furnished her." The language of this advertisement implies that Phillis Wheatley and Africa were inseparably linked in the minds of eighteenth-century Englishmen:

> The Book here proposed for publication displays perhaps one of the greatest instances of pure, unassisted genius, that the world ever produced. The Author is a native of Africa, and left not that dark part of the habitable system, till she was eight years old. She is now no more than nineteen, and many of the Poems were penned before she arrived at near that age.
>
> They were wrote upon a variety of interesting subjects, and in a stile rather to be expected from those who . . . have had the happiness of a liberal education, than from one born in the wilds of Africa.[16]

Although Phillis Wheatley's poetical "genius" is "unassisted," this is no Romantic conception of the artist. Phillis Wheatley is not praised because she expresses her naked, unadorned self; she is praised because, deprived of a "liberal education," she intuitively knows the adornments of art.

This tradition of "natural genius" continues well into the nineteenth century and is the basis of Margaretta Odell's short biography of the African poet. A strange mixture of fact and fancy, Odell's *Memoir* (1834) is our major source of information about Phillis Wheatley's life. The myth which Odell expounds has its roots in eighteenth-century England. We learn, for instance, that as a young girl Phillis took to poetry as naturally as ducks take to water. Although people encouraged her to read and write, "nothing was forced upon her, nothing was suggested, or placed before her as a lure; her literary efforts were altogether the natural workings of her own mind." Also, she never had "any grammatical instructor, or knowledge of the structure or idiom of the English language, except which she imbibed from a perusal of the best English writers, and from mingling in polite circles. . . ." Furthermore, she was visited by visions in the night which awakened her and which she wrote down as poems. The next morning, she could not remember these dreams which had inspired her to write poetry.[17]

The extent to which Phillis Wheatley believed she was a "natural genius" is difficult to determine, but she did skillfully employ this public image of herself in her poetry. The appearance of the idea of "natural genius" in her poems presented a familiar paradox, as her age would have instantly recognized. In a poetical correspondence with Lieutenant Rochfort of His Majesty's Navy, Phillis Wheatley modestly disclaims the use of artifice, at the same time that she artfully defines the kind of poet she is and hopes to be.

Phillis Wheatley had written a poem, addressed to Rochfort, in which she had praised the sailor's martial valor, and Rochfort responded by sending her a poem of his own. In "The Answer," Rochfort eulogizes Phillis Wheatley by glorifying the country of her birth. Africa is depicted as a "happy land" where "shady forests . . . scarce know a bound." Here there are

> The artless grottos, and the soft retreats;
> "At once the lover and the muse's seats."
> Where nature taught, (tho strange it is to tell,)
> Her flowing pencil Europe to excell.
>
> (P. 84)

In these lines, Rochfort has romanticized Africa. Primitivistic and picturesque, this Africa is as unreal as the "dark continent" of the advertisement to *Poems on Various Subjects*. Rochfort sees Africa as the cause of Phillis Wheatley's power as a poet; the simple "artless" land has given birth to an "artless" poet. In later lines, he celebrates "Wheatley's song" as having "seraphic fire" and an "art, which art could ne'er acquire."

When Phillis Wheatley wrote a poetic reply to this poem, she employed the same motifs which Rochfort had used. She refers to Africa as a luxuriant "Eden." Then she humbly says of Rochfort's flattery:

> The generous plaudit 'tis not mine to claim,
> A muse untutor'd, and unknown to fame.
> (P. 86)

She laments further that her "pen . . . Can never rival, never equal thine," but she will nevertheless continue to study the best authors to improve her talent. She illustrates this thought by soaring into poetic flight:

> Then fix the humble Afric muse's seat
> At British Homer's and Sir Isaac's feet
> Those bards whose fame in deathless strains arise
> Creation's boast, and fav'rites of the skies.
> (P. 86)

It is easy to see that Rochfort and Phillis Wheatley are playing an elaborate game in these poems, with the assumptions on both sides well understood. Rochfort tells her that she is an "artless" poet, and she modestly agrees, only to prove his thesis that her "untutored" muse has the capacity for true "seraphic fire." She is the "artless" poet as wise *ingénue*.

It is worth noting that in the above passage, Phillis Wheatley says that she will worship at the shrines of Pope and Newton, two of the greatest "bards" of the age.[18] In section two of this paper, her indebtedness to Pope will become clear as she tries to establish a convincing poetical voice. In section three of this paper, her connection to both Pope and Newton will be demonstrated in her attempt to write a specific kind of poetry which her century admired. Phillis Wheatley seemed to feel no "anxiety of influence," to borrow a phrase from Harold Bloom, in her desire to emulate other "bards." It probably never occurred to her that her "seraphic fire" might be snuffed out by rank imitation. In truth, her poetry did sometimes succumb to formula and repetition, but her adoration of Pope in particular often resulted in a grace snatched beyond the reach of artificiality.

II

What Phillis Wheatley learned from Alexander Pope, her favorite author, was an ability to transform her real self into an imagined self, a *persona*, which functioned as a means to a precise end, rhetorical persuasion. Instead of being a liability, this imagined self became a poetic asset. Often it was used as the cornerstone of an argument which she was building in a poem, and since the imagined self was based upon assumptions about race and "natural genius" which she and her age understood, the poem was convincing to the people who read it. Whatever her real feelings, it was her imagined self which she showed to the world. Whatever the disadvantages, her imagined self made her eloquent in places where she might have been simply maudlin.

Let us look more closely at a poem in which Phillis Wheatley uses her imagined self for rhetorical purposes. In "To The Right Honourable William, Earl of Dartmouth, His Majesty's Principal Secretary of State for North America," she congratulates Dartmouth on his new political post and pleads with him to protect and preserve the rights of Americans, vis-à-vis England, in the New World. To reinforce her point, she makes an analogy between America's situation and her own:

> I, young in life, by seeming cruel fate
> Was snatch'd from *Afric's* fancy'd happy seat:
> What pangs excruciating must molest,
> What sorrows labour in my parent's breast?
> Steel'd was that soul and by no misery mov'd
> That from a father seiz'd his babe belov'd:
> Such, such my case. And can I then but pray
> Others may never feel tyrannic sway?
> (P. 34)

These lines have been alternately praised and blamed for their sincerity or lack of sincerity.[19] Saunders Redding specifically singles out the words "seeming cruel" and "fancy'd happy seat" to argue that Phillis Wheatley did not believe "either in the cruelty of the fate that had dragged thousands of her race into bondage in America nor in the happiness of their former freedom in Africa."[20] In other words, not only had Phillis Wheatley's poetic personality been enslaved by "neo-classicism," but also her political attitudes were the products of the culture which owned her.

Redding's argument is based upon a twentieth-century interpretation of the word "fancy'd." As we know from Dr. Johnson's dictionary (1755), the word "fancy" can be a synonym for "delusion," but it can also be a synonym for the "imagination" which, in Johnson's words, "forms to itself representations of things, persons, or scenes of being." In this definition, "fancy" is that part of the mind which makes images, which in turn have their origin in sense experience. An alternative reading of Phillis Wheatley's "Afric's fancy'd happy seat" might be "the happy seat" which other poets have pictured Africa to be—either from seeing it themselves or from seeing it in their imaginations. We know that Phillis Wheatley was aware of the primitivistic tradition in eighteenth-century England which often conceived of Africa as a fruitful paradise.[21] Not only did she use this idea in her poem to Rochfort, but we also know that in her poem "To Imagination" she used "fancy" and "imagination" interchangeably and that both words were placed in the context of the mind's ability to perceive a truth beyond one's own immediate experience.

Thus the entire passage above might be read as follows. I, Phillis Wheatley, now a Christian slave, was once taken from my native land, Africa, which others besides myself have recognized as a Golden World. Not only did it cause my father much grief but also it has given me an understanding of the word "freedom." Fortunately for me, everything worked out for the best, for now I am a Christian (the "fate" is only "seeming cruel"), but others like myself, the Americans of these Colonies, are being threatened by political tyranny.

In this poem, Phillis Wheatley has artfully used the pathos of her own past to persuade Dartmouth to assuage the wrongs done to the Americans by the British. This is neither the poetry of self-expression nor the poetry of cold elegance; rather it is the poetry of argument. As such, it is reminiscent—not in excellence but in intention—of some of the great poems of the Restoration and eighteenth century: "Absalom and Achitophel," "An Essay on Man," and "An Epistle to Dr. Arbuthnot."

"To the University of Cambridge, in New England" also illustrates Phillis Wheatley's ability to manipulate an imagined self for the sake of argument. This poem is addressed to the students at Harvard who are urged by this young black slave to mend their profligate ways. To underscore her didactic theme, Phillis Wheatley describes the world from which she came:

> 'Twas not long since I left my native shore
> The land of errors, and *Egyptian* gloom:
> Father of mercy, 'twas thy gracious hand
> Brought me in safety from those dark abodes.
> (P. 5)

This is a different picture of Africa from the one of carefree primitives; it is an Africa without Christianity and without civilization. Although this portrait is not flattering to her native land, it is rhetorically useful; it creates an ironic contrast between her lot and that of the Harvard students. The latter are Christians by birth, and because they have the privileges of class, they are offered a knowledge of the highest civilization which man has attained. Yet they are abusing this god-given gift—a gift which has been denied to members of Phillis Wheatley's race. A lowly African must remind them that they too, like all men, may be destroyed by sin:

> Ye blooming plants of human race devine
> An *Ethiop* tells you 'tis your greatest foe;
> Its transient sweetness turns to endless pain,
> And in immense perdition sinks the soul.
>   (P. 6)

The situation here is archetypal. Phillis Wheatley is like the Roman slave in antiquity who stands behind the general marching triumphantly into Rome and who whispers into his ear that he is mortal. In this situation, the simple savage *knows* more than the sophisticated Harvard students.

In another well-known poem, "On Being Brought From Africa to America," we see a similar rhetorical strategy. Phillis Wheatley begins by celebrating God's mercy in bringing her from her *"Pagan* land" to the New World: "Once I redemption neither sought nor knew." Nevertheless, she is aware that some Christians in America "view our sable race with scornful eye." These Americans see the Negro's color as "diabolic" and thus Phillis reminds them in the last two lines of the poem:

> Remember, *Christians, Negroes,* black as *Cain,*
> May be refin'd, and join th' angelic train.
>   (P. 7)

As Phillis Wheatley said in one of her letters, God "was no respecter of Persons."[22] Although the Negro appears to be Cain to white Americans,[23] he is not Cain in Christ's eyes. The italicized words not only emphasize the falsehood of the analogy but they also serve as a reminder that all human beings—including whites—need to be "refined" before they "join th' angelic train."

The quiet irony of these last two lines seem to echo Pope's "lo, the poor indian" passage in "An Essay on Man." In Pope's poem, civilized man thinks himself superior to the naive savage whose conception of the afterlife is unimaginative. For the "poor indian," Heaven is simply a place where "No fiends torment, no Christians thirst for Gold." Yet it is this very simplicity which serves as a satiric comment upon the actual behavior of those people who call themselves "Christians." By placing her imagined self in ironic juxtaposition to the "Christians" who would view her as "diabolic," Phillis Wheatley is making the same satiric point.

Pope was not her only tutor in the use of a *persona* to rhetorical advantage. One poem recently discovered in manuscript indicates that Phillis Wheatley was probably aware of John Dryden's poetry. "To Deism" is similar to "Religio Laici" in both theme and technique; both authors use the *persona* of the "layman" to attack the web-spinning sophistry of Deism. Phillis Wheatley appears in the poem as an unlettered African who nevertheless knows the fundamental truths of Christianity. Her antagonist, a Deist, is out to disprove the doctrines of revelation and the trinity at the risk of losing his own soul to win an argument. Like John Dryden, Phillis Wheatley cannot hide her indignation for such folly:

> Must Ethiopians be imploy'd for you
> [I] greatly rejoice if any good I do
> I ask O unbeliever satan's child
> Has not thy saviour been to [o] meek [&] mild . . . [24]

Phillis Wheatley weighs God's mercy against the Deist's reason and finds the latter light indeed; the Deist rejects the very attribute of God, His infinite mercy, which for his sake he ought to hope exists. For if the Savior had not been "meek [&] mild," He would have already damned the Deist to endless perdition for his impudence. Again like John Dryden, Phillis Wheatley suggests that only the direct, simple truth will cut through the tissue of labyrinthian ratiocination which has so entrapped the Deist.

III

Phillis Wheatley's mastery of poetic technique, such as her ability to shape a *persona* for rhetorical purposes, shows her to be a more artful poet than we have previously recognized. If, at times, her elegies seem only a cut above "The Ode to Stephen Dowling Bots" in

Huckleberry Finn, at other times she eloquently wrote in the "sublime" mode which so fascinated her age. As a religious poet, she found the "sublime" a perfect vehicle for expressing transcendent emotions. As an artist, she responded to the secular theories of the "sublime," a kind of poetry which tried to be grandiloquent rather than clear, astonishing in its effects rather than logical. In this verse, whether sacred or profane, Milton and the Old Testament were influences upon her but so was Alexander Pope.

Phillis Wheatley's critics have had difficulty in explaining her indebtedness to Pope, and thus they tend to bury him under the generalizations which they make about "neo-classicism."[25] Actually, we are told by Margaretta Odell that Phillis Wheatley specifically admired "Pope's Homer."[26] This fact is significant, for Pope's preface to *The Iliad* and translation of it helped to create the critical opinion in the eighteenth century that Homer was the master of "sublimity."[27]

The "sublime" reached the zenith of its popularity around the same time that Phillis Wheatley began writing poetry.[28] A rash of essays on the subject appeared in the 1750s and 60s (the most famous being Edmund Burke's essay on *The Sublime and the Beautiful* in 1757), and Edward Young's final version of *Night Thoughts* (1746) and James Thomson's revised *Seasons* (1744) became models for poets hoping to write in this exciting poetic style. Mark Akenside, Thomas Gray, William Collins, Thomas and Joseph Warton, James Macpherson and others all wrote their poetry between 1740 and 1773, and if Phillis Wheatley was reading the best English writers, as she and Margaretta Odell say she was, then she was probably also aware of the writings of her contemporaries.

One essay dealing indirectly with the "sublime" has a special relevance to our subject. In 1756, Joseph Warton wrote "An Essay on the Genius and Writings of Pope," in which he argued that whereas Pope excels in the poetry of wit, he is nevertheless not one of our greatest poets because "he does not . . . ravish and transport his reader." Warton insists that "The Sublime and the Pathetic are the two chief nerves of all genuine poesy." And he asks, "What is there transcendently sublime or pathetic in Pope?"[29]

Phillis Wheatley could have answered this question, because she saw another facet of Pope's poetry besides the familiar one of social satire. In "To Maecenas," she describes herself as a humble poet who wishes to soar in exalted flight. Homer, she says, is her model, but she laments that she cannot "paint" with his power. Homer makes lightning "blaze across the vaulted skies," and causes the thunder to shake "the heavenly plains," and as she reads his lines: "A deep-felt horror thrills through my veins." She too would fly like both Homer and Virgil but complains:

> . . . here I sit, and mourn a grov'ling mind,
> That fain would mount, and ride upon the wind.
> (P. 3)

Not only is there an oblique reference to the Old Testament in the last line, but she is also remembering two lines from Pope's "An Essay on Man":

> Nor God alone in the still Calm we find;
> He mounts the Storm, and *walks upon the wind.*[30]

Phillis Wheatley identifies herself with Pope, because as the translator of Homer and as the author of "An Essay on Man," Pope is a poet who has already excelled in the "sublime" mode; in these two works, he has, as it were, mounted "the storm" and walked "upon the wind." To the pious young slave poet, for instance, "An Essay on Man" would be an example of the highest kind of "sublimity," for Pope's poem contains passages which grandly describe the vast, mysterious, awe-inspiring universe of God's creation.[31]

The "sublime" takes various forms in Phillis Wheatley's poetry. In "Goliath of Gath," she is consciously creating an epic character who terrifies us through our inability to imagine him as finite. In "On Imagination," she celebrates the imagination's capacity to seize upon what our senses cannot hold, the vast immensity of the universe. In "Ode to Neptune" and "To A Lady on Her Remarkable Preservation in an Hurricane in North-Carolina," she is concerned with the "natural sublime," the fact that some objects in nature such as storms and hurricanes fill us with terror because of their uncontrollable power. In "Niobe In Distress For Her Children Slain By Apollo," Phillis Wheatley is domesticating a mythological personage by treating her as a distressed mother. Not only is the poet's portrait contemporary in that this figure is a favorite one in the "Age of Sensibility," but Phillis Wheatley is also illustrating an aesthetic commonplace of the period: pathos is a branch of the "sublime."

If we examine two of her "sublime" poems, we shall see just how thoroughly Phillis Wheatley knew the taste of her age. In "Goliath of Gath," for instance, she illustrates Edmund Burke's famous dictum in *The Sublime and the Beautiful* that "to make anything very terrible, obscurity seems in general to be necessary."[32] Burke's point is that if a character is going to affect our imaginations with ideas of terror and power, the artist must not draw him too precisely. Hence, Phillis Wheatley describes Goliath as a "monster" stalking "the terror of the field" as he comes forth to meet the Hebrews. She mentions his "fierce deportment" and "gigantic frame," but never descends to particulars when she refers to his physical characteristics. Rather, she obliquely depicts Goliath by focusing upon his armor and weapons:

> A brazen helmet on his head was plac'd,
> A coat of mail his form terrific grac'd,
> The greaves his legs, the targe his shoulders prest:
> Dreadful in arms high-tow'ring o'er the rest
> A spear he proudly wav'd, whose iron head,
> Strange to relate, six hundred shekels weigh'd;
> He strode along, and shook the ample field,
> While *Phoebus* blaz'd refulgent on his shield:
> Through *Jacob's* race a chilling horror ran. . . .
>
> (P. 14)

Like Achilles in Book 22 of *The Iliad* and Satan in Book 1 of *Paradise Lost*, Goliath is terrifying because our sensory perceptions fail to contain him. If she had not read Edmund Burke, she at least knew about his psychological theory of the "sublime."

Goliath is meant to frighten us (like storms and hurricanes in nature), but the imagination in "To Imagination" is meant to bring us to an emotional state of religious awe. Following Mark Akenside's lead ("The Pleasures of the Imagination"—1744), Phillis Wheatley sees the infinite soul of man as a microcosm of God's infinite universe; only the imagination can capture a sense of that infinity:

> *Imagination*! who can sing thy force?
> Or who describe the swiftness of thy course?
> Soaring through air to find the bright abode,
> Th' empyreal palace of the thund'ring God,
> We on thy pinions can surpass the wind,
> And leave the rolling universe behind:
> From star to star the mental optics rove,
> Measure the skies, and range the realms above.
> There in one view we grasp the mighty whole,
> Or with new worlds amaze th' unbounded soul.
>
> (P. 30)

The imagination is a kind of mental eyesight ("optics") which allows us to penetrate the finite world and discover, to use Majorie Nicolson's phrase, "the aesthetics of the infinite."[33] In this context, it is no wonder that Phillis Wheatley referred to Sir Isaac Newton as one of the greatest "bards" of the age, for Newton's theories about the universe expanded God's world at the same time that they explained it.

IV

Although eighteenth-century England saw Phillis Wheatley as a "natural genius," she had larger plans for herself. She aspired to be an artist in the manner of Homer, Milton, and Pope. If we still complain that she failed as a poet because she did not express, with sufficient vehemence, her suffering black self, then we might do well to listen to Ralph Ellison, a contemporary black writer, who has argued against "unrelieved suffering" as the only basis of Afro-American art:

> . . . there is also an American Negro tradition which teaches one . . . to master and contain pain. It is a tradition which abhors as obscene any trading on one's own anguish for gain and sympathy; which springs not from a desire to deny the harshness of existence but from a will to deal with it as men at their best have always done. It takes fortitude to be a man and no less to be an artist. Perhaps it takes even more if the black man would be an artist.[34]

Phillis Wheatley could be called the founding mother of this tradition which Ellison describes, for the eighteenth century provided her with the tools to transmute her pain into art. She saw herself as a *poeta*, a maker of poems, and not as a suffering black slave who happened to be a poet. She may not have been a great poet, or even a good one, but she did write some good poems, and they were written because she had mastered the best which her century had to offer.

NOTES

1 In 1966, Julian Mason published a modern critical edition of Phillis Wheatley's poetry, including a biographical sketch and critical introduction. Since then several new letters and poems have been found. Two essays in particular have provided us with biographical information which Mason seemed to have missed: James R. Rawley, "The World of Phillis Wheatley," *New England Quarterly*, 50 (1977), 666–77; and William H. Robinson, "Phillis Wheatley in London," *College Language Association Journal*, 21 (1977), 187–201. Rawley's article also includes a list of recent discover-

ies in the Phillis Wheatley canon, and *PMLA* bibliographies from 1970 to the present show that our interest in the slave poet has not diminished. When referring specifically to Phillis Wheatley's poetry, I shall be using Mason's edition, *The Poems of Phillis Wheatley* (Chapel Hill: North Carolina Press, 1966). The reference to this edition will appear in the text.

2 See Winthrop Jordan, *White Over Black: American Attitudes Toward the Negro, 1550–1812* (1968; rpt. Baltimore: Penquin, 1969), p. 285.

3 See R. Lynn Matson, "Phillis Wheatley—Soul Sister," *Phylon*, 33 (1972), 222–30; and Terence Collins, "Phillis Wheatley: The Dark Side of Poetry," *Phylon*, 36 (1975), 78–88.

4 Saunders Redding, *To Make a Poet Black* (Chapel Hill: University of North Carolina Press, 1939), p. 11. M. A. Richmond, *Bid the Vassal Soar: Interpretative Essays on the Life and Poetry of Phillis Wheatley and George Horton* (Washington: Howard University Press, 1974), pp. 8, 131. See also Vernon Loggins, *The Negro Author: His Development in America to 1900* (1931; rpt. Port Washington, N.Y.: Kennikat, 1964), p. 16.

5 Mason, p. xxv.

6 See Dr. Johnson's dictionary, 1755 edition.

7 See Loggins, p. 29; Richmond, p. 131.

8 There are critics who have tried to rescue Phillis Wheatley from the charge of artificiality. They claim that we can find "personal elements" in her poetry if we only look hard enough. On the surface, this approach appears new, but in reality it is the first attitude turned on its head. On the one hand, we have a poetry whose artificiality hides the voice of the real poet; and on the other hand, we have an artificial poetry in which we can sometimes detect the poet's real personality. See Arthur P. Davis, "Personal Elements in the Poetry of Phillis Wheatley," *Phylon*, 14 (1953), 191–98. Davis' essay has influenced others. See Jean Wagner, *Black Poets of the United States*, trans. Kenneth Douglas (Urbana: University of Illinois Press, 1973), pp. 19–21. See also Matson, p. 224.

9 We know that Phillis Wheatley first tried to get her book published in Boston in 1772. See Muktar Ali Isani, "The First Proposed Edition of *Poems on Various Subjects* and the Phillis Wheatley Canon," *American Literature*, 49 (1977), p. 98. The project mysteriously failed. Robinson suggests that there was racist opposition to her book (p. 199); whereas Rawley argues that the project was dropped because her owners, John and Susannah Wheatley, thought that she could make more money from sales in England (pp. 675–76). An American edition of her poems was not published until 1789, five years after her death (Rawley, p. 677).

10 See Robinson.

11 See Jefferson Carter, "The Unlettered Muse: The Uneducated Poets and the Concept of Natural Genius in Eighteenth-Century England" (Diss. University of Arizona 1972), pp. 6,7. Although Carter does not discuss Phillis Wheatley, I am using his ideas when describing the eighteenth century's interest in "natural genius" and the "unlettered" poets.

12 Scott Elledge, *Eighteenth-Century Critical Essays* (Ithaca: Cornell University Press, 1961), I, 27–29.
13 Carter, p. 103.
14 Carter, pp. 69–238. As Carter points out, by 1786 the cult of "natural genius" was so widespread that the educated Robert Burns could exploit its popularity in his famous preface to the Kilmarnock poems.
15 According to Susannah Wheatley, when Phillis Wheatley's poems were first read to the Countess of Huntingdon, the latter would interrupt by saying, "Is not this, or that very fine? Do read another." See Kenneth Silverman, "Four New Letters by Phillis Wheatley," *Early American Literature*, 8 (1973–74), p. 269.
16 As quoted in Robinson's "Phillis Wheatley in London," p. 97. Robinson does not discuss the idea of "natural genius" in his article. Furthermore, he sees no purpose behind Lady Huntingdon's insertion of Phillis Wheatley's portrait in *Poems on Various Subjects* (p. 190).
17 *Memoir and Poems of Phillis Wheatley, A Native African and A Slave* (1838; facs. rpt. Miami: Mnemosyne, 1969), pp. 18, 20. The *Memoir* was published anonymously in 1834. For many years, its author was thought to be B. B. Thatcher. See M. A. Richmond, *Bid The Vassal Soar: Interpretative Essays on the Life and Poetry of Phillis Wheatley and George Horton* (Washington: Howard University Press, 1974), pp. 67–68.
18 Mason believes that Phillis Wheatley is referring to Milton in the phrase "British Homer's . . . feet" (p. 86n), but it is more likely that she is alluding to Pope. Pope's translations of Homer were famous throughout the century, and, as we shall see, they had a major influence upon her own poetry.
19 Loggins sees these lines as an indication that her "personality" does shine through her poetry, "even when she is most artificial" (p. 25). Richmond's response is that this personal note represents a "rare departure from Pope's classical strictures" (p. 29).
20 Redding, pp. 10, 11. I have singled out this criticism, because no one has answered Redding's objection to the words "fancy'd happy seat."
21 See Wylie Sypher, *Guinea's Captive Kings: British Anti-Slavery Literature of the XVIIIth Century* (1942; rpt. New York: Farrar, Straus, 1969), pp. 103–55. Sypher notes that the Negro as "Noble Savage" had strong roots in eighteenth-century English culture; whereas Winthrop Jordan points out that this tradition fell on barren soil in America (p. 27).
22 See Silverman, p. 265. Also, see Acts 10:34.
23 That the Negro's black skin is the mark worn by Cain seems to be a predominately American idea. See Jordan, pp. 42, 416.
24 Phil Lapsansky, "'Deism': An Unpublished Poem by Phillis Wheatley," *New England Quarterly*, 50 (1977), 519. Lapsansky does not mention the rather obvious connection to Dryden's poem.
25 For example, see Richmond: Phillis Wheatley's "ornate style was clearly an imitation of Alexander Pope's, which was then the fashion . . . " (p.

8). The word "ornate" tells us very little about Pope's influence and even less about his "style."

26 *Memoir*, p. 20.

27 See Pope's "Preface to the Translation of *The Iliad*" and his "Postscript to the Translation of *The Odyssey*" in *Eighteenth-Century Critical Essays*, I, 257–78, 291–300. Pope especially emphasized the "sublimity" and daring "Invention" of *The Iliad*. Also, see Samuel H. Monk, *The Sublime: A Study of Critical Theories in XVIII-Century England* (1935; rpt. Ann Arbor: University of Michigan Press, 1960), p. 103. In addition to being associated with "sublimity," Homer came to be seen by the mid 1750s as a "natural genius." See M. H. Abrams, *The Mirror and the Lamp: Romantic Theory and the Critical Tradition* (1953; rpt. New York: Norton, 1958), p. 188.

28 Monk, pp. 101–33.

29 *Eighteenth-Century Critical Essays*, II, 719.

30 "An Essay on Man," II, ll. 109–10. Also, see Psalms 104:3.

31 E.g., "An Essay on Man," I, ll. 22–32; I, ll. 247–58.

32 Edmund Burke, *A Philosophical Inquiry into . . . the Sublime and Beautiful*, in *Eighteenth-Century Poetry and Prose* (1939; rpt. New York: Ronald Press, 1956), p. 1166.

33 Marjorie Nicolson, *Mountain Gloom and Mountain Glory: The Development of the Aesthetics of the Infinite* (Ithaca: Cornell University Press, 1959). In *Newton Demands the Muse: Newton's "Optics" and the Eighteenth-Century Poets* (Princeton: Princeton University Press, 1946), Nicolson makes a connection between Newton's *Optics* and the poetry of the imagination which became popular in the 1740s. Phillis Wheatley's reference to "mental optics" may be another illustration of the impact of Newton's treatise on the poetry of the eighteenth century.

34 Ralph Ellison, *Shadow and Act* (1953; rpt. New York, Random House, 1966), p. 119. Also, see Henry-Louis Gates, "Dis and Dat: Dialect and the Descent," in *Afro-American Literature: The Reconstruction of Instruction* (New York: MLA, 1979), pp. 88–119. Gates' fascinating essay focuses upon the relationship of the African "mask" to Afro-American poetry. He does not discuss Phillis Wheatley's poetry, but some of the implications of his essay have relevance to her art. Perhaps Phillis Wheatley's poetical *persona* has its roots in African culture as well as in the artistic practices of eighteenth-century England.

Ut Pictura Poesis:

Smollett, Satire, and the Graphic Arts

ROBERT ADAMS DAY

Horace's famous phrase *ut pictura poesis* (usually detached from its rather limiting context in the *Ars poetica* and made into a maxim) was something of a catchword in eighteenth-century critical writings, both before and after Lessing's equally famous argument in *Laokoön* that the two modes of art were radically incompatible. But when we examine these discussions of the maxim's prescriptive or descriptive significance we are apt to feel an echo of Rasselas' distress on asking the philosopher what he meant by living according to nature, and discovering that "This was one of the sages whom he should understand less as he heard him longer."

In the practice of the arts, however, we find a quite different situation. Renaissance and later painters studiously reproduced on canvas the exact details of descriptive passages in Ovid or Ariosto, while *ekphrasis*, or the lengthy exposition of a painting, was a recognized branch of classical rhetoric, and highly detailed and realizable "instructions to the painter" grew into a genre as distinct and familiar to the eighteenth century as the progress poem.[1]

We might therefore think that the first great English novels would offer a rich field for investigating such practical applications of Horace's maxim. But when the reader in his turn becomes practical, and meticulously scrutinizes the *specific* details of color, shape, and positioning in the famous scenes of famous novels, he finds that though vivid they are few indeed—often single, in fact—and that a painter intent upon rendering the scene would have to do a great deal of original improvising around them.[2]

Nevertheless, if we wish to confine our working definition of *ut pictura poesis* to its expression in passages of fiction which virtually constitute sets of directions to a graphic artist, so that he could paint or draw a picture without having to resort to his imagination even in such matters as the exact placement of figures or the coloring of accessories, we can find one exemplary figure in the history of early English fiction—Tobias Smollett: and this for three reasons. First, among major eighteenth-century novelists (even including Sterne) Smollett abounds most in passages which really could be painted in great detail; second (again including Sterne), he seems to have the closest, liveliest, and most varied interest in the graphic arts; third, and most important, the history of his transactions with paintings and prints is the most complex, the best documented, and the most intensely personal. Moreover, it embodies a curious progression: from "instructions" to *ekphrasis* and then a return to instructions, but now vaguer, more blurred, and more varied in subject-matter than ever before. Further, we can see that this progression is governed by two factors: Smollett's distance from his material, in turn governed by the intensity of his personal feelings toward that material. At first a vigorous satirist of human nature in general, who constantly thinks in painterly terms, making the most brilliant use then known in prose fiction of detailed paintable scenes, by 1764 he has reversed his writer's rhetoric of the visual, and we find a ferocious political satirist who waits on the cartoonist for instructions, sometimes to the detriment of his art. The writer's servant has become his master, and it is not until *Humphry Clinker* that personal spleen has been purged, balance restored, and the novelist writes in firm control of a great panorama of caricatures, lively scenes, and placid landscapes. And to repeat, the key to the whole process lies in the word "personal."

The complete story of Smollett's relations with pictorial art needs a lengthy treatment which it has not had and which would require the space of a monograph; even his involvement with political cartoons needs preliminary explanation. But a few introductory points may be briefly made. Smollett certainly fancied himself as a connoisseur and critic of painting, architecture, and sculpture, as his *Travels* clearly show; and whether his judgments were "absurd," and those of a "choleric Philistine," as two critics have said, they were very firmly expressed and, as another has judged, at least "based on . . . common sense and intelligence."[3] His lengthy satirical treatment of Hogarth as the painter Pallet in *Peregrine Pickle* (which Hogarth seems never to have resented) bears eloquent testimony to what he thought about the old masters and about current affectations in critical terminology (chs. 46–70). (We should note parenthetically that these scenes and comments are balanced by an eloquent tribute to Hogarth's genius in the summary of George II's reign at the end of one of his volumes of history.)[4] But one need not be a competent critic or judge of painting to provide abundant materials for lively pictures.

Early and late Smollett's novels abounded in what Catherine Talbot in 1748 accurately called "very just, though very wretched descriptions"[5]—physiognomies and "frozen" yet highly detailed scenes. It was no accident that led him to compare himself defensively to "a Young painter indulging a vein of pleasantry" who had "sketched a kind of conversation-piece" with a bear, an owl, a monkey, and an ass shown as "an old, toothless, drunken soldier," a bespectacled newspaper-reader, and so on.[6] Smollett saw himself as a caricaturist in words. His worthy characters, male or female, were physically described in the tritest of saccharine clichés, as are the rare scenes of virtue and goodness. But when Lismahago's posteriors crawl by night down the fire-lit ladder in *Humphry Clinker* (Sir Thomas Bullford cruelly calls the scene "a fine Descent from the Cross"),[7] when Strap falls into the basement eating-house in *Roderick Random* (ch. 13), when the banqueting Ancients in *Peregrine Pickle* (ch. 48) fall over and bespatter one another (all scenes of descent, appropriate to comical satire), when Major Macleaver and Captain Minikin (ch. 41) smoke asafetida at each other in *Fathom* (a mock duel), postures, distances, and relationships of bodies are precisely visualized—and they are the frozen, puppetlike spatial relationships of slapstick comedy. Likewise, the famous descriptions of Crab, Lavement, and Captain Weazel in *Random* (chs. 7, 19, 11) and of Lismahago in *Clinker* (July 10), though unprecedentedly detailed, would if actually painted or drawn show outrageous enlargements and shrinkages of limbs and features as well as incredible discolorations—they go beyond even caricature. Here is Crab: "about five feet high, and ten round the belly; his face was as capacious as a full moon, and much of the complexion of a mulberry; his nose, resembling a powderhorn, was swelled to an enormous size, and studded all over with carbuncles; and his little grey eyes reflected the rays in such an oblique manner that, while he looked a person full in the face, one would have imagined he was admiring the buckle of his shoe" (ch. 7). We find nothing so preposterously lively (and grotesque) in other novelists until Blear-Eyed Moll in *Amelia* and Dr. Slop in *Shandy*—both very possibly in imitation of Smollett.

Whatever the genetic or environmental causes, then, the young Smollett is a born storyteller with a pronounced affinity, which singles him out from his contemporaries, for highly detailed and grotesque verbal caricature in the form of what I have called "instructions to the painter." Moreover, his young manhood coincides with the emergence—indeed the golden age—of the English political cartoon. Not uncommon in the Restoration, the trickle of cartoons became a flood in the reign of George II ("some Hundreds within this Month" wrote Thomas Gray in May 1742)[8] and began to abate only in Victoria's time. They were an instrument of political propaganda exceeding even pamphlets and newspapers in power and impact; several prosperous firms dealt entirely in such prints, and most important, literally everyone, literate or not, in London and the larger towns could form their audience. Most notably for our purposes here, these prints did not merely exaggerate physical features or behavioral habits of noted persons, nor merely identify them with animals or other grotesque figures: they routinely reduced political abstractions or events to ridiculously (or horribly) concrete terms. Thus Henry Pelham, the first minister, and his brother, the Duke of Newcastle, dissect a helpless, pinioned Britannia, whose blood is being greedily lapped up by a frenzied white horse, a figure taken from the arms of Hanover.[9] As the multi-volumed British Museum catalogue of these prints indicates, the complete political history of the times was rewritten in remorseless detail in their monstrous figures.

Enter Smollett. As we shall see, he was paying close attention to these prints; but during the 1750's, with his work on the *Universal History*, the *History of England* to 1748, and the *Critical Review*, he was becoming increasingly oriented toward political writing. The pictures of electioneering and of contemporary issues in *Sir Launcelot Greaves*, which began to appear serially in 1760, show this concern, though it is subordinated to the interest of the novel as a story, and partisan politics are but one of the areas which Sir Launcelot vainly endeavors to purify. About 1760, however, Smollett turned against the war policies of William Pitt; like many another Briton he had had enough of the costly European campaigns that the ministry supported.[10] And in the same year the youthful George III came to the throne and began his reign with its most disastrous mistake: he began to maneuver his Scots favorite, the Earl of Bute, toward supreme power. The resultant surge of popular hatred, cleverly manipulated by the opposition, released the greatest torrent of political propaganda that had ever been seen in England, including over 400 anti-Bute cartoons, one of which sold over 16,000 copies; fewer than a dozen attacked Bute's enemies.[11]

Smollett, who in 1762–63 wrote for the administration a weekly pro-Bute paper, *The Briton*, suggested in its pages that those responsible should be whipped and branded, and have their ears cut off.[12] Indeed, one need not be sympathetic to Bute to be shocked at the viciousness and grossness of these prints. They attack the Scots precisely in the manner of *Der Stürmer* belaboring the Jews; in particular they picture Bute as deriving his power from pleasuring the King's mother, the Dowager Princess of Wales (which is probably the main reason why the Court chose to ignore them).[13] But Smollett's indignation is not purely altruistic, for he himself figures in a dozen or so of these prints. He is pictured as a mountebank's zany, a hack scribbler, "Brother Small-wit," crouching behind Bute, a quack doctor, and a fisherman in troubled waters. He is brandishing manuscripts, asking Bute what to write, administering an enema to Britannia, and (literally) arse-kissing. He is flogged, shot with arrows, thrown down to Hell, eaten by the British Lion, and trampled by a dragon.[14] And, were all this not enough, in the spring of 1763 the Peace of Paris was ratified, ending the Seven Years' War, the *Briton* was thereupon unceremoniously terminated, Smollett received neither pension nor place from his "Perfidious Patron," and his much-loved only daughter died. He promptly departed for France, where he spent most of the next two years in recovering his health and balance, writing his *Travels* and a virulent political satire, *The History and Adventures of an Atom*.[15]

A good many things can be said about this book-length satire in narrative prose, which has been almost totally neglected by scholars until now.[16] It is a scathing denunciation of all the political and military leaders (and most of their subordinates) involved in the war, from its earliest stages in 1754 to its aftermath in 1763–68 with "Wilkes and liberty"; England, France, and Germany are converted into their geographical mirror-images of Japan, China, and "Tartary," and the satire is conducted in a manner reminiscent of Dr. Arbuthnot's *John Bull* pamphlets on the War of the Spanish Succession. But the most important aspect of Smollett's satire for our purposes is appropriately *ut pictura poesis*: this motto, to a degree so far as I know unique in English literature, accounts for both the book's nature and its history. The reasons for the *Atom*'s neglect become clear as soon as one has read it: it transforms in the manner of *Gulliver's Travels* a multitude of historical and political events now lost except to specialists; and it is the most thoroughly scatological book in English literature. But these two stumbling-blocks are accounted for as soon as one finds the key—English political cartoons, 1730–68. Smollett seems to

Figure 1: *The Evacuations. or An Emetic for Old English Glorys* [Nov. 3, 1762.]

FIGURES 1 AND 2, CARTOON ATTACKS ON LORDS BUTE AND SMOLLETT
FIGURES 3 AND 4, CARTOONS ON THE ROCHEFORT EXPEDITION

Figure 2: *The Scotch Broomstick & the Female Beesom, a German tale,* by Tawney Gesner, 1762.

303

Figure 3: *A New Map of Great Gotham & parts Adjacent* [September 20, 1757.]

Figure 4: *The Whiskers or Sᵣ Jⁿᵒ Suckling's Bugg-a-Bohs 1757* [by the Marquis Townshend, September 1757.]

have decided to turn his enemies' weapons against them, taking for his motto a rather restricted version of Horace: "As these pictures are, so my satire shall be." Indignation blinded him to the possibility that it might be dangerous to take the precept too literally.

We can see an indication of what was coming as early as 1760. Fielding might say, "Only the pencil of a Hogarth could portray," etc., to get out of doing a description, but in *Greaves* (ch. 12) Smollett casually mentions Hogarth's *Paul Before Felix Burlesqu'd* and clearly expects the reader to know the print, in which the Apostle's eloquence causes the Roman governor's bowels, in the Biblical phrase, to "turn to water." The allusion serves again in the *Atom*, as the Duke of Newcastle reacts to bad news.[17] With equal nonchalance Smollett compares the Privy Council to the figures in the *Table of Cebes*—an elaborate *ekphrasis* or exposition of an imaginary allegorical painting (*ut pictura poesis* again).[18] We cannot blame him for not counting on the illiteracy of posterity; surely half his readers had sweated in school through the elementary Greek and elementary moral preaching of the *Table*—but how many of us have? Few, I think, since the late Earl Wasserman was recently obliged to tell us in a learned journal what every schoolboy once knew. But Smollett could count on a ready chuckle, for instance, when he compared Newcastle to Cebes' emblem of Folly with her cup of delusion (as Pope had done with Walpole in the *Dunciad*).[19]

Scatology is another matter. Nowadays we can talk about it freely, and Smollett's predilection for it is almost as well known as Swift's; but the prints gave him ample precedent. Cloacina is their Muse to an extent that must be seen to be believed, as symbolic figures and royal, noble, and gentle personages bemire one another or freely give and take enemas. *Ut pictura poesis*: the *Atom*'s bowel movements are as rife as orgasms in hardcore pornography.

Turning one's nose elsewhere, the whole satiric fabric of the *Atom* is a tissue of hundreds of images from the prints. Let us consider two strategies and a liability in Smollett's method. The first is adoption. With politicians named Temple, Fox, and Pitt at their disposal, caricaturists had their work cut out for them, but they extrapolated ingeniously. Newcastle is a goose partly because he worked in tandem with Fox, and an old woman or old nurse because he is experienced and yet timorous and silly; thus he appears in the *Atom*. George II goes into infantile rages, turns his back on ministers, and kicks his hat about, because in fact he did. Admiral Anson is a duck or a sealion because of his naval exploits and a pun on the Latin for "duck," *anser*.[20] Arse-kissing goes back to a famous cartoon of Walpole's time, to say nothing of the Yahoos.[21] Newcastle is circumcised because he had originally sponsored the Jewish Naturalization Bill of 1753. Bute manipulates puppets from behind a curtain as Walpole had done before him. Pitt is Proteus because of his frequent reversals of principle, and a Colossus because he "doth bestride the narrow world," courtesy of Shakespeare. A military expedition is compared to well-born rakes out on the town, breaking windows by throwing guineas.[22] With all these received images Smollett merely performs his own *ekphrasis* by narrative development—the king honors favorites by kicking them in the breech, Newcastle turns into an old woman (though Smollett had already tried out this idea in the *Briton*).[23]

A second method of poetizing pictures is retaliation. Thus a print had showed Bute incubating eggs; Smollett makes Newcastle do it, appropriately, since he is already a goose and an old woman. A blindfolded George III is led about by Bute; the *Atom* has Pitt blindfolding George II so as to become a dictator. The quack doctor and the hydra, Smollett and Fox, are applied to Pitt and the House of Commons, which Pitt doses with soporific potions.[24]

As presented in summary these images may seem thoroughly effective; individually they are. But if we use, in laboratory parlance, *Gulliver's Travels* and a picture by Hogarth as controls, the difference at once becomes clear. Smollett uses *too many* pictures; they get in each other's way. Indeed, one of the reasons why Book III of *Gulliver* is often thought inferior is that too much is going on too rapidly. An elaborately allusive single picture, like Hogarth's *Strolling Actresses Dressing in a Barn*, with its myriad references to mythology, current events like the Licensing Act, the nature of the stage at the time, and with objects commenting ironically upon one another by juxtaposition, will sit still forever while it is explicated and while the eye travels from its surface to a text and back; the spatial relations of its figures will never alter.[25] But the reverse is not true, and here Lessing's objection—that painting functions in space, poetry in time—becomes fatal. He who reads must run, more especially in prose fiction; and a rapid-fire succession of detailed images borrowed from prints partly or wholly forgotten, commenting on events twelve years old and lost in the chaos of current history, places an intolerable burden of decoding and appreciative effort on the reader. Swift, with an animus no doubt equal to Smollett's against Walpole and the human race, wisely let a few simple pictures develop into his *poesis* of Flimnap and of the Houyhnhnms and Yahoos. The same contrast can be made between two undeniably great verse satires, *The Rape of the Lock* and *Absalom and Achitophel*: requiring too much detailed background of posterity can spoil the impact of a satire.

Let us take a single instance of Smollett's method to illustrate it and suggest its dangers. His account of the expensive and abortive expedition against Rochefort on the coast of Brittany in 1757 reads in part as follows:

> The commander of the first [expedition] disembarked upon a desolate island, demolished an unfinished cottage, and brought away a few bunches of wild grapes. He afterwards hovered on the Chinese coast; but was deterred from landing by a very singular phenomenon. In surveying the shore through spying glasses, he perceived the whole beach instantaneously fortified, as it were, with parapets of sand, which had escaped the naked eye; and at one particular part, there appeared a body of giants with very hideous features, peeping, as it were, from behind those parapets; from which circumstance the Japonese general concluded there was a very formidable ambuscade, which he thought it would be madness to encounter, and even folly to ascertain. One would imagine he had seen Homer's account of the Cyclops, and did not think himself safe, even at the distance of some miles from the shore; for he pressed the commander of the [fleet] to weigh anchor immediately, and retire to a place of more safety. I shall . . . let you into the whole secret. This great officer was deceived by the carelessness of the commissary, who instead of perspectives, had furnished him with glasses peculiar to Japan, that magnified and multiplied objects at the same time. They are called Phoberon-tia. The large parapets of sand were a couple of mole-hills; and the gigantic faces of grim aspect, were the posteriors of an old woman sacrificing *sub dio* to the powers of digestion.[26]

What are we to make of this Swiftian exercise in folly and futility, and why these details? In fact the English fleet demolished a half-finished fort on the Ile d'Aix at the mouth of the Garonne, and the "grapes" may refer to the biblical account of the spies sent into Canaan, who brought back grapes and said that they had seen giants in the land.[27] *Phoberontia* is Greek; it means "things greatly to be dreaded" or "bugaboos." A little historical research tells us that the captain of the ship *Viper* said that he had seen hastily-thrown-up fortifications on the shore, and many troops, when there were none. But the mystery is solved by two cartoons: in one a group of old women on shore derisively expose their buttocks to the commander-in-chief, General Mordaunt, who is looking through a telescope; in another a Frenchman calls out to the fleet, "Take our grapes, just let us have the rice, tobacco, indigo, and sugar," a reference to the idea that England's efforts should have been directed against the French possessions in the Caribbean.[28] Doing the research necessary to uncover these matters is pleasant enough if one likes research; the joke is funny; we must admire Smollett's pains and ingenuity; but notoriously our reaction to a joke that must be explained is lukewarm at best. A more important question—how many readers in 1769, twelve years after the expedition, could react as Smollett wanted? His delight in contriving all this is evident, but there is another, a personal motive: Smollett's attack on a pamphlet by Admiral Knowles, one of the leaders of the Rochefort expedition, had led in 1759 to his conviction for libel, a fine, and a short but humiliating stay in the King's Bench prison.[29] It is easy to picture Smollett's vindictive pleasure in assembling this grotesque picture of his enemy; but the common reader, alas, cannot share his savage glee.

Fortunately, Smollett's double involvement with politics and the pictorial arts ended at this point in his life. In the midst of the tumults that followed the sensational Middlesex elections of early 1768, when John Wilkes was three times returned and three times refused admission to Parliament, and when many feared revolution, Smollett made his final decision to quit England; whether because of his health or because of feelings of "epistemological alienation" and "a personal sense of dissolution of the external world . . . felt by members of both parties, for the empire and against it," we cannot know. Dropping the *Atom* off at the printer's in the autumn of 1768, however, and leaving England for "perpetual Exile" in Italy seem to have purged his spleen of its artistically damaging components.[30] But he had not lost his interest in satire or in caricature. The pictures of Tabby and Lismahago in *Humphry Clinker*, scenes such as the Duke of Newcastle's levee or the Pump Room at Bath, descriptions such as the exterior and interior of Mr. Baynard's house, are fully as lively and detailed as anything in *Random* or *Pickle*. Yet the idyllic descriptions of Scotland's scenery strike a new note. They are at once vaguer, more "picturesque" in the Radcliffian sense, than any scenes he had described before, and (for the acerbic Smollett seen in all his earlier work) verging on the sentimental in their direct evocation of unalloyed beauty. Impressionistic criticism might attribute these new tones to Smollett's love of his native land and to the mellowing of middle age; but more concrete causes also played a part. Smollett was distanced from his material in two ways, as he had never been before. He had not seen Scotland since 1766, and he was writing in

Italy; but it has been shown in convincing detail that he worked up many of his scenic descriptions from material compiled in earlier years for *The Present State of All Nations*, well before his last visit to Scotland.[31]

Smollett, like D. H. Lawrence, whom he resembles in indignation, in energy, and in many other ways, was always stimulated by vigorous personal involvement in what he wrote. When his "generous indignation," as he called it in *Roderick Random*, was dispersed over a broad satiric spectrum of human vice and folly, his pictorial impulse was channeled into caricature. When that impulse was narrowed too greatly, and heavily tinged with feelings of revenge, it reversed itself into *ekphrasis* to the detriment of art, and allowed the painter (or draughtsman) to dominate the poet. But when the picture-making faculty was exercised at a distance in time and space, reinforced by loving nostalgia, and limited by written materials that had grown vague in evocative power by the passage of some years, the result was *Humphry Clinker*. Restored estates, sunny landscapes and picturesque Scottish scenery, reconcilements and the restoration of health, gave a happy ending to Smollett's tempestuous affair with *ut pictura poesis*.

NOTES

1 See, for example, David Rosand, "*Ut Pictor Poeta*: Meaning in Titian's *Poesie*," *New Literary History*, 3 (1972), 527–46; Jean H. Hagstrum, "Verbal and Visual Caricature in the Age of Dryden, Swift, and Pope," *England in the Restoration and Early Eighteenth Century*, ed. H. T. Swedenberg, Jr. (Berkeley and Los Angeles: University of California Press, 1972), pp. 173–96.

2 Using Richardson as an example, the famous description of Clarissa's room in the spunging-house (Belford to Lovelace, July 17) might indeed be painted with accuracy; but if we compare Highmore's illustrations to *Pamela* with the scenes Richardson writes, we discover that the author has provided no more than a few telling details—the fabric of a dressing-gown, a sunflower, the theatrical posture of one figure; the rest comes from the painter. Notable exceptions are indeed found in Sterne—Trim's posture during his sermon (II, 17) or Walter Shandy's in despair on his bed (III, 29); but Defoe, *pace* Ian Watt and others, is not an exception. The vivid scene between Moll Flanders and her Bath lover, for example, tells us that he pours golden guineas from a little drawer in a cabinet into her lap (suggesting Zeus and Danaë, by the way), but only that; all other details, including positioning and grouping, would have to be supplied by the artist.

3 See Robert D. Spector, "Smollett's Traveller," *Tobias Smollett: Bicentennial Essays Presented to Lewis M. Knapp*, ed. G. S. Rousseau and P.-G. Boucé (New York: Oxford University Press, 1971), pp. 243–44.

4 *The History of England*, 5 vols. (London: Cadell, 1790), V, 384–85; and see Ronald Paulson, "Smollett and Hogarth," *Studies in English Literature*, 4 (1964), 351–59.

5 *A Series of Letters between Mrs. Elizabeth Carter and Miss Catherine Talbot*, 2 vols. (London: Rivington, 1808), I, 166.

6 "Apologue" prefixed to the 1754 (Dublin) and subsequent editions of *Roderick Random*.

7 Jery Melford to Sir Watkin Phillips, Oct. 3; the description also includes, from the jargon of art criticism, the terms *costume, aspect*, "lights and shadows," *groupe*, and *caricature*.

8 Quoted by George Kahrl, "Smollett as a Caricaturist," in *Bicentennial Essays*, p. 173.

9 "The Conduct of the Two B[rothe]rs," No. 3069 in the British Musem *Catalogue of Political and Personal Satires*, ed. Frederic G. Stephens, 4 vols. (London: 1870–73).

10 See Lewis M. Knapp, "Smollett and the Elder Pitt," *Modern Language Notes*, 59 (1944), 250–57.

11 See M. Dorothy George, *English Political Caricature*, 2 vols. (Oxford: Oxford University Press, 1959), I, 119–40; and for details of the prints, Herbert M. Atherton, *Political Prints in the Age of Hogarth* (Oxford: Clarendon Press, 1974), pp. 208–27.

12 No. 32 (Jan. 1, 1763), p. 190.

13 See Atherton, pp. 218–21.

14 These prints are among Nos. 3853–4079.

15 The attribution of the *Atom* and the dating of its composition are discussed in my article "The Authorship of the *Atom*," forthcoming in *Philological Quarterly*.

16 The only treatments in print that go beyond passing mention are Arnold Whitridge, *Tobias Smollett* (Brooklyn: privately printed, 1925); James R. Foster, "Smollett and the Atom," *PMLA*, 68 (1953), 1032–46; Louis L. Martz, *The Later Career of Tobias Smollett* (New Haven: Yale University Press, 1942). Two unpublished dissertations dealing with the *Atom* are Henry B. Prickitt, "The Political Writings and Opinions of Tobias Smollett," Diss. Harvard 1952; Wayne J. Douglass, "Smollett and the Sordid Knaves," Diss. University of Florida, 1976.

17 *The History and Adventures of an Atom*, 2 vols. (London: Robinson and Roberts, 1769), I, 94. The print is No. 3173 in the British Museum *Catalogue*.

18 *Atom*, I, 67–68.

19 Earl R. Wasserman, "Johnson's *Rasselas*: Implicit Contexts," *Journal of English and Germanic Philology*, 74 (1975), 1–25; *Dunciad* (1744 version), IV, ll. 517 ff.

20 See Nos. 2326, 2327, 2862, 3330, 3373, 3385, 3487, 3558.

21 This print is called "Idol-Worship or the Way to Preferment." It is reproduced in Atherton, fig. 28. See *Gulliver's Travels*, Bk. IV, ch. 7.

22 See Nos. 3205, 4049, 4163, 4162.

23 See Nos. 2857, 4133, and *Briton*, no. 30 (Dec. 18, 1762), p. 175.

24 No. 4163 and *Atom*, 2, 115; No. 4245 and *Atom*, 2, 4; No. 3917 and *Atom*, I, passim.

25 See Stanley Meltzoff, "Rhetoric, Semiotics, and Linguistics Look at the *Strolling Actresses* of Hogarth," *New Literary History*, 9 (1978), 561–79.

26 *Atom*, I, 183–87.

27 Numbers 13:23, 32. The demolition occurred on Sept. 23, 1757.

28 See historical notes to Nos. 3616 and 3625, in the *Catalogue*. The latter, subtitled with reference to the captain of the *Viper* "Sir Jnº Suckling's Bugga-Boh's," is doubtless, by way of Smollett's knowledge of Greek, the source for his word "*Pho-beron-tia*."

29 See Lewis M. Knapp, *Tobias Smollett: Doctor of Men and Manners* (Princeton: Princeton University Press, 1949), pp. 230–37.

30 Ronald Paulson, "The Pictorial Circuit & Related Structures in 18th-Century England," *The Varied Pattern: Studies in the 18th Century* (Toronto: A. M. Hakkert, 1971), p. 137, n. 36. (Paulson's article is a valuable discussion of the pervasive despair of the 1760's that is reflected in many tracts and pamphlets, as well as paintings and other graphics.) On the mob violence and disruption that followed the Wilkes campaign, see George Rudé, *Wilkes and Liberty* (Oxford: Oxford University Press, 1962). Smollett used the phrase "perpetual Exile" in a letter to David Hume written on Aug. 31, 1768, apparently shortly before his departure; *The Letters of Tobias Smollett*, ed. Lewis M. Knapp (Oxford: Clarendon Press, 1970), p. 136.

31 See Martz, *Later Career*, pp. 136–46.

Photo credits: Figs. 1–4 courtesy of the Trustees of the British Museum.

Jane Austen: A Romantic, Systematic, or Realistic Approach to Medicine?

TOBY A. OLSHIN

While it is the object of this paper to deal with the nature of Jane Austen's attitude toward medicine, it appears necessary first to note that it was a subject on which she *had* an attitude. Her nephew, J. E. Austen-Leigh, assures us in his *Memoir*: "She was always very careful not to meddle with matters which she did not thoroughly understand. She never touched upon politics, law, or medicine, subjects which some novel writers have ventured on rather too boldly, and have treated, perhaps, with more brilliancy than accuracy."[1] But she did, in fact, touch upon the subject of medicine, and with both brilliancy and accuracy. The brilliancy, of course, lies in the deft and subtle strokes with which a character such as Mr. Perry gives the medical response Mr. Woodhouse is eager to hear:

> [Mr. Woodhouse] earnestly tried to dissuade them from having any wedding cake at all, and when that proved vain, as earnestly tried to prevent any body's eating it. He had been at the pains of consulting Mr. Perry, the apothecary, on the subject . . . and, upon being applied to, he could not but acknowledge . . . that wedding cake might certainly disagree with many—perhaps with most people, unless taken moderately . . . but . . . there was a strange rumor . . . of all the little Perrys being seen with a slice of wedding cake in their hands. . . .[2]

313

It is, though, the accuracy of her portrayal of the medicine of her day with which I should like to deal in detail. Medicine, never a simple subject, was an especially complicated one during the eighteenth century in that it was very visibly undergoing a process of change. The great scientific discoveries of the nineteenth century lay ahead, and the eighteenth-century physician, apothecary, and surgeon frequently found themselves confronting clinical problems with which they could not deal effectively. The choice of diagnosis and subsequent therapy was influenced by two approaches which were problematic both in themselves and in the nature of their combination.[3] On the one hand, the clinician might choose what I shall here call the romantic or empirical approach; on the other, he might choose a rationalist, systematic, or anti-romantic, path. In her portrayal of medical practice and her attitude toward medicine, Jane Austen seems to reflect the ambivalence and uncertainty of her contemporaries: she touches upon both approaches, allowing us to make a number of pertinent inferences about her perceptions of medical complexities and the way in which they contribute to the tensions of her novels.

Several familiar aspects of romanticism are to be seen in one approach to medicine. There was, first of all, an interest in foreign diseases, although their exotic character—as described in case histories—served to mask the fact that no real understanding of their etiology existed.[4] Instead, one was asked to trust nature for cures for these and other diseases, and this idea—especially relevant in connection with Jane Austen—appears to have been enthusiastically supported by the clergy.[5] The romantic involvement of the senses, too, proved itself useful both to physician and patient. Dr. Richard Mead, writing in *The Influence of the Sun and Moon upon Human Bodies*, says, "I praise reasoning [in medicine], when it is grounded upon such principles as fall under our senses . . . and draws conclusions from manifest premises."[6] The patient's senses, on the other hand, were to be appealed to at a fundamental level: plenty of milk and vegetables plus a carefully planned course of Bath water were frequently prescribed by Dr. George Cheyne, especially since he himself had recovered, on such a treatment, from what one medical historian calls "a dark incumbrance of the soul."[7] The benefits of bathing and of drinking mineral water were noted, and the spa at Bath and the hot well at Bristol made those two places rival far more traditional medical centers.[8]

The real difficulty lay in making accurate discriminations among clinical syndromes, and diagnosis and treatment were hindered, if not defeated, by a lack of precision; there were only a few clearly delineated diagnostic categories.[9] This categorization, or system-making, became suspect, and instead, very broad and general diagnostic groupings were used to match the very broad and general "natural" romantic therapies. We may contrast the immense confidence that went into the making of John Quincy's title "Historical Certainty, Moral Certainty, and Demonstration" (in *Medicina Statica*, 1737)[10] with Christoph Hufeland's warning "*Natura sanat, medicus curat morbos*"; (nature cures disease, the physician merely does what he can to facilitate the operations of nature).[11] A historian of the period quotes Wordsworth's "Healthy as a Shepherd-Boy" as highly descriptive of contemporary attitudes: those who broke nature's laws, broke God's laws. At least one group of clinicians felt that until medicine could become a true science, it should help nature by establishing hygienic conditions for the sick. There were no cures except those nature could effect, and medicine—so said these therapeutic nihilists—did not know how to heal.[12]

Although the romantic attitude toward disease and cure existed side by side with the anti-romantic in the actual fact of medical practice, it was, in a sense, a reaction against it. The administration of heavy dosages of drugs, the application of purges, diaphoretic agents, and enemas had become routine. A number of theoretical structures were erected which indicated their prescription, but since no one system served as a unified field theory, a growing skepticism linked itself to the very unpleasantness of the drugs and procedures themselves, and an emphasis on the "natural way" was the result. However, the search for systems, and the appropriate medicines and treatments connected to these systems, went on. Newton's *Principia* served as the model: each nosologist hoped that he could show that medicine was as exact as mathematics. A major difficulty confronting those who tried classification was that they could not always distinguish between a disease and a symptom. Yet, the practitioner had to work from what the nosologists had accomplished and had to appear to the patient to have an intellectual basis for his advice if he were to have a reliably systematic stance—and yet the nosology was inadequate.[13]

The problem, then, was that each of the approaches was badly flawed; each undercut the substantive position of the other. The romantic or empirical attitude was too general in its diagnosis, and except for water, food, and air cures, essentially threw up its hands before illness. The anti-romantic or systematic attitude was hampered by the lack of a truly valid nosology, and frequently, by an insistence that an existing one was, in fact, correct. The outcome—

from the patient's standpoint—was that the doctor did not appear to be a real authority, and the patient (or observer) would need to fluctuate from one position to the other.[14] The particular difficulties of the period, then, provide a valuable context in which to view Jane Austen's novels: our understanding of a number of incidents and characters is considerably deepened, and certain—potentially melodramatic—scenes of anxiety are shown to have a basis in contemporary reality.

Following the course of Marianne's illness in *Sense and Sensibility* allows us to assess both the romantic and anti-romantic attitudes and to see the way in which their interplay serves to diminish the authority of the medical profession.[15] Elinor is the first to prescribe for what the narrator has described as "an aching head, a weakened stomach, and a general nervous faintness." This illness is to be cured by the offer of wine (*S&S*, 185). The "nervous complaint" continues, however, despite this romantic treatment. Later on, Marianne catches a severe cold, and once again laymen feel free to treat: "Prescriptions poured in from all quarters . . . a good night's rest was to cure her entirely . . . Elinor prevailed on her . . . to try one or two of the simplest remedies" (*S&S*, 306). It is, though, when the prediction that she will recover the next morning fails to come true that something *seemingly* more efficacious is tried: Mr. Harris, the apothecary, is summoned. As the representative of the systematic school, he makes his prediction: "A very few days would restore her sister to health" (*S&S*, 307). He rescues the prognosis from the triviality of optimism, though, by mentioning the words "putrid" and "'infection'" (*S&S*, 307).

These terms were part of a classification of disease that had been established by Boerhaave and later elaborated upon by the English nosologist John Huxham (1694–1768). Fever was seen as an illness, not a symptom, and its "putrid" characteristic indicated that it was severe and contagious.[16] The Palmers take their children and flee because they respect the apothecary's diagnosis of "putridness," but Elinor continues to believe that the illness will be a short one. Three days later, Mr. Harris's optimism and Elinor's are rewarded: both look like good prognosticators. But the illness, in fact, grows worse, and Elinor—confronted with Marianne's sudden "feverish wildness" (*S&S*, 311) feels terror.[17] Wisely—considering the state of medicine at the time—Elinor sends for both the apothecary and their mother, the second act indicative of the amount of faith she has in the first.

It is at this point that the utter impotence of *both* medical approaches stands starkly revealed. Elinor and her lay prescriptions are certainly valueless, but the apothecary, who is hours late in coming, incorrectly predicts the course of the illness; his new medications are no more successful than the others were, and yet he once again "had still something more to try, some fresh application, of whose success he was almost as confident as the last" (*S&S*, 313). Elinor, however, is now "almost hopeless" until the inexplicable moment when Marianne's pulse rate changes. Without predictable reason, without documented cause, the cure is effected: the illness has simply followed its course, and Mr. Harris confesses to finding himself surveying a recovery "surpassing his expectation" (*S&S*, 314).

The same pattern of events occurs in miniature when first Mrs. Jennings, and then the apothecary Mr. Donovan, diagnose the Palmer infant's dermatitis as "red-gum" or teething rash (*S&S*, 257). Charlotte is reassured only by the apothecary's diagnosis, but the reader is shown that any layman can try his hand at the systematic approach with a success that matches that of the professional.

Again, in *Northanger Abbey*, the romantic position is mocked, and the anti-romantic is shown as ineffectual. Mrs. Allen, the proponent of the benefits of Bath, is herself a rather foolish figure in whom the reader can have limited trust. When Mr. Allen "was ordered to Bath for the benefit of a gouty constitution" (*NA*, 17), Mrs. Allen accepts the opportunity for social adventure; she invites Catherine to go along and is grateful for the interlude from boredom:

> I tell Mr. Allen, when he talks of being sick of it, that I am sure he should not complain, for it is so very agreeable a place that it is much better to be here than at home at this dull time of year. I tell him he is quite in luck to be sent here for his health. (*NA*, 54)

And, of course, the essential plot of the novel shows Bath to be a place where more human happiness is brought about by Hymen than by hydrotherapy.

Even though Henry Tilney is a far more trustworthy narrator than Mrs. Allen, the events he describes do not serve to increase the reader's trust in the anti-romantic stance:

> My mother's illness . . . the seizure which ended in her death *was* sudden. The malady itself, one from which she had often suffered, a bilious fever—its cause therefore constitutional. On the third day . . . a physician attended her, a very respectable man, and one in whom she had always placed great confidence. Upon his opinion

of her danger, two others were called in the next day, and remained in almost constant attendance for four-and-twenty hours. On the fifth day she died. (*NA*, 197)

Henry notes, apparently with some conviction, that the "cause" of a "bilious fever" is "constitutional." The nosologists of the period did not, in fact, see an infectious agent as causal, although Sir John Pringle (1707–82), classifying "bilious fever" among the "diseases" he described, insisted that "it has never been proved that either the autumnal fevers or fluxes originally proceed from a redundant or a corrupted bile."[18] The point, though, is that Jane Austen makes a substantial effort to document the blind helplessness of the medical profession: the faith of Mrs. Tilney in her own physician is misplaced, and the "almost constant attendance" of all three physicians is unavailing.

The course of Jane's illness, so important to the plot of *Pride and Prejudice*, allows us, primarily, to watch her effect on Bingley increase but also serves to diminish our impression of the "scientific" diagnosis. When Jane writes, "'They insist also on my seeing Mr. Jones'" (*P&P*, 31), we are to infer that the unpredictable course of illness and potential ineffectiveness of the apothecary justify Elizabeth's "feeling really anxious" (*P&P*, 32). By the time of Elizabeth's arrival, Jane is "very feverish" (*P&P*, 33), and the voice of science is presented to the reader in a way not appropriate to decreasing our fear for Jane:

> The apothecary came, and having examined his patient, said, as might be supposed, that she had caught a violent cold, and that they must endeavour to get the better of it; advised her to return to bed, and promised her some draughts. (*P&P*, 33)

That any observant layman could make the diagnosis is implied in the phrase "as might be supposed," but the most pointed comment on the faith the reader is to have in the apothecary comes next: "The advice was followed readily, for the feverish symptoms increased, and her head ached acutely" (*P&P*, 33). And once again, the illness proceeds—inexplicably—through its unpredictable stages: she is by no means better (*P&P*,35) and is, that evening, "very poorly" (*P&P*, 37); the next morning, she can be described by "a tolerable answer" (*P&P*, 41)—although Mr. Jones feels she can still not travel; she continues, "though slowly, to mend" (*P&P*, 47), and by the late afternoon of the following day, is "so much recovered as to intend leaving her room for a couple of hours that evening" (*P&P*, 53).

This physical illness which allows Jane and Bingley to become intimate parallels the much briefer moment of emotional travail in which Darcy and Elizabeth glimpse each other's hearts. When Elizabeth receives the letter telling her that Lydia has eloped with Wickham, she does not reveal its contents to Darcy but simply asks him to find her uncle, Mr. Gardiner. He observes, though, that she is "unable to support herself, and looking . . . miserably ill." Immediately, and appropriately, he offers the romantic cure: "Is there nothing you could take . . . ? A glass of wine;—shall I get you one?—You are very ill" (*P&P*, 276). Although the apothecary's self-assurance deserves much less regard than Darcy's "compassionate silence" (*P&P*, 277), the wine will be as ineffectual in curing Elizabeth as the draughts were in curing Jane. Medical uncertainties here are a haunting donnée, and our understanding of this adds an enriching chiaroscuro touch to the famous "light, and bright, and sparkling."[19]

In *Mansfield Park*, Edmund replicates Darcy in his offer of the romantic treatment. Fanny's headache, caused by "stooping among the roses" (*MP*, 73) and "walking across the hot park" (*MP*, 72), has not been helped by Lady Bertram's of an ancient remedy, aromatic vinegar (*MP*, 72). Edmund, though, offers a glass of Madeira (*MP*, 74) which is restorative—but Jane Austen points out that it is the symbolism of the Madeira and not the wine itself which has helped her: "Edmund's kindness" effects "the sudden change" (*MP*, 74).

Contemporary science is as unsuccessful in curing Tom's illness as it has been in helping the characters in the earlier novels. He, too, catches the "fever"; this time, though, it is thought to be caused by "a neglected fall, and a good deal of drinking" (*MP*, 426). Under the care of a physician, "his disorder increased considerably" (*MP*, 426), and he is then "dangerously ill" (*MP*, 427). No physician prohibits him from being moved from London back to Mansfield, and the narrator implies a lack of judgment:

> Tom's extreme impatience to be removed to Mansfield . . . had probably induced his being conveyed thither too early, as a return of fever came on, and for a week he was in a more alarming state than ever. (MP, 427)

Again, the indeterminate nature of the illness terrifies those who must observe it and can do nothing: even the indolent Lady Bertram experiences "real feeling and alarm" (*MP*, 427), and upon Tom's return home, "They were all very seriously frightened" (*MP*, 427). In this setting, with Tom "in his suffering, helpless state" (*MP*, 429), the physician serves only to increase anxiety: Edmund writes to Fanny of "the apprehensions which he and his father had imbibed from the physician. . . . They were apprehensive for his lungs" (*MP*, 429). "Strong hectic symptoms" (*MP*, 429) follow the fever; time passes, but "Tom's amendment was alarmingly slow" (*MP*, 430). Unpredictably, he suffers a relapse when he hears of Maria's elopement (*MP*, 451), and again Lady Bertram feels "alarms" (*MP*, 451). Finally, after months have passed, we learn that Tom "gradually regained his health" (*MP*, 462). Although Jane Austen gives much attention to his changed moral state, she gives none whatsoever to the physicians who had treated him. We are, I contend, to infer that the illness has a destined path of its own before which all attitudes are impotent; one should feel only fear, and then ultimately, gratitude or acceptance.

The inverse version of this statement is well demonstrated by *Emma*. Emma's health is one of the chief attributes of her character; it is surely one of the "best blessings of existence" (*E*, 5) noted in the novel's opening sentence. She is always "perfectly well" and "hardly knew what indisposition was" (*E*, 336).[20] The unremitting course of her health is as inexplicable as the course of any illness. Mr. Woodhouse's opinions—favoring gruel (*E*, 105), closed windows (*E*, 251), sea air (*E*, 106), and diluted wine (*E*, 25) while opposing both bathing (*E*, 102) and suppers (*E*, 25)—represent Jane Austen's satiric views of the romantic attitude. There is no evidence to show that any of these treatments is at all beneficial, and Mr. Woodhouse is portrayed as one who uses hypochondriasis for self-dramatization.

Mr. Perry and Mr. Wingfield, the apothecaries, fare no better. Mr. Perry is bilious (*E*, 101) and cannot cure himself, and even Mr. Wingfield's most devoted patient—Isabella—cannot with certainty attribute her daughter's cure to his "excellent embrocation" (*E*, 102). Perry never appears to offer a cure for Harriet's ulcerated sore throat (*E*, 125), and Emma—although Harriet has been her constant companion—never catches it.

In *Persuasion*, the two accidents which occur show again Jane Austen's perception of the uncertainty of clinical skills based, as they are, on incomplete information; the point is that life is lived on the very edge of terror. When little Charles Musgrove falls, the family responds "with the most alarming ideas" (*P*, 53). Although they themselves are able to make the diagnosis—"His collar-bone was found to be dislocated, and . . . injury received in the back . . ." (*P*, 53)—they send for the apothecary because "their apprehensions were the worse for being vague" (*P*, 54). But the apothecary, although he is able to replace the collar bone, generates further uncertainty:

> . . . [T]hough Mr. Robinson felt and felt, and rubbed, and looked grave, and spoke low words both to the father and the aunt, still they were all to hope the best, and to be able to part and eat their dinner in tolerable ease of mind . . . .(*P*, 54)

The following day, "Mr. Robinson found nothing to increase alarm" but admits, "It must be a work of time to ascertain that no injury had been done to the spine" (*P*, 55).

The portrait of Louisa Musgrove's surgeon is a somewhat more serious one. He is not a figure of satire—he is neither pompous nor greedy, and he even comes promptly when called. Primarily, though, the dignity that lies in his very brief portrayal derives from his admission of his helplessness and limited understanding:

> They were sick with horror while he examined; but he was not hopeless. The head had received a severe contusion, but he had seen greater injuries recovered from: he was by no means hopeless; he spoke cheerfully. . . . [H]e did not regard it as a desperate case . . . . (*P*, 112)

Somehow, Louisa recovers, and we may conclude that luck played a large role.

Mrs. Smith's luck, though, was not the equal of Louisa's, and the medical connection allows us to see her as a character well integrated into the pattern of the novel.[21] Her luck—since that appears to be as much a therapeutic agent as any—makes a striking contrast: time and "severe rheumatic fever . . . setting in her legs" (*P*, 152) had changed "the fine-looking, well grown Miss Hamilton, in all the glow of health and confidence of superiority into [the] poor, infirm, helpless [Mrs. Smith]" (*P*, 153). Although Captain Wentworth eventually succeeds in arranging her economic affairs, neither physician nor Bath water ever succeeds in curing her.

The novels' portrayals of illnesses and injuries provide remarkable demonstrations of Jane Austen's technical abilities when they are seen as an outgrowth of the medical realities of the period. Unlike the clinician, the novelist was in a position of therapeutic power, and we can watch her arranging matters so that the "right" characters are punctually saved and the "wrong" efficiently eliminated. The narrator of *Mansfield Park*, here certainly speaking in *propria persona* tells us: " . . . I [am] impatient to restore everybody, not greatly in fault themselves, to tolerable comfort, and to have done with all the rest" (*MP*, 461). All the novels bear this out: Jane Bennett's cold is timed to allow Bingley to increase his devotion to her, Marianne Dashwood's fever brings about the confession of the conscience-stricken Willoughby, Mr. Allen's gout gives Catherine an opportunity to go to Bath, Tom Bertram's illness allows him time for maturation and moral growth, Harriet Smith's sore throat enables Mr. Elton to be alone with Emma, and even the notorious arrangement for the death of Richard Musgrove serves to enrich the portrayal of Captain Wentworth.

The clinician, though, cannot "restore everybody," and what achieves comic dimensions in the novels gains poignancy in the letters. The impotence of the medical profession, the uselessness of both the romantic and systematic attitudes, is even more clearly dramatized there. Mr. Perry's subjection to his wife's therapeutic intervention when he agrees to set up a carriage for his health (*E*, 344–45) makes him a figure of mockery in *Emma*.[22] When, however, that same carriage-cure is ineffectual in life, Jane Austen's absolute rejection of the attitude which prescribed it takes on a note of seriousness:[23]

> My aunt does not enter into particulars, but she does not write in spirits, and we imagine that she has never entirely got the better of her disorder in the winter. Mrs. Welby takes her out airing in her barouche, which gives her a headache—a comfortable proof, I suppose, of the uselessness of the new carriage when they have got it. (*Letters*, No. 72)

When her brother Henry is ill, the difficulties in making a specific diagnosis and prognosis show up clearly. Regretting "the uncertainty of all this," she writes to Cassandra:

> Henry calls himself stronger every day & Mr. H[aden] keeps on approving his pulse which seems generally better than ever—but still they will not let him be well. The fever is not yet quite removed. The Medicine he takes (the same as before you went) is chiefly to improve his Stomach, & only a little aperient. He is so well, that I cannot think why he is not perfectly well. I should not have supposed his Stomach at all disordered but *there* the fever speaks probably; but he has no headake, no sickness, no pains, no Indigestions. (*Letters*, No. 117)

The point is that befuddlement reigns: Mr. Haden's treatment, supposedly based on an understanding of the ailment, has failed to cure it.

In the letters as in the fiction, following the course of an illness allows us to see her assessment of the patient's helplessness. Her father's final hours are carefully detailed:

He was taken ill on Saturday morning, exactly in the same way as heretofore, an oppression in the head, with fever, violent tremulousness, & the greatest degree of Feebleness. The same remedy of Cupping, which had before been so successful was immediately applied to—but without such happy effects. The attack was more violent, & at first he seemed scarcely at all relieved [sic] by the operation. Towards the Evening however he got better, had a tolerable night & yesterday morning was so greatly amended as to get up & join us at breakfast as usual, & walk about with only the help of a stick, & every symptom was then so favourable that when Bowen saw him at one, he felt sure of his doing perfectly well. But as the day advanced, all these comfortable appearances gradually changed; the fever grew stronger than ever, & when Bowen saw him at ten at night, he pronounc'd his situation to be most alarming. At nine this morning he came again—& by his desire a Physician was called in;—Dr. Gibbs—But it was then absolutely a lost case—. Dr. Gibbs said that nothing but a Miracle could save him, and about Twenty minutes after Ten he drew his last gasp. (*Letters*, No. 40)

As in the fiction, the physician who confesses his powerlessness is saved from satire.[24]

One could argue, of course, that her father's death was not an occasion likely to have provoked satire—even on this intensely felt and certainly related subject of medical impotence. Yet, on the subject of her own death, the mockery of those who insist they know the answer continues undiminished:

Mr. Lyford says he will cure me, & if he fails I shall draw up a Memorial and lay it before the Dean & Chapter, & have no doubt of redress from that Pious, Learned, and Disinterested Body.[25] (*Letters*, No. 146)

That clinicians can be satirized for their greed, their pomposity, and their self-aggrandizement is no surprise; such a tradition in literature is an ancient one. Jane Austen's touch, though, adds this dimension: because these men know so little and we turn to them expecting so much, life becomes a perpetually terrifying uncertainty with only a scrim of knowledge to hide the abyss. Neither the romantic nor the rationalistic view will do, and Jane Austen rejected both: she saw the very general dietary and bathing cures as laughable, and the trust in existing systems of disease classification as misplaced. She was—in her attitude toward these views, neither romantic nor rationalistic, but rather wryly, acceptingly, and ironically—correct.

NOTES

1 James Edward Austen-Leigh, *Memoir of Jane Austen* (1871; rpt. Oxford: Clarendon Press, 1926), pp. 15–16. Austen-Leigh is one of the first, but certainly not the last, to speak of Jane Austen's "limitations"; for a valuable defense of these as strengths, see Donald Greene, "The Myth of Limitation," in Joel Weinsheimer, ed., *Jane Austen Today* (Athens, Ga.: University of Georgia Press, 1975), pp. 142–72.

2 All quotations from Jane Austen's novels are from *The Novels of Jane Austen: The Text Based on Collation of the Early Editions*, ed. R. W. Chapman, 3rd ed. (London: Oxford University Press, 1932–34), 5 vols. The citation above is from *Emma*, p. 19; further references are included parenthetically in the text.

3 G. S. Rousseau, "'Sowing the Wind and Reaping the Whirlwind': Aspects of Change in Eighteenth-Century Medicine," in Paul J. Korshin, ed., *Studies in Change and Revolution: Aspects of English Intellectual History 1640–1800* (Menston, Yorkshire: Scolar Press, 1972), p. 143. Rousseau's description of the dual current in medicine has provided a most useful background for my work. He, however, uses the terms "rationalist" and "empirical" while I have used "systematic" and "romantic," primarily because the latter is a term so entrenched in literary discussion as to make comment unnecessary. For remarks on Jane Austen's own use of the term, see Norman Page, *The Language of Jane Austen* (Oxford: Basil Blackwell, 1972), p. 11.

4 Lester S. King, M.D., *The Medical World of the Eighteenth Century* (Chicago: University of Chicago Press, 1958), p. 201.

5 Rousseau, pp. 141 and 150. For discussions of other aspects of Jane Austen's romanticism, see L. J. Swingle, "The Perfect Happiness of the Union: Jane Austen's *Emma* and English Romanticism," *The Wordsworth Circle*, 8 (1976), 312–20; and Gene W. Ruoff, "Anne Elliot's Dowry: Reflections on the Ending of *Persuasion*," *The Wordsworth Circle*, 8 (1976), 342–51.

6 Preface to *The Influence of the Sun and Moon upon Human Bodies* (1748), p. iv; quoted in Rousseau, p. 140.

7 E. S. Turner, *Call the Doctor: A Social History of Medical Men* (New York: St. Martin's Press, 1959), p. 73.

8 Turner, p. 74. Turner briefly details the growth of spas during this period.

9 King, p. 130.

10 *Medicina Statica* (1737), p. 8; quoted by Rousseau, p. 147.

11 Albert H. Buck, M.D., *The Dawn of Modern Medicine* (New Haven: Yale University Press, 1920), p. 33. The anecdote concerning Hufeland is presented by Buck without attribution.

12 For a discussion of these romantic attitudes in a social context, see Owsei Temkin, *The Double Face of Janus and Other Essays in the History of Medicine* (Baltimore: The Johns Hopkins University Press, 1977), pp. 431–35.

13 King draws attention to the problems in the development of an accurate nosology, pp. 193–226.

14 For a discussion of how the physician himself fluctuates, see Rousseau, pp. 131–34.

15 A. Walton Litz takes note of "Jane Austen's obvious admiration . . . for Marianne's vitality. . . ." That it is *she* who becomes ill adds to the poignancy of the situation. See *Jane Austen: A Study of Her Artistic Development* (New York: Oxford University Press, 1965), p. 78.

16 King, p. 130. "Fever" was a popular diagnosis in the eighteenth century, and there were various disputes over its classifications; see pp. 123–55.

17 Designations such as "putridness" appeared frequently but were not, of course, clinically accurate. King notes: "Huxham's classification was rather confused. He did not stress specificity, but he did achieve certain vague clinical groupings. These he tried to correlate with other data, but his knowledge was too fragmentary for successful definition or circumscriptions. He ended with a very imperfect cross-classification in which there was great fluidity and little precision" (p. 133). Because "putrid fever" struck and killed with rapidity, it is significant that this documents from the standpoint of medical history an insight noted by three critics about the uncertainty of life which lies just below the surface of structured English society: Lionel Trilling, *The Opposing Self* (New York: Viking Press, 1955), p. 207; John K. Mathison, "*Northanger Abbey* and Jane Austen's Conception of the Value of Fiction," *ELH*, 24 (1957), 138–52; Litz, p. 63.

18 *Observations on the Diseases of the Army* (London, 1774), p. 77, n.; quoted in King, p. 134.

19 All quotations from Jane Austen's letters are from *Jane Austen's Letters to her Sister Cassandra and Others*, ed. R. W. Chapman, 2nd ed. (London: Oxford University Press, 1952). The quotation above is from No. 77; further references will be parenthetical.

20 See the discussion of Emma's health as metaphor in Albert E. Wilhelm, "Three Word Clusters in *Emma*," *Studies in the Novel*, 7 (1975), 49–60.

21 The medical connection provides an additional factor integrating the problematic Mrs. Smith into the novel. See also Barbara Hardy, *A Reading of Jane Austen* (New York: New York University Press, 1976), p. 134; and the older but still valid discussion by Mary Lascelles, *Jane Austen and Her Art* (London: Oxford University Press, 1939), pp. 192–94.

22 Mr. Perry's carriage has, of course, an additional function in the novel: it serves as a clue to Jane Fairfax's correspondence with Frank Churchill.

23 This does not falsify the premise on which the parallel between the letters and the novels is based here. That the letters do, in fact, provide a somewhat looser, less disciplined vehicle for self-expression seems obvious, but I cannot agree that they fail to share the novels' "unifying vision of life." For such a view, see Robert Alan Donovan, "The Mind of Jane Austen," *Jane Austen Today*, pp. 109–26.

24 Jane Austen erred in attributing his earlier cure to successful cupping. See

King, p. 87, for a description of the way in which cupping was based on an incorrect hypothesis.

25 The diagnosis of her final illness—Addison's disease—was not made until 147 years after her death. See Sir Zachary Cope, "Jane Austen's Last Illness," *British Medical Journal*, 2 (1964), rpt. in Arnold Sorsby, ed., *Tenements of Clay: An Anthology of Medical Biographical Essays* (New York: Scribner's, 1974), pp. 174–79.

Montesquieu's Interpreters: A Polemical Essay

MARK HULLIUNG

The Need for a Critique of Montesquieu's Interpreters

Anyone who writes an interpretive book on Montesquieu premised on the assumption that the secondary literature may well be more an obstacle than an aid in the search for truth is under an obligation to explain where and why he believes so many able scholars have gone wrong.[1] My purpose in the present essay is to honor my duty to the secondary literature by taking it to task.

The literature on Montesquieu is possibly the least satisfactory body of interpretive works dealing with a major political thinker. Taken in the large, the mass of books, essays, and articles written on Montesquieu is so wanting that even at this late date his powerful claim to membership in the ranks of the greatest political theorists remains inadequately acknowledged. When scholars call out the honor roll of the foremost political minds, Plato to Marx, the name Montesquieu either is omitted or is included as an act of magnanimity. Truth be told, the Montesquieu of the secondary literature, even when sympathetically portrayed, is more fitting company for, say, Harrington, an influential second-rater, than for the likes of Rousseau or Hegel, thinkers who are their own history by virtue of their preeminent intellectual accomplishments. And if Montesquieu's intellectual stature has been so seriously misjudged, we should not be

327

surprised to find that his ideological convictions have also been misunderstood, his intentions misread, and his thought obscured by a secondary literature, passed from generation to generation, which contains as many layers of cumulative error as of cumulative knowledge.

Neither an exhaustive book-by-book critique of the secondary literature nor a bibliographical essay will be attempted here, but rather a paper organized around various "fallacies" of Montesquieu interpretation. My objectives are to designate categories of fallacies, to demonstrate that these fallacies are in fact fallacies, to cite representative examples from the secondary literature, and finally to suggest reasons, whenever possible, why interpreters have missed the mark in the past and may continue to do so in the future.

Montesquieu's Interpreters: Sins of Commission and Omission

Aristocratic Liberal or Feudal Reactionary? Was Montesquieu an "aristocratic liberal" or was he a "feudal reactionary"? Much ink has been spilled over this question—enough to testify that the majority of Montesquieu's interpreters believe the essence of his ideological commitments, his *parti pris*, is surely contained in one or another of these alternatives. J. J. Chevallier has written a very succinct, Elie Carcassonne a very comprehensive, account of Montesquieu the "aristocratic liberal"—the sworn enemy of royal absolutism, the dedicated friend of constitutional monarchy, the godfather of all persons of liberal persuasion.[2] On the other hand, Albert Mathiez, Louis Althusser, Franz Neumann, and Franklin Ford may be numbered among those convinced that Montesquieu was a "feudal reactionary" whose thrusts at despotic monarchy were taken with an aristocratic saber in hand: unmasked, Montesquieu stands exposed as the defender of privilege, inequality, and class oppression; for the heart and soul of his constitutionalism—so they argue—is an apology for the feudal society of which he was a beneficiary.[3]

It seems safe to say that the proponents of the "feudal reactionary" thesis have gained the upper hand. Theirs has been the pleasure of playing the game of ideological "unmasking," a process in which they can by turns be righteously indignant (for example, Mathiez) or urbanely forgiving (for example, Ford) in the face of Montesquieu's supposedly regressive opinions. Theirs also has been the enviable lot of taking credit for tying the history of ideas to social history, thereby saving us from an "idealist" interpretation of Montesquieu wherein ideas originally intended as rationalizations of a set of "material" conditions are later divorced from—and elevated ethereally above—those circumstances. Subjected to critical scrutiny, Montesquieu is merely a large-minded theorist of narrow-minded interests, no matter how much cosmetic surgery his scholarly defenders, the proponents of the "aristocratic liberal" thesis, perform on his visage. So say the triumphant advocates of the "feudal reactionary" interpretation.

Yet the victory of Mathiez over Carcassonne is purely pyrrhic, and a curse on both their houses is long overdue. Despite the animosity which has highlighted their debate, the proponents of the "aristocratic liberal" and "feudal reactionary" theses, viewed from a distance, are strikingly similar, strikingly wrong, and wrong for the same reasons. Brothers under the skin, they have stood together, and now it is time for them to fall together. Each assumes, incorrectly, that Montesquieu favored virtually all aspects of the old regime except absolute monarchy: in either interpretation Montesquieu figures as the enthusiastic supporter of aristocracy, of feudalism, of "intermediary bodies." Against these views it is necessary to object that Montesquieu attacked all of the old order, its social as well as its political structure. A country that failed to break the power of its First and Second Estates, he warned, was likely to go the way of Spain—the way of Inquisition, of economic stagnation. Conversely, a country which did break the power of its intermediary bodies, and of its absolute monarch as well, would be following in the footsteps of England, the most free and progressive of nations.[4] Montesquieu's thought does indeed "express" the old regime, as we have so often heard; it does so, however, not passively but through actively analyzing and explaining the old order; it does so, furthermore, through indicting and offering an enlightened alternative to the pre-revolutionary status quo.

"Aristocratic liberal" or "feudal reactionary?" Montesquieu was neither, and we are unlikely to do him justice until we delete both this question and the methodological assumptions which underlie it, namely, that the social history of ideas is either unimportant or impossible to write, or else is all-important and is properly written by discovering the social situation which a set of ideas "reflects." So long as our choice is "materialism" or "idealism," reductionism or platonic abstraction, the interpretive process is bound to yield disappointing results. A different tactic must be pursued. Henceforth encounters with the thoughts of a great mind should be undertaken in the realization, contra Marx, that ideas can be "reflections on" rather than "reflexes of the life process"; whence it will follow that we should stop working inward from the social world to thought which reputedly "mirrors" it, and start working outward from thought to the social world it apprehends.[5] The history of ideas will then enrich, but not disappear into, social history. Ideas will not be isolated from their social context, nor will their logical, analytical, or revelatory powers be neglected. The twin pitfalls of "idealism" and "materialism" will be averted.

The Comparative Study of Societies and Polities. Most students of Montesquieu's pioneering efforts in the use of comparative method argue one point above all: his objective in juxtaposing images of oriental and occidental countries was to sing the praises of the Robe, Sword, and clergy. Monarchy in the West, according to him, was one-man rule underwritten by the corporate bodies and privileged social groups—the "intermediary powers"—of feudal society: the estates, parlements, provincial assemblies, and semi-autonomous cities. Eastern monarchy, in dramatic contrast, was one-man rule in the absence of feudalism and hence in the presence of fear, purge, and social chaos. The message is unmistakable: succeed in subtracting feudalism from the French monarchy, Richelieu, and you will have created a despotic desert in the Western world. Once again we have Montesquieu presented as the champion of the old regime.

But Montesquieu was far from believing that the retention of intermediary bodies was sufficient reason for rejoicing, or their expulsion sufficient reason for despairing. Not at all: intermediary bodies had been removed from the English monarchy with admirable consequences, and retained by the Spanish monarchy with disastrous consequences, he insisted. The England which Montesquieu presented to the world as a pattern country was not, as has usually been maintained, a constitutional monarchy combined with intermediary bodies; it was constitutional monarchy, undeniably, but without intermediary bodies: "The English, to favor their liberty, have abolished all the intermediate powers of which their monarchy was composed." Not for want of clarity on Montesquieu's part has his position been misconstrued: "Abolish the privileges of the lords, the clergy, and cities in a monarchy, and you will soon have a popular state, or else a despotic government."[6] Again and again commentators have called our attention to the words "despotic government" in the foregoing quotation while ignoring the words "popular government" and their explicit referent, Montesquieu's beloved England. If a purge of intermediary bodies can lead to the worst of possibilities, despotism, it can also lead to the best, England's "system" of liberty. An aristocracy that was no longer a feudal nobility, a clergy tolerant, liberal, and removed from the political assemblies, an entrepreneurial ethic suffused throughout all social ranks—such were the benefits England reaped upon entering a post-feudal, post-old regime era of history.

Spain's significance as a pattern country equal in importance to England in Montesquieu's thought has gone unnoticed in the secondary literature—and this in spite of his lifelong fascination with Iberian affairs. Drawing attention to the Spaniards was for Montesquieu a means of complementing his comments on the British. If England's was the glory that potentially awaited a Western monarchy that crushed its feudal bodies, then Spain's was the degradation that threatened a monarchy whose feudal bodies continued to flourish. Inquisition, economic retardation, political weakness, and national decline were the fruits of Spain's tenacious clerical and aristocratic estates. Not an imported tyranny of exotic origin but rather a home-grown despotism—a despotism caused by the retention not the overthrow of feudal society—was what plagued Spain and menaced France. Montesquieu's comparative method yielded a vision of society and politics drastically at odds with the old regime—and drastically at odds with the opinions attributed to him by his interpreters.[7]

Precisely why Montesquieu's findings as a comparative analyst have been slighted[8] or misunderstood is not easy to determine. A certain relative neglect of the topic of comparative method can, however, be suggested as a tendency among students of the political classics. The theory of the social contract arouses much more interest today, doubtless because many contemporary political theorists are moral philosophers in search of ethical concepts that can be adapted to current dilemmas. Problems of political science are not their concern. Others do care about political science and its historical roots, but usually they assume that the social sciences did not exist before the French Revolution. That leaves Montesquieu nowhere.

Poor fellow, he does not even enjoy the consolation of good prospects, and especially not when it comes to an appreciation of his comparative method. At a time such as ours when there are those, armed with computers, who are eager to revive the nineteenth-century positivist quest for cross-cultural laws, it is perhaps inevitable that their critics (Alasdair MacIntyre, Peter Winch, for example[9]) should revive the nineteenth-century historicist claim that each nation is unique and comparison impossible. Montesquieu, however, knew nothing about positivism or historicism, but a great deal about Aristotle's *Politics*, including the comparative logic of genus and species which the master applied to Greek constitutions. An infusion of the concept of "feudalism" into the Aristotelian logic of *per genus et differentiam* was Montesquieu's intent. Applied to the West, feudalism supplied the generic term of comparative analysis, the common denominator; comparability of Western nations was assured because they were, differences notwithstanding, so many statements of the historical logic of feudalism.[10] Applied to East and West, feudalism supplied the term which differentiated types of royal absolutism, the oriental variety being unchecked, the occidental checked, by corporate bodies.

Neither the most outspoken contemporary advocates of comparative method, the neo-positivists, nor its most outspoken opponents, the neo-historicists, belong to the classical, Aristotelian world of ideas Montesquieu inhabited. His intellectual tradition is before theirs in time, between theirs in argumentation—comparative generalizations, yes, global laws, no—and feasibly above theirs in good sense. Together, the neo-positivists and neo-historicists block our awareness that another way once existed, with Aristotle and Montesquieu as its foremost representatives.

The History of Feudalism. Interpretations of Montesquieu's history of feudal laws usually go wrong at the very outset. According to the prevalent assumption, Montesquieu shared Boulainvilliers' and Dubos' belief that the origins of French history set the moral standard by which to judge succeeding ages. Not so for Montesquieu, to whom the entire debate over the past stood in obvious need of elevation to a higher plane.

Changing the ideologically inspired pseudo-histories of Boulainvilliers and Dubos into a social history of the rise of feudalism was Montesquieu's purpose. The *Germania* of Tacitus was his constant companion throughout the execution of his project, because its depiction of barbaric mores furnished him with the clue he needed to explain the gradual, unplanned, unintended erosion of the remains of Roman municipal institutions during the First Race. Germanic mores also were a vital element in the gradual development of feudal institutions and in the coming of age of a new *esprit général*, that of "honor." In the crudely accusatory histories of Boulainvilliers and Dubos—both authors under the domination of the past—the crucial term was usurpation, whereas for Montesquieu, a mature social historian, it was social evolution.

For all his objectivity Montesquieu did, of course, make moral judgments about feudal history. As related by him, the story of feudalism contained chapters on good and on evil, and on simultaneous good and evil. The constitutionalism of the Middle Ages was good, its class oppression evil; the England of his period was good, Spain was evil, yet both countries were mature offspring of the same feudal parents. For better and for worse, the Western world was defined by its feudal past, even England with its post-feudal society was, since its constitutional polity dated from feudal times. Morally as well as empirically, Montesquieu's vision transcended Boulainvilliers' and Dubos'.[11]

Marc Bloch's intelligent remarks on Books XXX–XXXI of the *Spirit of the Laws*, Robert Shackleton's discussion of Montesquieu's rigorous handling of sources, and E. H. Price's brief but able sketch of the meanings of "fundamental law" are contributions to Montesquieu studies which deserve applause.[12] Their research stands in marked contrast to the familiar pattern in which it is taken for granted that a member of the nobility could not have undertaken the task of writing a history of feudal laws for a reason other than the vindication of aristocratic privileges. In the "feudal reactionary" reading of Montesquieu, the brilliance of his treatment of the past cannot begin to come to light; the debunking process will not permit it. And debunking is so much easier than analyzing.

Monarchist or Republican? For most scholars the possibility that Montesquieu was not a monarchist is simply unthinkable. In their different ways, advocates of both the "aristocratic liberal" and the "feudal reactionary" theses visualize a Montesquieu so busy rendering the French monarchy responsive to aristocratic needs that it could never have occurred to him to question government centered in a single person. From another direction, J. Robert Loy, in his perceptive introduction to the *Persian Letters*, suggests that Montesquieu lived in a time of transition, thrived on change, but clung to monarchy as the one stationary point in an otherwise fluid society.[13] Still others pin the monarchical label on Montesquieu by a process of elimination: he despised despotism, his republics pertained to a bygone classical era,[14] so monarchies naturally won his approval, if only for want of a suitable alternative. It matters little, then, that he was as enamored of republican "virtue" as he was contemptuous of monarchical "honor"[15]; for the latter alone was available as a bulwark against despotic "fear."

Missing in all these readings of Montesquieu is an adequate account of his painstaking search for republics of post-classical vintage in the modern world. While taking the Grand Tour, he sought out the republics of Italy with keen interest, only to be disappointed. One and all those Italian cities, not excepting the much heralded Venetian republic, were scenes of degradation: not a hint of civic virtue was in evidence among them, nor did their histories of economic prowess have much to do with the eighteenth-century present. No, it was not Italy but Holland which stoked the fires of Montesquieu's republican imagination. A confederate republic, Holland was something antiquity never had been: a republic on a massive scale, or rather a series of republics loosely linked together at the national level—an arrangement which permitted her to combine the brute size of a monarchy with the smallness which had always been thought essential to the republican, participatory way of life. Serious problems of coordination abounded, but Holland could nevertheless boast second place among nations in freedom and roughly the same in economic productivity.[16]

First place in freedom, wealth, and most everything desirable went to England, a "republic disguised under the form of monarchy."[17] So said Montesquieu, invoking (consciously?) a formula dear to English republicans ever since the Restoration. Neither a city-state republic nor a confederate republic, England was an utterly novel phenomenon, a national republic. Holland's problems of inadequate centralization were not present in England, where, if anything, Montesquieu found too much centralization in national political institutions—the outcome, perhaps, of seventeenth-century upheavals. Carefully planned checks and balances were much needed in England as substitutes for the unplanned decentralization of power of days long past.

England's society was as remarkable as her political structure. A frenzied search for commercial success was a wave rolling across all Englishmen, even the nobles; and in its wake came individualism, independence, social mobility, and a blurring of class lines. Confederates rather than fellow-citizens, Englishmen were unlike ancient Romans or Spartans: not to the taste of the English was the preoccupation with things political, the downgrading of private life, so marked in the republics of antiquity. Yet the English would not abide the silencing of political speech, the enshrouding of things political behind a veil of secrecy, that was characteristic of monarchical politics. On the contrary, all Englishmen talked politics; all, if Montesquieu had his way, would even do some politicking—in particular, they would serve on the first democratic judiciary this side of ancient Athens.[18]

There is reason to hope that scholarly research is on the verge of bringing the republican identity of Montesquieu into prominence. Studies of neo-classical, neo-republican thought in early modern Europe—the Renaissance to the French Revolution—have been flourishing in recent years. Hans Baron's provocative account of "civic humanism" in Renaissance Italy has gained the attention it so richly deserves. Zera Fink's old but still useful account of English republicanism has been updated and embellished by J. G. A. Pocock in an ambitious effort to span time and space from Machiavelli to Harrington to the American founding fathers. Isaac Kramnick's study of Bolingbroke should be of great interest to students of Montesquieu, since it may be used to throw light on the Frenchman's republican interpretation of England.[19]

Economics. As an economist, Montesquieu's reflections were far-reaching and highly significant. Numbered among his accomplishments were contributions to formal economic theory, the sociology of economics, and international political economy. His suggestion that interest rates are decided by the supply and demand of money; his radical argument that economic progress is the special preserve of modern republics with open, liberal, and democratic societies; his appreciation of laissez-faire, both in its enlightening influence on domestic politics, and in its Janus-faced impact on international relations, where it curtails the violence of states but ruins poor nations—such are representative examples of his discoveries in different branches of economic thought.[20]

Obviously any comprehensive interpretation must come to grips with Montesquieu the economist; and yet scholars such as Mathiez, Althusser, Neumann, and Ford write almost as if Montesquieu never scribbled a line on economics. Not surprisingly, these are the same scholars who decipher Montesquieu's political commitments by pointing to his social class. Now they compound their initial error. If Montesquieu by virtue of his aristocratic status was the defender of aristocratic society, it follows that he could not have had much to say about economics, the science of the rising bourgeoisie. Melvin Richter reduces this misinterpretation to absurdity: ostensibly a kind of *Montesquieu par lui-même*, his commentary is in reality so much *Montesquieu par la littérature secondaire* that whenever he stumbles on evidence showing Montesquieu did not adhere to a feudal world-view, it immediately becomes proof that the author of the *Spirit of the Laws* was "confused."[21]

Not all of Montesquieu's interpreters have ignored his economic writings; rather the pattern has been one in which scholars of each generation have had to rediscover Montesquieu the economist—they have had, time and again, to begin at the beginning. Most recently we are indebted to N. E. Devletoglou and Thomas L. Pangle for calling our attention to the economic thought of Montesquieu.[22] But that their efforts have not decisively broken the pattern of discovery followed by forgetfulness is all too evident when one looks at two recently published books of selections from the *Spirit of the Laws*, neither of which includes any of Books XX–XXII, which contain the crux of Montesquieu's economic ideas.[23]

International Relations. Very little has been written about Montesquieu's theory of international relations. This sin of omission is glaring, since his works, from beginning to end, reveal a preoccupation with foreign affairs. The *Considerations on the Grandeur of the Romans* deals with the foreign policy of an ancient republic, the *Reflections on Universal Monarchy* with the foreign policy of modern monarchies; and considerable sections of the *Spirit of the Laws* recapitulate and extend his earlier findings. Always his concern is the same, and is evident as early as the *Persian Letters*: the problem of imperialism. Wherever he looked, Montesquieu saw the powers of Europe carving out empires; deeply disturbed, he could not rest until he had explained the imperialistic urge and found a rationale by means of which rulers might conceivably be convinced that restraint was in their interests, expansion was not.[24]

Only at a superficial level does the secondary literature recognize that Montesquieu had something to say about international relations. After duly recording his scattered moral outbursts against senseless wars, Montesquieu's interpreters fall silent. Both their frequent silences and their occasional words have a foundation in the study of political theory such as it is conducted today. Among political theorists, international relations is a much too neglected subject, and when the political theorist does find time to study the interaction of states, it is usually with an explicitly moral question in mind—under what conditions is a war just, for example. Montesquieu's efforts as a theoretician of international relations being empirical in appearance, they have lain dormant in the secondary literature. And ironically so, for a closer examination would reveal all the normative intent anyone could possibly seek, provided we understand that he aimed to promote morality without being moralistic. His explanatory models of imperialism were deliberately drawn up so as to exude a covertly moral message, a message all the more powerful for being stated in the language of power rather than morals. With dexterity and unflagging energy he drove home his message, moral in motive but coldly political in rhetoric, that imperialism drains monarchy of its powers.

How very far we have yet to travel in Montesquieu studies has been inadvertently attested by Badreddine Kassem, who somehow has managed to create a jingoistic Montesquieu. His edition of the *Oeuvres complètes* must be printed upside down.[25]

Politics and Morals. Like a thirsty man in sight of a well, Montesquieu's interpreters have raced to Book I of the *Esprit des lois*, hoping to quench their thirst for knowledge of what he had to say about "is" and "ought," empirical and normative. Whatever moral judgments the later Books contain are then referred back to Book I, and Montesquieu is graded for consistency and inconsistency. Despite the brevity of Book I's statements on natural law, despite the blatant contradiction between its a priori definition of justice on the one hand and Montesquieu's epistemological skepticism and cultural relativism on the other, Book I continues to enjoy a privileged position in the secondary literature on Montesquieu. It is time for Book I to suffer a demotion.

Everyone knows Montesquieu wanted to believe, contra Hobbes, in a justice superior to human conventions, those notorious carriers of evil. As early as the *Traité des devoirs* he may be seen advocating the anti-Hobbesian notion of transcendental justice which eventually found its way into Book I of the *Lois*. A direct plea via natural law philosophy for a more just and humane world was, then, characteristic of Montesquieu. It was not, however, the only characteristic of Montesquieu's moral thought, nor the most significant. In the *Traité* he was already visibly dissatisfied with a moralistic morality, as can be seen in the section entitled "De la politique."[26] Here emerged the Montesquieu of the future. Rather than plead the cause of justice, he sought to disprove the cause of injustice; that is, he set out to destroy from within the reason of state ideology, which, judging actions solely by consequences, suspended all considerations of justice. Out to prove that injustice is poor policy, Montesquieu quickly transformed his treatise on duties into a demonstration of the political inutility of "la politique," the "science of ruse and artifice."[27] Machiavellism, he argued with the aid of historical examples, simply did not measure up to Machiavellian standards. It did not work.[28]

Over the course of his subsequent writings Montesquieu doggedly continued his indirect assault on injustice. In the *Persian Letters* he demonstrated that a despotic society, a society thoroughly unjust, was disastrous for every last one of its members, not excepting the despot. In the *Considerations* he argued that the corruption of the Roman republic was the consequence of its unjust imperialism. Then followed the *Spirit of the Laws* in which he maintained that the injustice of monarchical imperialism led to consequences antithetical to the intentions of its perpetrators. Indeed, the best way to pursue power was to follow the program of Enlightenment: trade instead of guns, constitutional government, laissez-faire, social welfare. By the time Montesquieu had finished deliberately confounding the terminologies of freedom and power, no one could discern the difference between them.[29]

Of course, an over-emphasis on the significance of Book I is not the only reason interpreters have misunderstood the links Montesquieu drew between politics and morals. Equally blameworthy and responsible is their insistence on viewing him through the lenses of the philosophies of a later day. Some, for whom the distinction between fact and value is essential, take him to task for confusing "is" and "ought," never realizing that Montesquieu's moral philosophy was a systematic effort to exploit that very confusion.[30] Others, of whom Meinecke is the outstanding example, express regret that Montesquieu's incipient historicism stopped short of purging all elements of the Enlightenment's universal morality.[31] What could be more misleading? Meinecke's historicist morality, his vicious Hegelian success philosophy, would have struck Montesquieu as the reincarnation of Hobbism—whatever is, is right. For as long as the ethics of power served the ends of the Enlightenment Montesquieu was willing to abide by it, but not for a moment longer.

The positivists, too, have misled us. Theirs is a Montesquieu struggling to shake off his classical, moralistic heritage, notably the search for the ideal polity, in order to devote himself to a value-free study of real regimes. Wrong again, a value-free political science would have seemed value-less to Montesquieu; moreover, his political science was not an anticipation of that of positivism but rather an extension of Aristotle's, an outgrowth of the very classical tradition Durkheim would have us believe Montesquieu was repudiating.[32] Durkheim forgot that Aristotle had supplemented his depiction of the abstractly best polity with an astute account of the workings of different types of existing polities. Montesquieu updated both Aristotle's empirical method and his habit of forcing moral conclusions from political science, as in Aristotle's contention—later Montesquieu's in the *Considerations*— that an expansionary polis was necessarily self-destructive.

The pattern is obvious: each school of modern philosophy, claiming Montesquieu as its forerunner, has distorted his thoughts on politics and morals.

The Problem of Generalization

"Montesquieu the positivist," "Montesquieu the historicist"—these phrases tell us very little about Montesquieu but a great deal about the methods of his interpreters. To wit, such formulas suggest that his modern readers, often overly eager for generalization, generalize improperly. Interpreters read history backwards, tearing Montesquieu out of his context and congratulating him for discoveries—the founding of positivism or historicism—he never made nor had any interest in making. They over-state his break with the past by fixating on his supposed links with intellectual traditions which succeeded him, while systematically ignoring those traditions which preceded him and gave him intellectual nourishment.

Inevitably a reaction to such false modernization arises and breeds its own excesses. Mark Waddicor's hits at the positivist interpretation of Montesquieu are most welcome, as is his stress on the empirical ingredient in the natural law tradition.[33] But his conclusion, that Montesquieu is therefore best understood as a culminating point of natural law thought, is less deserving of praise. Citing phrases parallel to Montesquieu's in the literature of natural law reveals the essence of Montesquieu about as much as Allan Gilbert's citations to the literature *On Princely Rule* reveal the genius of Machiavelli,[34] which is to say, hardly at all. A victim of spurious continuity, Montesquieu begins to lose his individuality; his most distinctive innovations are constantly on the verge of disappearing into previous thinkers of minor stature. Properly situated, Montesquieu is neither a positivist *ex nihilo*—the first cause uncaused of later positivist thinkers—nor is he a significant link in an unbroken transmission of natural law philosophy through the ages. Rather, he is part of the tradition of classical, Aristotelian political science, and of its sporadic, discontinuous revival in early modern Europe, notably by Machiavelli, Bodin, and Harrington.

Improper generalizations are not the only obstacle to an appreciation of Montesquieu. An absence of generalization, or a bias against generalization, may well be the pattern of future research. Atonement for past mistakes, as is so often the case, may lead to the rise of new errors, the reverse side of the old. The danger is that books on Montesquieu may henceforth be graded as scholarly and proper to the extent they lack the generalizations which render findings meaningful. Unhistorical books written on topics in intellectual history (studies of "perennial questions"), books containing histories of relationships between thinkers who were scarcely aware of one another (studies of "influence"), books telling stories of intellectual goings-on that never happened (studies of "anticipation") have been very common in the discipline of intellectual history; and in Quentin Skinner's telling critiques they have received their just deserts.[35] Should, however, Skinner's attacks inadvertently signal the rise of a new generation of erudites without purpose or vision, Montesquieu among others will suffer. Conceivably, more and more will be said about less and less in his works. Skinner, the self-conscious thinker, may have unwittingly paved the way for the dominance of unself-conscious thinkers, mere chroniclers.

Nearest at hand, a generalization-killing fear of treating Montesquieu's thought as a whole easily follows from Skinner's strictures. The assumption of unity in the works of political philosophers is arbitrary, Skinner has complained. Generalization is thereby attained, but falsely so, since the various works of a given philosopher were spread out over a lifetime and written with different purposes in mind.[36] Surely Skinner's point is well taken, but we must be on guard against substituting an a priori assumption of disunity for the previous assumption of unity. In Montesquieu's case the chronological, work-by-work approach is not mandatory and can be pernicious; applied to him, Skinner's critique run wild would lead to an unnecessary dismemberment of the *Oeuvres complètes*. For Montesquieu's thought truly is a whole. Already in the *Persian Letters* his thought is mature: the model of oriental despotism is fully articulated; the civic nature of the ancient republic receives brief but definite mention; monarchy is linked with aristocratic "honor" and luxury; England is saved and Spain is damned.[37] Much, of course, can be learned by studying the *Persian Letters*, *Considerations*, and *Spirit of the Laws* one by one, in isolation from one another; but many of the finest riches of Montesquieu's mind can only be experienced by empathy with the amazing persistence and unity of his vision. His lifelong dedication to the refutation of injustice through covert means is a case in point.

Lastly, the process of seeing Montesquieu's work as a whole confers this benefit: it acts as a check against interpretations of particular works. Every so often one hears, for instance, that Roxane's rebellion at the end of *Persian Letters* is a premonition of the French Revolution.[38] Would it not be more accurate to understand her suicide as an early statement of the lesson Montesquieu taught most systematically in the *Spirit of the Laws*, that oriental despotism can sustain nothing of worth and is inimical even to the interests of the despot?

The rehabilitation of generalization can be carried much further.

Strange as it may seem to some historians, there is something to be said for reading intellectual history anachronistically, so long as we know what we are doing. As historians we want to enter into the minds of thinkers of another era; we want to identify the questions a thinker asked, the concepts at his disposal, the intellectual tradition in which he asserted his being. But we also need to know what a thinker could not say, think, or conceptualize. From the vantage point of the present, we see that Bodin and Montesquieu could not think the thoughts on bureaucratic monarchy which Hegel and Weber, Prussia in mind, were later to think. The language of administration available to Bodin turns out to be the language of fiefs and benefices, an inept language for fostering his would-be ideal of a depersonalized monarchical rule. A glance at Prussia, Hegel, and Weber makes all the difference: it highlights Bodin's plight in a way that an effort simply to view him in terms of his own age could never do.[39]

Another legitimate and rewarding method of generalization is that of abstracting the form of past political thought and applying it to the content of contemporary realities. Moral philosophers very frequently do just that; examinations of obligation or justice written today are commonly argued within a framework drawn from the social contractualists Hobbes, Locke, Rousseau, and Kant. For such purposes the intention of Hobbes or Locke, or what they were understood to mean in their day, is beside the point; instead, our proper concern, as philosophers rather than historians, is with the uses to which we can put their seventeenth-century concepts. Likewise the Aristotelian variety of political science which Montesquieu favored can be applied to the realities of the twentieth-century. Gaetano Mosca did so at the turn of the century, Samuel Huntington did so very recently in an essay entitled "Political Order and Political Decay." Both Mosca and Huntington emphasize the primacy of politics; according to them decay, degeneration, *stasis* is the natural condition of societies, economically developed or not, which lack sound political structures. For both, the building of political institutions is consequently the first task of creative politics. Both men know their Aristotle and use him effectively, one by modernizing the Aristotelian notion of polity, the other by adding to Aristotle the modern idea of the political party.[40]

Whatever our concern as we read the classics of political thought, Plato to Marx, whether we approach them as historians, as moral philosophers, or as political scientists, generalizations that matter are waiting to be made if only we will make them.

Afterword

To be critical of the secondary literature on Montesquieu is not to be ungrateful. Jean Starobinski's comments on Montesquieu are full of his customary intelligence; Robert Shackleton has put us all in debt to his biographical labors; Roger Oake's essays are always rewarding; Albert O. Hirschman's study of "arguments for capitalism before its triumph" is sprinkled with discerning remarks on Montesquieu; and many other scholars have toiled long, hard, and profitably in the realm of Montesquieu studies.[41] But as long as the hereditary errors which pervade the secondary literature persist, each step forward will be matched by a step backward.

NOTES

This paper was presented on April 19, 1979 to the American Society for Eighteenth-Century Studies. I wish to thank Robert Shackleton and Lester Crocker for their astute comments.

1 Mark Hulliung, *Montesquieu and the Old Regime* (Berkeley, 1976).
2 J. J. Chevallier, "Montesquieu ou le libéralisme aristocratique," *Revue internationale de la philosophie*, 9, (1955), 330–45; Elie Carcassonne, *Montesquieu et le problème de la constitution française au XVIIIe siècle* (Paris, 1926). The understanding of Montesquieu as an aristocratic liberal descends to contemporary scholars from the liberals of the French Restoration: Guizot, Constant, and Madame de Staël.
3 Albert Mathiez, "La place de Montesquieu dans l'histoire des doctrines politiques du XVIIIe siècle," *Annales historiques de la Révolution française*, 7 (1930), 97–112; Louis Althusser, *Montesquieu, la politique et l'histoire* (Paris, 1959); Franz Neumann, "Montesquieu," ch. 4 of *The Democratic and the Authoritarian State* (Glencoe, 1957); Franklin Ford, *Robe and Sword* (New York, 1965), ch. 12. The understanding of Montesquieu as a feudal reactionary descends to contemporary scholars from Voltaire, whose view was not shared by his fellow-*philosophes*.
4 Hulliung, *Montesquieu and the Old Regime*, ch. II, 4; ch. IV, 1.
5 Cf. J. G. A. Pocock, *Politics, Language and Time* (New York, 1971), p. 36.
6 Both quotations are from the *Spirit of the Laws*, II, 4 (Nugent translation).
7 On Spain and England, and their significance for France: Hulliung, *Montesquieu and the Old Regime*, ch. II, 2, 4; ch. IV, 1; ch. VII.
8 Surprisingly few scholars deal directly and at length with Montesquieu's comparative method. A recent exception is Melvin Richter, "Comparative Political Analysis in Montesquieu and Tocqueville," *Comparative Politics*, 1

(Jan. 1969), 129–60; but his essay is expository rather than analytical.

9 Alasdair MacIntyre, "Is a Science of Comparative Politics Possible?" in *Against the Self-Images of the Age* (New York, 1971), ch. 22; Peter Winch, "Understanding a Primitive Society," *American Philosophical Quarterly*, 1 (Oct. 1964), 307–24.

10 Cf. Louis Hartz's claim, thoroughly in the spirit of Montesquieu, that comparative histories of European countries can be written thanks to a shared feudal factor. *The Liberal Tradition in America* (New York, 1955), pp. 25–26.

11 Hulliung, *Montesquieu and the Old Regime*, ch. III.

12 Marc Bloch, *Feudal Society* (Chicago, 1964), pp. xvii, 190, 426, 441; Robert Shackleton, *Montesquieu: A Critical Biography* (Oxford, 1963), ch. XV; E. H. Price, "Montesquieu's Historical Conception of the Fundamental Law," *Romanic Review*, 38 (1947), 234–42.

13 J. Robert Loy, "Introduction" to *The Persian Letters* (New York, 1961), p. 29.

14 Robert Shackleton, "La genèse de *l'Esprit des lois*," *Revue d'histoire littéraire de la France* (Oct. 1952), pp. 425–38, argues (p. 432) that Montesquieu believed "virtue" was irrelevant in the modern world. Many other scholars hold similar views.

15 I do not mean to suggest that all scholars have taken note of Montesquieu's attack on "honor." Far from it, the assumption that Montesquieu was a defender of aristocratic society has frequently blinded his interpreters to this very obvious point. Or, as in the case of Henry J. Merry, Montesquieu's hits at "honor," though recognized, are treated as eccentric. *Montesquieu's System of Natural Government* (West Lafayette, 1970), p. 214.

16 Hulliung, *Montesquieu and the Old Regime*, ch. IV, 1.

17 *Spirit of the Laws*, V, 19. Nannerl O. Keohane, "Virtuous Republics and Glorious Monarchies: Two Models in Montesquieu's Political Thought," *Political Studies*, 20 (Dec. 1972), 383–96, is mistaken, I believe, in her attempt to dismiss this phrase (p. 393n). Her assumption that for Montesquieu republics and monarchies are mutually exclusive is belied time and again by his comments on England. Moreover, as an avid reader of the classics Montesquieu knew his Polybius, according to whom a monarchical element could and should be incorporated into a republican political structure.

18 Hulliung, *Montesquieu and the Old Regime*, ch. II, 4; ch. IV, 1; Epilogue, 1.

19 Hans Baron, *The Crisis of the Early Italian Renaissance* (Princeton, 1966); Z. S. Fink, *The Classical Republicans* (Evanston, 1945); J. G. A. Pocock, *The Machiavellian Moment* (Princeton, 1975); Isaac F. Kramnick, *Bolingbroke and His Circle* (Cambridge, Mass., 1968).

20 Hulliung, *Montesquieu and the Old Regime*, ch. VII, 2–3.

21 See, for example, his comment on Montesquieu's use of Mandeville. Melvin Richter, *The Political Theory of Montesquieu* (Cambridge, 1977), p. 43.

22 N. E. Devletoglou, "Montesquieu and the Wealth of Nations," *The Cana-*

dian Journal of Economics and Political Science, 29 (Feb. 1963), 1–25; Thomas L. Pangle, *Montesquieu's Philosophy of Liberalism* (Chicago, 1973), ch. 7. In both of these works the benefits of international trade, as seen by Montesquieu, are stressed; its liabilities for poor countries, a subject of equal importance to him, are neglected.

23 Richter, *The Political Theory of Montesquieu*; David Wallace Carrithers, ed., *The Spirit of Laws* (Berkeley, 1977).

24 Hulliung, *Montesquieu and the Old Regime*, chs. VI–VII.

25 Badreddine Kassem, *Décadence et absolutisme dans l'oeuvre de Montesquieu* (Paris, 1960), pp. 125, 143.

26 *Oeuvres complètes* (Paris, 1949), I, 108–19.

27 *Oeuvres complètes*, I, 110.

28 Studies of the relationship of Montesquieu to Machiavelli, even when they overcome the antithesis of power politician versus humanitarian, fail to underscore the extent to which Montesquieu assumed Machiavellian poses in order to promote humanitarian ends; e.g., E. Levi-Malvano, *Montesquieu e Machiavelli* (Paris, 1912); Robert Shackleton, "Montesquieu and Machiavelli: A Reappraisal," *Comparative Literature Studies* (1964), pp. 1–13.

29 Hulliung, *Montesquieu and the Old Regime*, chs. V–VII.

30 E.g., Richter, *The Political Theory of Montesquieu*, p. 27.

31 Friedrich Meinecke, *Historism: The Rise of a New Historical Outlook*, trans. J. E. Anderson (London, 1972), ch. 3.

32 Emile Durkheim, *Montesquieu and Rousseau: Forerunners of Sociology* (Ann Arbor, 1965).

33 Mark H. Waddicor, *Montesquieu and the Philosophy of Natural Law* (The Hague, 1970).

34 Allan Gilbert, *Machiavelli's Prince and Its Forerunners: The Prince as a Typical Book* de Regimine Principum (New York, 1968). J. R. Hale's one-sentence comment is more illuminating than Gilbert's entire book: "Because of its formal resemblance to old manuals *Of Princely Government*, Machiavelli's *Prince* was like a bomb in a prayer-book." *Machiavelli and Renaissance Italy* (New York, 1966), p. 30.

35 E.g., Quentin Skinner, "Meaning and Understanding in the History of Ideas," *History and Theory*, 8, no. 1 (1969), 3–53.

36 Skinner, "Meaning and Understanding . . . ," pp. 16–20.

37 *Lettres persanes*, XIX, XXXIV, LXIII, LXXX, LXXXVIII, LXXXIX, CII, CIII on oriental despotism; LXXXIX on the ancient republic; LXXXVIII, LXXXIX, XC on honor; XCIX, CVI on luxury; CIV, CXXXVI on England; XLV, LXXVIII, CXVIII, CXXI, CXXXVI on Spain.

38 E.g., Marshall Berman, *The Politics of Authenticity* (New York, 1970), p. 8; Pangle, *Montesquieu's Philosophy of Liberalism*, p. 217.

39 Hulliung, *Montesquieu and the Old Regime*, ch. IV, 2.

40 Gaetano Mosca, *The Ruling Class* (New York, 1939); Samuel P. Huntington, *Political Order in Changing Societies* (Yale, 1968), ch. 1.

41 Jean Starobinski, *Montesquieu par lui-même* (Paris, 1966); Robert Shackleton, *Montesquieu: A Critical Biography*; Roger B. Oake, "Montesquieu's Religious Ideas," *Journal of the History of Ideas*, 14 (Oct. 1953), 548–60; "Montesquieu's Analysis of Roman History," *Journal of the History of Ideas*, 16 (Jan. 1955), 44–60; Albert O. Hirschman, *The Passions and The Interests: Political Arguments for Capitalism before its Triumph* (Princeton, 1977).

Who Is Boswell's Johnson?

WILLIAM R. SIEBENSCHUH

In view of much recent scholarship this is not an idle question. The validity and value of Boswell's portrait of Johnson in the *Life* have come under serious attack. Boswell's once famous ability to gather facts is now debatable; his ability to understand the facts he had is being called deficient. And his marvelous dramatizations of Johnson are being called distortions.[1] Although the *Life* has been considered one of the world's greatest biographies for nearly two centuries, it is now being argued that it is not really biography at all.[2] To even begin to defend Boswell, if that is possible, each of these charges must be faced and dealt with somehow. My purpose, in this brief paper, is not to attempt ultimate statements, but to suggest some lines along with such defense of Boswell might be made.

The questions concerning Boswell's ability to gather and assess his facts are the easiest to confront directly. Much has to be conceded here, but there are really no surprises. For a long time, it has been more or less clear that there was a great deal about Johnson's life that Boswell knew little about or didn't understand. The wealth of new biographical studies of Johnson simply makes it clearer than ever before exactly what and how much there was.[3] Some of Boswell's blind spots are important; there is no question about it. There is, for example, the clear evidence of severe mental breakdown, which Boswell dismisses as a serious possibility. There is the role of the Thrales, which Boswell does not give nearly the importance that it obviously had. There are the subjects that Boswell is known to have been aware of and that he doctored in the final version of the *Life*: Johnson's problems with his wife, his earthy, bawdy sides, etc. And there is John-son's complicated psyche into which biographers such as Walter Jack-son Bate have probed much further than Boswell could have.

Added together, this is a substantial amount of material that is either missing from the *Life* or inadequately treated in it. Some would argue that the list should be longer. It is foolish to deny that these problems exist. But Boswell's ignorance of aspects of Johnson's life and character are only fatal flaws in his book if his primary achieve-ment as a biographer is considered to be his facts. His major contri-bution as a biographer is not his facts; it never really has been. His achievement is his vision of Johnson, the imaginative possession of him that his book allows us to have. That vision is, in fact, a "ver-sion," not a compilation, photograph, or tape recording. It is an inter-pretation and it will not be superseded by new facts because there is no such thing as an ultimate interpretive biography of a man like Johnson. There will always be a continuing dialogue between his life—a central core of known facts and shared assumptions—and a more or less constant succession of minds that will strike up new relationships with him and confer different degrees of significance upon his works and deeds. We don't go to the *Life* to get factual in-formation to assimilate; we go to the *Life* to see and hear Johnson. Boswell's version can be added to but not replaced by new knowl-edge unless it is of the sort that totally invalidates his image of Johnson.

This, however, is exactly what some are willing to argue that it does. They suggest that the Johnson we see in the *Life* is far more a romantic and fictional creation of Boswell's, a response primarily to his own needs, than an historically accurate image. Certainly there is an element of this in the portrait of the *Life*, that "involuntary trib-ute," as it has been called, "of a great human weakness to a great human strength."[4] But this has been known or suspected for a long time, and to invalidate the portrait of Johnson on these grounds seems extreme. It is throwing the baby out with the bathwater. If we do that, then we probably ought to throw out all the other contem-porary portraits as well—Sir John Hawkins', Mrs. Thrale's, Kearsley's, Hannah More's, the lot of them—because the man we see rolling about in Boswell's book is certainly the same man we see moving about in theirs.

All biographical portraits have limitations because they are written by human beings. Attacking Boswell's personal limitations and ig-norance of certain facts is valid enough if one wants to argue that we need more than just Boswell's *Life of Johnson* if we want to know Johnson fully. That is certainly true, but if it is a limitation that must be acknowledged, it ought not to be a death sentence. It is not the most serious problem. The greatest problem with the book is the success of Boswell's art. The most serious threat to his reputation as a biographer is his use in a biography of methods we normally associate with fiction. Boswell's greatest achievement, his dramatic ability to bring Johnson to life, is now, potentially, his greatest liability.[5] The use of fictional methods in a factual work is one of the most basic generic taboos, and if we concede, as surely we must, that Boswell depends heavily on fictional techniques in his portrait of Johnson in the *Life*, then defending his methods as valid biographical practice means challenging some of the most automatic assumptions we make about the nature of biography.

To defend Boswell against attack in this quarter, we need to have a clear idea of exactly what he does and does not do. First of all, though it seems obvious, we need to remind ourselves that although Boswell may sometimes idealize, it cannot be argued sensibly that he invented Johnson or all of the things about Johnson's character that we love in the *Life*. As many have pointed out, he couldn't have. He may romanticize, but he doesn't invent whole cloth. He doesn't invent the facts of Johnson's life or his moral courage and intellectual powers. If the *Life* had never been written, the broad contours of Johnson's character would have been projected forcefully by his own works, letters, and diaries. We would be able, easily, to create an image of him based on our readings of his works, and it would be a powerful image. Some would argue that it would be a far superior image to the one we get in the *Life*.[6] It might well be in the sense that it would be more balanced, less sharply focused on Boswell's own interests. Yet it is hard to imagine that the image of Johnson projected by his works alone would be radically different from the kind we can get from the works of other literary figures whose lives we can find out about, whose letters we can read for ourselves, to whose journals we can have access, and who don't make the kind of impression on us that Boswell's Johnson does. We might know Johnson and we would certainly admire him, but we wouldn't possess him in the same way.

Boswell doesn't just make the physical man accessible to our imaginations; he makes the personal greatness accessible too.[7] That is his great achievement in the *Life*. Because of Boswell's unorthodox biographer's methods, we don't just intellectually understand the nature of Johnson's greatness; we experience it vicariously—the way we would if he were a fictional hero. We get out of ourselves and are enlarged by him as we learn about him.

The causes of this are many. Some have always been understood, and some have often been misunderstood. Obviously, one of the reasons Boswell's Johnson stays in our minds so clearly is that since Boswell's method is dramatic, we see Johnson more concretely than the subjects of most other biographies. This has always been pointed out, and it is extremely important. Yet as strong and obvious an argument as this is, it isn't enough to explain the full impression Boswell's Johnson produces. There is a good deal more to it than just a superabundance of concrete detail, and a good way to check this is to go to any other biography in which Johnson is described physically. Read the descriptions carefully, supply the appropriate "Sirs" and "Aye, Sirs," and then imagine Johnson described in the same way as often as we see him in Boswell. The result is in no way comparable.

The same is true of the famous conversations. These are often cited as the single most important element in the book, but for the wrong reason. They are far more than priceless transcripts. A great many contemporaries recorded Johnson's *bons mots*, or the famous "tossings and gorings." All modern biographers retell the most famous stories. Johnson doesn't sound the same; the reason is not attributable simply to the fact that Boswell was a transcendently good dramatist, or even to the well-known fact that he practically *became* Johnson when he wrote some of the conversations. The physical descriptions, the dramatizations, and the conversations in Boswell are effective precisely because they are always important in some greater context; because their importance lies outside themselves in the truth about Johnson that they symbolize.

In Boswell it is Johnson's character that we are seeing visually, not just his body; it is what he stands for, not just what he looked or sounded like. In the *Life*, Johnson's actions and his statements never occur in a vacuum. (Comparison with Mrs. Piozzi and especially any of the less important biographers is instructive in this regard.)[8] Nearly every important scene or conversation is part of the collective interpretive statement that Boswell is making, but we are seldom conscious that these kinds of connections are being made for us. We don't imagine we are experiencing a biographer's comment, only his data,[9] and the truths we encounter about Johnson have all the freshness of discovery and the clarity of the visual image.

Boswell's Johnson appeals to us on many different levels, and one of the most important things he does is to be what most of us want to be but aren't, to do what most of us wish we could do but cannot. Of the many memorable moments in the *Life*, think how often the ones we remember longest and retell with the greatest pleasure are the ones in which Johnson puts somebody in his place, shoulders impertinence aside, clears the air of cant. "Well, [said he,] we had a good talk." BOSWELL. "Yes, Sir; you tossed and gored several persons." "Sir, [to a foolish and impertinent fellow] I have found you an argument. I am not obliged to find you an understanding." [to Boswell] "My dear friend, clear your *mind* of cant. You may *talk* as other people do; you may say to a man, 'Sir, I am your most humble servant.' You are *not* his most humble servant."

Everyone has his favorites. Johnson is, in the *Life*, a lesson in self-assertion. He is always adequate, always ready. He doesn't truckle; he doesn't mouth cant; he doesn't suffer impertinence. He doesn't wake up in the middle of the night and think of what he should have said; he says it. He doesn't make excuses later about why he didn't speak up—he thunders. Boswell certainly doesn't invent this quality about him; it is confirmed by most contemporary sources.[10] But he does raise it into high relief; he does give it to us dramatically and thus allow us to experience this aspect of Johnson's greatness vicariously. And this is crucial. When we read the *Life*, we can do through Johnson what few of us can do with any regularity in our own lives.

How is all this different from saying that Boswell's Johnson does for us what any good hero in a work of fiction does? It isn't, except in one extremely important sense. Johnson is made to do for us some of the things that fictional heroes do, but the book we encounter him in is not fiction and does not strike us as such. In that apparent paradox lies the reason why the *Life* is different from virtually all other biographies. Put most simply, Boswell does dramatically what other biographers do analytically. It is wrongheaded, I think, to assume that such imaginative creation or objectification is automatically synonymous with distortion. It can be, but it need not. In Boswell's hands, it is objectification by dramatic means of the same coherent image of the subject that any good biographer has. What it gives us that is unique is a startlingly out-of-the-ordinary relationship, as readers, with the subject of a biography. It puts us in a relationship with Johnson that approximates the relationship we have with a fictional hero, but the hero has the impact of truth, not fiction. We can be greater and better than we are through the medium of Boswell's Johnson, because while we imagine that we are assimilating information about him, we are in fact acting out some of our favorite fantasies without reacting to them as if they were fantasies. They aren't "untruths" about Johnson simply because they appeal to us at this level, and seeing Johnson this way doesn't diminish the validity of the portrait; it complicates and enriches the experience of the reader.

The pleasure of such vicarious enjoyment is qualitatively different from the pleasure we get from the wit of, say, Wilde or Shaw. We can assimilate knowledge about them and perhaps remember what they said but we can't *be* them through the medium of the biographer's art, and we are not encouraged to want to do so for the same reasons. We may think privately that to call fox-hunting the unspeakable in pursuit of the inedible is clever. But the wit of other men, even very witty men, usually exists for us in a vacuum. When we think of the sparks struck out of Johnson in Boswell, we remember the dramatic and therefore the human and the moral context. (It is no accident that Hamilton's observations on Johnson's death are more moving in Boswell than in the original. The effect of context is the difference.) Boswell's Johnson is not only a proof of Johnson's greatness; he is a perpetual affirmation of something in us, not, perhaps, of what we always are but of what we are capable of being. Yet, as a rule, we do not put the book down with the sense that it is art and our own lives are something else. And rightly so, because we have not been seeing a fiction but instead, I think, imagining a truth.

The crucial question is "Is this possible?" Can it be argued legitimately that fictional methods can successfully be used to make factual statements? According to most standard views of the nature of the genre, the answer would have to be "No." It would presumably be inevitable that aesthetic considerations would begin to take precedence over the impulse towards factual accuracy. Boswell would dramatize what he wanted to see and not what was actually there. He is undeniably guilty of this sort of thing in his journals (think of the Louisa episode); how do we know it isn't a serious problem in the *Life*?

It may be, but we don't know as much about the subject as we need to know, because until recently we haven't asked the right questions. The most common fears and assumptions about what must happen when fictional techniques are used in factual works are valid enough as generalizations. When they are proved, as they often have been, by means of extreme examples (Carlyle's most excessive prose or badly executed novelistic histories) they can seem unquestionable. But of course they aren't more absolute or unquestionable than any other broad generalizations, and they have seldom been tested rigorously in particular works.

The history of critical response to the *Life* is a perfect example of this. Until the flurry of reassessments following the discovery of the *Boswell Papers*, the *Life* was considered a monument to indefatigable research and "fact gathering."[11] The great conversational moments were considered to be marvelously dramatized tape recordings (Boswell's amazing accuracy was always stressed). As long as the factuality could be insisted upon, the dramatic achievements could be praised unreservedly. Although it has since been shown to be incorrect, it was argued confidently that there was little or no change between Boswell's original journal entries, taken on the spot, and their introduction, virtually without any change, into the final version of the *Life*.[12] Yet in the last two decades, Boswell has been shown to have depended far less on facts and far more on fictional techniques than was ever imagined before,[13] and reaction has been swift and utterly predictable. In direct proportion as Boswell has been shown to have depended on fictional techniques, his validity and value as a biographer have been attacked and doubted.

These doubts may or may not turn out to be fully justified, but at the moment I don't think we know enough about the possible uses of fictional methods in factual works, or about what Boswell actually does in the *Life* to know. Until very recently the subject has not been confronted directly at all. The debate has just begun; clear battle lines are being drawn. But more evidence is needed before any conclusions can be arrived at. Many will disagree, but I think that it is not only possible but likely that Boswell gives us great biography precisely because he uses fictional techniques. To prove this, if it can be proved, a good deal of new work will have to be done. The subject is enormous—far greater than the scope of this paper allows—and I would like here to suggest some likely sources of new evidence.

I have suggested that Boswell does dramatically what more traditional biographers do analytically. This is an obvious place to begin. His dramatizations are his interpretive statements, and at times they are relatively sophisticated. Presumably, either this shouldn't be possible or it shouldn't be effective. The tendency of Boswell's art, some have suggested, is not to give a sophisticated portrait but to oversimplify and stereotype Johnson,[14] to give us a portrait that is vivid but, of necessity, shallow. Boswell is no psychoanalyst, and he has his famous limitations. But this argument is far truer of the *Tour* than of the *Life*.[15] Within the limits of his ability to consciously or intuitively understand Johnson, I believe Boswell's dramatic art in the *Life* adds depth and dimension to the portrait of Johnson rather than reducing it.

Think, for example, of all that is contracted into the famous Wilkes episode: Johnson's awareness, when it is too late, of the nature of the trap Boswell has sprung on him; Johnson's discomfiture and his triumph over himself and the situation; his truce with Wilkes and the triumph of "civility" as they discover subjects about which they can agree or talk safely. Think of Johnson's awareness of Wilkes' awareness of the situation as they both decide to roast Boswell for being a Scot, and Johnson comically punishes Boswell for a crime for which he has obviously forgiven him. The interplay of different facets of Johnson's character in this essentially comic but nevertheless complex social situation is anything but shallow.

It is too easy, I think, to write off a great scene like this as a case of Boswell's "pitting" two of his favorite alter egos against one another and then writing up what he wanted to see. It's possible, of course. But we need to remind ourselves anew that although Boswell had all the disadvantages of being very close to his subject, he had all the advantages as well. At our distance we can argue reasonably that we see more than Boswell did. We do in many ways. Better minds than his, with better conceptual tools and far more information, have been brought to bear on Johnson's works, life, and character, and they have discovered much. But Boswell saw and knew Johnson and talked with him. That used to be one of the *Life*'s strongest selling points and, although it doesn't guarantee anything, it bears remembering. However few the days were that Boswell actually spent in Johnson's company, there was a firm personal relationship there, one taken completely seriously by Johnson. It seems dangerous in the extreme to assume, at the distance of two centuries, not only that we routinely see more than Boswell did but that Boswell's tendency was automatically to fictionalize.

In this regard, there is another fact we need to remember. It has been suggested, notably by Professor Bertrand Bronson, that Johnson had his own needs and his own reasons for continuing Boswell's friendship.[16] This is extremely important because we can't know for certain how Johnson acted around Boswell or whether he didn't actually play some of the roles that Boswell puts him in. We know that, naturally, Johnson played different parts in different company. He certainly does so in his correspondence: the early letters to Cave are careful, modest, sometimes highly deferential; there is none of the aggressive dignity of the letter to Chesterfield, and no one expects that there should have been. In Johnson's most famous letters to Boswell ("Resolve and pursue your resolution, choose and pursue your choice") he takes a tone and plays a role that he would never have played with Burke. It would be pointless to go too far with this kind of speculative argument, but it is only sensible to admit that we are not any more immune to the tendency to see things in Johnson that we want or need to see than Boswell, Macaulay, or anyone else. Some of the most famous and delightful moments in the *Life* may be more accurate than we think and contain a good deal more than we know.

That is another problem and, I think, another fertile field for new exploration of the book: How do we "know" things about Johnson in the *Life*? When Boswell is at his best, his dramatically most brilliant and sophisticated, he seldom analyzes formally. He dramatizes. Because he depends so heavily on fictional methods, he places a far greater burden of understanding and interpretation on us, the readers, than a standard biography would. It has been argued in the past, and is being argued now, that too great a burden of interpretation is left to us.[17] Twenty or thirty years ago, it was even suggested that the *Life* was like the unassembled pieces of mosaic, a kit from which an image of Johnson could be built.[18] Of course, the *Life* is a good deal more than that. It has been argued convincingly that Boswell shaped his greatest dramatic moments carefully and had a coherent image of Johnson to which they all more or less conform.[19] It is an image that the *Life* has consistently projected to too many people for too many years to be the result of pure chance. Boswell's success in his dramatic "characterization" of Johnson, in which he gives us an active, imaginative role to play as readers, is exactly the sort of thing we would immediately praise a novelist or dramatist for doing. We don't quibble about the burden of inference when we read a work of fiction; we assume it gladly and accept it as a central part of our experience of the book. At times it is a central part of the experience of reading the *Life* as well. We are sceptical because we don't expect it in a biography. Yet this became a problem only when we realized that we were doing it. Can a biographer successfully make important interpretive statements metaphorically or dramatically? I think we know far more about what *should* happen than what *does* happen in a book like the *Life*.

Another subject that needs close investigation is the role that Boswell's dramatic instincts alone may have played in the *Life*. That Boswell had an intuitive understanding of Johnson's character that sometimes exceeded his conscious understanding is not as widely recognized as, I think, it ought to be. Consider, for example, the role of his artist's imagination in the following well-known passage from the *Life*, in which Johnson indulges in some strange humor at the expense of his friend Sir Robert Chambers. It bears full quotation because, although it is strikingly dramatized, the most important fact about the whole episode is that Boswell clearly did not understand what it was that he was seeing. Chambers has just drawn up a will for Bennet Langton and something strikes Johnson as extraordinarily comical about the incident. "I have known him," writes Boswell, "at times exceedingly diverted at what seemed to others a very small sport."

> He now laughed immoderately, without any reason, that we could perceive, at our friend's making his will; called him *testator*, and added, "I dare say, he thinks he has done a mighty thing. He won't stay till he gets home to his seat in the country, to produce this wonderful deed: he'll call up the landlord of the first inn on the road; and, after a suitable preface upon mortality and the uncertainty of life, will tell him that he should not delay in making his will; and here, Sir, he will say, is my will . . . and he will read it to him (laughing all the time). He believes that he has made this will; but he did not make it; you, Chambers, made it for him. I trust you had more conscience than to make him say, 'being of sound understanding'; ha, ha, ha! I hope he has left me a legacy. I'd have his will turned into a ballad."
>
> In this playful manner did he run on, exulting in his own pleasantry, which certainly was not such as might be expected from the author of the *Rambler*. . . . Mr. Chambers did not by any means relish this jocularity . . . and seemed impatient till he got rid of us. Johnson could not stop his merriment, but continued it all the way till we got without the Temple-gate. He then burst into such a fit of laughter, that he appeared to be almost in a convulsion; and in order to support himself, laid hold of one of the posts at the side of the foot pavement, and sent forth peals so loud, that in the silence of the night his voice seemed to resound from Temple-bar to Fleet-ditch.[20]

The most remarkable thing about this episode is that Boswell put it in the *Life* at all. It doesn't handily fit any of the stereotypes he is accused of reducing Johnson to; if anything, it complicates. And it would have been easy enough to omit it entirely; a good many other things were omitted. It could, alternatively, have been summarized with complete truth to history if Boswell had said something like, "Dr. Johnson made Sir Robert Chambers and me uneasy by laughing at Bennet Langton, whose will Chambers had just drawn up." Boswell instinctively deals with the incident as a novelist might have, and produces an effect substantially different from that of either a summary or an analysis.

He formally downplays its importance, suggesting only that he preserves it at all so that "my readers may be acquainted with even the slight and occasional characteristics of so eminent a man." But he treats it dramatically as more than just a "slight and occasional characteristic." His references to Johnson's laughter, Chambers' reaction, and Johnson's need to hold onto the posts at the side of the pavement visually emphasize the unusual—and manic—quality of the scene. The extended concluding image (Johnson's huge peals of laughter echoing through the silent streets) confers dramatic importance on the moment even if it does not explain it; and Boswell's instincts as an artist-biographer are surely correct. The episode is tantalizing because it is atypical. Johnson's thunderbolts usually come in the form of cleverer verbal wit. They are usually reserved for relative intellectual or literary equals, and Sir Robert Chambers doesn't really fit either category—nor does Bennet Langton.

Boswell's treatment of this episode and his decision to include it in the *Life* tell us, I think, something important about both his practice and his motives. Such a dramatization does indeed put the burden of interpretation squarely on the reader; it must in this instance, because Boswell cannot interpret it for him. But his treatment of it is not neutral or a complete abdication of a biographer's responsibility. He doesn't walk away from it, or simply hand us a blurred photograph from which we or experts may derive information. There is an element of this, but the dramatic choices Boswell makes explore if they don't explain. They correctly call attention not only to the importance of the moment but to the most important aspects of it. Instead of simplifying stereotypically, Boswell's art does here what dramatic art can always do; it complicates and suspends multiple possibilities. Walter Jackson Bate writes a brilliant analysis of Johnson's sense of humor, using Boswell's account of this incident as an important bit of evidence.[21] And this is significant. The success of Bate's analysis based on this passage depends in part, of course, on the knowledge, intelligence, and remarkable understanding of Johnson that he brings to it himself. But it also depends on the existence of the episode treated in this way. Boswell's "evidence" doesn't speak for itself entirely; Boswell's art makes it possible for it to speak. His art preserves Johnson in a way that is different from either stereotype or photograph. There is not, as yet, adequate conceptual terminology to describe exactly what it is that he does. This is the problem and another challenge the book now poses.

All this has been brave talk, but of course there are problems. It can be argued cogently that talking about art of which Boswell is not fully conscious is not talking about art at all. Many of the above speculations are exactly that: as yet unproved speculations. Boswell can be said to allow us to "imagine a truth" only if we believe his own imaginings to be truthful,[22] and this is still a matter of debate. There is little doubt now, surely, that there *is* a mythical Johnson who is not exactly the same as the historical Johnson and that Boswell is most certainly the "alleged perpetrator" of that myth. But is all to be thrown out because discrepancies can be discovered? I would say no. I don't think it is fair to say that Boswell's use of fictional methods cannot produce valid biographical statement until we have first seriously entertained the possibility that fictional methods *can* result in valid biographical statement. Some extremely cogent negative arguments have recently been made and will continue to be heard; conclusive defenses of Boswell are yet to be made and will require rigorous reexamination of the *Life*. New terminology may have to be invented and new generic possibilities raised. Ultimate proof may not be possible. Yet the need to try to find it is compelling. I am not ready flatly to echo the sentiment that if Johnson has to be someone's version, he might as well be Boswell's. But if a book long considered the world's greatest biography can suddenly be called no biography at all, then what is at issue is not just an estimate of the *Life* but our definition of biography itself. If we are forced to work within the confines of a definition of biography that is so narrow that it excludes the *Life of Johnson*, then surely what we need is not just a reexamination of the *Life* but a new and better definition of biography.

NOTES

1 The most immediate and concentrated revaluation of the *Life* is Richard Schwartz's *Boswell's Johnson* (Madison: University of Wisconsin Press, 1978), p. 127. In it, Schwartz argues each of these positions with vigor. But *Boswell's Johnson* is simply the fullest expression to date of a school of thought about Boswell, Johnson, and the *Life* argued most persistently and ably by Donald Greene, especially in works like "The Development

of the Johnson Canon," *Restoration and 18th-Century Literature: Essays in Honor of Alan Dugald McKillop* (Chicago, 1963), pp. 407–25; "The Uses of Autobiography in the Eighteenth Century," in Phillip B. Daghlian, ed., *Essays in Eighteenth-Century Biography* (Bloomington: Indiana University Press, 1968); and "'Tis a Pretty Book, Mr. Boswell, But—," unpublished paper.

2 Schwartz, pp. 101–2.

3 Of course the process of finding out more about Johnson has been going on more or less continuously. I refer here most specifically to the substantial efforts of research and analysis such as the late James L. Clifford's *Young Sam Johnson* (New York, 1955) and the companion volume, soon to be published, that completed Clifford's study of the years before Boswell met Johnson, and Walter Jackson Bate's *Samuel Johnson* (New York, 1977).

4 Bertrand Bronson, "Boswell's Boswell," in *Johnson Agonistes and Other Essays* (Berkeley: University of California Press, 1965), p. 76.

5 The clearest articulation of this point of view is Schwartz, p. 92, but the idea is echoed in Greene's suggestion ("The Johnsonian Canon") that Johnson is a "character in Boswell's book" (p. 407).

6 Both Schwartz and Greene argue this position actively: Schwartz throughout *Boswell's Johnson* and Green especially in "The Uses of Autobiography in the 18th Century."

7 See my more elaborate argument in this vein in *Form and Purpose in Boswell's Biographical Works* (Berkeley: University of California Press, 1971) and "The Relationship between Factual Accuracy and Literary Art in the *Life of Johnson*," *Modern Philology*, 74 (1977), 273–88.

8 For an excellent comparison of Boswell and Mrs. Piozzi in this regard, see Ralph Rader, "Literary Form in Factual Narrative: The Example of Boswell's Johnson," in Daghlian, and Siebenschuh, *Form and Purpose*.

9 For a more extended discussion of the phenomenon, see Siebenschuh, "The Relationship between Factual Accuracy and Literary Art in the *Life of Johnson*."

10 Most, if not all, of the personal qualities we may imagine that Boswell idealizes or enlarges in the *Life* can be found in the other major biographers and collections of reminiscence and anecdote. It is not the facts themselves but the way we are made to experience them that is different about Boswell's Johnson.

11 This was the standard view echoed in all the general studies of biography in the early decades of this century. Particularly pure versions can be found in Mark Longaker's *English Biography in the 18th Century* (Philadelphia, 1931) and Donald Stauffer's *The Art of Biography in 18th-Century England* (Princeton, 1941).

12 This was the point of view of the earliest students of the Malahide Papers. See especially, Geoffrey Scott's introduction to *The Private Papers of James Boswell from Malahide Castle in the Collection of Lt. Colonel Ralph Heyward Isham*, ed. Geoffrey Scott (I–VI) and Frederick A. Pottle (VII–XVIII) (Mt. Vernon, New York: privately printed, 1928–34). The review of the first

books of the *Malahide Papers* (R. W. Chapman in *Times Literary Supplement*, 6 Feb. 1930) echoes the same idea.

13 The discovery and analysis of Boswell's use of literary and dramatic techniques usually associated with fiction has been going on over the last decades. Besides the works already mentioned—my own, B. H. Bronson's, and Ralph Rader's—are W. K. Wimsatt's "James Boswell: The Man and the Journal," *Yale Review*, 49 (1959), 80–92; David L. Passler, *Time, Form, and Style in Boswell's Life of Johnson* (New Haven: Yale University Press, 1929); and Paul Alkon, "Boswellian Time," *Studies in Burke and His Time*, 14 (1973), 239–56.

14 See especially Schwartz, chs. 4 and 5.

15 For an extended discussion of the differences between Boswell's treatment of Johnson in the *Tour* and the *Life*, see my *Form and Purpose in Boswell's Biographical Works*.

16 See Bertrand Bronson's excellent essay "Samuel Johnson and James Boswell," in *Facets of the Enlightenment* (Berkeley: University of California Press, 1968).

17 This is an argument implied in Donald Stauffer and in Bronson ("Samuel Johnson and James Boswell") and asserted aggressively by Richard Schwartz, see especially ch. 5.

18 Stauffer, pp. 445–46.

19 Ralph Rader makes an excellent case for this view in "Literary Form and Factual Narrative."

20 James Boswell, *The Life of Johnson*, ed. G. B. Hill, 6 vols, rev. and enl. L. F. Powell (Oxford, 1964), II, 261–62.

21 Walter Jackson Bate, *Samuel Johnson* (New York: Harcourt Brace Jovanovich, 1977), pp. 486–87.

22 A point of which I was reminded in a long and thoughtful letter by Bertrand H. Bronson after he had seen an earlier draft of this essay.

Pediatric Practice at the London Foundling Hospital

RUTH K. McCLURE

The title of my paper is, admittedly, anachronistic: the word *pediatrics* did not come into use until the late nineteenth century. In eighteenth-century England neither the word nor the specialty itself existed. Physicians received no training in the diagnosis and treatment of children's diseases. Everyone assumed that any qualified practitioner could treat all patients who came his way, whether they were young or old. But, in fact, many physicians preferred not to attend child patients if they could avoid it.[1]

Nevertheless, when the Foundling Hospital in London opened its doors in 1741, at least four eminent physicians and two surgeons immediately offered their services to the infant foundlings. And all through the century leading members of the medical profession responded to the needs of these children, who, sooner or later, suffered all the normal illnesses of eighteenth-century children and some that the more fortunate escaped. The common run of ailments included smallpox, measles, fevers, and chincough. In addition, the physicians had to deal with venereal diseases, scabies, scald heads, scrofula, and illnesses caused by diet deficiencies.

Everyone worried about smallpox. In the eighteenth century it was chiefly a disease of infants and children under three years of age. As Dr. John Coakley Lettsom remarked late in the century, "most born in London have smallpox before they are seven."[2] Between 1721 and 1760 smallpox caused ten percent of all deaths in London and left

361

many who recovered blind.[3] It was no respecter of social status. But the aristocracy and persons of the middling sort could, if they chose, fend off the disease by inoculation, a technique that Lady Mary Wortley Montague had popularized upon her return to England from Constantinople in 1718. Because inoculation, unlike vaccination, induced a case of smallpox in the recipient, the procedure was hazardous. It required the combined services of a physician, a surgeon, and an apothecary. The preparation of the patient with purges and emetics, bleeding and blisters, could take a month, and the recovery period might last five to six weeks.[4] In short, it was expensive.

Yet inoculation was one of the earliest preventative measures adopted by the Governors of the Foundling Hospital. Three years after admitting the first foundlings, they asked Dr. Richard Conyers, the Hospital's physician, to inoculate some of the children. The outcome of this experiment proved so satisfactory that the Governors decided to make it a rule to inoculate all of the children on their return to the Hospital from the country where they were nursed from admission to age three or four. By the end of April 1755, 211 children had been inoculated with only one loss of life.[5]

The action of the Governors in having the foundlings inoculated at such an early age was indeed forward-looking. The smallpox hospitals for the poor, established in London between 1746 and 1768, did not inoculate children under seven years of age,[6] and many children of well-to-do families were not inoculated earlier. Doubtless the strong approval of Dr. Richard Mead and Sir Hans Sloane influenced their fellow Governors.[7] But they were less willing to embrace the new method of vaccination when Jenner published a report on his work in 1798, and the Hospital's physician was still inoculating the children in the usual way during the autumn of 1799.

In spite of these efforts, some children died of smallpox contracted in the natural way, usually while at nurse in the country. But deaths from a great variety of fevers outnumbered any other category specified in the Hospital's records. This was to be expected, since fevers caused eight out of ten deaths in the eighteenth century. But of what diseases these fevers were symptomatic I cannot say. The records mention eruptive fever, spotted fever, inward fever, putrid fever, purple fever, worm fever, nervous fever, and uncategorized fever. In 1763 an epidemic of "eruptive fever" accompanied by "ulcerous sore throats" swept the Hospital: 150 children lay in the infirmary at one time; at least 9 died. Almost certainly this was scarlet fever or scarlatina. And in 1787 another epidemic of scarlet fever struck down over a hundred children, a number of whom died. Probably some of the fevers were typhus or typhoid. Some may have been cases of diphtheria, which was largely unrecognized until mid-nineteenth century. And from the fact that on several occasions the records list the cause of death as water on the brain, we might also suspect epidemic meningitis.[8]

Next to fevers, measles was the great killer. From time to time epidemics of measles ravaged the Hospital. In 1768 seven out of the 101 who were stricken died, and in 1770 so many children were suffering from measles in the spring that the Governors suspended all apprenticing.[9]

Chincough, which we know as whooping cough, presented a continuing problem and frequently proved fatal. The Governors often sent children so afflicted to the country for nursing. Consumptive children and those weakened by measles were also sent to the country to recuperate. Undoubtedly, this was done on the recommendation of Dr. Mead, for he believed that change of air was essential in cases of measles.[10]

No less worrisome were the decisions that had to be made by the Governors whenever the need arose for operations on children suffering from stones in the bladder or requiring amputation of limbs. An operation was a hazardous procedure in the eighteenth century, for surgery, performed without anaesthesia, was accompanied by high mortality from septic infection and loss of blood—transfusions were not given. Because of the uncertainty of the outcome and the intense fear induced in the patient, most people thought of operations as a last resort, and the foundlings did not differ from other folk in such feelings. In 1774 when Baron de Wenzell offered to remove cataracts from the eyes of a blind foundling, the boy's "irresolution prevented the Operation." He remained blind for the rest of his life rather than submit to a procedure that might well have given him sight, for seven years earlier the Baron had successfully removed cataracts from both eyes of the Duke of Bedford, the Hospital's president.[11]

Less likely to cause death but more demanding of prolonged care on a day-to-day basis were those conditions described as the itch, "scrophulous" symptoms, scald head, inflammations or weakness of the eyes, and scorbutic eruptions. The itch (scabies) unquestionably gave the most trouble. A highly contagious rash accompanied by violent itching but no fever, it could break out anywhere on the body except the face. It was caused by a parasitic mite easily spread through clothing, bedding, or personal contact, which made control of the disease almost impossible in any institution.

Scrofula, or the King's Evil, was a tuberculous condition of the lymphatic glands in the neck. Sometimes it also affected joints and bones, and its inflamed, ulcerated swellings, when healed, almost always left ugly scars. Scald head was a contagious ringworm of the scalp characterized by pustular patches that broke open and formed scabs. These would thicken and spread until the incrustations enveloped the whole head and face like a mask.[12]

The Governors exerted every effort to prevent the spread of these contagious diseases. Separation of the sick from the well began within a few months after the opening of the Hospital and continued throughout the century.[13] During the period of the General Reception—that is, from 1756 to 1760—the problem of caring for sick infants and of isolating them took on the aspect of nightmare. The Hospital's infirmary wards lacked the capacity to deal with the numbers involved, so that it became necessary to transform four buildings near the Hospital into specialized infirmaries, some serving to isolate children with infectious diseases and others as a place for convalescent children.[14]

Undoubtedly the Governors were influenced in these policies, too, by Dr. Mead, who as early as 1720, had advocated the separation of the sick from the well and the observance of strict cleanliness at all times.[15] The Governors achieved isolation more easily than cleanliness. From time to time they waged combat against rats; lice and nits in the children's hair; stinks arising from tubs of wet diapers; poor ventilation; uncleaned privies; inadequate sewers; and drains without traps. They dealt with bedbugs by engaging a "Bugg Docter" at a cost of 4s. a bed, "no Cure no Money," and tried to make sure that lazy servants and nurses did not neglect the cleaning of the wards as well as the twice-a-day scrubbing of the children's hands and faces.[16] But total cleanliness was a goal never fully attained.

One of the buildings converted into an infirmary in 1759 was located at nearby Powis Wells—a chalybeate spring that was supposed to have curative powers. For that reason, it was used to isolate and treat children suffering from scrofula, scald heads, diseases of the eyes, and the scorbutic eruptions symptomatic of scurvy, a disease caused by a deficiency in vitamin C. This was not the only indicator of dietary deficiency: we find records of many cases of lameness, crooked legs, and other deformities, as well as purchases of supports for weak legs, all of which strongly indicate the existence of rickets—a disease attributable to vitamin D deficiency. In addition, the many cases of blindness and of weak or diseased eyes—"The Children in general seem to be extremely subject to distempered eyes," commented the Subcommittee's minutes in 1759—support the premise that the children's diet did not contain sufficient vitamin A.[17] From this evidence and from my analysis of the Hospital's tables of diet, which show serious deficiencies in calcium, and vitamins A, C, and D, I have concluded that the children were, in certain respects, malnourished.

The Governors were in no way to blame for this state of affairs. They wanted the children's diet to be ample and nutritious and considered it to be so because it had been prescribed by the Hospital's physicians. They went to great lengths to ensure the quality of the food. And it was a far more adequate diet than children in other institutions or children of poor parents received. But the Governors and the Hospital's physicians had no way of thinking, as we do today, in terms of calories, minerals, and vitamins, so that their efforts to prevent disease through a healthy diet fell somewhat short of their goal.

More successful was the Governors' policy of selective admission. From the Hospital's opening in 1741 to the beginning of the General Reception in 1756, and from the termination of the General Reception in 1760 to the end of the century, every child presented for admission was thoroughly examined to determine whether it had any illness. This procedure very effectively screened out children afflicted with congenital syphilis, who could, if admitted, pass the disease on to their nurses. Unfortunately, such screening was impossible during the period of the General Reception because Parliament had undertaken the support of the institution on the condition that it receive all children offered. As a consequence, in March 1759 the Governors found so many children infected with venereal disease that they considered for a time the possibility of taking over a ward in the Lock Hospital for their treatment. This they did not do, but during the next seventeen months they paid for the treatment of at least fourteen children in the Lock Hospital. Many of the infants did not survive the treatment, which was salivation produced by the use of mercury.[18]

The key to day-to-day care of the children lay in the quality of the nursing and the degree of supervision exercised by the apothecary, who, in the beginning, visited the Hospital once a day. The General Reception, however, made necessary the employment of a resident apothecary, and in 1759 Robert McClellan was engaged at a salary of £50 a year. When he retired in 1797 the Governors decided that the Hospital no longer required an apothecary in residence and appointed a visiting apothecary.[19]

Until 1759 the visiting apothecary made up all medicines in his own shop or obtained them from Apothecaries' Hall, but when McClellan came to live in the Hospital, an apothecary's shop was fitted up for his use. When he retired, the shop contained 390 different drugs, and such pieces of equipment as pewter syringes and a "tobacco clyster machine." Among the drugs in the shop that we might find familiar were: camphor, digitalis, jalap, opium, sal ammonia, ipecac, myrrh, alcohol, silver nitrate, calomel, magnesia, and rhubarb.[20]

Despite the repertory of drugs, the state of eighteenth-century knowledge about their true properties was such that few specifics existed: Peruvian bark (quinine) for malaria, mercury for syphilis, and sulphur for the itch. Although the apothecary used all of the drugs in his shop in various combinations to treat the children, no doubt most of them had little effect on the course of the diseases for which they were given, but, unless they contained metallic substances, such as antimony, they probably did little harm. On the other hand, the common practices of purging, inducing vomiting, and blood-letting in the treatment of fevers, all of which were believed necessary to expel the cause of the illness, may have served only to weaken further children already critically ill.[21] Nevertheless, blood-letting by the use of leeches was practiced at the Hospital as late as 1790.

From the directions that the physicians prepared for the use of medicines in the branch hospitals, we also learn that they recommended for fever "the fever powder of our own dispensatory, an Occasional Clyster [i.e., enema], and Bark in Intermittents"; for worms, "Wormseed—the best Medicine, Quicksilver, Rhubarb, & sometimes a little common Aloes, Crude Antimony, . . . and Magnesia"; for diarrhea and dysentery, "a vomit of Ipecacuana, especially in the beginning, Hartshorn drink, Nutmeg, Rhubarb at Intervals." The Hospital also supplied the country inspectors with rhubarb and magnesia to treat their infant charges for "watery gripes," probably because Dr. Cadogan thought so highly of *magnesia alba* as a remedy for "green Stools, Gripes and Purgings." In this, he was following the recommendations of Dr. Walter Harris, whose treatise, *De morbis acutis infantum*, published in 1689, was the accepted authority on the diseases of children for a hundred years. Harris held that there was a single cause for all infant's diseases: acidity, and that "the whole Art of Cure turns entirely on subduing the Acid."[22] Contrary to modern ideas about the harmfulness of excessive use of laxatives, eighteenth-century opinion held that a good purge was helpful in the treatment of almost any ailment and probably a general preventative of disease—a notion that accounts for Mr. McClellan's practice of dosing all the children in a ward with physic every three weeks, taking the wards by turns.[23]

One of the most difficult problems to confront the Governors was what to do about deformed, blind, mentally retarded, epileptic, or otherwise handicapped children. Largely because of the policy of indiscriminate admission during the General Reception, the Governors found themselves burdened with many children afflicted with congenital defects, as well as those who had incurred permanent damage through malnourishment, neglect, or abuse at the hands of their parents. Where any form of cure held out hope, the Governors tried it. They sent one paralytic girl to the hospital at Bath for treatment and another to be "electrified." They purchased trusses, leg braces, spectacles, and special shoes for children whom these devices might help. But for the blind, the epileptic, and the mentally retarded there was no help.

The care of such afflicted children, even in infancy, was attended with difficulties, and often the Governors had to pay the country nurses premiums to take them. Then, as the children grew older, the Governors discovered that many could not be apprenticed even though they offered larger fees with them. Tailors and shoemakers sometimes took lame boys, and some blind children with musical talent could be trained as singers and organists, but no one wanted the deformed girls. One solution was to employ the handicapped children in the Hospital at whatever tasks they could perform and, as they grew older, to pay them servants' wages.[24] In 1771 there were over ninety handicapped children in the Hospital's care. By 1790 death had removed many of them, but twenty-seven of the girls still remained in the Hospital. Most of them could perform some work, but four were incapable of any employment at all.[25] Ten of the girls were classified as having "weak understanding" or being "Ideotical," a situation that invited difficulties of several kinds, not the least of which was the pregnancy of one thirty-three-year-old idiot woman, who had been seduced by several of the older boys.[26]

Fortunately, the Governors could call upon the best medical opinion of the time from among their own number to aid them in the many difficult decisions affecting the children's health. There was, first of all, Dr. Richard Mead, who, like many other fashionable physicians, visited only his most socially prominent patients and prescribed for lesser folk without seeing them on the basis of the description of symptoms furnished him by their attending apothecaries. The

foundlings, however, received his personal attention. Another celebrated physician who gave advice in the early years was Sir Hans
Sloane, who also served for thirty-six years as physician to the children in Christ's Hospital. Dr. Richard Conyers, the Hospital's first
official physician, had written his doctoral thesis at Leyden on the
diseases of children. His successor, Dr. William Cadogan, wrote *An
Essay Upon Nursing and the Management of Children From their Birth to
Three Years of Age*, which the Governors published in 1748, and which
became the Hospital's bible. Later in the century, the Hospital was
served from 1762 to 1787 by Sir William Watson. Dr. John Mayo, who
officiated as the Hospital's physician at the end of the century, also
acted as physician to the Princess of Wales.

During the entire century, then, the children enjoyed the advantage of medical supervision by some of the most eminent physicians
of the time. And, considering all the evidence, it seems safe to say
that the standard of health care that the Governors provided for the
foundlings not only exceeded that available to the offspring of the
poor but, in many ways, exceeded that which their own children
normally received. Certainly no Governor maintained an apothecary
in residence in his own home, nor would his children's health have
benefited from regular weekly supervision by such distinguished
physicians. The Governors, it would seem, having rescued the children from almost certain death, felt an overwhelming compulsion to
exert every means to preserve them, even if it entailed lifelong care.
To do so, after all, justified the Foundling Hospital's existence.

NOTES

This paper is, for the most part, based on several chapters of my book *Coram's
Children: The London Foundling Hospital in the Eighteenth Century*, to be published by the Yale University Press in 1980.

1 According to Dr. Walter Harris, because " . . . sick Children, and especially Infants, give no other Light into the Knowledge of their Diseases,
than what we are able to discover from their uneasy Cries, and the uncertain Tokens of their Crossness . . . several Physicians of the first Rank
have openly declared to me, that they go very unwillingly to take care of
the Diseases of Children, especially of such as are newly born" (*A Treatise
of the Acute Diseases of Infants*, trans. John Martyn [London: T. Astley,
1742], p. 3). The first person to recognize the need for special training in
the diseases of children was Dr. Andrew Wilson in his tract, *Aphorisms*

Composed for a Text to practical Lectures on the Constitution and Diseases of Children, published in 1783.

2 Quoted in Charles Creighton, *A History of Epidemics in Britain*, 2d ed. (London: Frank Cass, 1965), II, 511.

3 Ibid., II, 531, 556.

4 Ibid., II, 504; Lester S. King, *The Medical World of the Eighteenth Century* (1958; reprint ed., Huntington, N. Y.: Robert E. Krieger, 1971), pp. 321–22.

5 *An Account of the Hospital for the Maintenance and Education of Exposed and Deserted Young Children* (London: privately printed, 1759), p. xiii; Foundling Hospital General Court Minutes I, 108; Foundling Hospital General Committee Minutes III, 55; IV, 270. The General Court and General Committee Minutes of the Foundling Hospital are at the Thomas Coram Foundation for Children, London. The General Committee Minutes will hereafter be referred to as FH Gen. Com.

6 Creighton, *History of Epidemics*, II, 506. Horace Walpole, for example, was not inoculated until he was seven.

7 Dr. Mead's *A Discourse of the Small-Pox and Measles* (London: J. Reason, 1747) contains a strong argument in favor of inoculation. Sir Hans Sloane had been interested in the procedure as early as 1716 and did much to popularize it. See E. St. John Brooks, *Sir Hans Sloane, the Great Collector and his Circle* (London: Batchworth Press, 1954), pp. 88–93.

8 Secretary of the Foundling Hospital to Dr. Lee, June 10, 1763, Secretary's Letter Books III, 238; Memorandum Books for Admission and Disposal of Children; Register of Grown Up Children. All of the foregoing are in the Foundling Hospital Records at the Greater London Record Office, hereafter referred to as GLRO. See also *The Information and Complaint made to the Last General Court . . . By Dr. Mayo . . . with the Proceedings of the Committee of Enquiry thereon* (London: privately printed, 1790), pp. 6–7; Creighton, *History of Epidemics*, II, 678–79, 706–7, 714; G. Melvyn Howe, *Man, Environment and Disease in Britain* (New York: Barnes and Noble, 1972), pp. 145–48.

9 FH Gen. Com. XII, 280; Memorandum Book for Admission and Disposal of Children, vol. I; Treatment and Prescription Book for Measles, 1766–1800; both GLRO.

10 Mead, *Discourse of the Small-Pox and Measles*, pp. 70–72; FH Gen. Com. VI, 34; Rough Books of Inspection, 1741–1838, vol. I, GLRO.

11 FH Gen. Com. XIV, 335; *Yale Edition of Horace Walpole's Correspondence*, ed. W. S. Lewis et al. (New Haven: Yale University Press, 1937–), XXII, 567 and n. 12; British Museum Additional Manuscript 32,987, ff. 212–13; *The Letters and Journals of Lady Mary Coke*, ed. James A. Home (Edinburgh: privately printed, 1889–96), II, 164, 172; C. D. O'Malley, "The English Physician in the Earlier Eighteenth Century," in H. T. Swedenberg, Jr., ed., *England in the Restoration and Early Eighteenth Century* (Berkeley and Los Angeles: University of California Press, 1972), p. 148.

12 Robert Hooper, *Lexicon Medicum, or Medical Dictionary*, 6th ed. (London: A. and R. Spottiswoode, 1831), pp. 1001–5.

13 FH Gen. Com. IV, 18; V, 263; Memorandum Book for Admission and Disposal of Children, vol. I, sub July 13, 1741, GLRO.

14 FH Gen. Com. V, 188; VII, 35, 67; XI, 18; Foundling Hospital Subcommittee Minutes II, 91, 114, 134; III, 91–92, 232–33. The Subcommittee Minutes are in the Foundling Hospital Records at the Greater London Record Office and will hereafter be referred to as FH Subcom.

15 Richard Mead, *A Short Discourse concerning Pestilential Contagion, and the Methods to be used to Prevent it*, 2d ed. (London: S. Buckley and R. Smith, 1720), pp. 39, 41.

16 FH Gen. Com. IV, 68–69, 73, 166; XVII, 333, 342; XIX, 65–67; FH Subcom. III, 103–4; V, 31, 126, 129; XII, 151; Letter from Lady Vere, Jan. 13, 1753, Secretary's Correspondence In, 1753; Report of W. L. Kingsman, May 27, 1790, and Report of J. Holliday, July 21, 1790, Visiting Committee's Reports, 1790–91; the last three items are GLRO.

17 FH Gen. Com. VI, 213; XVI, 6; FH Subcom. IX, 59–60, 174, 212; List of Children in Ackworth Hospital [a branch of the London Foundling Hospital] mentioning how each child is employed and also the Infirmities those labour under which render them unfit to be placed out Apprentice, June 6, 1771, Secretary's Correspondence In, 1771–72, GLRO; James Nelson, *An Essay on the Government of Children Under Three General Heads: Viz. Health, Manners and Education*, 2d ed. (London: R. and J. Dodsley, 1756), p. 96; J. C. Drummond and Anne Wilbraham, *The Englishman's Food: A History of Five Centuries of English Diet* (London: Jonathan Cape, 1939), pp. 322–23, 325; Miriam E. Lowenberg et al., *Food & Man* (New York: John Wiley and Sons, 1968), pp. 19, 188, 191, 193.

18 FH Gen. Com. V, 129–30; VII, 22, 58, 172, 201, 394; Statement of Account with the Lock Hospital, 1758–92 bundle, Secretary's Miscellaneous, GLRO. The Lock Hospital was established in 1746 for the treatment of venereal diseases.

19 FH Gen. Com. I, 155–57; VI, 318; XXII, 67–69.

20 FH Subcom. III, 111; Inventory of Medicines in the Apothecary's Shop, 1798, Medical Miscellaneous, GLRO.

21 O'Malley, "The English Physician," p. 154; King, *Medical World*, pp. 128–29.

22 Harris, *Treatise of Acute Diseases*, p. 39.

23 FH Gen. Com. V, 206, 298; FH Subcom. II, 146–48; III, 18–19; William Cadogan, *An Essay Upon Nursing and the Management of Children From their Birth to Three Years of Age*, 6th ed. (London: J. Roberts, 1753), pp. 32–33.

24 FH Gen. Com. VI, 97–98, 175, 213; VII, 408–9; X, 38; XIII, 213; XIV, 208, 257; XV, 52, 231; XVI, 100, 178; XXII, 62, 113, 148; XXIII, 90, 97; FH Subcom. II, 236; Bill of G. Grafton, Oct. 29, 1796, and Bill of William and James Lauries, April 1, 1797, Minutes of Committee of Accounts, 1795–1843, vol. I, GLRO.

25 FH Subcom. IX, 174, 212–13; List of Children in Ackworth Hospital; List of Handicapped Children, Dec. 8, 1794, ca. 1770–92 bundle, Secretary's Miscellaneous, GLRO; A List of such Foundling Children who from various Causes could never be placed out of the Hospital to provide for themselves, Visiting Committee's Reports, GLRO.
26 Report of John Wilmot, May 20, 1790, and Report of B. Filmer, June 21, 1790, Visiting Committee's Reports, GLRO.

Science, Medicine, Religion:
Three Views of Health Care in France
on the Eve of the French Revolution

LOUIS S. GREENBAUM

The spring of 1787 found Parisians in a fever of hospital-building projects. The inhabitants of the City of Light, who only shortly before had consigned their faddish delight to animal magnetism, dirigible balloons, and the *Marriage of Figaro*, now dug deep into their pockets to build a new municipal hospital, the Hôtel-Dieu, ordered by King Louis XVI's law of June 22, 1787.[1] Two million pounds were subscribed in a few months by patricians and commoners in a universal outpouring of sentiment to close down the redoubtable fortress of suffering,[2] standing for a thousand years astride Notre-Dame cathedral, and huddling a population of 3,000—larger than 84 percent of the cities of France[3]—in cramped, unsanitary quarters. The legislation which ordered the Hôtel-Dieu out of the central city into four new locations, was the culmination of efforts reaching back as far as King Francis I[4] and widely urged after a great fire of 1772 engulfed one of its two wings.[5] The enormity of this tragedy set off a lively, far-reaching debate on optimum health-delivery systems. Public interest was nurtured by the Enlightenment humanitarian movement of the 1780s[6] and by crises posed by unprecedented numbers of hospital clients, the urban poor, whose ranks were swelled and whose physical condition aggravated by the socio-economic conditions of the period (demographic shifts to the capital, unemployment, inadequate and infected housing, malnutrition, high accident rates and labor-related diseases, promiscuity, illegitimacy, and crime).[7]

The pre-Revolutionary hospital question has recently been taken up by Michel Foucault and a regiment of co-workers,[8] whose focus, however, is conspicuously one-sided. For, as this paper proposes to show, there was not one government policy at work in 1787, but two. And there was not merely one group which agitated for a drastic revision of service within the Hôtel-Dieu, but three. Our object, unlike that of Foucault's *Machines à Guérir*, is not to define the hospital question as a compound of technical components alone, but rather to illuminate its human and institutional dimensions, involving, as students of the Old Regime since Tocqueville have come to expect, a dialectic of competing forces, policies, and coalitions.

This paper wishes to call attention to three orientations to healthcare—all prominently represented before the public. Each addressed the problem in different terms. But all agreed that the municipal hospital must continue to be the principal vehicle of the administration of health services, despite widespread public prejudice against hospitals, the prevailing popularity of the neighborhood hospice, and persuasive physiocratic theories of dehospitalization and home care advanced by Dupont de Nemours and Condorcet.[9]

The first, advanced by scientists of the Paris Academy of Sciences, held that the hospital was a uniquely therapeutic instrument. Since the Hôtel-Dieu, they argued, had evolved in response to no settled objectives, and since its appalling mortality, raging epidemics, and irremediable abuses prevented this function, it should be levelled and rebuilt according to the lights of science and medicine. The second was held by a group of physicians and surgeons working inside the Hôtel-Dieu, responsible for patients whose daily health needs could not await the advent of some perfect institution in a dim future. Unwilling to scrap the only hospital the sick of Paris were likely to know, and mindful that an insolvent government could not come up with the millions to build four new hôtels-Dieu, these medical reformers labored to improve conditions along two models: the military hospital, where sweeping medical and administrative innovations had been introduced in the name of economy and efficiency, and the clinic, where controlled bedside procedures had been tested and latest knowledge applied to patients and outpatients in the interest of medical progress and instruction. A third position came from the nurses of the Hôtel-Dieu, a powerful, entrenched group of Augustinian nuns who believed themselves to have a stake equal to scientists and doctors whose reforms they implacably fought in favor of their own. In a moment of supreme challenge they lodged a suit of protest before the highest tribunal of the land and sounded the swan song of the long regnant conception of the hospital as a center of Christian charity. They emphasized a system of health-care which exalted man's spiritual needs, the obligation to provide shelter for everyone, and to temper the brutal, impersonal mechanisms of scientific medicine.

I

On December 10, 1785, the Paris Academy of Sciences appointed an eminent committee under the chairmanship of the astronomer Jean-Sylvain Bailly to investigate the municipal hospital, part of a cleverly orchestrated campaign by the Baron de Breteuil, Minister of the Royal Household and the Department of Paris, to revamp the central city and to remove its supreme obstacle, the Hôtel-Dieu.[10] The committee worked for nearly three years, publishing three reports[11] which thrust hospitals and health care, as never before, in the limelight of public scrutiny.[12] It formulated a model of a new kind of hospital, in pavilion form, which incorporated innovations in physics, chemistry, pathological anatomy, surgery, medical technology, sanitation, architecture, and hospital administration, realized all over Europe and America in the course of the next century.[13]

The work of the Academy committee must be located in several contexts to which this paper can only briefly allude: (1) The Enlightenment humanitarian movement, to make Paris a safer place by ridding the city of a hospital which instead of extinguishing disease, reducing morbidity, and lowering mortality, raised them, "a plague which constantly desolates the capital . . . a cause of depopulation which can be destroyed."[14] Such a hospital made a shambles of the dignity and worth of the indigent sick upon whom depended the fortunes of family and society: "The sentiments of humanity, charity and patriotism reclaim the rights of suffering man," herded ignobly three to six in a bed, deprived of the simplest rest enjoyed by horses and cows in barns, cats and dogs in houses.[15] (2) The collaboration of science and government along a broad front of public health reform[16] illustrates the scientists' heightened consciousness of the social consequences of poverty and disease, the mobilization of scientific knowledge for their alleviation, the growing emphasis on utilitarian thought, and the increasing concern of scientists with political economy. The committee held that the Paris Hôtel-Dieu, with purportedly the highest death-rate in Europe, not only deprived the state of thousands of productive citizens each year but retarded population growth and reduced the nation's work force upon which depended its strength and wealth.[17] (3) "Medical police," the conviction that the maintenance of a healthy population was the duty of the state.[18] Only by an interventionist role, only by nationalizing and secularizing the hospital, by laying down standards by which charity and dependency would be transformed into the right of every citizen to health and public assistance[19] could the hospital be made an effective curative force instead of the generator of physical and social maladies long decried by critics like Montesquieu, Voltaire, Diderot, Marmontel, Dupont de Nemours, and others.[20] The reformed hospital could practice social justice, for it would provide the indigent sick with the best care and latest technology, heretofore available only to the rich.[21] The hospital treasury was part of the public domain, as Turgot had advocated,[22] and like every other public institution the hospital owed a regular accounting to the nation.[23]

While the scientists insisted that they were not "seeking to move" but only "to expose facts and figures,"[24] they brought the full weight of their recommendations down on the side of liberal opinion to relocate the Hôtel-Dieu, from whose doors and records they had three times been turned away.[25] They exploited the prestige science enjoyed in French society and the widely-shared hope that the Academy might help transform the quality of life,[26] the "lens where various objects for reform which the eye of the government seizes and embraces come together."[27] Parisians were impressed that hospital procedures could be reduced to analytical-quantitative precision and that the committee advanced statistico-mathematical evidence for all its assertions, "the first time that arithmetic made people cry."[28] The scientists calculated the number of beds (4800) necessary for a city of 600,000, the actual bed count of the hospital and the numbers of patients inside, and even those preempted by hospital nurses. They arrived at global hospital mortality (1:4) as well as that of delivering mothers (1:15); measured body heat; air volume necessary to sustain life; per diem patient cost; average case duration; proportion of men to women. They laid equal stress on Newtonian experimentation and observation, incorporating data gathered by one of their members, the surgeon and anatomist Jacques Tenon, to describe the unendurable conditions within the hospital.[29]

The committee's point of departure was to disencumber the hospital of all past associations as a refuge of indigence and confinement. Viewed rather as a "factory"[30] or "healing machine"[31] for patient-citizens, the hospital and its location, design, construction, organization and operation need not be left, as in the past, to accident, convention, or expediency. On the contrary, these questions were empirically both determinable and verifiable: "A hospital that one erects today must be, in an enlightened century like ours, the result of acquired knowledge. It must unite all the aid that the latest science can offer for the relief of sickness."[32] Cross-infection, afflicting both patients and the neighborhood population, was the central focus. Physics, chemistry, architecture showed the way to overcome contagion. Health conditions could be improved by appropriate devices of topography, construction, air-renewal, hygiene, water supply, paving, and other details worked out in part in the Academy's earlier proposals of 1780 for the building of prisons.[33] Physiological principles afforded a new explanation of the therapeutic purpose of the single bed, the symbol of the dignity and the equality of treatment of each patient, and by extension of the hospital itself. Human stature determined the dimension of the bed and from that the size of wards and the design of staircases.[34]

How effectively the hospital accomplished its curative mission could also be measured: by case duration and cost efficiency.[35] Since the average admission remained twice as long and patient cost averaged one-third more than other hospitals, owing to deficient facilities and services, the Hôtel-Dieu was the most costly and inefficient of Paris hospitals. Salubrity could be computed by mortality relative to admissions. Here the hospital stood doubly condemned, for its faults not only prevented recovery but also spread maladies to patients who did not have them upon entry and propagated miasms outside. The Hôtel-Dieu therefore was also the unhealthiest of all hospitals.[36]

The committee's advocacy of four general hospitals made up of small, isolated pavilions was a compromise between the neighborhood hospice, then much in vogue, but which could not furnish the services of the general hospital, and the large, undifferentiated monolith, which inevitably bred the vices of the Hôtel-Dieu. Sympathetic in principle to home care in lieu of the hospital, the committee dismissed it in the end as unworkable.

In its last report of March 1788 the committee gave expression to current Anglomania and propagandized emulable health-policy of England, visited on the morrow of the new Anglo-French entente by two committee members, Tenon and Coulomb, whose hospital voyage the British celebrated as the "commercial treaty of humanity."[37]

The scientists boldly urged substantial public financing of hospitals on the English example, the adoption of the dispensary, and the practice of cleanliness. They concluded with an extraordinary appeal to supranational cooperation in the interest of health using the model of scientific research: "Human knowledge is today the product of the efforts of all peoples of Europe. The great work of our hospitals will be the result of general enlightenment, which all nations must share without pretension on the part of the giver or jealousy on the part of the receiver."[38]

The close cooperation of the Academy hospital committee and government illustrates the dependence of scientific reform on the credit of the sponsoring minister. Breteuil was an eighteenth-century Haussmann, who sponsored an ambitious program of public-health reform and urban renewal which leaned heavily on scientific expertise. Breteuil's plans for the Hôtel-Dieu brought him into conflict with other departments. Ministerial rivalry betrayed the same bewildering confusion, duplication, and contradiction within the branches of monarchy as existed in its laws, taxes, and institutions.[39] The Breteuil-sponsored legislation of 1787 was a direct repudiation of hitherto prevailing government policy promulgated by Necker in the law of April 22, 1781,[40] which had ordered the rebuilding and expansion of the Hôtel-Dieu *in situ*. This law, in turn, was a reversal of earlier legislation of Louis XV of May 1773,[41] which had ordered the removal of the hospital out of the center after the 1772 fire but which never had been put into effect. The 1781 law, honored by Necker's successors through Calonne, was administered by the Department of Hospitals, part of the Contrôle général des finances. Antoine-Louis de Chaumont de La Millière, head of service of the hospitals within the general-control of finances, and his lieutenant, Jean Colombier, General Inspector of civil hospitals and prisons,[42] worked closely inside the Hôtel-Dieu with administration and architects and conferred vast government credits for its reconstruction.[43]

While the king's law of 1787, ordering four new hospitals, seemed to imperil the Hôtel-Dieu and appeared to the public a repudiation of the 1781 law, Colombier did not cease his efforts. On the contrary, and in the teeth of the open challenge of Breteuil and the Academy, he published grandiose claims about space available in the rebuilt wing, paraded its single beds and other improvements,[44] and redoubled efforts to accelerate its opening on August 1, 1787.[45] With Breteuil's enemies Necker and Calonne safely out of the way,[46] the Minister of Paris moved in April 1788 to transfer the authority enjoyed by the Department of Hospitals to a permanent committee within the

Academy of Sciences, which fell within the jurisdiction of his ministry, and which he had served as past president.[47]

Breteuil's unexpected disgrace two months later and the withdrawal of ministerial support for the project of the four hospitals brought to an end the noble dream of Bailly and his fellow scientists. The moneys of the hospital subscriptions and lottery were sequestered by a desperate Loménie de Brienne,[48] First Minister of a government tottering on the abyss of revolution.

II

While Breteuil's propaganda campaign dramatized the united determination of Crown, citizenry, and science to replace a Hôtel-Dieu purportedly beyond redemption, nothing was known to Parisians of an equally heroic, but invisible, struggle of rehabilitation going on inside led by Colombier and the great surgeon Pierre-Joseph Desault.

Colombier, distinguished military physician and reformer,[49] was a key lieutenant in Necker's attempts to reform the Paris hospitals between 1777 and 1781.[50] He collaborated with the minister's famous wife in establishing the model parish hospice of La Charité and himself founded the Paris venereal hospital.[51] Colombier entered the Hôtel-Dieu in 1781 as Necker's representative with marked deference to the power of its officers and with the clear understanding that change inside the vast monolith could not happen without the approval of its administration, jealous guardians of the hospital's vast patrimonial, institutional, and corporate power against encroachments both of Crown and lay reformers.[52] The daily operations of the Hôtel-Dieu and the promulgation of hospital regulations were entrusted to twelve prominent citizens of Paris, magistrates, financiers, and lawyers of the various tribunals of Paris who enjoyed life tenure. Their policies and directives were ratified at regular meetings by a board of governors, seven trustees who exercised legal authority for the hospital, dignitaries of church (Archbishop of Paris), Crown (Lieutenant of Police), magistracy (First President of the Paris Parlement, Attorney-General of the same body, First President of the *Cour des aides*, First President of the *Chambre des comptes*) and the City of Paris (Provost of Merchants). The hospital suffered severe problems of diminishing revenues, the inflation of food cost (which amounted to 60 percent of its total budget)[53] and services, and management which was both wasteful and anarchic.[54] Colombier and La Millière exercised their authority skillfully, gradually winning over a distrustful administration which increasingly became dependent on them against attacks of hostile critics, an inimical public, and tempestuous rifts within its own house. For eight years, from 1781 until his death in 1789, literally from exhaustion on one of his regional hospital inspection tours, Colombier proposed and supervised myriad details of rebuilding and refurnishing the Hôtel-Dieu. He reconciled opposing demands of doctors, nurses, and officers and accommodated the Augustinian nuns in rebuilding their chapel, infirmary, dormitories, and novitiate (which took up a significant portion of the new building), designed and supervised construction of wards, laundries, kitchens, fixtures, beds, transferred various services between wings, planned a new obstetrics service, and promulgated regulations for their operation.[55]

In July 1787 Colombier secured the adoption of a comprehensive code of fifty-seven articles regulating for the first time in the Hôtel-Dieu[56] the full range of medical intervention—admission, examination, diagnosis, feeding, treatment, and discharge—to be subject to rigorous regulation and faithful recording in patient case-records. These procedures were defined as medical functions and were vested in the hands of staff physicians and surgeons under whose direction the nurses would serve. Based on precedents of military medicine,[57] widely hailed by contemporaries like Chamousset, Cabanis, Tenon, Chambon de Montaux, and others as a model for civil hospital reform,[58] treatment would be based on carefully maintained journals (under seven columns). The case record which registered where and how each patient was being treated and the progress of his disease denoted the preeminence of medicine and the doctor[59] within the hospital setting as well as the individuality of each case. The regulations provided for regular visiting of patients, collaboration of physicians, surgeons, nurses, and pharmacists, stringent regulation of food services, pharmacy, and laundry, the introduction of lay nurses, and the speedy discharge of convalescents.

The 1787 code depended for its implementation on the cooperation of the medical staff, physicians and surgeons, who functioned separately in the hospital as they had outside for 1,600 years.[60] Despite reforms in 1735 and 1771,[61] the eight physicians and seven assistants continued to be delinquent in fulfilling their principal obligation of twice daily visiting 2,500 patients, "the greatest number" of whom never saw a doctor in twenty-four hours.[62] Some physicians defied this requirement altogether or ran through the wards in fifteen minutes. Though the Colombier reforms significantly increased both the numbers and salaries of physicians, this did not keep them from disliking and envying Desault and his staff of 107 surgeons, practitioners of the progressive branch of French medicine,[63] and from resisting the reform provisions of Colombier's code,[64] which accorded surgeons greater prominence and responsibility in caring for the sick.

The mainstay of the government's attempt to reform the Hôtel-Dieu was Pierre-Joseph Desault, chief surgeon since 1786, formerly first-surgeon of the Charité, the second hospital of the capital, professor of the College of Surgery's *école pratique* and hospice. It was at the Hôtel-Dieu that a foremost founder of the clinical method of French medicine would transform the teaching of surgery.[65] Desault's foremost ambition was to make the city hospital, whose surgery wards performed more operations than any other hospital in Europe,[66] the outstanding surgery school of the continent,[67] and to provide needed surgeons for the state. This policy received the full endorsement of the administration.[68] Desault secured authorization to transform the surgery wards, dependencies and chapel into a unified clinic which emphasized carefully controlled surgical care and the formation of surgical practitioners. With the announced thesis that "health is the principal object in the design of a ward,"[69] he seized the initiative for a rational reorganization of surgical services: accommodating patients in single beds, carefully regulating the regime of feeding, bedside teaching, case-recording which denoted the evolution of maladies and effectiveness of treatment and which yielded clinical data used for teaching and published by Desault and his students in their *Journal de Chirurgie*. Surgical operations were discontinued in wards in favor of a newly constructed amphitheater,[70] the central component of Desault's surgical teaching. A dissection facility and a dispensary to treat the public were also added.[71]

III

Colombier's administrative regulations and Desault's surgical reforms unleashed a storm of hostility from the nursing sisters, who commanded a staff of 400.[72] The Augustinians rejected the new rules, which robbed them of sovereignty over patients, from admission to discharge, privileges they claimed had been theirs for 1100 years. They were now subject to surveillance by the medical staff—instead of the other way around, and were forced to relinquish key services (kitchens, laundry, pharmacy) formerly under their direction. The nuns were subjected to the further humiliation of sharing power with lay nurses brought in by the new rules. The Augustinians' ire was directed principally against Desault, whom they perceived as the instigator of the new code which brought hundreds of surgery apprentices and outside students, whose conduct they deemed disrespectful, promiscuous, and anti-Catholic,[73] into what already before the Revolution had become an important teaching hospital.

The administration's refusal to satisfy the nuns' grievances against the new rules pitted nurses and surgeons in bitter conflict. When the sisters' appeals to the king, his ministers, and their own temporal and spiritual superiors (Archbishop of Paris, Cathedral Chapter) failed, all of them having requested the nuns to obey the rules,[74] they defiantly commenced legal proceedings before the Paris Parlement. Their suit demanded parity with the administration in running the hospital, a free hand in managing patients, and the return of their historic strongholds.[75]

The Augustinian sisters entered the forum of public debate on the hospitals by the publication of a widely-circulated sixty-four-page brochure.[76] Its object was to enlist public sympathy for the nuns' suit against an administration which they claimed had degraded and persecuted them. The pamphlet denigrated the new health-delivery procedures of the Hôtel-Dieu after 1787 and the surgeons who practiced them, accusing them of incompetence, malpractice, and misconduct.

What was the root cause of the sisters' protest? In essence they realized that adoption of the new rule signalled the end of a thousand-year tradition of Christian hospitality. On two fronts—the hospital and the patients—there was no ground for compromise if the nuns were to remain true to their vows and rule.[77] They considered the doctors "outsiders" who sold their services and who, lacking spiritual vocation, could not be genuinely concerned for the welfare of the sick. They conceived the hospital as a "hospice of religion" which belonged to them and to the poor.[78] They reviled the therapeutic institution to which men came for the cure of specific disorders.[79] To them the aged, hungry, infirm, destitute—those to whom Christ had ministered—deserved a place equal to the sick. All hospital planning which reduced space, controlled admission, introduced single beds, confined service to acute and chronic cases, abridged sacred ministrations were abhorrent, since the object of charity was to turn no one away, to lavish the gifts of the house in the name of God, to pack the hospital with as many deserving souls as possible. Nor could this position be logically repudiated by the administration of the hospital bound to honor ancient practice of admitting all who came to its doors. In the bitter winter of 1788–89 which occasioned terrible crowding, it gave in to the sisters' repeated importunity by ordering the replacement of single beds by large ones in several wards over the protests of the doctors.[80]

The second prime consideration was the patient. The sisters deemed themselves divinely appointed servants of the suffering Christ whom they saw mirrored in each sick man.[81] Nursing was a vocation for the attainment of their own salvation as well as that of the patients. Hence the soul came before the body. Nursing meant not merely service in the wards—feeding, comforting, surveillance— but education—teaching religion, sacraments, morality, converting whenever possible and preparing the sick for death—each in direct emulation of scriptural or sacramental authority. None of these services was, strictly speaking, medical. The only washing of patients provided in their rule was at admission, and that in honor of Christ.[82] Patients' hands and mouths were cleaned at mealtime for the reception of the host, in emulation of the Lord's Supper. To honor God the sister was enjoined to practice love and kindness, to answer the call of the sick "as to the voice of Jesus Christ her husband." The bed, which for the doctors was the indispensable resort of each patient's rest and rehabilitation, the space where controlled treatment and clinical teaching could be practiced from precise data *in situ*, was for the sisters the sacramental setting within which to practice piety, to instruct, to inspire, to convert, to fill with as many needy as possible.

The sisters saw their consoling presence, the particular endowments of their sex, the reinforcement of the spirit and psychotherapeutic concern for the total well-being of the patient as superior to prevailing medicine which they believed—nor were they alone in this—to be imperfect and often ineffectual.[83] Their admission of everyone, their indulgence of patients by overfeeding and frequent snacks, without regard to ailment or to doctors' directives, their suppressing or even vetoing prescribed medication were formally decried by the physicians of the Hôtel-Dieu in 1756 and 1780[84] and by Desault after 1787.[85] Another source of contention was that they kept convalescents on in the hospital, often well beyond the term of cure, in clear defiance of house rules, out of piety, favoritism, or to help with domestic chores, including the crushing hospital laundry. The convalescents became a major source of expense as well as friction and occasioned the economy drives of the Colombier code which transferred the kitchens and laundry to lay direction, just as clinical procedures had been conferred upon the doctors.

Not everyone shared the Augustinians' blinding vision of their piety. The First-Surgeon accused the nuns of cruelty and neglect of patients, of quarrelling constantly among themselves and abusing lay nurses.[86] The hospital administration established that in pressing their claims against Desault and the surgeons the sisters had lied and suppressed evidence.[87] Only at the Revolution and before the National Assembly did the lay nurses and orderlies of the Hôtel-Dieu feel sufficiently free to seek redress of what they considered to be dictatorship and persecution at the hands of the nuns.[88]

In April 1789, after two years of boycotting the rules and doing everything possible to prevent their implementation, the sisters threatened bodily intervention against workmen sent to prepare the new surgery wards.[89] The administration, on the verge of resignation,[90] conceded that discipline had broken down inside the hospital and invoked the intervention of Necker,[91] once again called to the head of government. The hospital administrators were driven to the wall, their direction of the hospital explicitly challenged by the nurses and ignored by the physicians, stymied by a humiliating suit before the Paris Parlement in which a powerful member of their board of trustees, Omer Joly de Fleury, legal officer of the Hôtel-Dieu, who was also Attorney-General of the Parlement, was not only sympathetic to the sisters but also allowed their case to drag on without adjudication.[92] Facing the challenges of the new legislation of the four hospitals, which avowedly claimed the will of the king and populace of Paris, and dislocated finances which threatened bankruptcy,[93] the administration conceded a position of enormous importance: "The Hôtel-Dieu is a public institution belonging to the state whose administration must be directed wholly by public authority."[94] Thus before the Revolution made this policy official, the administration of the Hôtel-Dieu espoused a position essentially consonant with Bailly and his colleagues of the Academy of Sciences. In siding with Colombier and Desault against the sisters, the administration, again before the Revolution, laid the groundwork for the future development of the hospital, as a center not merely to treat patients but also to study disease and to train students.

When the Revolutionaries changed the name of the hospital from Hôtel-Dieu, literally "House of God," to "Grand Hospice d'Humanité," this signalized the passage from a hospital governed in accord with religious, corporate, and charitable purposes to a secular, public, state-supported health center. By drastically reducing numbers of patients, by legislating space and bed requirements, by regulating diet, by recruiting lay nurses and orderlies, by exalting the supremacy of medicine and the reunited physician-surgeon within the hospital environment, the Revolution and Napoleon gave force to the reform propositions of the 1780s that hospital organization must be an arrangement of curative components in which unity and efficiency of service was essential at once to therapy and to progress of the medical art.[95]

Already before 1789 the confessional hospital championed by the Augustinian nurses found outside defenders from authorities neither in church nor state. Through a convergence of reform efforts of Academy scientists and hospital doctors, operating in separate contexts but nourished by common experimental emphases, the milieu was being prepared in the principal infirmary of the capital wherein the practice of hospital medicine would soon make Paris—and for the next fifty-five years—the center of the medical world.[96]

NOTES

1 *Arrêt du conseil d'Etat du roi, qui fixe l'établissement de quatre nouveaux hôpitaux pour la ville de Paris . . . du 22 juin 1787,* 6 pp.

2 Printed in Rondonneau de La Motte, *Essai historique sur l'Hôtel-Dieu de Paris* (Paris, 1787), pp. iii–iv.

3 A. Soboul, *La France à la veille de la Révolution: Economie et Société* (Paris, 1974), p. 65.

4 M. Fosseyeux, *L'Hôtel-Dieu de Paris au XVIIe et au XVIIIe siècle* (Paris, 1912), p. 214.

5 M. Batcave, "Projets de transfert de l'Hôtel-Dieu à l'Ile des Cygnes au XVIIIe siècle," *Bulletin de la Société d'Histoire d'Auteuil et de Passe,* 5 (1905, 192–96; M. Candille, "Les projets de translation de l'Hôtel Dieu de Paris hors de la Cité," *Revue de l'Assistance Publique à Paris,* 7 (1956), 743–52; 8 (1957), 239–63, 343–59, 433–49.

6 S. T. McCloy, *Government Assistance in Eighteenth-Century France* (Durham, 1946), and by the same author, *The Humanitarian Movement in Eighteenth-Century France* (Lexington, 1957).

7 These questions have been expanded in O. H. Hufton, *The Poor of Eighteenth-Century France, 1750–1789* (Oxford, 1974).

8 M. Foucault et al., *Les machines à guérir: Aux origines de l'Hôpital moderne* (Paris, 1976).

9 These questions are summarized in L. S. Greenbaum, "Health-Care and Hospital-Building in Eighteenth-Century France: Reform Proposals of Du Pont de Nemours and Condorcet," *Studies on Voltaire and the 18th Century,* no. 152 (1976), 895–930.

10 L. S. Greenbaum, "Jean-Sylvain Bailly, the Baron de Breteuil and the 'Four New Hospitals' of Paris," *Clio Medica,* 8 (1973), 261–84.

11 *Extrait des registres de l'Académie royale des sciences du 22 novembre 1786: Rapport des commissaires chargés, par l'Académie de l'examen du projet d'un nouvel Hôtel-Dieu* (Paris, 1786), 128 pp.; *Extrait des registres de l'Académie, des projets relatifs à l'établissement des quatre hôpitaux* (Paris, 1787), 15 pp.; *Extrait des registres de l'Académie royale des sciences du 12 mars 1788: Troisième rapport des commissaires chargés, par l'Académie, des projets relatifs à l'établissement des quatre hôpitaux* (Paris, 1788), 36 pp.

12 *Gazette de Santé*, Année 1788, 47. Cf. F. M. von Grimm, *Correspondance littéraire, philosophique et critique*, 14 (Paris, 1882), pp. 297–300; L.-P Bachaumont, *Mémoires secrets pour servir à l'histoire de la république des lettres en France depuis 1762 jusqu'à nos jours*, 24, p. 4; *Journal de Paris*, Jan. 3, 1787, 11; *Mercure de France*, Année 1787, 115.

13 D. Jetter, "Frankreichs Bemühen um bessere Spitäler," *Sudhoffs Archiv für Geschichte der Medizin*, 49 (1964), 164; J. D. Thompson and G. Goldin, *The Hospital: A Social and Architectural History* (New Haven, 1975), pp. 128–42.

14 *Extrait des registres . . . du 22 novembre 1786*, p. 82.

15 Ibid., pp. 23–25.

16 Cf. R. Rappaport, "Government Patronage of Science in Eighteenth-Century France," *History of Science*, 8 (1969), 119–36; A. J. Bourde, *Agronomie et agronomes en France au XVIIIe siècle*, 3 vols. (Paris, 1967); L. S. Greenbaum, "The Humanitarianism of Antoine-Laurent Lavoisier," *Studies on Voltaire and the 18th Century*, no. 88 (1972), 651–75.

17 *Extrait des registres . . . du 22 novembre 1786*, p. 80.

18 Cf. G. Rosen, "Cameralism and the Concept of Medical Police," *Bulletin of the History of Medicine*, 27 (1953), 21–42; E. Lesky, "Johann Peter Frank and Social Medicine," *Annales Cisalpines d'Histoire Sociale*, 4 (1973), 137–44.

19 *Extrait des registres . . . du 22 novembre 1786*, p. 105.

20 Voltaire, article *"charité,"* *Dictionnaire philosophique, Oeuvres complètes de Voltaire*, Kehl ed. (n.p., 1785), vol. 49, pp. 239–47; Diderot, article *"hôpital,"* *Encyclopédie* (Paris, 1765), vol. 8, pp. 293–94; Montesquieu, *Esprit des lois*, liv. 23, ch. 29, ed. Pléiade (Paris, 1951), vol. 2, p. 712; J.-F. Marmontel, *La voix des pauvres* (Paris, 1773); Du Pont de Nemours, *Idées sur les secours à donner aux pauvres malades dans une grande ville* (Paris, 1786).

21 *Troisième rapport des commissaires . . . du 12 mars 1788*, p. 11.

22 Article *"fondation,"* *Encyclopédie* (1757), vol. 7, p. 73.

23 *Extrait des registres . . . du 22 novembre 1786*, p. 106.

24 Ibid., p. 21.

25 Ibid., pp. 2–3.

26 S. Mercier, *Tableau de Paris*, 2 (Amsterdam, 1782), 76–78; cf. Dupont de Nemours, *Nouvelles éphémérides économiques* (1775), cited in R. Dujarric de la Rivière, *E. I. Dupont de Nemours, élève de Lavoisier* (Paris, 1954), p. 71.

27 Mercier, *Tableau de Paris*, 11 (Amsterdam, 1789), 161.

28 Ibid.

29 L. S. Greenbaum, "'Measure of Civilization': The Hospital Thought of Jacques Tenon on the Eve of the French Revolution," *Bulletin of the History of Medicine*, 49 (1975), 43–56.

30 J. Tenon, Bibliothèque Nationale MS, Nouv. Acq. 11357, fol. 19. Cf. Greenbaum, "Measure of Civilization," 46.

31 J.-B. Le Roy, "Précis d'un ouvrage sur les hôpitaux, dans lequel on expose les principes résultant des observations de physique et de médecine qu'on doit avoir en vue dans la construction de ces édifices, avec un projet d'hôpital disposé d'après ces principes," *Mémoires de l'Académie Royale des Sciences*, 1787 (Paris, 1789), 585–600. Cf. L. S. Greenbaum, "Tempest in the Academy: Jean-Baptiste Le Roy, the Paris Academy of Sciences and the Project of a new Hôtel-Dieu," *Archives internationales d'histoire des sciences*, 24 (1974), 122–40.

32 *Extrait des registres . . . du 22 novembre*, 1786, p. 2.

33 "Rapport fait à l'Académie royale des sciences, sur les prisons, le 17 mars 1780 par MM. du Hamel, de Montigny, Le Roy, Tenon, Tillet et Lavoisier," *Mémoires de l'Académie Royale des Sciences*, 1780 (Paris, 1784), 409–24.

34 J. Tenon, *Mémoires sur les hôpitaux de Paris* (Paris, 1788), pp. 144 ff.

35 *Extrait des registres . . . du 22 novembre*, 1786, p. 98.

36 Ibid., pp. 85–86.

37 L. S. Greenbaum, "'The Commercial Treaty of Humanity': La tournée des hôpitaux anglais par Jacques Tenon en 1787," *Revue d'histoire des sciences*, 24 (1971), 317–50.

38 *Troisième rapport des commissaires . . . du 12 mars 1788*, p. 19.

39 "Because there was no machinery for coordinating the actions of ministers, they proceeded, as Necker once observed, like the heads of sovereign states at war with each other. Because the powers of no authorities were precisely defined, and could be interfered with by the monarchs at their good pleasure on the advice of whoever gained their confidence, there were continual conflicts of jurisdiction. Because as a matter of principle the monarchs set all their servants at loggerheads by encouraging them to spy on each other, and because there was no established routine for presenting matters for the monarch's decision, he was continually bombarded by contradictory opinions on matters which increasingly became too complicated for him to understand. As a result no consistent line of policy could ever be formulated." (C. B. A. Behrens, *The Ancien Régime* [New York, 1967], p. 117).

40 J. Isambert et al., eds., *Recueil général des anciennes lois françaises*, 27 (Paris, 1827), 11–14; *Lettres patentes du roi concernant l'Hôtel-Dieu de Paris: Données à Versailles le 22 avril 1781*, 8 pp.

41 *Récit de ce qui s'est passé tendant à la construction d'un nouvel Hôtel-Dieu année 1773* (Paris, 1773).

42 This was a post of inspection and surveillance, extending and centralizing authority of the state to the reform and improvement of hospitals all over the nation. Colombier brought vast administrative, financial and technical competence, evaluating hospitals and services, auditing finances and hospital practice, furnishing knowledge, recommending changes, mediating quarrels, promising government assistance. (Article *"hôpital," Encyclopédie méthodique*, section *Jurisprudence* [Paris, 1791], vol. 10, p. 507; N. M. Cla-

vareau, *Mémoires sur les hôpitaux civils de Paris* [Paris, 1805], p. 190; C. Bloch, *L'Assistance et l'Etat en France à la veille de la Révolution* [Paris, 1908], p. 319; E. Lallemand, *Quinze années de réformes hospitalières, 1774–1789* [Paris, 1898], p. 5 ff.; C. Boyer, *Les Hôpitaux de Carcassonne à la fin de l'Ancien Régime d'après des documents inédits: Les Papiers de l'inspecteur Jean Colombier, 1785–1786* [Carcassonne, 1937]; J.-P Gutton, *La Société et les pauvres: L'Exemple de la généralité de Lyon, 1534–1789* [Paris, 1970], p. 461 ff.); T. M. Adams, "Medicine and Bureaucracy: Jean Colombier's Regulation for the French *Dépôts de Mendicité* (1785)," *Bulletin of the History of Medicine*, 52 (1979), 529–41.

43 *Délibérations de l'ancien bureau de l'Hôtel-Dieu de Paris*, ed. M. Briele, 2 (Paris, 1883), 92–252.

44 *Relevé des principales erreurs contenues dans le mémoire relatif à la translation de l'Hôtel-Dieu et examen du projet du sieur Poyet qui est à la suite* (Paris, 1785), 15 pp.

45 Archives de l'Assistance Publique de Paris, "Registre des délibérations du bureau de l'Hôtel-Dieu de Paris," Année 1787 (vol. 157), fols. 470 ff.

46 Bachaumont, *Mémoires secrets*, vol. 34, p. 387; *Mémoires du baron de Bésenval*, 2 (Paris, 1821), 231, 246–47; *Mémoires de Marmontel*, ed. M. Tourneux, 3 (Paris, 1891), 128–29.

47 Archives Nationales de France (Paris), 0^1 499 (1788), fol. 188; Greenbaum, "Bailly . . . Baron de Breteuil," p. 272; Archives de l'Académie des Sciences de Paris, "Registre de l'Académie royale des Sciences, 1787," fol. 1; cf. Greenbaum, "Bailly . . . Baron de Breteuil," p. 264.

48 Discours de Dupont de Nemours devant l'Assemblée Nationale, sur les banques en général (Paris, 1789), cited in J. Egret, *La préRévolution française* (Paris, 1962), p. 313.

49 P.-L.-M.-J. Gallot-Lavallée, *Un hygiéniste au XVIIIe siècle: Jean Colombier* (Paris, 1913).

50 Archives nationales F^{15} 226, 227, 230, 245; F^{17} 1310–50; Bibliothèque Nationale, Fonds Fr. 6801; Cf. Clavareau, *Mémoires sur les hôpitaux civils de Paris*, p. 190; Lallemand, *Quinze années de réformes hospitalières*, p. 5.

51 J. Necker, *De l'administration des finances de France*, 3 (Paris, 1784), 176–200; A. Tuetey, *L'Assistance publique à Paris pendant la Révolution*, 1 (Paris, 1895), lv; A. Gervais, *Histoire de l'hôpital Necker, 1778–1885* (Paris, 1885), p. 10.

52 Many of these ideas had previously been defined by Colombier in his *Code de médecine militaire, pour le service de terre*, 2 (Paris, 1772), i–ii, 1–142, and his *Médecine militaire ou traité des maladies*, 1 (Paris, 1778), 74–116. Cf. J. des Cilleuls, "Un réformateur de l'hygiène militaire sous l'ancien régime: Jean Colombier, inspecteur général des hôpitaux (1736–1789)," *La France médicale*, 54 (1907), 409–11, and J. des Cilleuls, J. Hassenforder, et al., *Le Service de santé militaire de ses origines à nos jours* (Paris, 1961), pp. 73–74.

53 Costs of wine, flour bakery, and kitchens amounted to 830,289 livres out of a total expenditure of 1,339,474 livres. (Derouville, *Compte général des*

recettes et dépenses de l'Hôtel-Dieu de Paris pendant trente-neuf années commencé le premier janvier 1750 et fini le 31 décembre 1788 avec l'état des revenus de l'Hôtel-Dieu (Paris, 1789), pp. 16–19.

54 Fosseyeux, *Hôtel-Dieu de Paris . . . au XVIIIe siècle*, pp. 197–210.

55 *Délibérations de . . . l'Hôtel-Dieu de Paris*, p. 195; "Registre des délibérations du bureau de l'Hôtel-Dieu," fol. 468 ff.

56 *Délibérations de . . . l'Hôtel-Dieu de Paris*, p. 219.

57 Especially the law of May 2, 1781. *Ordonnance du roi portant règlement général concernant les hôpitaux militaires du 2 mai 1781* (Paris, 1781), 192 pp.

58 "Mémoire sur les hôpitaux militaires," *Oeuvres complettes [sic] de M. de Chamousset*, ed. Abbé Cotton des Houssayes, 2 (Paris, 1773), 1–24; Cabanis, *Observations sur les hôpitaux* (Paris, 1790), pp. 20–29; Tenon, *Mémoires sur les hôpitaux de Paris*, pp. 324–27; Chambon de Montaux, *Moyens de rendre les hôpitaux plus utiles à la nation* (Paris, 1787), pp. 97–100; Dulaurens, *Essai sur les établissemens nécessaires et les moins dispendieux pour rendre le service des malades dans les hôpitaux vraiment utile à l'humanité* (Paris, 1787), pp. 37–51. Cf. M. Foucault, *The Birth of the Clinic: An Archaeology of Medical Perception*, trans. A. Smith, (New York, 1973), pp. 28–30.

59 For convenience, I am using the term "doctor" in its post-1794 sense, meaning *both* physicians and surgeons.

60 E. H. Ackerknecht, *Medicine at the Paris Hospital, 1794–1848* (Baltimore, 1967), p. xii.

61 *Délibérations de . . . l'Hôtel-Dieu de Paris*, vol. 1, pp. 321–27; vol. 2, pp. 13–18.

62 Ibid., p. 16.

63 P. Huard, "L'enseignement médico-chirurgical," in R. Taton, ed., *Enseignement et diffusion des sciences en France au XVIIIe siècle* (Paris, 1964), pp. 171–236. For the background of eighteenth-century surgery in France, cf. T. Gelfand, "The Training of Surgeons in 18th-Century Paris and Its Influence on Medical Education," Diss. Johns Hopkins 1973; M.-J. Imbault-Huart, *L'Ecole pratique de dissection de Paris de 1750 à 1822 ou l'influence du concept de médecine pratique et de médecine d'observation dans l'enseignement médico-chirurgical au XVIIIe siècle et au début du XIXe siècle* (Paris, 1973).

64 "Registre des délibérations . . . de l'Hôtel-Dieu de Paris," vol. 1787, fol. 540; Bibliothèque Nationale, MS, Joly de Fleury 1211, letter of March 5, 1789.

65 O. Temkin, "The Role of Surgery in the Rise of Modern Medical Thought," *The Double Face of Janus and Other Essays in the History of Medicine* (Baltimore, 1977), p. 495; P. Huard, "Pierre Desault, 1738–1795, chirurgien de l'Hôtel-Dieu, professeur de l'Ecole de santé de Paris," in *Biographies médicales et scientifiques* (Paris, 1972), pp. 119–80, for complete bibliography.

66 Tenon, *Mémoires des hôpitaux de Paris*, p. 223.

67 In 1791 Desault claimed that more "real surgeons" were produced in his school in four years than during the previous century in the Hôtel-Dieu

(letter reproduced in T. Gelfand, "A Confrontation over Clinical Instruction at the Hôtel-Dieu of Paris during the French Revolution," *Journal of the History of Medicine*, 28 (1973), 272; Archives Nationales, AD.VIII.30., "Prospectus de l'école de chirurgie, établie au grand hospice d'humanité" (Paris, n.d.).

68 *Délibérations de . . . l'Hôtel-Dieu de Paris*, p. 247.

69 "Registre des délibérations . . . de l'Hôtel-Dieu de Paris," vol. 1788, fol. 606, January 2, 1788.

70 Ibid., fols. 6–7; *Délibérations de . . . l'Hôtel-Dieu de Paris*, p. 222.

71 For the hospital within a wider context of institutional discipline and surveillance, cf. M. Foucault, *Discipline and Punishment: The Birth of the Prison*, trans. A. Sheridan, (New York, 1977), pp. 184–92.

72 This is part of a larger question examined by L. S. Greenbaum, "Nurses and Doctors in Conflict: Piety and Medicine in the Paris Hôtel-Dieu on the Eve of the French Revolution," *Clio Medica*, 13 (1979), 247–67, based on the archives of the Augustinian nuns of the Hôtel-Dieu of Paris.

73 Letters of the Prioress to the Attorney-General of the Paris Parlement, March, 1788. Bibl. Natl. Joly de Fleury, 1211, fols. 250–52.

74 Archives Nationales F15 233; Also Archives Nationales, "Chapitre de Notre-Dame: Délibérations," Année 1787, LL 232⁴⁰ (2), fols. 200, 213.

75 Bibl. Natl. Joly de Fleury 1211, fols. 168–69.

76 *Mémoire pour les prieure et religieuses hospitalières de l'Hôtel-Dieu de Paris contre Mrs. les administrateurs du temporel dudit Hôtel-Dieu* (Paris, 1788).

77 Archives des Religieuses Augustines de l'Hôtel-Dieu de Paris. "Constitutions faites en 1652 pour les religieuses de l'Hôtel-Dieu de Paris par le Chapitre de Paris leur supérieur et revues en 1725," 578 fols. On the general background of the Augustine sisters, cf. A. Chevalier, *L'Hôtel-Dieu de Paris et les soeurs augustines, 650 à 1810* (Paris, 1901); J. Boussoulade, *Moniales et hospitalières dans la tourmente révolutionnaire* (Paris, 1962); A. Tenneson, *Les Religieuses hospitalières de l'Hôtel-Dieu de Paris, 651 à 1947* (Paris, 1958); D. Weiner, "The French Revolution, Napoleon and the Nursing Profession," *Bulletin of the History of Medicine*, 46 (1975), 274–305; L. S. Greenbaum, "Hospitals, Scientists and Clergy in 18th-Century France: An Unpublished letter of Gaspard Monge to Jacques Tenon on the Hôtel-Dieu of Beaune (1786)," *Episteme* (1975), 51–59.

78 *Mémoire pour les prieure et religieuses*, p. 52.

79 "Perish the murderous system born in this selfish century, whereby the poor are now only admitted into the hospital to prevent their death, and they should be thrown out just as soon as they cease to be afflicted with sickness. No sooner did this opinion find a single partisan than it is already being practiced in the Hôtel-Dieu of Paris. The nuns hasten to rise up against these fatal maxims." (*Mémoire pour les prieure et religieuses*, p. 52).

80 "Registre des délibérations . . . de l'Hôtel-Dieu de Paris," vol. 1788, fols. 619, 624, 632.

81 "Constitutions faites . . . pour les religieuses de l'Hôtel-Dieu," fol. 177.
82 *Exercice du jour pour les religieuses de l'Hôtel-Dieu de Paris* (Paris, 1637), p. 27.
83 "It is to women and especially to those who by their vocation are devoted to the continual care of the sick to whom is reserved that empire so sweet that nature and religion have given them over the sick, that Providence confers on them. Who better than they know how to console despair, to temper chagrin, to calm anxiety . . . constantly at bedside talking, consoling, does she not more often influence healing than the application of medicines that almost never aid nature." (Bibl. Natl. Joly de Fleury 1211, fol. 163.)
84 *Délibérations de . . . l'Hôtel-Dieu de Paris*, pp. 215–19.
85 The surgeons could not make their rounds without encountering the sisters' feedings: 5:30 A.M. soup; 9:00 wine; 9:45 meat (called "dinner"); 12:30 snack; 3:00 bread; 4:00 wine; 4:45 meat or soup; 8:00–9:00 snack and boiled eggs (*Délibérations de . . . l'Hôtel-Dieu de Paris*, p. 243.)
86 Ibid., p. 243
87 Ibid., pp. 245–49.
88 Ibid., pp. 286–87.
89 *Délibérations de . . . l'Hôtel-Dieu de Paris*, p. 250.
90 Ibid., p. 230.
91 Bibl. Natl. Joly de Fleury 1211, fols. 292–93.
92 Ibid., fol. 186.
93 Fosseyeux, *Hôtel-Dieu de Paris . . . au XVIIIe siècle*, p. 210.
94 "Registre des délibérations . . . de l'Hôtel-Dieu de Paris," Feb. 20, 1788, fol. 229.
95 G. Rosen, "Hospitals, Medical Care and Social Policy in the French Revolution," *Bulletin of the History of Medicine*, 30 (1956), 124–39; Ackerknecht, *Medicine at the Paris Hospital*, pp. 15–22, 129–47; M. Rochaix, *Essai sur l'évolution des questions hospitalières de la fin de l'ancien régime à nos jours* (Paris, 1959); J. Imbert, *Le Droit hospitalier de la Révolution et de L'Empire (Paris, 1954); L. MacAuliffe, La Révolution et les hôpitaux de Paris*, (Paris, 1905); Clavareau, *Mémoire sur les hôpitaux civils de Paris*, pp. 50–84; R. Mandrou, "Un problème de diététique à l'Hôtel-Dieu de Paris à la veille de la Révolution," *Actes du 93e Congrès national des sociétés savantes (1968): Section d'histoire moderne et contemporaine*, 1 (Paris, 1971), 125–37.
96 Ackerknecht, *Medicine at the Paris Hospital*, p. xi.

Is Childbirth Any Place for a Woman?
The Decline of Midwifery in
Eighteenth-Century England

BARBARA BRANDON SCHNORRENBERG

For many centuries, the normal assistant for all women in child-birth was a midwife. In the eighteenth century, however, the profession of midwifery began to decline markedly in England. By the nineteenth century midwives were mostly women of little education and generally no social status; their patients were the same. For the middle and upper classes, the stereotype of the midwife was the fat, dirty, drunken old woman whose image culminated with Dickens's Sairey Gamp in *Martin Chuzzlewit*. She is an old literary type, found in stories at least since the late Middle Ages, who still appears in popular novels about old and ignorant times. This view of the midwife has also passed from fiction into fact to encompass all midwives in all periods in many serious works. The latest evidence of this can be found in Lawrence Stone's *The Family, Sex, and Marriage*.[1] How the profession of midwifery sank to this state is the subject of this paper. There were three major factors that depressed the role and reputation of the midwife in England during the eighteenth century. The least important of these was the increase in scientific knowledge and medical skill. Far more important were the professionalization of medical practitioners and the emergence of what we usually call "Victorian" ideas of the role, abilities, and status of women.

At the beginning of the eighteenth century, the position of the midwife in Britain seemed fairly secure.[2] Any woman could set herself up in practice as a midwife. She was supposed to have a license, issued by a bishop; its qualifications were concerned with good moral character rather than knowledge or experience in the job. Since the enforcement of licensing was the responsibility of the church courts, little was done to pursue it, especially after the Restoration.[3] The midwife's training was primarily through experience. The best served an apprenticeship with an established midwife, and some even received instruction from physicians. Various handbooks and treatises on midwifery and related subjects were also available, although the value of these was sometimes questionable. Certainly one of the most valid criticisms of English midwifery was its lack of any kind of required training and regulation.[4]

In the seventeenth century there had been attempts to remedy this situation. Under the Commonwealth the licensing of midwives had been placed in the hands of the physicians, but this change, which might have meant more training, lapsed in 1660. In the first half of the seventeenth century, members of the prominent family of man-midwives, Peter Chamberlen I and Peter II, attempted to establish a corporation for midwives which would have regulated itself and enforced requirements for training. But these proposals were opposed by both midwives and physicians and so came to nothing.[5] Whether licensed or not, however, the midwife who read the available literature and who received training under a reputable midwife or physician had practical education as good as most males.

The midwife was seldom involved in any kind of prenatal care. She was called in when labor began, having perhaps been consulted shortly before about supplies or equipment she might need for the delivery. At the beginning of the eighteenth century there were essentially no provisions for delivery in hospitals; only in the second quarter of the century did lying-in hospitals and wards begin to be established in London, primarily for poor but respectable (married) women.[6] If the delivery was a normal one, all went well; the labor after all in such cases is that of the mother. If, however, things began to go wrong, the midwife was limited in what she could do. The better trained could use manual manipulation, but the midwife had no instruments. If things got really bad, the only recourse was to call in the physician or man-midwife. This provided another ground for criticism of the midwife; it was often said that she waited so late that even the skill of the physician was inadequate to save the mother or child. However, an examination of midwifery literature will show that he might well know little more than the midwife. The main difference between them was that the male, whether physician or man-midwife, used instruments.

By the early eighteenth century there were several basic texts for midwifery in circulation, and their number increased markedly throughout the century.[7] They reveal, however, the deficiencies of eighteenth-century medicine in general. What could be discovered by gross observation was clear and well understood. They could chart the development of the foetus and the various presentations of the child ready to be born. The finest of anatomical drawings, William Hunter's *The Anatomy of the Gravid Uterus*, appeared in 1774. But eighteenth-century physicians did not really understand the process of conception, the relation of the menses to reproduction, ova production, the causes of miscarriages. They were beginning to make some connections between such things as diet and exercise and a successful pregnancy and delivery, though all still believed firmly in the danger of marking the unborn child through the mother's external experiences.[8] All writers assumed that the midwife would officiate at a normal birth, though they urged that in difficult situations the physician be called in earlier rather than later.

The physician had instruments. In really abnormal births, the health of the mother was more important than that of the child. As Caesarian sections were universally fatal, they were not performed on living women. When natural childbirth failed, the physician used various instruments to crush and dismember the foetus in order to achieve its expulsion. More humane and more useful was the obstetrical forceps, which came into general use in the eighteenth century.[9] There are vague references in earlier literature to the use of forceps, but it appears that the efficient and practical prototype was developed in the seventeenth century by the Chamberlen family, man-midwives who came to England as Huguenot refugees in the later sixteenth century. They served the royal family and others; as they perfected the forceps they became widely known among their fellow professionals on the continent as well as in England. The exact design of the Chamberlen forceps was a highly guarded secret, although by the beginning of the eighteenth century various versions were being tried by other men. By about 1725 to 1730 the basic design had been developed and put to use by several practitioners, and by mid-century forceps were in general use among man-midwives.

The man-midwife was in a special category in England. Owing to the peculiar system of medical education and organization, they were a varied group. Whereas on the continent and in Scotland men practicing midwifery received standard university medical training, this was not necessarily true in England. Some of the men who practiced mainly in the area of obstetrics and gynaecology were university graduates; others were trained in the same way as their female counterparts. None of the Chamberlens, for example, held an English medical degree; those who did have university training received it on the continent. By the middle of the eighteenth century, graduates of Scottish universities dominated the man-midwife practitioners, especially in London.[10]

The whole system, if it can be dignified by such a term, of English medical education and professional organization and licensing was, by the eighteenth century, in need of major reform. Licensed medical men were divided into three separate organizations, but the actual practice of each was by no means so clearly divided or separated. The least prestigious group was the apothecaries. Although their original function had been to dispense drugs, by the eighteenth century many were serving, particularly in the provinces and among the urban poor, as general practitioners and even surgeons. They were trained by the apprenticeship system, not by formal education, and officially could charge only for drugs, not for attendance on a sick person. The regulatory body for the apothecaries was the Society of Apothecaries, which was essentially a London mercantile gild. Surgery was also controlled by what had originally been a London livery company, the Barber-Surgeons. By the eighteenth century the two functions of barber and surgeon had clearly divided; in 1745 the Surgeons Company separated from the older organization. In 1800 they were chartered by the King as the Royal College of Surgeons. The surgeons were not university-trained; a man could not be licensed as both a surgeon and a physician. The surgeons were the least numerous and probably the least important practitioners, especially outside the metropolitan area. Finally there were the physicians, organized under the Royal College of Physicians. The College, based in London like the other two companies, dominated the practice of its branch of medicine throughout the country. The College of Physicians was governed by the Fellows; admission to this body was by written and oral examination, which often seemed more concerned with the candidate's knowledge of Latin and whether he had an Oxford or Cambridge degree than with his medical knowledge. The Fellows administered examinations for the licensing of members of the College; the charter restricted licentiates to graduates of the two English universities. By the eighteenth century the Fellows had permission to grant licenses to others who might qualify, thus including the graduates of continental and Scottish universities if they chose to do so. To practice medicine in London and vicinity, a physician had to hold the College's license.[11]

The problem lay particularly in the limitation of the leadership of the profession to graduates of Oxford and Cambridge. Major changes in the study and teaching and the whole concept of medicine began in the seventeenth century and continued throughout the eighteenth. These emphasized an empirical approach to medical questions and a clinical approach to medical training. On the continent and in Scotland these ideas took hold, but England lagged far behind.[12] Some hospitals were founded, and by the mid-eighteenth century there were private medical schools in London offering lectures in anatomy and other medical subjects and training their students in the hospitals. But at Oxford and Cambridge, medical education continued in almost the same fashion as it had existed in the seventeenth century.[13] Nevertheless, the graduates of these two universities provided the political and organizational leadership of the medical profession. The often better trained and more skillful foreign or Scottish graduate was thus limited in his opportunity to achieve the fullest professional recognition.

There were also social implications in the question of any change in the organization of English physicians. Society assumed that a graduate of Oxford or Cambridge was a gentleman. Since the College of Physicians was controlled by these graduates, medicine was a gentlemanly profession, though it certainly ranked behind the church, the law, the military, or the civil service in the numbers it attracted and in prestige value.[14] But by the second half of the eighteenth century, English society itself was changing. The old order was being challenged, not just by political radicals but also by increasing industrialization. Those who were making the new society valued education and empirical results.[15] They were mostly outside the traditional establishment, and as their voice grew stronger, criticisms of the ruling class increased. There was demand for political reform and for change in various aspects of society. The gentleman physician whose main qualification was his Latin and his university degree was often a target. Obvious literary examples are Dr. Slop in *Tristram Shandy* and a number of doctors in the works of Tobias Smollett, himself a Scottish physician.[16]

Midwifery training and the relation of man-midwives to women midwives became a part of the larger issue of reform of medical education and licensing and the changing society of later-eighteenth-century England. Both men and women were practicing midwifery; no woman had a medical degree, and only some had acquired adequate training. Most of the man-midwives in London were not members of the College of Physicians; many had Scottish degrees, some were members of the Company of Surgeons. The College of Physicians had apparently recognized the problem of the man-midwife; in 1726 John Maubray and five other man-midwives were summoned before its Censorial Comitia for practicing without a license. Two years later another man-midwife was summoned; he argued that his profession did not need the College's license, and nothing more was heard on the subject for some years. In 1749 lectures on midwifery for men, sponsored by the College, were begun.[17]

By the forties a number of very distinguished man-midwives were practicing in London. The most important of these was William Smellie, a Scotsman whose teaching and writing on midwifery made him probably the most influential practitioner of the century. Older than Smellie were Frank Nicholls, the College's first lecturer on midwifery, and Sir Richard Manningham, also a College Fellow and the founder of a lying-in hospital. Students of Smellie were numerous; of them the most important was undoubtedly William Hunter, holder of a Scottish degree, anatomist as well as man-midwife.[18] Both Smellie and Hunter favored giving the same sort of lectures and clinical training to midwives as to men and had themselves begun private lectures and demonstrations for women. In 1752, with their endorsement, a proposal came before the College of Physicians to set up instruction for women in midwifery and to require this instruction before a midwife could get an episcopal license, but it was voted down.[19] Meanwhile Smellie published his *Treatise on the Theory and Practice of Midwifery* in 1751, followed by case history volumes in 1754 and 1764.[20] Smellie died in 1763; his place as the leading man-midwife was taken by Hunter. Aside from his *Anatomy of the Gravid Uterus*, Hunter made no original professional contribution. He was concerned with his own advancement, both financially and socially, so mixed in the leading political and intellectual circles of London. He became the fashionable man-midwife; he attended Queen Charlotte at the birth of her first son (later George IV) and at the births of the subsequent thirteen royal children. He died in 1783, before the birth of the Queen's fifteenth child. At the royal lyings-in, however, Hunter was not allowed in the room, where a midwife actually helped at the delivery. He also attended most of the nobility, including Lady Hester Pitt at the birth of the younger William Pitt.[21]

In 1767 the question of the relation of man-midwives to the College of Physicians again surfaced. Dr. Letch, a man-midwife, was rejected as a licentiate. He then went to the Court of King's Bench, asking the College to show cause for its actions. The Court found in favor of the College, but its judgement was tempered with a warning that the College ought to reform its practices. Meanwhile a number of licentiates of the College, including Hunter, formed the Society of Collegiate Physicians. The Society was closed to Fellows of the College of Physicians; its announced aim was the reform of the College. Twenty-three of these licentiates applied for admission as Fellows and were denied. The Society tried to debate with the Fellows, but this degenerated into an exchange of threats. The Society's members hired a gang from the neighborhood of the College's quarters and attempted to use force to break down the door to gain physical as well as paper admission. This action, known as the Battle or Siege of Warwick Lane, was clearly illegal, and the matter returned to the courts. There followed several lawsuits over the next years; in every case the College won, but always with strong advice from the judges to reform. These warnings finally took effect; in the seventies the College admitted some licentiates as Fellows and opened the possibility of more to come. The Society continued in existence, hearing papers and exchanging views until 1798, but its effectiveness as a reforming body declined rapidly after the mid-seventies.[22]

In the first reforms of the College, man-midwives were specifically exempted from the possibility of becoming Fellows.[23] Hunter, for example, who was admitted to the licentiate in 1758 on the strength of his Scottish degree, never became a Fellow. By the end of the seventies, however, the College had apparently decided that man-midwifery was there to stay. In 1783 they resolved to grant licenses to those qualified in midwifery only, for an entrance fee of £20. The number of those applying was small, but ten man-midwives were admitted to the College, including Thomas Denman, who succeeded Hunter as the fashionable man-midwife and whose training was entirely clinical.[24] Only a few man-midwives finally joined the College, although it was a far more prestigious body than the Company of Surgeons, which had been and continued to be the organization for many man-midwives. Those who attended royalty and society, such as Denman, Michael Underwood who attended the birth of Princess Charlotte, daughter of George IV, and Richard Croft, Denman's son-in-law, who let Charlotte die in childbirth, were all members of the College before it ceased to license man-midwives in 1804.[25]

As man-midwifery became socially respectable, these practitioners looked for a less awkward and contradictory name for themselves. Maubray, in his book of 1724, suggested that the man-midwife be called an "Andro-Boethogynist, or Man-Helper of Women"; it is not surprising that this name did not catch on. There was considerable use of the French term "accoucheur" in the eighteenth century, but doubtless many were not happy with the connotations a French word might carry. The term obstetrician seems to have come into use about 1828 and was apparently rapidly adopted by men to put themselves further from the midwives.[26]

In winning their own professional and social respectability, the man-midwives helped to depress the status and opportunities of their female counterparts. More and more by the end of the century, midwives attended the lower classes, who could not pay adequately; therefore, the lack of rewards meant the profession attracted fewer educated and qualified women. Of course there were exceptions, mainly London midwives who actually attended the births of royal children and who wrote books of instruction for their fellow practitioners.[27] Most of these books were positive statements of what a midwife could and ought to do. The bulk of the writing about midwifery, however, was increasingly vituperative criticism of men for taking over the profession. Although by the end of the century the best midwives were also using forceps, the most obvious ground for attack was the male's use of instruments. Actually the best men, such as Smellie and Hunter, were against their indiscriminate use. In 1751 Dr. Frank Nicholls published *A Petition of the Unborn-Babes*,[28] which accused man-midwives of killing both mothers and children by the misuse of instruments. It was said that Nicholls was paid for this support by the current royal midwife, but he was clearly sympathetic to the woman, for it was he who proposed in 1752 that the College offer lectures for midwives.[29]

The most vehement attack on man-midwives appeared in 1760, Elizabeth Nihell's *A Treatise on the Art of Midwifery, Setting forth Various Abuses therein, Especially as to the Practice with Instruments: the Whole Serving to put all Rational Inquirers in a fair Way of very safely forming their own Judgement upon the Question; Which it is best to employ, In Cases of Pregnancy and Lying-in, a Man-Midwife; or, a Midwife.* Nihell was a midwife who had studied and worked for two years at the Hôtel-Dieu in Paris, where French midwives were trained. Her husband was an apothecary, and of course there were those who said he really wrote the book. Nihell's language was intemperate and her target ill-chosen, for much of her attack was against Smellie. An example of her style and views can be seen in her summary of her three essential points.

The *first*, is that the origin of the men, insinuating themselves into the practice of midwifery, has absolutely no foundation in the plea of superior safety, and, consequently, can have no right to exact so great a sacrifice as that of decency and modesty.

The *second*, for that they were reduced first to forge the phantom of incapacity in the women, and next the necessity of murderous instruments, as some color for their mercenary intrusion. And, in truth, the faculty of using those instruments is the sole tenure of their usurped office.

The *third*, their disagreement among themselves about, which are the instruments to be preferred; a doubt which, the practices tried upon the lives and limbs of so many women and children trusted to them, have not yet, it seems, resolved even to this day.[30]

Her work was reviewed at length and extremely unfavorably in the *Critical Review*, probably by its editor Tobias Smollett. The review began by proposing that she adopt as a motto *Ex nihilo nihil fit*, and went on to attack her views of "the whole body of male-practitioners, as ruffians who never let slip the smallest opportunity of tearing and massacring their patients with iron and steel instruments." Among her other points were that women were more sympathetic in their attendance on those in labor, and midwives on the whole were better trained than their male counterparts. The *Critical Review* denied these claims.[31] Nihell replied in *An Answer to the Critical Review for March, 1760, Upon the Article of Mrs. Nihell's Treatise on the Art of Midwifery.*[32] The *Critical Review* noticed this refutation in a brief but sprightly call for an end to the exchange, saying "you have delivered yourself of a monstrous birth, that fully evinces your dexterity in the obstetric art: may it, however, be the last of our begetting!"[33] It is difficult to believe that the kind of attack Nihell made did much to improve the reputation of midwives.

Besides the unwarranted use of instruments, the other main attack on man-midwives was made on the grounds of propriety. Nihell raised this issue, which, as instruments were more accepted by women as well as men, became a key question in the employment of man-midwives. Especially by the end of the century, as what we usually refer to as "Victorian" attitudes about the purity and privacy of a woman's body came to be widely held,[34] the issue was raised as to whether a woman ought to let a man see and touch her. Midwives argued that they would not compromise a woman's purity. Stories of patients seduced by their male physicians, of poor women in lying-in hospitals being subjected to the harassment of examination by countless medical students, were repeated in various versions. Man-midwifery, along with boarding schools for girls, novels, and dancing (all French in origin), were ruining English women. Once women were lost, all society would crumble.[35] This Victorian attitude toward "touching," as it was usually called, did not, however, save the mid-wife. Rather it led to nineteenth-century gynaecology and obstetrics, with male physicians diagnosing and prescribing for women whom they had not really examined and whose propriety forbade them to describe their own condition adequately.[36] While concern for female modesty did not save the midwife as the primary agent of delivery care, other aspects of the "Victorian" view of women were certainly influential in her decline. A lady does not work, and no decent woman would voluntarily involve herself in such a physical (even sexual) and messy affair as childbirth. Therefore, the kind of woman who became a midwife was for yet another reason uneducated and lower-class, and thus even less likely to be engaged by the middle and upper classes.

One of the complaints of midwives against their male counterparts was that the men were taking away women's work. All through the eighteenth century this complaint was made about many occupations; midwifery is another example of women's loss of employment in pre-industrial society. The reasons men gave for their own advance were all what would now be called male chauvinism. A woman is more delicate than a man, less able to engage in strenuous activity. Therefore, was a midwife physically fit to do her job? Although the nineteenth-century millowners argued that women's delicate and sensitive fingers made them more fitted to work in the textile mills for less money than men, the man-midwives argued that these fingers were not sensitive enough to manipulate obstetrical instruments. Since women's minds could not comprehend the mysteries of science, they could hardly be qualified to be obstetricians in the modern world. These arguments were in the end the most critical in the decline of the midwife. Women were excluded from the universities, the teaching hospitals (except as patients), from the professional organizations. Medicine, like other professions, was a male preserve, to be guarded jealously against incursion from illogical, unscientific, weak women. If medicine was to be scientific, it must be male. This is an attitude which has not died easily.

NOTES

1 *The Family, Sex and Marriage in England 1500–1800* (New York: Harper and Row, 1977), pp. 72–73, 79. Even so respected a medical historian as George Rosen makes these assumptions in "A Slaughter of Innocents: Aspects of Child Health in the Eighteenth-Century City," *Studies in Eighteenth-Century Culture*, vol. 5 (Madison: University of Wisconsin Press, 1976), pp. 293–316.

2 General accounts of midwives and midwifery in the eighteenth century vary in value. Jean Donnison, *Midwives and Medical Men* (New York: Schocken Books, 1977) is concerned primarily with the nineteenth century; however, she has an extensive introductory section on the earlier period. This is also the best-documented account of midwives. Other surveys include Kate Campbell Hurd Mead, *A History of Women in Medicine* (Haddam, Conn.: Haddam Press, 1938), pp. 460–77; Gustave J. Witkowski, *Accoucheurs et sages-femmes célèbres* (Paris: G. Sternheil, n. d.); James Hobson Aveling, *English Midwives: Their History and Prospects* (London: J. and A. Churchill, 1872; rpt., London, Hugh K. Elliott, 1967); Herbert Ritchie Spencer, *The History of British Midwifery 1650 to 1800* (London, John Bale Sons and Danielson, 1927; rpt., New York, AMS Press, 1978), really about British writing on obstetrics; Thomas Rogers Forbes, *The Midwife and the Witch* (New Haven: Yale University Press, 1966); Barbara Ehrenreich and Diedre English, *Witches, Midwives, and Nurses* (Old Westbury, N.Y.: Feminist Press, 1973), a stridently feminist account; J. Elise Gordon, "British Midwives through the Centuries 3: From the 18th Century to Today," *Midwife and Health Visitor*, 3 (1967), 275–81; M. Olive Haydon, "English Midwives in Three Centuries," *Maternity and Child Welfare*, 3 (1919), 407–9; Alice Clark, *Working Life of Women in the Seventeenth Century* (London: George Routledge, 1919), pp. 265–85; Hilda Smith, "Gynecology and Ideology in Seventeenth-Century England," in Berenice A. Carroll, ed., *Liberating Women's History* (Urbana, Ill.: University of Illinois Press, 1976), pp. 97–114.

3 See Aveling, Clark, and other sources cited above. Also see Thomas Rogers Forbes, "The Regulation of English Midwives in the Sixteenth and Seventeenth Centuries," *Medical History*, 8 (1964), 235–44, and "The Regulation of English Midwives in the Eighteenth and Nineteenth Centuries," *Medical History*, 15 (1971), 352–62; Thomas G. Benedek, "The Changing Relationship between Midwives and Physicians during the Renaissance," *Bulletin of the History of Medicine*, 51 (1977), 550–64.

4 Compare what happened to midwifery in France. See Richard A. Petrelli, "The Regulation of French Midwifery during the *Ancien Régime*," *Journal of the History of Medicine and Allied Sciences*, 26 (1971), 276–92.

5 Donnison, *Midwives and Medical Men*; Aveling, *English Midwives*; James Hobson Aveling, *The Chamberlens and the Midwifery Forceps: Memorials of the Family and an Essay on the Invention of the Instrument* (London, J. and A.

Churchill, 1882; rpt., New York, AMS Press, 1977); Smith, "Gynecology and Ideology."

6 G. C. Peachey, "Notes upon the Provision for Lying-in Women in London up to the Middle of the Eighteenth Century," *Proceedings of the Royal Society of Medicine*, 17 (1923–24): Section of Epidemiology and State Medicine, 72–76; J. E. Donnison, "Note on the Foundation of Queen Charlotte's Hospital," *Medical History*, 15 (1971), 398–400; Donnison, *Midwives and Medical Men*, pp. 25–28.

7 A useful survey of the various writers on the subject can be found in Irving S. Cutter and Henry R. Viets, *A Short History of Midwifery* (Philadelphia: W. B. Saunders, 1964), pp. 10–44. Shorter and less-exhaustive summaries are John Byers, "The Evolution of Obstetric Medicine; With Illustrations from Some Old Midwifery Books," *British Medical Journal*, 15 June 1912, pp. 1345–50; Walter Radcliffe, *Milestones in Midwifery* (Bristol: John Wright, 1967); Miles H. Phillips, "Men-Midwives of the Past," *Bristol Medico-Chirugical Journal*, 52 (Summer 1935), 83–102; Ritchie Spencer, *History of British Midwifery*.

8 This summary can be detailed from the secondary works cited above as well as contemporary works. I have read those available in the Lawrence Reynolds Collection, Lister Hill Library, University of Alabama in Birmingham: François Mauriceau, *Traité des maladies des femmes grosses . . .* , 4th ed. (Paris: Chez Laurent d'Henry, 1694. The first edition of this work was published in 1668; an English translation by Hugh Chamberlen appeared in 1672, titled *The Diseases of Women with Child and in Childbed*); John Maubray, *The Female Physician . . .* (London: James Holland, 1724); William Buchan, *Domestic Medicine*, 3rd American ed. (Norwich, Conn.: John Trumbull, 1778; first published in Edinburgh in 1769). In the Rare Book Room, Medical History Section, Medical School Library, University of Rochester: Alexander Hamilton, *Outlines of the Theory and Practice of Midwifery*, 3rd ed. (London: T. Kay, 1791); John Burton, *An Essay Towards a Complete New System of Midwifery* (London: James Hodges, 1751). On microfilm from the National Library of Medicine: Paul Portal, *Midwives, or the True Manner of Assisting a Woman in Childbearing: . . .* (London: S. Crouch and J. Taylor, 1705); John Memis, *The Midwife's Pocket Companion: or a Practical Treatise of Midwifery . . .* (London: Edward and Charles Dilly, 1765). See also Kenneth Dewhurst, "Locke's Midwifery Notes," *The Lancet*, 4 Sept. 1954, 490–91; Michael K. Eshleman, "Diet during Pregnancy in the Sixteenth and Seventeenth Centuries," *Journal of the History of Medicine and Allied Sciences*, 30 (1975), 23–39.

9 Cutter and Viets, *Short History*, pp. 44–69; Aveling, *The Chamberlens*; Kedarnath Das, *Obstetric Forceps: Its History and Evolution* (St. Louis: C. V. Mosby, 1929); Donald T. Atkinson, *Magic, Myth and Medicine* (Cleveland: World Publishing Co., 1956), pp. 163–66; John H. Peel, "Milestones in Midwifery," *Postgraduate Medical Journal*, Nov. 1947, pp. 523–29; Alban Doran, "Burton ("Dr. Slop"): His Forceps and His Foes," *Journal of Obstet-*

rics and Gynaecology of the British Empire, 23 (1913), 3–24, 65–86; and "Dusée: His Forceps and His Contemporaries," ibid., 22 (1912), 119–42, 203–7.

10 William F. Mengert, "The Origin of the Male Midwife," *Annals of Medical History*, ns, 4 (1932), 453–65; R. W. Johnstone, "Scotland's Contribution to the Progress of Midwifery in the Early Eighteenth and Nineteenth Centuries," *Journal of Obstetrics and Gynaecology of the British Empire*, 57 (1950), 583–94; Howard D. King, "The Evolution of the Male Midwife, with Some Remarks on the Obstetrical Literature of Other Ages," *American Journal of Obstetrics*, 77 (1918), 177–86; George Bancroft-Livingstone, "Louise de la Vallière and the Birth of the Man-Midwife," *Journal of Obstetrics and Gynaecology of the British Empire*, 63 (1956), 261–67; Steven A. Brody, "The Life and Times of Sir Fielding Ould: Man-Midwife and Master Physician," *Bulletin of the History of Medicine*, 52 (1978), 228–50.

11 On these three companies and medical practice, see S. W. F. Holloway, "The Apothecaries' Act: A Reinterpretation," *Medical History*, 10 (1966), 107–29, 221–36; Zachary Cope, *The Royal College of Surgeons of England: A History* (Springfield, Ill.: Charles C. Thomas, 1959); George Norman Clark, *A History of the Royal College of Physicians of London*, 2 vols. (Oxford: Clarendon Press, 1964–66); Frederick N. L. Poynter, *The Evolution of Medical Practice in Britain* (London: Pitman Medical Publishing Co., 1961); W. J. Bishop, "The Evolution of the General Practitioner in England," in E. Ashworth Underwood, ed., *Science, Medicine and History: Essays on the Evolution of Scientific Thought and Medical Practice written in honour of Charles Singer*, 2 vols. (London: Oxford University Press, 1953), II, 351–57; Joseph F. Kett, "Provincial Medical Practice in England: 1730–1815," *Journal of the History of Medicine and Allied Sciences*, 19 (1964), 17–29; Bernice Hamilton, "The Medical Professions in the Eighteenth Century," *Economic History Review*, 2nd ser., 4 (1951), 141–69.

12 Lester S. King, *The Road to Medical Enlightenment: 1650–1695* (London: Macdonald, 1970) and *The Medical World of the Eighteenth Century* (Chicago: University of Chicago Press, 1958); Albert H. Buck, *The Dawn of Modern Medicine* (New Haven: Yale University Press, 1920); Michael Kraus, "American and European Medicine in the Eighteenth Century," *Bulletin of the History of Medicine*, 8 (1940), 679–95; G. S. Rousseau, "'Sowing the Wind and Reaping the Whirlwind': Aspects of Change in Eighteenth-Century Medicine," in Paul J. Korshin, ed., *Studies in Change and Revolution: Aspects of English Intellectual History, 1640–1800* (London: Scolar Press, 1972), pp. 129–59; William R. LeFanu, "The Lost Half-Century in English Medicine, 1700–1750," *Bulletin of the History of Medicine*, 46 (1972), 319–48; Arnold Chaplin, *Medicine in England during the Reign of George III* (London, Henry Kimpton, 1919; rpt., New York, AMS Press, 1977).

13 Phyllis Allen, "Medical Education in 17th-Century England," *Journal of the History of Medicine and Allied Sciences*, 1 (1946), 115–43; James L. Axtell, "Education and Status in Stuart England: The London Physician," *History*

of Education Quarterly, 10 (1970), 141–59; A. H. T. Robb-Smith, "Medical Education at Oxford and Cambridge Prior to 1850," in Frederick N. L. Poynter, ed., *The Evolution of Medical Education in Britain* (Baltimore: Williams and Wilkins, 1966), pp. 19–52; Arnold Chaplin, "The History of Medical Education in the Universities of Oxford and Cambridge, 1500–1850," *Proceedings of the Royal Society of Medicine*, 13 (1919–20): pt. 3, Section of the History of Medicine, 83–107; Charles Singer and S. W. F. Holloway, "Early Medical Education in England in Relation to the Pre-History of London University," *Medical History*, 4 (1960), 1–17; Charles Newman, *The Evolution of Medical Education in the Nineteenth Century* (London: Oxford University Press, 1957), pp. 1–55.

14 Axtell, "Education and Status"; Edward Hughes, "The Professions in the Eighteenth Century," *Durham University Journal*, ns, 13 (1951–52), 46–55; N. D. Jewson, "Medical Knowledge and the Patronage System in 18th-Century England," *Sociology*, 8 (1974), 369–85.

15 J. H. Plumb, "Reason and Unreason in the Eighteenth Century: The English Experience," in *In the Light of History* (Boston: Houghton Mifflin, 1972), pp. 3–24.

16 William White, "A Survey of the Social Implications of the History of Medicine in Great Britain, 1742–1867," *Annals of Medical History*, ns, 10 (1938), 279–300; Rousseau, "Sowing the Wind and Reaping the Whirlwind"; Doran, "Burton ('Dr. Slop')"; W. H. Allport, "Tristram Shandy and Obstetrics," *American Journal of Obstetrics and Diseases of Women and Children*, 65 (1912), 612–17; Arthur H. Cash, "The Birth of Tristram Shandy: Sterne and Dr. Burton," in R. F. Brissenden, ed., *Studies in the Eighteenth Century* (Toronto: University of Toronto Press, 1968), pp. 133–54; G. S. Rousseau, "Pineapples, Pregnancy, Pica, and Peregrine Pickle," in G. S. Rousseau and P. G. Boucé, ed., *Tobias Smollett Bicentennial Essays Presented to Lewis M. Knapp* (New York: Oxford University Press, 1971), pp. 79–109; Cecil K. Drinker, "Doctor Smollett," *Annals of Medical History*, 7 (1925), 31–47; E. Ashworth Underwood, "Medicine and Science in the Writings of Smollett," *Proceedings of the Royal Society of Medicine*, 30 (1937), 961–74; Claude E. Jones, "Tobias Smollett (1721–1771)—The Doctor as Man of Letters," *Journal of the History of Medicine and Allied Sciences*, 12 (1957), 337–48.

17 Clark, *Royal College of Physicians*, II, 502–3.

18 Cutter and Viets, *Short History*, pp. 15–38; Johnstone, "Scotland's Contribution"; George C. Peachey, "William Hunter's Obstetrical Career," *Annals of Medical History*, ns, 2 (1930), 476–79.

19 Clark, *Royal College of Physicians*, II, 504–5; William Hunter to William Cullen, London, 22 Feb. 1752, John Thomson, *An Account of the Life, Lectures, and Writings of William Cullen M.D.*, 2 vols. (Edinburgh: William Blackwood, 1859), I, 543–44.

20 Tobias Smollett was a friend of Smellie; in the fifties and sixties, while editor of the *Critical Review*, he also edited and supervised the publication of Smellie's work. Jones, "Tobias Smollett"; Lewis M. Knapp, *Tobias Smol-*

lett, Doctor of Men and Manners (Princeton: Princeton University Press, 1949); Claude E. Jones, "Tobias Smollett on the 'Separation of the Pubic Joint in Pregnancy,'" *Medical Life*, 41 (1934), 302–5; G. S. Rousseau, "Tobias Smollett: Doctor by Design, Writer by Choice," *Journal of the American Medical Association*, 216 (1971), 85–89.

21 Johnstone, "Scotland's Contribution"; Gordon, "British Midwives"; Jane M. Oppenheimer, *New Aspects of John and William Hunter* (New York: Henry Schuman, 1946); Charles W. F. Illingworth, "William Hunter's Influence on Obstetrics," *Scottish Medical Journal*, 15 (1970), 58–60; Cutter and Viets, *Short History*, pp. 33–37; Olwen Hedley, *Queen Charlotte* (London: John Murray, 1975).

22 Iwan Waddington, "The Struggle to Reform the Royal College of Physicians, 1767–1771: A Sociological Analysis," *Medical History*, 17 (1973), 107–26; Lloyd G. Stevenson, "The Siege of Warwick Lane: Together with a Brief History of the Society of Collegiate Physicians (1767–1798)," *Journal of the History of Medicine and Allied Sciences*, 7 (1952), 105–21; R. Hingston Fox, *Dr. John Fothergill and His Friends* (London: Macmillan, 1919), pp. 143–51.

23 Dr. William Watson to Dr. John Fothergill, London, 16 Sept. 1771, Thomson, *Account of William Cullen*, I, 657–60.

24 Clark, *Royal College of Physicians*, II, 588–89; Forbes "The Regulation of English Midwives in the Eighteenth and Nineteenth Centuries"; Cutter and Viets, *Short History*, pp. 41–42, 185–86.

25 Clark, *Royal College of Physicians*, II, 636–37; Cutter and Viets, *Short History*, pp. 187–88; W. J. Maloney, "Michael Underwood: A Surgeon Practicing Midwifery from 1764 to 1784," *Journal of the History of Medicine and Allied Sciences*, 5 (1950), 289–314.

26 Forbes, "The Regulation of English Midwives in the Eighteenth and Nineteenth Centuries."

27 Mead, *Women in Medicine*, pp. 472–77; Gordon, "British Midwives"; Witkowski, *Accoucheurs et sages-femmes*; Aveling, *English Midwives*, pp. 118–29.

28 *The Petition of the Unborn-Babes to the Censors of the Royal College of Physicians of London* (London: M. Cooper, 1751).

29 Clark, *Royal College of Physicians*, II, 503–5; Donnison, *Midwives and Medical Men*, p. 32; Gordon, "British Midwives."

30 Nihell, *Treatise . . .* (London: A. Morley, 1760), pp. xii–xiii.

31 9 (1760), 187–97.

32 London: A. Morley, 1760.

33 9 (1760), 412. See also Aveling, *English Midwives*, pp. 118–26; Philip J. Kluhoff, "Smollett's Defense of Dr. Smellie in *The Critical Review*," *Medical History*, 14 (1970), 31–41. Most of the other attacks on man-midwives used exactly the same material as Nihell with perhaps different emphases. For example, Philip Thicknesse, *Man-Midwifery Analyzed: and the Tendency of That Practice Detected and Exposed* (London: R. Davis, 1764), stresses the impropriety of men treating women.

34 On this point see Muriel Jaeger, *Before Victoria* (London: Chatto and Windus, 1956); Gordon Rattray Taylor, *The Angel Makers* (New York: E. P. Dutton, 1974); Keith Thomas, "The Double Standard," *Journal of the History of Ideas*, 20 (1959), 195–216.

35 Donnison, *Midwives and Medical Men*, pp. 28–31; Mengert, "The Origins of the Male Midwife." Nihell and Thicknesse make many of these points as well.

36 Regina Morantz, "The Lady and her Physician," in Mary S. Hartman and Lois Banner, eds., *Clio's Consciousness Raised* (New York: Harper and Row, 1974), pp. 38–53; Jane B. Donegan, "Man-Midwifery and the Delicacy of the Sexes," in Carol V. R. George, ed., *"Remember the Ladies": New Perspectives on Women in American History* (Syracuse, N.Y.: Syracuse University Press, 1975), pp. 90–109; John S. and Robin M. Haller, *The Physician and Sexuality in Victorian America* (Urbana: University of Illinois Press, 1974). While these works deal with the United States, the results of these practices were the same everywhere.

A Case Study of Defoe's
Domestic Conduct Manuals Suggested by
The Family, Sex and Marriage
in England, 1500–1800

LAURA A. CURTIS

In his seminal book *The Family, Sex and Marriage in England, 1500–1800*, Lawrence Stone locates the origin of family life as we know it today in the late seventeenth and early eighteenth century. He distinguishes the modern family from its patriarchal predecessor by its closer, warmer relations and more equal distribution of power between husband and wife and parents and children. This new structure Stone calls "affective individualism."

Underlying affective individualism were cultural values not, however, entirely new. Similar values had appeared briefly in earlier periods of other societies, but always among the wealthy urban professional and entrepreneurial bourgeoisie. What enabled these ideas to persist in England, Stone argues, was their germination among the "squirarchy," the predominant class politically, culturally, and socially, with a "near monopoly of high prestige and status."[1] The incorporation of the values of affective individualism among the landed elite in a new and appropriate family structure was unprecedented in Western history.

Not only did the gentry adopt the family structure of the wealthy urban bourgeoisie; it allied itself culturally with its city cousins in a common desire "to pursue whatever was the fashionable mode."[2] The result was a "homogeneous social unit" that constituted a "carrier elite" for disseminating the ideas of affective individualism throughout the entire English population. "Thanks to the extraordinary homogeneity of English elite society, and the ease of cultural and social connections between the landed classes and the wealthy bourgeoisie from the late seventeenth century," asserts Stone, "the latter's ideas about domestic behavior soon spread to the squirarchy, with Locke's *Some Thoughts upon Education* and Addison's *Spectator* as the key instruments of their propagation."[3]

Although critics have challenged various of Stone's theories, so far as I know, no one has as yet questioned his assertion that there was an essential identity of belief between the urban upper middle classes and the squirarchy. I propose, therefore, to focus more closely upon the horizontal movement taken for granted by Stone, in an effort to determine more precisely what ideas were being transmitted and to whom. Instead of dealing in detail with "universally read didactic writers like Locke, Addison, Steele and others," the importance of whose writing in creating fashion Stone points out is "impossible to overestimate,"[4] I will concentrate on Daniel Defoe, the importance of whose highly popular domestic conduct manuals is only too frequently underestimated because, like much of his most influential anonymous writing, they were not generally attributed to him by his contemporaries, and the identity of their author was totally unknown to most later readers.

Close examination of Defoe's works reveals: (1) the model of family structure he popularized so widely is closer to late seventeenth century Nonconformist structure than to affective individualism; (2) the sequence in readership he projected for his manuals between 1715 and 1722 was increasingly the country gentry but decreasingly the wealthy and fashionable London upper middle class; and (3) Defoe's advice on domestic conduct is closer to Locke, who wrote to the middle-aged country gentleman, than to Addison, who wrote to the young, wealthy, and fashionable urban bourgeois. These conclusions suggest the need for modification of Stone's striking generalizations about the history of family structure in England: the late seventeenth-century Nonconformist family seems to have endured as a model for the gentry, with affective individualism gaining adherents mainly among wealthy urban professionals and entrepreneurs.

Furthermore, close examination of the ideas, the characters, and the style of writing in Defoe's domestic conduct manuals between

1715 and 1722 puts into question the orthodoxy of literary historians that Defoe, "a member of the vigorous and durable group of Noncon-formist tradesmen," spoke "for and to the members of his own class."[5] Instead, analysis of the domestic conduct manuals suggests that the anonymous Defoe was widely read by many social classes and that twentieth-century scholars may be only just discovering the truth of his reiterated claim to being a "universal" writer.[6]

My discussion of Defoe's domestic conduct manuals begins with his ideas about family relationships and continues with the religious and social classes of his projected readership, comparing Defoe's ideas and readership with those of Locke and Addison. It concludes with analysis of the psychology and style of speech Defoe uses to differentiate the upper classes from others in his manuals. The dis-cussion is interdisciplinary, in the sense that it draws upon scholar-ship from literature and from social history,[7] applying the discoveries of each to illuminate the other, and using the methods of both disci-plines. Therefore, analysis of style—variations in diction, imagery, and syntax signaling to readers the age, sex, and class of individual characters—is as important to the argument as historical facts, ana-lysis of ideas about family structure, and correct application of ter-minology used by Stone.

Defoe's first didactic treatise, *The Family Instructor*, was published in March 1715. The first of his works to be reprinted in the United States, the book went through ten editions before he died in 1731 and, according to John Robert Moore, "became the most popular book of domestic instruction in a century which took delight in di-dactic writings."[8] A second volume appeared in 1718, and a third volume, entitled *A New Family Instructor*, in September 1727. The 1718 volume was not as popular as the first, reaching only a third edition by 1728. *A New Family Instructor* seems not to have sold very well, and since its subject is theology rather than domestic relations, I am not including it with the others. I do include the 1722 *Religious Courtship*, however, because it concentrates upon the selection of a marriage partner and therefore belongs in the same general category of didactic works as the *Family Instructors*. Although it had a slow start, not reaching a second edition until 1729, it was ultimately suc-cessful; by 1789 there had been twenty-one editions.[9]

Affective relations and allocation of power within the family are the topics most pertinent to Stone's classification of structure; accord-ingly, my discussion of the ideas popularized in Defoe's domestic conduct manuals centers upon these topics. The "personal affection, companionship and friendship" between husband and wife signaling the companionate marriage to Stone are basic in Defoe's models of ideal families, as he reiterates through examples of how one partner should react to the other's moods of depression. For instance, both husband and wife whose parental adventures dominate the 1715 *Family Instructor* decide individually that they have been derelict in their duty to provide religious instruction to their children. Seeing his wife melancholy and tearstained, the husband asks her to share her sorrow with him. The wife demurs, explaining that since her affliction concerns the two of them, she does not wish to make him as sad as she is by revealing its cause. The husband replies:

> *My Dear*, there is no Affliction can befal thee, but either I must be wanting in Affection to thee, *which I never was yet*, or concern for my own Happiness, since ever since we have been One by Consent or by Contract, I have had but one Interest, one Wish, and one Desire with you, and this not by Duty only, but by Inclination. (p. 68)

The same point is echoed on a similar occasion by another couple later on in the volume. In the second case, the husband is the sorrowful one. The social level of the couple is slightly lower, and so the sentiment is expressed in more concrete nouns:

> *Husb.* I wish I had not this Secret to conceal, it is a Burden too heavy for me.
> *Wife* Then let me bear some of it for thee, *my Dear*, cannot I lighten the load, by taking some of it upon my self? I would bear any Burden to remove it from you. (p. 297)

A polite variation on the same theme, this time in the subjunctive mood, occurs in *Religious Courtship*, where a young woman reports to her sister that, seeing her pensive, her suitor, a country gentleman, told her that

> he took himself to be so much interested in me *now*, as to be concerned in all my Griefs; and he claimed to know, if any thing afflicted me, that he might bear his Share in it. (p. 40)

Not content simply to dramatize his point, Defoe explains his rationale of mutual assistance in an authorial comment in the 1715 *Family Instructor* on the meaning of the word "Help-meet"; he concentrates upon communication between partners in times of stress, particularly in periods of depression: " . . . that Party that is discourag'd and dejected *to Day*, and receives Support and Encouragements, Relief and Direction from the Counsel and comforting Assistance *of the other*, shall be restor'd and comforted, and perhaps enabled *the next time* to give the same Encouragement, Counsel, Advice and Comfort to the other, who may in like manner be sunk under his own Fears and Temptations" (p. 81).

Again and again throughout the manuals, often in different styles appropriate to the age and class of each speaker, Defoe reminds married couples that they should not repeat the mistake of Adam and Eve, attempting to evade responsibility by shifting the blame for their own faults onto their partner; a companionate marriage requires the sharing of responsibility.

Almost as pervasive as emotional support between husband and wife, comradeship among siblings is customary in Defoe's domestic conduct manuals. If we are to believe Levin Schücking, historian of the Puritan family in English literature, we must conclude that such comradeship was rare in the paternalistic families characteristic of Puritanism.[10] On the other hand, it could not have been uncommon in the moderate type of American Puritan family identified by Philip Greven in his 1977 *Protestant Temperament*,[11] a type which bears a striking resemblance to the late-seventeenth-century English Nonconformist family.

An amusing parallel to the mutual assistance of the religious mother and father of the 1715 *Family Instructor* (see page 412 above) is the behavior of the irreligious oldest brother and sister. Coming to fetch his eighteen-year-old sister for the Sabbath day ride in the park just forbidden to the young lady by her newly converted mother, the unsuspecting older brother finds his companion unaccountably upset. He asks her to tell him what is disturbing her:

> *Sist.* I *wont*; don't trouble me, *I won't tell you*, let me alone. (Sobs and cries still.)
> *Bro.* Prethee what is the matter, *Sister*? Why, you will spoil your Face, you won't be fit to go to the Park; *come*, I came to have you *go out*, we will all go to the Park.
> *Sist.* Ay, so you may if you can.
> *Bro.* If *I can!* what do you mean by that? I have order'd *Thomas* to get the Coach ready.
> *Sist.* It's no matter for that, I can assure you *he won't do it.*
> *Bro.* I'll Cane the Rascal if he don't, *and that presently too*; come, do you wipe your Eyes, and don't pretend to go Abroad with a blubber'd Face. (p. 86)

The brother's nineteen-year-old masculine echo of his father attempting to comfort his mother is characterized by directness and vigor, conveyed by his translating emotions into physical terms: what his father perceived as his wife's "affliction," the brother perceives as his sister's "blubber'd Face," and what his father proposed to ameliorate by the sharing of emotion, the brother proposes to cure by thrashing the coachman. Like his father, who counts upon the support of his wife to strengthen him in the task of reforming the religious life of his family, the oldest son counts upon the support of his sister to strengthen him in his resistance to this reform:

> Well, I'll go up to my *Sister*, she is an honest resolute Girl, if she will but stand up to me, we will *take our Fate together*. What can *my Father* do? Sure we are too big for his Correction. . . . (p. 159)

Another example of sibling comradeship occurs in *Religious Court-ship*, where the relation between older and younger sisters is moving and dramatically convincing: the older girl offers advice and counsel to the younger and does her best to protect her from their father's wrath. Their comradeship is echoed in the older generation by their father and sister.

In terms of warmth and intimacy of relations, then, the Defoean family clearly belongs to the category of affective individualism. In terms of allocation of power, however, classification is more difficult. Although the principles that the wife is subordinate to the husband and that children must always obey their parents underlie all three of the manuals, the practices described in complex specific situations engendered by Defoe's reliance upon dramatic dialogue do not always coincide with these principles. The husband of the second lead couple in the 1715 *Family Instructor*, in need of advice from his wife, presumably expresses Defoe's own pragmatism about the appropriate balance of power between husband and wife:

> *Husb. My Dear*, what can I do?
> *Wife My Dear*, you are no ignorant Person, you do not want to have me say what you can do, you know what you ought to do, it is not my Part to teach you your Duty.
> *Husb.* Abate that Nicety for once, *my Dear*, and make no Scruple to say what you think is my Duty to my Servants; tho' you do not think it your Part to teach me my Duty, you may be a Means to convince me, that something was my Duty which I did not think was my Duty before; and I may learn from you what you do not set up to teach; There need not be so much Shyness between a Wife and her Husband, that for Fear of taking too much upon you to teach me, you should omit a kind Hint to me of what you think I ought to do. (p. 302)

In the 1718 *Family Instructor*, there is even a case in which the wife assumes control of her family and eventually manages to have her sons displace their father in the family business because her husband, continually overcome by violent fits of rage, has become incompetent. She is careful always to act with punctilious deference to her husband and to train her sons to do the same, but external formalities cannot conceal the real source of power in the family.

The relation between parents and children is more authoritarian than that between husbands and wives, but it cannot be classified as simple paternalism: fathers and mothers hold only an empty title as long as they do not behave in a manner appropriate to their position of authority. Evidently Defoe believed this notion unconventional enough to offend some of his readers, for in the author's notes on the first dialogue in the 1715 *Family Instructor*, he explains that it was necessary for fictional reasons (verisimilitude in motivating the conversion of father and mother) to have the tiny son frequently "fall . . . upon the Father with a Charge of not instructing him" (p. 41). Throughout the 1715 volume he dramatizes many similar instances of children reproving parents and apprentices reproving masters for neglect of religious duty, although he is always careful to include in the dialogue itself some form of excuse for this temerity. Father and mother, master and mistress, openly acknowledge the justice of these reproofs from inferiors. On one such occasion the mother says to her rebellious older daughter, "Tho' that is very unnatural and unmannerly in you to reproach me with it, yet I confess, it is but too just upon me, *and I deserve it*" (p. 114). How such self indictment might be regarded by less pious or more fashionable readers is demonstrated by the scornful comments of the older brother and sister about their father's self-abasement and religious enthusiasm. The sister observes that since their father has himself kept fashionable company, he must be well aware of the insults her brother will have to endure from friends as a result of any radical reformation:

> *Bro.* Why, that is true too; but he is so bewitch'd with *this new Whimsie* of having neglected the Education of his Children, and the Government of *his Family*, that he is coming to Confession *even to us*; he talks of asking God forgiveness for it, and I know not what, *a deal of such Stuff*; I am perswaded he will bring his whole Family into Confusion. . . .
>
> *Sis.* I wish they would but hear Reason; *if they would let us alone*, we would let their Reformation go on as it will.
>
> *Bro.* But I see it will not be done; *my Father* is so over submissive in his Confessions, and so warm in his Proceedings, that I doubt he

will also be obstinate, *for nothing is more so* than these Enthusiastick
Fits of Repentence.
    Sis. What a Tale is this! HE repents, and WE must perform the
Pennance. . . . (p. 169)

The ideal balance between parental authority and filial liberty popularized in Defoe's conduct manuals is perhaps best illustrated by a
conversation about marriage between a father and his youngest
daughter in the 1722 *Religious Courtship*. The right of all three daughters in this work to exercise a veto over their father's choice of suitor
is accepted by everyone in the story, including the father himself.
The real conflict is about the qualifications for marriage: that the suitors be attractive to the daughters is as much taken for granted as that
they be financially acceptable; but the point of Defoe's polemic is that
attractiveness must include, in addition to a pleasant personality,
good manners, and physical presentability, religious compatibility.
Knowing that his investigation of the religious background of his
daughter's suitor has been perfunctory, the father is uncomfortable at
her attempt to shift the responsibility for a final decision onto his
shoulders. It is clear that Defoe regards the daughter's proclamation
of the principle of absolute submission to paternal orders as down-
right irresponsible:

    Da. Well, Sir, if you are satisfy'd, I have no more to say.
    Fa. Nay, Child, why dost thou put it so all upon me? I believe he
is a good Man, and religious enough; I didn't bring him up, nor I
han't ask'd him how religious he is; I do not enter into those Things
with Folks; every one's Religion is to himself.
    Da. Well, Sir, if you are satisfy'd, I must be satisfy'd to be sure.
    Fa. Nay, I would have you be satisfy'd too, Child; can't you ask
him what Religion he is of? (p. 223)

In spite of the balance he prescribes between parental authority
and filial liberty, much of Defoe's advice on child-rearing is a gentler
and more liberal version of the Puritan patriarchal attitude Stone dislikes, describing it as "one of concern and love, which rejected physical punishment but substituted for it overwhelming psychological
pressures of prayer, moralizing, and threats of damnation."[12] Actually, psychological pressure must have represented an innovation;
Defoe assumes that brute force is the norm among his readers, for
the point he stresses about correction of children is that exhortation
and instruction should always precede and possibly avert beating.[13]
Like Locke, Defoe regards physical punishment as a last resort, in-

dispensable for young children, undesirable for older ones, but in any event to be applied judiciously as a form of instruction, never as an outlet for a parent's anger.

Permissiveness seems to have been almost unheard of by Defoe; he supplies only one example (in the 1718 *Family Instructor*) of a foolishly doting father, who eventually learns from suffering not to be overly indulgent. One form of permissiveness apparently familiar before the rise of affective individualism, however, was the preferential treatment of a favorite child. Defoe deplores this as a common practice, explaining and demonstrating that the parent is usually punished for his foolishness by the eventual ungratefulness of the child he has preferred to his others.

Defoe's attitude toward parental authority and filial duty can best be summarized by the case of the 1715 family, where Defoe believes the father to be in the right when he insists that his children accommodate themselves to his regimen of family worship. The rebellious older brother and sister are clearly in the wrong, and Defoe insists they must eventually submit and beg their father's pardon. Nevertheless, he goes a long way toward justifying their rebellion by causing other characters to comment adversely on the father's abrupt, even tyrannical manner of introducing a new routine to young adults accustomed to a fashionable social life. In theory the father is right, but in practice, pragmatic consideration makes the application of pure theory inhumane and even counterproductive.

The Puritan strain in Defoe's domestic conduct manuals is unmistakable, but his Puritanism is not really typical of the version associated with patriarchy. In its respect for the opinion of each family member, its rejection of violence as a means of persuasion, and its appeal to conscience, it resembles the Puritanism of Richard Baxter espoused by Defoe's patron Robert Harley, the country gentleman who served Queen Anne as Lord Treasurer. In its program for the religious education of children, it resembles Locke's educational doctrine, described and classified by Stone in this way:

> Locke warned parents against excessive permissiveness, or "fondness" as he called it, but he argued that education had to be a stage process adapted to the growing capacities and self-development of the child. At birth the infant is merely like an animal, without ideas or morals and ready to receive any imprint, but later, as he develops both a will and a conscience, the treatment of him has to change accordingly. . . . Locke was clearly not an apostle of childish autonomy and parental permissiveness, but he differed widely from those theorists earlier in the century who advised constant distance and

coldness, and the enforcement of deference and obedience by the use of force. After infancy, he advocated psychological manipulation rather than physical coercion.[14]

Indeed, the Defoean family seems to belong to a category of structure that Stone has not succeeded in fitting comfortably into his taxonomy. His description of patriarchy is formulated from examples of extremely authoritarian and repressive Puritan families, the evangelical type contrasted by Philip Greven to the moderate type.[15] Since Stone feels that the individual introspection characteristic of Puritanism is incompatible with the toleration for diversity that later became the norm in England, he is forced to posit a hedonistic family structure capable of generating the national spirit of toleration. For this purpose the late-seventeenth-century middle class Nonconformist type of family of which Defoe's models appear typical seems inadequate to Stone. Accordingly, he leaves it in limbo, suggesting that it merged in some undetermined way with a new and fashionable affective individualism. When he asserts, "Puritanism persisted as a viewpoint adhered to by a minority,"[16] Stone is limiting Puritanism after the early eighteenth century to a patriarchal family structure he can prove to be outmoded.

But when we consider the popularity with readers throughout the eighteenth century of Defoe's manuals, we cannot help but wonder if Stone has not been too hasty in dismissing the family structure portrayed in those manuals. Defoe complains in his preface to the 1715 *Family Instructor* that the practice of family prayers is on the decline. If his complaint was accurate, as Stone insists it was, it is difficult to account for the success of his books, which deal mainly with conflicts aroused by the introduction of family prayers and by religious incompatibility between marriage partners, except on the improbable supposition that readers were willing to overlook the subject for the sake of excellent practical advice, couched in exciting dramatic dialogues, about managing family disputes. Even that supposition would have to be rejected if one accepted Stone's assertion that the decline of family prayers coincided with the decline of domestic patriarchy itself;[17] after all, Defoe's advice is appropriate only in a context of the family structure he depicts, which is clearly not that of the affective individualism Stone posits as successor to patriarchy.

A concrete indication that the Puritanism of Defoe's family conduct manuals appealed to a broader readership than a minority of Nonconformist adherents of patriarchy appears in his preface to the 1715

Family Instructor: "There is no room to inquire here who this tract is directed to, or who it is written by, whether by Church of England man, or Dissenter; it is evident both need it, it may be useful to both, and it is written with charity to, and for the benefit of both" (p. 3).

In addition, complaints about the poor quality of the first printing turn out to arise from problems caused by Defoe's insistence upon the last-minute insertion of a new section stressing the value of both Dissenting and Anglican positions on the common basis of Christianity.[18] The most memorable story in the 1718 *Family Instructor* is about an Anglican family: the brother is a Member of Parliament and an uncle is a minister of the Church of England. Indeed, the family is so overwhelmingly Establishment that Defoe feels impelled at one point to mention the high regard of two of his characters for the learning of the local Presbyterian minister, presumably to remind his readership of the existence of Nonconformists. In *Religious Courtship* the central conflict between Protestantism and Catholicism clearly involves the Anglican variety of Protestantism. Defoe's emphasis upon religious beliefs and practices common to Dissenters and Anglicans as well as his depiction of generally Church of England families argues, therefore, that the family structure portrayed in his best-selling domestic conduct manuals was not confined in appeal to Nonconformists.

Finally, Defoe's ecumenical domestic conduct manuals were not limited in their appeal to the social class generally associated with Nonconformists—the middle and lower middle ranks of the urban middle classes. Speculation about his readership makes it seem likely that the manuals appealed as much to the squirarchy as to the Nonconformist urban middle classes but less strongly to the fashionable and wealthy urban professional and entrepreneurial bourgeoisie. If this speculation is accurate, we would have to conclude that a family structure somewhere between patriarchy and affective individualism was what became most acceptable to the predominant squirarchy in eighteenth-century England and that the cultural alliance between the landed elite and the urban bourgeoisie did not rest as solidly upon shared values of affective individualism as Stone has claimed.

What we can say definitely about the readership of Defoe's manuals is based upon our knowledge of his career, our observation of the social background he provided for the families he portrayed, and Defoe's own comments. Since he wrote these works after the most active part of his career in politics had ended, and since he relied upon his pen for his livelihood, he must have expected to profit from the sale of the manuals. By 1715 Defoe was no novice at directing different writings to different audiences; recognized as one of the foremost political and economic pamphleteers and journalists of his day, he had had over twenty years of experience, ten of them working for ministries of Queen Anne, about five as the favorite writer of Robert Harley, the leading statesman of the period. The sequence of classes Defoe chooses to represent in 1715, 1718, and 1722, is accordingly an important clue to the readership he projected for his manuals. In the 1715 *Family Instructor*, the featured family belongs to the wealthy and fashionable London upper middle class.[19] The two second lead families are urban but not from London; they represent the middle and lower middle ranks of the middling classes, their occupations are shopkeeping and handicraft-trading. In the 1718 *Family Instructor* the feature story concerns a family of the country gentry closely connected with a titled parliamentary family; the minor story, supposedly about a wealthy London upper middle class family, is remarkably deficient in the sociological detail characterizing the 1715 family of the same class. The urban upper middle class has been upstaged by the squirarchy, and the urban middle and lower middle class has been squeezed together as undifferentiated extras in a crowded series of vignettes demonstrating the evils of disciplining children in anger. Defoe emphasizes the social difference between the 1715 and 1718 volumes in his preface to the 1718 *Family Instructor*: " . . . The whole Scene now presented, is so perfectly new, so entirely differing from all that went before, *and so eminently directed to another Species of Readers*, that it seems to be more new than it would have been, if no other Part had been publish'd before it" (my italics, p. iii).

Although the 1718 volume did not sell as well as that of 1715, the feature story must have accounted for the success it did have, for in his 1722 *Religious Courtship* Defoe concentrates upon families from the gentry, but he improves the manual over his 1718 volume by unifying it around a central theme. *Religious Courtship* treats the adventures of a family with three marriageable daughters. The father of the family, a Londoner who has retired to the suburbs, is an ex-merchant of the highest social category for a businessman—he has dealt in foreign trade.[20] Significantly, however, in the light of Stone's assumption of homogeneity between gentry and urban upper middle classes, the father is not of London origin, not one of the successful merchants whose alliances with the gentry Defoe refers to so proudly in other contexts. Instead, considering his readers, Defoe prudently makes him a younger son, brother to a baronet, a gentleman who was apprenticed as a young man to the most prestigious trade possible. His daughters' suitors include a lord of the manor, oldest son to a Sir

Thomas, and a fabulously wealthy Italianate English Catholic, who as a merchant has resided for many years in Italy and now associates with Italian ambassadors and noblemen.

Defoe's increasing emphasis upon the squirarchy in his domestic conduct manuals[21] does not prove definitively that these works were designed for or did appeal to that class: fiction of both Richardson and Fielding, who differed widely in social origins, featured the gentry, presumably because as the most prestigious, it was the most interesting class to a readership of a lower social level—upper middle as well as middle and lower middle classes. But domestic conduct manuals are read for utilitarian purposes, and it would therefore be more appropriate to compare Defoe's works with the didactic writings of Addison and Locke designated by Stone as key instruments in propagating the domestic conduct ideas of the wealthy bourgeoisie among the landed classes (see page 410 above) than with fiction.

The readers to whom Locke directed *Some Thoughts Concerning Education* were the solid, middle-aged landed gentleman and his wife;[22] the reader to whom Addison directed his *Spectator* was the youthful, wealthy, and fashionable urbanite.[23] Whereas the *Spectator* treats marital and parental issues from the point of view of young people,[24] concentrating upon courtship and the social life of newly married couples, Locke discusses education from the point of view of estate-owning parents of established families, interested primarily in the best method of educating their beloved sons. Defoe's program for educating children in religion is close to Locke's program for educating children in virtue. Like Locke, Defoe speaks from the point of view of parents. The general tone of Defoe's domestic conduct manuals clashes with Addison but harmonizes with Locke.

If comparison with the didactic writings of Locke and Addison suggests that Defoe's manuals could easily have appealed to the squirarchy, comparison with other of Defoe's writings suggests that he was well acquainted with the tastes of this readership. In the 1718 and 1722 volumes Defoe launches further into the exploration of obsessive psychological states than in any of his works other than the 1724 fiction *Roxana*, which treats the aristocracy in some detail. In the main story of the 1718 *Family Instructor* conflict arises between a husband and wife because the wife, an atheist, objects to her husband's conducting family prayers. Although in recounting his troubles to a friend, the husband claims that he made so unwise a marriage because he was attracted by his wife's money, the tone of the quarrels Defoe dramatizes suggests instead the extravagant emotions of concealed sexual warfare. The husband's passion for his wife and her

struggle not to be mastered by it underlie her opposition to his conduct of family worship and the excessive and irrational form taken
by her rebellion. The basis of the husband's uxoriousness, except on
the one issue of family worship, is suggested when his wife attempts
to make him go to bed with her instead of conducting evening prayers at his usual hour. Breaking from her with a promise to return
shortly, the husband overhears his wife say as he leaves, "I'll promise
you I'll desire you less than I have done" (p. 79). After the wife leaves
home and has lived for some time with a dissolute friend whose favorite fashionable phrase is "Poison it!" she becomes so obsessed
with the desire for revenge on a husband whose power over her
emotions she cannot shake off, that the words take hold of her imagination, and she broods about applying them literally to her husband.

A similarly odd hypnotic state occurs in the 1722 *Religious Courtship*, where the sister who discovers she has inadvertently married a
Catholic seems trapped in a nightmarish state of paralysis while her
husband attempts to convert her. She describes at length the sinister
vitality of a diamond cross given to her by her husband, as she begins
to feel that the object to which he and his friends pay homage has
some occult power over her. It is significant that Defoe confines these
cases to families of great wealth and high social status: the 1718 wife
is the sister of the £2,000-a-year Member of Parliament, Sir Richard;
and the 1722 wife is daughter to a younger brother of a baronet and
wife to a fabulously wealthy merchant and financier.

Defoe sometimes varies his middle style—lively, idiomatic, concrete, and witty—by the simple device of inserting imagery suitable
to the social class. Two examples from the 1718 *Family Instructor* are
remarks by Sir Richard using the figures of Privy Council and duels
that reflect his social and political experience:

> Oh these Wives, says he smiling, are such Bosom Friends! There's
> my wife, says he, pointing to his Lady, is just such another Privy-
> Counsel-keeper. (p. 23)
> Pray Brother, says Sir Richard [preparing to reply to a belligerent
> statement from his sister], leave it to me; it's my Quarrel, and I'll
> have no Seconds. (p. 25)

But in several instances, including his descriptions of the peculiar
psychological states I have mentioned, Defoe alters the dialogue
completely, removing concrete nouns, refusing to separate and analyze ideas, and using ambiguous diction in order to suggest the polite
and polished conversation characteristic of upper class speakers. The

conversation is frequently sinister because the words conceal instead of revealing the motives of the speaker. In the 1722 *Religious Courtship*, for instance, when the Catholic merchant's widow tells her father and sister about a diamond cross given to her by her husband, she recounts the incident as follows:

> *Wid.* I stood up and thank'd him, with a kind of Ceremony; but told him, I wish'd it had been rather in any other Form. Why, my Dear, says he, should not the two most valuable Forms in the World be placed together? I told him, that as he plac'd a religious value upon it, he should have it rather in another Place. He told me, my Breast should be his Altar; and so he might adore with a double Delight; I told him, I thought he was a little prophane; and since I did not place the same Value upon it, or make the same Use of it, as he did, I might give him Offence by meer Necessity, and make that Difference which we had both avoided with so much Care, break in upon us in a Case not to be resisted. He answer'd, No, my Dear, I am not going to bribe your Principles, much less force them: Put you what Value you think fit upon it, and give me the like Liberty; I told him, I hop'd I should not undervalue it as his Present, if he did not overvalue it upon another Account. He return'd warmly, My Dear, the last is impossible; and for the first, 'tis a Trifle; give it but Leave to hang where I have plac'd it, that's all the Respect I ask you to show it on my Account. (pp. 267–68)

The most sustained example of this kind of conversation occurs in Defoe's 1717 *Minutes of the Negotiations of Monsr. Mesnager . . .* , a work purporting to reveal the inside story of the diplomatic negotiations that led to the treaties of Utrecht ending the War of the Spanish Succession. The English characters in the Mesnager *Minutes* are prominent statesmen from the highest ranks of the aristocracy, including Queen Anne herself. Clearly, then, Defoe associated this style, which he uses in parts of his 1718 *Family Instructor* and his 1722 *Religious Courtship*, with the upper classes.

The disappearance from his domestic conduct manuals of lower and middling ranks of the urban middle classes as well as of the wealthy urban bourgeoisie, and the increasing emphasis on families belonging to the squirarchy; the preponderance of Anglican families; the psychological explorations of obsessive and hypnotic states; and the experiments with a different style of speech, not only in the domestic conduct manuals, but also in the Mesnager *Minutes* directed at Members of Parliament and of the government in order to convince them that Robert Harley, Earl of Oxford, was innocent of treason, all suggest that Defoe was consciously directing his family conduct manuals to the country gentry he believed would be interested in them. The similarity in point of view and in educational doctrine to Locke's *Some Thoughts Concerning Education* suggests that Defoe was correct in gauging this interest.

But it is doubtful that Defoe's call to family prayers and his insistent condemnation of play-going and card-playing, indeed the whole ethos of his responsible model families, would have appealed to the fashionable and wealthy urban professional and entrepreneurial bourgeoisie whose alliance with the squirarchy Lawrence Stone predicates as the disseminating force of the new family structure of affective individualism. Addison's *Spectator*, on the other hand, in its unblushing (and ungentlemanly) assertion of gentility, its frank appeal to the rich, its declaration of intent to mold fashion, and its ridicule of rusticity, must have spoken directly to the wealthy London family Defoe drops from his manuals after 1715. As J. H. Plumb points out, Addison and Steele wrote to the modish middle class that wished "to feel smug and superior to provincial rusticity and old world manners."[25]

We can best recognize the difference between the mores of Defoe's and Addison's readers by noticing that although both writers discuss marital compatibility, the qualification of agreement in religious outlook does not appear at all in such discussions in the *Spectator*. Yet since Defoe's 1722 *Religious Courtship* went through at least twenty-one editions during the course of the eighteenth century, religious compatibility appears to have persisted as a topic of interest in spite of the sneers of the fashionable. Defoe's general call to family prayers may well have been especially attractive to country gentlemen, who would tend to retain some conservative social practices after they had become outmoded in urban surroundings. After all, Robert Harley, Defoe's closest political connection, was a quintessential country gentleman with whom the writer shared many affinities of temperament and who came from a family very particular about the performance of domestic worship.

As late as 1814, in *Mansfield Park*, the discontinuation of domestic worship by the deceased father of a wealthy Northampton family is deplored by the heroine. The clash between the system of family governance adhered to by the country gentry and the affective individualism espoused by the modish upper middle class is one of the central themes of Jane Austen's novel. Persistence in the early nineteenth century of the discord we have perceived in the early eighteenth century between Addisonians and Lockeans is summed up in the thoughts of one of Austen's characters, a fashionable young man:

"He had known many disagreeable fathers before, and had often been struck with the inconveniences they occasioned, but never in the whole course of his life, had he seen one of that class, so unintelligibly moral, so infamously tyrannical, as Sir Thomas."

In spite of the tendentiousness of some of its theses, in particular the one asserting an identity of outlook on family structure between squirarchy and urban upper middle class, and the one assuming the demise of the late-seventeenth-century Nonconformist family model, *The Family, Sex and Marriage in England, 1500–1800* is a seminal book. It has the potential to provide a framework for new case studies of many writers and for new general studies redefining the term "middle class" in the eighteenth century;[26] in the present instance it has guided the discussion of ideas in important but neglected works by a major English writer and has suggested a social context in which to place those ideas and works. In addition to its germinative effect upon scholarship, Stone's book can also have a specifying effect, illustrated in this study by the differentiation of a variety of accents among Defoe's speakers, most strikingly the accent of the upper classes. Recognition of his upper class style has an expansive effect in its own turn, challenging the orthodoxy that Defoe wrote mainly for Nonconformist "tradesmen" and suggesting a series of more precise literary studies of his different styles and historical studies of the social variety represented in Defoe's picture of early eighteenth-century England.

NOTES

1 Lawrence Stone, *The Family, Sex and Marriage in England 1500–1800* (New York: Harper & Row, 1977), pp. 260–61.
2 Ibid., p. 394.
3 Ibid., p. 261.
4 Ibid., p. 394.
5 *Norton Anthology of English Literature*, 3rd ed. (New York: W. W. Norton, 1974), I, 1854, 1855.
6 Speaking of himself through the mouth of M. Mesnager in 1717, Defoe writes, " . . . and frequently his books were said to be written by one great lord, or one eminent author or other. . . ." In his 1718 *Vindication of the Press* Defoe speaks of the ambition of authors "to acquire a universal Character in Writing . . . " (p. 17).
7 See the discussion of the term "interdisciplinary" in the East Central ASECS *Newsletter*, No. 1 (Jan. 1979), p. 2.

8 John Robert Moore, *Daniel Defoe, Citizen of the Modern World* (Chicago: University of Chicago Press, 1958), p. 218.

9 William Lee, *Daniel Defoe: His Life, and Recently Discovered Writings* (London: John Camden Holten, 1869), I, 357.

10 Levin Schücking, *The Puritan Family*, trans. Brian Battershaw (New York: Schocken Books, 1970), pp. 89–91. But judging from his total misinterpretation of an incident in *Religious Courtship*, Schücking's theoretical notion of the Puritan family apparently preceded his empirical investigation of its image in literature.

11 Published in New York by Alfred Knopf.

12 Stone, *Family*, p. 451.

13 The section on punishment appears in the 1718 *Family Instructor*. Defoe's vignettes feature families of the middle and lower ranks of the urban middle classes, many of which would probably have been Nonconformist.

14 Stone, *Family*, p. 407.

15 In his *Protestant Temperament* Greven classifies early American families on the basis of temperament: evangelical, moderate, and genteel. His taxonomy is derived almost entirely from American materials, but his moderate type resembles the families depicted by Defoe. This resemblance is significant in view of the popularity of Defoe's 1715 *Family Instructor* in America.

16 Stone, *Family*, p. 224.

17 Ibid., p. 246.

18 Dessagene C. Ewing, "The First Printing of Defoe's *Family Instructor*," *Papers of the Bibliographical Society of America*, 65 (1971), 272.

19 Defoe supplies many sociological details about the wealthy and fashionable London family featured in his 1715 *Family Instructor*. They own a coach, employ a footman, amuse themselves by going to card-playing parties and to plays, and take outings in the Mall. Both older sons have attended university; the younger of the two is preparing for the law. The older, who has his own estate of £200 a year, regards it as insufficient, without supplementation from his father, to permit him to live like a gentleman. He is planning to go on the Grand Tour of the Continent. This young man and his oldest sister associate with titled friends. What is lacking from the social picture is the occupation of the father, neither specified nor hinted at by Defoe. Since he rarely fails to supply this information for artisans, craftsmen, shopkeepers, wholesale men, or merchants, I assume he meant his readers to infer the father was either a professional, perhaps even a writer, or a rentier of the class identified by Alan Everitt as "pseudo-gentry." (See "Social Mobility in Early Modern England," *Past and Present*, 33 [April 1966], 71–72.) Except for the London residence, the pseudo-gentry is the more likely of the two, because the father is clearly not a *nouveau riche* writer like Defoe, having himself as a young man led a fashionable social life like that of his older children.

20 Defoe analyzes in his preface to the 1725 *Complete English Tradesman* the current local meanings of the word "tradesman" and sets out the hierarchy among traders, explaining that only foreign traders are properly referred to as "merchants," by way of "honourable distinction." Dorothy Marshall explains how difficult it was to decide whether or not any specific merchant or banker should be classified as a gentleman; those trading occupations were very genteel. (*English People in the Eighteenth Century* [London: Longmans Green, 1956], pp. 54–56.)

21 David Cressey shows, in his "Levels of Illiteracy in England, 1530–1730," *The Historical Journal*, 20, i (1977), that Norwich yeomen were a surprisingly literate group, more so even than tradesmen and craftsmen. He points out that they "were the natural audience for certain types of printed materials. Almanacs, guides to good husbandry, even books of etiquette, appear to have a yeoman readership in mind and such books are occasionally mentioned in a yeoman's probate inventory" (p. 7). Mildred Campbell mentions one such etiquette book as William Gouge's *Of Domesticall Duties*. If an early Stuart yeoman was interested in one of the most popular domestic conduct manuals of his day, we can assume his eighteenth-century descendant would have been interested also. Yet Defoe's *Family Instructors* and *Religious Courtship* give no indication of his interest in such a readership, probably because a more dependable country market, both in terms of literacy and of ability to buy, was the gentry. (Mildred Campbell, *The English Yeoman under Elizabeth and the Early Stuarts*, [London, 1967].)

22 Throughout the work Locke discusses education exclusively from this point of view. He says in concluding: "Though I am now come to a conclusion of what obvious remarks have suggested to me concerning education, I would not have it thought, that I look on it as a just treatise on this subject. There are a thousand other things that may need consideration. . . . Each man's mind has some peculiarity, as well as his face, that distinguishes him from all others; and there are possibly scarce two children, who can be conducted by the same method. Besides that, I think a prince, a nobleman, and an ordinary gentleman's son, should have different ways of breeding. But having had here only some general views, in reference to the main end and aims in education, and those designed for a gentleman's son, whom, being then very little, I considered only as white paper, or wax, to be moulded and fashioned as one pleases; I have touched little more than those heads, which I judged necessary for the breeding of a young gentleman of his condition. . . ." (*John Locke on Education*, ed. Peter Gay [New York: Bureau of Publications, Teachers College, Columbia University, 1964], p. 176.)

23 Addison writes in No. 488, September 19, 1712, responding to complaints about a rise in price of individual issues of the *Spectator*: "In the next place, if my readers will not go to the price of buying my papers by retail, let them have patience, and they may buy them in the lump without the

burden of a tax upon them. My speculations, when they are sold single, like cherries upon the stick, are delights for the rich and wealthy: after some time they come to market in greater quantities, and are every ordinary man's money. The truth of it is, they have a certain flavour at their first appearance, from several accidental circumstances of time, place, and person, which they may lose if they are not taken early; but, in this case, every reader is to consider, whether it is not better for him to be half a year behind-hand with the fashionable and polite part of the world, than to strain himself beyond his circumstances." (*The Works of Joseph Addison* [New York: Harper & Brothers, 1845], II, 244.)

24 Stone points out that by the early eighteenth century, many had accepted the principle that children had the right to veto marital partners chosen for them by their parents. Defoe insists upon this principle in *Religious Courtship*. But discussions in the *Spectator* emphasize, not the power of veto, but the positive initiative of young people.

Another indication of the younger generation perspective of the *Spectator* is that behavior inappropriate to one's age is illustrated by examples of mothers and fathers who refuse to recognize they are no longer young and insist upon monopolizing the social spotlight that by nature belongs now to their grown children.

25 J. H. Plumb, "The Public, Literature, and the Arts in the Eighteenth Century," in M. R. Marrus, ed., *The Emergence of Leisure* (New York: Harper & Row, 1974), p. 18.

26 What we now refer to by various synonyms all implying "middle class" had no clear existence in Defoe's period at the beginning of the eighteenth century. Even later, according to Frank O'Gorman, "it was minutely divided and sub-divided at the level of occupational groups." (Letter to the author of Feb. 3, 1978.)

Note: All citations from Defoe's domestic conduct manuals have been taken from British Library films of the editions of the years specified in this article.

Rereading The Rape of the Lock

Pope and the Paradox of Female Power

ELLEN POLLAK

One would be hard pressed to think of a major work of English literature predating the advent of the novel that portrays its heroine as more manifest a center of its fictional universe than Pope's *Rape of the Lock*. And yet one would be equally hard pressed to find another work which so completely reifies the proposition that women are marginal beings. In the present discussion I shall analyze this seeming paradox[1] in the *Rape* between Belinda's centrality and marginality—an apparent contradiction inherent also in the fictional dominance of those three eponymous heroines of the early English novel, Moll Flanders, Pamela, and Clarissa.

Standing as it does at the threshold of those revolutions in English thought and culture that produced the novel, and embodying the dominant themes of that emergent genre though still within the framework of a traditional poetic form, Pope's symbolic fable of Belinda and the Baron seems a critical starting place for analysis of the feminocentric novel in England. Indeed, as Leo Braudy has asked in a recent study of *Clarissa*, "What connection is there between the barren Baron and the loveless Lovelace . . . ?"[2]

Pope's fictive history of a single virgin's severed hair is nothing less than emblematic of the birth of the female as a social being in eighteenth-century English culture. In it, Belinda functions as a type of Everywoman and the battle between the sylphs and gnomes as a psychomachic framework in which the drama of woman's sexual and

429

social initiation is forever reenacted. Though couched in an allusive context that calls for a "Christian Greco-Roman" readership,[3] the poem already contains the main features of that bourgeois sexual ideology which Pierre Fauchery has identified as characteristic of the early European novel.[4] Most notably, it mythologizes female destiny as a natural continuum between virginity and defloration. Writing of Richardson's *Clarissa*, Fauchery remarks on the binary relationship between virginity and rape so typically exploited in eighteenth-century prose fiction, and his observations shed an interesting retrospective light on Pope's mock-epic synthesis of classical and contemporary sexual themes:

> Rape, in the imaginary society of the century, is presented as the potential destiny of every woman; but it maintains with virginity one of those antithetical relations in which contradiction becomes attraction. Chastity attracts rape as the sacred invites defilement.[5]

One almost immediately senses the relevance of this formulation for a culture where virginity had ambiguous moral status and where singleness was scorned.[6] Both "purity" and its loss are natural and necessary phases of female life as Pope conceives it, and together they embody the truth about woman as she exists in his version of natural and social order; at base, she is impure, and any willful effort to contravene this ontological given can but incur a violent self-restitution of the axioms of female fate.

Historians of the novel commonly subscribe to what one might call a "Whig" leisure time interpretation of women's history. Conceiving of the social and economic developments of the late seventeenth and early eighteenth centuries largely teleologically, in terms of the great literary achievements produced by 1750, they tend to emphasize the benefits for women represented by increased literacy and leisure time while ignoring the more negative effects of British economic growth on the lives and status of women.

In fact, however, the rise of bourgeois culture in England meant middle-class women's rise to economic superfluity. Under the influence of expanding commercial interests, the patriarchal system of household industry in which women of the upper and middle classes had traditionally played an active and often indispensable role was undergoing a process of erosion. With movement of economic activity outside of the home and the substitution of an individual for a family wage, the earning power of English women significantly declined.[7]

At the same time, an important shift in emphasis in prevailing definitions of ideal womanhood occurred. While Elizabethan books of domestic conduct had concerned themselves seriously with women's competent performance of agricultural, industrial, and managerial tasks, the feminine conduct books that became popular in the second half of the seventeenth century were distinguished by an advocacy of purely passive female virtues.[8] As the burden of productivity fell increasingly on men, associating them predominantly with the secular world of business and work, woman became the embodiment of spiritual value, exemplifying at her best a passive (and, indeed, in the context of a prevailing Protestant ethic a paradoxically "Catholic") ideal. Married, loyal, modest, good-natured, and obliging, she was to tolerate idleness cheerfully—without *ennui*, expense, or recourse to pedantry. Properly woman was a pawn in the struggle for estate accumulation, a procreative vessel for the perpetuation of property and its heirs; and any deviance from this norm of radical self-denial was, by definition, a form of narcissism and a lack of "femininity."[9]

Polarization by gender of secular versus spiritual interests finds expression in the popular literature of the age in fictive as well as prescriptive contexts. It is reflected in the persecuted maidens of periodical fiction[10] and in the work of Mary Manley, which repeatedly exploits the myth of union between the chaste female embodiment of religious values and the amoral male aristocrat who proves her ruin—if she does not first prove his salvation.[11] The best known and most fully imagined versions of this myth are, of course, Richardson's *Pamela* and *Clarissa*; but as John Richetti's work has shown, they were by no means the first.[12] Even Moll Flanders, by the lesson of her deviance from a passive ideal of woman, functions as an emblem of its axiomatic nature.[13]

Pope's feminine ideal is embodied in *To a Lady* in his portrait of Martha Blount, whose "virtue" depends on a functional dichotomy between femaleness and femininity, according to which Martha's true charm—that is, her "femininity"—is represented not as a raw but as a mediated form of femaleness (270–80); and this same mediation of femaleness that is a *fait accompli* in Martha is given dramatic expression in the *Rape* in the chronology or "progress" of Belinda's beauty from a state of strident intactness to one of stellarized dismemberment.[14] A woman of sober beauty, like Martha, is in a sense more "natural" than Belinda, who receives canonization only after she has been "naturalized" or shorn of the emblem and the product of her art. But, paradoxically, this process of "naturalization" is at the same time the process of Belinda's "socialization" as a female—in a word, of her "femininization." And it is not insignificant that the symbolic loss of the Belle's much-coveted virginity is realized in the form of a castration or literal *cutting off* of that bodily part of her associated most strongly with those "masculine" attributes of the coquette—her power, skill, and pride.[15]

The notion of "the natural" in Pope's text is admittedly complex, since as Clarissa makes clear in her speech in Canto V, Pope's ideal of "femininity" itself involves a form of "Pow'r" and the skill to use it well (V, 29). But there is a crucial distinction to be made between Belinda's "artfulness" and that which either Martha represents or Clarissa recommends, and this distinction rests squarely on Belinda's resistance to the demands of wedlock—or, to put the matter in Clarissa's terms, on the coquette's refusal to accept with good humor the premise that loss is an inherent ("natural") feature of the female predicament (V, 30). What Clarissa is saying is that if one seeks to dominate men by coquettish rejection, one loses by dying single; and she values this loss more dearly than the loss of one's virginity, the gracious and passive yielding of which in marriage is, in her view, the stuff of woman's "virtue" and the paradoxical basis of her "gain." It is fitting, then, that the consecrated lock—which bears Belinda's name—can become a vehicle for the heroine's immortalization only *after* it has been (in this case forcibly) given up.[16]

For Belinda, the passage from girlhood to womanhood—from the simply "female" to the truly "feminine"—must involve not merely a giving up of sexual independence, but of all other forms of independence as well; her chastity is a complex metaphor for these. Her maturation is envisioned not as a coming into selfhood, but rather as an abdication of the impulse to autonomy in every aspect of existence. Pope builds the "naturalness" or inevitability of this circumstance into the very structure of reality in the *Rape*. As Wasserman has observed, Belinda may want to avoid wedlock and its concomitant subjugation of the female, but her intention is inexorably doomed; in the terms of Pope's poetic universe, her chastity is a challenge to the intrusion of reality itself.[17]

Belinda, in short, would shirk her proper function as a woman. By contrast to Pope's model of female health, she is an empty vessel laden down with a cargo of disembodied objects, and her pathology is reflected in the "hysterick" Cave of Spleen. But though Pope criticizes the sterility of a world in which the signs of things have actually become substitutes for the things themselves, where virtue has been reduced to reputation and men themselves to swordknots, where in effect people live in a materialistic and metonymic void, he never does controvert the premise that female sexuality is a material property over which man has a natural claim. The apparent contradiction between this premise and his satire on commercial values, rather, is afforded an enabling balance in his work. In the linear progression of the poem, Belinda as an image of strength and wholeness gives way to Belinda as an image of impotent disarray. But in Pope's symbolic system these two contradictory images are not so much one another's negations as they are complementary and mutually sustaining facades of Pope's objectification of the female.

At the root of the paradox of female power in Pope is the premise that female sexuality is responsible for the exercise of desire in both men and women. For, indeed, at the dramatic center of the *Rape*, where the Baron performs the action of a desiring subject—

> Th'Adventrous *Baron* the bright Locks admir'd,
> He saw, he wish'd, and to the Prize aspir'd . . .
>   (II, 29–30)

—Belinda is defined as both the object and the source of that desire:

> This Nymph, to the Destruction of Mankind,
> Nourish'd two Locks, which graceful hung behind
> In equal Curls, and well conspir'd to deck
> With shining Ringlets the smooth Iv'ry Neck,
> Love in these Labyrinths his Slaves detains,
> And mighty Hearts are held in slender Chains.
> . . . .
> Fair Tresses Man's Imperial Race insnare,
> And Beauty draws us with a single Hair.
>   (II, 19–28)

In the absence of any concept of female autonomy, Belinda's self-involvement and apparent indifference to the Baron are an automatic challenge to assault, her "ravishing" beauty a passive-aggressive inducement to revenge.[18] Though the agency of the drama is located in the Baron, its motivation is situated in her.

Belinda's status as a prime motivating force in the *Rape* is established in a variety of ways. In her glory she is likened to the sun, the bright center of attention around whom "Fair Nymphs and well-drest Youths" (II, 5) gather as mere satellites to envy and admire and over whom, saint-like, she impartially extends the benevolence of her smiles (II, 14). She is a priestess at whose altar "the various Off'rings of the World" unite (I, 130), a Goddess whose "awful Beauty" assumes a grace beyond the reach of art (I, 139). In her "mighty Rage" toward "little Men" she is compared to Juno herself, the very Queen of Heaven who drove the good Aeneas through so many toils and perils (I, 11–12). Yet even as they work to exalt Pope's heroine, these tributes to her majesty are occasions for belittlement: in the magnanimity of her gaze, she is fickle and self-centered; in her self-adoration, she performs the "Rites of Pride" (I, 128); and where Juno, likened by Virgil to a temperamental woman, has at least the fact of her Godhead to sustain the human metaphor, this toyshop belle ultimately shrinks under the invocation of divinity. In the world of the *Rape* "mighty Contests rise from trivial Things" (I, 2), whether Pope means by these temperamental women themselves or the male impertinences that manage to offend them.

The same principle of mock-heroic deflation that controls Pope's use of metaphor also determines the larger shape of his drama. For while as a center of attraction and attention in the *Rape*'s social and economic universe Belinda functions as a veritable Prime Mover, what she sets in motion is a process which involves her own subduing and subordination on almost every level. By her very mode of being she enacts a self-destruction which, though mediated by the Baron, begins and ends with her.

The reflexiveness of Belinda's rhetorical and dramatic function is best exemplified in the subtle process by which the female passes from subject to object in the *Rape*. Portrayed as an essential subject, or Logos, a maker of worlds with the power to command trumps (III, 46) as well as smiles (II, 52), indeed whose own smile commands the world, Belinda is a gravitational force about whom all the gay universe revolves. But this subjective identity is no sooner asserted than it is exposed as a bogus identity and the very synecdochic power by which Belinda as creative force becomes a symbol for all creation transforms her from an original to a generated term in a grammar of motives where man is always the subject. As a "Vessel" (II, 47) carrying all the "glitt'ring Spoil" (I, 132) of the world, she herself is identified with that world and, like nature, is to be conquered, ransacked, and possessed by commercial man. Like the sunbeams that tremble jewel-like on London's "floating Tydes" (II, 48), she shines with "Glories" on "the Bosom of the Silver *Thames*" (II, 4) and wears a "sparkling *Cross*" on her own bosom, at once the bearer of ornament and an ornament herself (II, 7). Decked "with all that Land and Sea afford" (V, 11), she is both the trophy of men's exploits and their manikin, a compulsive consumer who not only receives but testifies to British national wealth.

In short, Belinda's narcissism, while satirized according to propriety as unfeminine and subversive, is also glorified as keeping commerce in motion. As Louis Landa's analysis of the "lady of quality" in terms of economic attitudes of the age suggests, Belinda as coquette occupies as basic and indispensable a place in the providential order assumed by mercantile rationalism as ever Martha Blount did in her role as domestic ideal.[19] The belle's vain indulgences at the mirror of her toilette, as Pope only half-ironically asserts, are her form of idle "Labours" (III, 24) in a vision of society where female self-involvement is ultimately justified and, in the process, robbed of independent force by being brought into line with male economic needs. Woman's display of beauty is identified with man's display of booty, her enslavement of and ultimate triumph over man through her powers of attraction with his blissful "living Death" (V, 61,68). While according to rational analysis Pope's coquette is a "masculinized" female, by symbolic accretion she is a complex manifestation of male prowess itself—its inspiration, its conquered object, its result.

Of all the works regarded by the modern critical establishment as classics of English poetry, Pope's *Rape of the Lock* is perhaps the most liberal in its use of that synecdochic principle by which a part is made to stand for the whole. In it, woman—whom it defines as a mere appendage to man, her world a mere corner of his—represents the whole world in what amounts to a large-scale repetition of that more basic equation by which Belinda's lock, the symbol of her chastity, becomes a proxy for Belinda herself, what Kenneth Burke would call a "fetishistic surrogate" for the whole woman.[20] Now the equation by which Belinda's lock equals her chastity provides a crucial cross-link in this ever-expanding spiral of synecdoche between Pope's criticism of the sterile "fetishism" of the *beau monde* on the one hand and his positive assertion of a normative ideal of woman on the other. For if, as Pope portrays it, female chastity (that is, sexuality) is something over which man has a rightful claim, then the lock must, by association, be understood at least transiently as a common property of Belinda and the Baron. Moreover, just as this part of her which is all of her is really part of him (and here the notion of the lock as phallus is relevant), so in "wedlock" (the term is never actually used in the poem and yet it functions as a silent pun throughout) the good wife is the rightful possession of her husband and a natural extension of him.[21]

In fact, throughout the *Rape* Pope is engaging in extended play on the notion, already conventional in his day but to which his own work gave new force, that woman's entire value is tied up with her identity as a piece of property transferable among men. In *Tatler* no. 199, Steele expressed consternation over the materialism of his age in much the same spirit that Pope's *Rape* portrays the displaced values of a world that sets more stock in appearances than realities, where the fall of a china jar is given the same weight as the loss of a lady's honor. Palamede has deceived Caelia into a bigamous union which has "ruined" her, and Bickerstaff reflects:

> It seems a wonderful inconsistence in the distribution of public jus-
> tice, that a man who robs a woman of an ear-ring or a jewel, should
> be punished with death; but one, who by false arts and insinuations
> should take from her, her very self, is only to suffer disgrace.[22]

While the *Tatler*'s reference to Palamede's crime as the theft of a woman's "very self" would seem to underscore the enormity of his offense, actually it depends on a trivialization of the intrinsic offen- siveness of the act. For while Bickerstaff condemns a hierarchy of values that sets a piece of jewelry above a woman's bodily and emo- tional integrity, he nonetheless manages to speak of female chastity not only as a synecdochic substitute for a woman's whole self but also as a precious piece of property. Similarly in Pope, where seduc- tion and ravishment ("Fraud" and "Force" [II, 34]) are viewed as in- terchangeable means to a single possessive end, rape—in fact a form of bodily assault—is reduced through the metaphor of Belinda's sto- len lock to a form of petty larceny.

Ultimately, by placing woman in the same category as her jewels, Pope collapses the distinction between female self-display and the condition of being displayed by another. Thalestris balks at the rape on precisely these grounds. Do Belinda's effort, art, and endurance exist only for the sake of being appropriated as tokens of male enter- prise?

> Was it for this you took such constant Care
> The *Bodkin, Comb,* and *Essence* to prepare;
> For this your Locks in Paper-Durance bound,
> For this with tort'ring Irons wreath'd around?
> For this with Fillets strain'd your tender Head,
> And bravely bore the double Loads of Lead?
> Gods! shall the Ravisher display your Hair,
> While the Fops envy, and the Ladies stare!
> (IV, 97–104)

For Thalestris these questions are rhetorical and their implied answer is consistently "Certainly not!" Indeed, through a pun on the term "Head," Pope treats Belinda's cosmetic arts, as he did in Canto I, as Beauty's Arms—a kind of chastity belt designed to protect Belinda *from* not *for* the Baron. The coquette's conscious intention has never been to relinquish her place in the sun to him. In terms of the unwinding of Belinda's built-in destiny as a woman, however, the answer to Thalestris' question is flatly "Yes." To shine for man's sake— or to reflect his light—is woman's trial on earth, and Pope has designed his heroine to symbolize this fact. As Steele said in terms which resonate with the imagery of the *Rape*, when women

> place their Ambition on Circumstances wherein to excell, 'tis no addition to what is truly Commendable. Where can this end, but as it frequently does in their placing all their Industry, Pleasure, and Ambition on things, which will naturally make the Gratifications of Life last, at best no longer than Youth and a good Fortune? . . . But when they consider themselves, as they ought, no other than an additional Part of the Species, (for their own Happiness and Comfort, as well as that of those for whom they were born) their Ambition to excell will be directed accordingly; and they will in no part of their Lives want Opportunities of being Shining Ornaments to their Fathers, Husbands, Brothers or Children.[23]

But the concept of display works on another level besides the literal one involving the question of who will wear Belinda's lock. It also works on a figurative level strongly suggested by the language of the second part of Thalestris' indignant peroration:

> *Honour* forbid! at whose unrival'd Shrine
> Ease, Pleasure, Virtue, All, our Sex resign
> Methinks already I your Tears survey,
> Already hear the horrid Things they say,
> Already see you a degraded Toast,
> And all your Honour in a Whisper lost!
> How shall I, then, your helpless Fame defend?
> 'Twill then be Infamy to seem your Friend!
> And shall this Prize, th'inestimable Prize,
> Expos'd thro' Crystal to the gazing Eyes,
> And heighten'd by the Diamond's circling Rays,
> On that Rapacious Hand for ever blaze?
> (IV, 105–16)

Pope is using Thalestris to mock the gay world's regard for honorable appearances over true virtue, but he is also constructing a genital image in the last lines of her speech, which suggests an important link implict throughout the *Rape* between the concept of display and the sexual act itself.[24] Perceived in terms of its sexual subsurface, the poem's central dramatic struggle over who displays the lock can be read as an elaborate camouflage for the submerged but stubborn question of which gender properly initiates sexual intercourse.[25]

Images of display and sexual activity converge for Pope in the verb "to spread." The term is used a total of eight times in the entire poem, and all of these instances significantly occur in Cantos III and IV with a definite concentration of usage in and around the actual description of the cutting of the lock. In Belinda we find the link between "spreading" and "display" in the ornithographic allusion contained in the term "coquette," which derives its meaning from the strutting and displaying habits of the cock. Images of spreading fans, plumes and hands, moreover, recur throughout the poem in the sylphs' "careful Plumes display'd" over Belinda's lap (III, 115), Thalestris' spread hands (IV, 95), Belinda's spread cards (III, 31), and the Baron's triumphantly spread fingers with the sacred lock upon them (IV, 139–40).[26]

In Pope's description of the game of Ombre, the Queen of Spades—otherwise known, the Appendix tells us, as "the Queen of Swords"—"invades" Belinda's King of Clubs, who is described as having "Giant Limbs in State unwieldy spread" (III, 65–72).[27] The episode is important because, while it embodies in microcosm a reversal of gender traits that operates throughout the *Rape*,[28] it quite visibly sets that reversal within a corrective context. It is the Baron, after all, who both possesses and plays the aggressor card that threatens to conquer Belinda; and, indeed, his Queen seems to function as a mirror-image of that other "warlike Amazon," Belinda herself, who in the broader drama enacts her own defeat while unconsciously inviting the Baron's triumph.

Thus, although Belinda's victory at cards is a transient fulfillment of her subversively "masculine" power, it also manages to foreshadow the maiden's final defeat and does so in terms which covertly allude to the specifically sexual form that defeat will take. The "livid Paleness" that "spreads o'er all her Look" (III, 90) not only contains a clue to this sexualized interpretation in its use of the familiar key verb, but as Rudat's study of the poem's allusive context would suggest, it intends a silent association between the "approaching Ill" of the lock's removal and the loss of Belinda's "virgin blood."[29]

> At this, the Blood the Virgin's Cheek forsook,
> A livid Paleness spreads o'er all her Look;
> She sees, and trembles at th'approaching Ill,
> Just in the Jaws of Ruin, and *Codille*.
>
> (III, 89–92)

But the verb "to spread" continues to multiply, appearing again thirty-two lines later in connection with the "fatal" shears that clip the lock. Clarissa, it will be remembered, has bestowed the "two-edg'd Weapon" on the Baron:

> So Ladies in Romance assist their Knight,
> Present the Spear, and arm him for the Fight.
> He takes the Gift with rev'rence, and extends
> The little Engine on his Finger's Ends,
> This just behind *Belinda*'s Neck he spread,
> As o'er the Fragrant Steams she bends her Head.
>
> (III, 129–34)

Given Pope's passing comparison of the scissors to "a Spear" as well as the fact that the Baron wears them on his fingers (where he later wears the phallic lock), it is difficult to resist an association with Fanny Hill's frequent references to the male genital as an "engine" or "machine." Still, in Pope's version of the phallic sword, male and female symbolism seem curiously and significantly combined. Indeed, in the very next stanza the Baron's "little Engine" is described as a "glitt'ring *Forfex*" whose wide-spread stance is distinctly suggestive of female anatomy:

> The Peer now spreads the glitt'ring *Forfex* wide,
> T'inclose the Lock: now joins it, to divide.
>
> (III, 147–48)

The most likely inference to make regarding the intertwining of sexual metaphors in the image of the scissors is that Pope means to symbolize the coming together of man and woman in sexual union. But it seems worthy of special notice that male and female involvement in sexual activity as Pope portrays it at this central point in his poem are *both* under the agency of the Baron; as Pope insinuates later by his ambiguous reference to the Baron's "Steel" as "unresisted" (III, 178), Belinda's tacit cooperation is entirely passive.

As activator of the scissors, in short, the Baron is the subject of the verb "to spread," which on the level of the poem's sexual symbolism suggests an appropriation of female sexuality on the part of the male not unlike the male appropriation of female self-display we observed earlier. Indeed, the complex link between display and sexuality reasserts itself at the moment of the rape in Pope's sudden and arresting allusion to the Baron as "Peer" in a line plainly suggestive of male voyeurism.[30]

Pope's division of the functions of motivation and agency between Belinda and the Baron is thus brilliantly carried through his poem down to the very description of the gesture by which the lock is cut. Designed to mimic the motion of sex, this description embodies two complementary assertions of fact: (1) that spreading and enclosure take place simultaneously in sex and (2) that a closed position is accompanied by the division of sexual partners. But Pope's description of the cutting of the lock has an even broader inclusiveness than this in its yoking of the principles of joining and division. For it not only recalls Belinda's distant, rejecting—in a word, closed—attitude toward men, but it reasserts the motivational connection between that evasiveness and the ultimate consummation of the rape. In one and the same conceit, two joining-separations are contained: the literal severing of the lock, which *is* consummation itself, and the identification of this consummation with the female aloofness that motivates it. In short, through the highly sophisticated use of a couplet counterpoint which itself seems to mimic a scissor motion, the evasion and completion of sex are brought into congruence with one another just as the *Rape* as a whole attempts to fashion a congruence between Belinda's far-ranging "influence" and the Baron's assault upon her.

Pope, thus, may create a metaphorical framework in which Belinda is an all-pervasive force, a prime mover and a symbol for the world; but it is the concrete specificity of the Baron's literal deed that we find at the true heart of this poem and the structure and syntax of which determine everything around it. In so far as "spreading" behavior is engaged in by Belinda for her own sake, it is condemned as an arrogation of masculinity. In so far as such behavior is contained within the broader context of male display and male spreading, however, it is legitimized. By virtue of anatomical fact, Pope's key verb may be inexorably gender-related, but at the hub of his poem he resolutely establishes a syntax in which woman is not its proper subject, but its object.

NOTES

1 By Cleanth Brooks's criteria ("The Case of Miss Arabella Fermor," in *The Well Wrought Urn* [New York: Harcourt Brace Jovanovich, 1947], pp. 80–104), it is a paradox which reflects the "both/and" quality of Pope's art, his supple and accommodating breadth of mind—what Maynard Mack identifies as the two-way-lookingness of Pope's mock-epic form ("'Wit and Poetry and Pope': Some Observations on his Imagery," in *Pope and his Contemporaries: Essays Presented to George Sherburn* [Oxford: Clarendon Press, 1949], pp. 20–40). By contrast, I shall argue that the paradox is ideologically consistent; that, in effect, it functions as a rhetorical vehicle for an essentially univocal statement about women.

2 "Penetration and Impenetrability in *Clarissa*," in [John] Phillip Harth, ed., *New Approaches to Eighteenth-Century Literature* (New York: Columbia University Press, 1974), p. 177.

3 Earl Wasserman, "The Limits of Allusion in *The Rape of the Lock*," *Journal of English and Germanic Philology*, 65 (1966), 426.

4 Pierre Fauchery, *La Destinée féminine dans le roman européen du dix-huitième siècle 1713–1807: Essai de gynécomythie romanesque* (Paris: Armand Colin, 1972).

5 Translated and quoted by Nancy Miller in "The Exquisite Cadavers: Women in Eighteenth-Century Fiction," *Diacritics*, 5, no. 4 (Winter 1975), p. 39. Miller's excellent review article is useful for its summary of Fauchery's arguments, its translations of portions of his text, and its critique of his conclusions.

6 See William Haller, "'Hail Wedded Love,'" *ELH*, 13 (June 1946), 81, and Ian Watt, *The Rise of the Novel: Studies in Defoe, Richardson and Fielding* (Berkeley: University of California Press, 1957), p. 145.

7 Alice Clark, *Working Life of Women in the Seventeenth Century* (London: George Routledge & Sons, 1919; rpt. New York: Augustus M. Kelley, 1968). In her review article "'Women's History' in Transition: The European Case," *Feminist Studies*, 3 (Spring-Summer 1976), 83–103, Natalie Zemon Davis offers a useful critique on Clark, attempting to balance the book's basic strengths against its inevitable limitations given its early publication date, its Fabian bias, and its status as a ground-breaking work in the economic history of women. Davis' suggestions for revising Clark—a process which has only just begun—should be of interest to anyone seeking a more detailed analysis of the history of women in early modern Europe. Nonetheless, Clark emerges from Davis' scrutiny as essentially sound and still the best existing work on the subject to date.

8 See, for example, [Richard Allestree], *The Ladies Calling* (London, 1673), and George Savile, Marquis of Halifax, *The Lady's New-Years Gift; or, Advice to a Daughter* (London, 1688).

9 Such seventeenth-century changes in property law as the strict settlement, a legal device which enabled landowners not only to project plans

for their estates onto future generations but also to entail all their property in each generation on a single heir, helped to exacerbate the damaging effects of bastardy on the lineal descent of family wealth and thus contributed to an intensification of social anxiety over the conjugal chastity of woman. See H. J. Habakkuk, "Marriage Settlements in the Eighteenth Century," *Transactions of the Royal Historical Society*, 4th series, 32 (1950), 15–30.

10 See, for example, *The Tatler*, nos. 45 and 198.

11 Manley's most notable piece was her scandal novel *Secret Memoirs and Manners of Several Persons of Quality of Both Sexes: From the New Atalantis, an Island in the Mediterranean* (1709–10), more commonly known as *The New Atalantis*.

12 *Popular Fiction Before Richardson: Narrative Patterns 1700–1739* (Oxford: Clarendon Press, 1969).

13 Miriam Lerenbaum comments on Moll's underlying passivity in "Moll Flanders: A Woman on her own Account," in Arlyn Diamond and Lee R. Edwards, eds., *The Authority of Experience: Essays in Feminist Criticism* (Amherst: University of Massachusetts Press, 1977), pp. 101–17. See also Nancy Miller's chapter on *Moll Flanders* in *The Heroine's Text: Readings in the French and English Novel 1722–1782* (New York: Columbia University Press, forthcoming 1980).

14 All references to Pope's poems, cited by line number in the text, are to *The Twickenham Edition of the Poems of Alexander Pope*, gen. ed. John Butt (New Haven: Yale University Press; London: Methuen, 1939–61), vols. II and III, ii.

15 One thinks of Samson here. Stanley Edgar Hyman also refers to Belinda's "rape" as a ritual initiation in "The Rape of the Lock," *Hudson Review*, 13 (1960), 411.

16 Clarissa's speech is of unequivocal importance in any reading of the *Rape*, but the confines of space prevent me from offering a full explication of it here. I deal with this subject in another context, where I rely heavily on John Trimble's analysis of Clarissa as at once a mouthpiece for Pope and (as an envious prude competing with Belinda for the Baron's favors) yet another object of satiric diminution ("Clarissa's Role in *The Rape of the Lock*," *Texas Studies in Literature and Language*, 15 [1947], 673–91). Pope, I argue, not only exploits a tautological view of female virtue in this speech but at the same time uses the convention of female rivalry as a strategy for enabling the recurrent deflation of female power ("Perspectives on a Myth: Women in the Verse of Swift and Pope," Diss. Columbia University, 1979, ch. 9).

17 Wasserman, pp. 436, 438.

18 For an interesting commentary on the idea of a woman's beauty "ravishing" a man, see Susan Gubar, "The Female Monster in Augustan Satire," *Signs: Journal of Women in Culture and Society*, 3, no. 2 (1978), 387. For my response to Gubar's article (which contains portions of the present essay),

see ibid., no. 3 (Spring 1978), 728–32. Judith Wilt's discussion of the lexical relationship between "ravishment" and "rape" in "He Could Go No Farther: A Modest Proposal about Lovelace and Clarissa," *PMLA*, 92 (1977), 19–20, is also of interest in this connection.

19 "Of Silkworms and Farthingales and the Will of God," in R. F. Brissenden, ed., *Studies in the Eighteenth Century* (Toronto: University of Toronto, 1973), II, 259–77, and "Pope's Belinda, the General Emporie of the World, and the Wondrous Worm," *South Atlantic Quarterly*, 70 (Spring 1971), 215–35.

20 *The Philosophy of Literary Form*, 2nd ed. (Baton Rouge: Louisiana State University Press, 1967), p. 30. Jeffrey Meyers actually analyzes the Baron as a fetishist in "The Personality of Belinda's Baron: Pope's 'The Rape of the Lock,'" *American Imago*, 26 (1969), 71–77. See also on the subject of fetishism Peggy Kamuf, "Inside Julie's Closet," *The Romanic Review*, 69, no. 4 (Nov. 1978), 296–306. This fascinating study of the fetish as it functions in Rousseau has striking implications for the analysis of other eighteenth-century texts.

21 The latent notion of Belinda as phallus is an interesting correlate to the popular Freudian notion, extrapolated from analyses of Victorian femininity, that the child is the symbolic phallus of the woman. According to the latter notion, it is the child, in effect, which makes a woman "feminine" in terms of "normal" psychosexual development. As the fulfillment of her womanhood, it bestows on her the power appropriate to her sphere. By the same token, it is the woman that makes a man "masculine" according to what Elizabeth Janeway, in *Man's World, Woman's Place: A Study in Social Mythology* (New York: William Morrow, 1971), calls the "regular, orthodox bargain by which men run the world and allow women to rule in their own place" (p. 56): "What [a woman] is offered," writes Janeway, "is the knowledge that by her submission she does what the man cannot do alone: she bestows on him his full status. Her submission makes him a man" (p. 48).

22 A. Chalmers, ed., *British Essayists* (New York, 1809), IV, 283.

23 *Spectator*, no 342 (Bond ed., III, 272).

24 The link is already evident in Thalestris' earlier lines quoted above—"For this with Fillets strain'd your tender Head, / And bravely bore the double Loads of Lead?" For, through yet another interpretation of his pun on "Head" here, Pope effects an identification of chastity's arms with their nemesis. As he fashions it, Belinda's putting on of armor is a version of self-torture—not only metaphorically but also because, indirectly, it is her beauty that instigates her "rape." As the couplet suggests, the coquette's strength must always, inescapably, embody her suffering of sexual assault.

25 Wolfgang Rudat, who has studied this subsurface in terms of the *Rape*'s allusive context in "Belinda's 'Painted Vessel': Allusive Technique in *The Rape of the Lock*," *Tennessee Studies in Literature*, 19 (1974), 49–55, actually

discovers an etymological basis for Pope's use of container-ship imagery as vaginal symbols. Rudat sees the "painted Vessel" that competes with the sun in Pope as part of a parody of Shakespeare's passage on Cleopatra's barge that burns on the water. Here the lock—like a ship, another symbol for Belinda's genitals—blazes like a sun and an ornament on the Baron's fingers. Rudat's findings are illuminating, but his conclusion that Pope's sexual symbolism is evidence of the "exuberance" of the eighteenth century seems to me an unfortunate judgment. Pope's implicit trivialization of rape and his portrayal of woman as its victim-aggressor seem precarious grounds on which to base his age's exuberance. In the present essay I intend an alternative analysis of Pope's sexual imagery.

26 It is of incidental interest that the verb "to splay," meaning "to spread or extend," derives from the word "display."

27 For descriptions of these cards, see Appendix C to the Twickenham *Rape*, pp. 391–92.

28 See Ralph Cohen, "The Reversal of Gender in 'The Rape of The Lock,'" *South Atlantic Bulletin*, 37, no. 4 (1972), 54–60.

29 Rudat, pp. 53–55.

30 In "Rousseau's Politics of Visibility" (*Diacritics*, 5, no. 4 [Winter 1975]) Peggy Kamuf translates Luce Irigaray's remarks on the importance of visual knowledge of genital discrepancies in Freud's work. A "phallomorphic sexual metaphoricity," writes Irigaray in *Speculum de l'autre femme* (Paris: Editions de Minuit, 1974), is the "reassuring accomplice" to "an over-investment in the eye, in an appropriation by the look." In her analysis of Rousseau, Kamuf establishes a link between the act of sex and the act of self-signification through language (i.e., self-representation) which parallels the link between sex and self-display in Pope. "As non-power, non-presence," she writes, "the feminine cannot pretend to a sign of transparent presence. There is *literally* no place for this absence, no manner for that lack to signify itself with a sign of plenitude. The feminine, in order to show itself, must usurp some other signifier, must find its presence in the absence of the other" (p. 54).

Changing Affective Life
in Eighteenth-Century England
and Samuel Richardson's Pamela

JUDITH LAURENCE-ANDERSON

For literary critics and many readers, a problem with England's first novel, Samuel Richardson's *Pamela* (1740), has always been understanding how any sensitive, religious woman could possibly marry a man who has been constantly abusive to her, both verbally and physically, who has kidnapped her and held her prisoner, and who has even tried to rape her on two occasions. We have to wait for *Clarissa* (1747–48) to receive an acceptable moral answer. On a psychological level, however, research into social history is steadily furnishing us with increasing insights about how much the emotional lives of our ancestors differed from our own. These insights, I believe, go a long way toward explaining, if not justifying, the conduct of both Pamela and Mr. B. The new realization that domestics played a very important role in the social structure of the past,[1] with as much as 40 percent of the population having been servants during adolescence, further aids our understanding of this novel. By choosing a young female servant as his single correspondent, Richardson could contrast earlier, more brutal attitudes toward women, children, and domestics with the new desire for companionate love and the respect for individual rights which were emerging in England at this time. Richardson's psychological intuition, moreover, led him to dramatize conflicts in sexual relationships which our society still has not fully resolved. For these reasons, *Pamela* records with psychological accuracy what it was like to be a young female domestic in the eighteenth century, and only when we fully understand the psychological tensions her experiences would have created can we ask why any sensitive, religious woman would marry a man who has tried to rape her twice.

Apart from the novel's obvious fairy-tale ending, there are many problems involved in the transfer from literature to social history.[2] No matter what amount of historical data is unearthed to get a glimpse of a real eighteenth-century Pamela, she still remains, after all, a literary character. With a novelist such as Richardson there are further problems; one must constantly explore not only what he deliberately set out to do, but also his unconscious intentions and his fantasy life.[3] This enmeshes the reader in a whole network of assumptions not only about Richardson but about his readers in the past and his readers today. In spite of these pitfalls, recent scholarly speculations about life in the eighteenth century are invaluable tools for the literary critic. Keeping in mind, therefore, that whatever I am going to say is problematic at best, I would like to hazard certain conjectures about changing emotional life in England in the eighteenth century and Richardson's *Pamela*.

To begin, most critics agree that *Pamela* reflects the growing individualism of eighteenth-century England. More recently, social historians have claimed that major changes in the quality of family relationships also occurred at this time, probably earlier in England than in other countries.[4]

Put very simply, their essential point is that love for one's spouse and one's children, as we think of it, has by no means been a historical absolute, but rather is a relatively new phenomenon in western culture, of the last two or three centuries. Before that, as we have learned, individuals tended to diffuse their emotional loyalties to a large group of relatives, kin, and neighbors rather than concentrate them on what is today called "the nuclear family."[5] Put another way, persons before the eighteenth century usually would not permit themselves to become too emotionally attached to single individuals, since death was all too frequent, and necessary psychic health required horizontal rather than vertical investment of affections. This meant that if a spouse or child died, they could more easily be replaced in one's emotional life. In certain ways, this parallels the description by Bruno Bettelheim, in *Children of the Dream*, of what happens in the emotional life of children raised in *kibbutzim*. Instead of concentrating on their parents, their emotions are diffused and less intense, with the peer group playing a particularly important role in establishing and maintaining community values. For persons in earlier history, we can substitute for the kibbutz's peer group the whole network of extended family, kin, and village neighbors. In both cases, child-rearing practices differing markedly from our own help or helped to create a personality less prone to intense emotional attachment to single individuals.

Three major practices employed in England before the eighteenth century helped to create this type of personality: widespread use of wet nurses; early separation from the parents when children were between ten and fourteen; and deliberate harshness to break the child's will, because of widespread belief in the devil and the child's intrinsically evil nature. As a result, children in the past were much less emotionally dependent upon their parents than so many middle-class children are in today's western society.

For many reasons, changes in attitudes toward human relationships, particularly domestic ones, took place in England at the end of the seventeenth century. One major impetus for this was the breakdown in religious orthodoxy, which eventually enabled many to view physical pleasure as a positive good rather than a possible path to eternal damnation. The breakdown in religious orthodoxy also changed attitudes toward human nature, at least in the upper classes, so that the child was no longer viewed as born evil, but rather, as Locke put it, as a *tabula rasa*, to receive impressions under careful parental guidance. The belief that children must be treated harshly remained fairly constant, however, in the lower classes. Calvin had decreed the death penalty for disobedient children, and several New England colonies actually had such laws on the books. We see the same harshness continuing in eighteenth- and nineteenth-century evangelical teaching. Wesley's teachings approve extreme physical severity to very young children. His own mother, incidentally, had begun beating her children when they were one year old to stop them from crying.[6]

Locke of course exerted the most profound influence on changing pedagogical thought in England in the eighteenth century, and most of Samuel Richardson's writing on education in his novels is drawn directly from Locke. Besides discussing at length Locke's theories in the sequel to *Pamela*, the heroine also explains in detail her reasons for opposing Mr. B.'s wish that the child be sent to a wet nurse. Pamela's wish to nurse her own baby reflects the intimacy between mother and infant openly coming into existence as reduced infant mortality made it less threatening to invest emotions in the new-born. Richardson, on the other hand, disapproves of the new leni-ency in child-rearing, and presents in all of his novels portrait after portrait of spoiled, strong-willed children whose actions as adults bring pain and sometimes destruction to others. In *Pamela*, Mr. B., his sister Lady Davers, and her nephew Jackie are all variants of this type.

Concomitant political thought in the eighteenth century, with its emphasis on individual rights, made abuses of authority once taken for granted now objectionable, and this ultimately led to changes in the basic social unit—the family. Since physical pleasure was no longer sinful, the general pursuit of happiness as a legitimate life goal became more acceptable, with domestic affection seen more and more as a primary mode of achieving such happiness. This gave pres-tige to sex, marriage, and the family as literary topics in the emerging novel, where they have remained dominant ever since.

Let us go back to *Pamela*. The book was intended as a fictional con-duct book for eighteenth-century servant women, but it actually re-cords in many ways aspects of the changing affective life we have been talking about. The first aspect I would like to discuss is that of changes taking place in the master-servant relationship. I do not have to point out that most masters did not marry the pretty servant girls they lusted after. But more to the point in understanding the psycho-logical tensions a real Pamela would have experienced is the fact that domestic service was going through a transitional period at this time. In the past, the master-servant relationship had been basically a fa-milial one. But in the eighteenth century, it was beginning to become the contractual relationship it has become today.[7] Because of this tran-sitional nature of domestic service, the employing class saw emerg-ing changes in older attitudes as threatening, and used a variety of propaganda methods, such as conduct manuals and sermons, to keep alive the earlier view of the relationship as a familial one. The moral dicta of the period keep stressing the parent-child nature of domestic service, with the parental employer viewed as responsible for the spiritual lives of his or her employees.[8] Servants, in turn, were continually urged to pay childlike obedience to their employers.[9] The parental role inculcated permitted physical punishment regardless of age or sex.[10]

Examining Pamela's position in the B. household, we see many elements of this earlier familial pattern.[11] To begin with, in keeping with the practice of sending children away from home very early, Pamela has been sent out to service before puberty, and has been raised by Lady B., who becomes a kindly surrogate mother. Lady B. makes an eligible companion of Pamela by teaching her all the arts of a gentlewoman, which would have been fine needlework, dancing, drawing, and deportment. Pamela is luckier than many eighteenth-century women in that Lady B. also teaches her how to read, write, and "cast accounts."

When the novel opens, though, Lady B. has died, leaving the fifteen-year old Pamela a bereft child, with all of the moral advice of her world encouraging her to look on her new master, Mr. B., as a father figure, a role which he eagerly adopts from the very first letter. The beginning of *Pamela*, however, also suggests more threatening aspects of the master-servant relationship for young women, which eighteenth-century readers would have spotted. B. tells Pamela he wants her to stay on to "take care of his linen," a particularly hazardous duty since it involved going alone to the man's bedroom. Similarly, the eighteenth-century Virginian William Byrd, while on a visit to England, casually records in his diary payments of two guineas to his first mistress, a Mrs. Alec, to make his shirts and ruffles and also to sleep with him; even after he had tired of her, he writes occasionally of having intercourse with her when she would bring his linen to his room.[12]

As is well known, the female servant was the primary sexual object before the twentieth century. In *Thinking About Women*, Mary Ellmann attributes the high incidence of variations on the master-servant relationship in novels such as *Moll Flanders*, *Pamela*, and *Jane Eyre* to the reality that female domestics, who constituted the largest occupational group for women until the twentieth century, were the most readily available sexual object in English society.[13] Female domestics were without economic and legal power. The psychological emphasis, moreover, on obedience to masters made them a very desirable combination of childlike obedience, sexual maturity, and minimal demand.

We need only glance at some diary entries to see how common was the abuse of female servants. For example, Robert Hooke, the scientific virtuoso, inventor, and architect, who never married, records from 1672 to 1680 how female servants were his primary sexual objects. From 1672 until 1673, he slept with his maid and seamstress Nell, even having intercourse with her two days after her marriage before she left to live in her own home. In October, he hired another maid named Doll, whom he forced to sleep with him, but she lasted only until March. Throughout June and July, he "wrestled," as he phrases it, with his next maid Bette, who did not give in until the end of July. Evidently her compliance was not altogether satisfactory, since he dismissed her in August for what he called "laziness."[14]

Because access to female domestics was so easy, a profligate such as Boswell, disregarding his continual bouts of gonorrhoea, nevertheless ranked common prostitutes above domestics as desirable sexual objects. Yet in spite of its extremely low moral reputation, domestic work was eagerly sought after by eighteenth-century women. Pamela's position as a lady's maid was the highest in the female servant hierarchy, assuring her of a relatively easy life if she worked in a household which employed many servants. As the Enclosure Acts and declining cottage industry drove more and more people off the land, throngs of young women flocked to growing urban areas, primarily London. Although work in the most menial positions was probably always available—as dishwashing is today—employment in decent working conditions became more and more difficult for women to secure in the eighteenth century. The rate of unemployment for women in London was the highest in the country,[15] and many women, unwilling to steal or become prostitutes, ended by starving or committing suicide. Henry Fielding, in one issue of the *Covent Garden Journal*, notes that suicides among the poor were more frequent for women than men.[16]

The high rate of unemployment for women in London enabled unscrupulous officials of registries, the eighteenth-century equivalent of our employment agencies, to send unknowing young victims to brothels. In the first scene of Hogarth's *The Harlot's Progress*, we see a bawd from a registry in the background as the notorious Colonel Charteris eyes young Moll Hackabout. *The Newgate Calendar* relates how Charteris would also employ his bawds to go directly to London Inns as wagons would arrive from the country loaded with young women hoping to find employment in domestic service.[17] Several Richardson scholars, by the way, mention Charteris as a possible model for Mr. B.[18]

Another problem created for young women by the industrial revolution in eighteenth-century England was the breakdown of village pressures on young men to marry the woman they had impregnated. The high illegitimacy rates Edward Shorter documents[19] indicate the much greater vulnerability young female workers in cities faced once they were removed from the familial structure of a close village network which had protected them in earlier times. Joan Scott and Louise Tilly refute Shorter's contention that these high illegitimacy rates during the industrial revolution represent changing sexual values for both sexes. Instead they argue that the older values still operated for women, but in circumstances where there was no way to enforce promises of marriage as there had been in the rural communities from which the majority of young female workers came. Instead, the loneliness and isolation these young women experienced encouraged them to form illicit liaisons, but the pressures on women in domestic service—the field most rural women entered—to remain unmarried forced many of them to abandon their illegitimate children.[20]

In many ways, this movement to the city ultimately led to more self-seeking attitudes and greater individualism, and we see in Pamela a young woman trying to combine earlier loyalty to familial values with the cautious self-reliance necessary for her survival. Critics of her so-called "calculations" and inordinate concern for physical chastity fail to recognize that for the Pamelas of the eighteenth century wary protection of their "virtue" literally meant economic survival, for pregnancy meant immediate dismissal without a letter of recommendation, or Character as it was then called. Pamela fears that B. will prevent his housekeeper, Mrs. Jervis, from giving her a good Character,[21] without which further decent employment would be very difficult to find. Prostitution was one of the few occupations in which an eighteenth-century woman could earn enough to live on, and Theresa McBride, in her research on French domestics, notes in one study how a majority of women who became prostitutes had been maids seduced by their employers and then dismissed when they had become pregnant.[22]

Besides the life of prostitution and crime Defoe's Moll Flanders resorted to, the few respectable occupations which would have been open to Pamela were needlework at home for a pittance, which Jane Austen's Mrs. Smith in *Persuasion* does to support herself, or else agricultural work. Pamela considers doing both, with the strong possibility of becoming a dairymaid—an occupation which, contrary to pastoral literary images, was actually one of the most arduous and unhealthy female jobs of the period.[23] Thus Pamela's willingness to become a dairymaid rather than submit to B. is no sign of romantic naiveté, but rather an indication to eighteenth-century readers of her extreme courage, something we may overlook in our tendency to idealize preindustrial rural life.

Richardson, in fact, as a self-made London printer who had lived close to its brutal underworld most of his life,[24] would have been very familiar with the problems of these poor, displaced countrywomen and, in writing *Pamela*, sought to create a self-help conduct manual to relieve their plight. In his manual, he stresses the ultimate need to rely on God through Pamela's refusal to commit suicide at the pond episode. Pamela's refusal to commit the crime Fielding noted as increasing among poor women was intended by the conventionally religious Richardson as the highpoint of the novel.

But as we said earlier, in analyzing literature as social history, one must consider not only an author's conscious intention, but also what he or she has created unconsciously. In this area, Richardson's psychological genius, which Samuel Johnson recognized immediately, led him to a deep understanding of the sexual and emotional tensions a young adolescent servant girl would actually experience in Pamela's situation.

We cannot be certain that a fifteen-year-old working-class woman in the eighteenth century would have achieved sexual maturation.[25] But if we grant that the relatively easy work load as a lady's maid and a good diet permitted Pamela to reach menarche, then at this crucial moment of sexual awakening, when she moreover has just lost a loving surrogate mother, she would be extremely susceptible to forming an emotional attachment to Mr. B. We have already noted encouragement for servants to view their employers as family. We have also considered the desperate poverty Pamela must return to if she leaves. A further point to note is that adolescents of the period were encouraged to try to gain favor with a potentially hostile adult world by acquiring as many pleasing ways as possible.[26] For all of these reasons, Richardson is able at the very outset to establish B. as a powerfully seductive father figure, capable of replacing the loving mother Pamela has just lost, and able to save her from the destitution she fears. B.'s selection of her to care for his linen, as we have mentioned, would warn eighteenth-century readers of his sexual intentions. Though Pamela is by nature suspicious—she wraps the coins B. gives her in paper when she sends them to her family so they will not "chink"—she is naive enough in the beginning not to recognize the sexual demands that will eventually be made, thus creating for the reading audience an engrossing tension which virtually took all literate Europe by storm.

Throughout the novel's early portions, B. constantly exercises his power over Pamela, and becomes verbally abusive whenever she rejects his sexual advances. Psychologically, this creates feelings of parental rejection which increasingly trouble and depress the young girl, who, in spite of her father's warning, cannot resist B.'s many attractions. Whenever he is kind to her, she responds like any grateful child, and must struggle with all her moral energy not to let her emotions control her.[27] When B. abducts her and holds her prisoner at his Lincolnshire estate, none of the authority figures in the neighborhood will lend her even token support, and she steadily becomes more and more depressed. But she resists suicide on the grounds of religious scruples, as we have already noted.

But going beyond Richardson's conscious intentions again, and back to what the novel dramatizes on a psychological level, we find that Richardson intuits B.'s attractions as the seductive father figure. To make a gigantic leap, but perhaps not so gigantic after all when we try to understand how Pamela can accept a man who has tried to rape her twice, recent studies reveal that there is a much higher incidence of father-daughter incest in all classes than many people realize. Whereas young males fear their avenging father, so that mother-son incest is relatively rare, no such protection exists for the young girl, who realizes this as she grows up and sees the power distribution in the world around her. The perceptive maturing girl sees that as a future adult, the easiest method of achieving desired power is indirectly by becoming the choice of some strong man. This recognition creates incestuous feelings in many women and the tendency to marry father figures rather than potential adult partners.[28]

B. certainly possesses the preponderance of power in his relationship with Pamela. He is older, stronger, infinitely wealthier, and his socio-economic position demands of Pamela childlike obedience. It is not too difficult then to see why Pamela can disregard his attempts to rape her. He is virtually the beloved father whose sexual advances are highly desirable tokens of attention, even though she obviously must resist them until they are properly married. In this light, Pamela's attitude, while it may not accord with abstract morality, is certainly understandable in the light of what we know today about psychology and sexual politics.

To conclude, then, Richardson's insistence that a young working woman has individual rights and is moreover capable of becoming a loving, companionate wife asserts the new attitudes toward human relationships coming into being in the England of his day. But B.'s abuses and Pamela's responses reflect earlier power relationships which continue to trouble the modern family. Numerous women still experience variations of the psychological tensions Richardson so brilliantly captures, and many are still seduced in one way or another by powerful figures such as Mr. B. For this reason, the first novel written in England dramatizes still-contemporary questions about sex, marriage, and the family.

454 / LAURENCE-ANDERSON

NOTES

1 Excellent scholarly research on French domestics has been done by Theresa Marie McBride, "Rural Tradition and the Process of Modernization: Domestic Servants in Nineteenth-Century France," Diss. Rutgers 1973 (rpt. Ann Arbor, Mich.: University Microfilms, 1977). Chapter 2 in Peter Laslett's *Family Life and Illicit Love in Earlier Generations* (New York: Cambridge University Press, 1977) also discusses women servants in the eighteenth century. J. Jean Hecht has written several studies on eighteenth-century English domestics: *The Domestic Servant Class in Eighteenth-Century England* (London: Routledge & Kegan Paul, 1956), and "Continental and Colonial Servants in Eighteenth-Century England," *Smith College Studies in History*, 5 (1954), 1–61. Hecht, however, bases his conclusions on evidence drawn almost entirely from the employers, which naturally reflects their biases. For example, he writes that black servants had a low reputation for fidelity and, accepting this, he offers as evidence the fact that Johnson's Frank Barber left twice: once to become an apothecary and once to try his luck at sea. Hecht sees both attempts as proof of "restlessness" rather than ambition (ibid., p. 44). Other scholars working on the subject of domestic service in the eighteenth century are Ann Kussmaul at the University of York, Toronto; Sheila Cooper, Department of History, University of Adelaide, Australia; and Evelyne Sullerot, ed., *Le Fait féminin* (Paris, 1978).

2 In *The World We Have Lost* (New York: Scribners, 1967), Laslett shows the fallacy of relying on Shakespeare's *Romeo and Juliet* for evidence that our ancestors married much earlier than we do. See "Births, Marriages and Deaths," pp. 81–94.

3 Peter Laslett, "The Wrong Way Through the Telescope: A Note on Literary Evidence in Sociology and in Historical Sociology," *British Journal of Sociology*, 27 (no. 3, Sept. 1976), 324–25.

4 Phillipe Ariès, *Centuries of Childhood*, trans. Robert Baldick (New York: Knopf, 1962); Peter Laslett, *The World We Have Lost*; Edward Shorter, *The Making of the Modern Family* (New York: Basic Books, 1975); an earlier summary of Shorter's major theories in "Illegitimacy, Sexual Revolution, and Social Change in Modern Europe," *The Family History*, ed. Theodore R. Rabb and Robert I. Rotberg (New York: Harper & Row, 1973); and Lawrence Stone, *The Family, Sex, and Marriage in England 1500–1800* (New York: Harper & Row, 1977).

5 Both Laslett and Shorter refute the popular contention that the preindustrial family was extended rather than "nuclear," primarily because of late marriage and early death, which kept the basic unit to parents and children.

6 Stone, *The Family*, p. 467.

7 Hecht, *The Domestic Servant Class.* McBride notes the same transition in France, but occurring throughout the nineteenth and even into the twentieth century.

8 William Darrell, for example, in *The Gentleman Instructed, in the Conduct of a Virtuous and Happy Life,* 9th ed. (London, 1720), advises that "though you are their Master, you are also their Father" (I, 87).

9 Patrick Delany, in *Twenty Sermons upon Social Duties and Their Opposite Vices,* writes in 1750 that "a servant is supposed to have no will of his own, where his master is concerned; but to submit himself entirely to the will of his master, and obey all of his lawful commands" (Hecht, p. 192).

10 The Reverend William Cole writes in his diary of a neighbor, a Dr. Pettingal, who "on calling his Maid, & her not coming so soon as he expected, went out & beat her very severely . . ." (ibid., p. 79).

11 Lawrence Stone claims that Pamela's mother was her teacher (p. 349), but Pamela, like most female domestics, has been sent from home early, and it is Lady B. who teaches her: "For, you know, my Lady, now with God, lov'd Singing and Dancing; and, as she would have it I had a Voice, she made me learn both; and often has she made me sing her an innocent Song, and a good Psalm too, and dance before her. And I must learn to flower and draw too, and to work fine Work with my Needle. . . ." All citations are to *Pamela: or, Virtue Rewarded,* ed. T. C. Duncan Eaves and Ben D. Kimpel (Boston: Houghton Mifflin, 1971), p. 77.

12 Stone, *The Family,* pp. 565–66.

13 Mary Ellmann, *Thinking About Women* (New York: Harcourt Brace Jovanovich, 1968), p. 1.

14 Stone, pp. 561–64.

15 Ivy Pinchbeck, *Women Workers and the Industrial Revolution, 1750–1850* (New York: Augustus M. Kelley, 1969), p. 3.

16 Pinchbeck cites June 26, 1752, as the date for this quotation, p. 3; however I could locate no such article for this date in the two-volume Yale edition by Gerard Edward Jensen of 1915. Fielding does evidence his concern for poor women in a number of discussions about the problems of prostitution in the *Covent Garden Journal.* He also discusses how difficult it is for former prostitutes to ever gain employment as domestics: "for who is there that will take into Service any of those Persons, tho' ever so willing to abandon their Debaucheries . . ." (II, 39).

17 *The Newgate Calendar: or Malefactors Bloody Register,* ed. Sandra Lee Kerman (New York: Capricorn Books, 1962), p. 118.

18 A. D. McKillip, *Samuel Richardson, Printer and Novelist* (Chapel Hill: University of Carolina Press, 1936), p. 32; Margaret Anne Doody, *A Natural Passion: A Study of Novels of Samuel Richardson* (Oxford: Clarendon Press, 1974), pp. 45–47.

19 See both *The Making of the Modern Family* and "Illegitimacy, Sexual Revolution, and Social Change in Modern Europe."

20 Joan Scott and Louise Tilly, "Woman's Work and the Family," *The Family in History*, ed. Charles E. Rosenberg (Philadelphia: University of Pennsylvania Press, 1975), pp. 168–70.

21 P. 46.

22 McBride also notes a higher percentage of suicides among women domestics than among the rest of the population in France, in a study for the years 1875–82, pp. 246–47. See pp. 132, 147–48, and 243.

23 For one thing, the cheese-making process went on around the clock, making the work-day an incredibly long eighteen or even twenty hours. Since cows were not milked in a barn as they usually are today, but in the fields, a dairy maid faced the additional difficulty of having to lug extremely heavy milk pails back to the cheese-making house. Once there, moreover, she frequently had to lift alone cheeses weighing anywhere from eighty to one hundred and forty pounds. So much for the weaker sex! When the Commissioners of 1843 investigated conditions of women agricultural workers, they found general good health in all occupations except among dairywomen, who suffered extremely from their long hours and over-exertion (Pinchbeck, pp. 13–14).

24 McKillop in *Samuel Richardson: Printer and Novelist*, and T. C. Duncan Eaves and Ben B. Kimpel, *Samuel Richardson, A Biography* (Oxford: Clarendon Press, 1971), both show that the area where Richardson lived and worked most of his life bordered on "criminal" sections of London.

25 Peter Laslett, "Age at Menarche in Europe since the Eighteenth Century," *The Family in History*.

26 Patricia Meyer Spacks, "Ambiguities of Pleasing: Some Attitudes Towards Youth," *The Eighteenth Century Views Its Present*, American Society for Eighteenth-Century Studies Annual Meeting, Chicago April 21, 1978.

27 Her first letter indicates keen pleasure from his attentions and praise. Even after he has kidnapped her and made her the prisoner of the odious Mrs. Jewkes and Colbrand, she is upset because she "cannot hate him . . ." (p. 157).

28 Judith Herman and Lisa Hirschman, "Father-Daughter Incest," *Signs: Journal of Women in Culture and Society*, 2 (no. 4, Summer 1977), 735–56.

The Fallen Woman, from the Perspective of Five Early Eighteenth-Century Women Novelists

JEAN B. KERN

That women novelists of the early eighteenth century moved away from the French romance and toward a more realistic novel of manners is demonstrable in a number of ways: by examining statements of purpose in prefaces and dedications where they emphasize their intent to "speak the truth"; by examining the plot and style of the novels themselves; by showing sociologically how society is reflected in their novels; or by focusing on a stereotypical character such as the old maid, the stepmother, or the female rake, and examining how women novelists gave a new realism to such characters as they groped to record the manners of their age. I have chosen in this paper to focus on the stereotype "fallen woman" as presented by five women novelists writing before 1726. Because my sample is small, I do not wish to overgeneralize my conclusions, but I do hope to correct some previous generalizations about the early women novelists.

First, I would call attention to an article by Maximillian E. Novak[1] who has warned against (1) carrying "notionalism" into a study of fiction, and (2) reading into novels fictional values that the author would not admire; on the other hand, he has urged that critics should be constantly aware of the past. What Novak seems to be suggesting is that studies of the novel should avoid reading into early fiction

457

ideas (his word is "notionalism") which are current in the twentieth century; at the same time they should reflect awareness of the age in which the novels were written. This wise caution is particularly useful to a limited study of these five women novelists in the first quarter of the eighteenth century. While they are not just women novelists to be looked at from the perspective of recent purely feminine criticism, they are conversely not writing in a vacuum about the position of a "fallen" woman in their own day. I have chosen a combination of literary history, including biographical detail where it is known, and a close look at the novels themselves to determine how their "fallen" women contribute realism to their novels of manners as these novelists relate their own experience in the society in which they lived. I have noted where they were conscious, in prefaces and dedications, of creating a new theory that fictions should be truthful. I have slighted structure and style except where the latter is realistic, because I am less interested in how good their novels are on an absolute scale than in what they say about a type character. While I found Lawrence Stone's *Family, Sex and Marriage in England 1500–1800* (London: Weidenfeld and Nicolson, 1977) extremely useful about the society of this first quarter of the eighteenth century—especially on the double moral standard which permitted sexual liaisons to men but not to women, my choice of working from five examples of women novelists who write of the "fallen" woman is a small addition to a sociological approach. Finally, this is not a short chapter in the history of women novelists, but an attempt to integrate literary history and close reading in order to examine how these women write of manners in fictional form.

As early as 1929, E. A. Baker was aware of their importance to the novel of manners: "The service they rendered was to have kept up a supply of novels and stories, which habituated a larger and larger public to find their amusement in the reading of fiction, and which, poor in quality as they were, provided the original form for the eighteenth century novel of manners."[2] Yet in spite of Baker's statement, these early women novelists have either been ignored or lumped together as imitators of French romance. Few appear in the *DNB*; of the five who are the subject of this paper, only Mary Manley and Eliza Haywood rate a notice, while Penelope Aubin, Mary Hearne, and the anonymous "Ma A" do not. Few, also, are the studies of their entire canon,[3] but many are the studies of the novel which dismiss them summarily.[4]

Recent interest in women writers as a result of the feminist criticism has returned attention to these early novelists, picking up where Joyce M. Horner, "The English Women Novelists and Their Connection with the Feminist Movement (1688–1797)," *Smith College Studies in Modern Languages*, 11, (nos. 1, 2, 3, 1930), and Brigid G. MacCarthy, *The Female Pen: Women Writers and Their Contribution to the English Novel 1621–1744*, 2 vols. (Cork: University Press, 1944), left off. Contemporary studies are much helped by the recent wave of reprinted novels from Garland Publishing Company, Scholars Facsimile Reprints, and the Augustan Reprint Society. The present accessibility of their novels inevitably raises some new questions: Did women authors view the "fallen" woman differently when writing in this first quarter of the century before the novel of manners was firmly established? How far were their views conditioned by their own experience? Were their promises to write of "events just as they happen'd" (see Mary Davys' Introduction to *The Works of Mary Davys*, London, 1725) self-conscious affirmations of female experience which they considered to have been neglected in the idealized heroines of romance? To answer whether these women were writing from a female perspective and out of their own experience, we should consider first what we already know about the "fallen" woman from male novelists.

We already know, as shown by Defoe, Fielding, or Richardson, the parameters of a woman who succumbed to passion either willingly (Moll Flanders, Molly Seagrim, Lady Bellaston) or by seduction or rape (Clarissa Harlowe). She becomes a prostitute or a tragic figure. The higher her station in society, the less chance there is for her to recover enough even to escape notice. Unless she is as resourceful as Moll, who eventually climbs into the lower middle class, her future is bleak. For Clarissa Harlowe the future is unthinkable; the loss of her chastity is the loss of virtue and consequently the loss of life. As Marlene Gates points out in "The Cult of Womanhood in Eighteenth-Century Thought," *Eighteenth-Century Studies*, 10 (Fall 1976), 21–39, the eighteenth-century Enlightenment placed little confidence in women's ability to control their sexuality; despite the idealization of women as guardians of morality from Richardson to Rousseau, there is insistence on the need for men to be masters in relations between the sexes. However, I found these five women novelists less anxious to submit to such mastery and more insistent on women as the real guardians of sexual morality in society. The examples of women novelists I chose from among the group that Baker celebrated as establishing the form of the novel of manners, deliberately including an anonymous female ("Ma A") as well as the unknown Mary Hearne along with Penelope Aubin, Mary Manley, and Eliza Haywood, in order to provide a sample not already preselected by Baker or others. While my choice may appear arbitrary, it was based on a great number of novels read for a study of the eighteenth-century novel of manners as written by women, and it was limited to five writing in the same time span—the first quarter of the century.

How, then, do these five women novelists portray a female character who succumbs to passion? In part, their treatment as could be expected depends on their own experience and their motivation for writing fiction, which is expressed in their prefaces and dedications. Whether they are sensational like Mary Manley or didactic like Penelope Aubin, their stated motivation is uniformly to encourage sexual virtue and abhor vice or the libertine mores of their time. Also they all acknowledge if not accept the double moral standard for men and women, but they differ sharply on whom to blame for the fate of the "fallen" woman. Aubin, the most didactic of the five, clearly blames women more than men and accepts the authority of husbands in sexual behavior. When in her novel *The Life and Adventures of the Lady Lucy* (1726) Frederick is killed by Albertus, who thinks he has found him in his wife's bed (actually it is the immoral Henrietta who has posed as his wife Lucy), Aubin's authorial voice regrets only that "a brave young gentleman, who was dear to his Prince and his Family" was killed "without any time for Repentance."[5] To the moral Mrs. Aubin, it is more important that Frederick died in sin than that he attempted to ruin a married woman. She exhorts all women to avoid Henrietta's fate and imitate Lucy, the faithful wife: "But I forget the Age I live in . . . when there is scarce any Truth, Honour or Conscience in Men, or Modesty and Sobriety in Women" (p. 130). She clearly does not expect sexual morality of men and gives only libertine women like Henrietta credit for wit and ingenuity. Women are to be sober, modest, and unthinking; men are to be honorable, truthful, but not necessarily chaste. Albertus has three sons by his mistress Gertrude during the nineteen years he is separated from his supposedly unfaithful wife Lucy, but he claims his illegitimate sons are exempt by their sex "from the Misfortunes yours [Gertrude's] is subject to" (p. 80)—a shocking if not incredible statement to a woman he has seduced. Mrs. Aubin, thus, accepts the double moral standard and charges only women with the responsibility for sexual morality.

Mary Manley, however, is not so easy on men in her avowed purpose to discourage vice. Because of her personal experience, she would never worry as Aubin did about Frederick dying in sin. After Manley's father's death, she was seduced at the age of fourteen by a cousin who lured her into a false marriage when he already had a wife. Manley tells her own story both as Delia in *The New Atalantis* (1709) and in *The History of Rivella* (1714).[6] As an older woman (it could be Manley herself) points out to a seduced younger one, "no Lady ever suffer'd herself to be truly touch'd, but from that moment she was blinded and undone; the first thing a Woman ought to consult was her Interest and Establishment in the World; that Love shou'd only be a handle towards it; when she left the pursuit of that to give her self to her Pleasures, Contempt and Sorrow were sure to be her Companions" (*The New Atalantis*, I, 345). This is patently the voice of experience to a "pauvre Fille trompez," for Manley after her "fall" was befriended briefly only by the King's mistress, the Duchess of Cleveland, and soon found herself excluded even from that society until she was forced to support herself by her writing. She defends the woman who is raped because "Frailty is not only excusable at *such a juncture*, but *indispensable*, especially with *Persons* [men] that are resolv'd to prevail whether *one* will or not" (*New Atalantis*, I, 663–64). The tone of this acknowledged sexuality combined with the awareness she shows of the greater physical strength and social advantage of men, reflects Manley's experience closely. She does not absolve the rapist as Mrs. Aubin does; in fact, Manley's own rapist, her cousin, is severely censured: "Certainly whoever *first* seduces a young *Virgin*, is answerable for all the Crimes and Misfortunes of her future Life; were he even to die for it . . . it would be a just Punishment to him" (*New Atalantis*, I, 726).

In her autobiographical *The History of Rivella* the narrator who relates Manley's story states the double standard thus: "*If she had been a Man, she had been without Fault*" (II, 743). The narrative device of using a male narrator in this novel gives added validity to this clearly stated double standard of morality. As Rivella/Manley pursues her career of sexual liaisons and complicated lawsuits, she, by chance, encounters her first seducer, "cover'd with Blushes and Confusion, not imagining what Business she had there, unless it was to expose him" (*Rivella*, II, 805). Her seducer and cousin is only worried about the charge of bigamy she could bring against him. (Stone, *Family, Sex and Marriage*, p. 35, indicates the prevalence of such bigamy before the Marriage Law of 1754 discouraged secret marriages.) To divert her attention from that, he even tries to trick Rivella out of some of her promised fee for helping to settle an estate with the appeal that it will help provide some money for their illegitimate child. Far from being disturbed by gossip about his rape of his cousin, once he recovers from his initial embarrassment, his only action is to continue to exploit the woman whose social position he had ruined. Curiously,

Manley slides over that initial ruin in a rather vague reference to "All those Misfortunes that have since attended her, in Point of Honour and the World's Opinion" (*Rivella*, II, 764). What seems most to preoccupy her in writing her autobiographical novel is how a fallen woman can support herself by (1) living with other men (her affair with John Tilly is readily admitted), (2) helping male friends through legal difficulties such as recovering an inheritance (the longest episode of *Rivella*), (3) writing *The Secret Manners and Memoirs* of her contemporaries, or (4) entering politics (Manley herself succeeded Swift as an editor of the Tory *Examiner*). Of the latter occupation, her male narrator reports, "She now agrees with me, that Politicks is not the Business of a Woman" (*Rivella*, II, 853), and adds that she intends to return to writing for the stage, a decision made when her printer and publishers of *The New Atalantis* are arrested and jailed, because "she could not bear to live and reproach herself with the Misery that might happen to those unfortunate People" (*Rivella*, II, 848). Thus the self-portrait which emerges is complicated by flashes of sympathy, fondness for intrigue (legal as well as sexual), flexibility in turning from one means of support to another, and frankly acknowledged sensuality. She even admits to being fond of flattery although she is hard-headed enough to recognize the hypocrisy of the flatterers: "The Casuists told her a Woman of her Wit had the Privilege of the other Sex, since all Things were pardonable to a *Lady, who could so well give Laws to others, yet was not obliged to keep them her self*" (*Rivella*, II, 780, italics hers). Manley well knew the casuistry of such an argument; all things were *not* pardonable to a Lady, although they appeared to be to the Gentleman who first ruined her.

If Robert A. Day is correct that Mary Manley is also the author of *Love upon Tick* (1724), an early epistolary novel published anonymously, she continued to show men as foolish gulls of passion (*Told in Letters* [Ann Arbor: University of Michigan Press, 1966], p. 41). I am not so certain that Manley is the author of this novel written ten years after *Rivella*, because the tone is much more satiric than her usual combination of scandal and sensualism. The technique is a direct authorial voice reporting the exchange of letters between the aging Urganda and a silly fop named Philander, who is tricked into thinking the letters come from a much younger widow. Urganda keeps the upper hand throughout, but her similarity to Rivella is only in a kind of ingenious flair for exploiting Philander's vanity. Urganda is not a "fallen" woman who like Rivella, Delia, and Manley herself is barred from ever regaining the position in society to which she was born.

Eliza Haywood, despite editing what has been called "the first magazine by and for women" (see Mary R. Mahl and Helene Koon, *The Female Spectator: English Women Writers before 1800* [Bloomington: Indiana University Press, 1977], p. 224), in which she prints fictive letters arguing "There is undoubtedly, no Sexes in Souls" (p. 227), resignedly admits "the Mode is against me" when she urges girls not to marry too young and parents not to shut their daughters away from mixed company so that they lack experience to distinguish a sincere lover from a deceiver. She is certain that any man would prefer having said of his wife that "She is a woman of admirable Understanding and Great Learning" (Mohl and Koon, *Female Spectator*, p. 236), but the men in her novel *The Rash Resolve* (1724)[7] do not bear out her confidence. Instead they engage in secret marriages (Emilius of the heroine Emanuela) or carry out seductions and elopements (the fop who runs off with Berillia and then murders her). Emanuela's naiveté is perhaps excused because she was raised in Puerto Rico, where she was allowed more freedom than her cousin Berillia, whose Spanish father first locks her up and then sends her into the country to separate her from her lover of whom he disapproves, but neither seducer is excused by Haywood. Emilius is not proud of Emanuela's "admirable Understanding and Great Learning" although she is described throughout as a paragon of virtue and accomplishments; he also fails to acknowledge her as his wife when her reputation is ruined by the jealous accusations of infidelity from Berillia. Emanuela is *not* a "fallen" woman, since she is sexually chaste before her secret marriage to Emilius, but her fate is no better than that of Berillia, who *is* "fallen." Emilius discards her before admitting their marriage and then chooses a wife of good family and fortune. Emanuela is forced to live in disgrace with her son, supporting herself by doing menial work for nuns in a convent. Even when Emilius and his new wife discover her and she is cleared of the charge of infidelity by Berillia's dying confession, Emanuela does not recover her social status but immediately dies of her grief once she knows her son will be raised by his father.

Haywood judges all men in this novel harshly. They are too rigid as fathers (like Berillia's), too dishonest (like Don Pedro, Emanuela's guardian in Puerto Rico, who steals her inheritance), or too coldbloodedly selfish about their own pleasure (like Emilius, who makes no attempt to test the false story of Emanuela's infidelity; instead, Emilius looks immediately for another wife, despite his former love for Emanuela). "Where is the man who dies for repeated Possession?" (p. 67) Haywood asks at this point, partly out of her own experience with an unhappy early marriage before she was twenty. Her own husband even advertised after she ran away that he would accept no debts incurred by her; thus she, too, was driven to support herself and her illegitimate children by writing plays and fiction in which "the pill of improvement supposed to be swallowed along with the sweets of diversion hardly ever consisted of good precepts or praiseworthy actions, but usually of a warning or a horrible example [like Emanuela and Berillia] of what to avoid" (Wicher, *Mrs. Eliza Haywood*, p. 18).

Both Haywood and Manley, unlike Aubin, emphasize those "sweets of diversion" in their sensual descriptions of sexual liaisons. They seem to have their cake while eating it too in pointing out the plight of the "fallen" woman but lingering over sensuous warm baths, filmy nightgowns, flower-scented gardens, and descriptions of smooth flesh; yet both these women had reason from personal experience to know the permanent disgrace of the "fallen" woman. Manley, particularly in *The History of Rivella*, describes herself as an attractive woman despite the fact that "from her Youth she inclin'd to Fat" (II, 744), by having her male narrator concentrate on the physical description of her eyes, her small feet, and her liveliness of expression. Again, this has more credibility coming from a male narrator who clearly knows what is sexually attractive to men. But neither Manley nor Haywood is as outrageously sensational as the sensual anonymous author of *The Prude* (1724), one "Ma A," who dedicated her novel to Eliza Haywood.[8] The prude, Elisinda, in this novel is ironically anything but. She is closer to a nymphomaniac with additional lesbian inclinations. Guided by her friend Stanissa, she poses hypocritically as a very devout lady who spends hours at her devotions, while actually she is sharing a servant's bed along with Stanissa before taking other and higher-born male lovers. The only man she cannot seduce is Lysander, her sister's suitor, and thus she decides to ruin his reputation. As so often in these early novels by women, the sisters are without parents (shades of *Evelina*), though the importance of parental guidance is never stressed in this novel as it is in Haywood's *The Rash Resolve*. What is stressed in this anonymous novel is Stanissa's opposition to marriage because a husband "has a Right to exact from you where you go, and how long you stay, and on the least Suspicion, you must move like Clock-work at his Will and Pleasure" (p. 18). Such cynical advice is followed by a warning that Elisinda's servants, who are at present her accomplices, would inform on her after a marriage. Stanissa concludes that "the Woman who expects Happiness in Marriage, must have an Understanding as conformable to that of her Husband, as Echo is to Sound, she is only to think the same thing o'er again, he has thought before; and love him with so entire a Fondness, as to imagine his very Follies superiour Perfections to the rest of Mankind" (p. 19). Stanissa's is the cynical voice of the experienced "fallen" woman who has tried the double moral standard and learned its inequities. Could she also be voicing the experience of "Ma A," the author?

The plot of Elisinda to win Lysander is not resolved in volume 1 of *The Prude*. However, parts II and III[9] continue her attempt to discredit her sister by planning to have her raped by her servant. Other women's stories are now interpolated to spin out the plot. Emelia, for example, to divert her friends on a long coach journey into the country, takes up seventy pages telling how she was seduced by Bellvile and then discarded after a secret marriage (p. 25) because he tired of her. Bellvile, who falsely charges her with infidelity to excuse his harsh treatment, later steals her infant son (p. 33), and she is forced to go to the Indies as a Lady's companion. Her comment, " 'Tis certain, Bellvile would not have dared to act so arch a piece of Treachery, had Redress been within my Power" (p. 41), shows her as helpless as Manley's Rivella to clear her reputation after a false marriage. Like Haywood's Emanuela, she cannot meet a charge of infidelity in the clandestine marriage, which the husband would not acknowledge. Stanissa's strong aversion to marriage in part I is now reinforced by a victim of marriage: "Were all the wrongs of our hapless Sex to be publish'd, the famous *Alexandrian* Library would be far too narrow to contain the Numberless Millions of our repeated wrongs from Mankind" (p. 44). The most interesting addition to the sensuality of Ma A's style in this particular story of Emelia is that the author relates Emelia's fall into the water and her rescue by Bellvile as a metaphor for her succumbing to a wave of passion: men, she says, "are all as smooth as summer's waters in pursuit, Beauty then concealing the ravenous Passions that closely lurk to devour the heedless believing Prey" (p. 12). Ma A's pretentious attempt to go beyond Stanissa's cynicism about marriage in part I by an effort to link nature and human nature, shows wives as victims—the "prey," to use her word, to passions which they cannot direct or control. This anonymous novel is, thus, the most outspoken advocate of sexual freedom for woman of any of these early novels by women.

Mary Hearne's *The Lovers' Week or the Six Days Adventures of Philander and Amaryllis* (1718)[10] is written by a woman about whom we know as little as about the anonymous author of *The Prude*. There is, in other words, no way of relating the author's experience to her treatment of the "fallen" woman, in this case the young Amaryllis, again a girl without parents who is under the supervision of an aunt as "censorious and ill-natur'd, as can be" (pp. 3–4). Amaryllis, like most of the heroines of these early novels, falls in love at first sight in a convention which these women novelists apparently borrowed from the theatre. On the third of the "Six Days" which she is recording as her own narrator, she keeps an assignation with Philander at what proves to be a bagnio, the eighteenth-century version of a massage parlor, where she is seduced, though hardly raped, because she admits her "open free Temper" kept her from inflicting pain on his passionate advances "out of a little affected Coyness of my Sex" (p. 14). Like the other frank women authors in the early eighteenth century, Hearne avoids any explicit description of the sexual act after she sets the scene following a relaxing bath in the bagnio. Her authorial comments are, in fact, comically cryptic: "He at length talk'd me to sleep" (p. 31), or on the next night, "We went to bed without anything remarkable happening that Night" (p. 48). By the sixth day, Philander has hidden his new mistress away in a country house outside London, from which seclusion she recounts her *Six Days*.

Her future is defined in the sequel, *The Female Deserters* (1719, bound in the same Garland reprint as *The Lovers' Week*), where Amaryllis continues her story by telling also that of another "fallen" woman, Callista, who is her neighbor; Callista and her lover, Torismund, furnish the only social life of Amaryllis and Philander in their post-fall Eden; these two "fallen" women have only each other to talk to when their lovers are off to Court in the city. Neatly telescoped inside Callista's story, which is already enclosed in the first-person account of Amaryllis, is the story of Callista's maid, Isabella, who is the most realistic of the three disgraced women about her future: "Have you not often seen, that when they have courted a Woman Years together, and gained their vile Ends, they have basely left them, and triumph'd over the Conquests they have made?" (p. 56). Isabella is of lower social status, which perhaps is why she sounds more like Pamela. For example, after the wife of a couple who has befriended the runaway Isabella dies, Isabella foresees trouble and moves out to take the position as maid to Callista "since," as she says, "generally Men are much more apt to laugh at Woman's folly, than anyways to help her in her Misfortune" (p. 70). A "fallen" woman may expect help from another woman, but from a man—only laughter.

In summary, I have chosen these novels arbitrarily from among the early eighteenth-century novels by women which I have read thus far in order to indicate the patterns of similarity in their writing about manners as they apply to the "fallen" woman. I have also attempted to relate their own experiences to their treatment of mores in their society. Two of these novelists are women who have often been dismissed as sensational scandal-mongers—Mary Manley and Eliza Haywood. One was a widow—Penelope Aubin. About the others we have no information. Of the group, only Aubin excuses the male sexual aggressor, although she agrees with the others that the "fallen" woman has no place in society after her fall. Manley, from her own fall "lacking of fourteen," and Haywood, after an early marriage to a clergyman fifteen years older than herself, are explicit in showing that the loss of chastity outside of legitimate wedlock is socially irretrievable. None of them deny sensuality to women, though a moralist like Aubin limits it to the evil Henrietta. Only the anonymous author of *The Prude* goes so far as to advise against marriage, trusting no men, not even husbands.

I conclude from even this amount of evidence that women novelists in this period 1700–1726 were, indeed, attempting to write of manners out of their experience, and that they were already turning away from French romances to write of "Facts" and "Truth" as they promised in their dedications and introductions, but that they clearly understood that sexual mores limited a woman more than a man.

E. A. Baker refers to such women as helping to shape the novels of Richardson and Fielding (III, 107), and William H. McBurney in an article on Aubin finds evidence that she directly influenced Richardson's *Pamela* as well as *Clarissa* ("Mrs. Penelope Aubin and the Early Eighteenth-Century English Novel," *Huntington Library Quarterly*, 20 [May 1957], 245–67). Whether they were writing key-novels to current scandals or imitating romances, whether they wrote in epistolary form or with the heavily authorial didacticism of Aubin, their unchaste woman has to hide behind hypocritical behavior (Elisinda in *The Prude*, Henrietta in *The Lady Lucy*, Berillia in *The Rash Resolve*), be hidden away from all but her "fallen" peers (Amaryllis in *The Lovers' Week*), or brazen it out in a tough male-dominated city life where her pen is her sole means of support (*Rivella* when she was too old and fat to attract more lovers). Thus all of these five women novelists, in turning away from French romances as models, write out of their experience in eighteenth-century society as they push their fiction towards a realistic novel of manners. Their treatment of the "fallen" woman is one measure of realism in their novels.

NOTES

1 "Some Notes Toward a History of Fictional Forms; from Aphra Behn to Daniel Defoe," *Novel*, VI, 2 (1973), 120–33.

2 *The History of the English Novel*, 10 Vols. (1929; rpt. New York, Barnes and Noble, 1961), III, 107. Baker is speaking particularly of Jane Barker, Mary Davys, Penelope Aubin, and Elizabeth Rowe in the passage quoted.

3 George F. Wicher, *The Life and Romance of Mrs. Eliza Haywood* (New York: Columbia University, 1915); William H. McBurney, "Mrs. Penelope Aubin and the Early Eighteenth-Century English Novel," *Huntington Library Quarterly*, 20 (May 1957), 245–67; Patricia Koster's Introduction to *The Novels of Mary Delariviere Manley* (Gainesville, Fla.: Scholars Facsimile Reprints, 1971); and recent Introductions to the Garland Foundations of the Novel series, exhaust such criticism of the five novelists discussed in this paper.

4 William Forsythe, *The Novels and Novelists of the Eighteenth Century in Illustration of the Manners and Morals of the Age* (London and Port Washington, N.Y.: Kennicot, 1871, reissued 1971), even avoids citation to prove the coarse manners these women depict: "Necessarily I cannot give quotations to show this, for in doing so I should myself offend" (p. 162).

5 Penelope Aubin, *The Life and Adventures of the Lady Lucy* (London: J. Darcy et al., 1726; reprinted, with an Introduction by Josephine Grieder, in the series Foundations of the Novel, New York, Garland Publishers, 1973), p. 63. All citations are to the latter edition.

6 *The Novels of Mary Delariviere Manley*, ed. Patricia Koster, 2 vols. (Gainesville, Fla.: Scholars Facsimile Reprints, 1971). All citations are to this edition.

7 Eliza Haywood, *The Rash Resolve* (London: D. Browne and S. Chapman, 1724; reprinted, edited by Josephine Grieder, in the series Foundations of the Novel, New York, Garland Publishers, 1973). Citation is to the latter edition.

8 Only vol. 1 of *The Prude a Novel by a Young Lady* (London: J. Roberts, 1724) has been reprinted in the series Foundations of the Novel. Citations to vol. 1 are to this edition, edited by Josephine Grieder (New York: Garland Publishers, 1973).

9 The British Library has Part II of this novel printed by J. Roberts (2nd ed., 1725) and Part III also printed by J. Roberts (1725, but not marked as 2nd. ed.). My references to Parts II and III are to these editions.

10 Mary Hearne, *The Lovers' Week or The Six Days Adventures of Philander and Amaryllis* (London: E. Curll, 1718) and *The Female Deserters* (London: E. Curll, 1719) are reprinted, edited by Josephine Grieder, in the series Foundations of the Novel, (New York: Garland Publishers, 1973). Citations are to the Garland reprints.

Executive Board, 1979–80

469

Institutional Members

of the American Society

for Eighteenth-Century Studies

Arizona State University
Appalachian State University
National Library of Australia
Bodleian Library, Oxford
Brooklyn College
Bryn Mawr College
University of Calgary
University of California, Berkeley
University of California, Davis
University of California, Irvine
University of California,
   Los Angeles/William Andrews
   Clark Memorial Library
University of California, Riverside
University of California, San Diego
Carleton University
The Catholic University of America
Art Institute of Chicago
University of Cincinnati
City College, CUNY
Claremont Graduate School
Cleveland State University
Colonial Williamsburg Foundation
University of Colorado,
   Denver Center
University of Connecticut
Dalhousie University
Delta State University
Detroit Institute of Arts,
   Founder's Society
Institute of Early American
   History and Culture
Emory University
Fordham University

Franklin and Marshall College
Librairie Gason, Verviers, Belgium
Georgia Institute of Technology
Georgia State University
University of Georgia
Herzog August Bibliothek,
   Wolfenbüttel
University of Illinois, Chicago Circle
Indiana University
The Johns Hopkins University
University of Kansas
University of Kentucky
Kimbell Art Museum, Fort Worth
Lehigh University
Lehman College, CUNY
The Lewis Walpole Library
Los Angeles County Museum of Art
University of Maryland
University of Massachusetts, Boston
McMaster University/Association
   for 18th Century Studies
The Metropolitan Museum of Art
University of Michigan, Ann Arbor
Michigan State University
The Minneapolis Institute of
   Fine Arts
University of Minnesota
University of Mississippi
Mississippi State University
Université de Montréal
Mount Saint Vincent University
University of New Brunswick
State University of New York,
   Binghamton

470

State University of New York,
  Fredonia
University of North Carolina,
  Chapel Hill
North Georgia College
Northern Illinois University
Northwestern University
The Ohio State University
University of Pennsylvania
University of Pittsburgh
Princeton University
Purdue University
Rice University
University of Rochester
Rockford College
Smith College
Smithsonian Institution
University of South Carolina
University of Southern
  Mississippi
Stanford University
Swarthmore College
Sweet Briar College
University of Tennessee
University of Texas
Texas Tech University

Toledo Museum of Art
Tulane University
University of Tulsa
University of Utrecht, Institute
  for Comparative and General
  Literature
University of Victoria
University of Virginia
Virginia Commonwealth
  University
The Voltaire Foundation
Washington University
Washington and Lee University
Westfälische Wilhelms-
  Universität, Munster
West Chester State College
West Virginia University
The Henry Francis Dupont
  Winterthur Museum
University of Wisconsin,
  Madison
University of Wisconsin,
  Milwaukee
Yale Center for British
  Art and British Studies
Yale University

Sponsoring Members

of the American Society

for Eighteenth-Century Studies

Margaret E. Adams
Mary-Margaret H. Barr
Rand Burnette
Joseph A. Byrnes
W. B. Carnochan
Chester Chapin
Henry S. Commager
Lester G. Crocker
Robert A. Day
John Dowling
Lee A. Elioseff
Charles N. Fifer
John Irwin Fischer &
    Panthea Reid Boughton
Philip M. Griffith
Walter Grossmann
Kay Hardesty
Donald M. Hassler
Lloyd E. Hawes
Robert R. Heitner
Robert H. Hopkins
Annibel Jenkins
Judith Keig
Victor Lange
J. Patrick Lee

I. Leonard Leeb
J. A. Levine
David Macaree
Roger Mandle
Michael J. Marcuse
Helen L. McGuffie
Robert D. Moynihan
Jean Perkins
R. G. Peterson
Gerard Reedy, S. J.
Thomas J. Regan
Walter E. Rex
Frederick G. Ribble
Edgar V. Roberts
Ronald C. Rosbottom
Ambrose Saricks
William C. Schrader III
Oliver F. Sigworth
J. E. Stockwell
George B. Tatum
Robert E. Taylor
H. L. Trobough
Robert W. Uphaus
Calhoun Winton

Index of Names